Women and Social R
in Modern Indi

MW00816983

Women and Social Reform in Modern India

A Reader

edited by

SUMIT SARKAR

&

TANIKA SARKAR

Indiana University Press
Bloomington and Indianapolis

This book is a publication of

Indiana University Press
601 North Morton Street
Bloomington, Indiana 47404-3797 USA

http://iupress.indiana.edu

Telephone orders	800-842-6796
Fax orders	812-855-7931
Orders by e-mail	iuporder@indiana.edu

The paper used in this publication meets the minimum requirements of American
National Standard for Information Sciences—Permanence of Paper for Printed
Library Materials, ANSI Z39.48-1984.

Manufactured in the United States of America

Cataloging information is available from the Library of Congress.

ISBN 978-0-253-35269-9 (cl.)
ISBN 978-0-253-22049-3 (pbk.)

1 2 3 4 5   13 12 11 10 09 08

Contents

Introduction

Tanika Sarkar and Sumit Sarkar

Colonial social reforms have long been a routinized part of our school, college, and university syllabi, written and taught more or less on similar lines at all three levels. Reforms conjure up, inevitably, the names of a few great individuals, almost invariably Hindu: upper-caste educated men from metropolitan cities, and one or two memorable women. This galaxy of remarkable persons identified and abolished abuses in social life, and their efforts ushered in more progressive gender relations—although we must remember that even though the reforms largely related to women and family relationships, the word 'gender' rarely occurs in the more conventional textbooks. We find little about reforms among Muslims or among 'lower castes'. Attention is centred on upper-caste women's education and on their marriage practices—which were altered largely through new laws: in particular those that banned widow burning, allowed widow remarriage, restricted child marriage.

To explain the emergence of reformers precisely from the early nineteenth century, three kinds of reasons are invoked in these historical writings: a new colonial education, purveyed through the state and Christian missionaries, that altered and modernized traditional social perceptions; new religious movements that revived and consolidated older humanitarian impulses; and, of course, the sudden availability of a pool of human greatness, eager to save the weak and the helpless. Little significant change has inflected such presentation of this theme over the years, and the social reform chapter usually occurs as a boring though easy interlude, interrupting the more exciting or taxing chapters on nationalist struggle and the colonial economy.

Even within its own terms, such a perspective on social reform could have broadened into an engagement with a number of connected themes. The invocation of the great reformist individuals could, for instance, have expanded into a discussion of their regional, class, and caste specificities, or of the way in which the variations in their social particulars shaped distinctive styles of work or varied the patterns of their social concerns. This, in turn, would have led into a consideration of variations within the new intelligentsia, and of the characteristics of the public spheres that emerged in metropolitan centres with the development of print culture, newspapers, and new modes of communication and association, all of which allowed the reformers to engage in sustained conversations and arguments with one another and with their orthodox opponents in the public domain. A description of the situation in the metropolitan centres would, then, need to expand into a discussion of how, over time, and with the progressive enlargement of the public sphere, smaller towns and new regions were incorporated within the larger debates on the 'women's question', leading to the development of new modes of argument and presentation. We need to know, moreover, what exactly was written about reforms in the newspapers, novels, and tracts, how the matter was performed in the public theatre, how public opinion was formed, pluralized, made contradictory and fractured, swerving people away, finally, from the rule of prescriptive texts and commands that may have been diverse but which, certainly, were authoritative and compelling.

The term 'middle class', so commonly deployed in textbook histories, is also surely in need of some problematization. The term has been in fairly wide use from the nineteenth century, in Indian-language equivalents such as *madhyabitta* in Bengali. It used to invoke, in those days, an optimistic analogy with the history of the English middle class as the presumed harbinger of economic and social progress. Paradoxically, in striking contrast with the English middle classes, the emergent Indian educated 'middle class' was rooted primarily in rent income from land, where production relations were far from capitalistic. This was combined with professions and office jobs in government or European business firms. The gap between that social group and indigenous entrepreneurship actually widened over time, most notably in Bengal.[1] The middle class, again, would have varied across regions and times, its links with commerce and industry being much more evident in Bombay—and to some extent in the United Provinces—for instance. Recent research also uncovers a kind of lower stratum, a 'low-life of literature' (to borrow a phrase by Robert Darnton about eighteenth-century France), typically clerical in its ambience, its values somewhat at odds with those of the well-known established reformers, writers, journalists, and politicians. The proliferation of cheap print resulted in a mass of tracts, plays, farces, and manuals which disclosed the characteristics of this more plebeian underworld. Little of this research, however, has found its way as yet into textbooks.[2]

We have moreover a recurrent use of the word 'debates' in connection with social reforms, without acquiring an understanding of how public debates—a very new historical development—could take place: Among whom? Through what concrete communication practices and technologies?

Second, when we discuss what was being done for women in those times, we rarely connect the 'abuses' to enduring systems or traditions of gender practices and their internal variations across times, classes and castes, labour patterns, and regions. For instance, when we address changes in widow immolation or widow remarriage practices, we do not study the larger domain of gender relations which sanctified immolation or which outlawed widow remarriage: What arguments were used? What else went with these specific norms that reformers did not address, what was said by the orthodox practitioners who defended such traditions? In other words, an exclusive focus on reformers—once they had already been installed as reformers—obscures the milieu they came from, and the large, powerful context of orthodoxy that they had to contend with. The focus on the specific achievements of reformers thus obscures the larger horizon of gender norms and practices.

Third, there is a very curious omission. Most reforms passed through the grid of state legislation. Yet, there is little engagement even with the law-making machinery and with the state under colonial governance, far less with the judicial courts that enforced the laws and dealt with disputes around the new laws. Most surprisingly, there is seldom any mention of the fact that the reforms related to the sphere of 'personal laws', Hindu, Muslim, Christian, and, later, Parsi. The colonial state had marked these out as parts of a domain that would be governed by the religious scriptures and customs of the various Indian communities, within which the state would only intervene if it could be definitively demonstrated that present practices deviated from more authentic norms. The state had demarcated a sphere of personal laws from the late eighteenth century, based on clear-cut assumptions about religious divisions. Colonial courts were instructed to apply such personal laws, and colonial lawmakers, too, rarely stepped out of such boundaries. Even though the entire domain was supposedly governed by both scripture and custom, in cases of conflict between the two, scripture was generally privileged in Bengal: which explains why Rammohan Roy and Ishwarchandra Vidya-sagar scoured ancient scripture to locate citations for their views. In Bombay Presidency, on the other hand, local custom was taken far more seriously from the late eighteenth century. Case law was compiled through detailed investigations among various caste heads; they were also compiled carefully as precedents. In the South, there was a recurrent vacillation between Sanskrit and brahmanical texts, and old vernacular texts, the latter sometimes seen as non-textualized custom. The separate marriage practices of Nayars and Tiyyas, for instance, and their matrilineal residential and property-owning tradi-tions, could be jettisoned as corrupt forms when, from the late nineteenth century, the community men themselves began to agitate for changes in marriage and property relations. In Punjab, customary laws of landholding 'tribes' were clearly privileged over the different textual traditions of Hindus, Muslims, and Sikhs. Similarly, the version of Shariati law—derived from a twelfth-century Arabic text, the Hedaya—that was made the paradigmatic Islamic law in the country provided no space for different marriage practices among Muslim communities like the Khojas, the Momins, and the Mapillas. It has often been said that the newly codified colonial laws stamped out customary variations and pluralities and froze the legal system. What emerged, rather, was a combination of centralization with sharpened distinctions, not a single uni-form pattern.

The legal framework, thus, set limits to the reformist enterprise. Reformers had to invent supple stratagems to bypass or manipulate the boundaries of the law, and so did the orthodoxy. It is pointless, as has often been done, to condemn the reformers for constantly appealing to old texts instead of going beyond them. What we find, instead, is a recurrent tension and play over varied texts, plural interpretations, and the invocation of custom. Instead of a permanent closure, therefore, there were repeated contestations within the realm of the various personal laws, and they never completely settled into a particular mould. By the mid-nineteenth century, for instance, Khoja and Memon marriage practices came to be recognized as a subdivision within Islamic law. Low-caste Hindu widows challenged inheritance regulations under the law of 1856 in the name of plural caste custom. In the interests of stable revenue flow and the quality of recruits from Punjabi Jat landholding communities into the British Indian Army, widows in Punjab were not allowed to marry outside the matrimonial family and were often coerced into levirate marriages even when they would have wanted to retain their widowhood with some property inheritance rights.

This, again, takes us into the problems of codification of scriptural citations and of customary usages, of judicial interpretations under the guidance of Brahman pandits and maulavis officially appointed by courts, and of the variety of contentious inter-pretations that would, eventually, alter the legal-judicial parameters that had been set initially. It should also lead us to a consideration of who exactly manned the courts and the legislatures: what happened when Indians finally pierced these preserves of colonial governance.

Finally, even apart from the invocation of the few remarkable women reformers that there were—like Pandita Ramabai—the theme of social reforms should take us into the zone of women's own intervention in the public sphere.[3] It is generally argued that male nationalists separated the two domains, public and private, into male and female spheres, respectively, achieving a resolution regarding the distribution by allotting the home to the woman and the world to the man with a seeming but counterfeit equity.[4] Actually, women—however few and exceptional—did begin to shape public opinion by writing about their lifeworlds even from within the domestic seclusion. Educated at home by fathers or husbands, and benefiting from the growth of print culture and vernacular prose that made writing easier for them, they published their views on women's entitlements, or the lack thereof, often with remarkable criticality. We also have the instance of Rashsundari Debi, an upper-caste rural housewife, who very secretly and fearfully taught herself to read and write, and later in the century published an autobiography—the first such venture in the Bengali language—to recount the history of her self-earned mastery over words. Tarabai Shinde of Maharashtra disclosed the hidden world of women with passionate anger, berating even liberal reformers for failing to address some of the crucial lacks in women's lives.

What is interesting is that such writings found a popular market in the new world of print, and the corpus grew. It was evidently thought that women did possess privileged knowledge about the domestic sphere, and, since social reforms revolved so much around the home, their views were eagerly read, if not always approved of. What is also important is the way in which the pattern of their concerns would be allied to, yet somewhat dislocated from, the major preoccupations of male reformers. By and large, male reformers addressed issues of marriage and widowhood, whereas a lot of women writers talked about the pain of premature patrilocality, of the need to acquire an education so that they could be independent of male intellectual tutelage, of the oppressively insensitive relatives that child brides found in their new matrimonial homes. Focusing on these figures—who do not constitute front-ranking reformers—we enter into the details of the domestic sphere and of women's experiences. We are also introduced to a new social category that was a crucial sign of modern times: that of the woman writer.

By the turn of the century, and precisely around the time when the male nationalist resolution into the 'home' as distinct from the 'world' was reaching its zenith with the rise of Extremist nationalism, women were doing even more unusual things. They attended schools which began to develop in the metropolitan cities from the mid-nineteenth century, and which took them away from the domestic confines and the control of kinship networks, giving them a public identity beyond the familial. They were also admitted into colleges and universities, receiving degrees in the sciences and arts, much earlier than English women were allowed those in Britain. Some of them went abroad for medical training and a few of them took up employment as teachers and doctors. Of course, they were fortunate to have exceptionally supportive families and they were blessed with class privilege. The vast majority of girls—like their male counterparts—were deprived of literacy because of dire poverty. At the same time, these upper- and middle-class women would earlier have been the most closely guarded of people, repositories of lineage honour, specially obliged to faithfully observe orthodox prescriptions of conduct. The new paradigm of female behaviour not only breached brahmanical and sharif lifeworlds. However modestly, it created an alternative trajectory of social respectability for women of lower castes and classes who often tended to emulate the behaviour of their social superiors—when they could afford it at all.

In the early decades of the twentieth century, their numbers had multiplied to the point when they set up networks among themselves. Gradually, women emerged as leaders in social reform, banding together, writing and petitioning for better health and childcare facilities, female education and maternal benefits, improved marriage and inheritance laws, suffrage. The trajectory of social reforms thus blends into the new world of women's political activism.

So we find that the hoary theme of social reforms takes us into entirely new domains which, in their turn, get reconfigured through their association with reforms. We enter into older prescriptive texts and schools of law and the regime of gender discipline that they prescribed. We consider the variations that caste practices would have introduced into the textual domain. We turn to new modes of public argument and their presentation in literary, journalistic, and performative genres: and into the spheres of legislatures and courts, of lawmaking and judicial disputes. And finally we move away to take a broad look at the new thrusts that develop into thinking, arguing, writing, and relating to the state. In other words, we revision colonialism and modernity in the light of the broad discussion of social reforms.

II

It is surprising that textbook presentations of social reform have not changed much over the years. Outside the classroom, a number of very significant historiographical shifts and debates have actually changed the nature of the field. We used to have an old, positive teleology about the nature of Indian modernity deriving predominantly from social reforms: their intention and their impact. Concerned with beating the West at its own game, the historian Jadunath Sarkar had proclaimed in the 1940s that Indians enjoyed a Renaissance far nobler than anything that had happened in Europe, for the Indian version was inflected by deep moral concern and was hence far more than a mere aesthetic efflorescence. The Marxist historian S.C. Sarkar traced back impulses of social and political freedom to nineteenth-century social-reform movements, which unfolded steadily into national emancipation and promised to eventuate into socialism.[5] Till the 1960s, when a new corpus of histories of the nationalist movement bloomed—largely as a reaction against the Cambridge School denigrations of nationalism—social reforms were a central axis of historical writings, especially in Bengal, supposedly the nerve centre of the reform movements.

In the early 1970s, largely in the light of contentions with the Cambridge School, and motivated by fresh and urgent critiques of colonial rule and of the 'development of underdevelopment' in intellectual and social life that imperialism inflicted, a new group of leftist historians turned to a review of social reform. They found much to dispute with: the elite subject position of reformers appeared significant, along with their compromises with colonialism, their investment of hope in its liberal promises. The distance of reformers from popular, low-caste religious movements with composite cultural styles and critiques of religious establishments was seen as crucially limiting their agenda and causing a severe social restriction of its reach among common people. Finally, the colonial context that reformers had to work within was underlined, along with the way its logic inverted the liberal possibilities that reform could amass in the imperial metropolis.[6] In the 1980s, a new and more final critique was added. Not only did the colonial context limit the social acceptance or even the content of the reformist agenda, but the endeavour was doomed in a more profound way. Had it fully succeeded, it would only have consolidated imperial mastery over Indians, since every modern enterprise for change and progress was suffused with Western knowledge forms and Enlightenment influence.[7]

In the late 1980s, finally, a feminist survey of reforms was initiated, partly under the influence of these postcolonial theories, and partly deriving from certain notions within feminist critiques of modernity. The new approach argued that modern notions of gender rights in the public domain were premised on a public–private split whereby private disempowerment and the subordination of women were masked and reinforced by the bestowal of public rights. More influential, however, was the Marxist–feminist influence, reworked in the Indian colonial context. It was argued that colonial rule introduced a capitalist regime into India and produced a modern but dependent bourgeoisie. This class recast its women and its gender practices to align itself more closely with the domesticity of the colonial masters and the ways of modern capitalists. A new form of patriarchy thus evolved which provided the rationale for reforms, not seriously questioning, but merely 'recasting', male domination.[8]

There is much truth in the new negative teleology of reforms—as there was in the older positive teleology. Certainly, the reforms were the first clear signs of guilty and self-critical introspection by a privileged, male, upper-caste, middle-class intelligentsia, compromised with colonial governance and yet convinced that the present order was not a just one, even when it benefited them. If they took no political risks, as later nationalists would, they took huge and painful social risks. Made outcaste by their families, kin groups, and community, threatened by an outraged orthodoxy, they often watched reformist gains peter out in the face of social ostracism and hostility, even when they had been enacted as state laws. We can map a trajectory of broadening social and political criticism, if not social change, from the time of reforms. If not directly connected with or created by the reforms, and even when contradicted by the class, caste, and political limits of the early reformers, there were complex, parallel, interanimating movements for rights: for self-determination against colonialism, for social justice for low castes, for the human rights of the labouring poor.

At the same time, the later critics of reform pointed out crucial and valid limits, both in reformist understanding and in their historical context. The criticism enriches our understanding of modernity as a complex and contradictory formation, not a linear model of steady progress.

Where the Left, postcolonial, and early feminist versions converge is over two shared absences in all three discourses. None of them has cleared any space for women's investment, agency or political activism in the reform agenda. It has, in fact, been suggested that nationalism imposed a closure on the 'women's question' by dividing up the world into female/home and male/world domains. However, a growing volume of research indicates that, increasingly, women assumed initiatives in leading reforms, as well as in forcing openings into the male and public sphere of politics of all sorts.

The other absence relates to a virtual ignoring of the world of the orthodoxy which exerted decisive influence on gender relations throughout the colonial era. Reforms inevitably ran into an impossible impasse, since orthodoxy ruled the social world. Reforms, when refigured in the light of orthodox discourses and discipline, begin to look very different from the timid, pallid and imitative agenda they are often made out to be.

Apart from a few significant works, there is a similar crucial absence of historical writing on the Hindu revivalism of the late nineteenth century.[9] A form of cultural nationalism, revivalism glorified older, pristine Hindu traditions uncritically and chauvinistically, attributing existing abuses to 'Muslim misrule' or to British misunderstanding. It would accept no colonial legislative intervention in Hindu gender practices. At the same time, movements with strong revivalist leanings did carry out certain reforms. The Arya Samaj, notably, espoused many of the reformist measures, not as legal change but as change effected within and by the new community of Aryas: widow remarriage, female education, a higher age of marriage. It had moreover to strenuously argue on behalf of such changes in the face of a rejuvenated North Indian orthodoxy embodied in the Sanatanist movement for a rigidly brahmanical gender and caste discipline. Why then do we distinguish revivalist from liberal reformers?

Many liberal reformers too, in order to gain social acceptability, had justified reforms as part of an older and more authentic scriptural tradition, reassuring the state that no genuine religious norm was being violated. In so far as they still asked for legal change, however, they sought to provide the woman with a legal personhood, with legal rights. Revivalists, on the other hand, offered the same kinds of changes as coming from the hands of male community leaders and the scriptures. The woman, recipient of social change, did not relate to the change as a right-holder. Moreover, the basis for revivalist change was quite different from that of liberal reform. It did not talk much about the sexual double standards that forbade female education or widow remarriage. It did not refer to the sexual and intellectual needs of the woman. It talked, rather, of the need to populate the community and to educate the girl child properly at home. The entire discourse gradually came to be framed within antagonism and competition *vis-à-vis* other Indian religious communities. In the Sikh reformist movements, too, women were encouraged to educate themselves and take a more active part in community life—not in the name of their own needs and rights but in order to invigorate the inevitably male-dominated community.

The last decades of the nineteenth century saw a political shift from Moderate nationalism, which criticized colonial policies but which asked for reforms and improvements within the existing framework of governance; this shifted to more strident and militant nationalist critiques. It often relied on revivalist Hinduism, and resisted social reform as well as any changes through interventions by the alien state. Traditional women came to be glorified as the last refuge of a threatened indigenous culture. Revivalism and a more militant nationalism thus fed on each other. Tilak, who had supported revivalists in their opposition to the Age of Consent Act of 1891, forced a split between the Congress and the National Social Conference in 1895 by disrupting the earlier practice of the two organizations holding conferences in the same physical space.

With the growth of the popular politics of the Gandhian Congress and mass movements under the leadership of radical men and women like Nehru, Subhas Bose, and Sarojini Naidu, the intimate interdependence between cultural nationalism and militant political nationalism waned. Gandhi himself was opposed to the practice of child marriage and accepted women's decision to enter Congress movements. Women acquired an equal place in all forms of struggle and women from all social strata joined such movements. Bose encouraged the formation of women's brigades within the Congress and even recruited women soldiers for his Azad Hind Fauj. Nehru promised universal franchise after Independence. Women's organizations, such as the All India Women's Conference—worked in a close relationship with the Congress movement. In the transformed political environment, Indian legislators in the Assembly moved a resolution against child marriage and, in 1929, the Child Marriage Restraint Act was passed without any great difficulty: a significant change from the anti-Age of Consent agitation only thirty years earlier, when a curtailment of premature conjugal cohabitation was seen as a destruction of faith and nation. The new legislative departure was a conjoined effect of the power of women's organization, a more liberal and activist Congress leadership, and the embarrassment and anger caused by a very racist account of Indian marriage practices by the American journalist Katherine Mayo. Significantly, the anger now led to reform initiated by nationalist Indians, not social conservatives.

The nineteenth century had been especially clamorous about Hindu social reforms. The main themes that characterized Hindu social reforms did not constitute problems within Muslim personal laws. These did not demand widow immolation and contained no strictures against widow remarriage. In fact, Faraizi reformers of the mid-nineteenth century attributed the prevalence of such norms among Muslims to Hindu influence, and encouraged Muslims to popularize widow remarriage. Similarly, the opening up of female education in Urdu in North India was undertaken largely to integrate women in seclusion with authentic Islamic teachings and to eradicate female rites and customs that Muslims shared with Hindus. Effects, however, outran original intentions, and, by the turn of the century, Muslim women in North and East India emerged as noted reformers in their own rights, introducing girls' schools, and criticizing absolute female seclusion. Later, a curious and ironic political development enabled further reforms. In the 1930s, as communalism gained ground, the Muslim League sought an entry into Punjab, then governed by the Unionist Party, by espousing scriptural female inheritance rights which, in Punjab, had been undermined in the name of 'tribal custom' among landholders (Hindu, Muslim. and Sikh), which denied land inheritance rights to women. Similar communal motives, once again, granted the right to initiate divorce to Muslim women in 1939. Faced with the threat of female apostasy, religious leaders chose to adopt elements from the Maliki School of Islamic law which was not otherwise practised in India. Communalism created competitive mobilization whereby women emerged as a significant constituency.

Recent historical work offers increasingly wide and complex perspectives, working into their analyses women's agency and the possibilities and constraints that the legal framework simultaneously held. Reforms are reviewed in the light of political change, class and labour patterns, caste movements, and literary and religious processes within the public sphere. Whereas the earlier focus was exclusively on Hindus, the new explorations are undertaken into gender relations and ideologies among all Indian religious communities. So, this is a felicitous moment to reopen discussion of social reforms in the area of gender relations.

We intend to follow up this collection with a subsequent volume on caste and social movements. For that reason, major subordinate-caste and Dalit reformers like Phule, Periyar, and Ambedkar find little or no place in the present work, which remains deliberately centred on middle-class reform. Our focus is on debates and movements around reform, and readers will not find here a comprehensive account of the broader dimensions of gender relationships, women's conditions, and sexuality. Our intention has been for the present to publish a selection of research articles, along with some excerpts from contemporary sources. The Introduction has been kept to a bare minimum to allow space for as large a volume on the subject as seemed possible.

III

The volume consists of research papers (Part A), and excerpts from contemporary documents (Part B).

Part A begins with two essays on widow immolation. Anand Yang provides a thick description and analysis of the practice of sati on the eve of the legal ban in 1829, on the basis of a careful study of the sources. This is followed by one of Lata Mani's very influential, if controversial, contributions, marked by an emphasis on certain basic similarities underlying the premises of British officials, Indian reformers, and Conservatives alike. For all of them, she suggests, the condition of women provided the site, or occasion, for developing a new stress on the textual basis of Hindu religious notions and practices.[10] Readers at this point have been given an opportunity to have a look at some excerpts from Rammohan's tracts against sati (Part B 1). It will be seen that one of these tracts moves away in conclusion from a purely textual exigesis to a powerful, humanistic critique of the everyday conditions of women in Hindu society, utterly remarkable for its times.

The extract by Geraldine Forbes which is placed next is about the education of women, and its far-reaching, and sometimes unexpected, consequences. It includes three case studies of pioneer educationists, two of them women, all of whom, unlike many others, worked independently of religious reform organizations.

This is followed by several essays on the thorny issue of widow marriage, possibly the central theme in the history of reform through much of the nineteenth century. Lucy Carroll studies the way in which the law permitting widow marriage unwittingly restricted the already existing rights to property of widows who remarried among certain subordinate castes, for whom there was no taboo on such unions. It provides data about alternative paths followed subsequently by law courts in various provinces while adjudicating the issue.

Two essays then focus on Vidyasagar and his times. Sekhar Bandopadhyay highlights the strength of orthodox opposition to Vidyasagar's efforts, a dimension which, as already mentioned, has generally been little studied in the historical literature on social reform. Sumit Sarkar attempts a detailed analysis of Vidyasagar's position within Brahmanical society and his reformist endeavours. Prem Chowdhry, like Carroll, focuses upon regional distinctions, where a peculiarly restricted kind of widow marriage was actually encouraged in the Punjab region by officials and menfolk alike, coercing women into levirate practices.

We then come to an essay woven around the outstanding figure of Pandita Ramabai. Gauri Viswanathan provides a sensitive account of the complexities of religious conversion and how these could at times lead to a certain embattled agency for a woman in the interstices between two orthodoxies.

With Chowdhry's essay on the Haryana region (then part of Punjab) and the excerpt about Ramabai, the volume has moved out from its earlier primary focus on Bengal. This widened spatial perspective continues through Madhu Kishwar's study of the specific features of Arya reformism, and John and Karen Leonard's evaluation of the leading Andhra reformer Viresalingam.

We are coming now towards the end of the nineteenth century, when the Age of Consent issue revealed a widespread shift in moods in a revivalist, anti-reform direction. Two essays deal with this controversy. Tanika Sarkar highlights the linkages between the Age of Consent furore and the emergence of an aggressive cultural nationalism which defined itself, from the perspective of women, as a realm of unfreedom rather than of liberty. Padma Anagol looks at the same theme from the perspective of the Bombay Presidency, and, like Carroll and Tanika Sarkar, highlights the importance of judicial archives in the study of social reform.

Five essays that follow move beyond the boundaries of Hindu society. Extracts from Kenneth Jones's survey of socio-religious movements look briefly at a range of late-nineteenth-century movements among Sikhs: the reformist Nirankaris and Namdharis, the Dev Samaj, and the Singh Sabha, the latter similar to the Aryas in its incorporation of reform within a basic emphasis on the purity and distinct identity of Sikhs. This is followed by four papers on Muslim social reform—a largely neglected subject. Gregory Kozlovski looks at rights to property of Muslim women under colonial Anglo-Muslim law. C.M. Naim examines the kind of values being sought to be inculcated among Muslim women through Urdu novels which combined encouragement of education and reading habits with correct morality. Gail Minault probes the rebellious figure of Sayyid Mumtaz Ali (editor of *Tahzib ur-Niswan*), the associate of Sayyid Ahmad Khan who did not share the Aligarh movement founder's conservatism on women's issues. The last essay in this group, by Faisal Devji, attempts an analysis of late-nineteenth-century Muslim movements for women's reform in terms of a *sharif* discourse aimed at setting up firm spatial boundaries around the community.

Four ensuing essays move to new regions and social spaces. Two articles on the South, by S. Anandhi and G. Arunima, deal with the women's question as foregrounded by the early phase of the Dravidian movement in Tamilnadu, and the marked specificities of the situation in Kerala, where the existence of matriliny among the Nairs and the prevalence of the custom of *sambandham* sexual relations meant that reform concentrated on the establishment, rather than the reform, of the patrilineal conjugal family. Virginius Xaxa offers a survey of gender relations among *adivasi* groups in Central and North East India, entered through a review of the historiography around that subject. The article by Saroj Parratt and John Parratt is a case study of a women's movement in the 1940s in Manipur, a region remarkable, down to present times, for the level of initiative and militancy displayed by women in popular movements for freedom and human rights.

Our selection has focused primarily on the nineteenth century, in that way sticking to the conventional stress in the literature so far. But Xaxa and the Parratts have already taken us into the twentieth, and indeed to some extent postcolonial times, and this temporal shift continues through the concluding two articles of Part A. Both focus upon legislative changes and their settings. Mrinalini Sinha looks at the contexts of the 1929 Sarda Act raising the minimum age for marriage. Reba Som examines parliamentary debates in the early postcolonial years and offers a critical review of the legislation that eventually became the present code of Hindu marriage and succession law, a significant advance shot through with the compromises that Nehru eventually agreed to make.

Part B comprises extracts from historical documents. Spatial constraints, along with the obvious problem of language, have made us restrict the number. The most interesting writings, particularly by women, were generally in the vernaculars, and the limits of time and absence of translation facilities have compelled a restriction to articles already in English translation. Within these constraints, and keeping in mind that there is a general, but quite misleading, common sense that women's reform in the nineteenth century consisted entirely of efforts by philanthropically motivated men, we have tried to include articles by reformist women rather than men: three of the extracts, therefore, are by women.

The first, from Rammohan's tracts on *sati*, is followed by passages from a remarkable pamphlet written in the early 1860s in Bengali, by Kailashbasini Devi. This illustrates the point made in the Introduction that women's writings advocating reform were often distinctive in seeking to cover a much wider area of the everyday lives of women and did not rest content with advocating marriage practices reformed through legislation. The next extract is from a work by a much better-known woman polemicist, Tarabai Shinde's *Stripurusha Tulana*. Then there are excerpts from the premier late-nineteenth-century reformer of western India, Mahadev Govind Ranade, who made the Indian Social Conference the main space for his endeavours, seeking to raise the reform question from the provincial to an all-Indian platform. The volume ends with a remarkable essay by Begum Rokeya, 'Nari-puja', 'The Worship of Woman', brilliantly ridiculing the widespread assumption that women have been held in high honour in traditional Hindu and Muslim society through the insistence on seclusion.

Notes

1. The dualism here was neatly expressed by the *Amrita Bazaar Patrika* of 9 December 1869: 'madhyabitta people are always considered the most useful group in any society. Our country's welfare depends to a large extent on this class. If there is ever to be a social or any other revolution in this country, it will be by the middle class. All the beneficial institutions or activities that we see in our country today have been started by this class . . . The livelihood of middle-class people comes from landed property and the services. Middle-class people are often "*gantidars*" [A form of intermediate tenures common in the central Bengal region from which the newspaper was then being published].'

2. Recent research highlighting distinctions within the middle class includes Veena Naregal, *Language Politics, Elites, and the Public Sphere* (Delhi: Permanent Black, 2001); Sumit Sarkar, 'Renaissance and Kaliyuga: Time, Myth and History in Colonial Bengal', in *Writing Social History* (Delhi: Oxford University Press, 1997); Tanika Sarkar, *Hindu Wife, Hindu Nation* (Delhi: Permanent Black, 2001), chapters 1, 2; Tithi Bhattacharya, *The Sentinels of Culture: Class, Education and the Colonial Intellectual in Bengal* (Delhi: Oxford University Press, 2005);

Judith Walsh, *Domesticity in Colonial India: What Woman Learned When Men Gave Her Advice* (Delhi: Oxford University Press, 2004); and Anindita Ghosh, *Power in Print: Popular Publishing and the Politics of Language and Culture in a Colonial Society* (Delhi: Oxford University Press, 2006).

3. For Maharashtra, this zone is explored in Meera Kosambi, *Crossing Thresholds: Feminist Essays in Social History* (Delhi: Permanent Black, 2007).

4. This is the very influential argument put forward by Partha Chatterjee, in his 'The Nationalist Resolution of the Woman's Question', in Kumkum Sangari and Sudesh Vaid, eds, *Recasting Women* (New Delhi: Kali for Women, 1989), and *The Nation and Its Fragments*, chapters 6, 7 (Delhi: Oxford University Press, 1994).

5. Jadunath Sarkar, *Dacca University History of Bengal* (Dacca, 1948); S.C. Sarkar, 'Notes on the Bengal Renaissance' (1946), and 'Rabindranath Tagore and the Renaissance in Bengal', reprinted in Sarkar, *Bengal Renaissance and Other Essays* (Delhi: Peoples' Publishing House, 1970).

6. See the essays of Barun De, Asok Sen, Sumit Sarkar, and Pradyumna Bhattacharya in V.C. Joshi (ed.), *Rammohan Roy and the Process of Modernization in India* (New Delhi, 1975); Asok Sen, *Iswarchandra Vidyasagar and His Elusive Milestones* (Calcutta: 1977).

7. Partha Chatterjee, *Nationalist Thought and the Colonial World: A Derivative Discourse?* (Delhi: Oxford University Press, 1986); Chatterjee, *The Nation and Its Fragments*, op. cit.

8. *Recasting Women*, op. cit., particularly its Introduction, by Kumkum Sangari and Sudesh Vaid.

9. One important exception here is Amiya P. Sen, *Hindu Revivalism in Bengal* (Delhi: Oxford University Press, 1993).

10. Lata Mani subsequently developed her argument through her contribution in *Recasting Women*, and finally in her book *Contentious Traditions: The Debate on Sati in Colonial India* (Berkeley: University of California Press, 1998).

PART A
Historical Research

1

Whose Sati?

Widow Burning in
Early-Nineteenth-Century India*

ANAND A. YANG

Intentionally interrogatory, the title of this essay emphasizes the speculative nature of my remarks regarding the phenomenon of sati. Derived from the Sanskrit term for pure or chaste (*sat*)—the very term 'sati', therefore, is a misnomer—sati has come to signify both the act of immolation of a wife on the funeral pyre of her husband (in some areas a widow was buried with her deceased husband or took poison) and the victim herself rather than its original meaning of a 'a virtuous woman'.[1] Generally, a woman was burnt together with her deceased husband, a practice termed *sahamarana* or *sahagamanan* (dying together with). But if concremation was not possible, such as when a husband died in a distant place or a woman's pregnancy required that she wait till after delivery, a sati conformed to the practice of *anumarana* or *anugamana*: burning with the husband's ashes or with some other memento representing him, for example, his sandals, turban, or piece of clothing.[2]

The title also has another meaning, a double trajectory: an interrogation of the historical literature on the subject and an interrogation of sati as a practice involving women of different times, places, and backgrounds. Both lines of inquiry seek to converge on the same objective: better questions *and* answers regarding the phenomenon of sati.

Hitherto, much of the literature on sati has tended to favour an institutional approach.[3] Not surprisingly, the most familiar aspect of sati is the British campaign against it culminating in the promulgation of Regulation XVII in 1829 'declaring the practice of suttee, or of burning or burying alive the widows of Hindus, illegal and punishable by the criminal courts.'[4] Viewed from this angle, the history of sati has been appropriated by some scholars to represent the beginnings of 'a deliberate policy of modernizing and westernizing Indian society', as embodied in the person and policies of Governor-General Lord Bentinck who directed the official campaign against sati, and in the emergence of a Bengal 'Renaissance' under the guiding hand of the 'Father of Modern India', Raja Rammohun Roy, who acted as the Indian architect of this and other social reforms.[5]

The legislative prohibition of sati has also 'become a founding moment in the history of women in modern India.' To continue in the words of this scholar,

*From *Journal of Women's History*, vol. I, no. 2 (Fall 1989): 8–33.

colonial rule, with its moral civilizing claims, is said to have provided the contexts for a thoroughgoing re-evaluation of Indian 'tradition' along lines more consonant with the 'modern' economy and society believed to have been the consequence of India's incorporation into the capitalist world system. In other words, even the most anti-imperialist amongst us has felt forced to acknowledge the 'positive' consequences of colonial rule for certain aspects of women's lives, if not in terms of actual practice, at least at the level of ideas about 'women's rights'.[6]

But as Lata Mani's deconstruction of the colonial discourse on sati reveals, women were neither the subjects nor the object of this discourse, 'but rather the grounds of the discourse on *sati*. . . . For the British, rescuing women becomes part of the civilizing mission. For the indigenous elite, protection of their status or its reform becomes an urgent necessity, in terms of the honor of the collective—religious or national.'[7]

For the political and ideological context in which the government campaign for social reforms was waged, whether focusing on sati, infanticide, *thagi* (ritual murder), or human sacrifice, aimed at entitling the British with the right to proclaim the superiority of their own values, and ultimately, to justify their right to rule. Only they could usher in the morality they found wanting in the indigenous civilization. Consider the tenor of the following government pronouncement on sati:

> Of the rite itself, of its horror and abomination not a word need be said. Every rational and civilized being must feel anxious for the termination of a practice so abhorrent from humanity. . . . But to the Christian and to the Englishman, who by tolerating sanctions, and by sanctioning incurs before God the responsibility of this inhuman and impious sacrifice not of one, but of thousands of victims, these feelings of anxiety must be and ought to be extreme. The whole and sole justification is state necessity—that is, the security of the British empire, and even that justification, would be, if at all, still very incomplete, if upon the continuance of the British rule did not entirely depend the future happiness and improvement of the numerous population of this eastern world.[8]

In part, the prevailing modes of inquiry have fashioned their own blinders because they have not until recently sought to penetrate the purdah of rhetoric imposed on sati, whether that made out of the fabric of discourse woven from the religious ideology sanctioning its practice, or that stitched together from the doctrines of policy makers and reformers seeking its abolition. In part, the peculiar emphases in the literature on sati reflect the predominant orientation of South Asian studies towards conventional political history rather than the 'new' social history.[9]

No wonder the history of sati is still being written—or perhaps better stated, being revised. And the fact that its full reconstruction is only now being attempted reflects not only the biases and limitations of the historical record but also of historians. Enough has been uncovered by the new scholarship to establish, as does the discussion below of sati as 'an invented and reinvented tradition', that the practice can no longer be merely ascribed to and explained away as a 'tradition' rooted in an immemorial past. On the contrary, recent scholarship has treated it more as an 'invented tradition' whose origins can be roughly dated and whose construction, institution, and development can be traced over historical time.

Another perspective, largely absent in the literature, is the focus of the human face of sati: neither the identities of those who committed sati, nor their reasons for seeking 'virtue' in death has received much attention. A notable exception—although raising more questions than providing answers—is the work of Ashis Nandy which unequivocally states that not only did the incidence of sati rise sharply in the late eighteenth century because of the effects of the British presence on certain sectors of Bengali society but also that the considerable surge can be traced to the upper-caste Bengali gentry (*bhadralok*) who resorted to sati as a means of compensating for the social and cultural price they paid for abiding by the new rules established by the British system rather than the traditionally prescribed norms. According to this psychocultural interpretation, 'the rite had anxiety-binding functions in groups rendered psychologically marginal by their exposure to western impact. These groups had come under pressure to demonstrate . . . their ritual purity and allegiance to traditional high culture. To many of them sati became an important proof of their conformity to older norms at a time when these norms had become shaky within.'[10]

This essay will attempt to identify the faces of sati victims by highlighting their social and economic conditions and circumstances. Such a characterization intends to examine the practice of sati as part of the fabric of the local society in which the widows lived, and such a portrait seeks to draw us closer to the subjects themselves and their subjectivity in playing out their lives as satis. Because of limitations of data, however, a complete portrait of the victims is not possible; the best close-up of these otherwise invisible women can only put faces on them, faces whose features can be partially filled in by considering their act as an 'option' bound by economic, social, and religious constraints.[11] The specific reasons for their sacrifice, however, cannot be fully determined from their perspective because their voices have not been preserved in historical documents; in fact, they appear largely as mute objects even in the most detailed of sources—colonial records of the early nineteenth century. Indeed, even their names have been 'grotesquely mistranscribed'. To continue in the words of Gayatri C. Spivak, 'one never encounters the testimony of the women's voice-consciousness. Such a testimony would not be ideology-transcendent or "fully" subjective, of course; but it would have constituted the ingredients for producing a counter sentence. As one goes [through] the records of the East India Company, one cannot put together a "voice".'[12]

In order to develop a more sharply focused portrait, this essay will rely on a local-level perspective based on data from the Bengal Presidency, an area which returned the highest reported cases of sati in British India. An extensive territory stretching across northeastern and northern India, this area (then encompassing the present-day Indian states of West Bengal, Bihar, Orissa, Uttar Pradesh [UP], and the new nation of Bangladesh) also represented a diversity of local contexts because it included several distinct cultural, linguistic, historical, and structural regions. Most studies regarding sati in Bengal have concentrated their attention on Bengal proper, particularly the area focusing on the metropolitan centre of Calcutta—Calcutta Division reported the highest number of satis in the Presidency. This essay, however, will also consider the local contexts of sati in the Gangetic plain area in the western peripheries of the Presidency, the Bhojpur-speaking region. In the Bhojpur districts of Gorakhpur and Ghazipur in UP, Saran and Shahabad in Bihar, and, to a lesser extent, in the premier city of the region, Banaras, the incidence of sati reached such significant proportions that only in Calcutta Division were there a greater number of cases.[13]

The Documentary Basis of Sati

Data exist to compile a portrait, albeit incomplete, of the many faces of sati in the early nineteenth century. As Bayly notes, 'the British obsession with sati was boundless. Thousands of pages of Parliamentary papers were given up to 4,000 immolations while the mortality of millions from disease and starvation was only mentioned incidentally.'[14] But these accounts 'cannot be read as photographic representations of reality' because they reflected the 'anxieties of the new rulers as much as of a practice of the people . . . ruled'.[15]

The documentary basis for this essay is the data collected annually on sati in British India prior to its prohibition in 1829. Drawn from local-level police records, much of the information for the period between 1815 and 1829 was compiled into parliamentary papers for the scrutiny of the authorities in England. District judicial and police records, were they to exist in their entirety, of course, would offer the most comprehensive official inventory of sati cases. Eyewitness accounts of sati can be found both in official reports and in contemporary memoirs and travelogues.

To track the growing British interest in documenting the phenomenon of sati is not only to comprehend the biases of the source materials but also to see the gradual development of a policy. From Poona in western India, from Banaras, and from Shahabad, in 1787, 1788 and 1789, respectively, came the first official reports of widow burning.[16] In response to the Shahabad administrator who had informed the authorities of his intervention in a sati case because he had mistakenly thought that the practice had been disallowed in the Calcutta area, the government spelled out its initial position on sati. Although approving his actions, the government directed him, in future, to 'exert all his private influence to dissuade', but not 'to prevent the observance of it by coercive measures, or by any exertion of his official powers'.[17]

Because official documentation was only kept if a sati raised questions relating to government policy and procedure, or to other matters requiring administrative attention,[18] systematic data do not exist for the early years of British rule although some local officials kept records of incidents they encountered in the course of their administrative rounds. Some sati reports also appeared in other guises. For instance, an 1801 account of a 'desperate affray' involving several hundred armed men in Shahabad, although filed as a record of a 'heinous crime', reports not only of the death of 16 men in the fighting but the subsequent satis of four widows.[19]

Sati surfaced again as an issue in 1803–4 when the missionary William Carey produced reports documenting the incidence of sati in the Calcutta area. Although appalled by the missionary accounts, and eager to prohibit the practice, Governor-General Lord Wellesley deferred taking decisive action in 1805 by turning the matter over for the consideration of the legal authorities.[20]

Until the promulgation of Regulation XVII of 1829, the main principles of the official policy on sati emanated from a directive issued by the Nizamat Adalat (head criminal court) in 1805. In providing the 'guidance' sought by a district magistrate who had rescued a 12-year-old girl from burning with her deceased husband, the

Nizamat Adalat refused to outlaw sati on the grounds that such a step was 'impracticable at the present time' and inconsistent 'with the principle invariably observed by the British government, of manifesting every possible indulgence to the religious opinions and prejudices of the natives'. This court also expressed concern about stirring up 'alarm and dissatisfaction in the minds of the Hindoo inhabitants of these provinces'.[21] Nevertheless, it asked judicial officials to secure advance notice of the occurrence of a sati, *then* to depute police officers to proceed personally to the site of the burning in order to ensure that the rite was performed voluntarily and not under the influence of intoxicants or drugs, and to establish that the 'youth' or the 'state of pregnancy' of a widow did not violate the norms of 'tradition'.[22]

In enacting these procedures, however, the government invariably played its hand cautiously, consulting with its Hindu pandits before setting up any rules regulating sati. Thus, the parameters of a 'legal' sati were drawn with the assistance of Pandit 'Ghunesham Surmono' who informed the court: 'Every woman of the four cast[e]s (brahmin, khetry, bues, and soodur) is permitted to burn herself with the body of her husband. . . . No woman having infant children, or being in a state of pregnancy, uncleanness, or under the age of puberty is permitted to burn with her husband; with the following exception, namely, that if a woman having infant children can provide for their support, through the means of another person, she is permitted to burn.'[23]

The issue of sati returned to the political limelight in 1812 when a local administrator sought instructions on 'whether a magistrate ought to take any and what steps to prevent Hindoo females from sacrificing themselves on the funeral piles of their husbands'.[24] The Nizamat Adalat's rejoinder was to revive its 1805 statement—largely a dead letter until then—to redraft the earlier instructions into 'Directions to be issued by Magistrates to the Police Daroghas', and to insert an additional proviso into the Draft specifying 16 years as the age of puberty.[25] The government also took this opportunity to remind local officials of its earlier orders enjoining them to gather information on satis occurring in their jurisdictions.

From a statistical and documentary viewpoint, systematic records begin in 1815 when annual reports on satis indicated name (of widow), age, caste, name and caste of husband, date of burning, name of police jurisdiction, and in a separate column entitled 'Remarks', 'any particular circumstances in the report of the police officers, which may appear to deserve notice'.[26] The 'Remarks' column allowed local officials to note whether or not a sati was legal by government's definition. Beginning in 1821, information was also gathered on the kind of sati committed: sahamarana or anumarana. The purpose behind this directive was to ensure that the customary and legal prohibition (first enacted in 1817) against Brahmin widows committing sati by anumarana was being enforced. Prior to the outright ban in 1829 the British strategy was to restrict the practice by tightening up the definition of a 'legal' sati—a definition for which they invariably sought and received the sanction of their 'authoritative' Indian advisers. In 1821 information on the economic backgrounds of the deceased husband was also collected; by 1824 data on husbands became a regular feature of sati reports.[27]

After the prohibition of sati in 1829, no doubt its practice did not fall into disuse entirely, although government vigilance and enforcement of severe punishments for offenders must have sharply reduced the number. Cases of sati also tapered off dramatically because the official ban on it—notwithstanding the fact that the implementation of legal sanctions was entrusted to a weak administrative infrastructure—proved to be enough of a blow to shake the foundations of an institution that enjoyed greater support in the spirit than in the actual practice; the number of widows who resorted to immolation never amounted to a sizeable proportion of the population. Furthermore, the attack on sati was launched with the active cooperation of Indian reformers. Thus, in the initial years after its prohibition, as police and crime reports indicate, the numbers were quickly down to only one or two in districts where there had formerly been considerably more.[28]

Sati: An Invented and Reinvented Tradition[29]

The Vedas, the religious hymns constituting the earliest literature of the Aryans who arrived in India in the centuries after 1700 BC, reveal no evidence of sati. The Rig Veda, however, refers to an act, appropriately termed a 'mimetic ceremony' where a 'widow lay on her husband's funeral pyre before it was lit but was raised from it by a male relative of her dead husband'.[30] A later, and probably deliberate, mistranslation (perhaps in the sixteenth century) was made in order to attain 'Vedic sanction for the act [of sati] by changing the word *agre*, to go forth into *agneh*, to the fire, in the specific verse.'[31]

That sati was not a practice in vogue in the early Vedic period is also suggested by the occurrences of widow remarriages which, apparently, were not uncommon. Vedic texts, furthermore, indicate the existence of a system of *niyoga* or levirate whereby a widow without male heirs was allowed to marry her husband's brother, an act designed to consolidate property.[32]

Nor is sati featured in the literature that developed in the wake of the Vedas, whether the Hindu expository texts stemming from the period 1,000 to 500 BC or the early Buddhist literature. Sati makes an occasional appearance in the popular religious texts of early Hinduism, the epics, but these are works that developed by continuous accretion over a thousand-year period beginning in the fifth century BC; some of the references to sati, moreover, have been attributed to later interpolations. Nor is there a clear-cut endorsement of sati in the prescriptive literature dating to the beginning of the Christian era. The codes associated with the names of Manu and Yajnavalkya, considered among the most authoritative of Hindu law books, for instance, prescribe austere and chaste lives for widows but issue no specific injunctions for them to become satis. Increasingly, however, in the first millennium AD, for instance, in the popular texts of later Hinduism, the Puranas, sati is mentioned as an option for widows. But so is a life of asceticism; other texts of this period, however, glorified sati.[33]

The 'virtue' of this practice was ostensibly defined by a religious logic that deemed a widow inauspicious for having outlived her husband—an abnormal circumstance said to have been brought about by her sinful nature in this, or a previous, life. A life of ascetic discipline could diminish the stigma with which widowhood branded her, but she was, nevertheless, considered a spiritual hazard to all around her except her own children. Closely related to this idea was the belief that an unattached woman, a woman without a husband, for instance, constituted a grave danger to her community because of the supposedly irrepressible sexual powers she possessed, a capacity which always had the potential to disrupt her ritually prescribed life of austerity. No wonder at least one writer

ancient texts don't really talk abt. sati

has considered sati 'an expression of the perceived superfluity of women who were considered unmarriageable in a social context where marriage was the only approved status for women'.[34] By becoming a sati, furthermore, a widow not only ended the threat she posed to the spiritual welfare of others but also reaped honour and merit—according to some religious texts enough to last 35 million years—for herself, her husband, and the families of her husband, her mother, and her father.[35]

The fact that sati is not featured in the earliest religious texts and is referred to infrequently in the later literature leading up to the Christian era is supported by historical information that tracks the first instance of sati only back to the fourth century BC. Such a chronology also reflects the changing status of women in Indian society. Although the characterization of the Vedic Age between 1700 and 500 BC as a 'golden age for women' is debatable, the decline in their status in the centuries thereafter is less a matter of dispute. As a recent review of the literature on women in South Asia notes, 'by 500 BC women were increasingly assigned the same low status as *sudras*, forbidden to wear the sacred thread, and excluded from the performance of sacrifice either as priests or as partners with their husbands'.[36]

But to attribute the rise of sati solely to the declining status of women—a position that eventuated ideologically in the model of a dutiful wife and of sati as the ultimate wifely act of duty—is to overstate the equation; nor does it adequately explain its uneven geographical spread. Just as sati lacked clearcut scriptural authority, so too did the paradigm of dutiful wife that represented only one construct of the feminine in Hindu ideology and, at that, one emanating from the priestly tradition of Brahmanic Hinduism. Hinduism, 'a composite of religious traditions in which diverse philosophical, sectarian, and cultic movements are loosely associated', has historically comprised two distinct ideological traditions: 'brahmanic Hinduism [that] has tended to objectify and exclude women . . . [and] nonbrahmanic Hindu traditions [that] have tended to provide for full recognition and active participation by women'.[37]

Furthermore, as Romila Thapar states, although the beginning of sati can be 'traced to the subordination of women in patriarchal society', changing 'systems of kinship and inheritance' and '[c]ontrol over female sexuality' were also factors in the rise of widow immolation. Moreover, the 'practice may have originated among societies in flux and become customary among those holding property such as the families of chiefs and kshatriyas. Once it was established as a custom associated with the kshatriyas it would continue to be so among those claiming kshatriya status as well'.[38]

Principally associated with high status and rank during its early history, particularly with families of kingly or warrior (Kshatriya) status or those aspiring for such status, sati, according to another version, became more widespread during the Muslim period when invasions and conquests precipitated its development as a means of preserving the honour of Hindu women. Its rise, in this interpretation, is therefore typically linked to 'wars of conquest and their inevitable toll on the women of the defeated groups'.[39] But evidence exists from western and southern India indicating that women were becoming satis in appreciable numbers well before the advent of Muslim rule; in some areas, the peaks in numbers were reached in the pre-Islamic period. According to one scholar, inscriptional and archaeological sources, including sati stones erected at the sites of immolation, suggest that the practice was increasing towards the end of the first and the beginning of the second millennium AD. This rise, moreover, occurred in areas characterized by internal conquests and competition, often involving traditional castes, newly emergent castes, and tribal groups. In this setting, competition for status may have made upper-caste practices such as sati more prevalent. That is, sati became valorized as a practice—a practice emphasizing the subordination of women—as groups with different conceptions regarding the status of women encountered one another. Thus, widow immolation 'may have been . . . a method of demarcating status'.[10]

The spread of sati across caste boundaries must also have been generated by Sanskritization—the process whereby lower castes aspire for higher position by emulating the 'customs, rituals, ideology, and way of life' of higher castes. Although the effect of Sanskritization is evident from the enormous range of castes who performed sati, the practice never became generalized throughout the subcontinent but was confined to certain areas: in the north, particularly to the Gangetic Valley, Punjab, and Rajasthan; in the west, to the southern Konkan region; and in the south, to Madurai and Vijayanagar.[41]

Whether its rise can be attributed to groups aspiring for Kshatriya status or of lower castes emulating the rituals of higher castes, sati clearly developed as a reinvented tradition, a tradition no longer confined to warrior widows whose husbands had died in battle. A crucial development in this regard may have been its adoption by Brahmins who, according to some religious texts, were specifically prohibited from taking up this practice.[42] Perhaps the Brahmin appropriation of this warrior practice represented yet another round in the ongoing 'inner conflict of tradition' that J.C. Heesterman regards as the 'pivot of Indian tradition': the 'irreconcilability of "brahmin" and king", who yet are dependent on each other, for the king will need the transcendent legitimation that only the brahmin can give. But the brahmin, however much he may need the king's material support, cannot enter into relations with the king, for this would involve him in the world of interdependence—a situation that would be fatal to the brahmin's transcendence.'[43] Surely, with the practice rooted in both the kingly and Brahmanical traditions, its constituency must have grown rapidly across spatial and social boundaries.

Certainly, in Bengal, where sati dates back to at least the twelfth century AD, Brahmins figured prominently among its practitioners. But from very early on, as vernacular sources indicate, it was not restricted to Brahmins, but observed by both upper and lower castes.[44] Perhaps its rise in Bengal was not unrelated to the growing reliance on marriage in the period between 1450 and 1800 as 'the way to sustain rank and the path to fame [for upper castes—Brahmins and Kayasths]'.[45] And, as the emphasis on marriage intensified, so must have the importance of sati as its structural concomitant. Not surprisingly, Brahmins took to this practice in great numbers; so did merchants and the writer caste of Kayasths who sought to emulate the ritual observances of the Brahmins. And once elevated to new heights as a status-conferring ritual, the next step was its practice by lower—artisan and entrepreneurial—castes who saw it as an avenue for attaining prestige and status in society.[46]

A practice once tied to the warrior ideal of the Kshatriya thus became a tradition appropriated by all of society. But in the process of widening its constituency, as the evidence from Bengal shows, sati emerged as a reinvented tradition. How novel the reinvented tradition was—assuming that the old tradition really was guided by a heroic ideal—is apparent from looking at sati in its 'new' context, a context in which it figures as an 'option' bound by the economic, social, and religious constraints of widowhood.[47]

Sati: Subjects and Subjectivity

Abraham Caldecott, writing in 1783, stated that had he not seen a sati with his own eyes he would 'have been apt to doubt the veracity of it, but the fact is so well established, and so many instances of the like nature have occurred . . . as leaves no doubt of the generality of the Practice all over Bengal'.[48] A few 'hard' estimates reinforce this impression of the 'generality of the Practice' for the pre-1815 period. William Carey's investigations in a 30-mile radius of Calcutta in 1803–4 showed that as many as 438 widows had committed sati over a 12-month period.[49] District records can also provide some information for the pre-1815 years, but if the numbers for Saran are any indication, these may not be reliable. For 1812, 1813, and 1814, Saran returned one, two, and five cases—a far cry from the 15 noted for 1815 when the administrative machinery was geared to the task of collecting such information. In the magistrate's words, the police did not pay attention 'to cases of this nature, and it is most probable that a small part only of those that actually took place . . . were reported.'[50] Much more consonant with later statistics is the estimate for Burdwan district that 114 cases occurred in 1811–12 and 1812–13.[51] Statistical investigations conducted in Bengal at roughly this same period reported an average of 25 satis a year for Shahabad and 13 for Gorakhpur.[52]

In the 10 years between 1815 and 1824, 6,632 cases of sati were reported for the three Presidencies of Bengal, Bombay, and Madras. Of these, 5,997 (90.4 per cent) occurred in Bengal.[53] In the 14 years between 1815 and 1828 (Table 1), a grand total of 8,134 cases of satis were reported for the Bengal Presidency. But as the data reveal, the practice was not uniformly observed across the region but predominated in specific areas. The division of Calcutta alone accounted for 5,119 cases, or almost 63 per cent of the Presidency total, followed by Banaras, Dacca, and Patna divisions in a distant second, third, and fourth position, respectively.

Further geographical breakdown of these figures shows (Table 2) that sati was practised throughout the districts of Calcutta Division, but unevenly elsewhere. In the predominantly Muslim Dacca Division in east Bengal, it was primarily confined to Dacca City, Tipperah, and Bakarganj—areas with large Hindu populations; in Banaras, the highest incidence was in Ghazipur and Gorakhpur; and in Patna Division, in Saran and Shahabad. Indeed, 90 per cent of the total cases reported for the Presidency occurred in the nine jurisdictions of Calcutta Division (which included Cuttack at this time) and the above-mentioned areas of east Bengal, UP, and Bihar.

Notwithstanding the bold arguments of Ashis Nandy, little evidence exists to suggest that a considerable surge in the incidence of sati occurred beginning in the late eighteenth century. That sati increased with the coming of the British rests on a statistical inference for which Nandy can muster little evidence other than to refer to a few contemporary observations to that effect. Not only is the pre-1815 data scanty, but even the usable 'hard numbers' are fraught with problems. Although sati was by its very nature a public art—for 'virtue' in that practice lay in part in exposing it to the gaze of a crowd—the emerging colonial government simply did not possess the administrative apparatus

Table 1: Sati Cases in Bengal Presidency, 1815–28

Division	1815	1816	1817	1818	1819	1820	1821	1822	1823	1824	1825	1826	1827	1828	Total
Calcutta*	253	289	442	544	421	370	392	328	340	373	398	324	337	308	5119
Dacca	31	24	52	58	55	51	52	45	40	40	101	65	49	47	710
Murshidabad	11	22	42	30	25	21	11	22	13	14	21	8	9	10	260
Patna†	20	29	49	57	40	42	59	70	49	42	38	43	55	55	689
Banaras	48	65	103	137	92	93	114	102	121	93	64	70	49	33	1153
Bareilly	15	13	19	13	17	20	15	16	12	10	17	8	18	10	203
Total	378	442	707	839	650	597	654	583	575	572	639	518	517	463	8134

Source: Compiled from Great Britain, Parliament, *Parliamentary Papers* (hereafter *PP*), 1821, 1823, 1824, 1825, 1826/27, 1830; Amitabha Mukhopadhyay, 'Sati as a Social Institution in Bengal,' *Bengal Past and Present* 76 (1951): 106.

*Includes the numbers for the Orissan 'districts' of Cuttack, Khurda, Puri, and Balasore, which then formed part of Calcutta Division. The totals for these districts varied from 9 in 1815 to a high of 45 in 1825.

†The tallies for Gorakhpur have been retained in the Banaras totals although that district was transferred to Patna Division in 1824.

Table 2: Sati Cases in Districts of Bengal Presidency, 1815–26

Presidency Division	1815	1816	1817	1818	1819	1820	1821	1822	1823	1824	1825	1826	Average
Burdwan	50	67	98	132	75	57	62	40	45	56	63	45	66
Hughli	72	51	112	141	115	93	95	79	81	91	104	98	94
Jessore	7	13	21	23	16	25	31	21	14	30	16	3	18
Jungle Mehals	34	39	43	61	31	18	39	24	27	16	9	11	29
Midnapur	4	11	7	22	13	12	6	16	15	22	22	15	14
Nadia	50	56	85	80	47	59	59	50	59	79	60	44	61
Suburbs of Calcutta	25	40	39	43	52	47	39	43	46	34	48	35	41
24-Parganas	2	3	20	31	39	26	33	25	21	22	26	20	22
Cuttack†	9	9	14	11	33	33	28	27	30	24	30	45	24
Dacca Division													
Dacca City	4	6	18	25	15	18	26	9	14	7	18	12	14
Tipperah	20	7	13	22	21	17	11	6	9	6	8	4	12
Bakarganj	no figures available				6	3	3	18	11	28	63	45	21
Patna Division													
Saran	12	16	25	23	10	11	15	12	7	12	15	10	14
Shahabad	4	9	14	25	17	19	39	36	30	18	20	22	21
Banaras Division													
Banaras City	13	12	16	15	18	11	12	10	18	16	17	15	14
Ghazipur	8	15	27	43	26	34	35	48	55	33	21	19	30
Gorakhpur	14	23	24	50	23	32	44	28	32	17	9	22	26

Source: Compiled from *PP, 1821, 1823, 1824, 1825, 1826/27, 1830.*

to extend far into any locality and, certainly, not to maintain a regular presence in the interior. Furthermore, with much of the personnel of the incipient Raj lodged in cities, and in a major town or two in localities where there were no cities, reporting was only as good as the administrative infrastructure. In short, the inherent biases built into the system of reporting favoured better coverage for towns than countryside, and, not surprisingly, nowhere was official representation better than in the heart of the emerging empire—Calcutta. Indeed, in some districts, away from metropolitan centres, local officials did not even make their first visit into the interior until 1815![54]

The social geography of sati (see Table 2) also indicates that the practice was not confined to the Calcutta area, but also prevailed in such districts far removed from the seat of the Presidency as Ghazipur, Gorakhpur, Saran, and Shahabad. Furthermore, to consider sati as an urban-based phenomenon centred on Calcutta ignores the sizeable territorial dimensions of Calcutta Division. Nandy's critics have rightly noted that even Raja Rammohan Roy's family village 'which may nowadays feel like "greater Calcutta" . . . is about sixty miles away as the crow flies, and before the railway age, when that distance took many hours to traverse, it was considered quite another area'.[55]

To explain the higher incidence of sati in the Calcutta area, Nandy offers a cultural analysis emphasizing that city's close integration into the British system and its urbanness, characteristics he contrasts with other parts of India where the practice was less common. Thus, he concludes that 'the rite was prevalent among passive people and not among the "bold and manly" type', an assertion which prompts him to emphasize 'the difference between the exposed easterners [Bengalis], feeling increasingly impotent ritually, and the unexposed northern and western parts of India, still mainly outside direct British rule and yet undisturbed in their traditional life style. It was also noticed by others that there had been only one instance of the wife of a dead Indian soldier of the colonial army committing sati.'[56] In elaborating on why he considers only one case of sati by a sepoy's wife 'crucial', Nandy writes:

> given that (1) traditionally sati had been associated with the so-called martial races, (2) the British Indian Army was drawn almost entirely from these races, and (3) the earlier epidemics of sati (such as the one in Rajasthan towards the end of the Mughal period and the one in South India during the decline of the Vijayanagar kingdom) had a clear kshatriya (martial or princely caste) connection. Offset these against the facts that Bengal did not have a proper kshatriya caste and that the region was marginal to mainstream Hinduism, and one is forced to conclude that the eighteenth century epidemic of sati was not a pure product of traditions and that it drew upon a different configuration of political, cultural and psychological forces.[57]

The post-1823 sati reports, which contain information on the profession of deceased husbands, however, do not support the assertion that only one dead sepoy's wife committed sati. Since the 'martial races' recruited into the Bengal Army were drawn not from the heart of the Presidency but from the Bhojpur region, it is in the data for those areas that the best prospects lie for finding cases of sati among the widows of sepoys. The information for Shahabad—a district which supplied a considerable number of men for the military—does not disappoint. Names of sepoy widows who burnt themselves appear repeatedly on its sati rosters: in 1824 Mussamut Dela, wife of Naik Tiwari, Brahmin, and M. Somerin, wife of Sahi Rai; in 1825 Nagbansi, wife of Adhir Singh, Rajput, Jethun, wife of Bissambhar Ojha, Brahmin and Hisabea, wife of Raghubans Rai,

Bhumihar Brahmin; in 1826 Musst. Fakania, Rajput, Musst. Dhupia, Rajput and Musst. Abhi Lakhi, Brahmin.[58]

Nandy may be right, however, in insisting that sati was rooted in a different tradition in the region of Bengal focusing on Calcutta. Certainly, the notion of sati in the Bhojpur region seems to have had much of a 'kshatriya connection' as evidenced not only in the roster of victims above but also in the above-mentioned account of a 'desperate affray' in Shahabad in which 16 men were killed and four widows committed sati subsequently. Consider also the place of pride given to the tradition of sati in the Choudhary family, a Patna family of Bhumihar Brahmins with a long history of military service.[59]

Some scholars have also sought to relate the high incidence of sati (and female infanticide) in Bengal to the extreme hypergamy of the higher castes (*kulinism*), the practice whereby women of high castes had to marry men of equivalent or higher status. Presumably, this practice so restricted the pool of appropriate bridegrooms that a few eligible high-caste males were able to accumulate many, often young, wives for whom the demise of their husband left no choice but for them to commit sati. The evidence regarding the geographical distribution of sati in Bengal, however, offers little conclusive proof because rates of sati were higher in the west than in the east (more in Calcutta than in Dacca Division), whereas kulinism was more predominant in the east than in the west.[60]

Another argument has been to relate the high incidence of sati to the existing system of law in Bengal, the Dayabhaga school of law. In contrast to the Mitakshara school of law, the Dayabhaga school allowed widows greater access to their deceased husbands' property for support although it did not favour their rights of inheritance. Whereas this 'might have encouraged heirs to do away with widows or to pressurize them into suicide' and may therefore explain the 'numbers of satis in Bengal by comparison with other parts of India . . . it hardly explains the great variation of incidence between the different districts and cities of Bengal'.[61]

Some correspondence can be established, however, between the incidence of sati and mortality rates: 'There is no doubt that the rite was a primitive Malthusian means of population control in famine-ridden Bengal. Previously, high mortality rates and prohibition of remarriage of widows had helped the society to limit the number of mothers to below the level of available fertile women. However, at times of scarcity, these controls became inadequate and . . . the widows at certain levels of consciousness seemed "useless" drags on resources.'[62] But if sati were 'a Malthusian form of population control, stimulated by a series of crop failures and widespread famines', as G. Morris Carstairs notes, 'it would surely have resulted in higher rates among the poorer castes, less well protected against starvation, than among the gentry.'[63]

Much more significant is the correlation between changing rates of sati and shifts in mortality rates due to epidemics. Consider especially the increase in numbers of sati during peak years of cholera epidemics: in Bengal this occurred in 1817 and 1818 when cholera had a devastating effect on mortality rates (see Table 1). The close correspondence between the geography of the epidemic and sati rates in affected districts further demonstrates this correlation. Note that the unusual rise in cases of sati in 1817 and 1818 was registered primarily in Calcutta Division—in and around Calcutta, Burdwan, Jessore, Nadia, and 24-Parganas—precisely those areas that were also the most seriously afflicted by cholera.[64] In other parts of the Presidency, too, where increases, although not on a par with those for Calcutta Division, were registered for 1817 and 1818, local officials attributed the rise 'to the mortality occasioned by the epidemic'.[65] Much the same conclusion was reached by the Banaras magistrate who plotted the rise in sati cases in his city in 1823, 1824, and 1825 with the 'extreme sickness and mortality' of those years.[66] Similarly, the noticeable increase in satis in Dacca Division in 1825, especially in Bakarganj (see Table 1), was attributed 'to the excessive mortality which occurred in the district, owing to the prevalence of cholera morbus'.[67]

According to an official report in 1824, the annual death rate in the Bengal Presidency (total population 50 million people) was one in 33, that is, approximately 1,500,000 people. A sixth of this total, or 250,000, represented the number of Hindu women who became widows. Rounding out to 600 the figure for those who burned themselves that year, the number of immolations constituted only 0.2 per cent of the overall number of widows.[68] By this calculation, the incidence of sati in Hughli, the district consistently reporting the highest number of cases in British India, added up to 1.2 per cent.[69]

Perhaps Banaras provides the best illustration of the limited incidence of sati, especially when the practice of sati is viewed against a backdrop of that city's reputation as a place to which 'large numbers of elderly people . . . [came] specifically to die . . . and so achieve immediate salvation'.[70] Thus, the Banaras magistrate noted with surprise—and in an obvious ethnocentric manner—that only 125 cases had occurred in the nine years between 1820 and 1828.

> Benares is one of the most sacred homes of Hinduism . . . in it the bigotry of the people is nurtured . . . it is peopled by the wealthiest and most scrupulous of Hindus . . . inhabited by crowds of every description of religious enthusiasts, the place where every Hindu is anxious to die, and the resort of all classes of rank of all ages, more especially those whose earthly career is drawing to its close. . . . At such a place then it would be expected the performance of this most inhuman rite would be frequent, and that its frequency would be in proportion to the peculiar sanctity of the spot, a sanctity immemorially acknowledged.[71]

The practice of sati, in short, was not only peculiar to certain regions of the subcontinent, but within those particular areas, taken up by only a small fraction of the widows. Although difficult to verify because the data say little about kinship ties between satis, this restricted scope of the rite probably indicates, as many scholars suspect, that it was a practice that must have been a tradition only in certain lineages.[72] The Choudhary family of Patna, for instance, honour and worship, 'along with their family gods', two satis, wives of one of their ancestors who 'immolated themselves on the funeral pyre at their Patna house on hearing of the death of their husband on the battlefield. . . . It is still believed that the lineage which was threatened at that time with extinction continues through their blessing.'[73]

Another aspect of the identity of sati victims in the early nineteenth century that explains the phenomenon better is their caste and economic backgrounds. Contrary to the conventional wisdom regarding the high-caste status of sati victims, a different portrait emerges from a close examination of the detailed information. Of the 575 cases reported in 1823, 234 were Brahmins (41 per cent), 35 Kshatriyas (six per cent), 14 Vaishyas (2 per cent), and 292 Sudras (51 per cent).[74]

That this configuration of nearly even representation of both high and low castes was not uncommon is also borne out by the figures for individual districts. Of the 52 victims in 24-Parganas in 1819, 20 were Brahmins, 10 Kayasthas, and two Vaidyas, and the rest comprising such low castes as Sadgope, Jogi, Kaivarta, Kansari, Suri, and Ahir (Goalla). The 141 cases enumerated for Hughli district in 1818 reveal a similar composition: other than 40 Brahmins, 26 Kayasthas, and 4 Vaidyas, the remaining 71 were of the lower castes.[75] The diversity of caste backgrounds of sati victims also shows up clearly in the details regarding the Bhojpur districts of Ghazipur, Gorakhpur, Saran, and Shahabad. While Saran's numbers include a disproportionately higher percentage of high-caste women among its satis, the figures for the other three districts conform more closely with those for the rest of the Presidency. But in Saran, too, lower-caste women followed the practice. Noticeably present among the 168 satis in that district between 1815 and 1826 are two Harijans (Untouchables): in 1816 Punbosia Chamar, the wife of Jodhi, and in 1818, Dukhni Chamar, the wife of Dohari. Such diversity in the caste composition of sati victims certainly does not authenticate Nandy's character-ization of sati as the expression of a rudderless upper-caste Bengal gentry seeking to anchor themselves in a period of flux by resorting to the 'traditional' practice of sati.

The caste backgrounds of satis in Banaras city, however, add up to a different pic-ture. An overwhelming majority were upper caste, particularly Brahmins. In 1821 all 12 satis were upper caste (11 Brahmins and one Rajput); only in 1816 and 1820 did the proportion fall below 70 per cent (66 and 63 per cent, respectively). No doubt, the caste profile for this city is skewed by the fact that people from other areas of the subcontinent converged on it to die there. Not surprisingly, then, many 'foreigners' stand out among the roster of sati victims, including such typically Bengali names as Biswas, Mukherjee, Chakravarty, Bhattacharya, and Banerjee, as well as the well-known Maratha name of Joshi and even a 'Moorleedhur', identified as a former resident of Nepal.[76]

A different light on the practice of sati is also cast by analysing the ages of its victims. Whereas many studies have tended to emphasize the young ages of widows in any given year, almost half of them were 50 and over, and two-thirds 40 years and more (see Table 4). In 1818, out of 839 cases 123, or 14.6 per cent, were 70 and over; but only 98, or 11.6 per cent, aged 25 or under. The overwhelming majority, as in other years, were 40 years and more. As the official report concluded in presenting these statistics, 'a great proportion of these acts of self-devotion have not taken place in youth, or even in the vigor of age; but a period when life, in the common course of nature, must have been near its close'.[77]

Almost every district also yields examples of women who had not only reached a ripe old age but who immolated themselves long after their husbands' demises. To draw on illustrations from Ghazipur's 1822 cases: 60-year-old Jhunia committed sati 15 years after her husband passed away; 70-year-old Karanja 40 years after her husband's death; 80-year-old Bhujagan 25 years after her husband's death; and 70-year-old Hulasi immolated herself on the funeral pyre of her son, 16 years after her husband Niamdhar Tiwari had died.[78] Equally striking are cases from other Bhojpur districts: Lagni burnt herself at the age of 90, 25 years after the death of her husband; Namao ascended the funeral pyre at the age of 80 following the absence of her husband, presumed dead, for a period of 15 years.[79]

Such characteristics of its victims suggest that sati was a form of ritual suicide[80] con-ditioned at least in part by personal considerations. The economic conditions of many widows further underscores this colouring. Data collected on satis from 1822 onwards reveal that many widows came from impoverished families. Of the 40 cases reported for Burdwan in 1822, only three or four of the deceased 'left any considerable property . . . the

Table 3: Caste Composition of Sati Victims in Bhojpur Districts, 1815–1826

	1815	1816	1817	1818	1819	1820	1821	1822	1823	1824	1825	1826
Ghazipur Upper Caste	2	7	13	19	14	17	13	16	32	25	13	13
% of total	(25)	(46)	(48)	(42)	(50)	(50)	(37)	(34)	(54)	(75)	(61)	(68)
Gorakhpur Upper Castes	8	16	14	28	14	16	24	15	18	14	7	16
% of total	(57)	(69)	(58)	(56)	(60)	(50)	(54)	(53)	(56)	(82)	(77)	(72)
Saran Upper Castes	8	12	11	3	6	7	12	9	6	6	12	6
% of total	(73)	(63)	(79)	(57)	(60)	(64)	(80)	(75)	(86)	(50)	(80)	(60)
Shahabad Upper Castes	1	5	9	13	9	11	29	21	18	10	13	12
% of total	(25)	(56)	(64)	(52)	(50)	(58)	(51)	(58)	(60)	(55)	(65)	(55)

Source: Compiled from *PP, 1821, 1823, 1824, 1825, 1826/27, 1830.*

Table 4: Age Composition of Sati Victims in Bengal Presidency in 1825 and 1826

	0–19	20–9	30–9	40–9	50–9	60–9	70–9	80–9	90–9	100+	Total
1825	17	98	104	122	110	112	46	26	3	1	639
	(2.7)	(15.3)	(16.3)	(19.1)	(17.2)	(17.5)	(7.2)	(4.1)	(.5)	(.1)	100%
1826	20	104	70	77	84	81	53	24	3	2	518
	(4)	(20)	(13.5)	(14.9)	(16.2)	(15.6)	(10.2)	(4.6)	(.6)	(.4)	100%

Source: Compiled from *PP*, 1830, vol. 28: pp. 113–18, 208–13.

greater proportion were in a state of poverty'. Similar observations were filed for other districts that year: Hughli's 79 satis followed 25 husbands who had died in 'opulent circumstances, thirteen in middling, and forty-one in poor circumstances'; Bakarganj's 18 cases involved only five deceased husbands who were 'in respectable circumstances, all the rest died indigent'.[81]

The high representation of poor widows who took their lives after the demise of their husbands is again borne out by the statistics for 1823. Hughli's 81 cases involved 37 husbands who were 'poor, sixteen in middling, and twenty-four in opulent circumstances'; Jessore's 14 incidents involved six husbands in 'good [condition], three in middling, and five in bad circumstances'; Jungle Mehals' 27 cases included 10 said to be 'poor, the rest were generally in moderate circumstances'; and 'the greater part' of the 31 cases in Cuttack 'appear to have been in low circumstances'.[82]

Much the same conclusions regarding the advanced age and impoverished conditions of sati victims emerges from the information collected for 1826 when almost every district report turned in full details on these subjects. Burdwan's report on 45 satis referred to women who 'generally speaking . . . have attained mature ages, and their deceased husbands to have been in low circumstances'; Hughli's 98 cases evoked the observation that the 'greater proportion of the husbands appear to have been in poor or middling circumstances'; Nadia's 45 'female sacrifices . . . [involved] parties . . . for the most part . . . in poor circumstances; and the widows were, generally speaking, of an advanced age'.[83]

Furthermore, even in the best of circumstances, the practice of sati was shaped by other considerations. For it existed in a milieu in which widowhood was regarded as the final and lowest stage in the life of a woman, a stage sometimes termed 'cold sati'.[84] In other words, a widow was regarded as 'a marginal entity in society':

> She was not allowed to wear the insignia of her active married state, that is, her clothes and her jewelery, but wore rags. In some cases her hair was shorn. She was not permitted to partake in family meals, could only sleep on the ground and in all ways was kept separate from the active social world of the living. She was treated by the family and the rest of society as unclean, and polluting, and her marginality was enforced by these pollution taboos. She was expected to devote the rest of her life to asceticism and worship of the gods, especially Siva, and her dead husband.[85]

Thus, viewed from the perspective of widows in early nineteenth-century India, the 'option' of becoming a sati was not only conditioned by their economic and social circumstances but also by the 'virtue they earned in gaining long-term spiritual rewards for themselves and their families and by the deliverance they attained by closing out their lives as the 'symbolically dead,'[86] a role to which they were consigned. As an alternative to life as a 'cold sati', a life of marginal existence and symbolic death that was made more precarious for many by advancing age and poverty, self-immolation was an act of ritual suicide that terminated their 'after lives' of certain misery as widows.[87]

Notes

This is a much travelled essay that has benefited from many readings and suggestions. An excerpt from an earlier version appeared in *Manushi* 42–3 (1987): 26–9.

1. This essay follows the now common usage of the term to refer to both the act of widow burning as well as the woman victim. To differentiate between the two, some writers use suttee, the Anglicized term for sati, to refer to the practice and sati to the victim. E.g., see V.N. Datta, *Sati: A Historical, Social and Philosophical Enquiry into the Hindu Rite of Widow Burning* (New Delhi: Manohar, 1988), 1. See also Datta, *Sati*, 2, regarding the prevalence of widow immolation in other parts of the world.

2. Edward Thompson, *Suttee* (Boston: Houghton Mifflin, 1928), 15; Upendra Thakur, *The History of Suicide in India: An Introduction* (Delhi: Munshiram Manoharlal, 1963), 141–2.

3. E.g., see Thompson, *Suttee*; R.K. Saxena, *Social Reforms: Infanticide and Sati* (New Delhi: Trimurti Publications, 1975); Amitabha Mukhopadhyay, 'Sati as a Social Institution in Bengal', *Bengal Past and Present* 76 (1951): 99–105.

4. 'Sati: Regulation XVII, AD 1829 . . .', in *The Correspondence of Lord William Cavendish Bentinck, vol. 1: 1828–1831*, ed. C.H. Philips (Oxford: Oxford University Press, 1977), 360.

5. John Rosseli, *Lord William Bentinck: The Making of a Liberal Imperialist, 1774–1839* (Brighton: Sussex University Press, 1974), 208–14; Rajat K. Ray, 'Introduction', in *Rammohun Roy and the Process of Modernization in India*, ed. V.C. Joshi (Delhi: Vikas, 1975), 1–20.

6. Lata Mani, 'Contentious Traditions: The Debate on Sati in Colonial India', *Cultural Critique* (1987): 119–20.

7. Ibid., 153. British attitudes towards sati were also characterized by a 'deep ambivalence'. See Veena Das, 'Gender Studies, Cross-Cultural Comparison and the Colonial Organization of Knowledge', *Berkshire Review* 58 (1986): 68.

8. 'Government circular on sati addressed to military officers', 10 Nov. 1828, in *Correspondence of Bentinck*, 91.

9. Hanna Papanek, 'False Specialization and the Purdah of Scholarship—A Review Article', *Journal of Asian Studies* 44 (1984): 127–48. A significant departure from the conventional modes of interpretation is the work of Lata Mani (cited in notes 6 and 47).

10. Ashis Nandy, 'Sati: A Nineteenth Century Tale of Women, Violence and Protest', in *Rammohun Roy*, ed. Joshi, 174–5.

11. See Helena Znaniecka Lopata, ed., *Widows*, 2 vols (Durham: Duke University Press, 1987), for a study emphasizing the significance of the social context of widowhood in shaping the 'after life' of widows in positive or negative ways. Also see Betty Potash, ed., *Widows in African Societies: Choices and Constraints* (Stanford: Stanford University Press, 1986) for an anthropological analysis of the lives of widows and their options, choices, and strategies.

12. See Gayatri C. Spivak, 'Can the Subaltern Speak? Speculations on Widow-Sacrifice', *Wedge* 7/8 (1985): 120–30, for a provocative discussion of the 'muting' of subaltern women in the colonial discourse.

13. On the Bhojpur region, see Gyan Pandey, 'Rallying Round the Cow: Sectarian Strife in the Bhojpur Region, c. 1888–1917', in *Subaltern Studies II: Writings on South Asian History and Society*, ed. Ranajit Guha (Delhi: Oxford University Press, 1983), 60–129. See also Robert I. Crane, ed., *Regions and Regionalism in South Asian Studies: An Exploratory Study* (Duke University, Monograph and Occasional Paper Series, Monograph No. 5, 1967).

14. C.A. Bayly, 'From Ritual to Ceremony: Death Ritual and Society in Hindu North India since 1600', in *Mirrors of Morality: Studies in the Social History of Death*, ed. Joachim Whaley (New York: St. Martin's Press, 1981), 174.

15. Das, 'Gender and Colonial Knowledge', 69.

16. Great Britain, Parliament, *Parliamentary Papers* (hereafter *PP*) (Commons), *1821*, vol. 1, 3–22.

17. Ibid., 22.

18. See, e.g., Magistrate, Nadia, to Secty., Judicial, 30 Oct. 1803, Bengal Criminal Judicial Consultations, 5 Nov. to 29 Dec. 1803, 3 Nov., no. 10.

19. Collector, Shahabad, to Board of Revenue, 29 Sept. 1801, Bengal Revenue Consultations, 2 Sept. to 29 Oct. 1801, Oct. 22, no. 13.

20. Thompson, *Suttee*, 61.

21. Acting Register of the Nizamat Adalat (N.A.) to Secty., Judicial, 5 June 1806, in *PP, 1821*, vol. 18, 27.

22. Police officers were also ordered to submit information on sati cases in their monthly reports to the magistrates, ibid., 28.

23. In the four-fold division of Aryan society, Brahmins or priests constituted the highest order followed by Kshatriyas or warriors, Vaishyas or merchants and artisans, and Sudras or serfs. According to this pandit, if a woman reneged on her intention to commit sati before pronouncing the *sankalpa*, or resolution to die, she faced no punishments. However, if she had already announced her sankalpa and performed other ceremonies but refused to ascend the funeral pyre, then her decision could only be rectified by her 'undergoing a severe penance'. 'Question to the Pundit the Nizamut Adawlut', in ibid., 28–9.

24. Magistrate, Bundelkhand, to Register, N.A., 3 Aug. 1813, ibid., 32.

25. Register, N.A., to Chief Secty., 11 March 1813, ibid.

26. *PP, 1821*, vol. 18, 44.

27. *PP, 1823*, vol. 17, 7–26; *PP, 1824*, vol. 23, 76; *PP, 1825*, vol. 24; *PP, 1826/27*, vol. 20. A column entitled 'Profession, and Circumstances of the Husband' was added to the 1824 report.

28. Commissioner, Patna, to Secty., Judicial, 15 Oct. 1834, Bengal Criminal Judicial Consultations, 26 Jan. to 9 Feb. 1836, 26 Jan, no. 22.

29. This section draws on the highly suggestive and provocative ideas of Eric Hobsbawm, 'Introduction: Inventing Traditions', in *The Invention of Tradition*, ed. Hobsbawm and Terence Ranger (Cambridge: Cambridge University Press, 1983), 1–14.

30. Romila Thapar, 'In History', *Seminar* 342 (1988): 15. See also the other essays in this important and informative special issue on sati.

31. Ibid. Whether or not sati was referred to and endorsed by the Vedas is a subject of some disputation. See, e.g., Datta, *Sati*, 2–3.

32. Thapar, 'In History', 15; A.L. Basham, *The Wonder That was India* (New York: Grove Press, 1959), 186–7.

33. P. Thomas, *Indian Women through the Ages* (Bombay: Asia Publishing House, 1964), 217–24; Datta, *Sati*, 3–4; Benoy Bhusan Roy, *Socioeconomic Impact of Sati in Bengal and the Role of Raja Rammohun Roy* (Calcutta: Naya Prokash, 1987), 1–2; Thapar, 'In History', 15–16.

34. Dorothy Stein, 'Burning Widows, Burning Brides: The Perils of Daughterhood in India', *Pacific Affairs* 61 (1988): 465, and her 'Women to Burn: Suttee as a Normative Institution', *Signs* 4 (1978): 253–68; and Richard Lannoy, *The Speaking Tree: A Study of Indian Culture and Society* (London: Oxford University Press, 1971), 114–18, regarding the belief that women have a greater need of sexual satisfaction than men.

35. Thakur, *Suicide in India*, 126–45; Basham, *The Wonder That was India*, 186–8.

36. Barbara N. Ramusack, 'Women in South and Southeast Asia', in *Restoring Women to History* (Bloomington: Organization of American Historians, 1988), 4. Sudras were said to be the servants of the three higher orders.

37. Sandra P. Robinson, 'Hindu Paradigms of Women: Image and Values', in *Women, Religion and Social Change*, ed. Yvonne Yazbeck Haddad and Ellison Banks Findly (Albany: State University of New York Press, 1985), 183. See also Susan S. Wadley, 'Women and the Hindu Tradition', *Signs* 3 (1977): 113–25.

38. Thapar, 'In History', 15.

39. Vina Mazumdar, 'Comment on Suttee', *Signs* 4 (1978): 273. See also Sanjukta Gupta and Richard Gombrich, 'Another View of Widow-burning and Womanliness in Indian Public Culture', *Journal of Commonwealth and Comparative Politics* 22 (1984): 255–6 for an argument that Hindu emphasis on the chastity of women was reinforced under Muslim rule because Muslim rulers posed a threat to the purity of Hindu women and because Muslim culture placed an even higher premium on chastity as 'virtually the sole repository of family honor'.

40. Thapar, 'In History', 16.

41. Mukhopadhyay, 'Sati in Bengal', 100; Kenneth Ballhatchet, *Social Policy and Social Change in Western India 1817–1830* (London: Oxford University Press, 1957), 291. See also Ray, 'Introduction', 3–5 regarding the 'spread of sati as a Sanskritizing rite'; and M.N. Srinivas, *Social Change in Modern India* (Berkeley: University of California Press, 1969), 6 for a standard definition of Sanskritization.

42. Thapar, 'In History', 17.

43. *The Inner Conflict of Tradition: Essays in Indian Ritual, Kingship, and Society* (Chicago: University of Chicago Press, 1985), 15.

44. Mukhopadhyay, 'Sati in Bengal', 99–101; Zakiuddin Ahmad, 'Sati in Eighteenth Century Bengal', *Journal of the Asiatic Society of Pakistan* 13 (1968): 149–50; Thompson, *Suttee*, 15–43.

45. Ronald B. Inden, *Marriage and Rank in Bengali Culture: A History of Caste and Clan in Middle-Period Bengal* (Berkeley: University of California Press, 1976), 82.

46. Bayly, 'From Ritual to Ceremony', 175; Thapar, 'In History', 17.

47. No wonder the practice in the eighteenth and nineteenth centuries is often seen as an involuntary act, more akin to murder than ritual suicide. E.g., Datta, *Sati*, 216–19. Note also that in the nineteenth-century debate over sati the British followed legal and Brahminical precedents and ignored the multivocal nature of the discourse on sati. See Lata Mani, 'Production of an Official Discourse on Sati in Early Nineteenth Century Bengal', *Economic and Political Weekly* 21 (1986): 32–40.

48. Caldecott to Petter, 14 Sept. 1783, Caldecott Manuscript, Eur. Mss. D. 778, India Office Library and Records, London.

49. S. Pearce Carey, *William Carey* (London: Hodder & Stoughton, 1923), 209.

50. Acting Magistrate, Saran, to Acting Suptd. of Police, Lower Provinces, 20 Feb. 1819, Saran District Records, Letters Issued, 11-4-1816 to 17-6-1819, Bihar State Archives, Patna.

51. Magistrate to Register, N.A., 18 Dec. 1813, *PP*, *1821*, vol. 18, 37.

52. Francis Buchanan, *An Account of the District of Shahabad in 1812–13* (Patna: Patna Law Press, 1934), 213; Montgomery Martin, *Eastern India*, vol. 2, *Bhagalpur, Gorakhpur* (1938; reprint ed., Delhi: Cosmo Publications, 1976), 475.

53. Mukhopadhyay, 'Sati in Bengal', 105. These numbers do not include satis occurring in such areas as Punjab and Rajasthan that were then territories not completely under British control but where the practice was prevalent. On Rajasthan, see Saxena, *Social Reforms*, 57–147. On sati in the Bombay Presidency, see Ballhatchet, *Social Policy in India*, 275–91.

54. Anand A. Yang, *The Limited Raj: Agrarian Relations in Saran District, India, 1793–1920* (Berkeley: University of California Press, 1989); Basudeb Chattopadhyay, 'The Penetration of Authority in the Interior: A Case-study of the Zamindari of Nakashipara, 1850–1860', *Peasant Studies* 12 (1985): 151–69. See also Nandy, 'Sati', 174–5.

55. Gupta and Gombrich, 'Another View of Widow-burning', 254.

56. Nandy, 'Sati,' 175.

57. Ashis Nandy, 'Cultures of Politics and Politics of Cultures', *Journal of Commonwealth and Comparative Politics* 22 (1984): 265.

58. Wherever possible, I have attempted to correct the 'grotesquely mistranscribed' names. Compiled from *PP*, *1826/27*, vol. 20, 108; *PP*, *1830*, vol. 28, 30, 93–100, 189–91. The 1830 identifications of sepoy widows also lists Musst. Una of Ghazipur and Musst. Gurua of Kanpur. See also Buchanan, *Shahabad*, 153 for an estimate that at least 4,680, and as many as 12,000 men from Shahabad were serving in the military in 1812–13.

59. 'A Short History of the Chaudhary Family, Patna City (translated from the Hindi of Pandit Rampratap Pandey)', in Babu Ramgopal Singh Chowdhary, *Select Writings and Speeches of Babu Ramgopal Singh Chowdhary* (Bankipur: Express Press, 1917), ii. Bhumihar Brahmins, a dominant landholding caste in the region, sometimes termed Kshatriya Brahmins, have historically valorized their military and kingly identities. See M.A. Sherring, *Hindu Tribes and Castes* (1872; reprint ed., Delhi: Cosmo Publications, 1974), 39–54.

60. Gupta and Gombrich, 'Another View of Widow-burning', 256; Mukhopadhyay, 'Sati in Bengal', 108. Infanticide is said to stem from the same dynamic because the dearth of men of appropriate status also meant that high castes were faced with the dreadful prospect of raising unmarriageable daughters.

61. Bayly, 'From Rituals to Ceremony', 174. Such pressures have also been cited as reasons why many satis in Bengal should be seen as involuntary, i.e., as murder. E.g., see Ahmad, 'Sati in Bengal', 161–3.

62. Nandy, 'Sati', 171, goes on to argue that large-scale scarcities occurred in Bengal, such as the disastrous famine of 1770, after a period of about 150 years of relatively famine-free existence.

63. 'Ashis Nandy on the Inner World', *Journal of Commonwealth and Comparative Politics* 22 (1984): 259. Perhaps this was another dynamic in the generalization of the practice across social and economic liens.

64. James Jamesson, *Report on the Epidemic Cholera Morbus* (Calcutta: A.G. Balfour, 1820), 3–32, 167–74.

65. Magistrate, Patna, to Suptd., Police, 21 Dec. 1818, *PP, 1821*, vol. 18, 233.

66. Robert Hamilton to Captain Benson, 1 March 1829, in *Correspondence of Bentinck*, 175. For a similar trend in western India, see Ballhatchet, *Social Policy in India*, 275.

67. 'Extract from . . . suttee report . . . for the year 1825', *PP, 1830,* vol. 28.

68. 'Mr. Harington's Minute', with Governor-General's, 3 Dec. 1824, *PP, 1825*, vol. 24, 11.

69. I have used an 1822 population estimate of 1,239,150. See Durgaprasad Bhattacharya and Bibhavati Bhattacharya, eds., *Census of India, 1961: Report on the Population Estimates of India (1820–1830)* (New Delhi: Government of India, 1963), 71.

70. Bayly, 'From Ritual to Ceremony', 161.

71. Hamilton to Benson, 1 March 1829, *Correspondence of Bentinck*, 172.

72. Elizabeth Leigh Stutchbury, 'Blood, Fire and Meditation: Human Sacrifice and Widow Burning in Nineteenth Century India', in *Women in India and Nepal*, ed. Michael Allen and S.N. Mukherjee (Canberra: Australian National University Monographs on South Asia No. 8, 1982), 41.

73. 'History of the Chaudhary Family', in *Writings of Chowdhary*, ii.

74. *PP, 1825*, vol. 24, 153.

75. Mukhopadhyay, 'Sati', 108–9. Although upper-caste victims comprised approximately half the total number of satis in most districts, in proportion to the percentage of high to low castes in the overall population, they, of course, constituted a substantial proportion. Interpolating on the basis of the systematic census data of the late nineteenth century, one can assume that high castes typically represented eight to 20 per cent of the total population of most Bengal districts, their numbers standing higher in Bihar than in Bengal proper.

76. E.g., see *PP, 1821, 1823, 1825*. Nearly eight per cent of the population of Banaras, a centre of pilgrimage, were Marathas in 1820. See Bayly, 'From Ritual to Ceremony', 164–5.

77. 'Remarks . . . for the year 1818', 21 May 1819, *PP, 1821*, vol. 18, 222. For a different emphasis—on the youth of the victims—see Gupta and Gombrich, 'Another View of Widow-burning', 256.

78. *PP, 1825*, vol. 24, 67–70.

79. *PP, 1821*, vol. 18, 166–8.

80. For a discussion of sati as suicide and particularly Durkheim's views on this subject, see Raj S. Gandhi, 'Sati as Altruistic Suicide', *Contributions to Asian Studies* 10 (1977): 141–57; Arvind Sharma, 'Emile Durkheim on Suttee as Suicide', *International Journal of Contemporary Sociology* 15 (1978): 283–91.

81. *PP, 1825*, vol. 24, 76–7.

82. Ibid., 140–1. For a different profile, see the details regarding the 46 cases from the suburbs of Calcutta where the majority of the deceased husbands of satis were said to have 'been in good [economic] circumstances' (141).

83. *PP, 1830*, vol. 28, 138–9.

84. Susan Hill Gross and Marjorie Wall Bingham, *Women in India* (Hudson, Wisconsin: GEM Publications, 1980), 30.

85. Stutchbury, 'Widow Burning in India', 37; Stein, 'Women to Burn,' 254–5.

86. See Lina M. Fruzzetti, *The Gift of a Virgin: Women, Marriage, and Ritual in a Bengali Society* (New Brunswick: Rutgers University Press, 1982), 103–7 for an excellent discussion of the present-day status of the widow. Also Manisha Roy, *Bengali Women* (Chicago: University of Chicago Press, 1975), 146–7.

87. Nor have the conditions and ideologies favouring sati completely disappeared in twentieth-century India. Thousands were present at the recent burning of 17-year-old Roop Kanwar, a bride of eight months, who immolated herself on her husband's funeral pyre in Rajasthan on 4 Sept. 1987. For the literature—and some shocking pronouncement—on this incident, see, e.g., the special issues of *Manushi* 42–3 (1987); *Seminar* 342 (1988); and *Economic and Political Weekly*, 7 Nov. 1987 and 14 Nov. 1987.

2

Production of an Official Discourse on Sati in Early-Nineteenth-Century Bengal*

Lata Mani

Nineteenth-century British India was marked by a series of debates on reforming the status of women. The first, and most sensational public debate, was concerned with outlawing sati: the practice, prevalent predominantly among high-caste Hindus, of the immolation of widows on the funeral pyres of their husbands. These immolations were sometimes voluntary and at other times coerced. The official debate centred around the issue of the tolerance of such a practice in a 'British India'.

The literature on sati[1] and more generally on social reform in the colonial period has largely adopted the framework of modernization theory. Reform here is conceptualized as a product both of the impulse to 'moderate' that supposedly characterized the officials of this period and the demands of a small but increasingly vocal 'westernized', urban indigenous male elite. Officials who initiated and defended 'progressive' legislation like the abolition of sati, have been loosely called 'Anglicists'. They have been marked off from their 'Orientalist' forerunners and colleagues, said to have been more 'Hindooized' and wary of interventions in indigenous culture not prompted by the needs of colonial rule. The abolition of sati in 1829 is said to signal the rise of Anglicists whose victory is seen to culminate in the great debate on English *versus* vernacular education in the mid 1830s.[2]

However, I will argue that a number of important issues are obscured in a characterization of the official debate on sati as one between 'preservationists' and impatient westernizers. Firstly, the fact that the debate was primarily about the feasibility rather than the desirability of abolition is overlooked. Secondly, that which is common in the analyses of Indian society in the arguments of those for and against abolition remains hidden. Finally, I will argue the case for abolition is not, in fact, elaborated on the grounds that such a characterization implies. Rather than arguing for the outlawing of sati as a cruel or barbarous act, as one might expect of a true 'modernizer', officials in favour of abolition were at pains to illustrate that such a move was entirely consonant with the principle of upholding indigenous tradition. Their strategy was to point to the questionable scriptural sanction for sati and to the fact that, for one reason or another,

*From *Economic and Political Weekly*, vol. XXI, no. 17, 'Review of Women Studies' (April 1986): WS 32–40.

they believed its contemporary practice transgressed its original and therefore 'true' scriptural meaning.

I. Discourse as an Ideological Tool

In this paper I have treated the debate on sati as a discourse. My use of the term and a discussion of the value of this approach is presented below. Briefly, however, in analysing the debate as discourse, I focus on how knowledge about sati was produced. In particular, I examine assumptions about sati, Indian society and colonial subjects on which this discourse depended and also the role of indigenous people in its production. Several interlocking assumptions informed this discourse. Chief among these was the hegemonic status accorded by colonial officials to brahmanic scriptures in the organization of social life. The corollary to this was to assume an unquestioning submission of indigenous people to the dictates of scripture and thus to posit an absence of conscious individual will. Widows in particular are represented as having no subjectivity and as doubly victimized by their ignorance of the scriptures and its consequence, their reliance on brahmin pundits. The latter are portrayed as self-interested interpreters of the sacred texts. As for sati itself, there is a repeated insistence on a scriptural sanction for the practice, although this claim is increasingly contested as the debate develops.

Analysis of the discourse also clarifies how selected natives, especially brahmin pundits, were deeply implicated in its production, albeit in a subordinated role. As I will illustrate, pundits' statements were interpreted and deployed in ways that produced a distinctively colonial concepton of sati.[3] Examining the production of discourse clarifies what was privileged and what was marginalized in the process. Thus it becomes possible to contest the conclusions about sati drawn by colonial officials.

This paper falls within the category of historical studies that is concerned with the contribution of imperialism to what is known about colonial and ex-colonial societies; with reconstituting what B.S. Cohn has called a 'colonial sociology of knowledge'.[4] Building on the work of Foucault on the collaboration of power/knowledge in the production of discourse[5] and Said[6] with specific reference to discourses on the Orient, this study begins with the premise that what is known about colonial and ex-colonial societies is itself a colonial legacy. This problem is not merely confined to knowledge of what is designated 'the colonial period'. As Romila Thapar states: 'A major contradiction in our understanding of the entire Indian past is that this understanding is derived from the interpretations of Indian history made in the last two hundred years.'[7] Needless to say such understandings were forged in situations that reflect the vicissitudes of a 'colonial' representation of reality and the needs of colonial power.

Acknowledgement of the complex history of received ideas is not new. The production in recent years of 'workers' history', 'women's history' or 'subaltern studies'[8] implies the partiality, even bias, of existing accounts. An argument for women's history, for instance, is based on the need to remedy a situation in which history has largely meant the history of men. Obviously, accounts of women or workers do not function only in an additive way but transform our understanding of society as a whole.

I suggest, however, that an analysis of discourse is a different proposition, which goes beyond producing 'indigenous' or 'oppositional' accounts, whether nationalist, Marxist or feminist. Rather, discourse analysis focuses on that which is stable and persistent in the ordering of social reality in each of these accounts. Thus it can point to assumptions shared by those who claim to be opposed to each other or are conceptualized in this manner, whether nationalists and colonialists or Orientalists and Anglicists.

In a sense the term discourse as used by Focault and Said is similar in scope to the Marxist notion of ideology: a public, institutionalised set of constraints on what is 'truth' and 'knowledge'. Discourse is, however, the more useful analytical tool: for it retains the dialogical processes implied by speech and requires at least two parties. I believe it is useful to speak of a 'colonial discourse' on sati rather than a colonial ideology, precisely because knowledge about colonial society was produced through interaction between colonialists—officials, scholars, missionaries—and certain selected natives. The 'interaction' was often 'interrogation' and always transversed by power. Discourse signals the back-and-forth of these power-laden encounters more sensitively than ideology, for the latter seems to have gathered about it notions of rigidity and monological, even hegemonic, production. The concept of discourse also embodies the possibility of several simultaneous discourses. It makes for the analysis of missionary, official and indigenous discourses as autonomous although engaged with each other in relations of dialogue and struggle.

In this paper I examine the production of an official discourse on sati. A complete analysis of colonial discourses on sati would require, in addition, attention to missionary and indigenous discourses for both were important in the debate on abolition. This essay represents only the beginning of such an enterprise.

Such a critical reading of historical materials is not the province of intellectual history alone. Given that these discourses were spawned by considerations of social policy and informed practice, they are of equal concern to social historians. As for colonial subjects confronting the colonial legacy, such a critical reading offers a way of reinterpreting tradition, history and identity.

II. Sati: A Legislative History?

As a subject covered by criminal law, colonial policy on sati was formulated between the Governor General and Council and officials at various levels of the criminal justice system in Bengal: magistrates, police officials, the provincial court—Nizamat Adalat—and the superior court—Sadr Nizamat Adalat. Also involved was the Privy Council at the apex of East India Company hierarchy in London. Finally, given the supposed scriptural sanction for sati, brahmin pundits also became crucial participants. Appointed to the civil courts under Warren Hastings in 1772 to interpret scriptural law in civil matters— marriage, divorce, inheritance, succession—pundits were called upon to elaborate the dictates of scripture on all aspects of sati. Residents of Calcutta were beyond the purview of this debate since the city fell under the jurisdiction of British law and sati had been outlawed there in 1798.

The history of legislation on sati is relatively straightforward. In all, only one regulation and three circulars were actually promulgated between the first recorded query on the official position on sati in February 1789 and its prohibition in December 1829. The first official position on sati was articulated in response to a clarification sought by M.H. Brooke, Collector of Shahabad District. In the absence of any official instructions on the subject, and on the strength of its illegality in Calcutta city, Brooke had prohibited the burning of a widow and sought government approval for his decision. The Governor General commended his action but urged him to use private influence rather than official authority in dissuading natives from sati, claiming:

> The public prohibition of a ceremony authorised by the tenets of the religion of the Hindus, and from the observance of which they have never yet been restricted by the ruling power would in all probability tend to increase rather than diminish their veneration for it.[10]

He continued that he hoped in the course of time natives would 'discern the fallacy of the principle which have given rise to this practice, and that it will of itself gradually fall into disuse'.[11] The Governor General cites no support for his claim of a religious sanction for sati.

The issue was raised again in 1805 when Elphinstone, acting magistrate of the Zillah of Behar, reported his intervention in a case where an intoxicated 12-year-old was being coerced into the pyre. Like Brooke, he sought instructions from the Governor General and his Council. The secretary of the government referred the issue to the Nizamat Adalat, asking how far and in what ways the practice of sati was founded in the scripture, stating that if scriptural sanction precluded abolition, measures might be taken to prevent coercion and such abuses as the intoxication of widows.

The Nizamat Adalat in turn referred the matter to its pundit, Ghanshyam Surmono. The pundit responded in March 1805 but not until 29 April 1813, some eight years later, was his exposition of the scriptural position on sati issued in the form of instructions to the District Magistrates.

Based on an official reading of Surmono's interpretation of the texts, the instructions declared sati to be a practice founded in the religious beliefs of Hindus. It was clarified that the practice was intended to be voluntary and, if performed, was expected to ensure an after-life together for the widow and her husband. The circular also stated that a widow who had taken a vow to commit sati was permitted to change her mind without loss of caste, providing she performed a penance. The preface to the instructions clarified that given the scriptural status on sati and the government's commitment to the principle of religious tolerance, sati would be permitted: 'in those cases in which it is countenanced by their religion; and [prevented] in others in which it is by the same authority prohibited.'[12] Sati was thus to be prohibited in all cases in which the widow was less than 16 years of age, or was pregnant or intoxicated or in any other way coerced. Magistrates were also instructed to transmit to the Nizamat Adalat details of each sati committed in their jurisdictions, including any prohibitive measures they might have taken.

This circular, promulgated on 29 April 1813, was the only significant regulation introduced until the practice was outlawed. Three more circulars were issued, but these were merely further refinements prompted by the queries of District Magistrates on what constituted a legal sati. Its 'legality' supposedly conferred by its scriptural origin had been confirmed by the regulation of 1813. Queries were forwarded by the Nizamat Adalat to their resident pundits, requesting them to provide *vyawasthas* in conformity with the scriptures.[13] Thus a circular was promulgated in September 1813 that authorized *jogis* (a tribe of weavers supposedly the survivors of wandering mendicants) to bury their dead, since the scriptures reportedly forbade burning in their case.[14] It was similarly decreed in 1815 that women with children under three might commit sati only if arrangements had been made for the maintenance of their children. The 1815 circular also specified that brahmin women could only burn along with their husbands by performing the rite of *sahamarana*, while women of other castes were also permitted *anoomarana*, in which the widow burned at a later date together with an article belonging to the husband. Finally, this circular instructed magistrates to submit an annual report of satis in their districts to the Sadr Nizamat Adalat, specifying for each sati: the name of the widow, her age, her caste, the name and caste of the husband, the date of burning and the police jurisdiction in which it occurred. An additional column was provided for recording any remarks that the magistrate thought deserving of attention. A third circular, issued in 1822, instructed that information on the husband's profession and circumstances also be included for each sati.[16] Although no further regulations were issued, the following years witnessed intense debate on abolition. The debate was rekindled every year when the Nizamat Adalat analysed the annual returns of sati and examined for each incident the conduct of the district magistrate and police officers.

The question of abolition raised the related issues of desirability and feasibility. Colonial officials were unanimous on the desirability of abolition in the abstract, although they were fearful of violating the principle of religious tolerance. Needless to say, the latter concern was itself linked to the feasibility or political costs of intervention. Given their belief in the centrality of religion in the lives of Hindus, officials feared that any interference would produce repercussions that might endanger the East India Company's economic and political stakes in India. The tactic of gathering scriptural evidence was thus an attempt to challenge sati in such a way as to preclude a threat to public order. Indeed it had become clear in consulting with the pundits that the older scriptures made no mention of sati, but rather glorified ascetic widowhood. Even more recent texts did not enjoin sati but merely recommended it. The use of scriptures by officials for and against abolition will be discussed more fully below.

Meanwhile, a dramatic increase in sati lent urgency to the debate. In the first three years of data collection alone the number of satis nearly tripled from 378 to 839. Although the figures declined after 1819–20, they never fell to the levels first recorded in 1815, but fluctuated between an annual incidence of 500 and 600.

Over the years the Nizamat Adalat proposed various explanations for this rise. Initially it claimed that the rise could merely reflect more refined counting. In 1817–18 it argued, somewhat weakly, that the figures reflected the cholera epidemic that had ravaged parts of Bengal. Some officials, however, proposed a more convincing, albeit sinister, explanation pointing out that the government circular might have made people aware of more circumstances under which sati might be performed. Suspicion grew that the rise was somehow linked to government interposition. W. Ewer, Acting Superintendent of Police in the Lower Provinces, argued that 'authorising a practice is not the way to effect its gradual abolition'.[17] Courtney Smith, Nizamat Adalat judge, echoed Ewer's sentiment that government attention had given 'a sort of interest and celebrity to the sacrifice'.[18] He recommended that all circulars be rescinded since they had a tendency 'to modify, systematise or legalise the usage' and made it appear as though 'a legal suttee was . . . better than an illegal one'.[19]

Not all officials agreed with Ewer and Smith. Some Nizamat Adalat judges like C.T. Sealy and A.B. Todd resisted the implication that the circulars were interventionist and insisted that they merely implemented the law as embedded in the scriptures. Others asked for an even more rigorous enforcement of scriptural law. For instance, in 1828 Cracroft, Magistrate of Dacca, even went so far as to recommend that only widows from families with pure caste status be permitted to perform sati. Cracroft suggested that such a rigorous interpretation of caste would reduce sati by ninety per cent since few families if any would meet this standard.[20] In 1823, Harrington proposed circumventing the scriptures, suggesting that sati need not be outlawed outright but that brahmin pundits and relatives might be prosecuted as principals or accomplices in homicide.

Officials advocating further legislation, however, were in a minority. The general view was that in the context of a sustained high incidence of sati, anything short of total prohibition would be unwise. Yet this appeared out of the question. In the meantime, it was hoped that the spread of education and the example of the high caste, educated, westernized Hindus would serve to make the practice unpopular. Indigenous opposition to sati had been growing since 1818, when Rammohun Roy, chief campaigner and symbol of the native lobby against sati published his first tract against the practice.

However, in general, faith in the progressive influence of higher caste, better educated Hindus was misplaced, for the practice was predominantly theirs.[21] The regional distribution of sati also made it difficult to sustain in the hope that a great exposure to western influence would result in its popularity declining. For 63 per cent of satis between 1815 and 1828 were committed in the Calcutta Division around Calcutta city, the seat of colonial power. Indeed this high figure may in part be accounted for by Hindu residents of Calcutta going outside the city to commit sati, which was illegal within its boundaries.

The regionally skewed distribution of satis prompted some magistrates like H.B. Melville in 1823 and W.B. Bayley in 1827 to propose abolition in certain districts. Others used the regional variation as evidence that sati was a localized, temporal phenomenon and not a universal religious one. Further, already by 1818, it had become evident that the scriptural sanction for sati was not clearcut. In March 1824, the Court of Directors sitting in London, drawing almost exclusively on official correspondence and Nizamat Adalat proceedings on sati, came to the conclusion that these papers themselves were replete with arguments on the basis of which abolition could be justified. In particular, the directors highlighted the following: the questionable scriptural status of sati, the violation of scriptural rules in its performance, the inefficacy of current regulation, the support for abolition among Indians, the confidence of some magistrates that sati could be abolished safely, the incompatibility of sati with principles of morality and reason. The Court of Directors however conceded that the final decision must rest with the authorities in India since only they could evaluate the political consequences of such action.

Indeed it was in India that legislation to outlaw sati was finally initiated by Governor General Lord William Bentinck in December 1829. Bentinck had little more information than his predecessors, either on sati or on the probable effects of such legislation, although he had gathered military intelligence that such legislation would not provoke disquiet among the armed forces. What Bentinck did possess was a combination of the will to outlaw sati and the benefits of a greater political stability of the East India Company whose control had now been extended across Rajputana, Central India and Nepal. A new confidence and energy was reflected in Bentinck's Minute on sati: 'Now that we are supreme, my opinion is decidedly in favour of an open, avowed and general prohibition, resting altogether upon the moral goodness of the act and our power to enforce it'.[22] The desirability of abolition had never been at issue. Its feasibility had proved to be the thorny question, Bentinck settled the issue once and for all.

Sati either by burning or burial was outlawed and made punishable by the criminal courts. *Zamindars* and *talukdars* were made responsible for immediate communication to the police of intention to perform sati, any lapse being made punishable by a fine or imprisonment. The Nizamat Adalat was authorized to impose the death sentence on active participants in sati if the crime was gruesome enough to render them unworthy of mercy. It is not known to what extent the legislative act succeeded in putting out the flaming pyres. Statistics were no longer collected and thus it is impossible to evaluate the effects of abolition. What abolition did achieve was an official resolution in one instance of the conflict between political expediency and the civilizing mission of colonization.

III. The Discourse and Its Assumptions

The one feature that is clear even from this brief legislative history is that the abolition of sati was complicated by official insistence on its scriptural status. Whatever their views on the feasibility of abolition, all colonial officials shared to a greater or lesser degree three interdependent ideas: the centrality of religion, the submission of indigenous people to its dictates and the 'religious' basis of sati. Those against abolition argued that prohibition of sati was likely to incite native resistance. As the Nizamat Adalat put it: 'Such a measure would, in all probability, excite a considerable degree of alarm and dissatisfaction in the minds of the Hindoo inhabitants of these provinces.'[23] Officials in favour of abolition also developed arguments reflecting the view of Hindu society generated by these same assumptions. For instance, Judge E. Watson's argument for the feasibility of abolition rested on the precedent of Regulation 8 of 1799 which, by declaring female infanticide, child sacrifice and the burial of lepers capital offences, had similarly, in his view, violated religious principles. It is in this sense that I assert that officials on both sides of the debate shared the same universe of discourse.

Walter Ewer, Superintendent of Police in the Lower Provinces, made a different kind of argument for abolition. As a thorough and systematic analysis which sums up the arguments of officials over the years, it is worth detailed attention.[24] Ewer took the position that the contemporary practice of sati bore little resemblance to its scriptural model as a voluntary act of devotion carried out for the spiritual benefit of the widow and the deceased. Rather, in his view, widows were coerced and sati was performed most often for the material gain of surviving relatives. Ewer suggested that relatives might save the expense of maintaining the widow and 'irritation' of her legal right over the family estate. Also said to apply pressure on the widow by extolling the virtues and rewards of sati were 'hungry brahmins' greedy for the money due to them for officiating on such occasions.

Even if the widow succeeded in resisting the combined force of relatives and pundits, Ewer held that she would not be spared by the crowd. According to him, 'the entire population of the village will turn out to assist in dragging her to the bank of the river, and in keeping her down on the pile'.[25] For the crowd, sati was said to offer the lure of a spectacle. 'None of the holy exultation that formerly accompanied the departure of a martyr, but all the savage merriment which, in our days, accompanies a boxing match or a full-bait.'[26] Ewer thus concludes that 'the widow is scarcely ever a free agent at the performance of the suttee'.[27] According to Ewer, such scriptural transgressions as the coercion of widows or the performance of sati for material gain could either be the result of ignorance of scriptures or reflect conscious design on the part of relatives and pundits: in the former case sati could be abolished without provoking indigenous outrage; in the latter case, sati could not be considered a sacred act and could safely be abolished.

It is clear that, according to Ewer, when Hindus acted 'religiously', they did not act consciously. In other words, true 'religious' action was synonymous with a passive, unquestioning obedience. Thus, if the widow is construed as a victim of pundits and relatives, they in turn are seen by Ewer to act in two mutually exclusive ways: either 'consciously', that is 'irreligiously', or 'passively', that is 'religiously'. Hence Ewer nowhere suggests that pundits and relatives could manipulate religion to their own ends. As for the widow, she is not offered any possibility of ever exercising her will. Ewer submitted that left to herself, the widow would 'turn with natural instinct and horror from the thought of suttee'.[28] However, in his view, given her ignorance and weak mental and physical capacity it took little persuasion to turn any apprehension into a reluctant consent.

Ewer resolved the issue of the feasibility of abolition further by problematizing the assumption of a scriptural sanction for sati. He pointed to the heterogeneity of the scriptures on the issue; Manu 'the parent of Hindoo jurisprudence' did not even mention sati, but instead glorified ascetic widowhood. It is important to note that what unites both the 'temporal' and 'scriptural' aspects of Ewer's arguments is the privileging of religion and the assumption of a complete native submission to its force.

This analysis was not that of Ewer alone. Maloney, Acting Magistrate of Burdwan, similarly emphasized that the decision of widows to commit sati stems not 'from their having reasoned themselves into a conviction of the purity of the act itself, as from a kind of infatuation produced by the absurdities poured into their ears by ignorant brahmins.'[29] For Maloney, as for Ewer, the widow is always a victim and the pundit always corrupt. Maloney, like Ewer, also concedes the possibility of a 'good' sati that is voluntary and the product of reason; but only in the abstract. In reality, the widow is uneducated and presumed to be incapable of both reason and independent action.

This accent on 'will' in the analyses of Ewer and Maloney, testifies to the ambivalence which lies at the heart of the colonial attitude to sati. It suggests that within the general and avowed disapproval of the practice, there operated notions of 'good' and 'bad' satis. 'Good' satis were those that were seen to be true to an official reading of the scriptures. And the critical factor in determining official attitude was the issue of the widow's will. Thus the Nizamat Adalat instructed magistrates to pay close attention to the demeanour of the widow as she approached the pyre so that officials could intercept at the merest suggestion of coercion. Magistrates accordingly recorded in the annual returns on sati such remarks as the following: 'the widow voluntarily sacrificed herself', 'ascended the pyre of her own free will', burnt 'without in anyway inebriated and in conformity with the Shaster'.

Such guarded acceptance of 'good' satis is also evident in the suggestions of Harrington and Elliot that legislation should cover not the widow, who should be left free to commit sati, but brahmins and others who aided or unduly influenced her. Such an act it was argued would prevent coercion, with the additional merit that: 'No law obligatory on the consciences of the Hindoos will be infringed, and the women desirous of manifesting the excess of their conjugal love will be left at liberty to do so.'[30] Officials like Elliot, quoted above, approved of sati as long as it was an act of free will. This view also reflected in a non-horrified announcement of two satis in the *Calcutta Gazette* as late as 1827, by which time it was officially maintained that feasibility was the only reason for tolerating sati. It described the widows respectively as 'having abandoned with cheerfulness and her own free will, this perishable frame', and as 'having burnt herself with him in their presence with a swelling heart and a smiling countenance'.[31] Other officials dismissed out of hand the possibility of such voluntary satis and insisted with Ewer that widows were incapable of consenting and must therefore be protected.

It is evident that the arguments in favour of prohibiting sati were not primarily concerned with its cruelty or 'barbarity' though many officials did maintain that sati was horrid, even as an act of volition. It is also clear that officials in favour of legislative prohibition were not interventionists, contemptuous of indigenous culture, nor advocates of change in the name of 'progress' or Christian principles. On the contrary, officials in favour of abolition were arguing that such action was consistent with the policy of upholding indigenous religious tradition, even that such a policy necessitated intervention. And indeed this was how the regenerating mission of colonization was conceptualized: not as the imposition of a new Christian moral order but as the recuperation and enforcement of the 'truths' of indigenous tradition. In this regard, it is interesting that Elliot suggested a preamble to the legislation outlawing sati, explaining government policy on indigenous customs and appealing to scriptural authority for abolition through apposite quotations from the texts. In his opinion this would:

> . . . remove the evil from the less learned, who would thus be led to lament the ignorance in which they have hitherto been held enslaved by their bigoted priests, and at the same time to rejoice in the mercy and wisdom of a government which blends humanity with justice, and consults at once the interests and prejudices of its subjects, by recalling them from practices revolting, and pronounced erroneous even by their own authorities.[32]

This conception of colonial subjects held the majority to be ignorant of their 'religion'. Religion was equated with scripture. Knowledge of the scriptures was held to be largely the monopoly of brahmin pundits. Their knowledge was however believed to be corrupt and self-serving. The civilizing mission of colonization was thus seen to lie in protecting the 'weak' against the 'artful'; in giving back to the natives the truths of their own 'little read and less understood Shaster'.[33]

The arguments of abolitionists were thus developed within the ambit of 'religion'. The pros and cons of sati were systematically debated as doctrinal considerations. In this sense the debate on abolition might be fruitfully interpreted as, in part, a conflict over scriptural interpretation. In employing scriptures to support their view the abolitionists in effect resurrected the vyawasthas of pundits that had been marginalized in earlier official readings of the scriptures. In particular, they re-examined the discussions between officials and pundits leading to the formulation of the 1813 regulations. These previously marginalized vyawasthas were now reactivated by officials both as testimony

of the safety of abolition and as index of the ignorance of natives. Official debt to the
pundits in interpreting the texts was not acknowledged. This gives us a clue to the role
of the pundits in the production of official knowledge about sati, a theme that will be
taken up in the next section.

In the meantime, as we already know, official commitment to enforcing indigenous
faith and penalizing its violation in the practice of sati did not lead to a decline in its
incidence. This was regarded as native misunderstanding of colonial intention and
construed as further evidence of Hindu 'bigotry'. Proposals were made for closer supervision although in the event none were implemented. It is striking that officials did not
acknowledge the 'inconsistencies' between their interpretation of the place of scripture
in native life, and natives' own behaviour, let alone revise their view. If anything, it appears as though such inconsistencies served to reaffirm their assumptions.

In summary, the official view of sati rested on three interlocking assumptions:
the hegemony of religious texts, a total indigenous submission to their dictates and
the religious basis of sati. However, a re-examination of Parliamentary papers makes it
possible to contest each of these assumptions.

To begin with, the insistence on textual hegemony is challenged by the enormous
regional variation in the mode of committing sati. The vyawasthas of pundits had
elaborated differences by village and district, even caste and occupation in the performance
of sati. 'In certain villages of Burdwan a district in Bengal the following ceremonies are
observed.'[34] Or, 'In some villages situated in Benares, the following practices obtain
among the widows of merchants and other traders.'[35] Local influence predominated in
every aspect of sati. For instance the pundits pointed out, 'She then proceeds to the place
of sacrifice . . . having previously worshipped the peculiar deities of the city or village.'[36]
In the face of such diversity the pundits concluded, 'The ceremonies practically
observed, differ as to the various tribes and districts.'[37] Colonial officials acknowledged
these differences and instructed magistrates to allow natives 'to follow the established
authority and usage of the province in which they reside'.[38] However, such diversity was
regarded as 'peripheral' to the 'central' principle of textual hegemony.

Similarly, regional variation in the incidence of sati was not taken as a challenge to
the assumption of the hegemony of religion even though it did count as evidence of a
material basis for sati. Colonial officials did not completely ignore the fact of such variation. The regulation of 1813 recognized that in some districts sati had almost entirely
ceased while in others it was confined almost exclusively to certain castes. Despite this,
colonial officials decided to pursue a course of tolerance because in their opinion, in
most provinces, 'all castes of Hindoos would be extremely tenacious of its continuance'.[39]
Whatever the justification for concluding thus in 1813, such insistence was hardly
tenable once systematic data collection on sati was begun in 1815. For it quickly became
apparent that 66 per cent of satis were carried out between the districts surrounding
Calcutta city and the Shahabad, Ghazipur and Sarun districts. This indicates either that
sati was not a solely 'religious' practice as the officials maintained, or that religion was
not hegemonic—another colonial assumption—or both. However, officials interpreted
regional variation to imply that although sati was primarily a religious practice, other
factors might be at play. Therefore, as late as 1827, with 11 years of data at hand, W.B.
Bayley could continue to be puzzled by what he called 'anomalies' in the annual report

of satis. He wrote to the court seeking an explanation 'in regard to the following extra-ordinary discrepancies in the results exhibited by the present statement. In the district of Backergunj 63 instances of suttee are reported, and in the adjacent district of Dacca Telalpore only 2.'[40] These could only be 'extraordinary discrepancies' because Bayley, like other officials continued to maintain, despite evidence to the contrary, that religion had a uniformly powerful influence in native life.

If the hegemony of religious texts and its corollary, an unthinking native obedience to scripture, is called into question by regional variation in the incidence and mode of performing sati, the representation of widows as perennial victims is similarly debatable. For one thing the Parliamentary papers contain several accounts of women acting on their own behalf. Some of them did so when they resisted being coerced into the pyre. The annual reports of sati include many instances of women being coerced. Represent-ations of such incidents, however, stress not the resistance of women but the barbarity of Hindu males in their coercion.

Women also expressed their will when they resisted being prevented from jumping into the flames. One such case reported by Magistrate W. Wright in 1819 is worth recounting. A child widow, Mussummat Seeta had suddenly decided at age 15, some nine years after her husband's death, to commit sati. She resolved to die through the rite of anoomarana with a stringed instrument that had belonged to her husband. According to Wright, her parents, in-laws and police officers sought in vain to dissuade her. Wright records that the widow 'continually made use of the expression: "All your remonstrances are perfectly unavailing; it is now necessary for me to become suttee; if you persist in your remonstrances I will curse you."'[41] The relatives, supposedly fearing the legendary curse of the sati, are said to have complied with her wishes and built the pyre. Her parting words were reported to have been, "Set fire to the pile; if you refuse to do so, I will curse you".'[42] Colonial officials systematically ignored such evidence of the widows as subjects with a will of their own. Although they conceded the possibility of a 'voluntary' sati, these were interpreted not as evidence of the will of the widow, but testimony of her subjection to religion. The widow thus nowhere appears as a full subject. If she resisted, she was considered a victim of Hindu, male barbarity. If she appeared to consent, she was seen to be a victim of religion. Colonial representations further reinforced such a view of the widow as helpless by 'infantilizing' the typical sati. The widow is quite often described as a 'tender child'. Analysis of sati by age fails to confirm such a picture, for a majority of satis were undertaken by women well past childhood. In 1818, for example, 64 per cent of satis were above 40 years of age.

In highlighting the absence of women's subjectivity in colonial representations of sati, my intention is not to imply that women acted voluntarily or argue that sati could be an act of 'free will'. Their subjectivities were probably complex and inconsistent. In any case they are not accessible to us. As for whether or not relatives were self-interested or brahmins bigoted, such questions can also only be addressed with reference to specific cases. My purpose in raising the issue of the widow's subjectivity is rather to point out that the ubiquitous characterization of the widow as victim was not borne out by the experience of colonial officials as recounted by them in the Parliamentary papers.

It is not the widow alone who is represented as passive, for all colonial subjects, male and female, are portrayed as finally subordinated to religion. The Nizamat Adalat stated this view quite dramatically in the context of discussing the Hindu practice of burying lepers. Reviewing a case that had come to their notice, they exclaimed, 'no example can be of any avail. Their motives were above all human control.'[43]

IV. Production of Knowledge about Sati: Interaction and Interrogation

Information about sati was generated at the instance, one is tempted to say insistence, of colonial officials posing questions to pundits resident at the courts. The pundits were instructed to respond with 'a reply in conformity with the scriptures'.[44] The working of colonial power is nowhere more visible than in this process. It is worth examining one such interaction in detail.

In 1805, as noted earlier, the question of scriptural sanction for sati was first put to the pundits of the Nizamat Adalat. Specifically they were asked 'whether a woman is enjoined by the Shaster voluntarily to burn herself with the body of her husband, or is prohibited; and what are the conditions prescribed by the Shaster on such occasions?'[45] The pundit responded as follows:

> Having duly considered the question proposed by the court, I now answer it to the best of my knowledge:- every woman of the four castes (brahmin, khetry, bues and soodur) is permitted to burn herself with the body of her husband, provided she has no infant children, nor is pregnant, nor in a state of uncleanness, nor under the age of puberty; or in any of which cases she is not allowed to burn herself with her husband's body.[46]

The pundit specified that women with infant children could burn provided they made arrangements for the care of such infants. Further, he added that coercion, overt or subtle, was forbidden. In support of his opinion, he quoted the following texts:

> This rests upon the authority of Anjira, Vijasa and Vrihaspati, Mooni.
> 'There are three millions and a half of hairs upon the human body, and every woman who burns herself with the body of her husband, will reside with him in heaven during a like number of years.'
> 'In the same manner, as a snake-catcher drags a snake from his hole, so does a woman who burns herself draw her husband out of hell; and she afterwards resides with him in heaven.'
> The exceptions above cited, respecting women in a state of pregnancy or uncleanness, and adolescence, were communicated by Oorub and others to the mother of Sagar Raja.[47]

The question posed to the pundit was whether sati was enjoined by the scriptural texts. The pundit in effect responded that the texts did not enjoin but merely permitted sati in certain instances, drawing on quotes which spoke of the rewards sati would bring to widows and their husbands. That the scriptures permit sati can only be inferred from the above passage. Nevertheless on the basis of this rather elusive response the Nizamat Adalat concluded:

> The practice, generally speaking, being thus recognised and *encouraged* by the doctrines of the Hindoo religion, it appears evident that the course which the British government should follow, according to the principle of religious tolerance . . . is to allow the practice in those cases in which it is countenanced by their religion; and to prevent it in others in which it is by the same authority prohibited (emphasis mine).[48]

Two moves have been made from the pundit's actual words to arrive at this conclusion. The pundit claims that he has answered the question 'to the best of my knowledge'. However, his response is treated as an altogether authoritative one. Further, permission by inference is transformed into scriptural 'recognition' and 'encouragement' of sati. Colonial policy on sati was thus formulated on the basis of an interpretation of the pundit's replies by the officials who put the questions. It was a result of this encounter which produced the only legislative enactment on sati until its eventual abolition. The statement itself was also repeatedly recalled by officials arguing against abolition. Certainly, permission to commit sati was more explicit elsewhere in the scriptures. However, at issue here is not the scriptural accuracy of the pundit's response so much as the arbitrariness so typical of the official interpretation of vyawasthas.

This example embodies many of the basic principles by which a body of information about sati generated. Questions to pundits were intended to establish clarity on all aspects of sati. Pundits were required to comb the scriptures and produce unambiguous scriptural support. For instance, in April 1813, a pundit was required to specify the meaning of the phrase 'tender years' in his statement that 'a woman having a child of tender years is wholly inhibited from becoming a suttee'.[49] Inferential conclusions were only acceptable where explicit documentation was impossible. Thus, for example, the Sadr Nizamat Adalat had to be content with inferential scriptural support for the burial of *jogis*. The matter had been referred to the Sadr Nizamat Adalat by the magistrate of the provincial Dacca court, since the pundit at that court had in their view unsatisfactorily claimed that 'This is an act which is founded merely on practice'.[50] The Sadr Nizamat Adalat pundits produced inferential support in their response. In this context they also argued that the scriptures themselves gave equal support to custom and usage. However, despite official insistence on faithfulness to the scriptures, colonial officials continued to prefer explicit scriptural injunction.[51] It was for this reason that the Sadr Nizamat Adalat reprimanded a district pundit for referring 'to the custom of a country, upon a point which is expressly provided for by law'.[52]

Over the years, through such continual and intensive questioning, criteria for an officially sanctioned sati were generated. It had to be voluntary. Brahmin women were permitted only sahamarana. Non-brahmin women could burn through sahamarana or anoomarana. Sati was forbidden to women under 16 and to women with infants less than three years. Women of the jogi tribe were permitted to bury themselves.

Although scriptural authority was claimed for this model, a careful reading of the Parliamentary papers tells quite another story. For example, colonial officials treated vyawasthas as truthful exegeses of the scriptures in an absolute sense and enforced them legally. By contrast, it is clear from reading these vyawasthas that pundits issuing them believed them to be interpretive. However, not all vyawasthas were accorded such legitimacy; rather, colonial officials selectively privileged some and marginalized others.

Pundits attested to the interpretive nature of vyawasthas in several ways. Vyawasthas were often prefaced with such declarations as:

> Having inspected the paper drawn up by the chief judge of this court we proceed to furnish a reply *to the best of our ability* (emphasis mine).[53]
> Having considered the question proposed by the court I now answer it *to the best of my knowledge* (emphasis mine).[54]

Similarly, they characterised their replies as opinions: 'The authorities for the above opinion are as follows'. The interpretive character of the *vyawasthas* was also evident from the way in which the scriptures were used:

In support of the above *may be adduced* the following authorities (emphasis mine).[55]

In the above sentence by using the words 'she who ascends', the author *must have had in contemplation* those who declined to do so (emphasis mine).[56]

From the above quoted passage of the Mitateshura, *it would appear that* this was an act fit for all women to perform (emphasis mine).[57]

It is clear from the above that vyawasthas did not claim to pronounce either scriptural truth or the only possible response to a given question.[58]

The corpus of texts designated 'the scriptures' also made such a claim difficult to maintain. The scriptures were an enormous body of texts composed at different times. They included the *srutis*, the *dharmashastras* or *smritis* and *nibandhas*. The *srutis* were believed to be a pre-scriptural transcription of a revealed oral discourse anterior to the category of historicity. The *dharmashastras* or *smritis* were mnemic and historico-social texts supposedly transcribed by the sages under the authority of Hindu kings. The principal *shastras* are products of named and thus 'historical' subjects: Manu, Yajnavalkya and Narada. The commentaries and digests were treatises interpreting and expounding the *shastras* and mainly produced between the eleventh and eighteenth centuries. Different commentaries were held to be authoritative in different regions. It is no wonder then that two pundits could issue vyawasthas on the same point and quote different texts or different passages from the same text to support their statements.

The fact that the various texts were authored at different periods also accounted for their heterogeneity on many points, not least of which was the scriptural sanction for sati. Colonial response to such heterogeneity took three forms. Sometimes diversity was selectively recognized, as in the determination and enforcement of the appropriate modes of committing sati for brahmin and non-brahmin widows. At other times it was acknowledged for practical reasons but not 'resolved', as in the considered tolerance of regional variation in the mode of conducting sati: whether the widow's body was placed to the left or right of the corpse, the direction of the pyre, and so on. A third response was to marginalize certain vyawasthas. A telling example of such strategic marginalization is the fate of Mrityunjoy Vidyalankar's vyawastha, relegated to the appendix of the Nizamat Adalat proceedings of 1817, with no more than a mention in the main text. This vyawastha systematically called into question the colonial rationale of a scriptural sanction for sati and questioned its status as an act of virtue. Vidyalankar pointed out that as a form of suicide it was debatable whether sati was consonant with the *srutis* which forbade any wilful abridgement of life. Further he noted that the ultimate goal of all Hindus was selfless absorption in a divine essence, a union which was said to flow not from action like sati, performed with a view to reward, but from devotion and contemplation of the divine. Given this a life of austerity and sexual abstinence, as implied by ascetic widowhood, emerged as an equally if not more meritorious act.

Vidyalankar's vyawastha contained sufficient scriptural justification for prohibiting sati. It was however ignored. Continual reinscription of sati into a scriptural tradition despite evidence to the contrary points to the arbitrariness of meanings imposed by a colonial reading of vyawasthas. If the construct of sati thus produced is specifically 'colonial', it can also be argued that 'religion' in this discourse emerges merely as that part of culture that colonial power chooses not to interdict. If for some reason it was decided to prohibit a practice the strategy was to discount its claim to being 'religious' in a colonial reading of the scriptures. In the end this is what happened in the case of sati. Of course it was not quite as simple as this for as we have seen, sati's scriptural status was problematized long before the practice was prohibited. Ultimately abolition was legislated when it was deemed feasible. However, this was not the basis on which the discourse was articulated.

In the meantime, while sati was still conceptualized as 'religious' official policy, whatever its claim to non-interference, was to ensure adherence to the official conception of a 'true' sati. A coherent, unambiguous definition of sati was an essential prerequisite to this policy. We have already traced how such clarity was achieved. Attentiveness to the details of practice was another aspect of this policy. Official watchfulness was made possible by the systematic collection and tabulation of data on each sati. In addition to personal data on the widow and her deceased husband, the time, place and mode of burning, magistrates were also given explicit instructions to 'not allow the most minute particular to escape observation'.[59] Such details ensured that no infraction, whether on the part of officials or natives, could escape the official eye. Thus, for instance, in the review of satis for 1819, the magistrate of Shahabad was reprimanded for preventing an illegal sati by persuasion where he could have employed force. Magistrates were also censured for being overzealous. Thus in 1819, the magistrate for Bheerbhoom district was criticized for requiring previous intimation for performing sati when there was no order to this effect on the statute books. Given the importance of detail to such 'a penal mapping of the social body',[60] magistrates were compelled to record details and reprimanded for reports that were 'totally destitute of remark'.[61] The consistency of the Nizamat Adalat on this score drew the approval of the Governor General and his Council who commended them in 1820 on the 'minuteness with which the Nizamat Adaulut have entered on the examination of the returns from the several districts'.[62]

There is no doubt that despite the professed colonial policy of religious non-interference, the process by which knowledge on sati was produced for legal enforcement ensured that the concept of sati generated was distinctly 'colonial'. As the examples above indicate, despite the involvement of brahmin pundits, the privilege of the final authoritative interpretation of their vyawasthas was appropriated by colonial officials. For it was Nizamat Adalat judges, the Governor General and his Council who determined which vyawasthas were 'essential' and which 'peripheral'. The position of the brahmin pundits was ambiguous. The fact of being native simultaneously privileged and devalued them as reliable sources. They were critical to making the scriptures accessible to colonial officials. But they were also the 'artful classes' against whom it was the mission of colonization to protect 'the simple'.

This process by which this construct of sati was produced exemplifies the textualized nature of the discourse. Here I draw on the work of Paul Ricoeur.[63] Ricoeur illustrates the process of textualization, analysing what happens to 'discourse' or 'speech' when it becomes 'textualized' for instance, in language, action or ritual. Contrasting discourse with language, Ricoeur points out that discourse is realized temporally, it has a subject who speaks, 'a world which it claims to describe, to express or to represent',[64] and a person who is being addressed. In the example at hand, the pundit's vyawastha is analogous to discourse. Vyawasthas, like speech, had as their reference a specific context, as opinions expressed by the pundits on specific situations which took into account particular needs.

The textualization of such discourse, according to Ricoeur, results in the fixation of meaning, its dissociation from any authorial intention, the display of non-ostensive references and a universal range of addresses. The colonial rewriting/reinterpretation of the pundits' vyawasthas as invariant scriptural truths and their enforcement as law is analogous to the textualization of discourse. Opinions pronounced on particular cases became rules applicable to all cases. Thus the meaning of sati became 'fixed'; in other words, a sati that met certain criteria could be identified as authentic. Once 'textualized', in this instance through systematic writing, colonial officials could and did interpret the vyawasthas in ways that both reflected and did not reflect the intentions of pundits. Given that a statement of the particular became generalized, it obviously no longer had as its reference the initial interaction that produced it. Finally, the enforcement of vyawasthas as law automatically extended their relevance beyond those whose situation had initially elicited them.

The textualization of the pundits' discourse on sati also had as a consequence the elimination of human agency. If vyawasthas grounded in specific contexts were made autonomous the result was also to create an 'imaginative construct' that did not re-present any particular sati. This ideal typical representation of sati denied the possibility of sati as the conscious enactment of a social practice. Such erasure of human agency effectively put the operation of Hindu culture into a timeless present in which passive natives remained eternally yoked to religion. In this context it is interesting that many of the descriptions of sati written and used by abolitionists in their arguments are narratives of sati the phenomenon, not of any specific incident.

The following description of a 'typical sati' by the magistrate R.M. Bird is a perfectly textualized example:

> If it were desired to portray a scene which should thrill with horror every heart, not entirely dead to the touch of human sympathy, it would suffice to describe a father, regardless of the affection of his tender child, in having already suffered one of the severest miseries which flesh is heir to, with tearless eye leading forth a spectacle to the assembled multitude, who with barbarous cries demand the sacrifice, and unrelentingly delivering up the unconscious and unresisting victim to an untimely death, accompanied by the most cruel tortures.[65]

Bird here describes sati in which the widow, relatives and spectators all play parts which are predictable given what has been said here about colonial representation of each of their roles. That such textualization also denies the widow subjectivity has also been noted.

In Ricoeur's expanded sense of the term 'textualization', cultures are 'textualized' in a number of ways. Myths, folklore, epics, rituals and other artifacts express and reiterate to a society its cultural values. Ricoeur and Geertz[66] among others have interpreted such cultural expressions in the manner of texts. In arguing that the colonial discourse textualized sati, I am not suggesting that Indian society was not textualized in the pre-colonial period, merely that the colonial mode of textualizing was one that privileged writing and that such writing produced consequences of domination, including those discussed in this paper.

Finally, of course, the discourse on sati is a discourse of power. It illustrates dramatically Foucault's compelling thesis that knowledge is produced within the matrix of power and that power operates through the deployment of knowledge. The relationship between the colonial official and pundit was clearly interwoven by power while the production and accumulation of knowledge about sati enabled both attention to detail and the redefinition and redistribution of sati into its 'legal' and 'illegal' forms.

V. Conclusion

In this paper I have examined the first of the nineteenth-century debates on the status of women in India. These debates arose in the context of determining an appropriate colonial policy on such matters as sati which were seen to mark the depressed position of women in Indian society, the reform of which was held to be part of the regenerating mission of colonization. I have treated the debate as discourse and focused on the assumptions about Indian society crucial to this analysis—the hegemony of religious texts, native obedience to its injunctions, and a scriptural sanction for sati—all of which are problematized by material in the Parliamentary papers.

For instance, diversity in the mode of carrying out sati and regional variation in its incidence highlight the fact that textual tradition was actively negotiated. Similarly, both the resistance of some widows to coercion and what appears as the willingness of others to commit sati signal the fact that women had a will of their own and acted on their own behalf. Finally, whatever the official claims for sati as a practice founded in the Hindu faith, attention to the process by which knowledge about sati was produced illustrates that officials interpreted the responses of pundits in particular ways, with the consequence that the construct of sati that was legally enforced was specifically 'colonial'. Officials employed a number of tactics in reading the vyawasthas of pundits. Among these are the following: they privileged vyawasthas based on religious texts over those that drew on custom. They also insisted that pundits produce explicit scriptural injunction and would accept inference only where such unambiguous support could not be generated. Of course, such tactics were not used with any consistency. Some vyawasthas (like that of Vidyalankar) were simply ignored. Thus, whatever their insistence on having arrived at a concept of sati that was true to the scriptures, we can state with assurance that the process attests mainly to the arbitrariness of meanings imposed by official reading of vyawasthas.

However arbitrary or contingent nineteenth-century official interpretations might have been, some of these assumptions remain with us today, both in the scholarship on sati or more generally in our understanding of Indian society. It is the remarkable endurance of some of these ideas that confirms the contemporary relevance of this investigation. For example, much of the scholarly work on sati reproduces the notion of sati as an essentially religious practice.[67] One consequence of this is to assume a transhistorical significance for the phenomenon, a perspective that precludes the possibility of sati being the product of different factors at different times. Dorothy Stein even goes so far as to suggest that the concept of sati might be more important than its practice.[68]

Such an approach lacks explanatory value; it cannot, for example, explain regional variation in the incidence of sati. Not all academic work shares this perspective. Although he does not say so himself, Sharma's article on the history of western response to sati conclusively documents first, that the meaning of sati was historically variable and second, that its meaning was bitterly contested in the nineteenth century.[69] Also, in Ashis Nandy's work, we have the beginnings of an analysis of sati as a practice rooted in temporal and spatial contexts.[70]

The discourse on sati was by no means the first time colonial officials accorded primary significance to religion. The codification of scriptural law as civil law in 1772 had already enshrined its importance.[71] The enforcement of scriptural law as civil law had extended the applicability of brahmanic scripture hitherto limited to the twice-born castes to all colonial subjects. Thus was established a particular relationship between scripture and society, a relationship which was bolstered each time, as in the case of sati in Bengal, colonial officials privileged as authentic the scriptural tradition and marginalized the importance of custom.

I suggest that this designation of the scriptural tradition as 'true' was to have an important bearing on the nineteenth-century debates on the status of women. For these debates were a mode through which colonial power was both enforced and contested. Colonial officials sought to justify interference in indigenous tradition, even colonial rule itself, on the basis of women's low position in indigenous tradition as also in contemporary society. Divergent indigenous male elite responses to this challenge were to argue either that such poor treatment was contrary to tradition—Roy's strategy in the case of sati—or that women approved of their traditional lot—the conservative Hindu response—or that this tradition was bankrupt—the view among others of Henry Derozio. In all three instances, the official equation of tradition with scripture was reproduced. In other words, arguments for and against social reform were articulated, at least in part, upon a peculiarly colonial construction of tradition. Put another way, official discourse shaped the nature of indigenous counter discourses in quite specific ways.

Finally, analysis of the official discourse on sati suggests a less sharp distinction than has hitherto been proposed between Orientalists and Anglicists. The commonalities underlying their perspectives are significant. As such, the issue is raised of the extent to which the Anglicist programme for social engineering was determined by the Orientalist analysis of Indian society.

Notes

1. For a straightforward history of colonial state policy, A. Mukhopadhyay, 'Sati as a Social Institution in Bengal', *Bengal Past and Present*, 75, pp. 99–115; K. Mittra, 'Suppression of Suttee in the Province of Cuttack', *Bengal Past and Present*, 46, pp. 125–31; G. Seed, 'The Abolition of Suttee in Bengal', *History*, October 1955, pp. 286–99. For a 'colonial' account, E.J. Thompson, *Suttee: A Historical and Philosophical Enquiry into the Hindu Rite of Widow Burning*, London, Allen and Unwin, 1928. For a general but very suggestive history of western responses, A. Sharma, 'Suttee: A Study in Western Reactions', in his *Threshold of Hindu-Buddhist Studies*, Calcutta, Minerva, 1978, pp. 83–111. For a provocative psycho-social analysis, A. Nandy, 'Sati: A Nineteenth Century Tale of Women, Violence and Protest', in V.C. Joshi (ed.),

Rammohun Roy and the Process of Modernisation in India, Delhi, Vikas, 1975, pp. 168–94. For contemporary feminist analyses, D.K. Stein, 'Women to Burn: Suttee as a Normative Institution', *Signs*, 4(2), 1978, pp. 253–68; M. Daly, *Gyn/Ecology*, Boston, Beacon, 1978.

2. For a succinct formulation of this perspective as it relates to sati, C.A. Bayly, 'From Ritual to Ceremony: Death Ritual in Hindu North India', in J. Whaley (ed.), *Mirrors of Mortality: Studies in the Social History of Death*, London, Europa, 1981, pp. 173–4.

3. I am arguing that this conception was distinctly 'colonial' not by means of comparison with some pre-colonial conception of sati but rather, as will become clear in the course of the paper, with reference to the way a particular knowledge about sati was produced under colonialism.

4. B.S. Cohn in a lecture at University of California, Santa Cruz, February 1981.

5. M. Foucault, *Discipline and Punish*, New York, Vintage, 1979.

6. E. Said, *Orientalism*, New York, Vintage, 1979.

7. R. Thapar, *The Past and Prejudice*, National Book Trust of India, 1975, p. 3.

8. R. Guha (ed.), *Subaltern Studies I: Writings on South Asian History and Society*, Delhi, Oxford University Press, 1982.

9. There is a substantial literature on the history of law under colonialism, a discussion of which is beyond the scope of this paper. See especially: J.D.M. Derrett, *Religion, Law and the State in India*, London, Faber and Faber, 1968, chs 8, 9; Lloyd I. Rudolph and Suzanne H. Rudolph, *The Modernity of Tradition*, Part III, Chicago, University of Chicago Press, 1967, B.S. Cohn, 'Anthropological Notes on Disputes and Law in India', *American Anthropologist*, 67, December 1965, pp. 88–122; D.A. Washbrook, 'Law, State and Agrarian Society in Colonial India', *Modern Asian Studies*, 15(3), 1981, pp. 649–721. Also noteworthy is A. Appadurai's discussion of law in his *Worship and Conflict under Colonial Rule*, Cambridge, Cambridge University Press, 1981.

10. Parliamentary Papers on Hindu Widows (hereafter *PP*), 1821, xviii, p. 316.

11. Loc. cit.

12. Ibid., pp. 322–6.

13. *Vyawasthas* were the written legal opinions submitted by pundits in response to such questions. See also Note 58.

14. *PP*, 1821, pp. 332–3.

15. Ibid., pp. 335–8.

16. *PP*, 1824, xxiii, p. 353.

17. *PP*, 1821, p. 513.

18. *PP*, 1824, p. 378.

19. Loc. cit.

20. *PP*, 1830, xxviii, pp. 1009–11.

21. Analysis of sati by caste for 1823 is as follows: brahmin: 234; kayasth: 25; vaisya: 14; sudra: 292 (*PP*, 1825). It is clear that the practice was disproportionately high among the numerically smaller brahmin caste.

22. J.K. Majumdar (ed.), *Raja Rammohun Roy and Progressive Movements in India: A Selection from Records, 1775–1845*, Calcutta, 1941, p. 141.

23. *PP*, 1821, p. 321.

24. Ibid., pp. 521–3.

25. Loc. cit.

26. Loc. cit.

27. Loc. cit.

28. Loc. cit.

29. Ibid., p. 529.

30. *PP*, 1830, p. 918.

31. *PP*, 1828, xxiii, p. 169.

32. *PP*, 1830, p. 918.

33. *PP*, 1821, p. 532.

34. Ibid., p. 410.
35. Ibid., p. 411.
36. Loc. cit.
37. Ibid., p. 412.
38. Ibid., p. 424.
39. Ibid., p. 321.
40. *PP*, 1830, p. 906.
41. *PP*, 1821, p. 506.
42. Ibid., p. 507.
43. Ibid., p. 404.
44. Ibid., p. 400.
45. Ibid., p. 322.
46. Loc. cit.
47. Loc. cit.
48. Ibid., p. 325.
49. Ibid., p. 322.
50. Ibid., p. 406.
51. The undermining of custom and customary law was not particular to sati but was a general feature of colonial rule and has been noted among others by Derrett, op. cit.; Rudolph and Rudolph, op. cit.; Appadurai, op. cit.
52. Ibid., p. 134.
53. Ibid., pp. 408–9.
54. Ibid., p. 322.
55. Ibid., p. 407.
56. Loc. cit.
57. Loc. cit.
58. In this context it is interesting to note that the dictionary definition of vyawastha tells its own tale of colonial legacy. Vyawastha is variously defined as 'settlement', 'decision', 'statute', 'rule', 'law', 'legal decision' or opinion applied to the written extracts from the codes of law or adjustment of contradictory passages in different codes. Source: A Sanskrit–English Dictionary compiled by Sir Monier Williams.
59. *PP*, 1821, p. 327.
60. Foucault, op. cit., p. 78.
61. *PP*, 1821, p. 344.
62. *PP*, 1823, xvii, p. 354.
63. P. Ricoeur, 'The Model of the Text: Meaningful Action Considered as a Text', *Social Research*, 1971, 38, p. 3.
64. Ricoeur, op. cit., p. 531.
65. *PP*, 1825, xxiv, p. 243.
66. C. Geertz, 'Deep Play: Notes on the Balinese Cockfight', *Daedalus*, 1972, 101, pp. 1–37.
67. Mitra, Mukhopadhyay, Seed, Stein, Thompson, op. cit.
68. Stein, op. cit.
69. Sharma, op. cit.
70. Nandy, op. cit.
71. B.S. Cohn, 'Notes on the History and Study of Indian Society and Culture', in *Structure and Change in Indian Society*, Singer and Cohn (eds), Chicago, Aldine, 1968, p. 10.

3

Education for Women*

GERALDINE FORBES

mong the earliest women's memoirs from the nineteenth century are stories of a passionate desire to learn to read. Rassundari Devi, born *c.* 1809, taught herself to read by stealing precious moments from her housework and the responsibilities of caring for 12 children. Later, she described her craving for knowledge:

> I was so immersed in the sea of housework that I was not conscious of what I was going through day and night. After some time the desire to learn how to read properly grew very strong in me, I was angry with myself for wanting to read books. Girls did not read . . . That was one of the bad aspects of the old system. The other aspects were not so bad. People used to despise women of learning . . . In fact, older women used to show a great deal of displeasure if they saw a piece of paper in the hands of a woman. But somehow I could not accept this.[1]

Rassundari's progress was slow but she learned to read, to write, and finally wrote about her own experiences.

Haimavati Sen (*c.* 1866–1932), born a half-century later, recalled her childhood in Khulna District of East Bengal:

> The outer quarters were my resort, that is where I spent all my time; during the office hours I stayed in the school room. The teacher was very fond of me. I greatly enjoyed listening to the lessons. But I had no right to education. Though I lived like a boy in every respect, in matters of education I remained a woman. It is a popular superstition in our country that women, if educated, have to suffer widowhood; hence that path was entirely closed for me. But I was inspired by an eager wish God had planted in my heart.[2]

Fortunately, a sub-inspector visited the school and heard Haimavati answer the questions her brothers missed. The sub-inspector spoke to her father and Haimavati became a regular pupil.

Pandita Ramabai (1858–1922) was awarded the title 'Pandita' in recognition of her great learning. Ramabai's first teacher was her mother. Anant Padmanabha Dongre, Ramabai's father, was a great Vedic scholar who decided to educate his wife over the objections of the community. Ramabai's rigorous education began at age eight and continued until she was 14. She memorized the *Bhagavata Purana* and the *Bhagavad Gita*;

*From Geraldine Forbes, *Women in Modern India* (*New Cambridge History of India*, vol. IV, no. 2) (Cambridge: Cambridge University Press, 1996), pp. 32–63.

then studied Sanskrit grammar and vocabulary. At this time her family was travelling from one pilgrimage site to another and Ramabai learned first-hand how various sects practised Hinduism.[3]

One cannot generalize from these three cases about women's desire to learn. But given conventional notions about the impropriety, even danger, of women's education we can be certain these headstrong women were a minority. In his Report on the State of Education in Bengal (1836) William Adam wrote: 'A superstitious feeling is alleged to exist in the majority of Hindu families, principally cherished by the women and not discouraged by the men, that a girl taught to read and write will soon after marriage become a widow.' Adam also commented on the fear, shared by Hindus and Muslims, that a 'knowledge of letters' might facilitate female intrigue.[4] Because Hindu women were totally dependent on fathers, then husbands, and finally sons for support, they said prayers and performed rituals to ensure longevity for these men. If learning to read would lead to a husband's death, then pursuing knowledge was tantamount to suicide. This was a sex-segregated world; men and women did different work and occupied separate spaces. Women interacted primarily with women and it was women who enforced the prohibition against female education. Many of the women who learned to read before the 1870s have reported hiding their accomplishments from other women. Even if mothers were lenient with daughters, mothers-in-law and the other women in the father-in-law's home were seldom as kind. It is difficult to impute motives to the women who vehemently opposed education. Subjects of a harsh patrilineal, patriarchal system they were not in a position to oppose prevailing codes. Their survival depended on upholding the status quo and an educated stranger in their midst posed an obvious threat. Those women and girls who were eager to learn had no recourse but to look to the men who controlled their lives.

Missionaries began the first girls' school but their efforts were soon rivalled by Indian reformers. Despite their valiant efforts, there were no real advances in female education until the second half of the nineteenth century when the government offered financial support. Even then, efforts to organize girls' schools languished until the urban professional elite joined reformers in supporting formal education for girls. In the last quarter of the nineteenth century, institutions proliferated and the number of educated women grew steadily. The debate then turned to what was the most suitable type of education for women. Before the century was over a few women came forward to articulate their ideas about female education. By the twentieth century women were ready to design a curriculum and set up schools for girls.

Traditional Education

Traditionally education meant learning to read sacred literature. Among Hindus, members of the priestly caste, brahmins, were learned in all branches of sacred knowledge, while the other twice-born castes (kshatriyas and vaishyas) were given a less rigorous programme but also learned practical skills. Shudras and most women were not taught the sacred books but some women were taught to read. Some women from upper-class Vaisnavite families learned to read puranic literature.[5] Muslims girls were expected to learn the Quran and some accounting skills but the strict seclusion observed by upper-class families prohibited their daughters from attending schools. Consequently, what they learned about their religion they learned at home, either from their families or through tutors.[6] At the turn of the century there were only 11 Quran schools for girls in Bengal with 142 pupils.[7]

At the beginning of the nineteenth century, female literacy was extremely low in relation to male literacy. Male literacy, ranging from approximately 6 per cent in Bengal to 20 per cent in the Deccan, was also low in comparison with Western nations or Japan. Moreover, indigenous schools for boys were on the decline.[8] Boys attended three kinds of schools: small village schools which taught elementary reading and accounting; higher schools for Hindus, primarily brahmins, which taught Sanskrit grammar, lexicography and literature; and Persian and Arabic schools for Muslims. We do not know how many of these schools there were throughout India, but in Bengal there were approximately 100 traditional institutions per district with a total of 10,800 students. There were 164 Hindu schools in Poona in the 1820s. Aparna Basu contends that 'the state of higher learning among Hindus and Muslims resembled that which existed in Europe before the invention of printing'.[9]

Female education was informal and largely limited to practical matters. Women from respectable families often studied classical or vernacular literature as 'a pious recreation', and girls from propertied families received some education in keeping accounts.[10] But most females learned only the household arts.

English Education in India

English education was introduced into India because the East India Company needed clerks and translators. From 1813 the Company set aside some money for education, and after the Charter of 1833 English became the official language. In 1844 Lord Hardinge announced that English-educated Indians would be given preference for government appointments. Free-traders voiced their support for this policy believing it would help develop an Indian population loyal to the British. The missionaries joined the chorus of approval. Eager to convert Indians from influential families, missionaries recognized how much easier it would be with English as the language of professional advancement. Liberals believed in the civilizing influence of Western philosophy and literature. It was only at the end of the century that these men saw the dangerous side of education, that is, its tendency to promote nationalism and political unrest. Then, the government made attempts to control and even curtail education.[11]

Long before the government decided to sponsor English education, Indian gentlemen set up Hindu College in Calcutta. Opened in 1816, Hindu College was designed to prepare young Indian men for lucrative positions with the East India Company. In the first three decades of the twentieth century Hindu College and similar schools throughout British India depended on the patronage of wealthy Indians and were in direct competition with traditional schools teaching Sanskrit, Persian and Arabic. As economic patterns changed, patronage for traditional schools disappeared. At about the same time, bright young men decided to study English.[12]

In contrast to support for boys' schools, there was little interest in the education of girls. The colonial government, despite pressure exerted by missionaries and liberals, was unconcerned with female education. The missionaries were interested in female education and schools for girls because, they argued, women needed to be brought into the fold to make conversions permanent. But since men made the decisions, female education was ancillary.[13]

Unmarried female missionaries arrived in India in the 1840s and were assigned to work with women and children. These missionary women, educated and eager to prove their worth, concentrated on converting adult married Indian women to Christianity.[14] They gained entry to households as teachers where they read stories, taught needlework, and attempted to bring their charges to Christ. Rarely were they successful in gaining converts. When it became apparent that these zenana projects were unproductive, the mission authorities substituted girls' schools. Missionary women continued to teach and it was their students, Indian women from Christian families, who became teachers in a number of the new girls' schools.[15]

Early Schools for Girls

The opening of Hindu College in 1816 was closely followed by the founding of the Calcutta School Society to promote female education. Radha Kanta Deb, the secretary of this society, became a patron of female education and assisted in the formation of the Calcutta Female Juvenile Society (founded in 1819 by Baptists). In 1821, the School Society brought Miss Mary Anne Cooke to Calcutta but could not raise the money to open schools. The Church Missionary Society stepped in, employed Miss Cooke, and opened 30 schools for 'respectable' Hindu girls. These schools enjoyed the patronage of Hindu gentlemen and were staffed by brahmin pundits, but they failed to attract girls from the higher castes. The religious instruction deterred prestigious families while pupils from the lower classes or Christian families were lured to the school by gifts of clothing and other items.

The Church Missionary Society was more successful in South India where it opened its first boarding school for girls in Tirunelveli in 1821. By 1840 the Scottish Church Society could claim six schools with a clientele of 200 Hindu girls. By mid-century the missionaries in Madras were instructing nearly 8,000 girls, the majority of whom were Christians, in day schools and boarding schools.[16]

One of the most important schools for girls was the Hindu Balika Vidyalaya opened in 1849 in Calcutta by J.E. Drinkwater Bethune, legal member of the Governor-General's Council and president of the Council of Education. The school was secular, instruction was in Bengali, and the girls were transported in a carriage emblazoned with a Sanskrit verse declaring that a daughter's education was a father's religious duty. Pandit Vidyasagar was appointed school secretary. Bethune persuaded several prominent families to endorse this experiment and by 1850 there were eighty pupils. When Bethune died in 1851, support for the school declined. In 1863 the school had 93 girls aged five to seven, three-quarters of whom were the 'lowest class', a clear indication of continuing upper-caste prejudice against female education.[17]

Government Support of Female Education

Lord Dalhousie, Governor-General of India from 1848 to 1856, declared that no single change was likely to produce more important and beneficial consequences than female education.[18] Sir Charles Wood, president of the Board of Control from 1853 to 1855, issued an education despatch in 1854 that detailed a shift in government policy, from

providing higher education for the elites to support for mass education in the vernacular. This new focus on a total system of education was to include both sexes. The despatch read:

> The importance of female education in India cannot be over-rated; and we have observed
> with pleasure the evidence which is now afforded of an increased desire on the part of many
> of the natives to give a good education to their daughters. By this means a far greater
> proportional impulse is imparted to the educational and moral tone of the people than by
> the education of men.[19]

The moral and financial support of the colonial authorities was essential to the
spread of female education, but did not guarantee schools for girls. Unlike education for
males, education for females did not automatically enhance the prestige and financial
standing of the family. In fact, the opposite may have been true.

Indian norms and social customs made the British model of schooling difficult, if
not impossible. Deeply ingrained notions of sex segregation and, in some areas, of
complete seclusion, meant girls had to have female teachers and study in separate
institutions. The widely accepted ideal of youthful marriage limited a girl's school-
going years. Moreover, the demands on women for food production and nurturing left
little time for lessons and studying.

There was a third set of problems associated with the institutions for female education. Indians were unaccustomed to sending their daughters to 'schools' yet this was
the only practical method of accomplishing the task. Zenana education—education
given in the home—was expensive, cumbersome, and largely ineffectual. Schools were
the answer but what kind of schools? Who would teach? What would be taught? Which
families would choose to send their daughters to school and for how long? If girls were
married prior to puberty, could they continue their education as married women? The
leaders of Indian society had to respond to these questions—a far more difficult task
than providing moral and material support.

Reformed Hinduism and Female Education

The breakthrough came with the establishment of government schools, such as
Bethune's, and schools sponsored by reformist religious institutions. First the Brahmo
Samaj, and later the Prarthana Samaj, Arya Samaj, and Theosophical Society all sup-
ported female education.

In 1854 there were approximately 626 girls' schools (Bengal: 288, Madras: 256,
Bombay: 65, and NWFP and Oudh: 17) with a total of 21,755 students.[20] Obviously
these schools were very small and the total number of girls receiving this education was
minuscule in relation to the total population. Yet, a shift in attitudes towards female
education had taken place.

Indians supported female education because they wanted social and religious
reform, or social and financial mobility, or both. The founders of Hindu College and
other early schools for boys wanted to advance the opportunities of their own class. In
the case of female education, early supporters saw opportunities for social mobility as
the demand for educated brides increased. They were also motivated by a desire for social
reform, possible only if women as well as men were educated. Many Western-educated
Bengali gentlemen undoubtedly wanted to 'wean away their own wives and daughters'

from various forms of popular culture regarded as licentious and vulgar. This increased the social distance between the 'new women' and their less educated sisters and deprived educated middle-class women of an avenue of protest offered by street performers and popular songs.[21] The concern here was not with women as individuals, but with their development as companions to men, as 'scientific' nurturers, and as members of civil society.

Members of the Brahmo Samaj, the Bengal-based reform society, led the movement for female education and equality between the sexes. Keshub Chandra Sen, a Brahmo leader, lectured on the importance of female education in 1861 and the following year organized a society for males who supported reforms for women. In 1865, the Brahmo Samaj sponsored the first organization where women met for religious instruction, sewing lessons, and discussions of social issues.[22]

The topic of women's education led to a split in the Brahmo Samaj in 1866. That year, Navabidhan (Keshub Sen's breakaway group) welcomed Miss Mary Carpenter to Calcutta. Carpenter's mission was to encourage female education and she was quick to notice the short-age of suitable teachers.[23] She spoke publicly about the problem, presented her proposals to the Governor-General, and helped establish the National Indian Association to promote mutual understanding between Indian and English people. In 1872 Carpenter, Keshub Sen, and another English woman, Annette Akroyd, set up a normal school.[24] Later Akroyd broke with Keshub and worked with another group of Brahmos to establish the Hindu Mahila Vidyalaya (Hindu Girls' School). By 1878 this school had merged with the older Bethune School to become Bethune College, an affiliate of Calcutta University. In 1883 Kadambini Basu and Chandramukhi Basu received their BAs from Bethune, becoming the first women graduates in the British Empire.[25]

In Madras it was the Theosophical Society that encouraged female education. Speaking as a leader of the society, Annie Besant (1847–1933) asserted that in ancient times Hindu women were educated and moved freely in society. She urged a return to this 'golden age'. In England Besant had been identified with women's emancipation since her public lecture on women's suffrage in 1874.[26] Besant had been associated with a number of other movements in England before she read Madame Blavatsky's *Secret Doctrine* in 1889. She then decided to join the theosophists and make India her home. Madame Blavatsky, a founder of the Theosophical Society, viewed child marriage, child widowhood, and sati as perversions of the original Hindu doctrine.[27] When Besant first spoke in India in 1893, she spoke of the greatness of the Indian past and the need to regain that past. Later she focused on specific problems and by 1901 had written an article for the *Indian Ladies Magazine* on the 'Education of Women'. Besant warned that India's fate would be sealed if women were not educated. But Western education was not the answer; it would 'unsex' women. Indians should look to their own ideal of womanhood—the Goddess Durga.[28] Besant pledged her efforts to this reform and founded a women's college based on these principles.[29]

In North India female education was encouraged by the Arya Samaj, a reformist Hindu sect which followed the teachings of Swami Dayanand Saraswati. By the end of the nineteenth century, progressive Arya Samajists recognized the importance of involving women in their reform efforts. The Jullundar Samaj opened the Arya Kanya Pathshala (Girls' School) in 1890 with a lady principal in charge.[30]

The Kanya Mahavidyalaya (Girls' Higher School) of Jullundar was opened somewhat later. Both this high school and the elementary girls' school, firmly established by 1892, owed their existence to the efforts of Lala Devraj. He opened his first school for girls in the family home, supported it through the sale of 'waste paper', and staffed it with teachers who were partially compensated with food from his mother's kitchen. As public acceptance for the idea of female education grew so did the school's enrolment. Before long a cadre of experienced women teachers and school administrators had designed special instructional materials. This institution occupied a special place in the community and 'became a catalyst for various kinds of change relating to women in [the] Punjab'.[31]

The Progress of Women's Education

Between 1849, when Bethune School opened, and 1882, when the Indian Education (Hunter) Commission reviewed the progress of education in India, serious efforts had been made to develop primary schools for girls and teacher-training institutions. Higher education for women and co-education were still contentious issues.[32] Faced with the fact that 98 per cent of school-age girls were not in school, authors of the Hunter Commission Report recommended more liberal grants-in-aid for girls' schools than for boys' and special scholarships and prizes for girls. In the next two decades higher education expanded rapidly; whereas there were only six women in Indian universities in 1881–2, by the turn of the century there were 264. During the same time period secondary school enrolment rose from 2,054 to 41,582.[33]

The story of women's education in the period following the Hunter Commission and the end of the century can be told through the work of three pioneer educationalists—Pandita Ramabai Saraswati, founder of the Sharada Sadan in Bombay and Poona (1889), Mataji Tapaswini who began the Mahakali Pathshala of Calcutta (1893), and D.K. Karve who began a school for widows in Poona (1896). These three examples are particularly significant because they represent efforts to build female schools distinct from those of the religious reform organizations. These were not secular public schools in the contemporary sense; in fact, they were all narrowly caste-, class- and community-based. These three examples are especially worthy of attention because they highlight the involvement of women in structuring and defining female education.

Pandita Ramabai

Pandita Ramabai was truly remarkable as a pioneer in women's education and rebel champion of women's rights. Her father supervised her education and allowed her to remain unmarried. When her father and mother died, Ramabai was 16 years old, unmarried, and able to read Sanskrit. She and her brother travelled throughout India lecturing on female education and social reform. The Calcutta elite were enchanted and bestowed on her the name 'Saraswati'—the Goddess of Learning—and called her 'Pandita' because she seemed as learned as other brahmin pandits. Other audiences were outraged and they jeered and booed when she attempted to speak.[34]

Ramabai's brother died in Calcutta and she married his close friend, Bipen Behari Das Medhavi (a shudra by caste). The next year, at age 23, Ramabai gave birth to a daughter. Unfortunately her husband died the following year.

Returning to Poona, Ramabai began to work with reformers to educate women through the Arya Mahila Samaj (Aryan's Women's Society).[35] While in Poona she gave evidence before the Hunter Commission and stressed the urgent need for women doctors and teachers. Determined to learn English and study medicine, Ramabai sought help from members of the Anglo-Catholic Community of St Mary the Virgin whose mother house was at Wantage in Oxfordshire, England. They were able to give her some assistance while the balance of her expenses were met through the sale of *Stri Dharma Neeti* ('Morals for Women'), her book urging women to take charge of their own lives. Ramabai, her young daughter, and a travelling companion, Anandibai Bhagat, left for England in 1883. Soon after the three of them had settled at Wantage, Ramabai declared she was unwilling to convert to Christianity. Some months later Anandibai committed suicide (the records here become very elusive) leaving Ramabai extremely shaken.

Ramabai was only 25 years of age and had already watched her parents, her brother, her husband, and her closest friend die. It was at this time, alone with her small daughter in a strange country, that Ramabai decided to accept baptism.[36] She continued her studies until 1886 when she decided to sail for America to attend the graduation ceremonies of her cousin Anandibai Joshi.

To finance this trip and popularize her cause Ramabai wrote *The High Caste Hindu Women*. Ten thousand copies of this book were sold before Ramabai had left America. In 1887 Boston admirers set up a Ramabai Association to support her work in India. She travelled throughout the United States and Canada studying educational, philanthropic and charitable institutions and lecturing to various groups. By May of 1888, she had collected over $30,000 in the name of her association.[37]

In India Pandita Ramabai established Sharada Sadan (Home of Wisdom), a school for widows, in Bombay. This was to be a non-sectarian school where all the caste rules of brahmins were scrupulously observed. It attracted some high-caste Hindu widows, among them Godubai (renamed Anandibai after her marriage to D.K. Karve) but generally the Hindu community remained suspicious of Ramabai's motives.

Ramabai attempted to forestall criticism by forming an Executive Committee composed of reformers who were known as staunch Hindus. This plan did not work and less than one year later Bombay newspapers carried articles critical of Ramabai and her school. When financial problems forced her to move the school to Poona, the newspaper *Kesari* charged her with converting widows to Christianity. Ramabai's admitted crime was allowing widows to attend her personal prayer meetings. By 1893, 25 girls were withdrawn. But there was no dearth of widows in need of shelter and before long Ramabai had other students. By 1900 the Sharada Sadan had trained 80 women who were able to earn their own living through teaching or nursing.[38]

Ramabai's second school, Mukti, was established 30 miles outside of Poona at Kedgaon following the famine that began in 1897. She began taking women and children who were victims of famine into Sharada Sadan where she fed and clothed them, and enrolled them in her school. Attempting to control the plague, the government placed restrictions on the movement of people; in Poona the city magistrate placed a limit on the number of inmates in Sharada Sadan. Since she could not keep famine victims in Poona, Ramabai took her charges to Kedgaon where she had purchased 100 acres of land. By 1900 this venture had grown into a major institution housing 2,000 women and children attending school and involved in industrial training and production.

Financing for Mukti came from an American committee which willingly approved all her schemes.[39]

Given a free hand, Ramabai urged the inmates of her home to become Christians and developed a unique educational programme to suit their needs. Her own version of Christianity was doctrinally eclectic, combining ideas she had learned from the sisters at Wantage, and from Roman Catholic, Jewish and Indian Christian friends. Ramabai saw caste as the great flaw in Hindu society. It led to false valuing of the intellect and denigration of physical work. Caste association promoted narrow self-interest and inhibited the development of a democratic spirit.

Ramabai designed a remedial curriculum. Literature selected for its emphasis on moral models would engender a spirit of caring; classes in physiology and botany were included to teach students about their own bodies and the physical world in which they lived. Industrial training was included—in printing, carpentry, tailoring, masonry, wood-cutting, weaving and needlework—as well as training in farming and gardening. All students were required to join 'unions' or societies such as the Temperance Union or the Christian Endeavour Society in an effort to break down caste barriers and develop new loyalties based on interest. As members of these societies, the children learned simple parliamentary rules and were encouraged to take charge of their own affairs.[40]

Ramabai's educational work impressed contemporaries, but her connection with Christianity has obfuscated her contribution to women's education. An acknowledged Christian when hatred of the ruling power was growing daily, her work angered some of the most powerful men in western India. Ramabai believed the intensity of their anger was related to the fact that many of her pupils came from the higher castes. She argued that these men would have remained unconcerned if her work were confined to low-caste women.[41]

There were many issues that provoked Ramabai's sharp and unpopular comments. When she heard about the Rukhmabai case, she exploded in angry denunciations of both the British and Indian men. Rukhmabai, married as a child, had been tried and sentenced to prison (but was never imprisoned) because she refused to have a conjugal relationship with her husband. Ramabai wrote:

> Our only wonder is that a defenceless woman like Rukhmabai dared to raise her voice in the face of the powerful Hindu law, the mighty British Government, the 129,000,000 men, the 330,000,000 gods of the Hindus; all these have conspired together to crush her into nothingness. We cannot blame the English Government for not defending a helpless woman; it is only fulfilling its agreement made with the male population of India.[42]

Ramabai's greatest legacy was her effort, the first in India, to educate widows and the pupils she left behind to carry on her work.

Mataji Maharani Tapaswini

The Mahakali Pathshala (Great Mother Kali School) of Bengal stands in sharp contrast to Pandita Ramabai's school, with its missionary connection and foreign support. Founded in Calcutta in 1893 by Her Holiness Mataji Maharani Tapaswini, this school and its many branches has been styled a 'genuine Indian attempt' at developing female education.[43] This school received no financial assistance from foreigners and employed no foreign teachers. Founders of the institution accepted the 'school' model for female education, but opposed co-education and the use of one syllabus for both sexes. Their aim was to educate 'girls on strictly national lines in the hope that they might regenerate Hindu society.' This was a project consistent with those of nationalist 'revivalists', who, in the historian Tanika Sarkar's view, did not automatically oppose reform 'in the name of resisting colonial knowledge'.[44] Despite their differences with the liberal reformers, they too believed in the relationship between progress and female education and looked to a future where Indian women would play a large role in the affairs of the country.

Gangabai (Mataji Maharani Tapaswini), a brahmin woman of the Deccan who had learned Sanskrit and studied sacred literature, opened her first school with 30 pupils.[45] She had come to Calcutta with a mission: to promote female education in harmony with Hindu religious and moral principles. Unlike Pandita Ramabai, Gangabai believed that Hindu society could be regenerated from within. Her notion of an ideal education for women was translated into a syllabus which included: knowledge of sacred literature and history; an understanding of the myths and legends that spoke of the duties of the daughter, wife, daughter-in-law and mother; and practical skills such as cooking and sewing.[46] This syllabus was praised by 'Hindoo gentlemen of the middle-class' who believed that much of the female education then in existence 'demoralized and denationalized' young Hindu women.[47] Cooking lessons were especially popular in light of the prevalent belief that educated girls avoided the kitchen. Financial support for this institution grew rapidly and within 10 years there were 23 branches with 450 students. As the school expanded it published its own Bengali and Sanskrit textbooks. Gangabai turned more and more to supervision while the actual administration of the school was left in the hands of an illustrious board of trustees presided over by the Maharaja of Darbhanga, Bengal's largest landlord.

This school proved immensely popular. Patrons approved of the emphasis on religious injunctions, domestic skills, and strict purdah. Although the original curriculum included very little formal reading and writing, this gradually changed. In 1948 the Mahakali Pathshala was affiliated to Calcutta University and by that time all that remained of the original curriculum was the performance of a few pujas (religious rituals).[48] In the early years of the twentieth century the existence of this school and its popularity were regarded as indicators that the conservative elements of society, at least in Bengal, had given their approval to the concept of female education.[49]

Dhondo Keshav Karve

In the 1890s Dhondo Keshav Karve established a number of female schools in Poona. In his autobiography, *Looking Back*, Karve reconstructs his personal history to explain how his experiences led him to build a school for widows in 1896. Other accounts tell the story of Godubai Joshi (later Anandibai), a child widow who became Karve's second wife. She dreamed of setting up a widow's home soon after she became Pandita Ramabai's first pupil. What may well have been the culmination of the life-long dream of two people has been known as 'Karve's Home'. Anandibai joked about this when she was very old:

Sometimes in fun I tell him that although people call him Maharshi, some of the credit is due to me. For if I had not managed the family affairs and set him free to carry out his public activities, he could not have achieved to much.[50]

Karve's association with reform movements dated back to his college years. After graduation from Elphinstone College he taught mathematics in three different high schools in Bombay before accepting a position at Fergusson College in Poona. Here he was elected a life member of the Deccan Educational Society.[51] When his wife died, he decided he would marry a widow and chose Godubai, the 22-year-old sister of his college friend. People in his home town excommunicated him and persecuted his mother. These actions shocked Karve and caused him to question remarriage as a way of helping child widows. At the same time he became increasingly interested in education as a way of assisting widows to become financially independent. In 1896 he opened a shelter for widows that became a school.

The curriculum in this school was designed to make young widows employable and self-sufficient. Because schools for girls were scarce, Karve was asked to admit unmarried girls as well. To accommodate this new clientele, Karve set up the Mahila Vidyalaya (Girls' School) to develop 'good wives, good mothers, good neighbours'. He believed that widows needed an education 'that would make them economically independent and would enable them to think for themselves'[52] but unmarried girls needed an education that would reinforce their dependence.

Parvatibai Athavali, Anandibai's widowed sister, played an important role in the growth and expansion of Karve's schools. Married at age 11, Parvatibai became a widow at age 20, the third widowed daughter in her father's home. Rejecting all discussion of remarriage, Parvatibai declared her wish to study and 'do some work of importance'.[53] After receiving her education in Karve's school, she became a teacher and then the superintendent. Parvatibai, a voluntarily tonsured widow, orthodox in her food habits, spoke publicly against widow remarriage.[54] Through her, Karve gained credibility with conservatives who had previously characterized him as a radical because of his own remarriage. In her public lectures, Parvatibai insisted a woman's true mission in life was to marry. She supported the curriculum of Karve's school with instruction in the vernacular languages and emphasis on childcare and homecraft. Traditionally, these subjects had been taught by the older women in the households, but the increased complexity of women's work made formal education necessary.[55] Parvatibai warned women against rejecting their 'natural roles' to enter the tyrannical market place. Yet she had entered the market place and from her own account not unwillingly. She explained her own life as follows:

> I felt that a widow who had one or two children and who had had some actual experience of the happiness of domestic life, if she were able to do some work of importance would not be tempted to enter again into the duties of a married life. In accordance with this idea, I settled on my ideal of life.[56]

In her description of the ideal education for a woman and the ideal life-course, Parvatibai seemed to ignore the lesson of her own life. Like Karve, she regarded public roles for women as an aberration rather than the norm.

Karve spent much of his money on his institutions and even cashed in his life insurance policy of Rs 5,000 to raise funds for the home. Anandibai, now the mother of his child, was alarmed because she knew that if Karve died she would be refused even domestic employment. Many brahmin widows found employment as cooks or maid-servants but if they married a second time they were considered unclean. By her own account Anandibai, 'cried, quarrelled with him, abused him' but could not get him to budge. Karve was similarly neglectful of their day-to-day needs. Finally Anandibai realized that for survival she would have to seek employment. She completed a course in midwifery and earned enough to provide for the family's needs.[57]

Karve's third institution for women was the Women's University founded in 1916. He had heard of the Women's University in Japan and concluded that this model would be more suitable for India than the Western co-educational university. As president of the National Social Conference in 1915 he said: 'we must recognize that both national and social economy require that women should occupy a station of their own distinct from that of men . . . but that the office they have to fill is different, though equal— perhaps greater in importance.'[58] All courses at the Women's University were conducted in the vernacular, special subjects like home science were included, and it was 'possible for women to avoid difficult subjects like mathematics and physical science'.[59] This institution limped along for the first few years until it was adopted by Sir Vithaldas Thackersey who contributed Rs 1,500,000 in 1920 with the stipulation that the university be named after his mother (thereby becoming Shreemati Nathibai Damodar Thackersey Indian Women's University or SNDT) and relocated in Bombay.[60]

The Early Twentieth Century

By the turn of the century the number of schools for girls and school enrolment had risen dramatically. By the end of World War I, there were educational institutions for women in all parts of the country, and enrolments tripled at the school level and quintupled in universities.[61] Parents now had more options: they could choose the type of institution, the curriculum, even the language of instruction. These alternatives assuaged the fears of conservatives and liberals, the religious and the non-religious, those who desired radical change and traditionalists, anglophiles and anglophobes. Institution-builders like Karve had effectively argued that female education was the ideal method of smooth-ing over the rough spots in the transition from tradition to modernity and his successors continued to echo his reasoning:

> In the eyes of men of forethought and ambition, a woman trained on these lines to the profession of wifehood, is a far more desirable companion than an amateur wife. The training which a girl gets in her own home and under her own mother in India is admirable as far as it goes, but modern life has introduced many complexities to deal with for which a regular and systematic training is necessary.[62]

Maharani Tapaswini and K.D. Karve were educating young women from conservative homes to become, as they argued, better wives and mothers in a modern world. To gain the support of conservative communities, they developed curricula dominated by home science and religious lore. And their rhetoric matched their curricula. Karve may have educated young widows to be self-supporting but he was clear that unmarried girls needed to be taught how to become good wives and mothers. Maharani Tapaswini was not at all interested in education for employment.

Pandita Ramabai stands in direct contrast to these two educators. She was critical of her own society and renounced Hinduism to become a Christian. She built a successful school in terms of numbers but she relied for both material and psychological support on foreign missionaries. They sent her money and praised her while her own community ostracized her. Ramabai wanted to make women capable of supporting themselves. It was an appealing idea as long as her focus was lower-class women; upper-class/caste families were unwilling to contemplate economic independence for their wives and daughters.

Between 1900 and 1920 'new women', that is, women who were the beneficiaries of the social reforms and educational efforts of the nineteenth century, stepped forward to begin their own schools. They too were aware of conservative attitudes towards female education, but the picture had changed considerably. The demand for female education was growing steadily and what parents wanted, it seemed, was reassurance that these new schools observed 'traditional' customs. To illustrate the change I will sketch the educational effort of two women: Begum Rokeya and Sister Subbalakshmi.

Begum Rokeya Sakhawat Hossain

In 1909 Begum Rokeya Sakhawat Hossain (1880–1932) began an institution for Muslim girls in the district town of Bhagalpur, Bihar. She set up this school soon after her husband's death but his relations were offended. Driven out of her home by her stepdaughter, Begum Rokeya closed the school and moved to Calcutta where she opened another school, Sakhawat Memorial Girls' School, in 1911. Although this was not the first school set up by a Muslim woman for Muslim girls, Begum Rokeya's systematic and undaunted devotion to this project has earned her the title of pioneer. This school, with Urdu as its language of instruction, was designed and organized for students who observed purdah even though Begum Rokeya wrote and spoke publicly about the evils of this custom.[63]

Begum Rokeya was fortunate, by her own account, in having an elder brother and a husband who encouraged her interest in education. Her elder sister Karimunnessa had not been so lucky. When it was discovered that Karimunnessa had learned to read English, she was sent to live under the watchful eye of her grandmother until her marriage could be arranged. To be on the safe side, Rokeya's elder brother taught her to read English in the dead of night. Syed Sakhawat Hossain, her husband, was a widower who had been educated in the West. He looked to his young wife for companionship and soon after their wedding gave her lessons in English and encouraged her to write essays. At age 21, only three years after their marriage, Rokeya was publishing articles about women's condition. Over the years she wrote a number of articles, short stories, and novels in which she developed her ideas on the need to awaken women to their oppression and the role of education in this process.

In three of her essays, 'Ardhangi' ('The Female Half'), 'Griha' ('The House'), and 'Borka' (or *burqah*—'The Veil'), Rokeya commented on women's asymmetrical development, lack of economic means, and confinement for the sake of male honour. In 'Sugrihini' ('The Ideal Housewife') she pointed out that education would help women fulfil their traditional roles knowledgeably and professionally and hence contribute to the progress of the nation. Additionally, education would make it possible for women to grow and develop in step with their menfolk.

Begum Rokeya's school conformed, in curriculum and purdah restrictions, to the schools for Muslim girls in the Punjab and United Provinces.[64] Emphasis was placed on literacy and practical subjects such as handicrafts, home science and gardening. The curriculum in Begum Rokeya's school also included physical fitness training. But this was the only deviation from an educational programme designed to produce good wives and mothers: companions and help-mates to their husbands and teachers for their children.

The strictest rules of female seclusion were observed in transporting the girls to and from the school and there was only slight modification (curtains replacing closed shutters) when the young pupils vomitted and fainted in the hot, airless carriage.[65] Inside the school the girls covered their heads. This was a new form of modest attire, suitable for the modernizing women now entering new spaces where neither the burqah, designed as outdoor wear, nor the clothes worn inside the home were suitable. The new head coverings signified concern with both modesty and modernity.

While Begum Rokeya's school conformed to rules of female seclusion, she wrote stinging criticisms of the practice. In addition to her essay on the burqah, she wrote *Sultana's Dream* (1905), a short story in which women ran the world and men hid indoors, and *Avarodhbasini* ('The Secluded Ones') (1929), 47 serialized reports documenting the custom of purdah. Her satirical writings on female seclusion were meant to inform an audience ignorant of the real tragedy of purdah (her own aunt was killed by a train because she would not cry out for help). Seclusion, Begum Rokeya, wrote, 'is not a gaping wound, hurting people. It is rather a silent killer like carbon monoxide gas.'[66] She denied this custom had any basis in the Quran or Shari'ah (the Muslim religious law).

Rokeya's campaign was unpopular. Accused of being both pro-Christian and a Europhile, Rokeya attracted more hostility when she endorsed Katherine Mayo's *Mother India*. But her school remained open, attended by Muslim girls from good families. Apparently her central argument, that neglect of female education would ultimately threaten Islamic culture, struck a responsive chord.

Sister Subbalakshmi

At about the same time that Begum Rokeya opened her school for Muslim girls in Calcutta, Sister Subbalakshmi (1886–1969) established a school for young high-caste widows in Madras. Sister Subbalakshmi's concern was society's discarded child widows. Her plan was to transform these unfortunate and inauspicious women into useful and valued members of society.[67]

Prior to her own marriage at age 11, Subbalakshmi had received four and a half years of formal schooling. Her husband died shortly after their wedding and she returned to her parents' home in Rishyiyur, Tanjore District. Her parents decided not to burden her with all the restrictions normally placed on widows and instead arranged to send her to school. Their community reacted so violently that Subramania Iyer, Subbalakshmi's father, decided to move. In Madras, Subramania Iyer taught his daughter English at home and then sent her to a convent school. The nuns' dedication so impressed the young Subbalakshmi that she resolved to devote her life to educating widows. Although she never became a Christian, she was affectionately known as 'Sister Subbalakshmi' in recognition of her dedication to her chosen work.

Subbalakshmi completed her matriculation and enrolled in Presidency College, Madras University. As the first Hindu widow in Madras to study for a BA, she was threatened with excommunication, harassed in the streets, and ostracized in the classroom. By 1911 she had completed her BA degree and was ready to begin her life's work. She set up her first school in her father's home in a Madras suburb and began with a class of four brahmin widows.

Subbalakshmi's interest in helping widows coincided with that of Miss Christina Lynch (later Mrs Drysdale), the Irish feminist who was appointed inspectress of female education in Coimbatore. Miss Lynch was deeply troubled by the difficulty of finding 'suitable' (high-caste) teachers for the schools. At the same time she was aware that Madras had over 22,000 widows between the ages of five and 15, many of them brahmins. Meeting with Subbalakshmi's father, Miss Lynch explained that she had worked out a plan whereby the government would support a home for young brahmin widows willing to be trained as teachers. Meanwhile, Sister Subbalakshmi was pursuing the same scheme with her friends and relations. In 1912 the Sarada Ladies Union was formed as a women's club to provide its members with an opportunity to hear lectures, discuss new ideas and collect money for a brahmin girls' school.

In 1912 the government agreed to support a boarding school for training teachers. The government would pay the rent and give scholarships to three girls; the remainder of the operating expenses had to be met through donations and fees. In order to make this plan more acceptable to critics of education for Hindu widows, Miss Lynch proposed shifting the school from a liberal section of the city to the more orthodox Triplicane. This meant Subbalakshmi had to locate a 'home' for the widows. After an extensive search she finally settled on the Ice House, the old warehouse along the beach once used to store ice from Boston. The Ice House was slowly made habitable for the 35 girls who by this time had joined Subbalakshmi. As Sister Subbalakshmi commented, 'There was a lot of gossip and ill-talk' about the large number of girl widows and female staff who occupied the Ice House without male protection. The presence of so many inauspicious women walking about forced local people to modify their schedules. Subbalakshmi wrote:

> I remember how the orthodox elders in a well-to-do family wanted the bride-groom's procession either before 9 a.m. or after 10 a.m. so that there would be no contact (seeing) the widows on their way to school.[68]

The school's curriculum was set by the government. The aim was to train these women as teachers: first, they were prepared for regular classes, then they completed the syllabus for matriculation, and finally, they entered Queen Mary's College (begun in 1914 as the first college for women in Madras). In 1922 the Lady Willingdon Training College and Practice School, an institution for teacher training, opened with Sister Subbalakshmi as principal. At this institution Sister Subbalakshmi was able to implement some of her ideas on education. The college offered three programmes: post-graduate training for potential high-school teachers, secondary training for teaching through the eighth grade, and training for elementary teachers. English was emphasized (because teachers who knew English were in demand), some vocational subjects were required to instil the value of working with the hands, a training course in physical education was available and popular, and Hindu and Christian priests offered moral and religious instruction. Before long Sister Subbalakshmi was compelled to open Sarada Vidyalaya, a high school and boarding school for adult widows. This facility was necessary because the Ice House did not accept widows over age 18 even though the age of marriage was gradually shifting upward and the concept of widows working as teachers was gaining acceptance.

The boarding school was run in strict conformity with orthodox Hindu customs. In the early days of the school, Sister Subbalakshmi denounced remarriage. Her widowed aunt, V.S. Valambal Ammal, was described by a visitor to the home as a woman in 'disfigured [shorn hair] condition' wearing a white sari and performing a traditional puja (act of worship). Mrs Drysdale utilized her inspection tours to locate high-caste widows and would often pay the train fare of reluctant fathers who wanted to see for themselves how the institution was run.[69]

Sister Subbalakshmi understood the importance of running the boarding school for widows in accordance with orthodox customs and caste rules. At the same time her own life was one of rebellion against the accepted role for a widow. She defied caste rules by opening a school for the fisherfolk in the area of the Ice House. When she was warned that as a government servant she could not join the Women's Indian Association, Sister Subbalakshmi continued to attend branch meetings while scrupulously avoiding the more public annual conferences. When the Women's Indian Association and the All-India Women's Conference began their campaigns in support of the Child Marriage Restraint Bill, Sister Subbalakshmi lectured against the custom and gave evidence before the Joshi Committee about the harmful effects of youthful marriage. Her activities suggest that she was idealistic yet shrewd. She was willing to compromise as long as it served her long-range goals.

Spiritually, Sister Subbalakshmi was deeply attracted to Swami Vivekananda and the Ramakrishna Mission. She regarded Ramakrishna and his disciple Vivekananda as the first religious reformers to be deeply concerned with the woman question. Although the model of the Catholic nun attracted her in her childhood, as an adult Sister Subbalakshmi drew her spiritual sustenance and philosophy of action from reformed Hinduism.

Conclusions

What these examples accentuate is the extent to which successful experiments in female education were a product of the labour of educated Indian women. Many of the schools were geographically limited, communally bound, and caste-sensitive. They were schools for females only, the teachers were females, and curricula were geared to gender-specific socialization.

Looking at female education and its products in the second decade of the twentieth century one can begin to answer the question of how far female education had achieved the results desired by the three groups who had promoted it: the British rulers, Indian male reformers, and educated Indian women.

The British wanted their civil servants to have educated wives to further ensure their loyalty. Uneducated wives (or wives who were educated only in the vernacular and traditional subjects) would split the household into two worlds. Just as the British were certain that rebellious plots were hatched and nurtured in inaccessible zenanas, they believed English-educated Indian women would raise their children to be anglophiles. Despite this dream, education did not promote loyalty among women except those married to civil servants. They became help-mates to their husbands but there were some renegades even among this group. Many women became critics of British policy in India.

Reform-minded Indian men were interested in developing a progressive society. If women were educated, Indian society could no longer be characterized as decadent and backward. On a personal level, these men yearned for companionship and the support an educated woman could give them as they advanced professionally. They wanted women to take responsibility for helping the less fortunate members of their communities. On the national level, they envisioned women in charge of social reform while men pursued politics.

Educated women accompanied their husbands to their civil service postings, joined husbands who had left their ancestral homes, opened schools and entertained district magistrates. The two-person career was finally possible with the appearance of the carefully groomed, English-speaking wife. Women took over the task of social reform at a time when men were becoming obsessed with political action and worried that social reform might complicate the task of arousing the masses. While men feared education might cause women to 'go too far', female educators promised to graduate 'professionalized housewives.' The educational system was overwhelmingly conservative, but the education of women had unexpected and unanticipated consequences.

The first generation of educated women found a voice: they wrote about their lives and about the conditions of women. The second generation acted. They articulated the needs of women, critiqued their society and the foreign rulers, and developed their own institutions. That these institutions were often as conservative as those designed by men should not be taken as a sign that these women wished to preserve the status quo. Rather it should be taken as evidence that they understood their subordinate position very well.

Through their efforts to develop institutions women learned the limits of their power. Deviant behaviour was severely punished. Within households girls who wanted to learn were teased and ostracized. Those who attended schools were stoned in the streets and marginalized in the classroom if they attended boys' schools. They were harassed when they sought to practise their professions. By straining for new lives, 'new women' learned where the boundaries were and just how far they could go. But this was a dynamic process; women were becoming educated and then becoming the educators. The boundaries of the early nineteenth century had been stretched considerably by the early twentieth century. What was deviant behaviour for one generation was acceptable behaviour for the next. What is more important, by the early years of the twentieth century Indian women were full participants in the redefinition of their futures.

Notes

1. *Women Writing in India*, vol. 1, ed. Susie Tharu and K. Lalita (New York, Feminist Press, 1991), p. 199.
2. 'The Memoirs of Dr Haimavati Sen', trans. Tapan Raychaudhuri, ed. Geraldine Forbes and Tapan Raychaudhuri, unpublished ms., p. 15.

3. Nicol Macnicol, *Pandita Ramabai* (Calcutta, Association Press, 1926), pp. 11–13; 'Ramabai Pandita', *DNB*, vol. III, pp. 457–9.

4. Syed Nurullah and J.P. Naik, *History of Education in India During the British Period* (Bombay, Macmillan, 1943), p. 21; Meredith Borthwick, *The Changing Role of Women in Bengal, 1849–1905* (Princeton: Princeton University Press, 1984), pp. 60–1.

5. Aparna Basu, 'Mary Ann Cooke to Mother Theresa: Christian Missionary Women and the Indian Response,' *Women and Missions: Past and Present: Anthropological and Historical Perceptions*, ed. Fiona Bowie, Deborah Kirkwood and Shirley Ardener (Providence, R.I./Oxford, BERG, 1993), p. 190.

6. Sonia Nishat Amin, 'The Early Muslim Bhadramahila: The Growth of Learning and Creativity, 1876–1939', ed. Bharati Ray, *From the Seams of History: Essays in Indian Women*, ed. Bharati Ray (Delhi, Oxford University Press, 1995), p. 112.

7. Usha Chakraborty, *Condition of Bengali Women Around the Second Half of the Nineteenth Century* (Calcutta, Usha Chakraborty, 1963), p. 52.

8. Aparna Basu, *Essays in the History of Indian Education* (New Delhi, Concept Publishing Co., 1982), pp. 31–2; Syed Nurullah and J.P. Naik, *History of Education in India During the British Period*, pp. 12–13.

9. Basu, *Essays*, p. 33.

10. Kalikinkar Datta, *Survey of India's Social Life and Economic Condition in the Eighteenth Century (1707–1813)* (Calcutta, Firma K.L. Mukhopadhyay, 1961), pp. 23–4.

11. Basu, *Essays*, pp. 7–9.

12. Ibid., p. 14.

13. Harihar Das, *Life and Letters of Toru Dutt* (London, Humphrey Milford, 1921), p. 8.

14. Geraldine Forbes, 'In Search of the "Pure Heathen": Missionary Women in Nineteenth Century India', *EPW*, 21, no. 17 (26 April 1986), pp. ws2–ws8.

15. Glendora B. Paul, 'Emancipation and Education of Indian Women Since 1829', Ph.D. dissertation, University of Pittsburgh (1970).

16. Dr (Mrs) R. Vishalakshmi Neduncheziar, 'Education of Girls and Women in Tamilnadu,' *Status of Women Souvenir 1973* (Madras, Task Force Sub-Committee on Education, Tamil Nadu, 1975), no page numbers.

17. J.C. Bagal, *Women's Education in Eastern India: The First Phase* (Calcutta, The World Press Private Ltd., 1956), pp. 77–95; N.S. Bose, *The Indian Awakening and Bengal* (Calcutta, Firma K.L. Mukhopadhyay, 1969), pp. 188–9; 'Hindoo Women', *Calcutta Review*, 40 (1864), pp. 80–101; 'The Bethune Female School', *The Bengalee* (13 January 1863), p. 13; Borthwick, *Changing Role*, pp. 73–7.

18. Y.B. Mathur, *Women's Education in India, 1813–1966* (Bombay, Asia Publishing, 1973), p. 25.

19. Ibid., p. 29.

20. Ibid., p. 26.

21. Sumantha Banerjee, 'Marginalization of Women's Popular Culture in Nineteenth Century Bengal', *Recasting Women: Essays in Colonial History*, ed. Kumkum Sangari and Sudesh Vaid (New Brunswick, Rutgers University Press, 1990), pp. 130–1.

22. Borthwick, *Changing Role*, p. 219.

23. Mary Carpenter, *Six Months in India*, 2 vols (London, Longman, Green and Co., 1868), vol. II, pp. 142–5.

24. Lord Beveridge, *India Called Them* (London, George Allen and Unwin, 1974), p. 83.

25. David Kopf, 'The Brahmo Idea of Social Reform and the Problem of Female Emancipation in Bengal', *Bengal in the Nineteenth and Twentieth Century*, ed. J.R. McLane (East Lansing, Mich., Asian Studies Center, 1975), pp. 47–50.

26. Annie Besant, *The Political Status of Women*, 2nd edn. (London, C. Watts, 1885), pp. 1–11 (pamphlet).

27. H.P. Blavatsky, 'Hindu Widow-Marriage', *A Modern Panorama: A Collection of Fugitive Fragments* (London, T.S. Publishing Society, 1895), vol. I, p. 243.

28. 'Mrs. Besant on Indian Womanhood', *ILM*, 1, no. 7 (January 1902), pp. 195–7; 'Indian Women', *MR*, 25 (1919), pp. 271–2.

29. Arthur H. Nethercot, *The Last Four Lives of Annie Besant* (Chicago, University of Chicago Press, 1963), pp. 17, 55, 73; 'Annie Besant,' *DNB*, vol. I, pp. 51–3.

30. Kenneth W. Jones, *Arya Dharma: Hindu Consciousness in Nineteenth Century Punjab* (Delhi, Manohar, 1976), pp. 104–5.

31. Madhu Kishwar, 'Arya Samaj and Women's Education: Kanya Mahavidyalaya', *EPW*, 21, no. 17 (16 April 1986), pp. ws9–ws24; Kumari Lajjavati, 'A Pioneer in Women's Education', *ISR*, 45 (June 1, 1945), pp. 134–5.

32. Premila Thackersey, *Education of Women: A Key to Progress* (New Delhi, Ministry of Education and Youth Services, 1970), p. 6.

33. Thackersey, *Education of Women*, pp. 1–11; Mathur, *Women's Education in India*, pp. 40–4.

34. Jyotsna Kapur, 'Women and the Social Reform Movement in Maharashtra', M.Phil. thesis, Delhi University (1989), p. 79.

35. *The Letters and Correspondence of Pandita Ramabai*, compiled by Sister Geraldine, ed. A.B. Shah (Bombay, Maharashtra State Board of Literature and Culture, 1977), pp. 15–18; Rajas Krishna-rao Dongre and Josephine F. Patterson, *Pandita Ramabai: A Life of Faith and Prayer* (Madras, Christian Literature Society, 1969), pp. 6–10; Muriel Clark, *Pandita Ramabai* (London, Paternoster Bldg., 1920), pp. 24–5; 'Pandita Ramabai', *Men and Women of India*, 1, no. 6 (June 1905), pp. 316–19; Meera Kosambi, 'Women, Emancipation and Equality: Pandita Ramabai's Contribution to Women's Cause', *EPW*, 23, no. 44 (29 October 1988), pp. ws38–ws49; Meera Kosambi, *At the Intersection of Gender Reform and Religious Belief* (Bombay, SNDT, Research Center for Women's Studies, Gender Series, 1993).

36. *Letters and Correspondence*, p. 14.

37. Ibid., pp. xx–xxi.

38. Ibid., pp. 257–362.

39. Ibid., pp. 342–416.

40. Ibid., p. 412.

41. Ibid., p. 257.

42. Ibid., p. 257; Kosambi, 'Women, Emancipation and Equality', pp. ws44–ws45.

43. Minna S. Cowan, *The Education of the Women of India* (Edinburgh, Oliphant, Anderson and Ferrier, 1912), p. 113.

44. Tanika Sarkar, 'Rhetoric Against the Age of Consent', *EPW*, 28, no. 36 (4 September 1993), pp. 1869–78.

45. M.M. Kaur, *The Role of Women in the Freedom Movement (1857–1947)* (New Delhi, Sterling, 1968), p. 85. Kaur claims that Maharani Tapaswini was a niece of the Rani of Jhansi.

46. Kaur, *The Role of Women*, p. 145.

47. 'The Mahakali Pathshala', *The Statesman* (3 February 1985), p. 7.

48. Latika Ghose, 'Social and Educational Movements for Women and by Women, 1820–1950', *Bethune School and College Centenary Volume, 1849–1949*, ed. Dr Kalidas Nag (Calcutta, S.N. Guha Ray, 1950), p. 146; Cowan, *The Education of Women in India*, p. 113; 'The Mahakali Pathshala', p. 7.

49. *ILM*, 3, no. 1 (July 1903), p. 16; *ILM*, 3, no. 6 (December 1903), pp. 194–5.

50. D.D. Karve, ed. and trans. *The New Brahmins: Five Maharashtrian Families*, ed. assistance, Ellen E. McDonald (Berkeley, University of California Press, 1963), p. 79.

51. '(Maharshi) Dhondo Keshav Karve', *DNB*, vol. 1, pp. 299–301.

52. Quoted in D.D. Karve, *The New Brahmins*, p. 51.

53. Parvati Athavale, *My Story, The Autobiography of a Hindu Widow*, trans. Revd. Justin E. Abbott (New York, G.P. Putnam, 1930), p. 30.

54. Dhondo Keshav Karve, *Looking Back* (Poona, Hinge Stree-Shikshan Samastha, 1936), p. 75.

55. Athavale, *My Story*, p. 133.

56. Ibid., p. 30.

57. Karve, *Looking Back*, pp. 77–82.

58. Ibid., p. 104.

59. Ibid., pp. 95–106; D.D. Karve, *The New Brahmins*, p. 56.

60. G.L. Chakravarkar, *Dondo Keshav Karve* (New Delhi, Publications Division, Government of India, 1970), pp. 169–87.

61. Basu, *Essays*, p. 14.

62. 'Thackesay (*sic*) Women's University Convocation', Sir Visvesvaraya's convocation address, 29 June 1940, *IAR*, (January–June 1940), (Calcutta, Annual Register, n.d.), p. 438.

63. Sources on Begum Rokeya include *Inside Seclusion: The Avarodhbasini of Rokeya Sakhawat Hossain*, ed. and trans. Roshan Jahan (Dhaka, Bangladesh, BRAC Printers, 1981); Ghulam Murshid, *Reluctant Debutante* (Rajshahi, Bangladesh, Rajshahi University, 1983); Amin, 'The Early Muslim Bhadramahila', pp. 107–48; Sonia Nishat Amin, 'The World of Muslim Women in Colonial Bengal: 1876–1939', Ph.D. dissertation, University of Dhaka (1993); Sonia Nishat Amin, 'Rokeya Sakhawat Hossain and the Legacy of the "Bengal" Renaissance', *Journal of Asiatic Society*, Bangladesh, 34, no. 2 (December 1989), pp. 185–92; Sonia Nishat Amin, 'The New Woman in Literature and the Novels of Nojibur Rahman and Rokeya Sakhawat Hossain', *Infinite Variety: Women in Society and Literature*, ed. Firdous Azim and Niaz Zaman (Dhaka, University Press Limited, 1994), pp. 119–41.

64. Gail Minault, 'Purdah's Progress: The Beginning of School Education for Indian Muslim Women', *Individuals and Ideals in Modern India*, ed. J.P. Sharma (Calcutta, Firma K.L. Mukhopadhyaya, 1982), pp. 76–97.

65. Jahan, *Inside Seclusion*, pp. 33–5.

66. Ibid., p. 20.

67. Monica Felton, *A Child Widow's Story* (London, Victor Gollancz, 1966); *Women Pioneers in Education (Tamilnadu)* (Madras, Society for the Promotion of Education in India, 1975); interview with Mrs Soundarain, Madras (22 January 1976); letter from Rabindranath Tagore to Miss M.F. Prager, Eur. Mss., B 183, IOOLC; interview with Sister Sublakshami (*sic*) (10 December 1930), RWC, box 28; Malathi Ramanathan, *Sister R. Subbalakshmi: Social Reformer and Educationalist* (Bombay, Lok Vangmaya Griha, 1989).

68. By Sister Subbalakshmi, n.d., enclosed in a letter from R. Tagore, Eur. Mss., B 183, IOOLC.

69. Ibid.

$$\underline{4}$$

Law, Custom and Statutory Social Reform

The Hindu Widows' Remarriage Act of 1856*

LUCY CARROLL

Second marriages, after the death of the husband first espoused, are wholly unknown to the Hindu Law; though in practice, among the inferior castes, nothing is so common.—Sir William Hay Macnaghten, 1862.[1]

When the British assumed judicial responsibility in India, there were several diverse systems of law existing. Not only were there literary traditions of Hanafi and Ithna Ashari Muslim Law and the Dayabhaga and Mitakshara schools of Hindu Law, but there were also numerous practical traditions of Customary Law, applicable to caste, tribe, lineage or family group. In assuming judicial powers and responsibilities over Indian territory in the late eighteenth century, the British rulers promised their Indian subjects that the personal laws administered to them would be those of their own respective religious community—a promise reiterated in every act establishing further courts and expanding the jurisdiction of the legal system. For the Hindus (particularly upper-caste Hindus) this meant that the British-Indian courts assumed the responsibility of administering textual Hindu Law (Dayabhaga or Mitakshara as appropriate) in suits concerning such matters as marriage, adoption, succession, and legitimacy to which the parties were Hindus. In order to fulfil this promise, the British appointed Indian pandits to expound the Hindu Law and advise the courts on questions concerning Hindu Law coming before them; and undertook to collect, compile, and translate standard legal texts which were then recognized by the British-Indian legal system as authoritative. By the mid-nineteenth century the texts had replaced the pandits as the repositories of Hindu Law.

What about Customary Law, which by definition rests not in literary works but in the mores and behaviour of the people? The British-Indian courts gave lip-service to Customary Law, but in actual practice it was extremely difficult in most cases to prove custom in the face of the judicial presumption that Hindu (book) Law applied. The history of the British administration of Hindu Law is largely the story of the erosion of

*From *Indian Economic and Social History Review*, vol. 20, October–December 1983, pp. 363–88.

Customary Law in the face of a judicial preference for law that could be found in the (judicially recognized) texts.

At the same time, because the Government of India possessed legislative powers sufficient to change this personal law, Hindu Law as administered in the British-Indian courts could be altered by statute. The Hindu Widows' Remarriage Act of 1856 (Act XV of 1856) is an example of such statutory social reform. The judicial controversies that arose over the interpretation and application of this Act set in clear relief three different categories of law—Hindu Law, Customary Law, and Statutory Law—and illustrate the role of the judicial branch of the British Raj in the process of propagating values of orthodox Hinduism and 'Hinduizing' castes and tribes on the fringes of Hinduism.[2]

The Hindu Widows' Remarriage Act was enacted by the British-Indian government in response to the social reform agitation organized by Pandit Vidyasagar and others. Legislation was required because under the Hindu Law, as administered by the British-Indian courts, widow remarriage among higher-caste Hindus was prohibited and children of such a remarriage were illegitimate: the social reform movement thus required legal sanction.

The problem of widows—and especially of child widows—was largely a prerogative of the higher Hindu castes among whom child marriage was practised and remarriage prohibited. Irrevocably, eternally married as a mere child, the death of the husband she had perhaps never known left the wife a widow, an inauspicious being whose sins in a previous life had deprived her of her husband, and her parents-in-law of their son, in this one. Doomed to a life of prayer, fasting, and drudgery, unwelcome at the celebrations and auspicious occasions that are so much a part of Hindu family and community life, her lot was scarcely to be envied.

On the other hand, the lower, particularly Sudra, castes and the (so-called) 'Untouchables'—who represented approximately 80 per cent of the Hindu population—neither practised child marriage nor prohibited the remarriage of widows.

The Hindu Widow's Right of Succession

Before proceeding to a consideration of the Hindu Widows' Remarriage Act, it is necessary to establish a few general propositions concerning the Hindu widow's right of succession prior to the modifications introduced by the Hindu Women's Rights to Property Act (Act XVIII of 1937) and the Hindu Succession Act (Act XXX of 1956).

Prior to 1937, under both the Dayabhaga and the Mitakshara schools of Hindu Law, the widow only succeeded to her husband's estate in the absence of a son, son's son, or son's son's son of the deceased; and the estate which she took by succession to her husband was an estate which she held only for her lifetime; at her death it went not to her own heirs but to the nearest living heir of her deceased husband. According to the Dayabhaga school, the widow (given the absence of a son, son's son, or son's son's son) succeeded to her husband's share whether or not he was a member of an undivided coparcenary: according to the Mitakshara school, she succeeded to his estate only if he were separate and had simply a right to maintenance if he were a joint coparcener.

Under Hindu Law of both schools, it is only the chaste wife who is entitled to succeed to her husband's estate. It is further a rule of Anglo-Hindu Law, as laid down by the Privy Council in 1880, that once a widow has succeeded to her deceased husband's estate, she does not forfeit her right to the enjoyment of that estate until her death by living an unchaste life.[3]

The Hindu Widows' Remarriage Act
(Act XV of 1856)

The preamble and sections 1, 2, 5, and 6 of the Hindu Widows' Remarriage Act are as follows:

> Whereas it is known that, by the law as administered in the Civil Courts established in the territories in the possession and under the Government of the East India Company, Hindu widows with certain exceptions are held to be, by reason of their having been once married, incapable of contracting a second valid marriage, and the offspring of such widows by any second marriage are held to be illegitimate and incapable of inheriting property; and
>
> Whereas many Hindus believe that this imputed legal incapacity, although it is in accordance with established custom, is not in accordance with a true interpretation of the precepts of their religion, and desire that the civil law administered by the Courts of Justice shall no longer prevent those Hindus who may be so minded from adopting a different custom, in accordance with the dictates of their own conscience; and
>
> Where it is just to relieve all such Hindus from this legal incapacity of which they complain, and the removal of all legal obstacles to the marriage of Hindu widows will tend to the promotion of good morals and to the public welfare;

It is enacted as follows:

> 1. No marriage contracted between Hindus shall be invalid, and the issue of no such marriage shall be illegitimate, by reason of the woman having been previously married or betrothed to another person who was dead at the time of such marriage, any custom and any interpretation of Hindu Law to the contrary notwithstanding.
> 2. All rights and interests which any widow may have in her deceased husband's property by way of maintenance, or by inheritance to her husband or to his lineal successors, or by virtue of any will or testamentary disposition conferring upon her, without express permission to remarry, only a limited interest in such property, with no power of alienating the same, shall upon her re-marriage cease and determine as if she had then died; and the next heirs of her deceased husband or other persons entitled to the property on her death, shall thereupon succeed to the same. . . .
> 5. Except as in the three preceding sections is provided, a widow shall not by reason of her re-marriage forfeit any property or any right to which she would otherwise be entitled; and every widow who has re-married shall have the same rights of inheritance as she would have had, had such marriage been her first marriage.
> 6. Whatever words spoken, ceremonies performed or engagements made on the marriage of a Hindu female who has not been previously married, are sufficient to constitute a valid marriage, shall have the same effect, if spoken, performed or made on the marriage of a Hindu widow; and no marriage shall be declared invalid on the ground that such words, ceremonies or engagements are inapplicable to the case of a widow.

However clear the intent of the legislature may appear to the lay reader of the statute, when called upon to interpret these provisions, the judges of the British-Indian courts found the language of the legislature 'somewhat embarrassing';[4] 'somewhat ambiguous';[5] 'to some extent misleading';[6] 'not free from difficulty';[7] and 'curious'.[8] Substantiation of these characterizations of the wording of the Act is found in the fact that this humanely-inspired statute was responsible for more than three-quarters of a century of dramatic judicial controversy among the High Courts of the British-Indian legal system.

The main point of contention in the judicial controversies arising from the differing interpretations placed upon Act XV of 1856 by the various High Courts concerned the effect of the statute in regard to those castes which had, according to their own pre-existing customs, permitted widows to remarry. Although section 6 of the Act prescribes the ceremonies which would be regarded as solemnizing a valid widow marriage (thus indicating that the legislators believed themselves to be writing on *tabula rasa*, innovating a practice where none had existed before); and although the ceremonies so prescribed differed significantly from those observed among castes which had a custom of widow marriage, the High Courts of Bengal, Bombay and Madras held that section 2, involving forfeiture of the deceased husband's estate on remarriage, applied to all Hindu widows, whether or not the validity of their remarriage derived from the Act, and whether or not their marriages were solemnized by the ceremonies prescribed in section 6; or, alternatively, that if section 2 did not apply, the same forfeiture was enjoined by Hindu Law. The exception of this judicial trend was the High Court of Allahabad, which held consistently—and in the face of contrary rulings and open criticism from the other High Courts—that the Act of 1856 was inapplicable to individuals who were, prior to the passing of the Act, permitted by Customary Law to remarry.

Customary Law

The case of *Har Saran Das v. Nandi*,[9] decided by the Allahabad High Court in 1889, established what was to become the scrupulously observed precedent for this High Court and those lower courts subject to it.[10]

Nandi, the widow of a sweeper, succeeded to her deceased husband's interest in two *kothas* of land and subsequently remarried. Her deceased husband's brothers contested her right, following her remarriage, to the property. Two lower courts held that under section 2 of Act XV of 1856 all rights and interests which the widow had acquired from her deceased husband had been forfeited upon her remarriage. Justice Straight, writing the decision of the High Court, overruled the lower courts:

> It is admitted that the woman Nandi was of the sweeper caste, and in that caste there is no legal obstacle or hindrance, either by law or custom, or otherwise, nor is any suggested, against remarriage, and it must be taken that this condition of things has been existing in the caste for years past, and was existing in the year 1856. Accordingly, when Musammat Nandi married Bhujo, she did what in her caste never had been and was not prohibited by the law to which she was subject, and her marriage was a good and valid marriage. I do not think that, looking to the preamble to Act XV of 1856, which refers to Hindu widows, it was ever intended to apply to persons in the position of Musammat Nandi, or to place under disability or liability persons who could marry a second time before the Act was passed. The Act was passed for the purpose of enabling persons to marry who could not remarry before the Act, and s. 2 only applies to such persons. By her second marriage Musammat Nandi, in my opinion, did not forfeit her interest in the two kothas.[11]

The Allahabad High Court thus decided in favour of the remarried sweeper widow on the basis of Customary Law ('the law to which she was subject'). It was proved before the Court that custom sanctioned the remarriage of sweeper widows. The Court, however, neither heard nor asked for evidence on the Customary Law as to whether such a remarried widow retained her interest in her deceased husband's property; it simply ruled that she did not forfeit that interest under section 2 of Act XV as had been alleged in the suit.

On the other hand, in *Ranjit v. Radha Rai*[12] a custom entailing forfeiture upon remarriage among Kurmis was alleged but held not proved on the evidence; while in both *Ram Devi v. Kishen Dei*[13] and *Mangat v. Bharto*[14] it was proved that among the castes in question (Grihast Goshain and Jat, respectively) it was customary for a remarried widow to retain her interest in her deceased husband's estate.

It was, indeed, very rarely contended in cases before the Allahabad High Court that castes which permitted widow remarriage by Customary Law, by that same Customary Law deprived a remarried widow of her first husband's property. And, in the absence of proof of a custom of forfeiture, the Allahabad High Court refused to enjoin it. Chief Justice Sulaiman in 1932 summed up the Allahabad position on Customary Law as applied in widow remarriage cases as follows:

> When nothing more than a mere custom of remarriage is established, there is not presumption that under the Hindu Law she [i.e., the remarried widow] forfeits the estate. The party who is alleging that there has been a forfeiture must establish a further incidence of the custom that forfeiture is a necessary consequence [of remarriage]. Wherever such additional custom is established, she would, of course, lose the estate. . . . But where nothing more is established than a mere right to remarry under a custom, it cannot be presumed that forfeiture is a necessary consequence. The burden to prove a custom involving forfeiture is on the party asserting it, and in the absence of such proof, it must be held that she could remarry and retain the estate and not forfeit it. . . . [U]nless it is affirmatively established that in addition to the custom of remarriage there is the further custom of forfeiture of the husband's estate, she is entitled to retain the estate even after remarriage and till her death.[15]

The Allahabad position was therefore: (*a*) that Act XV of 1856 was not applicable to castes where Customary Law had permitted widow remarriage prior to 1856; and (*b*) that in order for a remarried widow subject to Customary Law to be deprived of property to which she had succeeded as heir of her first husband, a custom decreeing such forfeiture must be proved.

Individual judges of the Calcutta and Madras High Courts were willing to agree that Act XV of 1856 did not apply to widows 'who could without the aid of the Act marry according to the custom of their castes',[16] and that 'the word "remarriage" in the section [2] must be taken as meaning remarriage contracted under the Act'.[17] Nevertheless, these High Courts refused to follow the Allahabad precedent of *Har Saran Das v. Nandi* on the ground that 'although section 2 might not apply the same result might follow from an application of the fundamental rules of Hindu Law',[18] a fact which 'for some reason not apparent' the Allahabad High Court had not considered at all.[19]

Hindu Law

Judges of the British-Indian courts—judges both British and Indian—expounded freely on 'the Hindu Law', creating the impression that such an indigenous creation existed fully complete and ready to hand. This was really not the case, not only because statute had the power of changing Hindu Law as applied and enforced by the British-Indian courts (e.g., after Act XXI of 1850 excommunication from caste or religious apostasy no longer barred rights of inheritance under Hindu Law); but, even more importantly, because what was meant by the term 'Hindu Law' was altered by accretions of case-law (e.g., after the Privy Council ruling in *Moniram Kolita v. Keri Kolitani*[20] a Hindu widow did not forfeit her estate in her deceased husband's property by leading a notoriously unchaste life). Hindu Law as administered by the British-Indian courts was a mixture of Shastric Law, custom, and case-law, with a hardy dose of English legal concepts and notions, simplified and standardized for ease of application and administrative convenience. Not surprisingly, the end result contained several anomalies.

The case which provided the occasion for the exposition of what became the Calcutta precedent in regard to Act XV of 1856 and widow remarriage cases, *Matungini Gupta v. Ram Rutton Roy*,[21] arose out of somewhat unique circumstances. A childless widow, who had succeeded to her husband's property and subsequently converted to the reformist Brahmo Samaj sect, remarried under the provisions of Act III of 1872 (Special Marriage Act), having declared as required by that statute, that she did not profess the Hindu religion. The reversioner (next heir) sued for possession of the estate of the deceased husband, alleging that by her remarriage the widow had forfeited her interest in the property under section 2 of Act XV of 1856.[22]

The Court (Wilson, Prinsep, Banerji, JJ., referring opinion; Petheram, C.J., Wilson, Pigot, Ghose, and Prinsep, JJ., Full Bench) ruled, with Justice Prinsep dissenting,[23] that the widow forfeited. The majority disagreed, however, on whether the forfeiture occurred by virtue of the statute or by virtue of Hindu Law. Chief Justice Petheram interpreted section 2 of Act XV as applying to 'all persons who being Hindus become widows'; any person who had succeeded to property as a Hindu widow fell under the scope of the section when she remarried, regardless of whether or not she remarried as a Hindu. Justice Wilson held that both Hindu Law and Act XV applied and that both decreed forfeiture. Justice Banerji held that section 2 applied only to a widow who was a Hindu both at the time of succession and at the time of her remarriage and only to such widows as remarried under the Act. Nevertheless, according to Justice Banerji, although the widow had remarried independently of the Act and as a non-Hindu, she forfeited her interest in her deceased husband's estate by virtue of Hindu Law independently of the statute.

What then, precisely, was the Hindu Law that decreed the forfeiture? 'We cannot expect to find express texts on this point in the usual authorities on Hindu Law,' observed Justice Wilson, 'because second marriage was a thing they did not contemplate.'[24] Certainly all the texts speak of the widow enjoying the property until her death; indeed, the passage from Vrihaspati relied upon so heavily by Justices Wilson and Banerji ('Of him whose wife is not deceased half the body survives. How then should another take his property while half his person is alive?') speaks of the widow's right during her life, that is, until her death. But, arguing from this text that the widow inherits under Hindu Law because she is regarded as the surviving half of her deceased husband's body, Justice Wilson found it impossible to reconcile the idea of a widow continuing in the enjoyment of property so inherited when she 'ceases to be the wife or half the body of her late husband, and becomes the wife and half the body of another man'.[25] He supported his inference that under Hindu Law the estate of a widow must be forfeited on remarriage by remarking that 'where second marriages are sanctioned by custom, the further rule seems almost always to have been followed, that such remarriage entailed a forfeiture of the first husband's estate'; and concluding that the forfeiture section of Act XV indicated that the legislature considered forfeiture on remarriage 'to be in accordance with the principles of Hindu Law'.[26]

Of course, section 1 of Act XV was directly contrary to orthodox, textual Hindu Law; the necessity for legislative action derived from this very fact. Why then should it be assumed that section 2 was in accordance with Hindu Law? The observation that when custom permitted remarriage, it almost always also decreed forfeiture is not supported by the findings of fact in the courts of upper India where the question was actually considered.

Justice Banerji also based his contention of what the Hindu Law was concerning widow remarriage and forfeiture on inferences drawn from the 'half-his-body' metaphor:

> The widow's right of succession is based, according to the Dayabhaga, on the ground that she is half the body of her deceased husband, and is capable of conferring by her acts spiritual benefit on him. The widow takes her husband's estate, not because of past relationship, not because she was the wife of the deceased, but because of the continuing relationship, because she is still the *patni* (wife) of the deceased. . . . [I]t follows, as a necessary consequence, that the estate of a Hindu widow can last only so long as she continues to be the wife and half the body of her deceased husband; that is only so long as the relationship, by reason of which she inherits, continues, and the estate must be held to determine when she must cease to be the wife of her late husband and half his body by marrying another person.[27]

Although the 'half-his-body' metaphor is a quaint legal fiction, it is not the only text on the widow's right of succession to her sonless husband. Much more mundane is the statement of the law given in the Yajnayavalkya Smriti:

> Wife (widow), daughter, father, mother, brother, their sons, gotraja (of the same family), bandhus, disciple and Brahmacharias of the same school, each succeeding one is heir in the absence of the person immediately preceding him in the order of enumeration—this is the law in respect of the inheritance to the property of a sonless deceased person of whatever caste.[28]

Statutory Law

In 1896 a Full Bench of the Bombay High Court considered the application of Act XV of 1856 and overruled the decision of the same Court in *Parekh Ranochor v. Bai Vakhat*.[29] In the latter case it had been held that Section 2 of Act XV had no application to the case of a widow belonging to a caste among whom widow remarriage was permitted and the case had been remitted for determination as to whether the caste custom which permitted the widow to remarry also permitted her to retain her interest in the property of her first husband, or whether by custom such interest was forfeited upon remarriage.

The 1896 case, *Vithu v. Govinda*,[30] concerned a Sudra widow whose infant son had succeeded to her husband's/his father's property. The infant subsequently died and the estate passed to his mother, the widow. The mother, after succession to the estate, remarried (*c.* 1875); she and her alienee had been in possession since the death of the son. It was common ground that the caste of the widow permitted remarriage of widows; it was further found by the Subordinate Judge that according to the custom of the caste, remarriage did not entail forfeiture of property held by succession to the first husband.[31]

The Full Bench of the Bombay High Court (Farran, C.J., referring opinion; Farran, C.J., Parsons and Ranade, JJ., Full Bench) took its stand neither on Customary Law nor Hindu Law but on a very literal view of the wording of the enacting clauses of Act XV of 1856. In his referring judgment, Chief Justice Farran characterized Section 2 as a law which 'plainly extends to all Hindu widows irrespective of the castes to which they belong and to the special customs of such castes. It reads as a law of universal applicability.' He found nothing in the words of section 2 to support the notion that the legislature did not intend that section to be generally applicable, or that it intended it to apply only to those widows who were for the first time permitted to contract valid second marriages under the Act. Although the preamble indicated that the legislature, aware that some Hindu widows were permitted to remarry and some prohibited from doing so, desired to remove the disability affecting those widows prohibited from remarrying, he saw no reason for assuming that the Act applied only to those widows standing in need of such relief. The legislature might have chosen either of two means to secure their object of relief for widows barred from remarrying: 'First by passing a general act applicable to all Hindus alike, or secondly by passing an enabling act which would be applicable to such widows only as chose to avail themselves of its provisions. The Legislature has, we think, adopted the former method.' It was, the Chief Justice asserted, difficult to argue that the broad language of sections 1 and 2 'does not extend to all Hindus alike, whatever their caste or the interpretation of the Hindu Law authorized by their caste may be'.[32]

As to the Allahabad position, Chief Justice Farran had two comments:

(1) that it is an assumption without basis to attribute that absence of intention [i.e., the absence of intention 'to place under disability or liability persons who could marry a second time before the Act was passed'[33]] to the Legislature; it is equally probable that they intended to assimilate the Hindu Law in this particular in all castes and to make the law as administered accord with the true principles of Hindu Law; and (2) that it is not allowable to cut down the express provisions of a law by a consideration of the supposed intention of the Legislature in passing it.[34]

It could be argued, of course, that as between conflicting interpretations of a statute, it is a matter of prudence and justice to select that construction which is the least disabling, leaving it to the legislature to extend the liability if it so chooses in view of the judicial interpretation. The 'express provisions of the law' being, as every court dealing with the Act noted, ambiguous, a prudent construction might appear even more strongly enjoined; the remedy, if the legislature failed to secure its intention under such an interpretation, would lie with the legislature, not the courts.

In the decision of the Full Bench, Justice Ranade expanded upon the position taken by the Chief Justice in the referring opinion. Although Justice Ranade found that the preamble implied that the Act was not intended to apply to all classes of Hindu widows, nonetheless the enacting clauses 'are as general as they can well be, and there is no special section preserving to the castes in which remarriage was permitted full recognition of their customary rights'.[35] The apparent discrepancy between the preamble and the enacting clauses, Justice Ranade considered deliberate: while it was true that some castes permitted widow remarriage and some did not, it was, he considered, equally the case that in all castes where widow remarriage was permitted, forfeiture of the remarried widow's rights and interests in her first husband's property was the rule. In his view, the legislature had declared in the general language of section 2 what was in fact a rule already in force, and no new disability was thereby created. In support of the universal custom of forfeiture, Ranade cited Arthur Steele's *Law and Custom*,[36] a study confined to the castes of the Brahmin-dominated region around Poona, and ignored the finding of fact by the Subordinate Judge that according to the custom of the caste of the widow whose case was actually before the Court, remarriage did *not* entail forfeiture.

Justice Ranade conceded that the legislature had been mistaken in some of their assumptions underlying the Act: that is, (*a*) in assuming that the castes permitting remarriage were exceptions to a general rule of prohibition, while in fact the prohibition was confined to the upper castes or about 20 per cent of the population; (*b*) in assuming it necessary to prescribe ceremonies for celebrating a second marriage (*vide* section 6 of the Act); and (*c*) in prescribing remarriage ceremonies in the terms they did, for 'in this part of the country the customary ceremonies observed at a *pat* [second] marriage are different from those observed at a *lagna* or first marriage'. Nevertheless, he held that the legislature had been correct in its wording of section 2 and had in that section 'only declared what was a universal practice'.[37]

The difficulties and mistaken assumptions pointed out by Justice Ranade, however, only arise if one assumes that the legislature in Act XV was legislating for the whole of the Hindu population, and not simply providing an enabling act for the benefit of those sections of the population who, prior to 1856, neither recognized widow remarriage nor had available any ceremonial practices appropriate for such an occasion.

And, finally, Justice Ranade suggested that the legislature actually had before it the information from Steele's *Law and Custom* concerning the practice of widow remarriage in the Poona area and the custom of forfeiture among remarrying castes, and that it was on the basis of this information that the legislature enacted section 2 in broad general terms. It is, however, hardly likely that, if the legislature had studied Steele's volume and based section 2 on it, it would have at the same time confused *pat* and *lagna* marriage observances (*vide* Ranade's comments earlier).

Following the Farran/Ranade argument to its logical conclusion, the Madras High Court explicitly ruled that a custom of non-forfeiture could not be pleaded in the face of the statutory forfeiture enjoined by section 2 of Act XV: '[N]o plea of custom can prevail to violate an express statutory enactment to the contrary and any custom repugnant to such enactment will be held to have been swept away thereby.'[38]

The Allahabad Rejoinder

The dramatic conflict among the High Courts over the interpretation of Act XV—which really resolved into a conflict between the Allahabad High Court and the High Courts of Calcutta, Bombay, and Madras (the latter following both Calcutta and Bombay precedents)—continued until the question itself was superseded by the Hindu

Code legislation of independent India, almost exactly a century after the passage of the Hindu Widows' Remarriage Act.

In 1908 (*Gajadhar v. Kaunsilla*),[39] 1910 (*Mula v. Partab*),[40] and 1926 (*Mangat v. Bharto*),[41] individual judges of the Allahabad High Court appeared personally less impressed with the Customary Law position of their own Court than with the Hindu Law/Statutory Law traditions of the Presidency Courts. The power of precedent, however, served to overcome personal idiosyncrasies and to pull the wavering judges into line with the legal traditions of the bench on which they, for the moment, sat. The Allahabad tradition was maintained intact; no decision contrary to that tradition issued from any judge serving on the Allahabad High Court. The personal reservations of Justices Stanley, Banerji, Dalal and Pullan were more than compensated for by the strength and vigour of the Full Bench defence of the Allahabad tradition in 1932.

When *Bhola Umar v. Kausilla*[42] came before a Divisional Bench of the Allahabad High Court, the following question was referred to the Full Bench for decision: 'Does a Hindu widow, who remarried in accordance with a custom of her caste, forfeit thereby her rights in the estate of her first husband?' In reply, Chief Justice Sulaiman and Justices Mukerji and King picked up the gauntlet and proceeded to lecture those of the Wilson/Banerji and Farran/Ranade schools on the subjects of Hindu and Statutory Law.

While Justice Wilson had had difficulty in reconciling the notion of a widow retaining her inheritance from her first husband when she remarried and the assumption that under Hindu Law the widow inherited because she was regarded as the surviving half of her husband's body, Justice Mukerji had even greater difficulty in reconciling the notion that a widow inherited because she was half her husband's body with the actual practice of widow remarriage prevailing among many Hindu castes.

> If these people believed that a wife was one-half of the body of her husband and on the death of her husband one-half of his body survived in the widow, how could they possibly have allowed the widow to remarry. . . . It must follow that those people who allow their widows to make a valid remarriage *never believe* in the doctrine that a wife is one-half of the body of the husband and that the widow survives as one-half of his body.[43]

Was Hindu Law to be invoked and enforced by the British-Indian courts to penalize those who acted contrary to the religious ordinances of orthodox Hinduism because they were outside the charmed circle of the twice-born, for whom alone the sacred law was intended anyway? The textual Hindu Law was never intended for the Sudras.

> It was only the privilege of the first three classes, the Brahmins, the Kshatriyas and Vaishyas to read the Shastras and the sacred laws and to abide by them. . . . Indeed, Manu himself says in the clearest terms that his laws were meant mostly for the benefit of the three regenerate or higher classes and not for the Sudras.[44]

As the castes which permitted remarriage of their widows were generally Sudras, it was inappropriate to apply reasoning based on the general principles of Hindu Law—a law intended only for the upper castes—to decree forfeiture of the property the widow had inherited from her first husband.

On the other hand, Justice Mukerji continued, if it were assumed that 'the strict rule of Hindu Law applies to a caste which does not recognize the strict Hindu Law . . . the remarriage of a widow can only be regarded as an immoral act. The orthodox Hindus *would not recognize the marriage as valid*', although the caste and the British-Indian courts may do so.[45] According to the Privy Council Unchastity Case (*Moniram Kolita v. Keri Kolitani*[46]), unchastity in a widow does not divest her of her inheritance from her deceased husband once she has succeeded to the estate.

> Can it be an act of justice to say that living as the wife of one single man would be followed by a punishment, while the grossest immorality cannot be? It was argued that this may be so, but such is the Hindu Law. I, as a Hindu Judge, refuse to believe that such is the Hindu Law. I emphatically deny that such is the Hindu Law. The Hindu Law lays down, not at one place, but at many places, that the Shastras can never be interpreted apart from the dictates of conscience and reason.[47]

Chief Justice Sulaiman, concurring, denied both that the 'half-the-body' metaphor was the sole basis for the Hindu widow's right of succession, and that the efficacy of her acts of spiritual benefit to her deceased husband was a condition necessary for her continued enjoyment of his estate. The unchaste widow did not forfeit the estate vested in her, although her unchastity rendered her unable to secure through her acts spiritual benefit to her husband's soul. Relying upon the Privy Council's decision in the Unchastity Case, Chief Justice Sulaiman found it impossible to accept the situation whereby the courts would put 'a premium on unchastity' by holding that the widow 'can retain the property so long as she remains notoriously unchaste, but the moment she remarried she will forfeit it'. Particularly in the absence of an express text enjoining forfeiture on remarriage, 'the Hindu Law should be interpreted so as not to cause a shock to one's moral conscience'. Hindu Law did not contemplate remarriage and would not regard a remarriage as a valid marriage, but as a case of unchastity; under Hindu Law, as interpreted by the Privy Council, a widow's unchastity did not entail forfeiture of an estate once vested.[48]

The texts of Vrihat Manu and Katyayana, so much discussed in the Unchastity Case, established a clear right for the widow to hold the property until her death:

> The widow of a childless man, keeping unsullied her husband's bed, and preserving in religious observances, shall present his funeral oblation and obtain his entire share.
>
> Let the childless widow, keeping unsullied the bed of her Lord, and abiding with her venerable protector, enjoy with moderation the property until her death. After her let the heirs take it.

As interpreted by the Privy Council, the conditions contained in these texts concerned the right of succession to the estate and did not lay down conditions for its retention when once vested; violation of any or all of the conditions subsequent to succession did not involve forfeiture. Therefore, argued the Chief Justice, if the forfeiture section of Act XV did not apply, a correct application of Hindu Law did not entail forfeiture.

Justice King endorsed Mukerji's views on the application of strict Hindu Law:

> It appears to me that the general principles of strict Hindu Law could not be properly applicable to a caste in which a custom of remarriage is admitted. If the members of the caste recognized the remarriage of a widow as valid, then it follows that they do not accept

the theories of orthodox Hinduism which would make a legal remarriage impossible. If such theories are rejected by the caste for the purpose of permitting remarriage, it seems illogical to invoke the very same theories for the purpose of holding that if the widow does remarry, then she must forfeit her rights in her deceased husband's estate.[49]

And he took particular issue with Justice Ranade's Statutory Law position and his assumption, based on Steele's *Law and Custom*, that the custom of forfeiture among castes which permitted remarriage was universal and that the legislature, aware of this universal custom, had recognized it in section 2 of the Hindu Widows' Remarriage Act.

I do not think it can safely be inferred that even if the Legislature knew that among the tribes or castes of the Bombay Dekhan a custom was in force that a Hindu widow should forfeit her rights in her husband's estate upon her remarriage, this would furnish an adequate ground for enacting, in a statute applicable to the whole of British India, the rule that forfeiture of interest in her deceased husband's estate must be a necessary consequence of the remarriage of every Hindu widow, whatever the custom of her tribe or caste may be.

At least as far as the Northwestern Provinces were concerned, the rule of forfeiture was 'by no means universal . . . among those castes in which widows are permitted to remarry.' In the long series of Allahabad cases, where a custom of remarriage was alleged, it was seldom pleaded that custom decreed forfeiture; 'when it has been pleaded it has never been proved and in some cases a contrary custom has been proved affirmatively.'[50]

Social Consequences

By definition, social reform legislation is intended to have social consequences, to serve and facilitate ends deemed desirable. Obviously the social consequences of the Hindu Widows' Remarriage Act varied according to the geographical jurisdictions of the High Courts. Within the jurisdictions of the High Courts of Calcutta, Madras, and Bombay, the result was undoubtedly the displacement of Customary Law as regards remarriage and the establishment in its stead of Brahminical values which held widow marriage in disrepute and insisted on some penalty (in this case forfeiture of inheritance rights) being imposed for a breach of the preferred norm of the chaste, prayerful widow. I believe that this forms but a chapter in the much larger drama of the Brahminization of the low castes and the Hinduization of tribals that was an unintended, but, given the nature of the system itself, almost an inevitable consequence of the British administration of Hindu Law. An example of this process is conveniently provided by the Calcutta High Court in regard to the Rajbansis.

In 1885 *Fanindara Deb Raikat v. Rajeswar Dass*[51] reached the Privy Council on appeal from the Calcutta High Court. The case involved succession to the *gaddi* of the Baikantpur Raj. It was common ground that the family were descended from the Koch tribe, that they had been subject to Hindu influence, and that they had adopted some Hindu customs. The extent of this process of Hinduization was the point at issue: were they sufficiently Hinduised to be subject to Hindu Law or were they ruled by tribal and family custom?

The succession contest was drawn between the adopted son of the late Raikat and the nearest male agnate, whose claim was clear providing the late Raikat died sonless.

Hindu Law recognizes succession by adoption; for the adopted son it was contended that the family was governed by Hindu Law. Against this it was contended that although the family had come under Hindu influence, they did not observe the Shastras, and had retained and were 'still governed by many tribal and family customs inconsistent with that law', including the custom of exclusion of an adopted son from inheritance.[52] The District Judge held that adoption was contrary to the custom of the Baikantpur family and found in favour of the agnate. The Calcutta High Court (Morris and Tottenham, JJ.) held that Hindu Law was applicable to the case and that succession passed to the adopted son. Both the Indian courts held that the burden of proof rested with the agnate claiming the existence of a custom prohibiting adoption, although they differed in their judgments as to whether or not he had conclusively proved such a custom. In apportioning the onus of proof in the way they did, both Indian courts implicitly or explicitly took the position that Hindu Law applied unless and until a contrary family custom were proved in law.

The Privy Council turned the matter the other way up; given the non-Hindu origin of the family, the Privy Council refused to accept that the family was 'generally' governed by Hindu Law and threw the burden of proof upon the adopted son, who was then required to prove that the Hindu practice of adoption had been accepted by the non-Hindu family. On the basis of the history of the Raj family, which in 16 devolutions of the estate had seen no successions by adoption, 'though in three instances the circumstances were such [i.e., the Raja died sonless] as usually move Hindus to make an adoption', the Privy Council had no difficulty in holding that 'whatever Hindu customs may have been introduced into . . . [the family], the custom of succession by adoption has not been introduced'.[53]

Seven years later the Calcutta High Court heard another case involving Rajbansis, *Ram Das v. Chandra Dassia*,[54] on appeal from Rangpur. This involved an inheritance dispute between a daughter and her uncle (father's brother). The Bengal school of Hindu Law recognized the daughter's inheritance rights; tribal custom did not. The Calcutta High Court, which had held that Hindu Law applied to the Baikantpur Raj family, had no hesitation in holding this family likewise subject to Hindu Law—and no difficulty in distinguishing this case from the Baikantpur decision in the Privy Council. The Privy Council decision had been reached 'having regard to the origin and history of the family'; in the present case, 'of the history of the family nothing is known, and it is not likely that it has a history'! Witnesses called to testify to the law and custom of the family 'were ignorant, illiterate people who could not distinguish one system [of Hindu Law] from the other'.[55] The High Court held that the family were subject to Hindu Law and the daughter secured her inheritance.

A third Rajbansi case, *Santala Bewa v. Badaswari Dasi*,[56] reached the Calcutta High Court in 1923 and involved the question of widow remarriage. A daughter sued her deceased father's second wife, who had succeeded to his property, on the ground that as the widow had taken a dangua and thereby allegedly contracted a remarriage, she had forfeited the inheritance, and the daughter, as next heir of her father, was entitled to the property. The widow contended that among the Rajbansis custom decreed that a widow keeping a dangua did not forfeit property inherited from her deceased husband.

The Munsiff of Siliguri held that the family was non-Hindu by descent and origin and was governed not by Hindu Law but by custom. He further held that among the Rajbansis a widow may keep a dangua and that a widow so doing is permitted by custom to retain her former husband's property. The Deputy Commissioner of Darjeeling reserved the Munsiff's decision on the ground that the Calcutta High Court had previously held the Rajbansis to be Hindus and subject to Hindu Law. And Hindu Law, as interpreted in the strictly 'orthodox' tradition of the Calcutta High Court, divested remarried widows of any inheritance they had received from their first husbands, regardless of a custom of remarriage among the tribe or caste concerned.

The case was appealed to the Calcutta High Court. For the widow it was contended that: (*a*) Rajbansis were not Hindus and were not governed by Hindu Law but by custom; (*b*) according to Rajbansi custom a widow may keep a dangua and by such an action she does not compromise her interest in the property of her deceased husband; and (*c*) keeping a dangua is not equivalent to remarriage; at most such action may amount to unchastity but it is established in law that subsequent unchastity does not divest a widow of property already vested in her.

For the daughter it was urged that: (*a*) the Rajbansis were Hindus and governed by Hindu Law as held in previous decisions of the Calcutta High Court; (*b*) keeping a dangua was equivalent to remarriage; and (*c*) given the previous decisions of the Calcutta High Court on the forfeiture of property by remarried widows, a Rajbansi widow by keeping a dangua forfeited her interest in her first husband's property, even though there be a custom of remarriage and nonforfeiture.

The Calcutta High Court noted that widow remarriage was prevalent among the Rajbansis and that it took place without any ceremonies whatever.

> The peculiar circumstances under which widows are received by men as wives, amongst Rajbansis, have given rise to different names by which such women are known, such as *dangua* wife, *dhoka* wife, *pashua* wife. *Dang* means a stick or a blow dealt with a stick; when a widow lives by herself and a man goes to the house with a *dang* or stick in his hand and strikes a blow with it on the roof of the house, and so enters in and takes possession of the woman, such a woman is called a *dangua* wife.[57]

This is certainly a far cry from the provisions of section 6 of the Hindu Widows' Remarriage Act![58]

Writing in 1891 Risley had stated concerning the Rajbansis in the Darjeeling Terai that they

> make no secret at all of allowing a widow to remarry outside the degrees prohibited to her before her marriage, and subject to the further condition that she may not marry any of the elder relations of her late husband. Where a widow happens to be the head of the family, she enjoys the further privilege of choosing any man not within the prohibited degrees to live with her as her husband without going through any ceremony whatever. This looks like a survival, and may possibly furnish an explanation of the statement made by Buchanan about the Pani-Kochh that 'women who happen to be unmarried after they have grown up select a husband according to their own discretion', which by itself seems rather unlikely. If, however, we suppose the privilege to have been limited to women who had control of the property of their family, it bears a different aspect, and falls into line with several points of primitive practice in matters affecting property.[59]

These observations are particularly relevant as the parties to the suit before the Calcutta High Court were Rajbansis of Darjeeling and the widow who took a dangua had control of her late husband's property.

The Calcutta High Court, however, held that Rajbansis were governed by the 'ordinary Hindu Law, although there may be a custom prevailing amongst them which renders remarriage of widows possible'.[60] The Rajbansi widow was divested of her first husband's property, although the custom of her community allowed and permitted widow remarriage and although the Munsiff had found that custom also permitted a remarried Rajbansi widow to retain her first husband's property. In criticizing this decision, Justice Mukerji of the Allahabad High Court stated, quite rightly, that the Calcutta High Court, in coming to the decision it did, 'was not administering the law of the parties before the Court, but the law of a different people'.[61]

The judicial view of Indian society expounded by the Calcutta High Court appears to have been fundamentally incompatible with existing ethnographic evidence. Certainly such judicial imposition of Hindu Law must have been a potent force in expediting the centuries-old process of Brahminization and Hinduization among the castes and tribes on the cultural and geographical fringes of Hinduism. Particularly where, as among the Rajbansis, Hinduization (or 'Kshatriyization', or 'Sanskritization', if one prefers either of these terms) was a contemporary process actually in progress, judicial sanction of this nature amounted to partisan interference in the internal affairs of the group-category. Again the limitations of the 'caste-category'[62] approach to Indian social reality are illustrated. To quote further from Risley on the Rajbansis:

> The Rajbansis profess to marry their daughters as infants . . . but this custom has only recently been adopted, and it is difficult to ascertain to what extent it is really followed even among those sub-castes which profess to be pure Hindus. In the more primitive groups adult-marriage still prevails, and a breach of chastity before marriage is already condoned, though the tendency is continually towards the adoption of what is believed to be more orthodox usage. The same remark applies to the remarriage of widows. The Rajbansis in Rangpur if questioned on this point aver most positively that nothing of the sort is permitted; while their brethren in the Darjiling Terai make no secret of allowing a widow to remarry. . . . Curiously enough, the Rajbansis, who prohibit widow-marriage, nevertheless recognize divorce—a fact sufficient in itself to show, if further proof were wanting, that the former prohibition cannot have been long in force among them.[63]

Whether or not the decision to apply Hindu Law to the Rajbansis of Rangpur (*Ram Das v. Chandra Dassia*[64]) could possibly have been justified, the Rajbansis of Darjeeling were clearly a different cultural and social group, in spite of the fact that the same broad ascriptive designation was applied to both.

The partisan nature of the judicial attitude towards groups like the Rajbansis is illustrated by the fact that to prove a custom derogating from the textual, orthodox Hindu Law, strong and convincing evidence was required to prove to the satisfaction of the court that the custom pleaded was ancient, certain, and of invariable application. However, no such evidence was required to establish a 'custom' that coincided with (or approximated towards) the textual law. Even among the Rajbansi groups which observed it, the custom prohibiting widow remarriage was clearly far from 'ancient'; it was equally clearly far from being of 'invariable application' among the Rajbansi category as a whole. By the tests applied to prove custom, this supported 'custom' would have failed. But tests of custom were only applicable to customs in opposition to orthodox, textual law; they were not applicable to customs which were not at variance with that law. Among other things, this meant that, particularly in regard to matters which involved questions of personal legal status (e.g., marriage, divorce, adoption) and many aspects of property law (e.g., inheritance, succession, property rights of women), there was only one avenue of autonomous social change open, that is, change in the direction of conformity with the tenets of orthodox Hinduism. Change in any other direction required official sanction; the door to change could only be opened by legislation, such as the Hindu Widows' Remarriage Act. Yet even this Act in its application by the British-Indian courts, with the exception of the Allahabad High Court, was transformed into an instrument for the propagation and imposition of orthodox Hindu values.

It seems a fair comment to observe that the majority of the judges of the British-Indian courts—judges both British and Indian—shared a very Brahminical view of Indian society, derived in the one case from the legal texts which they studied and in the other from the texts as well as from family traditions and social circumstances, as most Indian judges were themselves Brahmins. Sitting on the High Court benches and moving in the society of the political and social elite, judges were far removed from the lives of the lower orders of society, from the beliefs and practices of the Sudra castes which permitted and recognized widow remarriage regardless of what the Brahminical texts might have to say on the matter of proper conduct befitting a widow.[65]

A second factor which undoubtedly contributed to the preference for orthodox Hindu Law was simply ease and convenience: it was much simpler for a busy court to refer to texts at hand than to undertake empirical investigations into the various and sundry local systems of Customary Law. Certainly the 'orthodox' tradition of the Calcutta High Court was, at least in part, a response to the difficulties inherent in a centralized judicial system attempting to deal with disputes arising in a social system characterized by a multitude of localized, largely autonomous groupings governed by their respective customs and *kulachar* (family practice). Coupled with a strong disinclination to decide cases on the basis of custom at variance with Hindu Law was an equally strong inclination to integrate these multitudinous groupings into a less complicated (and more easily administered) system of law, into a single overarching legal code.

That there was a vigorous and consistent alternative to the orthodox tradition of the Calcutta High Court is apparent from the long series (remarkably totally free of dissenting opinions) of decisions emanating from the up-country Allahabad High Court. In contrast to the Calcutta High Court's invocation of inferences from ancient texts which admittedly did not deal directly with the question in hand, and to the heavy-handed literalism of the Bombay High Court, the Allahabad decisions appear not only just and humane, but down-to-earth, in touch with what was actually going on down on the ground, with the lives, customs, and traditions of living people.

Within the jurisdiction of the Allahabad High Court, Customary Law was preserved—but it was also frozen. This was but an inevitable consequence of the codification or judicial recognition of custom. Once custom is recorded, it loses its ability to change, to evolve new refinements in the face of new situations. Within the jurisdiction of the Allahabad High Court 1856 became an arbitrary cut-off date. To prove a valid custom of widow remarriage, it was absolutely necessary to prove that the custom had existed prior to July 1856. No more recent custom of remarriage could be legally recognized. At least theoretically, for families and groups among the lower social strata, who as the

Calcutta High Court had noted in regard to the Rajbansi family, might well be ignorant, illiterate, and possessed of no (literary or documentary) history, the problem of proving a custom preceding the cut-off date became more difficult with every passing year.

It is also possible, of course—indeed, it is usually the desired objective of the legislators, particularly when the enactment relates to a social reform objective—that a consequence of legislation will be a change in the way people behave. Thus a new pattern of behaviour may be introduced which derives its legal validity not from recognized Customary Law but from the innovations introduced through changes in Statutory Law gradually influencing the way people actually conduct themselves and their affairs. In such a situation, a custom or pattern of behaviour going back three or four generations may be invalid under Customary Law. Such a problem of the validity of a new custom under Customary Law was presented to the Allahabad High Court in 1933 and 1937, that is, after Act XV had been in operation for approximately 80 years.

In *Bhola Umar v. Kausilla*[66] it was alleged that the remarried widow had forfeited all rights in her deceased husband's estate 'according to the custom of the caste [Umar Banya]'.[67] The Subordinate Judge held that the burden of proof of a custom of forfeiture lay on the party alleging it and that he had failed to prove the point. On appeal, the High Court held that the lower courts had failed to determine whether the validity of the widow's marriage derived from Customary Law or from Act XV, it only having been determined that the marriage was valid. The High Court commented:

> The practice of widow remarriage after 1856 in this community or in any other section of the Hindus may well be referrable to the provisions of the Hindu Widows' Remarriage Act and would not necessarily be indicative of an ancient custom existing before the passing of that Act. Unless, therefore, it is shown that the present practice is in pursuance of an ancient custom and not under the Act, the marriage of a widow cannot be held to be under the custom of the caste.[68]

If the custom were a 'new' custom, that is, one that came into existence after 1856 (or could not be proved to have existed before 1856), the assumption would be that the marriage derived its validity from Act XV of 1856 and the forfeiture clause of section 2 would apply. If the custom pre-dated 1856, there would be no forfeiture unless a further custom entailing forfeiture were proved. The High Court accordingly remitted the case for trial of the following issues:

(1) Whether, according to ancient custom, a widow belonging to the community of Umar Banyas could contract a valid remarriage before the passing of the Hindu Widows' Remarriage Act; and
(2) If the first issue is found in the affirmative, does such a widow forfeit her right in the property of her first husband according to the custom prevailing in the said community before 1856?[69]

The 1937 case, *Narain v. Mohan Singh*,[70] involved a Jat widow who had succeeded to her husband's property and subsequently remarried. She remained in possession of the property until her death. The suit arose following her death and the plaintiff, who was admittedly not the nearest reversioner at the time of her death, claimed that his ancestor had been the nearest reversioner at the time of her remarriage and had been from that date legally entitled to the property; and that he, as heir to this ancestor, was now its rightful owner. The lower courts held that the plaintiff had failed to prove a caste custom involving forfeiture on remarriage.

On appeal, the High Court was dissatisfied with the evidence in regard to both the alleged custom of remarriage and the alleged custom of forfeiture. On the one hand, the evidence as to a custom of re-marriage was

> ... nothing but a repetition of instances of remarriages deriving their validity from the Hindu Widows' Remarriage Act. To show that the custom now obtaining is not the result of the Act, but wholly apart from it, some evidence ought to be forthcoming to prove that the custom was in existence before the Act was passed.[71]

On the other hand, there were the plaintiff's 'allegations of forfeiture coming into existence in consequence of the Act [of 1856]'.[72] Accordingly, the High Court remitted the case to the lower court for retrial of the relevant issues of Customary Law.

Further findings in both these cases are unavailable.

In spite of the provocative suggestion in these two Allahabad cases that some castes may have accepted widow remarriage as a consequence of the Hindu Widows' Remarriage Act, it is difficult to come to any other conclusion than that, outside the jurisdiction of the Allahabad High Court, this humanely inspired statute was retrogressive in its social effects. Few women of the upper castes availed themselves of their new right to remarry, while those widows who, in the exercise of their customary rights, remarried independently of the Act, found themselves now subject to the forfeiture clause of section 2, regardless of their Customary Law which permitted a widow to remarry and certainly in many, if not most, cases permitted her also to retain property inherited from her first husband.

Postscript: The Law Today

The Hindu Women's Rights to Property Act (XVIII of 1937) gave the Hindu widow, who had previously been excluded from inheritance by the son, agnatic grandson, or agnatic great-grandson of her husband, a right to intestate succession equal to a son's share in regard to her husband's property liable to devolution by succession (i.e., separate and joint property under Dayabhaga and separate property under Mitakshara) and to the whole of her husband's interest in property liable to devolution by survivorship (i.e., Mitakshara joint family property). The estate which the widow took under this Act was a limited (life) estate, held during her lifetime with limited powers of alienation and descending on her death to the heirs of her deceased husband. This estate was subject to forfeiture on remarriage—unless the widow lived within the jurisdiction of the Allahabad High Court and was a member of a caste which by Customary Law permitted its widows to remarry and where it could not be proved (as it generally could not) that this same Customary Law divested remarried widows of the property of their first husbands.

The Hindu Succession Act (XXX of 1956) converted the limited (life) estate of a Hindu female into an estate of which she was the full and absolute owner (section 14). Although the Act specifically provides that heirs who are related to an intestate deceased by reason of being the widow of a predeceased son, the widow of a predeceased son of a predeceased son, or the widow of a brother are not entitled to succeed to the property if they have remarried at the time the succession opens (section 24), the Act does not provide for divesting such a widow, or the widow of the deceased himself, of the property to which she has succeeded if the widow should contract a remarriage after succeeding.

A widow succeeding to her husband's property after June 1956, or a widow who, having succeeded before this date, was in possession of such property when Act XXX of 1956 came into effect, became by virtue of that Act absolute owner of the property which prior to June 1956 she would have held as a limited estate.[73] Any such absolute estate held by a woman descends upon intestate succession in the first instance to her heirs, rather than to the closest living heirs of her husband as had been the case with the limited estate and was the course of succession prescribed in section 2 of Act XV of 1856.

The courts have held that section 2 of the Hindu Widows' Remarriage Act contemplates the forfeiture only of property held by the widow as a limited (life) estate and not of property of which she is absolute owner.[74] As the limited estate has for all practical purposes disappeared from intestate succession (it may still be established by will or gift), the applicability of the forfeiture clause of Act XV of 1856 has been severely curtailed.

Indeed, it would seem that the Hindu Widows' Remarriage Act, although not actually repealed, has been superseded by the Hindu Code legislation of independent India. Nothing in the Hindu Marriage Act (XVIII of 1955) restricts the remarriage of widows—section 5 provides that a marriage may be solemnized between any two Hindus if neither has a spouse living; the fact that one or both parties may have been betrothed or married previously is not listed among the factors preventing a valid marriage. Thus, there is no necessity for a widow wishing to remarry to have recourse to Act XV of 1856. Further, nothing in either the Hindu Marriage Act (1955) or the Hindu Succession Act (1956) provides for the forfeiting of property inherited by a woman from her first husband upon her subsequent remarriage.

The far-reaching legislative enactments of independent India have revolutionized the Hindu woman's rights in regard to succession and inheritance. Many of the prescriptions of the Shastric Law have been superseded by an emphasis on modernity, social emancipation, and equality of the sexes, and by the social exigencies of a new era. It is perhaps a sign of the times that a High Court judge, in holding that the forfeiture section of Act XV of 1856 did not apply to the absolute estate created by the Hindu Succession Act of exactly a century later, observed:

> In the present conditions women do earn and acquire property and husbands are entitled to inherit partially or wholly the property of their wives. There is no process providing for the forfeiture of the property inherited by a husband from a deceased wife on his contracting a remarriage.[75]

Although Hindu society and Indian public opinion are far from equating the remarriage of a widower with the remarriage of a widow, at least in law the remarried Hindu widow, after a century of penalty and forfeiture, is no longer in a worse legal position than the widow who lived in 'notorious unchastity' but wisely did not permit her paramour to make her an honest (and propertyless) woman.[76]

Notes

1. *Principles of Hindu and Mohammadan Law*, London, William and Norgate, 1862, p. 60.
2. See also Lucy Carroll, 'Colonial Perceptions of Indian Society and the Emergence of Caste(s) Associations', *Journal of Asian Studies*, 37 (1978): 233–50.

3. *Moniram Kolita v. Keri Kolithani*, ILR 5 Cal. 776 (P.C.).

4. L.S. Jackson, J., *Akora Suth v. Boreani*, 2 Bom. L.R. 199, p. 206.

5. E. Jackson, J., ibid., p. 203.

6. Ranade, J., *Vithu v. Govinda*, ILR 22 Bom. 321, p. 331.

7. Wallis, C.J., *Vitta Tayaramma v. Chatakondu Sivayya*, ILR 41 Mad. 1078, p. 1091.

8. Coutts, J., *Mst. Suraj Jote Kuer v. Mst. Attar Kumari*, ILR 1 Patna 706, p. 710.

9. ILR 11 Allah. 330; Straight and Brodhurst, JJ.

10. See also *Ranjit v. Radha Rani*, ILR 20 Allah. 476; *Khuddo v. Durga Prasad*, ILR 29 Allah. 122; *Gajadhar v. Kaunsilla*, ILR 31 Allah. 161; *Mula v. Partab*, ILR 32 Allah. 489; *Bhagwan Din v. Mst. Indrani*, AIR 1921 Oudh 233; *Narpat v. Mst. Janaka*, AIR 1921 Oudh 130; *Mangat v. Bharto*, ILR 49 Allah. 203; *Ram Lal v. Mst. Jawala*, ILR 3 Luck. 610; *Gajadhar v. Mst. Sukhdei*, ILR 5 Luck. 689; *Bal Krishna Sharma v. Paij Singh*, ILR 52 Allah. 705; *Bhola Umar v. Kausilla*, ILR 55 Allah. 24; *Ganga Saran Singh v. Mst. Sirtaji Kuer*, AIR 1935 Allah. 924.

11. ILR 11 Allah. 330, p. 332.

12. ILR 20 Allah. 476; Blair and Aikman, JJ.

13. AIR 1916 Allah. 193; Banerji and Piggott, JJ.

14. ILR 49 Allah. 203; Dalal and Pullan, JJ.

15. *Bhola Umar v. Kausilla*, ILR 55 Allah. 24, p. 49.

16. Wilson, J., *Matungini Gupta v. Ram Rutton Roy*, ILR 9 Cal. 289, p. 293.

17. Banerji, J., ibid., p. 296.

18. *Ganga Pershad Sahu v. Jhalo*, ILR 38 Cal. 862, p. 871; Mookerjee and Casperaz, JJ.

19. *Vitta Tayaramma v. Chatakondu*, ILR 41 Mad. 1078, p. 1085; Krishnan, J., referring opinion.

20. ILR 5 Cal. 776 (P.C.).

21. ILR 19 Cal. 289. See also: *Murugayi v. Viramakali*, ILR 1 Mad. 226; *Rasul Jehan Begum v. Ram Surun Singh*, ILR 22 Cal. 589; *Nitya Madhav Das v. Srinath Chandra Chuckerbutty*, 8 Cal. L.J. 542; *Gouri Churn Patni v. Sita Patni*, 14 Cal. W.N. 346.

22. For other cases involving conversion of a widow prior to remarriage see: *Ganga Saran Singh v. Mst. Sirtaji Kuer*, AIR 1935 Allah. 924; *Mohan Lal v. Mst. Bhudevi*, AIR 1954 Allah. 588; *Vitta Tayaramma v. Chatakondu Sivayya*, ILR 41 Mad. 1078; *Raghanath Shankar Dixit v. Lakshmibai*, ILR 59 Bom. 417; and *Abdul Aziz Khan v. Nirma*, ILR 35 Allah. 466.

23. Justice Prinsep, dissenting, held that as the remarriage was under Act III of 1872 and not as a Hindu widow under Act XV of 1856, section 2 of the latter Act was not applicable; and he was unable to accept the 'half-his-body' argument as ground for forfeiture when the widow remarried as a non-Hindu, given that neither change of religion (*vide* Act XXI of 1850) nor unchastity (*vide Moniram Kolita v. Keri Kolitani*, ILR 5 Cal. 776, P.C.)—either of which actions destroyed her ability to secure through her acts spiritual benefit to her deceased husband's soul—compromised her right to enjoyment of his estate (*Matungini Gupta v. Ram Rutton Roy*, ILR 19 Cal. 289, p. 300).

24. Ibid., p. 291.

25. Ibid., p. 292.

26. Ibid.

27. Ibid., p. 295.

28. Quoted by Seshagiri Aiyar, J., dissenting opinion, *Vitta Tayaramma v. Chatakondu Sivayya*, ILR 41 Mad. 1078, pp. 1095–6.

29. ILR 11 Bom. 119; Sargent, C.J., and Birdwood, J.

30. ILR 22 Bom. 321.

31. For other cases involving the widow who succeeded to her deceased husband's property as heir to their son, see *Akora Suth v. Boreani*, 2 Ben. L.R. 199; *Chamar Haru Dalmel v. Kashi*, ILR 26 Bom. 388; *Basappa v. Rayava*, ILR 29 Bom. 91; and *Lakshmana Sasamallo v. Siva Sasamallayani*, ILR 28 Mad. 425.

The distinction which was made by the Bombay, Calcutta, and Madras High Courts depended on whether or not the widow's remarriage preceded the son's death: the mother could inherit from her son if she had remarried during the son's lifetime; but if she remained a widow during her son's life, succeeded to the property on his death, and then remarried, she forfeited the property. Put another way, if the widow were actually in possession of the property of her deceased husband at the time of the remarriage, either as heir to her husband or to her son, she forfeited the property; if the property were vested in the son at the time of the remarriage, she did not compromise her rights as heir to the son in the event of his dying without wife or child surviving him.

32. *Vithu v. Govinda*, ILR 22 Bom. 321, pp. 326–7.
33. *Har Saran Das v. Nandi*, ILR 11 Allah. 330, p. 332.
34. *Vittu v. Govinda*, ILR 22 Bom. 321, p. 327.
35. Ibid., p. 300.
36. *The Law and Custom of Hindu Castes Within the Dekhun Provinces Subject to the Presidency of Bombay*, London: W.H. Allen and Co. (new edition, 1868). The Preface indicates that the original report was submitted in 1826.
37. *Vithu v. Govinda*, ILR 22 Bom. 321, p. 331.
38. *Gajapathi Naidu v. Jeevammal*, AIR 1929 Mad. 765; Pandalal, J.
39. ILR 31 Allah. 161; Stanley, C.J., and Banerji, J.
40. ILR 32 Allah. 489; Stanley, C.J., and Banerji, J.
41. ILR 49 Allah. 203; Dalal and Pullan, JJ.
42. ILR 55 Allah. 24.
43. Ibid., p. 36; italics in original.
44. Ibid., p. 38.
45. Ibid., p. 41; italics in original.
46. ILR 5 Cal. 776 (P.C.).
47. *Bhola Umar v. Kausilla*, ILR 55 Allah. 24, p. 42.
48. Ibid., pp. 46–8.
49. Ibid., pp. 59–60.
50. Ibid., pp. 56–7.
51. LR 121A 72 (ILR 11 Cal. 463 P.C.).
52. Ibid., p. 74.
53. Ibid., p. 87.
54. ILR 20 Cal. 409; Macpherson and Beverley, JJ.
55. Ibid., pp. 412–13.
56. ILR 50 Cal. 727; Ghose and Panton, JJ.
57. Ibid., p. 735.
58. See also *Ram Pearey v. Mst. Kailasha*, AIR 1930 Oudh 426; and *Tapoo v. Emperor*, AIR 1937 Sind 42.
59. H. Risley, *The Tribes and Castes of Bengal*, vol. I, Calcutta, Bengal Secretariat Press, 1891, p. 495.
60. *Santala Bewa v. Badaswari Dasi*, ILR 50 Cal. 727, p. 735.
61. *Bhola Umar v. Kausilla*, ILR 55 Allah. 24, p. 40.
62. See Lucy Carroll, 'Colonial Perceptions of Indian Society and the Emergence of Caste(s) Associations', loc. cit.; Bernard S. Cohn, 'Notes on the History of the Study of Indian Society and Culture', in M. Singer and B. Cohn, eds., *Structure and Change in Indian Society*, Chicago, Aldine, 1968.
63. H. Risley, op. cit., pp. 494–5.
64. ILR 20 Cal. 409; see note 63 above, pp. 37–8.
65. It is one of the many ironies of British India that while the Raj was morally justified by contrasting the alleged cultural superiority of western civilisation with the alleged social barbarism of India which the Europeans saw evidenced by such unenlightened practices as child marriage and the deplorable institutions of the child widow, nonetheless at the same time the judicial system of the Raj was sanctioning and enforcing Brahminical norms upon castes and tribes which were at best only marginally committed to these norms, and commonly actively committed to quite contrary norms.

66. ILR 58 Allah. 1034; Young and Naimat-ullah, JJ.
67. Ibid., p. 1035.
68. Ibid., p. 1038.
69. Ibid., p. 1040.
70. AIR 1937 Allah. 343; Naimat-ullah, J.
71. Ibid., p. 344.
72. Ibid. It may be noted that the Allahabad High Court, consistently with its entire approach to customs and Customary Law, here clearly implies that the same standard of proof would be required to prove an alleged custom which conformed with textual Hindu Law as to prove one derogating from that law.
73. *Punithavalli Ammal v. Ramalingam*, AIR 1970 S.C. 1730.
74. *Thangavelu Asari v. Lakshmi Ammal*, AIR 1957 Mad. 534; *Mst. Bhuri Bai v. Mst. Champi Bai*, AIR 1968 Raj. 139; *Pandurang Narayan Saluke v. Sindhu*, AIR 1971 Bom. 413; *Chinnappavu Naidu v. Meenakshi Ammal*, AIR 1971 Mad. 453; *Sasanka Bhowmick v. Amiya Bhowmick*, 78 CWN 1011; *Jagdish Mahton v. Mohammad Elahi*, AIR 1973 Pat. 170; *Smt. Sankaribala Dutta v. Smt. Asita Barani Dasi*, AIR 1977 Cal. 289.
75. *Mst. Bhuri Bai v. Mst. Champi Bai*, AIR 1968 Raj. 139, p. 145; L.N. Chhangani, J.
76. See *Parvati v. Bhiku*, 1867 Bom. HCR 25.

5

Caste, Widow-Remarriage, and the Reform of Popular Culture in Colonial Bengal*

SEKHAR BANDYOPADHYAY

Social reforms in Bengal in the nineteenth century affected many aspects of human relations and existential realities, the most important of them being gender relations and the condition of women. Yet, towards the close of the century a large section among the latter who were widows by civil status were still being 'forced' to live celibate and austere lives, despite the reform endeavours of men like Rammohun Roy, Iswar Chandra Vidyasagar and others. As the realities stand, while the former had succeeded in achieving his goal, the latter's mission ended in what has been described as an 'unavoidable defeat'.[1] Sati, the eradication of which was on Rammohun's reform agenda, was abolished by Regulation XVII of 1829. Widow-burning was made a penal offence, any violation of which would immediately invite the regulating hand of the state. Rammohun could thus save widows from being immolated with the help of the constant presence of state power and the law-enforcing apparatus. But Vidyasagar failed to see many widows remarried, as in this case the Act of 1856 only legalized their marriage, but could not make it socially acceptable; nor was it possible to enforce it with the help of the police force. So Vidyasagar had to depend ultimately on social consent, not on the power of the state, and it was here that his 'defeat' was quite manifest. But one might ask whether this was in fact avoidable or not.

It may also be argued that in retrospect the movement does not appear to have failed. That widow-remarriage has gained in social legitimacy today is partly due to this nineteenth-century reform endeavour. But it may be pointed out also that this legitimization has taken place only among the educated sections of the community and, even within that limited social sphere, it is not widespread. 'Everyone feels the evil and wishes that it could be removed', wrote *Hindu Patriot* in 1855, 'but the difficulty is how to meet the lion in his den.'[2] Widow-remarriage remains exceptional among the educated even today, as it was in the nineteenth and the early twentieth centuries. And contrary to the existing stereotypes, the uneducated and the lower orders are also ardent defenders of the taboo just as their social superiors are. This compels us to re-think this reform movement as a 'defeat', since the problem was complex and not one of education alone.

The existing literature[3] seeks to explain this 'defeat' by focusing mainly on the structural weaknesses of the reformist effort, but does not adequately emphasize the power of tradition that refused to be reformed. This paper is concerned mainly with the traditional culture of the Bengali Hindus, as it was to the realm of culture that the issue of widow-remarriage ultimately belonged. Culture, according to Peter Burke, is 'a system of shared meanings, attitudes and values, and the symbolic forms . . . in which they are expressed and embodied'.[4] Forms of marriage or social organization of human sexuality and relationship are therefore to be understood in terms of their cultural connotations and imputed social meanings. But culture is also multilayered, different social groups have different cultures. Usually, we assume a simple dichotomy between the two broad cultural traditions, the 'elite culture' and the 'popular culture', or to use E.P. Thompson's Marxian phraseology, between 'patrician' and 'plebeian' cultures.[5] But we need not assume a clinical disjunction between these two traditions, as there are constant interaction and overlapping, though of an unequal nature, between them. As a result of this process popular culture often accepts and internalizes the ideologies of the elites and assumes in some respects a common interface with their culture. This process of the 'reform of popular culture', which Peter Burke first talked about in relation to early modern Europe,[6] implies an imposition of certain elite cultural forms on the masses from above, rather than voluntary emulative behaviour of the socially mobile groups from below, as suggested in our familiar 'Sanskritization' discourse.[7] Martin Ingram has more recently defined the process in the following words:

> . . . the world of popular culture came under attack from elite groups (clergy, nobility and some middle class groups in town and country) who gradually attenuated and transformed many aspects of social life among the mass of the people. This 'reform of popular culture' combined attempts to suppress many popular activities and to modify the behaviour of the common people, . . . and the sponsoring of a new 'popular' or 'mass' culture which embodied the ideologies of the ruling elites.[8]

This concept[9] can be a useful tool for understanding and explaining the success or failure of the reforms proposed by men like Vidyasagar. The present paper will try to show that the taboo on widow-remarriage, which was adhered to by more people than is usually believed, was in itself the result of a 'reform of popular culture'. This first process of reform was so effective and of such antiquity, that the subsequent attempt at counter reform was bound to fail, given the weakness of the reform ideology and the vulnerability of the strategy to promote it.

II

One of the major contentions of the most recent feminist critique of the nineteenth-century reform movements is that the issues which had been picked up concerned mainly a small section of women. The reform endeavours therefore reflected only the paternalism of the elitist male reformers, concerned exclusively about their own class, and their eagerness to retain their patriarchal control over the private spheres of life.[10] The first premise of this feminist discourse, however, needs to be re-examined, for compulsory widow-celibacy, like many other similar customs, was more widely practised than indicated by the available cultural stereotypes, both old and recent.

In Bengal widow-remarriage was strictly forbidden among the upper castes and most of the middle-ranking castes in the nineteenth century. The 1891 list of castes that forbade widow-remarriage included, apart from the Brahmans, Kayasthas and Vaidyas of the upper stratum, the various trading castes, as well as the Sadgops, Sundis, Mahishyas, Telis, Mayras and Napits.[11] It was allowed among the lower castes, but they too appear to have shared the values of their social superiors. Widow-remarriage even when permitted, was looked down upon and was disparagingly referred to as *sanga* marriage, a practice prevalent in many other parts of India as well. Among the Namasudras of Bengal, for example, the married couples of a widow-remarriage occupied a lower place in the estimation of their caste fellows and were referred to as *Krishna-Paksha* (dark fortnight after full moon), while those married in a regular way were described as *Sukla-Paksha* (bright fortnight after new moon).[12] The very use of the terms 'dark' or 'bright' indicates the respective values attached by the community to the two forms of marriage. And by the beginning of the twentieth century, they too, like many other *antyaja jatis* around them had almost completely discontinued the practice and begun to conform to the traditional upper-caste behavioural norms of widowhood.[13] At the turn of the century, therefore, it was perhaps only the lowest menial groups like the 'Doms, Boonas, Bagdis and "low people" of various kinds' and the so-called 'aborigines' who practised widow-remarriage without any stigma attached to it, while the rest of the Bengali Hindu society strictly forbade this custom.[14] Nothing can be a better indicator of the failure or 'defeat' of the reform movement to introduce widow-remarriage.

Side by side, we also come across another social phenomenon the importance of which need not be minimized. And that was the increasing social legitimacy of widow-remarriage among the educated *bhadralok* who had been constructing in the nineteenth century new 'models of womanhood' to suit the socio-psychological as well as political needs of the time.[15] Even during Vidyasagar's lifetime, important groups in Calcutta, in addition to Young Bengal, and a significant section of the native press, like *Hindu Patriot, Tattvabodhini Patrika, Sambad Purnachandroday* or *Bamabodhini Patrika*, had lent full support to his reform movement.[16] As the bhadralok category kept on expanding across caste and local boundaries, this legitimacy became more and more broad-based. The Bengali bhadralok was never a closed status group incorporating only the members of the three traditional upper castes. In reality, as John McGuire's quantitative study has shown, in the latter half of the nineteenth century the Calcutta bhadralok community included individuals belonging to as many as 18 different castes.[17] In the early twentieth century, as there was further extension of education and literacy down the caste lines,[18] there were fresh entrants into this category. As the newcomers got access to the new literate culture of the educated urban bhadralok, they also began to accept and imbibe the reform ideology of the latter. To them widow-remarriage now appeared to be good conduct or *sadachar* while its prohibition became *kadachar* or bad conduct.[19] A symbolic acceptance of this innovation was taken as a signifier of their entrance into the new status groups. Certain sections of the Sadgops, Baruis, Gandhabaniks, Jogis, Rajbansis and Namasudras therefore sought to promote widow-remarriage at least for the minors. The educated Mahishyas also advocated remarriage of widows, though only for those who would be found incapable of practising *brahmacharya* or self-abnegation. And some of the progressive Jogis and Sadgops went even beyond such oral acceptance of the reform, and actually organized a few such marriages.[20] Such symbolic actions did not however mean that the innovation had acquired popular acceptance among such communities. The newly educated sections of these communities, the recent entrants into the bhadralok category, shared with the old members of the group the same dilemma as regards the actual practice of the reform. Since Vidyasagar himself had failed in his mission, a Sadgop rationalized his dilemma, what else could they be expected to achieve![21]

Thus as a direct legacy of the reform movement started by Vidyasagar to introduce widow-remarriage what we find during the decades immediately following his death are two parallel situations. Prohibition of widow-remarriage became a far more widely shared popular custom, while the innovation of widow-remarriage gained wider social legitimacy among the educated sections of society. But even those who had accepted the innovation refrained from practising it. This paradoxical situation constitutes a problematic that can be explained only with reference to the dynamics of popular culture in Bengal in the nineteenth and the early twentieth centuries.

III

Public control over private life as a dominant feature of Bengali Hindu society has had a long history. In this cultural milieu, marriage was not a consensual union between two individuals. It was indeed a concern of the whole community, as endogamy was one of the fundamental aspects of the caste system with a bearing on social rank. Transactional modalities, rituals and rites in a marriage were therefore parts of a public spectacle, supervised and often monitored by the community. The slightest deviation from the established norms invited public censure, while major violations meant more severe punishments, which usually took the form of social boycott of the erring families. Popular Hinduism in other words inculcated an ideology of discipline, which was enforced or maintained through a hierarchized structure of social authority that expressed itself through the idiom of caste. The caste system represented, according to a recent commentator, a cultural construction of power in Indian society.[22] That it was a system connotative only of a structure is essentially a colonial ethnographic stereotype. It was also a normative system which defined, determined and also legitimized the structure,[23] and this relationship is crucial for understanding the failure of the reform movement advocating widow-remarriage.

The *Hindu Patriot* in 1855 recognized without any reservation the rationality of the proposed reform of widow-remarriage. But for it the major problem was how 'to bring about so desirable an end as the removal of miseries of our helpless females without incurring the risk of losing caste with all its concomitant disadvantages. . . .'[24] The widow of the first proposed remarriage, who was subsequently let down by the prospective bridegroom, also complained that 'she had by such refusal lost her position in society and is now an outcast. . . .'[25] Even the observers who had participated in the first widow-remarriage ceremonies organized by Vidyasagar, 'were completely outcasted' by the large majority of bhadralok in Calcutta.[26] Social rebels like Dakshinaranjan Mukhopadhyay, who had committed a double sin by marrying outside his caste and by marrying a widow, also had to acquiesce ultimately to this social tyranny and had to migrate and seek refuge in a completely different and distant social environment of Awadh.[27] What appears to be crucial is the fear of 'losing caste', of being excommunicated by society, which intimidated people into surrendering to dominant social norms. The question therefore is what were the social implications of this phenomenon of 'losing caste' and how was the terror that it generated organized.

Caste as a normative system prescribed for each group in society, according to its rank, certain codes of conduct or *jati-dharma*,[28] which every individual had to perform in real life. This performance was believed to be the chief determinant of the quality of 'body spiritual', which determined a person's ritual as well as social rank and therefore took precedence over both the 'body individual' and 'body social'. Any deviation from such codes would lead to the fall from the ascribed rank, or loss of caste, which implied the denial of interaction with the local community and sometimes even of essential social services. The codes varied from group to group, but always there was a tendency of the lower groups changing and remoulding their behavioural patterns with reference to the elite model. The process which Alfred Lyall had once described as 'the gradual Brahmanisation of the aboriginal non-Aryan or casteless tribes' had reached such a point in Bengal in the mid-1880s that Herbert Risley could not detect any variance in customs and ceremonies of the different castes, high and low. He had to adopt, therefore, the method of anthropometric measurement in order to determine the origin of the inter-mediary and lower castes, who could thus be separated, somewhat arbitrarily, from the upper castes, to fit into his racial model of the Aryan–non-Aryan dichotomy in Hindu society.[29] The phenomenon which Lyall and Risley had observed in the nineteenth century was no doubt the reflection of the process of reform of popular culture, which had taken place apparently by volition and not by any visible application of power.

But this acculturation was not entirely voluntary; there was, as it appears, an element of compulsion in it. In order to get access to Hindu society and to move up in its status-ranking scale, acceptance of its behavioural norms was mandatory. These norms were essentially based on an ideology of hierarchy that legitimized the prime position of the Brahmans who, because of their monopoly over knowledge, both used to define such normative standards of social behaviour, as also arbitrated in cases of their violation. But the maintenance of social discipline, or the actual execution of the Brahmans' mandate, depended on an elaborate power structure within which every single individual had his or her own location. The primary unit within this structure was the extended family, which was always patriarchal, as patriarchy alone corresponded to the hierarchical ethos of Hindu society. The family household, as it appears from the late-nineteenth-century evidence, was organized in a hierarchical structure of obedience, in which every member was situated according to age, generation and gender, the supreme position of authority being held by the eldest male member, the patriarch or the *karta*.[30]

The lowest position, in terms of entitlement to rights and resources of the family, was held by the women, who were expected only to obey their husbands. An anonymous author wrote in a popular treatise entitled *Hindudharmaniti* (Principles of Hindu Religion) in 1794 Saka: 'The wife should follow her husband like his shadow; she should be like his friend in performing all religious duties; and like his maid she should carry out all his orders . . . The wife who retains her smile in spite of the harsh words and angry looks of her husband, is considered to have properly performed her sacred duties.'[31] What was thus defined as the dharma or the duties of an ideal wife virtually meant her unconditional surrender to the dictates of the husband, and this subjection would continue even beyond the death of the husband, as marriage was conceived to be a relationship of eternal bondage. As another pamphlet called *Hindu Narir Kartabya* (Duties of Hindu Women) noted in 1916: 'The duties of a widow are included among the duties of a wife. For marital relations among Hindus continue even beyond death.'[32] It was this eternalist concept of marriage which rationalized prohibition on widow-remarriage. But such restrictions were not applicable to the widowers. In Bengali Hindu society of the nineteenth century polyandry was unthinkable but polygamy was acceptable and in certain cases a legitimate social practice. A widower was therefore often encouraged to remarry, particularly for procreating progeny for the patriliny. Twentieth-century Bengali literature bears ample testimony to the existence of this social mentality.[33]

In the traditional social hierarchy of the Hindus, women and Sudras were the two lowest categories, as both were denied access to Vedic religious rites. Later on as sections of the Sudra *jatis* became socially mobile, gained access to elite culture, and became claimants to higher ritual status, they too began to conform to the patriarchal norms of the upper-caste elite families. Even the women of these castes were so deeply socialized into this essentially elite (or upper-caste) and male worldview that they too accepted without any question this patriarchal standard of morality. 'Devoted wives must always follow their husbands dead or alive,' wrote *Mahishya Mahila*, the journal of the Mahishya women, in 1911. 'If the husband was dead', it continued further, 'the widow, until her own death, should observe self-abnegation and should never even pronounce the name of any other man during her life time.' Because, 'it is only by serving the husband that a woman can reach the heaven'.[34] The prohibition on widow-remarriage, which thus virtually implied a total control over the mind and body of women by their husbands during their lifetime and even after, had become, as we have noted already, an almost universal practice in Bengal by the beginning of the twentieth century. This near-total acceptance of the moral code of widow celibacy was not just due to an imitative urge from below. It resulted from a long-drawn and often imperceptible process of the 'reform of popular culture' imposed from above.

The question that we had begun with, that is, how were these moral behavioural codes enforced, should now be answered. At an ideological level, these codes of behaviour derived their legitimacy from the injunction of the *shastra* or scriptures as interpreted by the Brahmans, who enjoyed, till the advent of print culture, a near-total monopoly over Sanskrit textual knowledge. Even when the printing press allowed a broader section of the people access to the scriptures, it was not the texts as such which were taken to the people,[35] but the commentaries written by these pundits which became more popular and widely read. Thus paradoxically, the spread of education or literacy in Bengal had led to a further traditionalization of society. The modernizing impact of education depends on its content, or as Bernard Cohn remarked on 'what people read after they have become literate'.[36] Even a cursory glance at the list of vernacular publications in the late nineteenth and the early twentieth centuries[37] would at once reveal that the average reading public in Bengal was more interested in traditional lore or the knowledge of the shastra, than in the new secular humanistic knowledge.

The educated Bengalis' infatuation with the shastra was, however, due mainly to the Orientalist tradition which had attached supreme importance to scriptures for understanding Indian society. Consequently, during the debate over sati, the competing discourses established the 'centrality' of brahmanic scriptures in determining the legitimacy of social customs.[38] Vidyasagar, an inheritor of this tradition and a Sanskrit scholar by training, also recognized the power of the shastra, from which he believed all social behavioural codes derived their legitimacy. His innovation of widow-remarriage would therefore acquire social acceptance, as his contention was, only if it could be supported by some scriptural maxims; because, as he noted, 'in this country people behaved in accordance with the dicta of the *shastra* and only the *shastra*'.[39] In his first treatise of widow-remarriage we find a massive effort to hunt for a supportive text from the available corpus of scriptural knowledge. But Vidyasagar by going according to the Orientalist tradition misunderstood his own society.

The shastra constituted only one element among many on the basis of which the moral-behavioural codes were constructed. The other elements were oral traditions and longstanding customary usages that gave Hinduism the character of a folklorized religion. Thus when Vidyasagar discovered in *Parasarasamhita* a maxim in support of his reform, the *Hindu Intelligencer* immediately pointed out that

> the views of Parasara, if they were such as have been interpreted to us by the author of the brochure under notice [i.e. Vidyasagar's first treatise on widow-remarriage], have never been adopted by the Hindus, and will continue to be discarded by the people of this country for a long time to come.[40]

Samachar Sudhabarshan also observed around the same time:

> Since the beginning of the Kali Yuga till date, the remarriage of Hindu widows has never been *heard of, nor seen*. And it is for this reason that people believe that widow-remarriage is against the *shastras* and the codes of good conduct.[41]

This statement needs to be emphasized as it implied that the popular perception that widow-remarriage did not conform to the accepted standards of moral conduct was not derived from any written tradition. It was based on hearsay or a longstanding oral tradition which a citation from an obsolete text could not invalidate. To the Hindus 'established custom is law' and in this case, the age-old, often believed to be 'eternal', custom was to debar widows from re-entering connubial relations.[42] An editorial in *Bamabodhini Patrika*, while discussing the futility of Vidyasagar's reform endeavour, very aptly summarized this situation:

> The common people neither follow reason, nor understand *shastra*; local customs also follow more or less the established tradition. These people hate widow-remarriage as a great sin, as they find it to be alien to their tradition.[43]

Vidyasagar had also realized, though much later, the power of oral tradition and customs and admitted it in his second treatise on widow-remarriage:

> . . . Most of the people in this country are ignorant of the *shastra*. Therefore when there is a debate on any issue concerning the *shastra*, they cannot evaluate the arguments of both sides to get at the actual truth.

As they remained 'slaves of local customs' or '*desachar*', they continued to prohibit widow-remarriage and thus 'ignored the injunctions of the *shastra*'. But local customs in this country changed from time to time and therefore Vidyasagar hoped that this inhuman custom could be changed, provided there was the right type of social consciousness.[44] But he himself failed to promote this consciousness, as neither he nor his associates were able to offer a radically new ideology—and they did not challenge the power structure that sustained the old custom.

But before we go into the limitations of the reform movement, it is essential to discuss the power structure that maintained social discipline and punished the errant in Bengali society. At the primary or family level, it was the karta who enforced the prescribed codes of behaviour on the individual members of his family. If he failed to do so, the family as a collective was held responsible for the violation or deviation and was liable to be excommunicated or ostracized. It could also be absolved, if the violation was involuntary, through the performance of *prayaschitta* or penance.[45] Such matters affecting families were the concerns of their immediate larger body, the clan or *goshthi* headed by the *goshthipati* who often adjudicated, with the advice of the clan elders, in such social disputes.[46] But the more serious matters, particularly those involving the possibility of excommunication, were referred to the higher authority, the caste council or the *jati panchayat*. Each caste had its own council which settled disputes relating to caste and family affairs and acted as the custodian of public morality. All these councils were however subservient to the larger *samaja*, which actually meant the hierarchy of castes living within a particular territory. In medieval Bengal, with minimum interference from the central state authority, the territorial chiefs or the Rajas, and below them the Zamindars, controlled the samajas. The Raja was the headman of his own caste council, as well as the head of all the councils in his chiefdom. He provided protection for his subjects, maintained law and order, settled caste and family disputes, and enforced the appropriate codes of social and moral behaviour. Thus, as Ronald Inden has shown, in a medieval Bengali Hindu chiefdom there existed different levels of leadership for social control. But all these levels were tied to each other in fixed vertical relationships and at the apex stood the Raja, the most powerful patron in the whole chiefdom.[47]

This medieval system of control possibly continued into the early British period, as it was present in the living memory of Bengalis even in the early twentieth century. A social historian of Bengal wrote in 1911:

> Previously some Brahman rajas like the Raja of Nadia, the Raja of Tahirpur, the Raja of Natore or the Raja of Susung, exerted immense influence on the Bengali Hindu society. The rules which they prescribed, in consultation with the chief *pundits* of the country, regarding ritual and social behaviour were obeyed by everybody.[48]

This Raja-pundit nexus, with one group enjoying monopoly over political power and the other a monopoly over scriptural knowledge, controlled popular culture in the medieval and early colonial periods. These power elites retained their control at the local level even in the nineteenth century, by adjusting themselves to the changes in the political structure of the country and in the organization of its social production. The nexus now started operating through a new institution called *dal*, which S.N. Mukherjee found to have, in the late eighteenth and the early nineteenth centuries, the same functions as those of the samajas in the earlier time.[49] The only difference was that while the control of the samajas was local or at the most territorial, that of the dal system was regional. Led by the absentee landlords and Rajas and guided by the priests and pundits, these dals operated from the colonial metropolis of Calcutta and stretched their controlling hands over the countryside. As a late-nineteenth-century observer notes, the dal in many respects performed the functions of the Rajas of the pre-colonial days.[50] The caste questions, which were theoretically under the jurisdiction of the colonial courts, remained for all practical purposes the prerogative of the *dalapatis*. It was on them that the interpretation, arbitration and modification of the customary laws depended almost entirely; only, they were advised in such matters by the knowledgeable pundits. While the dals usually operated at the local level, there emerged what McGuire has called a number of *supra-dals*, which were referred to variously as *sabhas* or samajas. Each consisted of a number of local dals and thus cut across the territorial boundaries of Calcutta and linked the city to the country. This dal system, which was generally used by the traditionalist elites as an apparatus of control over popular culture, continued to operate till about the end of the nineteenth century. Then, as McGuire has noted, it 'became increasingly more diffuse as capitalist development broke down the relationships upon which it was based. Yet this process of disintegration was long and complex.'[51]

The dal was gradually replaced by the various exclusive caste associations which began to emerge in Bengal in great numbers after 1905. These organizations, as recently discussed,[52] were also responsible for the process that has been described earlier as the 'reform of popular culture'. Through them more and more of upper-caste behavioural norms and notions of morality found acceptance and wider currency among people of the lower orders. The hegemonic culture set the limits for the imagination of the upwardly mobile lower-caste groups, who could not think of subverting the ritual order or repudiating its moral behavioural codes. Instead of inversion, which was rare and exceptional, we usually find co-option of these groups into the hegemonic cultural order and their acceptance or appropriation of upper-caste cultural symbols, which was mandatory, as we have discussed earlier, for being recognized as respectable in Hindu society. Any deviation from the prescribed norms led to the fall from the ascribed rank and this was monitored, as we have seen, through an efficient and ubiquitous control mechanism. As the *Hindu Patriot* had noted in 1855: 'Conservatism forms a principal feature in the character of the Hindu . . . The slightest breach of the established rules and practices is attended with serious consequences—the rash innovator is branded with infamy and discarded from all social intercourse.'[53] It was for this innate 'conservatism' of popular culture that even those who recognized the desirability of widow-remarriage could not actually practise it.

The power structure within Hindu society, together with its normative system, both based on the concept of hierarchy and expressed through the cultural idiom of caste, operated as a 'massive chain' that kept the entire society bound together. Important changes in the socio-economic structure were accommodated, but this was a gradual or slow and long-drawn process; the Sudra jatis, for example, were given more and more rights towards the turn of the century. Deviations from moral behavioural codes, on the other hand, were usually dealt with individually and were often pardoned after the performance of penance. The system, in other words, made piecemeal adjustments, but lacked the capacity to cushion and absorb the shock of any sudden or radical organizational reform. Like a 'massive chain', as a correspondent of the *Friend of India* had observed in the middle of the nineteenth century, 'Caste must exist in its entirety, or gradually cease altogether. . . .'[54] Destruction of any particular component of that chain would mean its losing the binding capacity and that would imply the loss of power and privilege for a traditionalist elite who had so long ruled society and controlled popular culture. Therefore, when the prohibition of *koolin* polygamy had been proposed, a panicky 'defender' of the system wrote a letter to the editor of the *Reformer* stating that if it was dropped by authority, it would lead to 'nothing short of great confusion and breach of peace. . .'.[55] Vidyasagar himself had to call in the police a number of times so that the widow-remarriage ceremonies which he organized could pass off smoothly.[56] The conservative press at the same time continued to threaten widows willing to remarry with the consequences of being ostracized.[57] The battle over widow-remarriage had thus become for the traditionalist elites a fight for a symbol of authority and domination. To lose the battle would mean the destruction of that 'massive chain' which had ensured their hegemony.

To fortify their position further, the traditionalist elites now began to argue that the caste system, both its structural and normative aspects taken together, was the essence of Hinduism, and so the destruction of the one would mean the annihilation of the other. In 1883, Shib Chandra Bose had observed in a cautious tone that '. . . though in every sense of the word an anti-social institution, it (caste) is nevertheless the main support of the Hindu religion. Take away this support and you destroy the very life and vitality of that religion. . . .'[58] Within a quarter of a century this sentiment came to be shared by a wide range of people in Bengal, from Chintaharan Chattopadhyay, a Brahman pundit of village Sundisar in Dacca district, to Sakharam Ganesh Deuskar, the celebrated history teacher of the Bengal national school. In 1910 Deuskar wrote in a little-known pamphlet: 'These days, to the people of this country, destruction of caste system has become synonymous with the destruction of Hinduism.'[59] Within a few months, Chattopadhyay noted in the same tone: 'Casteism is integrally related to Hinduism. For maintaining family life and Hindu identity, it is essential to preserve the caste system.'[60] Both of them belonged to the same elite group that was carefully building up this notion of an organic connection between caste and Hindutva. It was done to force people to adhere to the moral behavioural codes that legitimized the social hierarchy.

People down the ladder had also internalized this concept of hierarchy that imposed limits on their imagination. Talking about the caste feeling of the lower-caste people, an early-twentieth-century observer noted: 'A sort of instinctive dread of breaking caste puts the idea of doing without caste absolutely beyond the range of possibilities to their minds.'[61] Indeed, how their minds were conditioned becomes more clear from another observation of the same period:

> Each caste considers itself as only a petty member of a mighty body and it never entered into its head even in dreams to set itself in opposition to the central authority. Humble as it might be it was content to share the glory of belonging to the proud hierarchy. A man had no place unless he belonged to a caste; everyone therefore looked upon his caste as a valuable privilege, and no one would be foolhardy enough to lose this by offending the Brahmanical authority. . . .[62]

To lose caste would further mean losing religion, that is to say, a forced uprooting from the familiar social and cultural environment—a terrifying prospect for any individual or family. Some people braved the consequences, as there are instances of widows being converted to Islam or Christianity before actually getting remarried.[63] This meant that they had to get out of the control mechanism of Hindu society, before defying its cultural norms. But most people could not afford to do so because of the dreadful implications. *Samachar Sudhabarshan* could therefore boast: 'Widow-remarriage would mean violation of a part of the Hindu *shastras*, which we do not think most of the religious minded people would be courageous enough to risk.'[64]

IV

Vidyasagar was aware of and had consciously accepted this power structure of Hindu society and its ideology of hierarchy. In other words, he neither challenged the power structure, nor offered any radically different ideological alternative. This becomes apparent if we look at his two treatises on widow-remarriage as texts.

To some of his traditionalist contemporaries, Vidyasagar was the representative of the western educated intelligentsia. For the *Hindu Intelligencer*, he was 'the learned Principal of the Sanscrit [*sic*] College, who is regarded by foreigners as a man of enlarged views and deep research . . .'[65] And to the *Sambad Prabhakar*, his only achievement was the Anglicization of the Sanskrit College, which was not allowed to develop in the way that would have been most appropriate for it.[66] But whatever his popular image might have been, Vidyasagar's reformist ideology was not derived from the so called 'western' concepts of rationality or equality, as opposed to the traditionalist Hindu concept of hierarchy. At the very outset, in his first treatise on widow-remarriage, he had discarded the use of reason, for he believed that people were not amenable to reason and were only governed by shastra. So he went on interpreting and reinterpreting the shastra, trying to prove that his reform had sanctions within the corpus of traditional religious texts. In this he was not perhaps doing anything qualitatively very different from what the Nabadwip and Bhatpara pundits did when they issued *vyavastha* on various social issues.[67] The difference was only of degree: the vyavastha was applicable to individual cases, while Vidyasagar's reform had implications for the entire society.

When this method of referring to shastra failed, Vidyasagar in his second treatise appealed for a change of the local custom or *desachar*. While doing this, he argued.

> No one can prove that there has been no change in our customs since the first day of creation. . . . If an example is cited, you will be able to realize more easily to what extent the customs have changed in our country. In olden times, if a Sudra sat with a Brahman, there would have been no end to his crime. Now those very Sudras take the higher seats, and the Brahmans like obliging servants sit below.

This was, as Vidyasagar's footnote goes, 'against the *shastra*'. So at the end of his treatise he laments: 'Oh shastra! What a misfortune has befallen you! People who live their lives by indulging in activities which you have repeatedly identified as destructive of religion and caste are hailed as wise and pious, while those who even mention, not to speak of performance, the duty which you prescribe as an appropriate *dharma* [referring to widow-remarriage] are endlessly rebuked as atheist, irreligious and unwise.'[68] There could be no clearer statement vindicating the hierarchic ethos of the traditional

Hindu society. It was essentially within this discourse of hierarchy, despite occasional references to equal rights for women,[69] that Vidyasagar situated his reform proposal.

The notion of patriarchic control over women in Hindu society, as we have discussed earlier, emanated from this concept of an all-encompassing hierarchy. Vidyasagar had also accepted and internalized this notion. The language in which he phrased his reform proposal clearly revealed his concern to maintain the patriarchic control over female sexuality and family discipline. What we find in his two treatises is first of all a definite and honest statement of paternalistic sympathy for the miserable plight of the widows. But side by side, what is also writ large is a concern for the falling standards of public morality and the increasing social tendency towards adultery and foeticide, all due to the unsatiated sexual appetite of widowed women. Unable to lead a life of self-denial, they indulged in illicit sex and thus put to shame all the three lineages of their husband, father and mother. So it was necessary to regulate and direct this unbridled and wayward female sexuality into a socially legitimate channel, that is, marriage, and for this it was essential to remove the prohibition on widow-remarriage.[70] The reform, in other words, was meant to ensure social discipline and patriarchic control over women's bodies and desires.

Most of the educated contemporaries of Vidyasagar who supported his cause shared this basic hierarchic assumption of gender inequality and expressed the same concern for public morality. The growing sexual anarchy in society was attributed only to the inability of the widows to restrain their libido which, as even the more progressive *Tattvabodhini Patrika* apprehended, would affect other women in society and thus would completely destroy the family structure. The plea for widow-remarriage was no doubt coated in a language of equality. If men could remarry after the death of their wives, the *Patrika* asked, why could not widows do the same? But in the same breath it also argued in a sexist language that widow-remarriage was all the more necessary, as the libidinal urge of women was eight times greater than that of men. It was for this reason that all of them could not restrain their desires and brought infamy to Bengal.[71] A biological dimension was thus added to the concept of innate gender inequality. Other proponents of the reform also shared the same concern for falling standards of public morality and believed that what had further contributed to this social disorder were the other two evil institutions of child marriage and *koolin* polygamy,[72] which were also on the nineteenth-century reform agenda.

This assumption of innate and uncontrollable feminine sexuality, as James Mill had already shown, was embedded in Hindu cultural traditions.[73] And therefore, the ideology of reform as Vidyasagar and his supporters had defined it, appeared not as an alternative to but as a derivative from the ideology of hierarchy which the traditionalist elites of Hindu society had been propounding. It was natural therefore that this new reformist position would not find popular acceptance, unless sanctioned by these elites. Even those who had realized that the reform was a social necessity, could not raise their voice, as the *Tattvabodhini Patrika* commented, for fear of either offending the dalapatis or inviting public censure.[74] This was because Vidyasagar and the other protagonists of reform, instead of trying to subvert the power structure of Hindu society, sought the patronage of both the dalapati and the pundit themselves. Vidyasagar, for example, had accepted quite resignedly, that in this country people had to behave according to the words and dictates of the great men who were the interpreters of *dharma-shastra*.[75]

So he went to Radhakanta Deb and his dal for support and appeared in a public debate to argue his case against the rival pundits. He won the first round and got a shawl and favour from the almighty dalapati. Victory would have been his if the situation had not changed further. But soon the other dalapatis approached Deb and requested him to revise his decision to promote widow-remarriage. Vidyasagar was called for a second round of debate and here he lost, or he was perhaps meant to lose. The decision of the dalapati was reversed[76] and with this the fate of the reform movement was also sealed. Even those pundits who had earlier given a vyavastha in support of the marriage of the widowed daughter of Shyamcharan Das of Calcutta, now changed their minds and became opponents of widow-remarriage.[77] And the common people could hardly muster the courage to go against the shastra as interpreted to them by the pundits or defy the established customs as imposed upon them by the dalapatis.[78] No legislation had the power to break this massive chain.

Vidyasagar, in other words, had opted for the traditionalists' method of reforming popular culture, that is, of initiating and imposing reform from above. Crucial for the success of this method was the support of the hegemonic power of the traditionalist elites, in which he too had reposed his faith. The movement against koolin polygamy was successful as it received the support of some influential leaders of Hindu society, like the Maharaja of Burdwan, the Raja of Nadia and the Raja of Dinajpur. As *Friend of India* had noted, the Raja of Nadia was 'to Hinduism what Sir Harry Inglis was to Church of England' and the Raja of Dinajpur was 'a Hindoo of Hindoos'.[79] But widow-remarriage seemed to be too exotic a deviation from the established moral-behavioural codes of Hinduism to enjoy the favour of these elites. In the nineteenth-century cultural stereotype it appeared as a custom that violated the shastra; and it was complemented by another stereotype, that it was prevalent only among the lower orders. The *Hindu Intelligencer* wrote in 1855: 'This custom no longer prevails among the natives of the higher orders, . . . but it is still followed by those of the lower grades.'[80] For the *Samachar Sudhabarshan*, it was more specifically a custom of the '*antyja*' (low born) castes, 'prevalent only among the Hari, Methar, Dom, Chandal etc.'[81] Vidyasagar appeared to be proposing the adoption of the values of the unclean castes, who were at the bottom of society, by the Brahmans and the clean Sudras, who were the elites among the Bengali Hindus. He was asking the bhadralok to adopt a social practice that the *chotolok* had been pursuing since time immemorial. This must have looked like a reform of popular culture in the reverse direction—a 'counter reform'. The elites could only be expected to resist this effort.

The only alternative now left for Vidyasagar, which indeed he had already opted for, was to rely on a higher authority, that is, the colonial state. He had been pleading for a legislation, perhaps with the assumption that the state and social authority were the two mutually validating reflections of the same hierarchy. But this was a crucial misunderstanding of the relations of power in nineteenth-century Bengal, where the colonial state and the leaders of Hindu society still held sway over two mutually exclusive domains of power. The former occasionally tried to encroach upon the territory of the latter, but could never completely control it. Therefore, even if there was a law, there was no prospect of its being enforced without social consent. And this consent or cultural acquiescence of the people could only be ensured either through the support of the traditionalist elites or by completely breaking what we have described as the 'massive chain' of caste. Vidyasagar was denied the first, and his mind, like that of most of his contemporaries was culturally so conditioned that he could not even think of opting for the second alternative. He operated essentially within the ideological and functional boundaries imposed by the dominant power structure of Hindu society. The roots of his tragedy lay here; the reasons for the 'unavoidable defeat' of the reform movement.

V

However, as a result of Vidyasagar's campaign for reform, the question of widow-remarriage became an issue of public concern as well as a subject of controversy. This had long-term implications for Bengali society, as it became a symbol for the traditionalist elites, the acceptance or rejection of which was thought to have been inversely related to the diminution or continuance of their power. By taking the issue to the legislature, Vidyasagar had renewed the conflict over definition of boundary between the two domains of power of state and society. The traditionalists had already lost the first battle when Rammohun had the custom of sati abolished through the intervention of the state. As the *Hindu Patriot* had observed, the practice was discontinued only because it became 'penal at law'.[82] The leaders of Hindu society were no longer prepared to concede any further ground and the result was a stubborn resistance which sometimes even lapsed into violence. This critical response to the bill pending before the Legislative Council was adequately reflected when the *Eastern Star* noted:

> that the proposed legislative interference . . . is improper and quite uncalled for. The legislative body of the country, not being a representative assembly of the people for whom it legislates, is under the necessity of using great care and circumspection in the enactment of laws. . . . The legislative council cannot compel the natives to marry their widows, but it proposes to fix the stamp of legitimacy on the children born of Hindu widow. . . . The community will continue to look upon them as bastards, and as persons not born in lawful wedlock. The legislature cannot coerce the opinions of men, nor influence their social relations, at least not directly.[83]

The statement clearly questions the legitimacy of state power within the domain of social relations, where the will of the community was held to be the supreme authority. But this social opinion, as we have seen, was effectively manipulated by the powerful traditionalist elite group. And therefore, even when there was a law validating widow-remarriage, just as the *Samachar Darpan* had predicted four years before it was actually passed, there was no way to enforce it.[84] In the case of sati, what was being proposed was the abolition of an evil custom, which could be ensured through the intervention of the state. But widow-remarriage was an innovation, indeed a revolutionary one, which could not be introduced by government fiat. The law therefore remained a dead letter for several decades after Vidyasagar's death.

What was worse, widow celibacy gradually became a much more widely practised popular custom. The elites portrayed it as one of the most authentic symbols of the culture of the respectable, and the socially mobile sections of the lower orders readily appropriated it. There were some among the educated members of the lower castes who had notionally accepted the innovation, but they too shared the same patriarchal and moralist concerns[85] and refrained from practising it in real life. Neither could they popularize the reform among their respective communities, because of the obvious socio-cultural compulsions to adopt the dominant elites' behavioural codes, defined by the ideology of hierarchy. This was the ongoing or the usual process through which the traditionalist elites had been extending their hegemonic control over popular culture. It was beyond the power of Vidyasagar or his reformist compatriots to make a dent in their sphere of influence. This situation continued till about the middle of the twentieth century, when the war, the famine and Partition disrupted social bonds and destroyed in many cases the structure of the patriarchal family, making way for new values and fresh adjustments within the relations of power in Bengali society.

The final point to be mentioned about this reform movement is the marginality of women in the whole process. While Vidyasagar had started his crusade out of a sense of compassion for young widows, what followed subsequently was a battle for a cultural symbol, in which the plight of the widows had become a subsidiary concern for both the contending parties. It was never a concern for the opponents of the reform; even Vidyasagar's sympathetic self often got superseded by the orthodox social disciplinarian in him. And in the scriptural polemics, women did not even figure as objects. In the nineteenth- or the early-twentieth-century social world of Bengal, women had not as yet emerged as conscious subjects of history, trying to assert their own rights. If *Bamabodhini Patrika* represented the only feminine voice raised in support of the reform, it too accepted in a resigned mood the futility of the endeavour.[86]

On the other hand, women at the intermediate and bottom layers of the ritual hierarchy appear to have been so thoroughly socialized into the orthodox male world-view, that they not only accepted and promoted the dominant Hindu stereotypes of womanhood, but also opposed the idea of widow-remarriage. The *Mahishya Mahila*, a monthly journal for Mahishya women, edited by Krishnabhamini Biswas, is an ideal example at hand.[87] Even the Subarnabanik Mahila Sammilani, the first ever conference of about 500 women of the Subarnabanik caste, held in December 1925 under the supervision of the male leaders of their community, discussed strategies for the spread of female education and other issues concerning women, but did not dare to include widow-remarriage in their agenda.[88] This also explains the differential success achieved by the two reform programmes. The first reform for the spread of higher education had been relatively more successful, because its proponents, Vidyasagar included, had succeeded to a large extent in mobilizing female opinion in support of it. Some of the caste associations, as that of the Subarnabaniks mentioned above, had also ensured the active participation of women in this organized drive for female education. The *Mahishya Mahila* urged its literate women readers to educate their female neighbours and thus to spread literacy among the womenfolk of their community.[89] But none of the champions of widow-remarriage ever thought of mobilizing women's opinion in favour of the reform, not to speak of involving them as active participants in the actual reform process. This explains to a large extent the failure of their reform endeavour. And individual or independent voices of women, either in support of the reform or against it, have remained totally unrecorded, confirming only their marginality in this crucial social debate in colonial Bengal.

Notes

1. Asok Sen, *Ishwar Chandra Vidyasagar and His Elusive Milestones* (Calcutta, 1977), p. 6.
2. Benoy Ghosh, ed., *Selections from English Periodicals of 19th Century Bengal* (Calcutta, 1979), vol. III, p. 116 (hereafter *Selections*).
3. Asok Sen, *Ishwar Chandra Vidyasagar*; Amales Tripathi, *Vidyasagar, The Traditional Moderniser* (Calcutta, 1976).
4. Peter Burke, *Popular Culture in Early Modern Europe* (London, 1978), p. xi.
5. E.P. Thompson, 'Patrician Society, Plebeian Culture', *Journal of Social History*, vol. VII, 1974, p. 395.
6. Peter Burke, *Popular Culture*, pp. 207–43.
7. See M.N. Srinivas, *Social Change in Modern India* (Bombay, 1977), pp. 1–45.
8. Martin Ingram, 'The Reform of Popular Culture: Sex and Marriage in Early Modern England', in Barry Reay, ed., *Popular Culture in Seventeenth Century England* (London, 1988), pp. 129–30.
9. For more details, see Barry Reay, ibid., Introduction, pp. 17–22; also David Hall, Introduction, in S.L. Kaplan, ed., *Understanding Popular Culture* (Berlin, 1984).
10. For a comprehensive discussion of this recent critique, see Barbara N. Ramusack, 'From Symbol to Diversity: The Historical Literature on Women in India', *South Asia Research*, vol. 10, no. 2, November 1990, pp. 154ff.
11. *Census of India*, 1891, vol. III, The Report, p. 267.
12. Risley Collection, Eur. MSS. E. 295, vol. 3, pp. 258–9, vol. 4, p. 95, India Office Library, London.
13. Shyamlal Sen, *Jatitattva-Vivek* (The Caste Ethics, Barisal, 1797 Saka), p. 111.
14. H.H. Risley, *The Tribes and Castes of Bengal* (Reprint, Calcutta, 1981), vol. I, p. lxxxiv.
15. For details on the construction of these models, see Uma Chakrabarti, 'Whatever Happened to the Vedic *Dasi*? Orientalism, Nationalism and a Script for the Past', in Kumkum Sangari and Sudesh Vaid, eds, *Recasting Women: Essays in Indian Colonial History* (New Brunswick, New Jersey, 1990), pp. 27–87.
16. *Selections*, vol. III, p. 116; Benoy Ghosh, ed., *Samayikpatre Banglar Samajchitra* (Reflections of Bengali Society in Journals, Calcutta, 1980) (hereafter *Samajchitra*), vol. III, pp. 70–1, 166–7, vol. IV, pp. 157–66.
17. John McGuire, *The Making of a Colonial Mind: A Quantitative Study of the Bhadralok in Calcutta, 1857–1885* (Canberra, 1983), p. 22.
18. *Census of India*, 1911, vol. V, Part I, p. 373, Subsidiary Table VI.
19. Madhusudan Sarkar, 'Abar Bidhaba Bibaha Keno?' (Why Widow-Remarriage?), *Navyabharat*, vol. 25, no. 12, Chaitra, 1314 BS.
20. *Jogisakha*, Baisakh, Jaistha, Ashadh, Sraban, 1312 BS; *Bangiya Tili Samaj Patrika*, Chaitra-Baisakh 1332–3 BS, Magh-Falgun 1333 BS; *Kshatriya*, Chaitra 1332 BS; *Sadgop Patrika*, Baisakh 1330 BS, Sraban, Paush 1337 BS; *Tilir Gaurab*, Ashwin 1326 BS; *Bangiya Vaisya Barujibi Sabhar Chaturdas Barshik Karya-Bibaran* (Jessore, 1915), p. 55; *Subarnabanik Samachar*, Magh 1327 BS; *Gandhabanik*, Kartik-Agrahayan 1330 BS; *Mahishya Samaj*, Falgun 1328 BS, Jaistha 1329 BS.
21. *Subarnabanik Samachar*, Magh 1323 BS.
22. See Nicholas B. Dirks, *The Hollow Crown: Ethnohistory of an Indian Kingdom* (Cambridge, 1990), pp. 5–7.
23. For a detailed discussion on this aspect, see Sekhar Bandyopadhyay, *Caste, Politics and the Raj: Bengal 1872–1937* (Calcutta, 1990), pp. 1–51.
24. *Selections*, vol. III, p. 116.
25. Quoted in Asok Sen, *Ishwar Chandra Vidyasagar*, p. 58.
26. John McGuire, *The Making of a Colonial Mind*, p. 37.

27. Ibid., p. 40.
28. Ronald B. Inden, *Marriage and Rank in Bengali Culture* (New Delhi, 1976), pp. 14–21.
29. On the Application of Dr Toppinard's Anthropometric System to the Castes and Tribes of Bengal', by H.H. Risley, 8 March 1886, Government of Bengal, Financial (Miscellaneous) Proceedings, March 1887, pp. 83–5, West Bengal State Archives, Calcutta.
30. Shib Chandra Bose, *The Hindoos As They Are* (Second edition, Calcutta, 1883), pp. 2–3.
31. Anonymous, *Hindu Dharmaniti* (The Hindu Code of Ethics, Calcutta 1794 Saka), p. 8.
32. Jatindramohan Gupta, *Hindu Narir Kartabya* (The Duties of Hindu Women, Calcutta, 1323 BS), p. 108.
33. Cited in Bharati Ray, 'Do We Have a Choice? Widows of India with Special Reference to Bengal, 1900–1956', paper presented at the Berkshire Conference of Women Historians, June 1990 and at the Seventeenth International Conference of the Historical Sciences, August–September 1990.
34. *Mahishya Mahila*, vol. I, no. 3, 1318 BS.
35. Basumati Sahitya Mandir was one of the pioneering organizations responsible for the publication of such Smriti, Nyaya and Darshana texts published since the time of Rammohun Roy.
36. Bernard S. Cohn, *India: The Social Anthropology of a Civilization* (New Jersey, 1971), p. 100.
37. See, for example, National Library, India, *Author Catalogue of Printed Books in Bengali Language*, vols I–IV (Calcutta, 1959–63); also J.F. Blumhardt, ed., *Catalogue of the Library of the India Office*, vol. II, Part IV (London, 1905).
38. For a recent and excellent discussion on this aspect, see Lata Mani, 'Contentious Traditions: The Debate on Sati in Colonial India', in Kumkum Sangari and Sudesh Vaid eds, *Recasting Women*, pp. 88–126.
39. Iswarchandra Vidyasagar, *Bidhaba-Bibaha Prachalito Haoya Uchit Kina Etadbishayak Prastab* (Should Widow-remarriage be Introduced?), in Gopal Haldar, ed., *Vidyasagar Rachana Sangraha* (The Collected Works of Vidyasagar, Calcutta, 1972), vol. 2, pp. 21–2.
40. *Hindu Intelligencer*, 12 February 1855, *Selections*, vol. III, p. 112.
41. *Samachar Sudhabarshan*, 29 December 1855, *Samajchitra*, vol. III, p. 140.
42. *Hindu Patriot*, 15 February 1855, *Selections*, vol. III, p. 115; *Samachar Sudhabarshan*, 6 November 1855, *Samajchitra*, vol. III, p. 137.
43. *Bamabodhini Patrika*, Sraban 1277 BS, *Samajchitra*, vol. III, pp. 166–7.
44. Iswarchandra Vidyasagar, *Bidhaba-Bibaha Prachalito Haoya Uchit Kina Etadbishayak Prastab: Dwitiya Pustak*, in *Vidyasagar Rachana Sangraha*, vol. 2, pp. 36, 160–1.
45. Bani Chakraborti, *Samaj-Sanskarak Raghunandan* (Raghunandan, A Social Reformer, Calcutta, 1970), pp. 246–55, 259.
46. Umeshchandra Gupta, *Jatitattva-baridhi-dwitiya bhaag ba Ballal-Mohamudgar* (Calcutta, 1905), p. 441.
47. Ronald Inden, 'Hindu Chiefdom in Middle Bengali Literature', in Edward C. Dimock, Jr. ed., *Bengal: Literature and History* (East Lansing, Michigan, 1967), pp. 25ff.
48. Durga Chandra Sanyal, *Banglar Samajik Itihas* (The Social History of Bengal, Calcutta, 1317 BS), p. 450.
49. S.N. Mukherjee, *Calcutta: Myths and History* (Calcutta, 1971).
50. Shib Chandra Bose, *The Hindoos*, p. 167.
51. John McGuire, *The Making of a Colonial Mind*, pp. 30–5 (quotation from p. 35).
52. Sekhar Bandyopadhyay, *Caste, Politics*, Chapter III.
53. *Hindu Patriot*, 15 February 1855, *Selections*, vol. VIII, p. 116.
54. *Friend of India*, 5 June 1851, *Selections*, vol. III, pp. 44–5.
55. *Reformer*, 7 April 1833, *Selections*, vol. I, p. 170.
56. Subal Chandra Mitra, *Iswar Chandra Vidyasagar* (in Bengali) (Calcutta, 1902), p. 319.
57. *Samachar Sudhabarshan*, 29 December 1855, *Samajchitra*, vol. III, p. 140.
58. Shib Chandra Bose, *The Hindoos*, p. 163.

59. Sakharam Ganesh Deuskar, *Bangiya Hindujati ki Dhangsonmukh* (Is the Hindu Community in Bengal on a Path of Decline, Calcutta, 1317 BS), p. 116.
60. Chintaharan Chattopadhyay, *Brahman* (The Brahmin, Faridpur, 1317 bs), p. 19.
61. N. Sengupta, 'The Census and Caste', *The Dacca Review*, vol. 1, no. 6, September 1911, p. 200.
62. Jatindra Chandra Guha, 'Reform in the Hindu Society', *The Dacca Review*, vol. 1, no. 9, December 1911, pp. 284–5.
63. *Bamabodhini Patrika*, Jaistha 1277 BS, *Samajchitra*, vol. III, p. 165; *Census of India*, 1901, vol. VI, Part I, Appendix II.
64. *Samachar Sudhabarshan*, 6 November 1855, *Samajchitra*, vol. III, p. 137.
65. *Hindu Intelligencer*, 12 February 1855, *Selections*, vol. III, p. 112.
66. *Sambad Prabhakar*, 21 April 1265 BS, *Samajchitra*, vol. II, p. 177.
67. Indeed, some time before Vidyasagar wrote his first treatise, some of the *pundits* had given a *vyavastha* sanctioning the marriage of the widowed daughter of one Shyamacharan Das of Calcutta. See Iswarchandra Vidyasagar, *Bidhaba-Bibaha . . . Etadbishayak Prastab*, pp. 14–17.
68. Iswarchandra Vidyasagar, *Bidhaba-Bibaha . . . Dwitiya Pustak*, pp. 161, 164.
69. Iswarchandra Vidyasagar, *Ratnapariksha* in *Vidyasagar Rachana Sangraha*, vol. 2, p. 538.
70. Iswarchandra Vidyasagar, *Bidhaba-Bibaha . . . Etadbishyak Prastab*, p. 32 and *passim; Bidhaba-Bibaha . . . Dwitiya Pustak*, pp. 164–5 and *passim*.
71. *Tattvabodhini Patrika*, no. 140, Chaitra 1776 Saka, *Samajchitra*, vol. IV, pp. 158–62.
72. *Sangbad Purnachandroday*, 17 June 1851, *Sarbasubhakari Patrika*, no. 1, Bhadra, 1772 Saka; *Samachar Sudhabarshan*, 31 December 1855, *Samajchitra*, vol. III, pp. 70–1, 89, 140.
73. Uma Chakrabarti, 'Vedic *Dasi*', p. 35.
74. *Tattvabodhini Patrika*, p. 157.
75. Iswarchandra Vidyasagar, *Bidhaba-Bibaha . . . Etadbishayak Prastab*, p. 16.
76. For details, see John McGuire, *The Making of the Colonial Mind*, p. 33.
77. Iswarchandra Vidyasagar, *Bidhaba-Bibaha . . . Etadbishayak Prastab*, pp. 15–16.
78. *Sarbasubhakari Patrika*, no. 1, Bhadra 1772 Saka, *Samajchitra*, vol. III, pp. 82–3, 88.
79. *Friend of India*, 17 July 1856, *Selections*, vol. III, p. 93.
80. *Hindu Intelligencer*, 12 February 1855, *Selections*, vol. III, p. 113.
81. *Samachar Sudhabarshan*, 10 July 1855, 15 September 1855, *Samajchitra*, vol. III, pp. 134, 137.
82. *Hindu Patriot*, 15 February 1855, *Selections*, vol. III, p. 117.
83. *Eastern Star*, 8 December 1855, *Selections*, vol. III, p. 137.
84. *Samajchitra*, vol. III, p. 71.
85. Balaram Sarkar, *Namasudra Jnanabhandar* (About the Namasudras, Faridpur, 1911), pp. 80–3.
86. See note 43 above.
87. See note 34 above; for a more detailed discussion on *Mahishya Mahila*, see Chandrima Sinha, 'Mahishya Jatir Samajik Andolan O Mahishya Nari' (The Social Movement of the Mahishya Community and their Women), *Aitihasik*, vol. 3, no. 2, April–June 1981.
88. *Subarnabanik Samachar*, Paush 1333 BS.
89. *Mahishya Mahila*, vol. 1, no. 9, 1319 BS, pp. 108–12.

6

Vidyasagar and Brahmanical Society*

Sumit Sarkar

Vidyasagar never wrote a systematic treatise on education. The precise significance of his extremely innovative ideas and projects has to be reconstructed from scattered texts—official letters and notes,[1] school primers and textbooks written by him, and documents relating to Vidyasagar in the files of the government education department and archives of Sanskrit College.[2]

The changes Vidyasagar sought to make in Sanskrit College, as Assistant Secretary (1846–7) and later as Principal (1850–3), were not just about reforms in a particular institution, for they can be seen to imply ultimately a distinctive educational-cum-social philosophy. Even the innovations that might appear trivial today, such as Vidyasagar's insistence on punctuality and regular attendance by students and teachers,[3] acquire greater meaning when one remembers that clock time was no more than a generation or two old in India in the 1840s, having been a belated, colonial import. Its history has been surprisingly neglected in studies of colonial India. Bound up, as elsewhere, with new pressures for regularity and tighter work schedules, clocks and watches acquired somewhat distinct and varied implications through their links with structures of colonial power. The three principal early sites for time-discipline in colonial Bengal were educational institutions, government and mercantile offices and the railways.[4] Indigenous responses to it clearly had a differential character. Vidyasagar is a reminder that systematized, rule-bound education governed by clock time was widely perceived as indispensable for middle-class self-improvement under colonial conditions. Punctuality no doubt often remained a burden, but its normative role in schools and colleges was not questioned. Things were quite different in the alienated world of *chakri* or office work under foreign bosses, where disciplinary time entered into a distinctively late-nineteenth-century vision of Kaliyuga.[5]

Vidyasagar's plan of 16 December 1850 suggested a series of changes in the syllabus of Sanskrit College, all in a recognizably modern, rationalistic direction. It simultaneously sought to bring Sanskrit teaching into close contact with the development of both Bengali and English education. Thus, for Sanskrit grammar, which students so long had been forced to memorize through the very difficult *Mugdhabodha*, Vidyasagar suggested the learning of the basic rules 'dressed in the easiest Bengali', followed by graduated Sanskrit readings. (He would himself soon supply the appropriate Sanskrit grammar in Bengali, the *Vyakarana-Kaumudi*.) Training in English, too, was necessary, but only in the higher classes, to avoid the danger of getting swamped by it at the expense of the vernacular. Sanskrit College students, the plan emphasized, must 'acquire great proficiency in Bengali' and 'derive useful information' through it (for which he was already providing the wherewithal, through textbooks like *Jivancharit* and *Bodhoday*), 'and thereby have their views expanded before they commence their English studies'. They could also learn Jyotish (mathematics and astronomy) much more profitably through Bengali translations of contemporary English texts, instead of Lilavati and Bhaskaracharya, which Vidyasagar thought 'very meagre' by modern standards. Even more striking is the evident attempt to reduce the importance in the syllabus of the Smriti teachings of Raghunandan (whose texts constituted the principal barrier to reforms like widow remarriage or a higher age of consent throughout the nineteenth century) and the Navya-Nyaya of Raghunath Shiromani (whose logic Vidyasagar thought had been 'similar to that of schoolmen'). Along with Navya-Nyaya, the philosophical portions of the pre-Vidyasagar syllabus had a strong tilt towards Vedanta, characteristic of high-Hindu metaphysics since medieval times. It included texts specifically refuting 'the Bouddha or atheistical doctrine' and all other non-Vedantist schools. In their place, Vidyasagar wanted to introduce the *Sarvadarshanasangraha*, through which, he argued, the student would be able to see how 'the different systems have attacked each other, and have pointed out each other's errors and fallacies. Thus he would be able to judge for himself'—particularly since some courses in European philosophy would also be introduced.[6] In 1858 Vidyasagar brought out a critical edition of this fourteenth-century text of Madhavacharya, which he said had become a very rare manuscript.[7] It may not be irrelevant to note that the *Sarvadarshanasangraha* remains the primary source for the little information we have about the suppressed ancient Indian materialist tradition of Lokayata, associated with Carvaka.[8]

That the implications of Vidyasagar's reform plan went very much beyond mere syllabus revision becomes clear from his *Notes on the Sanskrit College* (12 April 1852), which summed up with admirable precision and logic the core of his educational perspectives. 'The creation of an enlightened Bengali Literature', Vidyasagar now declared, 'should be the first object of those who are entrusted with the superintendence of Education in Bengal.' This required the 'exertions of those . . . competent to collect the materials from European sources and . . . dress them in elegant, expressive and idiomatic Bengali.' But for this, Vidyasagar felt, mastery of Sanskrit was also essential, as 'more English scholars are altogether incapable of expressing their ideas in elegant and idiomatic Bengali. They are so much anglicized that it seems at present almost impossible for them to do so even if they later learn Sanskrit.' It is very clear then that 'if students of the Sanskrit College be made familiar with English Literature, they will prove the best and ablest contributors to an enlightened Bengali Literature'.[9]

In September 1853 Vidyasagar had to defend his syllabus against criticisms made of it by J.R. Ballantyne, Principal of Benaras Government Sanskrit College. In course of that exercise he had to formulate its underlying assumptions with greater clarity and polemical sharpness. Ballantyne had suggested a greater emphasis on the 'correspondences' between select aspects of European and Indian philosophical traditions as a way of reconciling the Brahmanical literati to the coming of Western ideas. This involved a very different pattern of choice between philosophical schools, than Vidyasagar's. The Benaras principal wanted less of Mill's *Logic*, the inclusion of Bishop Berkeley's *Inquiry*, and the introduction of a commentary written by Ballantyne himself which had emphasized the alleged similarities between that classic text of European philosophical Idealism, and Vedanta and Sankhya. This was the specific context for Vidyasagar's blunt and aggressive statement about Vedanta and Sankhya being 'false systems of philosophy': a remark that has been often torn out of context to indicate either Vidyasagar's laudable Westernized modernity, or (with some justice) his philosophical naivete and dogmatism. But Vidyasagar's position, it must be emphasized, was not an uncritical preference of Western to Indian thought, for Vidyasagar was equally dismissive of Berkeley. The really interesting thing about the reply to Ballantyne is the way it anticipated, and sought to refute, what by the late nineteenth century would become a central strategy of much Hindu revivalism, as well as of a brand of Orientalism from which it was often highly derivative.[10] 'Lately a feeling is manifesting itself among the learned of this part of India, specially in Calcutta and its neighbourhood, that when they hear of a Scientific truth, the germs of which may be traced out in their Shastras, instead of shewing any regard for that truth, they triumph and the superstitious regard for their own Shastras is redoubled.' Vidyasagar went on to make a most uncomplimentary characterization of the 'learned of India' as a 'body of men whose longstanding prejudices are unshakeable'— referring presumably to the traditional Brahman literati, not the Sanskrit College students he was trying to train in a new way. He went on to reiterate and expand the alternative cultural perspective he had outlined in April 1852. Instead of trying 'to reconcile the learned of the Country',

> what we require is to extend the benefit of education to the mass of the people. Let us establish a number of Vernacular schools, let us prepare a series of Vernacular class-books on useful and instructive subjects, let us raise up a band of men [who] should be perfect masters of their own language, possess a considerable amount of useful information and be free from the prejudices of their country. To raise up such a useful class of men is the object I have proposed to myself and to the accomplishment of which the whole energy of *our* Sanskrit College should be directed.[11]

Beginning, then, in 1844 with the suggestion for tackling the employment problem facing Sanskrit College graduates through giving them jobs in Hardinge's experimental village schools, Vidyasagar in course of a decade had progressed to an integrated plan for cultural renovation of the literati of Bengal. Considered in the perspective of conventional histories of education, Vidyasagar's scheme may be seen as a bringing together of Orientalist, Anglicist and Vernacularist positions, achieved through significant changes within each of them. Translated more meaningfully into social terms, it needs to be understood as an attempt to bridge the growing gap between the traditional pandits and the Westernized, English-educated intelligentsia: not through some kind of eclectic compromise, however, which roughly had been Ballantyne's advice, but by a determined effort to transform and get beyond both poles. Vidyasagar hoped to impart a fundamentally new vernacular-cum-rural turn to pandits and English-educated alike, and considerably broaden the social basis of the intelligentsia as a whole. That such a trend could unfold in mid-nineteenth-century Bengal, it needs to be added, should considerably complicate the Westernist–traditionalist dichotomy in terms of which so much colonial middle-class history has been conceptualized.

Vidyasagar had had ample opportunities of watching this rupture grow at first hand, for classes in Sanskrit College in his time took place in the same building as Hindu College, with the two institutions, however, carefully segregated from each other by walls. His class-friends would all be Brahmans (plus a few Vaidyas), mostly poor. Hindu College was catering to a more multi-caste clientele, including many sons of the relatively low-born Calcutta nouveaux riches, but it was at the same time considerably more exclusive in economic terms. Vidyasagar himself had managed to straddle both worlds, through mastering English and developing personal ties with a host of Hindu College products (including many of the Young Bengal variety), but he would have realized how insuperable the barriers might soon appear to many. And indeed the long-term consequences of the failure of Vidyasagar's dream have been very far-reaching. The logical implication of his educational strategy was a reunification of the literati on a basis oriented towards modernistic change, which would be at the same time geared towards mass vernacular education, and therefore at least potentially more democratic than pre-colonial Brahmanical culture. Instead, as the rift widened, the world of the old-fashioned pandits became increasingly narrow, immersed in futile grumbling about the many evils of Kaliyuga, often blindly conservative—while the 'Anglicized' have often swung between complete alienation and recurrent searches for 'roots' in (largely invented or spurious) 'traditions'. In total contrast to Vidyasagar's vision, the occasional unificatory moments have tended to develop around revivalist-nationalistic programmes—right down to our own times, one is tempted to add, in Hindutva's twin base among Vishwa Hindu Parishad sadhus and a Non-Resident Indian-oriented elite that is highly Westernized in a consumerist sense.

Two things were indispensable if Vidyasagar's plans were to succeed. There was the need for an 'enlightened Bengali Literature', in particular a vernacular discursive prose capable of tackling in a creative and attractive manner a much wider range of themes than had been possible or necessary in pre-colonial times. The other, interrelated, prerequisite was the rapid spread of vernacular education. The two together could help to constitute a public space open to argumentation, and based on expanding literacy and print culture.

The first condition was largely met, for this was an autonomous area where the intelligentsia could operate on its own, and where the coming of print culture enabled wide dissemination and created some possibilities for financial independence. Western education on the whole was a stimulus rather than hindrance to the development of indigenous languages, in significant contrast to what happened in some other parts of the colonized world. Vidyasagar's own seminal and multiple contributions to the development of modern Bengali prose have of course been very widely recognized. They ranged from mundane but necessary things like the introduction of standardized punctuation[12] and syntax, the careful compilation of glossaries of new terms for modern concepts,[13] to the creation of a style that was chaste, dignified, yet free from the inaccessible and excessively Sanskritized ornateness of the Bengali which many pandits still liked to use.[14] Rabindranath even felt this to have been Vidyasagar's greatest single achievement, and described it as an emancipation of the language simultaneously from 'rustic barbarism' and 'parochial scholasticism'.[15] And for a man capable of the considerable literary qualities of a text like *Sitar Banobas*, it must have been a major sacrifice to devote one's writing talents almost entirely to composing, as part of a deeply felt social commitment, school textbooks, adaptations and reform tracts.[16]

The expansion-cum-improvement of vernacular schools in villages required, however, considerable financial inputs from the state and/or the rural gentry, as well as active support from the literati, old and new. For a brief period in the mid 1850s the conjuncture appeared favourable for Vidyasagar's dream. Colonial educational policy was not quite the monolith, determined solely by Macaulay's notorious Minute of 1835, that is sometimes assumed nowadays. Bengal officials in the early 1850s had been impressed by the apparent success of the 'circle' experiment started in the North-Western Provinces under Thomason that had tried to set up a model school in each revenue district as a way of improving vernacular education. Wood's Education Despatch of 1854, though in the end contained within the 'filtration' framework, had also visualized some expansion in vernacular education through the grants-in-aid system by which costs would be shared between the government and local patrons.

Around 1855–6—the peak years also of his social reform drive—Vidyasagar was enjoying excellent relations with many high British officials in Bengal, from Lieutenant-Governor Halliday downwards. This had helped him to develop links with a number of prominent zamindars, in particular some 'improving' landlords like Joykrishna Mukhopadhyay of Uttarpara, who had recently acquired large estates in Hooghly district, and who around 1855 was combining efforts to promote new crops like potatoes and sugarcane with the establishment of both English and vernacular schools in the areas under his control.[17] Vidyasagar, finally, had become a major figure by the mid-1850s among the literati, both traditional and new: active in the Brahmo-led Tattwabodhini Sabha and Patrika, friends of many with Young Bengal antecedents, and yet numbering among his closest associates pandits like Madanmohan Tarkalankar, who helped him start the Sanskrit Press Depository, and Taranath Tarkavacaspati, who combined running a *tol* at Ambica-Kalna with far-flung business interests. The peak of Vidyasagar's educational and reform campaign seems to have coincided in fact with a last flurry of enterprising landlordism and middle-class entrepreneurship in Bengal.[18] Vidyasagar's, in other words, was not quite a lone venture in the Bengal society of the 1850s. A British Inspector of Schools would note in April 1859 that 'the learned Pundits of Sanskrit College have, as a body, been seized with a love of publishing books'. They had become interested 'in European Science and Literature' and 'were writing in a language that ordinary people may read'. Through their efforts, and particularly 'under the able superintendence of Ishur Chunder Vidyasagar', the Bengali language was becoming 'capable of being the elegant vehicle of scientific and other information'.[19]

In May 1855, Halliday appointed Vidyasagar Assistant Inspector of Schools for the four districts of Hooghly, Burdwan, Midnapur and Nadia, conjointly with his principalship of Sanskrit College, with a combined salary of Rs 500 a month. By the end of that year he had already established some 20 model schools, applying to Bengal Thomason's circle system, and also started a normal school to train village headmasters at Sanskrit College under the superintendence of his close friend, the rationalist Akshoykumar Dutta. In a parallel move Vidyasagar, who had already displayed his commitment to women's education by enthusiastically backing Bethune's school for daughters of respectable families in Calcutta in 1849, utilized his new official position to start 40 girls' schools in villages between November 1857 and June 1858.

Precision is needed about what exactly was new in these two initiatives of Vidya-sagar, for it is possible both to exaggerate or unduly downplay their significance. The surveys made in 1835–8 by William Adam, Rammohan's Unitarian friend, had found a fairly widespread system of indigenous vernacular education in the villages, with some 100,000 *pathshalas* for the 'indigent classes' in Bengal and Bihar, mostly under non-Brahman (often Kayastha) *gurumohasayas*. Adam discovered 'the desire to give education to their male children' to be 'deeply seated in the minds of parents even of the humblest classes', and thought that the pathshalas, of course quite radically modified and im-proved, could be 'the institutions—through which primarily, although not exclusively, we may hope to improve the morals and the intellect of the Native population'.[20] Vidya-sagar's plan of normal and model schools can be seen, therefore, as in a way a belated effort to implement Adam's suggestions.

The impressive number and apparent absence of direct Brahman control has led to an occasional romanticization of these pre-colonial schools, which in some ways fitted in better with rural conditions than the new system which colonial rule, actively helped by reformers like Vidyasagar, eventually established.[21] Poromesh Acharya has recently provided an important corrective here, emphasizing both the extremely limited nature of the education supplied by these schools even at their best, as well as the split-up and hierarchized nature of the entire indigenous educational system which allowed little scope for social mobility. Pathshala education, of course entirely in Bengali, was basically confined to writing, arithmetic, and a bit of revenue and commercial accounting. Read-ing was less important, since there were no printed textbooks and a necessarily very limited number of manuscripts—which put a premium on memorizing.[22] The pathshalas, in other words, were geared to the everyday needs of would-be petty zamindari officials, traders and better-off peasants: a source of strength, but also a limit. Adam's Reports were actually quite critical of the very limited content of indigenous elementary education.[23] The village school structure had little or nothing to do with the tols, *chatuspathis* and *madrasas*—centres of Sanskrit and Arabic or Persian learning which were the preserve of Brahman males and other learned groups. The educational apparatus consisted of 'separate classes of institutions without any link or relation of any kind, each catering to a distinct class or community'.[24] The relative absence of high castes from village schools was thus a mark of inferiorization and hierarchy (a crucial instance of *adhikari-bheda*, in fact, the principle which Ramakrishna had extolled and Vidyasagar questioned in their only conversation), not autonomy. The *Chanakya-slokas*, for instance, which pupils were often made to memorize in the pathshalas, combined maxims of worldly wisdom with frequent reaffirmations of Brahmanical supremacy: the Brahman was the guru of all other castes, it declared, just as the husband was guru to his wife.[25]

The changes Vidyasagar and other mid-nineteenth-century colonial officials sought to introduce in the pathshala involved expansion of its curriculum to include history, geography, ethics and natural philosophy (i.e. elementary science), much greater use of textbooks, promotion through examinations, and in general an integration within the theoretically 'complete and continuous' system that was being worked out for colonial education.[26] Hierarchies did not end, of course, particularly those based on economic or class differentials, and may even have been sharpened at times, both through the dichotomy in medium of instruction (English at higher levels) and by some of the changes brought about in the pathshalas.[27] At the same time, there was a new theoretical equality of opportunity independent of caste status, a chance for talented boys of families with some but not much resources to climb up a uniform educational ladder through personal grit, determination and self-discipline.

There was much more gradual and limited, but still strikingly new, opening for some girls, too, against formidable opposition, The widespread belief was that educated wives became widows, and while daughters in high-caste families could be occasionally taught a little within their parents' homes, the idea of sending them out to school was deeply shocking, and a very early marriage anyway obligatory. Conditions were no different in the villages: Adam's First Report made the categorical statement that 'there are no indigenous girls' schools'.[28] It is true that Radhakanta Deb, the great champion of sati against Rammohan and Bentinck and of ascetic widowhood against Vidyasagar, had been at the same time a promoter, of a kind, of the education of girls and is even said to have published a tract about it. This had specified, however, that only girls of poor parents could be sent out to school, while respectable families should have their daughters taught within the home—in both cases only till they were married off. A number of girls' schools were set up in Calcutta in the early 1820s, mostly at missionary initiative, but they were, significantly, located in the poorer parts of the city. The initiative then seems to have died out for a generation, and we may speculate whether the conservative consolidation against the ban on sati and Derozian iconoclasm may not have had something to do with this hiatus. What was striking about Bethune's endeavour in 1849 was that daughters of respectable families were now being encouraged to go out to a school, being transported there in a carriage that displayed a Sanskrit quotation said to have been hunted up by Vidyasagar.[29] In course of his drive for girls' schools in villages, too, Vidyasagar took special pride in those being attended by daughters of respectable, high-caste families, thus once again challenging directly conservative bhadralok prejudices.[30]

The characteristic features—and limits—of Vidyasagar's pedagogy are revealed most clearly through a glance at his primers and textbooks.[31] Three themes stand out. There is the motif of the poor boy making good through diligence, devoted effort, and single-minded pursuit of learning. *Jivancharit* and *Charitabali* use material from William and Robert Chambers' *Exemplary and Instructive Biography* (Edinburgh, 1846) to present brief life-histories of leading Western scientists, along with those of Grotius, Valentine Duval (a shepherd boy who rose to become a historian), and Jenkins (son of an African prince who managed to get a British education). The concentration on scientists (Copernicus, Galileo, Newton, Herschell Linnaeus) indicates Vidyasagar's rationalist preferences, and so perhaps is the insertion here of Grotius—founder of an international law which theoretically puts the same limits on the powers of all states, big or small, and prominent advocate of toleration in an age of religious bigotry. The life-histories are adaptations from English, yet a revealing displacement seems to be at work in many of the comments: diligence, which in the Western exemplars is by no means constricted to formal book-learning alone, tends inevitably, in the conditions of colonial, middle-class Bengal, to get focused solely on a single-minded pursuit of education. The biography of Duval ends with Vidyasagar remarking that *yatna* and *parisrama* (devoted effort and exertion) would have led the shepherd-boy nowhere had he not harnessed that devotion to learning.[32] The *Varnaparichay* and, even more, *Bodhoday* made the point sharper: 'Those who are diligent about becoming educated will live happy lives because they will be able to earn money.'[33]

The theme of improvement through education is inextricably bound up with a tremendous insistence on discipline, connoting both rigorous self-control and strict obedience to the commands of parents and teachers. The *Varnaparichay*, as Sibaji Bandopadhyay has emphasized in an important study, is structured throughout by a binary contrast between disciplined diligence and errant disobedience, culminating at the end of Part I in the opposition of Gopal who will succeed in life, and Rakhal who will never learn to read.[34] This is a discipline, it should be added, that is presented in terms utterly stark and bleak, abstracted from human affect and paternalistic glosses. Children are actually told in one lesson that they should always try to please their parents, for if the latter had not been kind enough to feed and clothe them, their sufferings would have known no limit.[35] The Utilitarian, materialistic tone of Vidyasagar's textbooks in fact provoked some contemporary criticism from both orthodox Hindus and some Christian missionaries.[36] These are understandable enough, but the peculiar bleakness of the world of *Varnaparichay* remains a bit puzzling: it is almost as if Vidyasagar sometimes is fighting a part of himself, suppressing an inner Rakhal, projecting the path of discipline and obedience as something made necessary by a heartless world.[37] *Varnaparichay* ends with a really strange and cruel tale, quite out of place one would think in a children's primer. Bhuban, an orphan boy spoilt by his loving aunt, becomes a thief, is condemned to be hanged, and as a parting 'gift' bites off his aunt's ear while saying goodbye.

Improvement, or social ascent, through stern discipline: but only up to a point, within limits set by existing property relations. *Bodhoday* affirms a highly status quoist version of a kind of labour theory of property: 'The things we see around us must belong to one or other person. An object belongs to whoever has worked to produce it, or has inherited it from his forefathers. No one else has any right to it. Whoever owns an object should continue to own it.' No respectable (*bhadra*) person should be a beggar, while having property is conducive to continuous effort. Vidyasagar's school texts are full of warnings about the immorality of theft: 'One shouldn't lay one's hand on something belonging to another person, even if one's life is at stake.'[38] There was, then, a clear class limit—and sometimes a caste frontier, too, though here it was more a question of expediency than believed-in principle. Vidyasagar had insisted in 1851 on opening Sanskrit College to Kayasthas, and in 1854 to other 'respectable castes'. But in 1855 he rejected as inexpedient a suggestion that a Subarnabanik student should also be admitted.[39] Though often very prosperous, he argued, 'in the scale of castes the class stands very low', and he did not want to further 'shock the prejudice of the orthodox Pundits of the Institution.'[40] Despite a concern for primary education in the countryside very rare among members of his class, Vidyasagar, it needs to be added, was probably not the unqualified advocate for mass enlightenment that later admirers have at times made him out to be. Hatcher has cited a letter of his written in September 1859, which argues that educating 'one boy in a proper style' was preferable to providing a smattering of learning to large numbers, for poor children would be taken out of school and put to work by their parents in any case.[41] Vidyasagar did set up a night school for 'sons of the cultivating class' in Birsingha in 1853, but this seems to have been a special gesture made for his home village, and not part of his overall schemes.[42]

Still it is possible to be over-harsh about Vidyasagar. Ranajit Guha has described his schoolbook morality as nothing but 'hard-baked, bourgeois individualism',[43] and certainly there are not only similarities but obvious connections (through Chambers, for instance) with nineteenth-century middle-class British ideologies of improvement as moulded by amalgams of Evangelicalism and Utilitarianism.[44] Texts like *Varnaparichay* comprise the part of Vidyasagar's work that might appear readily assimilable to today's very influential emphasis on 'disciplinary' projects, either derived from colonial discourses or running parallel with them.[45] Hatcher's book has effectively drawn attention, in significant contrast, to the possibility of the more indigenous roots of Vidyasagar's pedagogical values, in particular the traditions of *nitishastra*, embodied in texts like *Chanakya-slokas* and *Hitopadesha*, which also contained elements of an ethic of this-wordly improvement through strenuous learning.[46] But Hatcher, like the analysts of colonial discourse, remains within the parameters of a search for 'influence' or origins. What tends to remain unasked is the question of the precise social contexts which made the emphasis on discipline appear unavoidable. (Not necessarily pleasant or attractive: the bleak world of *Varnaparichay*, its almost Machiavellian realism and ruthlessness, perhaps signifies a recognition of necessity rather than blithe imitation or enthusiastic acceptance.) With the closing of opportunities for military careers and the decline of indigenous business enterprise, education in Bengal was, by the mid-nineteenth century, becoming virtually the sole channel for respectable upward mobility: education, further, of a far more formal, examination-centred kind, for which the old kind of pathshala, however much in tune with earlier conditions, was quite unsuited. Recruitment into services and professions was becoming increasingly dependent on examinations and educational degrees. The informal patronage that Vidyasagar could still distribute through his personal relations with top British officials would soon become a thing of the past. And, once again, instead of a homogenized 'middle class', a focus on its poorer elements seems helpful for situating Vidyasagar's initiatives. The strenuous moods of his school texts were not primarily meant for the gilded youth of Calcutta. They become meaningful only when placed in a context of genteel poverty, and here Vidyasagar's projects implied a striving for a real though limited expansion, an attempt, in the words of Asok Sen, to extend 'opportunities of education for the poorer gentry in small towns and villages of Bengal'.[47]

The attempt went some distance beyond them, perhaps, in terms of long-term appropriations by groups about whom Vidyasagar himself had shown little or no concern. Recent research has unearthed a mass of early-twentieth-century vernacular tracts composed by an emerging literati of Muslims and lower-caste authors located in obscure villages or small towns of rural Bengal.[48] They are imbued with an improvement ethic reminiscent often of Vidyasagar's combination of education with puritanical virtues and discipline, though there is also a greater focus on life outside the classroom, in particular on agricultural development. Given the continued, massive circulation of texts like *Varnaparichay*, one might even suspect a certain amount of direct, if unintended, influence.

Such developments lay much in the future in the 1850s. For Vidyasagar, the tragedy was that the favourable conjuncture that he had sought to utilize for major educational and other initiatives proved extremely short-lived. Educational administration was getting more bureaucratized under a brash young ICS Director of Public Instruction, Gordon Young, who did not get on with Vidyasagar. Much more important was a new mood of financial stringency, fairly obviously connected with counterinsurgency expenses in the wake of 1857. Vidyasagar had gone ahead in the early summer of 1857 in starting girls' schools in his four districts, on the strength of a verbal assurance from

Halliday that if 'the inhabitants would provide suitable school houses, the expenses for maintaining the schools would be met by the Government.' In the next year 'the Supreme Government . . . refused their sanction to their establishment except under the Grants-in-aid Rules. My labours have thus become fruitless and the interesting little schools will have to be closed immediately.'[49] Towards the end of 1858 Vidyasagar resigned in disgust from all his official posts.

Barriers of another kind, relating to the development of vernacular education for boys, become evident from an earlier report of Vidyasagar in January 1857. He had pointed out then that 'the success of Vernacular Education will depend materially upon the encouragement given in the way of providing the Alumni of these institutions with offices under Government'. Vidyasagar suggested that vernacular students should therefore be nominated 'to lower posts in the Judicial or Revenue Departments'—a proposal, needless to state, that was entirely ignored.

Colonial constraints—in the form of very material considerations and structures, not abstract ideas—are therefore entirely clear in the case of Vidyasagar's educational ventures. They had coalesced with the elite Brahmanical traditions of high castes, sometimes strengthening, but hardly creating them: for there is no evidence whatsoever of any major attempt at mass education (or organized efforts to improve the conditions of women, for that matter) by bhadralok men in pre-colonial times. The philanthropy of the more enterprising zamindars, on which too Vidyasagar had thought he could depend in the 1850s, was often a bit double-edged at its best,[50] and died away as en-hancement of rent became more difficult with the tenancy acts of 1859 and 1885. And deepening employment problems clearly constricted middle-class attitudes over time. Bhadralok protests poured in when Lieutenant-Governor Campbell suggested some diversion of funds from higher towards primary education in 1870.[51] Even anti-colonial nationalism did not change attitudes fundamentally. The 'national education' of the Swadeshi era concentrated on trying to float an alternative university, and certain inte-resting experiments in districts like Barisal and Faridpur to start autonomous nationalist-oriented village schools among Namashudras and Muslims, which had worried the government considerably, soon died away.[52]

A report of an inspector of schools just a few months after Vidyasagar's resignation can serve as an appropriate, if depressing, epitaph for this section. At Jowgong village near Boinchee, Burdwan district, where a girls' school founded by Vidyasagar was still getting an official grant of Rs 32 per month, 'not a girl, boy or pundit was in attendance' when it was visited on 25 January 1859. The inspector went from there to the neighbouring village of Koolingram, which, as we have seen, Vidyasagar had singled out for special mention in December 1857 as an instance of successful overcoming of the initial hostility of 'respectable men'.[53] A few girls could be seen there in January 1859, but 'the poor Pundit of the Girls' School had . . . no friends'. The headmaster of the boys' school was leading the opposition, and the girls' school had had to shift to another village a mile away.[54]

II

Many stories have been current about the origins of Vidyasagar's passionate concern for the plight of women, in a society where child marriage was normative, widow remarriage prohibited, austere widowhood stringently enforced among high and most intermediate castes, and polygamy considered prestigious among Kulin Brahmans, Kayasthas and Vaidyas. His mother first advised him to take up the cause of widows—according to one account. Others refer to first-hand experiences during visits to Birsingha in his college days: seeing a child-widow of his own age having to fast on *ekadosi*, and hearing about another forced into infanticide by parental command. He was particularly shocked when a favourite teacher of his at Sanskrit College, the elderly Vedanta scholar Sambhu-chandra Vacaspati, married a child to run his household for him a few months before his death. (Vidyasagar is said to have wept on meeting the child-bride, doomed to early and lifelong widowhood, and walked out of his teacher's house, refusing to touch water there henceforth.[55]) Two widows are prominent, as we have seen, in his own autobiographical fragment, but as exemplars of warmth and compassion rather than suffering.

What is common to all these anecdotes is an emphasis on personal experience that can be read as a confirmation of the inference I had drawn from Maheshchandra Deb's essay.[56] There are no references at all to any stimulus provided by Western models of marital relations. And, contrary to an interpretive model which today is very influential, all biographies about Vidyasagar agree that the counterposing of shastra against *deshachar*, texts versus customs, eventually the core of his widow remarriage and anti-polygamy tracts, came as deliberate strategy, formulated after he had become convinced that certain practices were harmful and evil.[57] Vidyasagar's reform tracts hardly bear out the assumption so often made nowadays that 'the discursive struggle in which the social reformers were engaged was over tradition and culture; women were simply the site of this contestation'.[58]

Vidyasagar's first essay on social reform, *Balyabibaher Dosh* (Evils of Child-Marriage, 1850), was marked in fact by a total absence of textual exegesis. Partly for that reason, it was also his most radical statement on gender relations, and it was able within the space of a few, brilliantly written pages to unfold an integrated, comprehensive critique of child marriage, arranged marriages, marital oppression, taboos against educating women, and the horrors and evils of austere widowhood.[59]

The essay began with a trenchant denunciation of *both* text and custom, shastra and *laukik vyavahara*. The two in combination have produced, and sustain, all that Vidyasagar found objectionable in existing marital practices. Throughout the essay, he judged the existing institutions and practices against an ideal norm of companionate conjugality based on adult mutual love (*pronoy*)—and that, Vidyasagar says, can flow only from a 'unity of minds'.[60] This is impossible if girls are married off at eight, nine, or ten—which happens because *smriti-shastras* have promised some imagined other-worldly boons from such action, and people are also afraid of flouting long-continuing custom. All marriages, further, are arranged by parents as advised by often corrupt *ghataks* (professional go-betweens), and the couple do not even see each other before the ceremony—and so 'in our country sincere marital love is rare: the husband is merely the breadwinner, the wife a domestic servant (*grihaparicharika*)'. Child marriage, again, is directly connected with women being kept without education, for, even if they had been taught a little at their parental homes, after marriage will begin life in an 'alien house (*paragriha*)', totally subjected to the authority of fathers and mothers-in-law, and filled with an endless round of 'cleaning the house, preparing beds, cooking, serving food, and other duties which would have to be learned with perfection'. The early marriage of girls

also increases the number of widows, 'and who has not witnessed first-hand the unbearable sufferings of widows? . . . All chance of pleasure must end as soon as their
husbands die . . . they will not be allowed a drop of water, even if critically ill, on days
of ritual fasting.' Never again would Vidyasagar condemn so uncompromisingly the
rules of austere widowhood, identify patrilocal marriage for women as life in an 'alien'
home, or indeed critique child marriage directly. These did not become part of his action
programmes, nor did he return to the interconnections he had worked out here between
the need to raise the age of marriage, promotion of women's education and improving
the lot of widows.

The major plank of Vidyasagar's argument in this pamphlet is thus individual and
conjugal happiness—but there is also a second register, of morality and social welfare—
that on the whole has figured more in social reform literature but remains somewhat
low-key here. The rigours of lifelong widowhood, imposed often on young girls, cause
much immorality and lead to abortions and infanticide. Children born of too early
marriage tend to be weak and unhealthy, nor can they get proper training from mothers
who have been kept uneducated. Young men married off in their teens neglect their
studies and are overburdened by the financial responsibilities of maintaining wife and
children: earning money has to become the sole aim of life, leading, once again, to immoral ways. Vidyasagar, interestingly, comes close for a moment here to what became
a standard late-nineteenth-century Kaliyuga theme, and figured often in Ramakrishna's
conversation as the link between *kamini, kanchan* and *chakri*—but then his argument
moved in a very different direction, prioritizing this-worldly happiness and welfare, not
devotion or asceticism. Ramakrishna would certainly not have shared his enthusiasm for
conjugal love.

Did the later, and very much better known, tracts advocating widow remarriage and
criticizing Kulin polygamy on largely textual grounds then mark a retreat for Vidyasagar,
with gender injustice becoming no more than a site for arguments about valid and
invalid tradition? Such a critique would be less than fair, for it fails to analyse the options
that were open (or not open) to Vidyasagar when formulating a specific programme of
reform and trying to organize a movement on its basis. The tract against child marriage
could be daringly radical and reject shastric exegesis, precisely because it was more of a
consciousness-raising exercise than a specific proposal for an immediate, concrete
reform. It raised no demand for a new law: did not need to, in strict logic, for of course
there was no law prohibiting adult marriage—as widow remarriage was prohibited and
its issue illegitimate till 1856. The basic point that has to be made is that under British
Indian law personal and family matters were supposed to be regulated in accordance
with the shastras for Hindus, and the shariat for Muslims.[61] Reform through external
state legislation, and reform-from-within through scriptural exegesis and community
debate, which today often get counterposed against each other (as in current controversies
about Muslim Personal Law, for instance), were actually interdependent in Vidyasagar's
time. He had to find shastric justifications for widow remarriage, if it was to become legal under 'Anglo-Hindu' law: reason and humanity alone would not be sufficient. The
intertwining of Brahmanical tradition and colonial law becomes clear when seen from
the opposite side, too. The petition organized by Raja Radhakanta Deb against the
Widow Marriage bill in March 1856 combined alternative interpretations of the

shastras and appeals to age-old custom with the argument that 'the proposed law is also at variance with the several Statutes of the British Parliament and the Regulations of the East India Company'.[62]

The author of *Balyabibaher Dosh* was not yet particularly important in official or elite Indian circles. The widow-remarriage tracts, in contrast, were published in 1855–6, at the peak of Vidyasagar's influence, and the plunge into shastric exegesis was obviously in significant part an attempt to convince leading pandits who, through their importance in the *sabhas* of big zamindars and at high-caste ritual occasions, could in turn help him get the support of the big men of Hindu society. Vidyasagar in other words was trying to utilize and manipulate, for reformist purposes, the traditions of the medieval raja–pandit nexus that had spilled over in modified forms into the Calcutta-based *dals* of the nineteenth century.[63] Soon after publishing his first tract justifying widow remarriage, Vidyasagar even tried to win over the Sobhabazar Raj, approaching Radhakanta Deb through a nephew who had become an ally of his. That attempt failed,[64] but he was able to get a substantial section of leading zamindars, along with a number of pandits like Taranath Tarkavacaspati and some Sanskrit College teachers, to line up with Brahmos and Young Bengal intellectuals in the petitions that were organized from October 1855 onwards asking for the legalization of widow remarriage.[65] Vidyasagar's subsequent campaign against Kulin polygamy in 1856–7 also got the support of many prominent zamindars: probably more easily, for in its extreme forms (Kulins with a hundred wives or more, many of whom never saw their husbands after marriage) this was an undeniable scandal, confined moreover to a limited circle of high-caste families claiming a peculiarly high status.[66] A law on the subject may well have been enacted but for the 1857 rebellion. In the late 1860s, when Vidyasagar revived the demand and published his two tracts against polygamy, support was forthcoming for a time even from the Sanatan Dharmarakshini Sabha that had lately been organized to defend Hindu orthodoxy.[67]

As Sekhar Bandopadhyay has emphasized, Vidyasagar's reform campaigns thus included an element of continuity with earlier ways of seeking change through *vyavasthas* (authoritative rulings on social matters) from prominent pandits.[68] There had been several attempts earlier to get individual widow marriages sanctioned in this way, notably one by Raja Rajballabh of Dacca in the mid eighteenth century, which had been blocked by the pandits of Maharaja Krishnachandra of Nadia. Shortly before Vidyasagar published his first tract on widow remarriage, Shyamacharan Das, a man of intermediate-caste (Nabasakh) status living in North Calcutta, had managed to get a favourable vyavastha for the remarriage of his widowed child from a number of leading pandits. (The ruling used a passage from Manu but was careful to limit permission for remarriage to Shudra widows who had remained virgins.[69])

Vidyasagar's tracts, then, were in a sense sophisticated vyavasthas, geared to an audience of fellow pandits and their patrons. But this was only one register among several on which he was playing. Right at the beginning of the first *Bidhaba-bibaha* pamphlet, there is a memorable appeal to a conception of public, vernacular space that is fundamentally new. This was the space that he was simultaneously trying to create, through vernacular prose and reformed elementary education, in endeavours that, like widow remarriage, attained their climax precisely around 1855–6. Tired of the endless controversy on the matter that had been so long confined to pandits animated by mutual jealousy, Vidyasagar declares he has decided to present his views 'in the language spoken by the people, to bring it to the notice of the general public [*sarbasadharan*]. Now let everyone read and discuss, in an impartial manner, whether widow marriage should be introduced or not.'[70] The shastric passages are therefore always translated, and the discussion, though inevitably complicated, is conveyed through a prose far simpler than what had been current in scholarly discussion in Bengali before Vidyasagar. And textual exegesis, ever so often, is interrupted by passages marked by deep compassion for suffering womankind, anger and a profound sense of male guilt. The best known of these is of course the eloquent condemnation of deshachar at the close of the second *Bidhaba-bibaha* tract, highlighting (in that order) the sufferings of widows and the flood of immorality and abortion which is caused by male cruelty sanctioned by that custom. As in the *Balya-bibaha* pamphlet, an implicitly positive recognition of the naturalness of physical, sexual needs underpins Vidyasagar's polemic: 'You think that with the death of the husband, the woman's body becomes like a stone.' The tract ends with the famous lines:

> Let not the unfortunate weaker sex [*abala*] be born in a country where the men have no pity, no dharma, no sense of right and wrong, no ability to discriminate between beneficial and harmful, where preservation of what has been customary is considered the only duty, the only dharma . . . By what sin do women come to be born in Bharatvarsha at all?[71]

There are other, less-known passages, too, that outstrip the limits of shastric interpretation. Space permits only one more reference. The first *Bahubibaha* pamphlet begins with the general proposition that women everywhere are subordinated to men, because 'they are physically weaker, and because social rules are so bad': 'But in no country are the conditions of women so bad as in our unfortunate land, due to the excessive barbarism, selfishness, and thoughtlessness of men.' And the long lists of Kulin men with many wives that Vidyasagar goes on to offer, giving precise names and locations, are interspersed with an angry sarcasm: 'The younger [of two Kulin sisters] has a husband aged 25–26. He has not so far managed to marry more than 32 times.'[72]

The more purely textual sections of the widow-marriage and anti-polygamy tracts are unlikely to attract many readers today: a pity, for they have a brilliance of their own. Vidyasagar displayed here a mastery over text and interpretive logic that was able to subvert, or appropriate for his own purposes, a number of standard orthodox arguments. The example of 'Kali-varjya' is particularly relevant for us, for once again we see Vidyasagar come close to the trope of Kaliyuga, and then move off in a completely different direction. Kali-varjya had been the method by which ancient texts had been modified or pruned, almost always in socially restrictive ways, and often with reference to controls over women, by medieval Smriti experts like Raghunandan.[73] Vidyasagar appropriated the same scholastic tool to prise open a textual space for widow marriage. The lynchpin of Vidyasagar's argument, as is well known, is a passage in *Parasara-samhita*, permitting the remarriage of women in five specific cases, one of which is the death of the husband.[74] But there were many contrary texts which had to be got out of the way. Vidyasagar eliminated the *puranas* among these through the argument that Parasara as a dharmashastra had to be given precedence over them, and then made maximum use of the claim, made in the *Parasara-samhita* itself; that this was the text specifically applicable to Kaliyuga:

the other texts, where they contradict it, are Kali-varjya. Vidyasagar's use of Parasara, and not, say, Manu, which had been cited by pandits to allow the remarriage of Shyamacharan Das' daughter, indicates his desire to open the space for widow remarriage to the maximum degree possible within the shastric mode of argument. (Manu, it will be recalled, had been read by the pandits to permit only the remarriage of Shudra widows who were also *akshata-yoni*, i.e. *virgo intacta*.) Vidyasagar's second tract specifically controverted the argument that remarriage is only permitted for low-caste widows, and he also quietly dropped all reference to virginity as a prerequisite.

The shastric rejection of polygamy seems to have been a more difficult task. With all his obvious enthusiasm for monogamous conjugality, Vidyasagar could not prove a complete case for strict monogamy from the Hindu scriptures. All that he could establish, mainly on the basis of Manu, was that the texts had laid down a number of specific conditions under which a man could take more than one wife—there was no unlimited and arbitrary right to multiple wives, as had become the practice among Kulins in Bengal.[75] The argument in the first tract against polygamy then shifts rather quickly to non-shastric grounds: a highly derogatory sketch of the history of Kulinism in Bengal, followed by statistics giving the names, ages, number of marriages, and locations of prominent polygamous men in Hooghly district.[76]

Vidyasagar's shastric arguments justifying widow remarriage and restricting polygamy provoked a flood of attempted refutations from pandits, mostly it seems from the Nadia-Jessore and 24 Parganas belt of solid Brahmanical orthodox scholarship, but joined in later by some erstwhile allies, notably Taranath Tarkavacaspati. Vidyasagar plunged with zest into the scholastic debate, making his sequels far longer than the initial tracts, and carrying on the battle right into his last days. Leafing through his voluminous replies to critics (the second tract against polygamy runs to nearly 200 closely printed pages in the edition I am using), one does at times get the impression of the reformer trapped in a scholastic morass, lost in an endless polemic of interest to fellow pandits alone, moving away in fact from that vision of widening, lay, public space that had animated him in 1850 and 1855. There is a sense of helpless anger, too, finding vent perhaps in bouts of violent, even vulgar, abuse that Vidyasagar sometimes published under pen-names, replying in kind to no doubt equal or greater scurrility on the other side.[77]

A more crucial problem lay in the built-in limits of a strategy of reform 'from within', by shastric exegesis. A number of areas dear to Vidyasagar's heart, as revealed by the 1850 pamphlet (notably, child- and arranged marriages) had to be left out as clearly validated by the scriptures, and the scholastic method also had a tendency to create problems for other, subsequent, reform agendas. Rammohan may have unwittingly added to Vidyasagar's difficulties by hunting up and publicizing the texts praising austere widowhood in order to controvert those that insisted on sati. Vidyasagar sought to eliminate one kind of polygamy which Manu had permitted (marrying a woman of lower caste) by emphasizing that in Kaliyuga intercaste marriage was strictly prohibited.[78] His polemic against Kulinism also used the argument that it often led to delayed marriages for girls in the absence of suitably high-status bridegrooms—and this, Vidyasagar emphasized, clearly contradicted the shastric command that marriage had to be consummated before the first menses.[79] Perhaps it was this passage in his own earlier writing that contributed to Vidyasagar's surprising ambiguity on the Age of Consent issue, when his opinion was officially asked for shortly before his death.[80] And finally, as Bankimchandra acutely pointed out in 1873 in a critique of Vidyasagar's demand for a law against polygamy, scriptural arguments were in a sense redundant, as Hindus guided themselves far more by customs, and texts at times prescribed rules which it would be quite impossible to implement strictly.[81]

We have been looking at Vidyasagar's reform initiatives so far in terms of texts and polemics. But this can be no more than a partial view, for with all its obvious limitations the issue of widow marriage did become for a time something like a movement, not confined to pandits or even always only to highly literate people. Vidyasagar, as is well known, did not stop with getting widow marriage legalized. From November 1856 onwards he went to enormous trouble, expenditure and sometimes real physical danger to organize widow marriages, and by 1867 had personally arranged about 60 of them.[82] Most of the big names, the rajas and zamindars who had joined him in petitioning the government for the law, quickly backed out, often defaulting on earlier commitments of financial help. He did continue to get enthusiastic and active support from a number of young men, most of them Brahmos, through the late 1850s and 1860s and beyond, and much of the information we do have about specific widow-marriage cases in fact comes from Brahmo biographies and histories.[83] During and just after the campaign for legalization of widow remarriage, interest and excitement was high enough to generate a large number of poems and songs, some ridiculing the move, others hailing it, and even 'cultivators, street-porters, cab-men and other lower-class people' indulged in them.[84] The best known of the verses is of course the one wishing long life to Vidyasagar, which appeared on the borders of some saris woven at Santipur. (As weavers have been a low-status group in caste society, this in itself is an indication of a reach beyond the bhadra-lok.) But more significant perhaps than such momentary excitement, yet peculiarly difficult to recuperate, are the long-term personal experiences into which a movement like widow marriage necessarily translated itself. For widow marriage meant, above all, young men, and girls growing up into young women, entering into a domesticity that flouted traditions, in the face of an enormous amount of everyday petty slander, persecution, ostracism.

Here our sources tend to fail us, for nearly all accounts stop with the first few highly publicized marriages in Calcutta, followed by some discussion of Vidyasagar as lonely, tragic hero. The flood of anecdotes, so voluminous on philanthropy, also narrows down quite suddenly. Indramitra's *Karunasagar Vidyasagar*, which brings together the largest number of anecdotes, is a collection of 737 pages: only 62 of them deal with widow marriage.

We can get a few stray and momentary glimpses, however, of developments that should have called into question a number of very well-established assumptions but have been almost entirely ignored. Vidyasagar has usually been seen as a reformer of urban, educated bhadralok society, whose work had Calcutta as its focus. Yet the *Tattva-bodhini Patrika* of Bhadra (August–September) 1858 contrasted the five widow marriages that had been achieved in Calcutta over the 20 months since the wedding of Srishchandra Vidyaratna in November 1856 with the seven in just two months in Hooghly villages (or very small towns) around Birsingha, beginning in June 1858. It mentioned Ramjibanpur, Khirpai, Chandrakona, Basuli; there were two more at Chandrakona next month, and the first widow marriage in Vidyasagar's home village in July 1852. By August 1862 *Somprakash* could report some 20 to 22 marriages in three years in this fairly small corner of Hooghly district, where Vidyasagar clearly had established some kind of a rural base.[85] Widow marriage, further, was not an entirely high-caste matter: thus Sambhuchandra Vidyaratna describes the '20–25' marriages that took place during 1864–5 as involving 'Brahmans, Kayasthas, Tantubay (weavers), Vaidyas, Telis, etc.'[86]

Vidyasagar's letter in *Hindoo Patriot* of July 1867 gives some hints about how the movement had been organized in the villages—as well as the kind of problems it was facing. Explaining why widow marriage had proved so expensive, Vidyasagar stated that apart from the heavy sums he had spent on the first wedding to establish its respectability, '*dals* or parties' were being 'maintained in several villages in the Mufassil', and anyone 'acquainted with the constitution of Hindoo society' would know that this was an expensive proposition 'even ordinarily'. But this was not an ordinary situation: many cases had been brought against 'the promoters of the movement in the Mufassil', and sometimes physical force was also being deployed. All this was demanding heavy litigation expenses.

Most remarkable of all, illuminating in concrete detail one instance of what Vidyasagar described in general terms in his letter, are the notes he had kept (in English) among his papers about a series of incidents in Kumarganj village, adjoining Birsingha. Long extracts from these are tucked away in a corner of Subolchandra's biography, but seem to have somehow gone unnoticed by later scholars.[87] The party at Kumargunj supporting widow marriage had been excluded from the ceremonies in the village Shiva temple at the time of 'Churrukpooja', at the end of the Bengali year. When they tried to enter the temple to offer puja separately, they 'were beaten back with great violence', and local police officials at first refused to record their complaints. Worse was to come, for then the 'Zamindar of the village Baboo Shib Narain Roy' of Jurul began 'oppressing with impunity those of the Royots of his Talook Comergunj who belong to the widow marriage party'. Shib Narayan sent durwans to forcibly round up the pro-reformers, who were dragged to his presence and 'dismissed with 10 strokes of shoes and a fine of Rs 10 each. . . . Several of them have left the village with their respective families.' The terror had a wider impact: 'The news having reached the inhabitants of pergonnas Burda and Chandrakona, those who are willing to marry their sons and daughters have fallen back, through fear of consequences.' Further, the zamindar was clearly being backed by not only subordinate police officials but the Deputy Magistrate of Jehanabad: the local state apparatus, in other words. Numerous complaints to the latter, including several lodged by Vidyasagar himself, had had no result. The Deputy Magistrate passed orders against continuation of the acts of oppression, but Vidyasagar had learnt from a friendly police *amla* that 'the Khan Bahadur' had told his subordinates to ignore these, render no help to the widow marriage party, but 'endeavour to give them trouble if possible. . . . It is notorious that Baboo Shib Narain Roy often calls on the Deputy Magistrate at an advanced hour of the night.' The net result was that 'the party at Coomergunge' which had 'consisted of about 60 families' was reduced to four or five. Vidyasagar concluded his notes in a mood of complete despair. As 'those who joined the cause at my solicitation and are suffering from their act' are not being relieved and their oppressors are going unpunished, 'I must leave the world, for what is the good of my remaining in it when there is no chance of success of the cause. I have resolved to devote my existence to it and if it fails, life would have no charm to me and existence would be useless.'

There is a little bit of data also in Vidyasagar's notes about the social composition of the two parties in the Kumargunj region. The Deputy Magistrate would of course be high caste, and the zamindar probably also so. Some names are given of Vidyasagar's 'Royot' supporters: Damoo, Sriharee, Nilcomal, Gopal and a 'Sreenibas Doss'. The one surname, as well as its absence in the other cases, suggests a subordinate, probably lower-caste status. But the peasants are clearly divided, for Vidyasagar's supporters at one point get beaten up by the 'Goallas [Sadgops] of the opposite Party'. An anthropological study of Birsingha in the 1950s located the Sadgops as an upwardly mobile jati, dominant in the neighbouring villages and becoming so in Vidyasagar's home village, where the other major groups were Brahmans and Bagdis.[88] One is tempted to speculate about a link between the 'Goalla' hostility to widow marriage and possible Sanskritizing aspirations at work already in the 1860s, but of course this is no more than guesswork.

The Kumargunj affair certainly raises some questions regarding the common stereotype about nineteenth-century social reform being an affair of the English-educated high bhadralok alone, generally backed by the foreign rulers and confined to issues which did not affect the rural masses. Despite Vidyasagar's contacts with leading British officials, an informal alliance between the state machinery at the local level and landlord power evidently frustrated all his initiatives in an area where he would have been most influential.[89] The implicit caste dimensions are equally interesting. In an important article some years ago, Lucy Carroll pointed out that for lower castes already practising widow marriage Act XV of 1856 could have been unwittingly retrogressive, and indeed in some ways represent a paradoxical extension of Brahmanical norms. It deprived widows who married of all succession rights to the property of the deceased husband, even though lower-caste customs had been more liberal in that respect at times.[90] But, at least in Bengal where Brahmanical norms had penetrated fairly deep into lower-caste society, it is dangerous to associate the 'popular' with any unqualified realm of freedom from upper-caste taboos and restrictions. The Kumargunj data seem rather to indicate that the ambiguities and divisions on reform issues could have their counterparts at other social levels, too, with some of the upwardly mobile seeking to 'Sanskritize' themselves by imposing greater controls on women, while at the same time the problems and misery caused by the widow-marriage ban could also stimulate quite contrary tendencies. In 1922, a big Namashudra conference broke up partly through a bitter controversy as to whether widow marriage should be prohibited or encouraged, and during the mid 1920s Digindranarayan Bhattacharya, the rebel Brahman closely identified with lower-caste movements, revived and indeed extended Vidyasagar's programme by campaigning against the practice of widows being made to go without water on ekadosi.[91]

Vidyasagar had sought respectability for widow marriage by making their forms as conventional as possible, and in his letter of July 1867 claimed to have spent no less than Rs 10,000 on the marriage of Srishchandra, giving massive presents to pandits, ghataks and kulins. The reference to go-betweens confirms the obvious: these were presumably all arranged marriages, independent of the bride's consent. Yet despite this strategic emphasis on conventionality, something entirely unconventional was happening, with implications that could at times go a bit beyond the norms set by the founder of the movement. In 'normal' marriages, the child or very young girl was doing what every rule and custom of her society told her to do: in widow marriage she, along with the man she was marrying, was engaged in a violation of norms which no amount of apparent conformity could really disguise. And though the emphasis was always on getting child-widows remarried, neither Vidyasagar's arguments nor the law itself made any mention of age of virginity being a condition. In practice, widows marrying again would have been likely to be of somewhat maturer age than first-time child-brides. It is unlikely that a socially dangerous second marriage could have been imposed on them.

Some of the verses composed during the height of the agitation do convey a real sense of rebellion: mostly in ridicule and outrage, but just occasionally in what seems to be celebration. Take some of the lines of the song said to have been inscribed on Santipur saris, of which only the first is commonly remembered. 'O when will that day dawn, when the law will be proclaimed/Orders will be passed in every district and region/Widow marriages will come in a rush/We will live happily, with husbands of our own choice/When will the day come, when the sufferings of widows will end.'[92]

That, of course, was optimistic imagination, not reality: but an autobiography by a little-known Brahmo from Bikrampur, Gurucharan Mahalanobis (1833–1916), does reveal an instance of woman's agency. Gurucharan, unusual among Brahmos in never having formal English education, married a widow in 1862. Remarkably, as described in detail by Gurucharan, he had known her for some time before the marriage, and it was she who had taken the initiative. Indeed, there is a hint of a bit of romantic competition over the young man between her and another young girl who had also lost her husband. Vidyasagar, Gurucharan reports, was quite pleased when told of these unusual happpenings, and commented that an intelligent person should never agree to marry someone s/he had never seen. He did not come to the wedding—for Gurucharan, as a fervent young Brahmo who had discarded his sacred thread, refused to follow the Hindu forms—but remained close to the Mahalanobis family.[93]

The limits of Vidyasagar's ideas and reform activities still remain clear, particularly from today's feminist perspectives. The problems did not consist only in the kind of inconsistencies that we have seen emerging from his reform-through-texts strategy. The fundamental impulse, as in all nineteenth-century male *stri-swadhinata* (women's freedom—'freeing women' would perhaps convey the implicit meaning better) initiatives, was 'protectionist' rather than egalitarian.[94] It sought through legal reform to improve the lot of the abala (weak), a term much in use in reformist discourses. Paternalist concern certainly differed from conventional patriarchal discipline, but it could slide towards ideologies of control. Vidyasagar was not entirely free, perhaps, from a certain fear of the 'over-independent' woman going beyond the bounds of (reformed and humanized) conjugality. All his tracts do have a moralizing strand, though to be sure usually on a minor key, which portrayed theoretically austere widowhood as in practice a realm of sexual license. (A license, it should be added immediately, that basically men enjoyed at the expense of widows, who would be left to bear the costs in terms of illicit abortion, infanticide and scandal: Vidyasagar's moralism did also have a point.) Such fears probably help to explain the most obvious limit, even contradiction, in Vidyasagar's programme. It made no attempt at all (unlike Digindranarayan later on) to improve the lot of the widow who could not, or maybe did not wish to, marry again. When his own daughter returned home as a widow, Vidyasagar is said to have imposed the same austerities on himself for some time. A moving tale, within limits: there is no report that Vidyasagar ever asked her to defy the traditional rules, the in-humanities of which had been a major impulse behind his entire reform drive. There are also a few indications that by the late 1860s and 1870s an increasingly frustrated and cynical Vidyasagar was falling behind some of the younger Brahmos in the extent to which he was prepared to endorse radical patterns of behaviour. He rejected Miss Carpenter's proposal for starting a normal school to train women teachers on the grounds that 'respectable Hindus' would not allow 'their grown-up female relatives to follow the profession of tuition', while 'unprotected and helpless widows', whose services might be available, might not be 'morally . . . fit agents for educational purposes'.[95] A last, very personal, inconsistency: there are many instances of husbands educating their wives in the nineteenth century, but Dinamoyee Devi, wife of the great educator and champion of companionate conjugality, seems to have remained virtually illiterate, spending much of her time looking after Vidyasagar's parents in Birsingha.

The failure, indeed absence of effort, to modify the conditions of most married women, as well as of widows who did not remarry, may help us to understand the somewhat paradoxical appeal of a figure like Ramakrishna by the closing decades of the century. The saint's conversations were full of references to the dangers flowing from womankind: yet middle-aged and elderly wives and widows flocked to Dakshineswar. Like the men caught in the toils of chakri, they sought solace from the burdens of household routine in the message of *grihastha bhakti*, which promised a certain distancing through the cultivation of an inner devotional space, even while remaining immersed outwardly in the mundane everyday. Similarly, the withering of hopes in the transformative potential of education, as pressures on the middle class increased, may have had something to do with the resonance of Ramakrishna's denigration of formal learning found precisely among the educated.[96]

The biggest limit of all, so far as prospects of change in gender relations were concerned, was of course the absence, as yet, of autonomous, organized women's initiatives. Domestic domination and injustice—located 'within the precincts of their own respective domiciles', to use again Maheshchandra Deb's clumsy but expressive phrase— has always been peculiarly difficult to organize against, which is one reason why self-conscious feminist movements and even perceptions have been fairly rare in history. A few of the preconditions for them did start to emerge in Vidyasagar's times, however, sometimes as distant consequences of his work.

The spread of women's education, combined with the questioning of norms that Vidyasagar had provoked, led on towards the beginnings of a female literary public sphere in the decade that immediately followed the peak of his educational and reform initiatives. Three instances will have to suffice. The *Bamabodhini Patrika* was founded in 1863, run by reformist Brahmo men but greatly stimulating writings by women.[97] The same year saw the publication of Kailasbashini Devi's *Hindu Mahilaganer Heenabastha*. Kailasbashini had initially become literate at the behest of her husband, but her learning process still included an element of subversion, for it had to be kept a secret from her parents-in-law. Its results, as her husband confessed in his preface to the book, had surprised him, for the text by this neo-literate woman had needed no correction from her erstwhile teacher. In the sheer range of its survey of women's disabilities *Hindu Mahilaganer Heenabastha* rivals Vidyasagar's polemic against child marriage, for it includes within its sweep unequal treatment from childhood onwards, keeping girls uneducated and immersed in female rituals (*vratas*) which Kailasbashini considered meaningless, marrying them off in childhood into loveless conjugality, and exposing them to the miseries of Kulin polygamy. The accounts of married life and austere widowhood are especially poignant: child-brides torn from parental homes live as if in a prison, she says, caged like birds and animals. The agony of widows observing ekadosi provoked Kailasbashini to remark that only God can understand the wonders of the Hindu religion.[98] And then in 1868 there was Rashsundari Devi's *Amar Jivan*, the product of the lone, heroic efforts of an obscure, otherwise entirely conventional housewife, who had learnt her letters in fear and secrecy and gone on to publish the first autobiography in the Bengali language.[99]

Vidyasagar failed, in so far as the number of widows daring to re-marry has remained almost negligible, and much social obloquy persists even today. But the legal reform he was able to push through, and even more the debates he provoked, did unsettle grossly unjust gender norms that had been part of a doxa of common sense, immune from rational debate and questioning. That, maybe, is where reformist efforts to change laws can help, even when they remain largely unimplemented, or much misapplied.

There is also a paradoxical way in which the extent of resistance to widow remarriage itself bears witness to the significance and radical implications of Vidyasagar's crusade. Whatever the degree of their continued prevalence in practice, child marriage and polygamy are no longer considered normative, but the widow who remarries still generally invites criticism or worse. Widow remarriage was, and remains, disturbing, because it had implications that went some distance beyond what is quite often assumed in feminist circles today to have been the outer limit of nineteenth-century male reformism; a notion of companionate marriage that in essence represented yet another form of control over feminine sexuality. Vidyasagar's campaign, and the law it was able to push through, implicitly challenged the basic Hindu notion of the pure woman as *ardhangini*, half her husband's body even after the latter's death (and hence entitled to a share in his property as long as she does not remarry), who is permitted to have sex in the entire course of her life with one male partner, her husband, alone. (Here lay also the core of the double standard in Hindu conjugality, for there was no corresponding restraint on men.) The subversion implied in Vidyasagar's work was that he achieved the legalization of the remarriage, not of child widows or virgins alone, but of adult women who would have had fullfledged sexual relations with their husbands, and may have borne children. The 'Great Unchastity Case' of 1873 drove the point home more sharply. It decided, going against general Hindu public opinion, that a widow who had not remarried but was proved to have committed 'adultery' subsequently (i.e. been 'unfaithful' to her deceased husband after his death) would retain her share of her husband's property. Vidyasagar, somewhat hesitantly, supported the majority judgement: 'I do not want to condone immorality. But how can property, once inherited, be taken away again?'[100] Bourgeois property right clearly triumphed in his mind in this case over customary norms of chastity.[101] It is also noteworthy that Vidyasagar's tracts on marriage sedulously avoided the standard language of describing the husband as the supreme, near-divine, preceptor of the wife. It emphasized repeatedly, rather, the dimension of mutuality, the meeting of adult minds and bodies. Vidyasagar obviously remained far from any questioning of the limits of ideal monogamous marriage, but he was still an uncompromising critic of double standards, and the weight he was prepared to give to theoretical equality of rights remains quite remarkable.[102]

The protectionist compassion of Vidyasagar was recuperable into socially innocuous philanthropy, and that quickly became, and remains, the dominant way of representing him. But his was a compassion associated above all with anger, and a deep sense of male guilt. It is this which distinguishes his widow-marriage campaign from apparently similar later moves, notably under Arya Samaj auspices, where there was a shift in emphasis to the need for breeding faster and better for religious community and/or country. Anger and guilt, too, have been often diffused or displaced on to external targets, in the heyday of anti-colonial nationalism, but also in much more recent times, through writings where Western 'post-Enlightenment modernity' becomes the primary polemical target.

We cannot afford to lose touch with Vidyasagar's anger and guilt, directed primarily towards gender relations in his own society. For we live in times when wives are regularly burnt for dowry, a lower-caste woman activist is raped for campaigning against child marriage, and the murderers of Roop Kanwar, burnt as sati at Deorala in 1987, are acquitted in court.

Notes

1. The most important of these are Vidyasagar's proposals for reorganizing Sanskrit College (16 December 1850), his notes on the Sanskrit College, drawn up at the request of Lieutenant-Governor Halliday (12 April 1852), and the controversy with J.R. Ballantyne, Principal, Benaras Sanskrit College, in 1853.
2. These have been usefully collated and published in Arabinda Guha, ed., *Unpublished Letters of Vidyasagar* (Calcutta, Ananda Publishers, 1971).
3. Vidyasagar introduced a pass system for students wanting to go out during college hours, and tried to shame latecomers among teachers by standing at the gate every morning 10:30. Chandicharan Bandopadhyay, *Vidyasagar* (Calcutta, 1895, 1969), pp. 92, 104–5.
4. Modern factories start getting important only in the later decades of the nineteenth century, and much of the workforce even then consisted of immigrants. Relatively few Bengali-speaking people were recruited into that other site of time-discipline—the modern colonial army.
5. For a fuller discussion, see Chapters 6 and 8 [of Sarkar's *Writing Social History*].
6. The full text of Vidyasagar's plan for the reorganization of Sanskrit College, submitted to F.J. Mouat, Secretary, Council of Education, on 16 December 1850, is included in Debkumar Basu, ed., *Vidyasagar Rachanabali*, vol. I (Calcutta, 1966, 1974), pp. 376–92. The quotations in this paragraph are taken from this report.
7. Ibid., pp. 364–5.
8. S.N. Dasgupta, *A History of Indian Philosophy*, vol. I (Cambridge, 1922); Debiprasad Chattopadhyay, *Lokayata: A Study in Ancient Indian Materialism* (New Delhi, People's Publishing House, 1959, 1978), Chapter I.
9. The text of the *Notes* has been reprinted in many places: I am using Indramitra, *Karunaisagar Vidyasagar* (Calcutta, 1969, 1992), pp. 652–4.
10. Ballantyne as Principal of Benaras Sanskrit College, interestingly, contributed quite directly to the later development of Hindu revivalism by insisting on the need to evolve a Sanskritized Hindi, distinct from Urdu. As early as 1847, he was advising his pupils that they should try to make the Hindi used by the pandits of the 'holy city' of Benaras 'the standard of all India'. 'It was the duty of himself and his brother Pundits not to leave the task of formulating the national language in the hands of the villag–ers, but to endeavour to get rid the unprofitable diversity of provincial dialects—.' This was in reply to a rather puzzled interjection of a student of his that it was difficult to understand 'what you Europeans mean by the term Hindi,

for there are hundreds of dialects . . . and what you call the Hindi will eventually merge in some future modification of the Oordoo, nor do we see any great cause of regret in this prospect'. Christopher R. King, 'Forging a New Linguistic Identity: The Hindi Movement in Banaras, 1868–1914', in Sandria B. Freitag, *Culture and Power in Banaras* (Delhi, Oxford University Press, 1990), pp. 184–5.

11. Vidyasagar to F.I. Mouat, replying to Ballantyne's observations, 7 September 1853. Text in Benoy Ghosh, *Vidyasagar o Bangali Samaj*, vols I, II, III (Calcutta, 1957, 1958, 1959; combined volume, Calcutta, Orient Longman, 1973), pp. 525–30.

12. Vidyasagar's introduction of commas and semi-colons made Bengali prose both more rigorous and more accessible, as a comparison, say, with Rammohan, immediately reveals. On the importance of punctuation, see the perceptive comments of Carolyn Steedman, who reminds us that even for written English, rules for punctuation were still 'in the process of being established' in the second half of the nineteenth century. *The Radical Soldier's Tale* (London, Routledge, 1988), p. 73, and *passim*.

13. Vidyasagar's *Jivancharit* (1849) included a list of the Bengali terms he was coining for words like 'colonial', 'prejudice', 'museum', 'natural law', 'theatre', 'revolution' and 'university'. Debkumar Basu, vol. I, pp. 234–6.

14. Many among the old-fashioned literati disliked Vidyasagar's Bengali. Chandicharan Bandopadhyay, p. 178, relates a story of Sanskrit scholars at a shastric debate in the palace of the zamindar of Krishnanagar ridiculing a pandit who had given a vyavastha (opinion on a point of religious law) in Bengali that seemed too close to Vidyasagar's: 'What have you done? This can be too easily understood!'

15. Rabindranath Tagore, *Vidyasagarcharit*, 13 Sravana 1902/1895; reprinted *Charitvapuja* (1907); *Rabindra-rachanabali*, vol. IV (Calcutta, Vishwabharati, 1940, 1975), p. 478.

16. Bankimchandra's remark in 1871 that 'beyond translating or primer-making Vidyasagar has done nothing' therefore appears peculiarly uncharitable. *Calcutta Review*, April 1871, quoted in Swapan Basu, *Samakale Vidyasagar* (Calcutta, 1993), p. 157.

17. In June 1855, for instance, Joykrishna and his brother proposed the starting of 14 village vernacular schools, and were able to obtain from the Lieutenant-Governor a grant-in-aid of Rs 189 a month for each. Nilmoni Mukherjee, *A Bengal Zamindar: Joykrishna Mukherjee of Uttarpara and His Times, 1808–1888* (Calcutta, Firma K.L. Mukhopadhyay, 1975), pp. 102, 160.

18. Thus the prominent Derozian Ramgopal Ghosh had prospered through rice trade with Burma, while Taranath Tarkavacaspati around 1860 was supplying imported yarn to 1200 weavers in Ambica-Kalna and Radhanagar, and exporting cloth to many places in north India. He was connected also with trade in timber and ghee. Such literati connections with successful business enterprise would become very rare after the 1850s. Benoy Ghosh, pp. 161–2.

19. H. Woodrow, Inspector of Schools, East Bengal, in General Report of Public Instruction, 1858–9, Appendix A, p. 30, cited in Arabinda Guha, ed., *Unpublished Letters of Vidyasagar*, p. 19.

20. William Adam, *First Report on the State of Education in Bengal, 1835*, ed. Anathnath Basu (Calcutta, Calcutta University, 1941), p. 7.

21. Thus the pathshalas used to have classes from early morning to ten, and again from three to sundown, and were often closed during the harvesting season: certainly arrangements far better suited to rural conditions and a hot climate than the 'modern' system. The changeover to a ten-to-four schedule was in the 1860s, after Vidyasagar had resigned his official positions, but it came about through the influence of the Normal School for gurus which he had started. Kazi Shahidullah, 'The Purpose and Impact of Government Policy on Pathshala Gurumohashoys in Nineteenth-Century Bengal', in Nigel Crook, ed., *The Transmission of Knowledge in South Asia* (Delhi, Oxford University Press, 1995), pp. 120, 122, 125.

22. One might recall in this context the terms which Vidyasagar's village teacher is said to have used when advising Thakurdas that his son should be taken to Calcutta and taught English: 'His handwriting is very beautiful.' Chandicharan Bandopadhyay, p. 23.

23. 'There is no text or schoolbook used containing any moral truths or liberal knowledge. . . .' Adam, p. 9.

24. Poromesh Acharya, 'Indigenous Education and Brahmanical Hegemony in Bengal', in Crook, p. 98.

25. Poromesh Acharya, pp. 105–11.

26. Brian A. Hatcher, *Idioms of Improvement: Vidyasagar and Cultural Encounter in Bengal* (Calcutta, Oxford University Press, 1996), p. 106; Poromesh Acharya, p. 98.

27. In 1863, a British official noticed a 'marked difference' in the appearance of pupils of 'improved', as compared to unreformed pathshalas. In the latter, cultivators' children were prominent, those of 'the better class of villagers' relatively rare. Normal school pupils in contrast were largely 'the Brahmin and writer-caste boys'. Report of Inspector Medlicott, Government of Bengal Educational Proceedings, No. 51, January 1863, cited in Kazi Shahidullah, p. 125. School fees in the new system were rigorously collected, and payable in cash only; school timings no longer made adjustments for agrarian rhythms; and the curriculum had become more abstract, detached from labour processes (e.g. the shift from zamindari and *mahajani* accounting to formal Western mathematics).

28. Adam. p. 7.

29. The above paragraph is based on Chandicharan Bandopadhyay, Chapter VII, and Benoy Ghosh, Chapter IV.

30. Vidyasagar's report to H. Woodrowe, Officiating Director of Public Instruction, 10 December 1857, emphasized the importance of the girls' school he had managed to start at Koolingram, Burdwan district, as those sending their daughters there 'are, for the most part, respectable men'. A later report of his claimed that with consistent government support he could have started girls' schools 'in almost every village in the districts under me, except perhaps the District of Nuddea'. The qualification is revealing, for Nadia was the citadel of Brahmanical learning and orthodoxy. Arabinda Guha, pp. 35, 36.

31. The key texts here include *Jivancharit* (1849), *Bodhoday* (1851), *Nitibodh* (1851: published in the name of Vidyasagar's close friend Rajkrishna Bandopadhyay, but with the first seven sections written by himself), *Charitabali* (1856), and, of course, *Varnaparichay* in two parts (April, June, 1855). *Varnaparichay* went through 152 editions totalling 3,500,000 copies in Vidyasagar's lifetime, and remained the standard Bengali primer right down to contemporary times. Sibaji Bandopadhyay, *Gopal-Rakhal Dvandvasamas: Upanibeshbad o Bangla Shishusahitya* (Calcutta, Papyrus, 1991), p. 135.

32. I owe this point to Hatcher, p. 181, who does not, however, make this distinction between Western exemplar and Indian adaptation explicit.

33. *Bodhoday*, in Gopal Haldar, ed, *Vidyasagar Rachanasangraha* (Calcutta, 1972), vol. I, p. 182. The theme, of course, has become a Bengali proverb: 'Lekhapara kore je garighora chare se.'

34. Sibaji Bandopadhyay, pp. 134–42, and *passim*.

35. *Varnaparichay*, Part ii, in T. Datta, ed., *Vidyasagar Rachanabali*, vol. I (Calcutta, 1994), p. 1264.

36. Biharilal Sarkar, *Vidyasagar* (Calcutta, 1895, 1900, 1910, 1922; ed., Asit Bandopadhyay, 1986), p. 153, was critical of *Bodhoday*, which had declared that sense impressions constitute the only source of knowledge, and defined matter as objects that can be perceived. The missionary leader John Murdoch objected to the use of the 'secularist' *Varnaparichay* in Christian schools. Swapan Basu, p. 130.

37. Vidyasagar's autobiographical fragment begins by recalling how disobedient he had been in his childhood and how often his father had had to scold or beat him: a relevant personal detail, but which does not, I feel, fully explain this tone.

38. *Bodhoday* (1851, 1886), in Debkumar Basu, ed., *Vidyasagar Rachanabali*, vol. I, pp. 282–3.

39. Subarnabaniks were a prosperous trading community in Bengal who had a surprisingly low-caste status: supposedly because they had offended Ballal Sen, eponymous founder of the specific caste structure of Bengal.

40. Letters dated 28 March 1851 and 21 November 1859, in Benoy Ghosh, pp. 542–5.

41. Letter to Rivers Thompson, 29 September 1859, cited in Hatcher, p. 111.

42. Vidyasagar also ran a free day-school and a girls' school at Birsingha, along with a charitable dispensary. His total expenses for these came to as much as Rs 500–600 a month. Subolchandra Mitra, *Life of Pandit Isvarchandra Vidyasagar* (Calcutta, 1902, 1975), pp. 240–1.

43. Ranajit Guha, *An Indian Historiography of India* (Calcutta, K.P. Bagchi, 1988), p. 61.

44. For later generations, Samuel Smiles' *Self-Help* has come to epitomize this ideology: here, however, there can have been no direct influence, since that text was published only in 1859.

45. See, for instance, Partha Chatterjee, ed., *Texts of Power: Emerging Disciplines in Colonial Bengal* (Calcutta, Samya, 1996). For a more nuanced version of a similar argument, see Sibaji Bandopadhyay.

46. A prize-winning Sanskrit poem by Vidyasagar in his student days, composed at a time (1838) when he had not mastered English, had already announced that 'though a man be weak, poor, or of low birth, through learning he earns the respect worthy of a king'. Hatcher, pp. 165–7.

47. Asok Sen, p. 42.

48. I am indebted for this point to the very original research of Pradip Kumar Dutta: 'Hindu–Muslim Relations in the Bengal of the 1920s' (unpublished thesis, Delhi University, 1996), Chapter II, and *passim*.

49. Extract from General Report of Public Instruction, 1858–9, Appendix A, in Arabinda Guha, p. 36.

50. There had been complaints in 1847 that Joykrishna Mukherjee was funding his Uttarpara English school by enhancing the rents of his tenants at Boinchee. Nilmoni Mukherjee, p. 108.

51. Asok Sen, pp. 38–9.

52. Sumit Sarkar, *Swadeshi Movement in Bengal 1903–1908* (New Delhi, 1973), Chapter IV.

53. See n. 21 above.

54. Report of E. Lodge, Inspector of Schools, South Bengal, 10 March 1859, cited in Arabinda Guha, pp. 50–1.

55. Chandicharan Bandopadhyay, pp. 59–61, rejects as inauthentic the story about his mother, and relates the tales about infanticide and Vacaspati. Subolchandra Mitra, p. 262, gives the story about ekadosi.

56. See above, footnote 39 and corresponding text [of Sarkar's *Writing Social History*].

57. Chandicharan Bandopadhyay, pp. 237–8, vividly describes sleepless nights spent by Vidyasagar hunting for shastric arguments to prove the case for widow remarriage, before he came across the Parasara passage he would make famous. The story may be overdramatized, as it seems unlikely that Vidyasagar would not have known about the passage earlier (see n. 73 below), but the essential point regarding the primacy of personal experience over text is reiterated by Subolchandra Mitra, p. 262, who adds that he 'rightly' took no public step before discovering the shastric justification.

58. Ratna Kapur and Brenda Cossman, *Subversive Sites: Feminist Engagements with Law in India* (New Delhi, Sage, 1996), p. 47, a pioneering feminist study of Indian legal discourse which unfortunately accepts at this point a little uncritically Lata Mani's thesis about the debate around sati. I have stated elsewhere my difficulties with Mani's argument, namely that nineteenth-century debates about the conditions of women were primarily a means to the end of establishing textualized versions of tradition, even when applied to Rammohan: see my 'Orientalism Revisited: Saidian Frameworks in the Writing of Indian History', *Oxford Literary Review*, 16, 1994.

59. *Sarvasubhakari*, 1850; Gopal Haldar, ed. *Vidyasagar Rachanabali*, vol. II (Calcutta. 1972), pp. 3–9. This was an article in a short-lived monthly brought out by some Hindu College friends of Vidyasagar; it was published anonymously, but there is complete unanimity among biographers and critics that the author was Ishwarchandra.

60. I intend to argue below that this implicit recognition of ideal conjugality as necessarily based on the union of adult minds and bodies is quite central to a proper assessment of Vidyasagar.

61. Warren Hastings' Regulations had laid down, in 1772 and again in 1780, that 'inheritance, marriage, caste and other religious usages or institutions were to be administered to Hindus

according to the laws of "Shaster".' Numerous changes were made, of course, but in consultation with indigenous experts (hence the need for 'judge-pandits' in courts)—till the 'assumption', made in 1864, that judicial knowledge of Hindu law was complete. In practice, occasional consultations continued even afterwards. J.D.M. Derrett, *Religion, Law and the State in India* (London, 1968), p. 233, and *passim*.

62. The petition, which obtained 36,764 signatures, went on to cite regulations enacted in 1772, 1793 and 1831, and the unanimous opinion of the judges of the Sadr courts given to the Law Commission of 1837 that legalization of widow remarriage would 'at once dislocate the whole framework of Hindu jurisprudence'. A similar combination is visible in the petition made by the 'Professors of the Hindu law' of 'Nuddea, Tribeni, Bhatpara, Bansberia, Calcutta, and other places' denouncing the efforts of a '*Modern* pandit, Vidyasagar', 'in conjunction with a few young men of the rising class'. For the texts of both these documents, see Subolchandra Mitra, pp. 302–17.

63. See the excellent discussion in Sekhar Bandopadhyay, pp. 22–3.

64. Radhakanta organized two shastric debates, but at the end of the second awarded the shawl that traditionally signified victory at such occasions to Brajanath Vidyaratna, leading Smriti expert of Nabadwip. Subolchandra Mitra, pp. 268–9. Brajanath remained one of Vidyasagar's most bitter and formidable antagonists down to the 1880s.

65. The signatories included the Maharajas of Burdwan and Nadia, and the heads of both branches of the Tagore family Debendranath and Prasannakumar), and the first petition was headed by the unimpeachably respectable and orthodox Joykrishna Mukherjee of Uttarpara. Altogether some 25,000 signatures could be collected for reform: less than the number collected by its opponents, but still fairly impressive. Chandicharan Bandopadhyay, pp. 255–6; Nilmoni Mukherjee, pp. 142–3.

66. Polygamy had become rampant because it often became the principal source of livelihood for Kulin young men, who would be paid handsome sums by the parents of daughters eager to move their families up in the hypergamous scale.

67. A support that Vidyasagar cited as a particularly telling argument in his favour in the introduction to his first *Bahubibaha* tract (1870). This also gives a brief history of the earlier campaigns against polygamy. Haldar, ed., *Vidyasagar Rachanabali*, vol. II, pp. 167–9.

68. Sekhar Bandopadhyay, p. 28.

69. Vidyasagar reprinted this vyavastha in the second edition of his initial widow-remarriage tract (1857), at the same time pointing to its subsequent repudiation by most of the signatories as a crass instance of opportunism. Haldar, ed., pp. 15–19. Chandicharan Bandopadhyay, pp. 224–5, lists a number of earlier attempts to get widow marriage accepted.

70. Ibid., p. 21.

71. Haldar, ed., pp. 164–5.

72. Ibid., pp. 171, 218–19.

73. Raghunandan had listed, among practices allowed by some dharmasastras but no longer permissible in the Kaliyuga, sea voyages, twice-born jatis marrying women of lower castes, going on too-distant pilgrimages, Brahmans using Shudra cooks—as well as a practice which had often been interpreted as widow marriage. The relevant passage was quoted, and glossed differently, by Vidyasagar in his first widow-marriage tract. Haldar, ed., p. 28.

74. 'A woman is permitted by the shastras to remarry if her husband has disappeared, has died, been found impotent, has abandoned the world, or has been outcasted.' Haldar, ed., p. 26. Biographers like Chandicharan Bandopadhyay, p. 237, present Vidyasagar's discovery of this text in dramatic terms, as coming in a revelation after many nights of sleepless study of the shastras. This seems a bit unlikely, as the Derozian journal *Bengal Spectator* had already referred to the passage in July 1842 while advocating widow remarriage. Indramitra, *Karunasagar Vidyasagar* (Calcutta, 1969, 1992), pp. 242–3. A Sanskrit scholar like Vidyasagar would surely have known his Parasara anyway: the real problem was how the texts contradicting this passage could be shown to be irrelevant.

75. The permitted grounds in Manu are nearly all highly gender-unequal: the husband could marry again, not only if his wife dies, but also if she is barren, bears daughters only, drinks, is unfaithful, extravagant, always ill and even if she talks back at him. Contrary to today's widespread communal stereotype which somehow associates Islam uniquely with many wives, the scriptural-cum-customary grounds for monogamy in Hindu traditions have been quite remarkably weak, and only postcolonial legislation has made a (partial) change. See the passages cited in Vidyasagar's two *Bahubibaha* tracts (1870, 1873), reprinted in Haldar, ed., pp. 173–5, 413–15.

76. One hundred and thirty-three are listed for Hooghly district, with the number of marriages ranging from 80 to five. A list follows for the single village of Janai, near Calcutta, with 64 names of men having from two to ten wives. Ibid., pp. 201–12.

77. See for instance the passage in *Ratnapariksha* (1886) where Vidyasagar, writing under the alias of 'Worthy Nephew', expresses regret that his earlier polemic has led to the death of 'Uncle Vidyaratna' (Brojobilas Vidyaratna, the Nadia Smriti scholar who had been opposing him from 1855), and now he doesn't know whether this should be classed as Brahman-slaughter or cow-slaughter. Haldar, ed., p. 512.

78. Ibid., p. 176.

79. Ibid., p. 188.

80. Vidyasagar found it impossible to support the bill in its existing form, as he thought fixing the minimum age of consent at 12 could go against the *garbhadan* rite immediately after menses. His alternative suggestion was to make consummation before first menses a penal offence, irrespective of age. As girls can menstruate very early, this would not have given protection against physical and emotional injury in many cases. Subolchandra Mitra, who enthusiastically gives long extracts from this note of 16 February 1891, rejects however a widespread opinion that it represented a kind of recantation of earlier attitudes: for two months before his death Vidyasagar warmly welcomed the marriage of the Brahmo activist Durgamohan Das (who had earlier tried to get his own widowed step-mother remarried) with a widow with several children. Mitra, pp. 652–5.

81. Bankim, however, used this potentially radical argument to reject Vidyasagar's demand for an anti-polygamy law, which he thought to be unnecessary. A passage in his article was quite prophetic in the way it anticipated what later became, and remains, a recurrent argument: it was unfair to pass a law curtailing Hindu (male) rights unless a similar restriction was imposed on Muslims too. *Bahubibaha* (*Bangadarshan*, 1280/1873), reprinted in Jogeshchandra Bagal, ed., *Bankim Rachanabali*, vol. II (Calcutta, 1954, 1969), pp. 314–19.

82. Vidyasagar mentioned this figure in a letter published in *Hindoo Patriot*, 1 July 1867, in connection with a proposal that had been made to raise a public fund to help him repay the debts he had incurred while organizing these marriages. He rejected the offer, but evidently felt it necessary to explain how so much had been spent.

83. In his preface to the third edition (1863) of his first widow-marriage tract, Vidyasagar referred to the excitement and agitation generated in the Dacca region by his pamphlet, necessitating the reprint. Vidyasagar is not known to have had many contacts in East Bengal, but the Brahmo movement acquired some of its principal bases in the areas of bhadralok concentration there, like Bikrampur, Barisal, and parts of Mymensingh and Sylhet.

84. Subolchandra Mitra, p. 279.

85. Indramitra, p. 292. Sambhuchandra Vidyaratna mentions 'nearly fifteen' widow remarriages organized in Jehanabad villages like Ramjibanpur, Chandrakona, Sola, Srinagar, Kalikapur and Khirpai in Asar-Sravana 1265 (June–July 1858). Numerous such marriages, he states, took place in this area down to 1865. Sambhuchandra Vidyaratna, *Vidyasagar-Jivacarit* (Calcutta, 1891; reprinted, ed. Kumud Kumar Bhattacharya, Calcutta, 1992), p. 104.

86. Sambhuchandra Vidyaratna, p. 116.

87. Subolchandra Mitra, pp. 511–16. There is a passing reference to the Kumarganj developments also in Biharilal Sarkar, p. 282. From Vidyasagar's autobiographical fragment, we learn that

Kumarganj was the weekly market-place (*hat*) for Birsingha, located in Chandrakona police-station, Jehanabad (Arambag) sub-division. There is no indication of date, but it must have been before 1869, when Vidyasagar left Birsingha permanently. Subolchandra places the extracts just after his account of Vidyasagar's relief work during the 1866 famine, and a date, *c.* 1867, seems indicated also by the reference in general terms to similar developments in the letter of 1 July 1867.

88. The study, made incidentally by a descendant of Vidyasagar, found the village Siva temple controlled by a Brahman family, surnamed Ray (a relation of Shib Narayan Roy, perhaps), who had land granted by the Maharaja of Burdwan. Village religious festivals were still the foci of social conflict. Gouranga Chattopadhyay, *Ranjana: A Village in West Bengal* (Calcutta, 1964).

89. There seems to have been a brief spell earlier where the local authority at Jehanabad had been helpful. Interestingly, the deputy magistrate who Sambhuchandra remembers as helping Vidyasagar then was the well-known Muslim intellectual Abdul Latif. Sambhuchandra Vidya-ratna, p. 104.

90. Lucy Carroll, 'Law, Custom and Statutory Social Reform: The Hindu Widow Remarriage Act of 1856', in J. Krishnamurty, ed., *Women in Colonial India: Essays in Survival, Work and the State* (Delhi: Oxford University Press, 1989).

91. Sekhar Bandopadhyay, 'Social Mobility in Bengal in the Late-19th-Early-20th Century' (unpublished thesis, Calcutta University, 1985), p. 480; Digindranarayan Bhattacharya, *Bidhabar Nirjala Ekadosi* (Serajgunj, 1923, 1926).

92. The full text of this song is given in Subolchandra Mitra, pp. 279–80.

93. Gurucharan Mahalanobis, ' Atmakatha', manuscript, *c. 1913:* pub. and ed. Nirmalkumari Mahalanobis (Calcutta, 1974), pp. 46–53.

94. See the useful theoretical distinctions drawn in Ratna Kapur and Brenda Cossman, pp. 22–33.

95. Vidyasagar to William Grey, 1 October 1867, reprinted in Subolchandra Mitra, p. 466.

96. See Chapter 8 of this book [*Writing Social History*].

97. Bharati Ray is editing a valuable collection of extracts from this journal: Ray, ed., *Sekaler Narishiksha: Bamabodhini Patrika, 1270–1329/1863–1922* (Calcutta, 1994).

98. Kailasbashini Devi, *Hindu Mahilaganer Heenabastha* (Calcutta, Gupta Press, 1863).

99. For Rashsundari, see Tanika Sarkar, 'A Book of Her Own, A Life of Her Own: Autobiography of a Nineteenth-Century Woman', *History Workshop Journal*, 36, 1993.

100. Biharilal Sarkar, p. 332.

101. My assessment of the significance of widow marriage has been greatly helped by Tanika Sarkar.

102. The second widow-remarriage tract, for instance, did some skilful bending of the shastras to reach the conclusion that 'carefully studied, the makers of the shastras may be seen to have wanted the same rules for men as for women'. Haldar, ed., p. 156.

7

Customs in a Peasant Economy
Women in Colonial Haryana*

PREM CHOWDHRY

In Haryana the control of women's behaviour through certain customs has been central to the affirmation of the solidarity of the dominant Jat peasant group. Such customs, emerging from the growth and demands of a patriarchy and interacting with specific geo-economic needs, have been largely constrictive for women. Further, when such customs came to be buttressed with the force of law by the colonial government, who became conscious agents in their perpetuation, the customs naturally became more binding upon Jat and other social groups in Haryana, making it either difficult or impossible for a woman to break out of their confines. The tenacious persistence of historically crystallized customs and attitudes made a mockery of attempts by women to contest these and often involved them in prolonged legal battles and open confrontations.

There is a peculiar contradiction in the dominant emergent customs and attitudes in rural Haryana in relation to women in the colonial period. On the one hand, the agrarian milieu shows the generally accepted indices of high status for women, that is, bride-price, widow-remarriage, polyandry or its own sexual variants and full economic participation in agricultural activities resting on a relatively greater similarity of function with men. On the other hand, it shows the region as also having indices of women's backwardness, that is, female infanticide in different forms resulting in an extremely unequal female sex ratio as compared to the male, purdah (seclusion) and the *ghunghat* (veil) custom, total neglect of and prejudice against female education, and the complete absence of women from any positions of power and decision making. This paper takes up the socio-economic aspects of such mutually contradictory indices, social customs and attitudes and analyses the dominant peasant cultural ethos which has accepted and sanctified them. In this connection, British administrative policy decisions as well as those of a reformist movement like the Arya Samaj, both of which sustained these customs, have also been examined. This paper also attempts to explore the social implications of these customs and the reasons behind the ostensibly 'liberal' attitudes towards women in the context of marriage, remarriage, sexuality, etc. All these factors are seen in the historical context of overall colonial domination, the adoption of certain policies which, although not directly connected with women, nevertheless had profound effects on issues specifically relating to women. As such, this study also highlights the role of the colonial administration and its attitudes in retaining and reinforcing the emergent dominant social ethos of the Haryana peasantry.

I. The Dominant Caste and the Peasant Ethos

In the agrarian milieu of the Haryana region of Punjab, the socio-cultural ethos came to be coloured and determined generally by the agriculturist castes, and in particular by the land-owning classes. Among the agriculturist castes, the Jats emerge as the 'dominant caste'.[1] The model of the dominant caste in a given region as described by M.N. Srinivas is apposite for the Jats in Haryana.[2] Economically and numerically stronger than any other caste, the Jats satisfied yet another norm of the 'dominant caste', that is, they did not occupy a low ritual status. Numerically they were found in very large numbers in the five districts of this region, viz., Ambala, Gurgaon, Hissar, Karnal and Rohtak, forming nearly one-third of the total population. They also held the bulk of agricultural land as proprietors. For instance, in Rohtak district in 1910, the Hindu Jats emerged as the owners of 60 per cent of the total cultivated land. In a very large number of 'Jat villages' of this region, they held a near monopoly of landownership ranging between 88 and 99 per cent. Besides, most other castes were in a relation of servitude to the landowning Jats who stood as the single largest receivers of services from the other castes. And, although the social status of Jats is somewhat difficult to define in terms of the ritualistic frame-work of caste hierarchies, the accepted social superiority of the Brahmin did not exist here or elsewhere in Punjab. The Brahmin could certainly be sacerdotally superior yet socially he was described as the 'lowest of the low'. Whatever superiority the Brahmin may have enjoyed declined severely by the early 1920s with the propagation and acceptance of the Arya Samaj, especially among the landowning Jats of this region. On the other hand, regarding the Jats, who ritually ranked in Punjab after the Brahmin, Rajput and Khatri, the Punjab Census of 1901 laid down 'there is no caste above the Jat'. In this agrarian society, the norms as seen to be operating and also as encouraged by the British did not conform to ritualistic concepts and were necessarily related to the amount of land that was in the possession of a particular caste. Seen as such the Jats clearly emerge as the 'dominant caste' in social, economic and numerical terms, as well as in the emerging politics of this region.[3]

This ubiquitous domination by a single caste (despite internal economic disparities) set the tone and shaped the customs and attitudes that became common in rural Haryana. The emergent customs followed by most Jats came to be accepted and projected for the entire region, especially as many of these customs could be seen to be followed by nearly all lower castes as well as classes.

II. Socio-economic Conditions: Their Significance
for Women

Haryana remained one of the most backward and underdeveloped regions of Punjab under the British. The needs of imperialism gave a very low priority to any improvement of agriculture in Haryana.[4] This region in any case had poorer resources as compared to most other parts of Punjab. Irrigation was extremely limited and British irrigational policies kept the region starved of this basic requirement which was the crucial de-terminant of agriculture. Apart from limited irrigation, pre-carious rainfall, recurrent floods due to periodic overflow of the river Jamuna, seasonal excesses and frequent *akal* (famines) spelt devastation for this region and its economy. Throughout, the official emphasis remained on low-value food-cum-fodder crops and the region continued to be seen as primarily suited for the supply of draught animals to the rest of Punjab as also to certain other parts of India.

In this chronic famine-ridden region, where large sections of the peasants tended to be subsistence or deficit producers, only a comparatively large holding could be economically viable. For example, in Rohtak district, a holding of at least 12 acres could be taken as an economic one.[5] This meant that only about 28 per cent of landhold-ings fell in this category.[6] The same was true, more or less, for the entire Haryana region. The *barani* (dependent on rainfall) nature of the region with its concomitant low-yielding inferior crops and chronic crop failures made for a subsistence economy and hand-to-mouth living for an overwhelming majority of landowners. Deficient in any kind of resources, the small landowners relied mostly upon their family labour and some hired labour, if the need arose. Such an economy reinforced covetousness for male progeny. A male child came to be as essential as the life-giving rain. A popular local saying maintained:

meehn aur bettya te koon dhappya sai[7]

(Who can be satisfied without rain and sons; for cultivation both are necessary.)

Moreover, given uncertain conditions, family labour requirements, and the high mort-ality rate, it was not considered either safe or sufficient to have only one male child:

ek ankh ka ke sulakshana,
ek poot ka ke sapoota[8]

(Just as a one-eyed man can hardly be called lucky, so also a man with only one son.)

Another proverb went on to maintain:

chohra mure nirbhag ka
chohri mure bhagwan ki[9]

(The son of an unfortunate dies, the daughter of a fortunate dies.)

This local proverb showing a marked preference for boys over girls, reflects the dominant social ethos. In very real terms this ethos manifested itself in the favourable male sex ratio. There was a great deal of difference in the male–female sex ratio at any given age not only in Haryana but all over Punjab.[10] The British administration ascribed this imbalance to a distant past, before the annexation of Punjab, when female infanticide had been practised to a large extent.[11] However, by the time of the 1901 Census they were not willing to give it any significant contributory role and ascribed the uneven sex ratio to other reasons like neglect of female children in earlier times (both pre-colonial and in the early years of British rule in Punjab), the high rate of mortality due to frequent child-bearing starting at a very early age, and the neglect of women of advanced age.

Additionally, in the all-too-frequent famines, droughts and epidemics, the first casualty were women.[12] All these factors undoubtedly combined to enable a different form of femicide to continue in order to keep the female ratio down, and resulted in Punjab having the smallest proportion of females as compared to the major Indian provinces under the British.[13]

The socio-economy of this region has been emphasized because of its special significance for women and not merely to rationalize or explain the low female sex ratio. The hard subsistence-level economy with total dependence on family labour for cultivation made women an economic asset. W.E. Purser and H.C. Fanshawe recognizing this, commented in their report on the revised land revenue settlement of the Rohtak district in 1880:

> Enquiry from people themselves, in almost every village of the district has shown that as long as a family has its proper complement of workers, male and female, it is well-to-do . . . where there is no woman in the family, the house is certain to fall into difficulties.[14]

Another graphic description of women's work showed:

> The women work as hard as the men if not harder. The heavy tasks of bringing in wood and fuel and water fall on them; they have to cook the food, and carry it daily to the fields; they have to watch the crops; to them the peeling of the sugarcane and picking of the cotton belongs; and when there is nothing else to do, they must always fill up the time by tasks with the spinning wheel.[15]

A large number of local proverbs show that certain agricultural tasks such as weeding fell exclusively on women. Two proverbs from Karnal can be cited here as examples:

> *main koli nahin duppatti*
> *keya chugegi kuppatti*

(Cotton says you did not weed me when I had two leaves above the ground, what do you expect to pick now, bad woman.)

> *jo wahin nalaye do patti*
> *to kya kamae kuppatti*[16]

(If weeding be not done when there are but two leaves, then what will you earn, worthless woman.)

To this may be added the extensive animal husbandry work. Animal husbandry was a necessary supplement to this region's subsistence-level economy. It meant tending, feeding, milking the cattle and making *lassi* (buttermilk) and *ghee* (refined butter). All this was the special preserve of women.

III. The Colonial View of Women: Utility to Agriculture

Hard work was a general feature all over rural Punjab. Yet, relatively speaking, due to the harsh, unyielding geo-economic conditions of Haryana, the women worked harder than elsewhere in the Punjab province. The British officials' observations bear this out:

It can be safely said that proportionately a large number of women are engaged in economic work in the Himalayan natural division than in the plains, and that in the latter the women of South-eastern districts such as Hissar, Rohtak and Gurgaon take a greater share of such work than the women of the Central districts with one or two exceptions. In the Himalayas, as well as in the South-east of the province, women take a large share in agricultural work and in some locations are believed to do it even better than their husbands. Women of North-western districts are also fairly active workers.[17]

Among these regional variations, women of certain caste groups were specially singled out for praise. For example, the Jatni (Jat woman) was hailed as an 'economic treasure' by British officials, who wrote a great deal applauding the 'help' she rendered to 'an ideal cultivator and a revenue payer', that is, the Jat.[18] The Jatni was universally praised thus:

bhali jati jatni ki khurpi hath
khel nivare apne khavind ke sath[19]

(Good kind Jatni, hoe in hand, weeds the fields in company with her husband.)

Another proverb maintained:

ran jatti, te hor sab chalti[20]

(A Jat wife for me, as all other women are a mere waste of money.)

The Rohtak Assessment Report of 1909 mentioned that a Jatni did not plough, dig or drive a cart, but there was no other form of agricultural labour which she did not perform. The women from other agricultural castes were also said to do as much work as the Jatni if not more.[21] Here one may include the women from lower castes as well. In fact, these women showed a higher number of female workers than the other castes.[22] Those specially mentioned were from among the Chamars, Chuhras and Jhimars. They were described by the officials as 'hard working',[23] but because they did not belong to the landowning castes their being 'economic assets' found no expression in official British accounts.

The caste groups who did not encourage their women to work outside home were the Bania, Khatri and Rajput among the Hindus, and the Pathan, Biloch, Sayyad, Shiekh and Ranghar or Rajput among the Muslims.[24] The colonial administrators' comments on these caste groups which were 'conspicuous' for having 'the smallest number of female workers' reveal their own attitude. For example, the Rajputs, both Hindu and Muslim, by the 'common consent' of various British officials were considered to be 'the worst cultivators in the Punjab' whose 'land revenue dues remained frequently in arrears'; the Rajput's regard for his *izzat* (honour) forbade him to take any help from his wife who remained in purdah and was generally considered to be 'an economic burden'.[25] The Brahmins were also considered to be 'inferior cultivators', because their women gave little or no assistance to the men in the fields beyond bringing them their meals.[26] For the same reason, the Pathans were considered 'bad cultivators' and 'very bad revenue payers'; the Biloch were described as 'poor cultivators and heavily indebted'.[27] The other castes being 'non-agriculturist castes', however, merited no mention.

Obviously, the British criterion for judging women was their usefulness to agriculture which was of supreme concern to them not only in terms of land revenue but also in terms of the general socio-economic stability and utility of this region. In fact, even the custom of purdah was seen from the point of view of women's non-availability for tasks other than the domestic as it led to women's seclusion and severely curtailed their availability for agricultural labour.[28] The British support to the social reformers' struggle against purdah therefore may well have emanated out of such concerns. Interestingly, this non-utilization of female labour was not only considered a handicap to the Indian peasant but was also considered to be one of the chief causes of Punjab poverty.[29] This fact made them take a very serious view of a social custom which prohibited women from sharing the work of their men. It was this custom which they felt could be substituted by the 'more progressive' western social norm. Comparing the two norms, British officials maintained in 1921:

> There is a vast waste of female labour, due primarily to custom and prejudice. In most other countries the proportion of female labour to the whole is high; while its efficiency is equal to the tasks performed; the contribution to the national dividend resulting from this forms an appreciable part of the whole. If there were in western countries a movement aiming at the exclusion of female labour for all except purely domestic tasks, that movement would endanger the whole economic fabric, and, if successful would involve those countries in ruin. The Punjab discards what in England and elsewhere is an absolutely necessary element in the maintenance of their civilization. The fact that there are tribes such as Brahmans and Rajputs which do not allow their womenfolk even to work in the fields is alone sufficient to explain their poverty. . . . In the course of generations the loss from the waste alone must have made material progress almost impossible. No European country could maintain its present standard of living without the assistance derived from female labour.[30]

The British officials' attempt to make 'deeply ingrained Indian minds' see the need for involving women in agricultural work by projecting their own western example of 'high present economic standards' was vastly frustrating. They confessed to experiencing 'great difficulty' in making Indians accept their reasoning and getting the desired results.[31]

IV. Marriage and Bride-price

The importance of women in the agrarian economy made marriage an acknowledged 'economic necessity'.[32] So much so that a man's inability to pay his revenue dues was put down to his unmarried status, since an '*akela adami*' (single man) was not expected to perform well agriculturally; and a widower was considered to be 'half paralysed'.[33]

Significantly, the so-called 'work qualities' of a prospective bride were looked for at the time of arranging marriages, the acknowledged requirement being, '*hath-paer ki mazboot honi chahiye, take khet-kivar ka kaam thik treh ho sake*'[34] (she should be physically strong, so that agricultural work can be performed well). The emphasis on these 'work qualities' also led them to disregard the girl's age, he,ight etc., with the result that the girl was quite frequently older and sometimes taller than the boy. This fact was made a virtue of and a local proverb eulogizing it maintained:

badi bahu bade bhag
chhota bandra ghane suhag[35]

(An older or taller wife brings luck, as also a shorter or younger bridegroom.)

The important role played by women in the economy led to a wide acceptance of the prevalent custom of sale and purchase of brides among the economically hard-up peasantry. In the nineteenth century, except among a few better-off families, this custom was observed to have been universal among the agriculturist castes as well as the lower castes.[36] Among the lower castes bride-price was well signified in a local proverb:

nai kis ka bhai
chhori bech leyava lugai[37]

(The *nai* [barber] is no one's friend, he sells his daughter to buy himself a wife.)

Although looked upon as a 'disgraceful custom' and admitted by Jats with a 'certain amount of apology and obvious sense of shame', it was a practice that was gaining ground everywhere in the first decade of the twentieth century.[38]

Regarding the price of brides, Malcolm Lyall Darling, one of the most distinguished of Punjab officials who made a thorough and comparative study of varied aspects of social life in different regions of Punjab, maintained that it rose steadily with the rise in prices:

> In the fifties a bride could be had for Rs. 50, but nowadays in neither hill nor plain can anything worth having be got for less than three or four hundred rupees, and a serious epidemic may considerably raise the price. In Rohtak, for instance, where in 1918 influenza carried off 10 percent of the people, the price rose from Rs. 500 to Rs. 2000. In Hissar, on the other hand, the prolonged drought of 1919–21 reduced it from Rs. 2000 to Rs. 500.[39]

In individual cases 'fancy prices' were paid, especially if the boy was handicapped in some way, or if he was considerably older or had an obvious defect of body or limb.[40]

It may be pointed out that payment of bride-price was one of the reasons why British officials denied that female infanticide existed in this region in any substantial way and offered other reasons for the low sex ratio of females. The situation was indeed apparently contradictory, especially as the official perception of bride-price conceived it as 'a compensation . . . for the family authority which was transferred to the husband'.[41] Similarly a recent article interprets bride-price as a 'compensatory payment to the family for the production loss they suffer on her departure'.[42] Yet, even this apparent economic worth did nothing to raise her status. In practice, bride-price was most common among the lower economic strata of agriculturists. It was this factor which was responsible for not elevating the custom to respectability. The middle-level agriculturist with some standing had to pay bride-price to marry his son (the bride generally came from the poorer families who charged a price) and gave a dowry to marry his daughter, as a better alliance within the caste was always sought.[43] No girl was allowed to marry outside the caste, the norm being '*Jat ki beti Jat ko*' (A Jat girl must marry a Jat). Since there were no recognized 'socially superior' clans as such, status was determined by the amount of land held, and in the arid Haryana region the coveted wish was to get daughters or sisters married where canal irrigation existed.[44] This combination of bride-price and dowry made the existence of females a financial drain. Those accepting bride-price were looked down upon for this very practice and consequently could hardly effect a change in the dominant attitude of the others towards women. In turn, they blamed the female species for being there at all, as a woman's existence meant bride-price and bride-price spelt ultimate shame to the family; izzat among the agriculturists scored over economics, even in financially deprived households. Females therefore meant drain—financial for some and moral and ethical for others. It is small wonder that bride-price even in its positive aspects could not represent high status for women in any real terms.

V. Widow-Remarriage or the Custom of *Karewa*

The agrarian needs which allowed bride-price also sanctified widow-remarriage. Like the former, this was also a feature which the agriculturist castes shared in common with the lower castes. However, the custom of widow-remarriage as followed here had special features of its own. Known as *karewa, karao*, or *chaddar andazi*, the custom was a throwback to the old Rig-vedic *niyog* (levirate marriage) which was prevalent in the geographical region of Haryana–Punjab and associated with the early Vedic Aryan settlements.[45] Karewa, a white sheet coloured at the corners, was thrown by the man over the widow's head, signifying his acceptance of her as his wife. This custom represented social consent for cohabitation. There could be certain variations.[46] For example, it could take the form of placing *churis* (glass bangles) on the widow's wrist in full assembly and sometimes even a gold *nath* (nose ring) in her nose and a red sheet over her head with a rupee tied in one of its corners. This could be followed by the distribution of *gur* (jaggery) or sweets. Significantly, this form of remarriage was not accompanied by any kind of religious ceremony, as no woman could be customarily married twice, that is, could go through the ceremony of *biah* (religious wedding). After karewa the widow merely resumed her jewels and coloured clothes which she had ceased to wear on her husband's death. So much so that sometimes mere cohabitation was considered sufficient to legitimize the relationship and it conferred all the rights of a valid marriage. However, for cohabitation to be accepted as remarriage it had to be cohabitation in the man's house. Mere visits to the woman were considered 'adulterous'.[47]

The Jats, as in other customs, led in the practice of karewa and other agriculturist castes (except the Rajputs) followed suit. Interestingly, among the Brahmins, the reports indicate that karewa was being followed.[48] Even in a far-flung district like Muzaffargarh, the Brahmins had declared their adherence to the Jat custom. The settlement officer of this district pointed out that there was scarcely a Brahmin there who had even the slightest knowledge of the Hindu law books or was acquainted with their names.[49] The Brahmins of this province, who were not a priestly class but were mostly landowners, consequently followed the dominant social custom of this region in preference to the sanskritic model of the other Brahmins who brooked no remarriage at all and upheld *sati* (widow immolation) instead. Among other Hindu castes, the 'low grade Khatris'[50] also followed this practice but others like the Bania and Kayastha did not do so, and among the Muslims nor did the Sayyads.[51] Castes that did not admit widow-remarriage were contemptuous of this practice and looked down upon those who practised it.[52]

The widespread acceptability of karewa is reflected in local proverbs:

aja beti lele phere
yo mergaya to aur bhotere[53]

(Come daughter get married, if this husband dies there are many more.)

Another one maintained:

ek kanya sabansar var[54]

(There are several bridegrooms available for one bride.)

Karewa, however, as a rule, was a levirate marriage in which the widow was accepted as wife by one of the younger brothers of the deceased husband; failing him the husband's older brother; failing him his agnatic first cousins, etc. In 1934, in the Ambala district there was also the case of a Jat who claimed validity of custom regarding karewa marriage with his widowed daughter-in-law.[55] The case was lost by the father-in-law, who then appealed to the Lahore High Court. The High Court also rejected it and maintained that the custom of karewa marriage between a Jat and his widowed daughter-in-law was invalid, 'being repugnant to the ideas of Jats'. However, this judgement did not apparently lay down a general rule of custom applicable to the entire province. In another case decided shortly afterwards in 1936, the Hoshiarpur district judge took a totally opposite view and held, on the evidence, that such a remarriage was valid by custom.[56] Significantly, it may be noticed that the customs could and were sought to be extended specially as they had come to have legal sanction. The father-in-law's claim to the karewa custom has to be seen as an attempt to retain the widow within the family for a variety of reasons (given later) ranging from control of property and of her sexuality to control of her options regarding marriage partners. The reigning ideology behind this control, recorded by E. Joseph, significantly laid down:

> A female, minor or adult, is always under guardianship, while single she is under the guardianship of her father, if he be dead, of other relatives, in the order given [all male members]. So too when married until her *muklawa*, when she comes under the guardianship of her husband; on his death until remarriage she is under the guardianship of his family, whether she be minor or major.[57]

Therefore, the widow's right as to whom she could marry was not only severely restricted, it could be settled only by her late husband's family. And although the widow could not be compelled to remarry, she was not free to marry without their consent. So complete was the control over the woman and on the question of her remarriage that it was freely admitted that the widow was often practically forced and made to yield to their wishes.[58] Any assertion to the contrary would be difficult to believe in a region which advocated:

zamin jor zoi ki
zor ghati hor ki[59]

(Land and wife can only be held through the use of force, when this fails they become another's.)

Karewa and the Question of Inheritance

The popularity of karewa among the overwhelming majority of land-owning classes emanated out of the need for retaining landed property within the family. The main reason for making the marriage arrangements inside the family was to transfer control of her deceased husband's land from the widow (who succeeded to a life estate in the absence of male lineal descendants) to his brother or to a patrilineal family member, because a widow who remarried lost all her rights to property, even if she married her husband's brother.[60] Remarriage therefore deprived her of even the limited right to land which she came to possess after her husband's death, that is, only a lifelong interest; ultimately the property passed to her husband's male line. In case she had children, her sons succeeded to the property and she had right only to suitable maintenance; her daughters and their issue had no right to inherit from the father. It was essential to deny the daughters any share in the inheritance in order to retain land within the immediate kinship group. The daughters were only entitled to maintenance and to be 'suitably betrothed and married'.[61]

However, even this limited right of the widow was seen as a menace, because she could claim a partition of the property on certain grounds, that is, when she could not secure the required maintenance.[62] But the onus of proving this was on her. This meant that the court either implicitly or explicitly took the position that the required maintenance was indeed being granted to her by her deceased husband's agnates. However, the fact that this view was contrary to reality was even acknowledged by the revenue officials. In their considered opinion the widow found it difficult to obtain her 'fair share of produce' as long as the holding remained undivided.[63] A separate possession meant that the widow could get it cultivated through someone else as she was customarily not allowed to undertake full agricultural operations herself. A popular proverb from Karnal maintained:

ikh ne bowen rand
aur paden sand[64]

(A widow may be able to sow sugarcane, but it needs a strong man [literally a bull] to press out the cane.)

A separate possession also produced a fear, 'often well founded', that it would lead to an 'attempt to alienate' the property.[65] The widow could alienate the property, though not sell it, for her own maintenance, for her daughter's wedding or for payment of revenue, all the reasons dubbed as 'strict necessity'. That a lot of women had started to utilize this proviso can be seen from the constant appeals made to the Deputy Commissioner, protesting against widows who were accused of alienating their property 'without necessity'.[66]

This self-assertion by widows in taking control of the economic resources after their husbands' death must have assumed such a proportion that, for a variety of reasons, government action against it became essential. J.M. Douie, compiler of *The Punjab Land Administration Manual*, advised the revenue officials that the widow's attempts to partition the land 'should be disallowed'.[67] (The widow's right to control land had been legalized under the Land Revenue Act because after her husband's death she was held responsible for the payment of government revenue dues.) However, since legally such advice could not have held much weight, the only solution to the fast growing claims to partition was, according to official instruction, to be sought in 'a firm anchoring of the widow in remarriage.' This, the *Manual* instructed, could be the 'only satisfactory arrangement against which she had no appeal'.[68]

Strengthening Karewa: Colonial Perception and Policy

Such advice was an inevitable outcome of the colonial policy followed in Punjab, because of its economic, political and military importance, too well known to bear a recount here. The imperial government had, right from the beginning, adopted the 'preservation of village community' as a settled policy for Punjab, To this end it advocated 'co-hering tribes' (rather than 'their break up') through the operation of their customary law as an essential prerequisite for controlling Punjab.[69] The general argument of British officials was that the mass of the agricultural population in this province did not follow either the Hindu or the Muslim law. Therefore, a general code of tribal custom was prepared by the settlement officers, who at each settlement had compiled the *rivaj-i-am* (record of customs and rights), in consultation with the village headmen of each principal landowning tribe in the district; these being acknowledgedly 'men of most influential families in the village'. Consequently the customs of the landowning class in regard to civil matters like succession, alienation, marriage, tenure of land, adoption and the like came to be settled primarily by the Punjab customary law, which then became the first rule of decisions.[70] However, the British perception of these customs, which they also made legally binding, is significant. For karewa they held:

> . . . most officers conversant with this tract of country have entertained, in the existence *sub rosa* of a system of polyandry. This institution is probably the first stage in development of a savage people after they have emerged from a mere animal condition of promiscuity. It is the concomitant of female infanticide. . . . The family is the first organisation, when all things, including the wife are owned in common. The eldest brother is the head of the house, but the younger brothers have their rights, and the universal survival of the karewa custom of widow-remarriage among the Jats shows how the younger brother (though now it is not necessarily always the younger brother or any real brother) succeeds to the headship of the family on elder's death.[71]

In Punjab, the fundamental political interest of the British transcended their less well-defined concern for 'social progress'. This 'low level' of civilization as signified by karewa had to be retained because the British concern lay in strengthening the hold of the existing peasant society over land; its break-up was inevitable if the widow was allowed to have her way.

The apprehension regarding the danger of social disequilibrium in Haryana was sharper because this region, with its insecure agricultural conditions, had provided the best recruiting ground for the British Indian Army. For example, in World War I, this region had contributed one-fifth of the total recruitment from the whole of Punjab.[72] And although the karewa custom contributed significantly to the unceasing heavy recruitment (despite the insecurity of life and the equally heavy rate of mortality) the agricultural interests of the recruits' families could not be allowed to be jeopardized by the ever-growing number of widows' claims. This could prove to be very costly to the imperial government and not only unsettle its military recruitment, but also the social equilibrium upon which its rule in the state was founded.

Moreover, even economically, such a demand, if conceded, would have only added to the fragmentation and sub-division of holdings and consequently to the fast-growing smaller uneconomic holdings in this region, as elsewhere in Punjab,[73] which were posing a direct threat to the agricultural prosperity of the province and so to the collection of revenue. In fact, the fast-spreading problem of the fragmentation of landholdings was serious enough for the Viceroy to order an inquiry in June 1936.[74] This fact had also led to government attempts at consolidation of holdings, the results of which were not noticeably fruitful.[75] The growing demands of the widows in this socio-economic milieu combined with an ever-growing population dependent on agriculture, was certain to further compound the problem. It became necessary to issue instructions and give out administrative guidelines in this connection. The district officials were therefore instructed: 'Often a young widow will present a petition to the Deputy Commissioner for sanction to marry a man of her choice, but with such application he is wise to have nothing to do.'[76]

A woman's resistance to the peasant culture of remarriage which was designed to retain her within the family of her deceased husband was not allowed to surface. Petitions nevertheless continued to be made. Petitions were also made by widows, and even courts moved, to deny that karewa had taken place. This resistance shows that many peasant women perceived the karewa custom to be a repressive one. So common was this resistance that British officials noted in 1921 that criminal proceedings were most frequently resorted to by the deceased husband's brother by lodging a complaint under section 498 of the Indian Penal Code to counter the widow's attempts to escape by asserting that a marriage by karewa or chaddar andazi had taken place whereas it was firmly denied and challenged by the widow.[77] It was very difficult for a widow to prove the contrary for, as pointed out earlier, even cohabitation could be and was recognized as karewa. Once marriage or remarriage status was accepted, on no account could a Hindu woman claim release from it.[78] As against this, there was no limit to the number of wives a man could have either through *shadi* (a caste marriage) or by karewa. He could also expel his wife for unchastity through a practice called *tyag* (renunciation) which practically amounted to divorce, and also for change of religion which was said to automatically dissolve the marriage.[79] The customary law of the land, backed by the full force of the colonial administrators, safeguarded the landed property from a woman's possession. Interestingly, not allowing women to inherit property was a view which found a sympathetic and even an enthusiastic chord among many British officials. A curious parallel observation about the situation of women prevailing 'back home' as compared to that in Punjab discloses the ambivalent attitude of British officials towards women:

> ... the proportion of females to males in England and Wales rises continuously from childhood to old age, indicative of the excessive care lavished on women in England qua women, and not merely qua child bearer. Social reformers may well stand aghast at the neglect of and the contempt for female life shown by all religious groups in the Punjab, but no less extensive, and, possibly fraught with serious consequences to the future of the race, is the excessive pampering of females in England. . .[80]

An attempt on their part to understand this 'great disproportion among females and males' resulted in the following conclusion:

> During the past half century there has been a steady tendency for females to acquire property and sums of money in their own right. Now, whereas, a man has through the force of tradition and social custom, a tendency to spend his money for the benefit of the woman, the woman has no traditional tendency to spend her money for the benefit of the man. The consequence is that, in enjoying the benefits of little comforts and luxuries, woman in England is steadily increasing her advantage over the man, and the effect of this process on the relative male and female mortality can hardly be negligible. In the Punjab the independent woman, i.e., the orphan daughter or widow, has under the customary law, only the right to maintenance, and she may never alienate the ancestral property except for necessity, the onus of proving which is put upon her.[81]

The 'dangers' of women inheriting and controlling property were evidently clear to those brought up in the British cultural milieu; they wanted no repetition of it in Punjab, The fact that the custom of karewa snatched away whatever little right of possession women in Haryana–Punjab had come to acquire as widows, was well known to them. They were fully aware of the nature and operation of this custom in relation to women. This can be seen from a perceptive observation of F. Cunningham, a British Barrister at Law; who compiled a draft gazetteer of Rohtak district in 1870–4. He wrote: '*Karewa* under these conditions may be called remarriage with reference to reasons affecting the women; but such unions often take place for causes which have regard to the men only.'[82] Widow-remarriage—a seemingly progressive feature—continued to be applauded by the British administrators. The practice, however, as it was encouraged to exist, merely reinforced the social ethos which safeguarded the land in the family, clan and community. The British administrators' own attitudes regarding female inheritance were closely identified with the primary concern of the colonial government which did not want to disturb the existing rural society of Punjab.

Widow-Remarriage: The Arya Samaj and the Brahminical Code

The Arya Samaj made its own contribution to the practice of karewa in this region. It provided a justification drawn from the most ancient Hindu texts and offered protection to those who accepted it. In actual practice, the Arya Samaj Jat *updeshiks* and *bhajniks* (preachers and singers) emphasized the Vedic derived niyog, that is, the levirate aspect of it, whereas widow-remarriage per se hardly formed a part of the programme they actually adopted. In fact, one of the major reasons for the popularity and acceptability of the Arya Samaj in this region was the legitimacy that it provided to this custom, which was looked down upon with great prejudice, and even horror, by the other upper-caste Hindus, especially by commercial castes. In fact the widow-remarriage programme of the Arya Samaj remained extremely restricted elsewhere in Punjab.[83] Among the followers of the Arya Samaj in Punjab, pre-dominantly the commercial castes, a distinction was drawn between virgin widows and those widows who had lived with their husbands or had children, The remarriage of the latter evoked very strong opposition, and remained socially unacceptable to many of the Arya Samajis themselves. In Haryana alone where the Arya Samaj merely legitimized its peculiar form (karewa), could widow-remarriage be called a huge success.

The peasant ethos of Haryana-Punjab sanctified widow-remarriage for reasons of its own and even celebrated it by maintaining:

titar pankhi badli
bidhwa kajal rekh
wuh barse yue ghar kare
ya mari nahin bisekh[84]

(Just as a cloud shaped like a partridge feather means that it is going to rain, so a widow using *kajal* [kohl] or paying attention to her toilette means that she is going to remarry.)

This was in sharp contrast to the high-caste Hindus who under the brahminical code prohibited widow-remarriage completely and considered the children of such a marriage as illegitimate. They had instead adopted an extremely repressive system for widows which condemned them to a living hell. Such a state, especially among the child-widows, had led to a wide-scale social reform agitation in Bengal, Maharashtra and the south as a response to which the Widow Remarriage Act, XV of 1856 was passed by the imperial government which legalized widow-remarriage. For rural Punjab this Act had no significance, as a form of widow-remarriage was not only being observed but was also legally recognized under the customary law of the land operable in the courts. As such this Act made no difference. However, like the generally forced levirate marriage of the peasant culture which successfully kept landed property intact in the family and within the patrilineal clan, the Widow Remarriage Act also successfully retained patrilineal hold over property by taking away from the widow her limited right over it in case of remarriage.[85] Interestingly, the social reformers, whether the Arya Samajis in the north, or the others in the east or south of India, were unanimous in emphasizing the remarriage of child-widows or virgins and were also unanimous in keeping a studied silence where inheritance and property matters were concerned.

VI. 'Liberal' Attitudes?

The agrarian milieu of Haryana which necessitated widow-remarriage, with its own peculiar features, also imparted a somewhat flexible attitude and wide social acquiescence to certain emergent practices involving women. In the given geo-economic background (the adverse female sex ratio, the prevalence of bride-price with the wife as an agricultural-labour asset) emerged the concept of the woman being married to a family rather than to an individual. Translated in terms of hard reality this concept meant that two or three brothers would share a wife;[86] thus began a systematic and extensive sexual exploitation of women. In 1904, P.J. Fagan, a district-level British official observed: 'It is not uncommon among Jats and lower castes for a woman to be shared in common by several brothers, though she's recognised as the wife of only the eldest of them.'[87] M.L. Darling, writing about the prevalence of this custom in the 1920s and identifying it as 'polyandry', similarly observed that the latter was not 'unknown'.[88] However, this kind of sexual exploitation did not always go unchallenged and at least one criminal case of adultery came up in the early twentieth century in which the accused cited in his plea the existence of this social custom which allowed him sexual access to his brother's wife.[89] Cases of worse sexual exploitation were also known. E. Joseph, recording the customary law of Rohtak district, observed:

> In point of fact the girl is often older than the boy. This is not an infrequent source of trouble that comes to the courts. . . . Certain villages which need not be named, have the evil reputation of deliberately getting girls older than their boy husbands in order that the father of the latter may have illicit enjoyment of them.[90]

From the sexual point of view, the two cases cited earlier, fathers-in-law wanting to marry their widowed daughters-in-law, may be taken as attempts to legitimize an already existing relationship.[91]

An oft-repeated story of those days, popular even now,[92] not only reveals this sexual exploitation to be common knowledge but also its acceptance, albeit in a humorous and highly exaggerated manner. The story concerns a new bride who had four or five *jeths* and *devars* (older and younger brothers-in-law). All of them had free sexual access to her. After 15 to 20 days of her marriage, the bride requested her mother-in-law to identify her husband from among them. Upon this the mother-in-law came out in the *gali* (narrow street) and started to howl loudly. When questioned, she replied: 'It's difficult for me to live in this house any more. I have been married for 40 years, yet even now I have never asked anyone to determine the identity of my husband. This bride of 15 days is already asking about hers.'

There were two other factors which seem to have provided grounds for the general acceptability of this custom. One was the emigration of men to seek work especially in the canal colonies (which offered better agricultural opportunities) as tenants or even as labourers and second, the wide-scale recruitment into the British Indian Army from this arid and famine-hit region. Both these factors meant that many married women had to live without their husbands for long stretches of time. On such occasions a man handed over his wife to his brother till he returned.[93] E. Joseph, the Deputy Commissioner and Settlement Officer of Rohtak district during 1905–10, writing about the 'liberal attitude' operating behind the acceptance of this practice, which also conveniently transferred the onus of desiring sexual favours on women, disclosed:

> A most respectable Jat of my acquaintance procured his son's resignation from the army because his wife could not be trusted alone, as he explained, all his younger sons were too small to assist in dealing with the difficulty.[94]

It was also considered a 'common practice' to beget children from a devar or jeth while the husband was away serving in the army.[95] This fact, a logical corollary of the sexually exploitative custom, had to be accepted in the rural society of the time. A popular local story is illustrative of this acceptance. The dialogues proceed as follows:

First man   : After how many years have you come home?
Second man : After three years.
First man   : And how old is your child?
Second man : Two years.
First man   : How come . . .?
Second man : (mildly) Well I had sent home my *dhoti*.[96]

Such is the reason why despite severe war casualties among the pick of the population and the absence of so large a proportion of the able-bodied men from their homes, the birth rate was not affected.

The sexual exploitation of menial (low-caste) women by other agriculturists was a common feature which does not need much comment. However, interestingly, the difficulties experienced in obtaining a wife for the reasons explained above, led many agriculturists of this region to take wives from among the lower castes as well. Although it never became a norm as such nor was practised on a wide scale, the economically hard-up agriculturists were known to take recourse to it. For example, a Jat was stated to marry almost any woman he could.[97] Frequently these were women from the Chamar caste.[98] However, a faint pretence was kept that the girl was of his caste and an equally faint acceptance followed. A local belief maintains:

Jat ek samunder hai aur jo bhi dariya es
samunder mein patti hai woh samunder ki hi bun jati hai[99]

(The Jat is like an ocean and whichever river falls into this ocean loses its identity and becomes the ocean itself.)

The children of a Churhi or a Chamaran, whoever was accepted as a wife by a Jat, were called Jats though many times they were ridiculed as *churhi ke* or *chamaran ke*.[100] Such general social acceptance, despite derogatory references, is due to the fact that these social groups could not afford to, and indeed did not, attach undue importance to caste purity in case it was breached by the man; a woman, as pointed out earlier, was not allowed this freedom. This is aptly referred to in a local proverb:

beeran ki kai jaat[101]

(Women have no caste)

Moreover, within this subsistence economy the social practice was rationalized by maintaining that '*roti to bun jagi, naam to chul jaga, dono ka guzara ho jaga*'[102] (at least the food will be cooked; the family name will be carried on, both will somehow manage to live together). This practice of taking wives from lower castes was greatly frowned upon by British officials who declared it 'a kind of disreputable matrimonial agency'.[103] Given to applauding the 'magnificent physique' of the so-called superior agriculturist castes in agrarian and military professions, they actually bemoaned its biological 'deterioration' because of this practice.[104]

VII. Some Further Indices of the Low Status of Women

Clearly, in Haryana a woman had come to be recognized and coveted as an economic necessity though only as a part of a man's property, and she was equated with food, a house and animals. A local proverb from Rohtak showed this:

santhi chaoul, bhains dudh, ghar kulwanti nar,
chauthe tarang ki, bihist nishani char[105]

(Red rice, buffalo milk, a good woman in the house, and a horse to ride, these four are heavenly things.)

Women provided labour for the peasant household, as well as for cultivation and for animal husbandry, all the while operating inside the male-dominated norms of the purdah culture—a culture of secluding women.[106] This culture represented a spatial boundary between man and woman, and was visible in Haryana in the normal six inches to a yard long ghunghat for the woman. However, the peasant economy, in which women provided an indispensable source of labour and thus could not be kept secluded, accommodated it by allowing her to work 'shoulder to shoulder' with her man, but only in a ghunghat. Even the progressive Arya Samaj was not known (in this region) to preach against women observing ghunghat.[107]

The ghunghat culture, as perhaps somewhat distinct from the purdah culture, accepted and took for granted women's extreme labour without affording them any freedom. This attitude can be seen to be operating in other spheres as well. For example, in education, a region which had considered literacy to be useless ('*kala akshar bhains barobar*',[108] that is, lack of literacy), was slowly realizing the importance of education, but only for boys. For the women it maintained:

beerbanni ghar kibanni[109]

(A woman who remains at home adorns it.)

Generally used in reference to education, it emphasized that a woman should remain a housewife only and not jeopardize her position by stepping out of the house. Education therefore was looked upon with suspicion and was associated with an inevitable crumbling of the social structure.[110] Even the Arya Samaj which did a great deal for women's education in Punjab,[111] was quiet in its Haryana region. The Arya Samaj established Gurukuls but primarily for boys. The Kanya Pathshalas for girls were negligible in number and experienced a perennial shortage of both teachers and students.[112]

This social attitude also kept women away from any decision-making process whether it was at home or in the wider sphere of *jaat-biradari* (caste-brotherhood), or in the village itself. At home they were never consulted even in matters of buying or selling of milch cattle, though cattle tending was generally an exclusive work domain of women.[113] And although women put in an equal if not larger share of work in the earning of money, its expenditure was the special and exclusive reserve of men, and was dictated to the minutest detail. An Ambala proverb maintained:

lekha mawari dhianda
bakhshisha lakh laketi[114]

(Even if one gives away lakhs in charity, a wife and a daughter must be held accountable.)

All that a woman had control over was merely a few rupees which her visiting relatives might have gifted to her.[115] Summing up this social milieu, the compiler of local customs in this region maintained:

> . . . in the present phase of customary law, especially among the Hindu Jat tribes, there is a strong disinclination to admit any independent power of the wife even over movables, however acquired by her, apart from the wishes of her husband, who generally exercises an unfettered control over her estate.[116]

The customary law prevailing among the agriculturists regarded the wife and anything associated with her, whether her ornaments or her earnings, if they existed, as the property of her husband, about which she had no independent voice at all.

The attitude of keeping women secluded from all decision making, as reflected at home, was also projected outside. The women were never a part of the caste or the village *panchayat* (village council) although certain issues relating to them were frequently brought to it for decision making. These matters concerned women who had made runaway marriages with other caste men or had simply run away with someone belonging to their own village.[117] Such self-assertion broke too many social norms and customs and was never accepted. The women were also not allowed to enter the village *chaupal*, that is, the place where the panchayat customarily sat. The guarding of the chaupal as forbidden ground for women symbolized their complete seclusion, subordination and inferiority.

VIII. Conclusion

From the above account emerges a picture of Haryanavi peasant women perhaps best exemplified in their high visibility as the full working partners of men—but only in a ghunghat. The reality of ghunghat culture exposes the apparent contradiction in the co-existence of indices of high status and of low status for women in the region. The indices of high status like bride-price, widow-remarriage, equal economic work partnership and a 'permissive' sexual climate, all emerge as customs evolved, dictated and enforced by the dominant peasantry of this region to suit its own peculiar socio-economic needs. They hardly had any relation to the needs of women. Therefore, in reality these indices were bereft of all validity as markers of high status and value. The customs encouraged by the British administrative policies, usually interpreted as indices of high status when combined with the discriminating practices also already operating, that is, the low-status indices, together became responsible for lowering the status of women in the colonial period. However, even within this tightly controlled peasant culture, as aided and abetted by the colonial government, occurred women's self-assertion and protest against a system in which they shared the work but not its fruits. This can be seen in the widow's determination to hold on to her limited right over landed property and the challenge which the women posed to her marriage or to her remarriage in its levirate form. Women's perception of peasant customs as repressive also exposes the claims of high-status indices. So outwardly the women of Haryana who have been projected as equal work companions of men and whose role has been celebrated by the British administrators, continued to remain men's inferior and subordinate counterparts—their status not above that of unpaid agricultural labourers.

It is perhaps needless to emphasize that once the socio-economic forces changed, the cultural ethos and the resultant customs and attitudes which these forces had moulded and determined also changed. This can be seen quite clearly in the wide-scale changes which have occurred in Haryana in the post-colonial period which have catapulted this region from a backward subsistence-level economy to the second richest state in India in the wake of the Green Revolution. These changes have had deep rooted socio-cultural effects especially in relation to women, in either completely or partially diluting many of the customs and social attitudes described above, in retaining or sharpening many others, or in introducing new ones. Apart from the wide-scale changes in the socio-economic sphere the role of the independent Indian state may also be underlined. Just as the colonial state's policies had selectively reinforced social norms and customs, the post-independence state policies have had a revolutionizing effect on rural society. A single example, the introduction of the Hindu Code Bill of 1956, is illustrative.

Two of its provisions had a direct bearing on Haryana's rural society. One was the Hindu Succession Act which gave equal right of succession to male and female heirs and the second was the divorce clause which allowed Hindu women for the first time the right to seek divorce on a variety of grounds. The effects of these acts, which reversed the hitherto carefully maintained traditions and customs of society, need to be studied in the framework of wider socio-economic changes. Briefly speaking, their effects can be seen, on the one hand, in the violent reaction of a greatly strengthened patriarchal society forging newer weapons for the social control of women involving even physical violence and bloodshed, and on the other hand, in the greater intensification of women's resistance seen, apart from other evidence of self-assertion, in the large influx of court cases involving inheritance, property and divorce. An understanding of the post-colonial period would require a separate study, which I propose to undertake later. Such a study alone would determine the extent and direction of change in various spheres involving women that is visible in the Haryana of today as compared to what existed in the colonial period.

Notes

This is a substantially revised version of my article, 'Socio-economic Dimensions of Certain Customs and Attitudes: Women of Haryana in the Colonial Period', *Economic and Political Weekly*. I wish to thank Uma Chakravarti, Sudesh Vaid and Kumkum Sangari for suggesting certain points for elaboraton.

1. The agriculturist castes of Haryana, as notified under the Punjab Alienation of Land Act, 1901, were: Jat, Rajput, Pathan, Sayyed, Gujar, Ahir, Biloch, Ror, Moghal, Mali, Taga, Saini, Chauhan, Main, Gaud Brahmin and Qoreshi.
2. For the concept and features of a 'dominant caste', see M.N. Srinivas, 'The Dominant Caste in Rampura', *American Anthropologist*, 61 (Feb. 1959), pp. 1–16. M.N. Srinivas specifically mentions Jats as the 'dominant caste' in Punjab-Haryana in his *Caste and Modern India and Other Essays* (Bombay: Asia Publishing House, 1962), p. 90.
3. For a detailed discussion on 'Jat dominance' in Haryana and for the different sources consulted, see Prem Chowdhry, 'Jat Domination in South-East Punjab: Socio-Economic Basis of Jat Politics in a Punjab District', *Indian Economic and Social History Review*, 19, nos. 3 & 4 (Oct.–Dec. 1983), pp. 325–46.

4. For details, see Prem Chowdhry, 'The Advantages of Backwardness: Colonial Policy and Agriculture in Haryana', *Indian Economic and Social History Review*, 23, no. 3 (Oct.–Dec. 1986), pp. 236–88.

5. *Rohtak District Gazetteer, 1910*, vol. 3 A (Lahore, 1911), p. 68.

6. Calculated from the Board of Economic Inquiry, *The Size and Distribution of Agricultural Holdings in the Punjab* (Lahore, 1925), p. 16.

7. Jainarayan Verma, *Haryanavi Lokoktiyan: Shastriye Vishaleshan* (Delhi: Adarsh Sahitya Prakashan, 1972), p. 123.

8. Ibid., p. 96.

9. Ibid., p. 30. The birth of a daughter was regarded as the equivalent of a decree of Rs 2000 against her father. See M.L. Darling, *The Punjab Peasant in Prosperity and Debt*, 2nd ed. (1925; rpt. New Delhi: Manohar Book Service, 1978), p. 5.

10. For details of female–male sex ratio, see *Census of India: Punjab, 1931*, vol.17, pt. i, Report, p. 157.

11. The British officials agreed that among Jats, especially the Sikh Jats and Rajputs, female infanticide had been widely prevalent at the time of annexation of the province, but by 1901, it had dwindled to insignificant numbers. By 1931, it was confined to some individual families or groups of families which, according to them, did not influence the sex ratio as such. See *Census of India: Punjab, 1931*, ibid., p. 154.

12. For details of these factors and other contributory reasons, see *Census of India: Punjab, 1931*, ibid., p. 156.

13. Ratio of females per thousand males in different provinces of British India in 1931: Punjab: 831; North West Frontier Provinces: 843; United Provinces: 906; Bihar and Orissa: 909; Bengal: 924; Madras: 1025; Bombay: 909; Central Provinces: 1000; Central India Agency: 948; Rajputana: 908. Although the proportion of the sexes was not uniform in different parts of Punjab or in the different castes (for example, the proportion of females among Jats had always been lower than among other castes), by and large the figures given for the whole of Punjab correspond to the detailed figures available for the different districts of Haryana. Source: *Census of India: Punjab, 1931*, ibid., p. 159. For the exact number of females per thousand males in different districts of Haryana, see subtable no. 1, p. 163.

14. W.E. Purser and H.C. Fanshawe, *Report on the Revised Land Revenue Settlement: Rohtak District, 1873–79* (Lahore, 1880), p. 65; hereafter *Revised Land Revenue Settlement, Rohtak*.

15. *Rohtak District Gazetteer, 1910*, p. 96.

16. R. Maconachie, ed. *Selected Agricultural Proverbs of the Punjab* (Delhi: Imperial Medical Hall Press, 1870), p. 264.

17. *Census of India: Punjab, 1931*, p. 217.

18. Darling, *Punjab Peasant*, p. 35.

19. *Revised Land Revenue Settlement, Rohtak*, p. 53.

20. Darling, *Punjab Peasant*, p. 35.

21. Ibid., p. 33.

22. *Census of India: Punjab, 1931*, p. 217.

23. Ibid., p. 217.

24. Ibid.

25. Darling, *Punjab Peasant*, p. 35. See also *The Settlement Report of the Ambala District*, 1893 (Lahore, 1893), p. 12.

26. *Rohtak District Gazetteer, 1910*, p. 77.

27. *Census of India: Punjab, 1931*, p. 217.

28. See Rushbrook William, Director, Central Bureau of Information, Govt. of India, *India in 1921–22* (Calcutta, Govt. Printing, 1922), p. 222.

29. *Census of India: Punjab and Delhi, 1921*, vol. 15, pt. i, Report, p. 363. Also see, *India in 1929–30* (Calcutta, 1931), p. 117.

30. *Census of India: Punjab and Delhi, 1921*, p. 363.

31. *India in 1929–30*, p. 119.

32. Darling, *Punjab Peasant*, p. 53.

33. Ibid., p. 53.

34. Personal interview with R.M. Hooda, Rohtak, 1 June 1986. Born in 1933, village Makrauli-Kalan, Rohtak Dist., a graduate from Jat College Rohtak (BA, LLB) R.M. Hooda has been practising law since 1962 at the district level. He has ancestral land, 4–5 acres, in the village.

35. Verma, *Haryanavi Lokoktiyan*, p. 43. The fact of the wife being older than the husband also arose out of levirate marriages, described later on, in which a much older widow married her *devar* (husband's younger brother), who could be younger than her by four to ten years.

36. Darling, *Punjab Peasant*, p. 49.

37. Shanker Lal Yadav, *Haryana Pradesh Ka Loksahitya* (Allahabad: Central Book Agency, 1960), p. 423.

38. *Rohtak District Gazetteer, 1910*, p. 85.

39. Darling, *Punjab Peasant*, p. 50.

40. *Rohtak District Gazetteer, 1910*, p. 91.

41. W.M. Rattingan, *A Digest of Civil Law for the Punjab Chiefly Based on the Customary Law as at Present Ascertained*, revised by Harbans Lal Sarin and Kundan Lal Pandit, 2nd ed. (1880; rpt. Allahabad: The University Book Agency, 1966), p. 737.

42. For an analytical study of bride-price and its socio-economic aspects, see Indira Rajaraman, 'Economics of Bride Price and Dowry', *Economic and Political Weekly* 18, no. 8 (19 Feb. 1983), pp. 275–9.

43. For details of similar cases in Gujarat, see Alice Clark, 'Limitation on Female Life Chances in Rural Central Gujarat', *Indian Economic and Social History Review*, 20, no. 1 (March 1983), pp. 1–25.

44. *Revised Land Revenue Settlement, Rohtak*, p. 49.

45. Niyog was a practice of levirate marriage. Later, as during the Mahabharata times, niyog came to signify cohabitation by the wife with men other than her husband under certain specific conditions like impotency of the husband and the 'moral' and 'religious duty' to beget sons to continue the family line. See, for instance, the case of Kunti.

46. For details, see C.L Tupper, *The Punjab Customary Law* (Calcutta: Govt. Printing, 1881), vol. 2, pp. 93, 123; see also E. Joseph, *Customary Law of the Rohtak District, 1910* (Lahore: Govt. Printing, 1911), p. 45.

47. Joseph, *Customary Law of Rohtak*, p. 46.

48. *Karnal District Gazetteer, 1976* (Chandigarh, 1976), p. 85.

49. Rattingan, *A Digest of Civil Law*, p. xvii.

50. *Census of India: Punjab and Delhi, 1911*, vol. 17, pt. I, Report, p. 219.

51. *Karnal District Gazetteer, 1976*, p. 85.

52. *Rohtak District Gazetteer, 1910*, p. 85. All those who were interviewed for this article also confirmed this.

53. *Revised Land Revenue Settlement, Rohtak*, p. 53. Generally said in relation to the Jats, this proverb highlights the social ease about widow-remarriage.

54. Verma, *Haryanavi Lokoktiyan*, p. 43.

55. Rattingan, *A Digest of Civil Law*, p. 82.

56. Ibid. Nothing more is known about this case.

57. Joseph, *Customary Law of Rohtak*, pp. 54–5. Until puberty a child-bride stayed on with her natal family; *muklawa*, which customarily took place several years after the wedding ceremony, was the entry and establishment of the wife in her husband's home when the marriage was consummated.

58. Ibid., p. 45.

59. Maconachie, *Agricultural Proverbs*, p. 280. This proverb is from Kangra, but according to R. Maconachie it revealed 'a universal sentiment' of Punjab.

60. *Rohtak District Gazetteer, 1910*, p. 90. In certain areas and among specific agricultural castes of Haryana and Punjab different forfeiture customs applied. The customary norm which was

to be operative in a particular case had to be decided by the court, on the basis of the custom applicable to the concerned parties. In any case the final result was the same, since the customary law prevailing amongst agricultural castes of Punjab regarded the wife's personal property as merged with that of the husband; he was also deemed entitled to all the wife's earnings and even her ornaments. In other words, the woman both by marriage and by remarriage lost all control over moveable and immoveable property. See Rattingan, *A Digest of Civil Law*, pp. 204, 427, 747.

61. *Hissar Dist. Gazetteer, 1907*, vol. 2 A (Lahore, 1907), p. 229.
62. Joseph, *Customary Law of Rohtak*, pp. 136–7.
63. Ibid., p. 40.
64. Maconachie, *Agricultural Proverbs*, p. 253.
65. J.M. Douie, *The Punjab Land Administration Manual*, 2nd ed. (1908; rpt. Chandigarh: Govt. of Punjab, 1971), pp. 270–1.
66. Joseph, *Customary Law of Rohtak*, pp. 70–1.
67. Douie, *Punjab Land Administration*, pp. 270–1.
68. Ibid.
69. Tupper, *Punjab Customary Law*, vol. 1, pp. 17–19.
70. Ibid., vol. 2, pp. 86–8, 99–100.
71. *Rohtak District Gazetteer, 1910*, p. 88.
72. M.S. Leigh, *The Punjab and the War* (Lahore: Govt. Printing, 1922), pp. 61–2.
73. See Inquiry conducted by M.L. Darling, Financial Commissioner of Punjab, dated 3 June 1936, *Darling Papers* (South Asian Centre, Cambridge), Box 5, F. No. 1.
74. Ibid. See letter of Laithwait, Private Secretary to the Viceroy, 3 June 1936. The village surveys undertaken by the Punjab Board of Economic Inquiry 1920–40, also showed that in seven out of eight villages, in different districts of this region, the average area per owner had decreased noticeably in the last 30 years.
75. Darling, *Punjab Peasant*, pp. 240–1, 251–3.
76. *Rohtak District Gazetteer, 1910*, p. 90.
77. *Census of India: Punjab and Delhi, 1921*, p. 244.
78. Joseph, *Customary Law of Rohtak*, pp. 40–1. See also *Gurgaon District Gazetteer, 1910* (Lahore, 1911), p. 58.
79. Joseph, *Customary Law of Rohtak*, pp. 35, 40.
80. *Census of India: Punjab and Delhi, 1921*, p. 234.
81. See views of Col. Forster, Director of Public Health, Punjab, in f.n., ibid., p. 234.
82. Cited in *Rohtak District Gazetteer, 1883–84* (Calcutta, n.d.), p. 51.
83. For details, see Kenneth W. Jones, *Arya Dharma: Hindu Consciousness in Nineteenth Century Punjab* (Delhi: Manohar Book Service, 1976), pp. 218–19.
84. Maconachie, *Agricultural Proverbs*, p. 46.
85. For the effects of customary law and Hindu law on widows and the remarriage question, see Lucy Carroll, 'Law, Custom and Statutory Social Reform: The Hindu Women's Remarriage Act of 1856', *Indian Economic and Social History Review*, 20, no. 4 (Oct.–Dec. 1983), pp. 363–89.
86. Darling, *Punjab Peasant*, p. 51. K.L. Rathi also confirmed the 'sharing of women among brothers' to be a 'common phenomenon' in the 1920s. He cited several cases in different villages in which there was only one married brother, but other brothers had free access to his wife. (Personal interview with K.L. Rathi, New Delhi, 24 May 1986. Born in 1912, village Rajlugarhi, Sonepat, K.L Rathi is currently practising law in the Supreme Court. His large joint family had been in possession of 100 bighas of land.) R.M. Hooda was also of the same opinion. He saw the stark poverty of the region as responsible for this practice (personal interview with R.M. Hooda).
87. *Hissar District Gazetteer, 1904* (Lahore, 1908), p. 65.
88. Darling, *Punjab Peasant*, p. 51.

89. *Rohtak District Gazetteer, 1910*, p. 88. Verdict given not known.
90. Joseph, *Customary Law of Rohtak*, p. 19.
91. R.M. Hooda also confirmed that this practice was widespread in the past. He, however, put the onus on the 'inability of the young immature husband to satisfy his fully physically mature wife'. According to him there were always some women who protested against the sexual demands of their fathers-in-law. Such women, he commented, were generally 'packed-off' to the parents—an act which was considered to be a matter of 'ultimate shame' for the natal family of the woman in question (personal interview with R.M. Hooda).
92. Personal interview with Smt. Chhotu Devi, village Dujjana, Rohtak district, 6 June 1986. Born in 1921, Chhotu Devi's late husband was a big landowner in Dujjana.
93. Darling, *Punjab Peasant*, p. 51.
94. *Rohtak District Gazetteer, 1910*, see f.n., p. 88.
95. Personal interview with R.M. Hooda.
96. Personal interview with Smt. Shanti Devi, Delhi, 9 June 1986. Born in 1921, Sonepat, Shanti Devi married a soldier who rose to the rank of a colonel in the Indian Army. A *dhoti* is a length of cloth worn as a lower garment by men.
97. Darling, *Punjab Peasant*, p. 51,
98. Joseph, *Customary Law of Rohtak*, p. 60. According to R.M. Hooda, low-caste women, especially from among the Chamars, worked shoulder to shoulder with the Jats in the fields. This led to 'sexual promiscuity' due to the innumerable opportunities for close physical proximity. Because of this a large number of children among the Chamars came to be fathered by Jats and an equally large number among Jats by the Chamars. This fact also led many Jats to take wives from among the Chamars. According to Hooda, this practice continues to this day (personal interview with R.M. Hooda). E. Joseph, the British Settlement Officer of Rohtak district, also mentions a case brought to his notice in which a Jat woman was physically involved with a Chuhra (menial), and she was thrown out of the house for this reason. See Joseph, *Customary Law of Rohtak*, p. 42.
99. Personal interview with K.L. Rathi.
100. Personal interview with Shamsher Singh, Rohtak, 23 May 1986; a Jat agriculturist, Shamsher Singh is the owner of 12½ bighas of good cultivable land in Haryana.
101. Verma, *Haryanavi Lokoktiyan*, p, 120.
102. Personal interview with Shamsher Singh.
103. *Census of India: Punjab and Delhi, 1911*, vol. 17, pt. I, Report, p. 216.
104. Darling, *Punjab Peasant*, p. 51.
105. *Land Revenue Settlement, Rohtak*, p. 54.
106. For details of purdah culture, see Uma Chakravarti, 'Pativrata', *Seminar*, no. 318 (Feb. 1986), pp. 17–20.
107. Personal interview with K.L. Rathi.
108. Verma, *Haryanavi Lokoktiyan*, p. 46.
109. Ibid., p. 46.
110. *Karnal District Gazetteer*, p. 87.
111. Kenneth W. Jones, *Arya Dharma*, pp. 107–8, 215–19. For the nature of education imparted to women by the Arya Samaj, see Madhu Kishwar, 'Arya Samaj and Women's Education: Kanya Mahavidalya, Jallandar'. Review of women studies in *The Economic and Political Weekly*, 21, no. 17 (26 April 1986), pp. 9–24.
112. Personal interview with K.L. Rathi.
113. Personal interview with R.M. Hooda.
114. Maconachie, *Agricultural Proverbs*, p. 209.
115. Personal interview with R.M. Hooda.
116. W.M. Rattingan, *A Digest of Civil Law*, p. 747.
117. Significantly, no marriage alliance was possible in the same village and consequently such cases were greatly frowned upon (personal interview with R.M. Hooda).

8

Silencing Heresy*

GAURI VISWANATHAN

Feminist Struggle and Religious Dissent

Pandita Ramabai (1858–1922), Christian convert and renowned social reformer, lived a life that was a prototype of feminist aspiration to succeeding generations of Indian women, but to her own generation her career appeared confusing, inconsistent and even contradictory. As a scholar of Hinduism who had profound quarrels with its philosophical premises, particularly with regard to women, and later as a Christian convert who rebelled against Christian dogma, Ramabai seemed always to be outside the system of which she was ostensibly a part. The travails of her early life reinforce this impression.

Born in 1858 to an upper-caste Chitpavan Brahmin family of Maharashtra, she survived a series of deaths in her immediate family, including the deaths of her parents, sister, brother, and husband, with a resilience steeled by her determination to turn misfortune into salvation for herself and other similarly afflicted women. (Years later, in 1921, she was to lose her only child Manorama, whose death would soon be followed by her own in 1922.) A peripatetic Sanskrit scholar for much of her early life, Ramabai's years of pilgrimage through the length and breadth of India mirrored the tragic rootlessness of her orphaned status, culminating eventually in her happy though brief intercaste marriage, then early widowhood, and finally espousal of women's causes—especially the plight of child widows—as her own personal mission. If, over the years, her life has tended to inspire hyperboles, such as A.B. Shah's extravagant description of her as 'the greatest woman produced by modern India and one of the greatest Indians in all history', such high praise is undoubtedly prompted by her achievement as an exceptionally learned woman and outspoken champion of women's rights and social reform.[1]

One of the few women of her time whose voice found its way into male-controlled public discourse, Ramabai quickly shot to fame as a passionate and enthusiastic spokeswoman for the amelioration of women's status in Hindu society. Publicly honoured by the Sanskrit scholars of Calcutta as a 'Pandita', or learned woman, she is nonetheless better known for influential works like *Morals for Women* (1882) and *The High Caste Hindu Woman* (1888), which are devastating critiques of Hindu patriarchy and the circumscribed lives to which upper-caste women were doomed. These diatribes earned her the wrath of orthodox sections of the Hindu public and the admiration of modernizing elites and social reformers. Both works express Ramabai's extreme disillusionment with the religion of her birth, particularly the false views of sublime philosophy that, to some extent, western Orientalism had helped promote. She importuned women in the west to resist the seductive subtleties of Hindu philosophy and resolutely look beyond them to unmask the thralldom in which Hindu women were held.

> I beg of my Western sisters not to be satisfied with the looking on the outside beauties of the grand philosophies, and not to be charmed with the long and interesting discourse of our educated men, but to open the trapdoors of the great monuments of the ancient Hindu intellect, and enter into the dark cellars where they will see the real working of the philosophies which they admire so much. There are thousands of priests and men, learned in the sacred lore, who are the spiritual rulers and guides of our people. They neglect and oppress the widows and devour widows' houses. . . . Thousands upon thousands of young widows and innocent children are suffering untold misery and dying helpless every year throughout the land, but not a philosopher or Mahatma has come out boldly to champion their cause and to help them. . . . Let not my Western sisters be charmed with the books and poems they read. There are many hard and bitter facts we have to accept and feel. All is not poetry with us. The prose we have to read in our lives is very hard. It cannot be understood by our learned brothers and comfortable sisters of the West.[2]

Refusing to be intimidated by accusations that such remarks merely confirmed the colonialist and missionary criticism of Hinduism's moral bankruptcy, Ramabai directed her ire against the guardians of a priestly tradition who obscured what she called the 'prose' of Hinduism's social hierarchy by turning it into a 'poetry' of refined moral sensibility.[3] Her disgust with Hinduism over its treatment of women made it impossible for her to accept religion as an exclusively philosophical system. This was an attitude to religion that would stay with her even when she had formally renounced Hinduism; even Christian missionaries never fully appreciated how repugnant she found a purely philosophical approach to religion. Thinking they had a better chance in winning her over by appealing to her logic and intellect, they turned to a view of Christianity as philosophy rather than historical revelation. In the long run, this approach bore consequences detrimental to their own interests.

Nor could Ramabai ever see religious devotion as purely personal salvation or search for solace in light of the ideological deployment of such a notion of religion for rationalizing women's subordination. *The High Caste Hindu Woman*, for instance, meticulously takes apart the various philosophical underpinnings of Hinduism and shows how they have succeeded in maintaining the low status of women in Indian society, such as propagating 'the popular belief among high-caste women that their husbands will die if they should read or should hold a pen in their fingers'.[4]

The path to Ramabai's rupture with Hinduism, however, was by no means a straightforward one, nor did her conversion to Christianity immediately follow her disillusionment with Hinduism. Attracted briefly while in Calcutta to reformist organizations like the Brahmo Samaj and the Prarthana Samaj, which had a practical agenda but were still focused on ridding Hinduism of outdated superstitions and rituals, Ramabai found that she could make her most enduring contributions not to debate and disputation but, rather, to the social welfare of women. That brought her back to her own native Maharashtra, where she revived a number of contacts with people active in establishing institutions for the benefit of women. She even appeared before the Hunter

Education Commission in 1882 to offer detailed recommendations for the improvement of female education. The momentum for reform certainly grew after her arrival in Maharashtra, but not quickly enough. Her plans to start a home and school for child widows and child wives in Poona received little support, and she was driven by a desire to go abroad to seek wider assistance from sympathetic organizations in the west.

While in Poona, she came in contact with Sister Geraldine, who had come to India from an English missionary order at Wantage, the Community of St Mary the Virgin. There were other missionaries from the same order in Poona who saw, in Ramabai, an eager and alert young woman intent on learning as much as she could about Christianity. Ironically, in these first few encounters with the missionaries, Ramabai's openness to Christian teaching came about primarily because she was interested in learning English in order to promote the education of women. With the missionaries' encouragement, Ramabai left for England on 20 April 1883 with her young daughter Manorama and, on her arrival there, was received by the sisters of the Wantage order, who welcomed her into St Mary's Home. Within five months of her arrival in England, Ramabai received baptism along with her daughter.

The simplicity of this chronology, however, does not come near to revealing the complex relationship Ramabai had to both Christianity and the missionaries in England. Some sense of this is already apparent in her initial interest in Christianity for pragmatic reasons, but the complexity extended to profound conflicts with Protestantism's position in England and the doubts that it engendered in her about the promise of Christian liberty offered by the scriptures, a promise that she found vitiated by the hierarchical government in which it was deeply mired. After all, it was the gender hierarchy of Hinduism that alienated her from the religion of her birth. Though Ramabai claimed she had no intention of converting to Christianity or any other religion at the time she went abroad, she had already begun to turn her back on Hinduism, decrying its cruel and heartless attitude to women. Yet when she joined the Wantage sisters and accepted their baptism, she discovered that the Christianity they propagated gave her little room to develop the sensibilities and spiritual inclinations that drove her flight from Hinduism.

Critical representations of Ramabai's feminism have tended to obscure the depth and intensity of her own spiritual struggle, either glossing over it as an incidental aspect of her feminism or as the instrumental medium through which she expressed her critique of Hindu patriarchy. Her anguished search for a personal God who is also a source of justice and love rarely finds a place in accounts of her battles with the Maharashtrian elite society. These accounts also invariably omit her protracted effort to define a conception of divinity that satisfied her craving for interpretive freedom. Ramabai's spirituality is accorded relevance only to the extent that it illuminates her protest against brahmanical ritualism and codification of women's social roles.

Receiving even less critical attention is the fact that Ramabai's developing religious sensibility enabled her also to critique the philosophical contradictions of British colonialism. Ramabai's search for a moral and theological framework of social critique did not merely serve her immediate purposes in disputing the gender disparities of brahmanism, but also provided her a point of entry into a devastating analysis of British colonialism. Her growing distance from the Trinity and other focal points of Anglican doctrine was compounded by her perception that other religious groups like Jews, Nonconformists, Wesleyans, Congregationalists, and Methodists were left outside the

Anglican fold as decisively as were colonial subjects. That she was able to attain this insight through a questioning of the theological inconsistencies in British Christianity—even as she affirmed her own faith in Christianity independently of the pressures of the English church—places her critique of colonialism uniquely in the framework of both Indian nationalism and English religious dissent.

It would be a mistake to regard Ramabai's Christian conversion as motivated entirely by assimilationist motives or to suggest that she was essentially rejecting her own cultural background in an act of identification with Western traditions of thought. Her learned readings in the religious literature of those who colonized her country helped her to see the divide between two possible meanings of religion as the source of cultural and national identity on the one hand and, on the other, as universal moral value. She reached startling insights about the distinctions between these meanings in a long and fractious correspondence with Sister Geraldine, her chief mentor in England. At one point, warned by the missionary that she was in danger of forfeiting divine grace through her arrogant questioning, Ramabai retorted that 'the door of the Universal Church of God is not shut against me, and I believe the Universal, the Holy Catholic Church is not confined within the walls of the Anglican Church'. Her response disaggregates religion from political, national institutions,[5] even as it also seeks out a subjective location for belief beyond the circumscribed world of Anglican doctrine. And though her use of the term 'Catholic Church' might lead one to conclude she was still narrowly focused on interpreting religion in institutional terms, the context of the passage as well as the repetition of the word 'Universal' suggest that she had a metaphorical and expansive understanding of Catholicism as an analytical concept signifying unity, as opposed to the divisions that produced institutions historically ranged against each other. This is further apparent in her attempt to detach religion from all forms of territorial associations, whereby 'Catholic' and 'universal' become interchangeable terms: 'Baptism and the solemn oath which we take before GOD do not belong exclusively to one person or to one church with particular belief or customs. They are Catholic, i.e., universal.'[6]

In her own critical practice, by which we must understand both her writing and her conversion, Ramabai further drove a wedge between these two ways of conceiving religion and, by converting, asserted a moral scale of values independent of the cultural systems of both her native and adopted religions. The warning issued to Ramabai by the missionary sisters 'against making . . . a self-chosen religion' reminds one that conversion is not necessarily a mode of assimilation to a predetermined reality, identity or system of thought.[7] Rather, conversion is a dynamic process that *creates* the ideal system to which the convert aspires. The self-styled construction of such a system is precisely what renders it heretical, and conversion's instrumentality in producing heresy marks it off dramatically from assimilationist goals.

In the absence of a perspective that accepts religious dissent as resistance not only to dogmatic interpretations but also the political structures that support them, Ramabai's conversion to Christianity is invariably written off as the source of a divided consciousness that alienated her from the nationalist stirrings of her fellow Indians. If Ramabai was considered a disloyal Indian by her Hindu peers because she converted, that impression has not been substantially countered by subsequent critical commentaries, which focus on her conversion as the axis along which she realigned herself with a colonialist agenda for women's reform. First, one will have to be deeply sceptical about the primary source for such a charge, which happens in this case to be missionary records. These reveal that Ramabai was clearly being trained, in true filtration style, to take up the task begun by missionaries in redeeming Hindu widows from their situation of destitution and social disgrace. Yet for this reason it is important to fragment and disperse the monumentality of the missionary archives in order to locate the dissonant voice of the subject herself. Does Ramabai see herself participating in a colonial reconstructionist scheme? Does her conversion signal her acceptance of missionary objectives for Indian women? Or does she place her conversion in the service of other objectives that, although focused on ameliorating women's position, did not necessarily partake of the missionaries' agenda for reform?

Although Ramabai's spiritual battles may have appeared to culminate in her conversion to Christianity in 1883, they never ceased, even with her apparent discovery of a more satisfying religious ethic. Her religious conversion was less a turning point than an intermediate stage in her pursuit of a moral goal that she believed Hinduism obscured by its denial of parity to women. Ramabai's search for religion encompassed a framework for her social activism that went far beyond the moral imperatives of contesting patriarchal oppression. In her restless striving for an ideal of human perfection she refused to accept that such an ideal could emerge either through institutional measures or from a system of philosophical thought based exclusively on human rationalism. Unlike other Hindu social reformers, such as Keshab Chander Sen in Bengal or M.G. Ranade in Maharashtra, she did not believe that Hinduism's egregious record in ensuring basic rights for women and other oppressed groups could be rectified by a materialistic ethic, professed by such reformist organizations as the Brahmo Samaj and the Prarthana Samaj. On the contrary, Ramabai rejected purely rational approaches to religious reform. Though she was initially drawn to these groups in her early gropings for religious alternatives to orthodox Hinduism, she was convinced they could not adequately illuminate pathways to basic philosophical dilemmas regarding such things as the apperception of supreme godhead. Since it was still necessary to deal with human authority as a mediating factor in perceiving divinity under these systems, Ramabai was persuaded that such dilemmas could only be resolved by private exertions of conscience and independent judgement. Her studious discrimination between the planes of the human and the divine meticulously separated obedience to the word of God (which she implicitly believed offered the path to salvation and liberty) from obedience to the law (which she considered to be the source of human enslavement). Her search for religion was essentially a search for viable ways of defining and realizing liberty far outside the boundaries of priestly intervention.

Ramabai's explicit quest for unconstrained spiritual freedom brings her squarely within an antinomian tradition of dissent particular to English history. For her careful distinction between two forms of obedience—to God and to the law—rehearses the antinomian rejection of 'Moral Law' as a product of institutional and priestly repression. Antinomian literature describes such repression as having the effect of removing the believer further and further from God's divine mercy and love; consequently, restoration to a position prior to one's estrangement from God means a repudiation of all forms of legal authority. As E.P. Thompson points out in his brilliant study of Blake and Muggletonianism, the term 'antinomian' itself means *against the law*, and is broad enough to include a range of oppositions to prescriptive dogmas. Primarily, antinomian doctrine takes its inspiration from Paul's letters to the Romans and to the Galatians. Apart from the fact that the Pauline emphasis on justification by faith resists a purely regulated form of worship involving ceremonial observances and rituals, its distinguishing attribute is its contestation of the imperatives of Mosaic Law. In its injunction to believers to obey moral commandments and follow the letter rather than the spirit of the law, Mosaic Law turns these commandments into what Thompson calls 'the necessary rules of government imposed upon a faithless and unregenerate people'.[8] Ramabai's admonition to her missionary mentors in England to respect her as a student 'not of letter alone but also of the spirit of religion' reproduces the language of Paul and salvages religious belief as personal testimony from the crude pit of religious ideology, which Ramabai came to see as a product of the instrumental rationality of the colonial English state.

Ramabai's disillusionment with the reduction of religious belief to a form of cultural and national identity is further aggravated by Sister Geraldine's comparison of the Christian kingdom to the English nation. By bringing the two within the same frame of reference, Geraldine establishes a bureaucratic worldliness in Christianity matching the complex requirements of the modern state:

> A corporate body . . . [such as] a nation, a municipality, a regiment, school or anything you like to name . . . must have its rulers, officers and discipline. If any member, or members, refuse to submit to its officers or otherwise set discipline at nought, they would be free to give up the rights and privileges of membership and go elsewhere. Now the Church is an invisible Kingdom with a visible and delegated Government. Christ is its King, and the Government which He has ordained for His Kingdom is that of Apostles or Bishops. We as members of Christ's Kingdom are not free to choose any other form of religious Government than this. If therefore any set up a self-chosen organisation or depart from His teaching, it is they who cut themselves off from the Church our Lord has founded and refuse to be governed in the way which He has appointed, and not the church which separates itself from them.[9]

The most interesting remark in this passage, of course, is the one that relates excommunication to civil disenfranchisement. In Sister Geraldine's presentation of the argument, what naturalizes the withholding of citizenship rights to non-Anglican groups, just as much as to colonial subjects, is their willing estrangement from the undivided community of God because of their refusal to submit to church authority. Heresy is an offence not pardonable by any but God; therefore, if non-Anglicans fail to be included in the body politic, the fault is theirs alone for stubbornly persisting in their misguided pride and false judgement. In Geraldine's stern reworking of church–state relations, the issue of obligatory citizenship rights is made irrelevant by a religious discourse that attaches criteria of sworn national allegiance to the practice of religious belief.

The antinomian rejection of 'Moral Law' laid the foundations for an antistatism that was to persist in English history. It also confirmed that challenges to English political life would invariably come from dissenting religious groups like the Anabaptists of the sixteenth century, to whom Pandita Ramabai is at one point disapprovingly compared by Sister Geraldine. The Anabaptists, declares Geraldine, 'taught polygamy and an entire freedom from all subjection to the civil as well as the ecclesiastical law'.[10] This allusion to an antistatist movement of English history—one that was not even contemporaneous but went back at least three centuries—suggests that Ramabai's rejection or authority is much greater than resistance to colonial subjection. Indeed, it is a rejection of the entire structure and content of civil and ecclesiastical law, which leaves no space for the articulation of belief outside doctrinal content or institutional constraints. Ramabai's repeated insistence on belief as inalienable choice openly repudiates the usurpation of her subjectivity by law or creed: 'When people decide anything for me, I call it interfering with my liberty, and am not willing to let them do it. I have a conscience, and mind, and a judgement of my own. I must be allowed to think for myself.'[11]

Ramabai's outsider position enables her to say this. Coming to an established religion from the outside allows her and other converts to interpret the new religion with a freedom not necessarily available to those already within the fold. She complains to Sister Geraldine that 'you have never gone through the same experience of choosing another religion for yourself, which was totally foreign to you, as I have. You, wise and experienced and old as you are, you cannot interpenetrate my poor feelings.'[12] Ramabai articulates a viewpoint that is not often heard in missionary literature: the convert's conflicted sense of cultural and spiritual change is compounded by the inability of missionaries to understand the reorientation of the convert's subjective reality. From the perspective of the missionaries, the challenges posed by choice are interpreted as wilful refashioning of reality. If Ramabai is typically seen as crossing a fine line between conversion and heresy and moving towards a 'diluted Christianity without Christ'—her spirited independence convinces her detractors that conversion, in her case, *is* heresy.

Ramabai's refusal to accept the command of law, coupled with her embrace of God as the only uncreated deity and Christ as a messenger but not surrogate of God, brought her into sharp conflict with her English mentors. The sisters, like many an Anglican divine who lambasted antinomianism as a smug recapitulation of the Calvinist heresy promising unmerited grace to the elect, warned Ramabai that she was reposing far too much confidence in her salvation without exerting any effort towards winning it through service and obedience to authority. Quoting Ruskin on unlimited liberty as being no different from licentiousness, Sister Geraldine turned the statement into its obverse to suggest that true liberty really implied obedience to law. Shortly after Ramabai's conversion, noting that she had grown more distant from her friends and community, Sister Geraldine and other missionaries concluded that her alienation was a mark of her developing pride. But Ramabai's own words suggest that the narrowly defined Christianity in which she had been trapped caused her to feel estranged from the spiritual longings she had been experiencing. The sisters' use of alienation as a metaphor for pernicious rootlessness and lack of meaningful community is transformed by Ramabai into a metaphor for the loss of intimate communion with God brought about by institutional regulation.

Ramabai's disagreement with Sister Geraldine regarding the existence of the Church before the Bible, however, is more than a young convert's refusal to accept a new religion on other people's terms.[13] Ramabai's often intemperate language appears to personalize her conflict with her mentor and sponsor, but the idiosyncratic tone of her responses is belied by her own careful, close reading of English religious history. But this kind of meticulous attention to church history is vehemently denied by Sister Geraldine, who interprets as pride what Ramabai puts forth as legitimate intellectual inquiry. Bishop Westcott, when informed of Ramabai's vexing recalcitrance, counsels Sister Geraldine that 'those dealing with her should seek to get her to believe rather than define'.[14]

The clash of perspectives between teacher and pupil is further exacerbated by the heady novitiate's refusal to allow a description of her turbulent state of mind as intransigent self-absorption; rather, by painting her situation as involving a loss of self, she castigated obedience to law as the source of a tragic self-estrangement. If Ramabai is accused of being smug, she turns the charge of complacency into a point of doctrine that distinguishes between divine election and personal belief—that is, between an offer of salvation on predestined grounds, as supported by Calvinism which Ramabai roundly rejects as disparaging of individual effort, and Pauline mysticism whose promise of salvation requires the believer to seek out personal truth in Christ's word. Ramabai thus overturns the charge that she is proud by denying Calvinist predeterminism and, instead, emphasizes the depth of her struggle for spiritual salvation as itself a process of Christian understanding.

On the other hand, the Anglican sisters, perceiving Ramabai's stance as dangerously presumptive in challenging the foundations of both Anglican doctrine and English law, remind her ominously that 'you have by your Baptism looked into this Law of Liberty'.[15] Their stress falls pointedly on the word *this*, which narrows down liberty to a prescriptive law sanctioned by church authority alone. Refusing to accept the regulated logic of such admonitions, which reduced liberty to an obligatory contradiction that included constraint as part of its self-definition, Ramabai heaped contempt on the missionaries' qualified notion of liberty as typifying 'the will of those who have authority to speak as expressing His will'.

> It seems to me that you are advising me under the WE to accept always the will of those who have authority, etc. This however I cannot accept. I have a conscience, and mind and a judgement of my own. I must myself think and do everything which GOD has given me the power of doing. . . . I am, it is true, a member of the Church of Christ, but am not bound to accept every word that falls down from the lips of priests or bishops. If it pleases you to call my word liberty as lawlessness you may do so, but as far as I know myself, I am not lawless. Obedience to the law and to the Word of God is quite different from perfect obedience to priests only.[16]

Ramabai's meticulous dismantling of her mentors' logic set up private interpretation not as an exalted alternative to institutional authority but rather a means of recapturing a lost affinity to God. Her God is less a product of human rationality (as the Brahmo Samajists believed) than a source of self-empowering reason. What ought to have been a point of little dispute between Ramabai and the missionaries, however, turned into a major disagreement because she used her God-given reason to construct her own religious system in which the Christian God is then placed (arbitrarily, according to the shocked sisters). Furthermore, her new system empties deity of established gender attributes as the first step towards an egalitarian order ensuring liberty. This is in contrast to the hierarchical religious scheme upheld by the missionaries, who acknowledge that 'in Christ she had learned that there was perfect liberty, and though there was necessarily a church order and subordination, yet in the Spirit, there was in Christ neither male nor female. It seemed going back to what she had been delivered from.'[17]

Yet, despite the obviously heretical components of Ramabai's Christianity, few critics are willing to see her conversion—or what Geraldine haughtily dismissed as her 'self-chosen religion'—as the site from which she chose to fight both British colonialism and Hindu patriarchy. Ram Bapat, for instance, who has written with considerable perspicacity about Pandita Ramabai's negotiation of the dialectics of faith and reason, sees her Christian conversion as a transitional moment in her fight against Hindu orthodoxy. He views her conversion as a crucial turning point in her resistance to the tradition that shaped her early life and established the foundations of her own deep learning in Sanskrit texts. In Bapat's reading Ramabai's point of reference for converting to Christianity remains Hinduism, despite her apparent attraction to the tenets of monotheism and the claims of mystical faith. He thus views her conversion as a reactive gesture against the retrograde features of Hinduism and patriarchal society, rather than as an act of will directing the self toward an exploration of the spiritual realm. If, however, the latter proposition is considered more seriously, it leads to the consideration that Ramabai's spiritual restlessness has less to do with Hindu religious reform than seeking out existential conditions of freedom from temporal bondage—conditions leading to the creation of a selfhood released from social restrictions. It is to this trajectory that we shall now turn our attention.

Ramabai's Early Upbringing

Ramabai's conversion to Christianity could not have been predicted from her early religious behaviour. Critics make much of her repeated insistence that she never intended to convert to Christianity, especially to a religion that she initially described as composed of meaningless and empty rituals. Perceiving no substantial difference between Christian and Hindu ceremonial worship, she writes sarcastically of the Christians she encountered in India, 'We did not see any image to which they paid homage but it seemed as though they were paying homage to the chairs before which they knelt.'[18] Christianity's own mysticism and ritualism appeared to be no more than a Westernized form of Hinduism. Ramabai's view that Christianity lacked a lively tradition of disputation on doctrine and dogma drew her initially to the Brahmo Samajists, who, as avowed social reformers, were dynamically engaged with debates on the nature of divine substance and theistic ideality. Certainly the instruction in Hindu religious texts that she received from her father did not prepare her for the questioning that later led her to reject Hinduism. Her father, Anant Shastri Dongre, believed it was imperative for women to read sacred texts, but he scrupulously excluded the Vedas as one of the required texts in Ramabai's Sanskrit education. As Meera Kosambi points out, it was not until Ramabai had encountered the monotheistic system of the Brahmo Samaj that she began to consider alternatives to the tradition-bound practices of Hinduism.[19] Yet not even the new attractions of a monotheistic faith can explain why Christianity should have so compelled her attention, particularly when there was every likelihood that, by converting, she would jeopardize her respected standing amongst her Hindu peers as a reformer and thinker.

The answer to this vexed question requires one to take a brief biographical detour, particularly in the circumstances of Ramabai's growing distance from a sense of affiliation to community, which her spiritual mentors in England noted as culminating in crisis around the time of her conversion: 'She was less free with her early friends, less confidential [*sic*]. She seemed somewhat less cordially disposed towards us, and to have a sense of distrust.'[20] Ramabai's utter isolation following the loss of all members of her family was certainly a factor contributing to her gradual detachment from community feeling. In the years following her parents' deaths, Ramabai travelled extensively across India with her sole surviving sibling, her older brother. Together, as pilgrims, they wandered from temple to temple, impressing people with their deep knowledge of Sanskrit texts and holding their own in learned conversations with pandits. Educated in the classical religious texts by her father, who was officially censured by a village council for exposing his wife and his daughters to the sacred texts, Ramabai was brought up in an atmosphere that was essentially oriented to the Dharmashastric Vedic tradition of Hinduism, the scriptural tradition of moral codes and precepts.

However, though providing the primary textual bases for legal and social identity, this tradition of moral precepts is only one of the many presentations of Hinduism, yet Ramabai remained fairly oblivious to popular expressions of other religious forms. Her subsequent disenchantment with Hinduism was entirely on the basis of the scriptural texts in which she received instruction from her parents, among which are the *Bhagavatapurana*, the *Bhagavad Gita*, the *Kaumudi*, the *Amarokosha* and other works in the oral tradition.[21] Thus, in spite of the fact that there were varying sets of religious scriptures, practices, and beliefs among Hindus, Ramabai held on to the conviction that 'no woman as a woman can get liberation' in the Hindu tradition, since she assumed that all the Hindu traditions treated the knowledge of the Veda, Vedanta, and Brahma as a necessary condition for religious salvation.[22] Her learning, though deep and wide, was limited largely to Sanskrit Bhagavata literature, and her impressions of the possibilities of female emancipation were confined to what this literature offered. Until she moved to Calcutta, where she acquired a new set of acquaintances in the reform-oriented Brahmo Samaj, Ramabai had not studied the Vedas, the Upanishads, the six systems of thought other than the *nyaya* (or analytical) system, nor the Dharmashastras. Nor was she familiar with the literatures even of the Varkari, the Lingayat or the northern Sant *sampradays* which offered the promise of salvation to the lower caste of shudras, women outcastes, and sinners, in total defiance of the Vedic scriptures and the Smritis (traditional texts). Thus, as Bapat argues, 'in spite of her bitter, pertinent and acute attacks on the fundamentals of the modernizing Hindu elitist world-views, she continued to operate within the confines of the same privileged discourse which was set up, first, by Western students of Hinduism, and then appropriated by the nationalist elites in India to meet their colonial or class interests and which valorized the Vedas and Smritis as the authoritative texts governing a monolithic Hindu order'.[23]

Ramabai's assessment of her early instruction helps explain her later antagonism to the reform of Hinduism along purely secular lines. Ramabai writes in her autobiographical tract, *My Testimony*, about the strictly religious emphasis of her classical training:

> My parents did not like us children to come in contact with the outside world. They wanted us to be strictly religious, and adhere to the old faith. Learning any other language except Sanskrit was out of [the] question. Secular education of any kind was looked upon as leading people to worldliness which would prevent them from getting into the way of *moksha* [salvation]. To learn the English language and to come into contact with *mlecchas*

[non-Hindus, or foreigners] was forbidden on the pain of losing caste and all hope of future happiness. So all that we could and did learn was the Sanskrit grammar and dictionaries with the Puranic and modern literature in that language. Most of this, including the grammar and dictionaries which are written in verse form, had to be committed to memory.[24]

Ram Bapat reads this passage as unassailable evidence of Ramabai's restrictive outlook within what he calls a 'high caste, high form of Hinduism'. And to some extent this is true. Anant Shastri's rejection of Shankara's monist philosophy of Advaitism and acceptance of Vaishnava doctrines did not necessarily mean that he welcomed dissenting traditions of low-caste protest, nor did it indicate his openness to other interpretations of Hinduism. As Bapat rightly points out, 'his revolt was rather expressive of the age-old contradictions and confrontations within the high caste, high form of Hinduism, rather than that of the emancipatory, egalitarian, popular Bhakti ethos emerging from below'.[25] Yet Bapat's evaluation of the 'patrician' aloofness of Anant Shastri's Vaishnavism assumes too quickly that bhakti, as an expression of religious dissent, is synonymous with anticasteism and low-caste protest, whereas in fact the mystical leanings of bhakti are perfectly consonant with the rigid orthodoxies of hierarchical brahmanism. Indeed, the accent on mystical unity in the *bhakti* tradition of worship does not preclude either the appropriation of bhakti by caste Hinduism or its accommodation by the requirements of upper-caste privilege.

In 1883 Pandita Ramabai, by then already a widow with a small child, set out for England. At the time of her departure she had already acquired a formidable reputation not only as a woman of profound classical learning but also as a social reformer of great perseverance and courage. But Ramabai had to pay a heavy price for her reformist activity: her espousal of widows' causes and her mobilization of (an essentially conservative) social conscience against child marriage earned her the wrath of Maharashtrian brahman society. Though it would not be accurate to say that she was driven out of India, nonetheless conditions in her home state of Maharashtra were too hostile for her to continue her relief efforts unhampered. Determined to study medicine, in order that her moral impulses for reform would be amply buttressed by a professional degree, Ramabai eagerly took up an offer made by the Community of St Mary the Virgin at Wantage, which promised to finance her higher studies. She paid her passage to England by publishing a book in Marathi, *Stree Dharma Niti*, translated into English as *Morals for Women*, which earned her both money and fame—far more than she or anyone else anticipated.

However, Ramabai's professional plans to study medicine abroad were quashed by her acute hearing problems, and she was instead channelled into a course of studies in English and natural science. The sisters of the Wantage community who sponsored her stay in England arranged for her to teach Marathi and Sanskrit at the Cheltenham Ladies College. In return for her own education in Western learning, Ramabai was expected to offer missionaries setting out for Poona the training in vernacular languages they needed for their proselytizing work. Here undisputedly was the case of the imported native informant, a prototype for upcoming generations of Indians travelling to England and America for higher studies, absorbing Western knowledge in exchange for 'native' languages. The exact terms of the exchange were to play a significant part much later, when Ramabai defied the accepted conventions and insisted on teaching missionaries more than the obligatory native languages. Far more shocking was her request that she also be allowed to teach English—and that, too, to young men, no less.

The Community of St Mary the Virgin was a small order of missionary sisters that had branches in western India, the largest and most important of which was in Poona. We have little information about the circumstances of their operation in England, though brief allusions in the letters indicate that they were in frequent communication with the Society for the Propagation of the Gospel, to whom they often sent novices and initiates from their own, much smaller order. Again, from the correspondence one has an impression that the order was challenged severely by the personal trials of missionaries: of failing health, inadequate resources, and the psychological demoralization caused by recalcitrant converts. At least one of the missionary sisters freely confessed that she suffered a nervous breakdown while working in the Indian missions. The frantic, almost hysterical tone of the correspondence between the missionaries—and between them and Pandita Ramabai—is partially explained by the stress these missionaries experienced in their effort to gain the most useful (that is, the most socially respectable) converts to continue mission work in India. Hence, the extraordinary investment in a high-caste learned woman like Pandita Ramabai, whose conversion was a prize acquisition and one not to be lost easily. Hence also the almost fastidious deference to her volatility and a willingness to mollify her at all costs, even when it clearly meant compromising the sisters' own Anglican principles.

Ramabai's ostensible motive in going to England for studies was to break what she called 'the bondage of social prejudice'—restrictions that were so great within India that 'higher principles of action' could only be pursued elsewhere.[26] But as her correspondence with the Wantage sisters shows, even as she disparaged the many strictures of Hindu patriarchy, she was no less critical of the orthodoxies governing the missionaries' conduct. Her letters reveal her alienation not only from Hindu society but also from the institutional culture of the religion to which she had converted. The letters further provide powerful insights into the lonely world of the convert, struggling to resist cooptation by both Hindu and Christian culture, even as she strove to recreate herself within a restrictive space offering little or no room for private manoeuvre. Sister Geraldine, Ramabai's chief mentor, was clearly aware that Ramabai was refashioning Christianity to her own requirements, far beyond what her sponsors desired for this young woman whom they aimed eventually to embrace within their fold: 'I fear she is willingly accepting a religion which has no claim to the name of Christianity, as she thinks it will commend itself more to the intelligence of her countrywomen than the revealed Truth, which latter will require for them a higher standard of moral and spiritual perfection than they would be willing to accept.'[27]

Because the correspondence between Ramabai and the missionaries elucidates Ramabai's construction of a belief system more systematically and coherently than any of her other better-known works, including her celebrated book *The High Caste Hindu Woman*, the primary text I shall focus on is A.B. Shah's edition of *The Letters and Correspondence of Pandita Ramabai*, a comprehensive collection of the correspondence between Ramabai and her missionary sponsors exchanged almost entirely during the time Ramabai spent in England. Unlike many missionary–convert interactions that form the basis for most scholarly analysis, this work registers the impressions of a new Christian convert writing from her location not in the colonies but in England. Ramabai's residence in England at the time she debated the missionaries gave her a closer perspective on English ecclesiastical history and its impact on the English state. Her letters powerfully reveal the fissures and dissensions within Anglican England, just as they also shed light on well-entrenched divisions in church history, which were by and large glossed over by the Anglican self-presentation of unity and strength required for efficacious missionary instruction. Ramabai's puncturing of the false certainties and presumed stability of mainstream Anglican orthodoxies paradoxically gave her an uncanny sense of release from the social constraints that bound her as a Hindu. Partly sensing this, the sisters with whom she was in communication found their own prose-lytizing ambitions uncomfortably compromised. For it was evident that, although to her English mentors' approving eyes Ramabai was loosening her ties with Hinduism and turning a suspicious and sceptical eye upon her native religion, yet her repudiation of Hinduism was accompanied at the same time by an intellectual resistance to accepting a version of Christianity handed down as scriptural authority. Chided by the sisters for her 'arrogant' independence, Ramabai angrily retorts that 'I have just with great efforts freed myself from the yoke of the Indian priestly tribe, so I am not at present willing to place myself under similar yoke by accepting everything which comes from the priests as authorised command of the Most High.'[28]

Ironically, Ramabai's departure from Hinduism is brought on by an independence the missionaries now wish to curb. Though the Wantage sisters initially believed that Ramabai's orphaned status and unen-cumbered situation would help them to transform her into whatever shape and form they desired, they found her rootlessness to be the source of an obstinate refusal to accept institutional will and authority. Their view that she offered 'fair promise of good at the outset of her career, but in consequence of having no restrictions is unprofitable to the world' disparaged her unattached status as the source of a pernicious intellectual ('heretical') independence. Their insistence on familial ties as the basis of temporal authority established dependence on a community or a family as a measure of one's usefulness, thus also confirming the family as a primary source of traditional, dependable and sustaining values. Unfettered liberty is the antithesis of a communitarian vision that Sister Geraldine locates at the heart of Christian enterprise, as she remarks in a pointed aside: 'The most unhappy person of my acquaintance, and one who has made shipwreck of her life is one who in independent circumstances and without family ties can do pretty much as she pleases.'[29]

If the single woman as a danger to society persists in the resolutely Victorian consciousness of Sister Geraldine, it was Ramabai's special insight that the persistently negative perceptions of women who chose to remain outside the family structure provided a rationale for the passing of retrograde British legislation, both in England and India. Referring to the infamous Rakhmabai decision of 1887 passed by the British Indian courts, which ordered a young woman Rakhmabai to return to her husband against her wishes, Ramabai remarked with great bitterness, 'A Hindu woman—*unless she be a widow and destitute of friends and relatives*—cannot follow even the dictates of her own conscience.'[30] Clearly Ramabai did not see widowhood as a condition of deprivation but rather understood that the absence of social ties also loosened obligatory ties to prevailing orthodoxies.

However, Ramabai's orphaned and widowed situation made her extremely culpable in the eyes of the missionaries. For her capacity of private judgement, which made her such a prime candidate for conversion, contributed at the same time to a questioning of all received notions and undercut the conceptions of priestly authority favoured by the Anglican order to which the Wantage missionaries belonged. In the absence of parents, husband, kinsfolk or community, Ramabai appeared to have the mobility that was the substance of heterodoxy. With the family as the undisputed touchstone of stable, orthodox values, the missionary order proceeded to turn into heretics single, unattached women like Ramabai, whose lack of ties to family or community made her extremely susceptible to the 'pride' of interpretative freedom. Not only did Ramabai's rejection of moral commandments puncture the family-based, community-oriented patriarchal authority of Mosaic Law, which the missionaries' beliefs affirmed, but such rejection was enabled by a slackening of all connections with a filiative order of things.

In other words, disruption of an affiliative model of the family becomes the source of a new and powerful assertion of antinomianism, in which unmediated faith in God challenges the moral prerogatives of obedience to law. The communitarian vision informing the missionaries' perspective required a web of alliances between women, family and community for the efficacious administration of religious law. The selflessness of community service is the norm of Christian liberty. Because this so clearly contradicted Ramabai's own sense of liberty as self-inspired devotion, her assertions cast a cloud of suspicion over the reasons for her conversion if, as seemed to be the case, she did not intend to serve Christianity in the same spirit as did the Wantage sisters. An early exchange between Ramabai and Sister Geraldine reveals that they had been talking at crosspurposes for a tragically long time, with Geraldine lauding Ramabai's conversion as having been inspired by the 'holy unselfish life' led by the missionaries. Ramabai breaks her silence on this representation of her conversion by finally responding to Canon William Butler:

> This is her opinion. I held my silence when I heard this, thinking that it was not of much consequence to discuss upon such points of question but now I see that the misunderstanding is growing too formidable not to be corrected.
>
> I was indeed impressed with the holy life of the Sisters, and their sublime unselfishness, and am so impressed to this moment, but I must say for the sake of truth that their life was not the cause of my accepting the faith of Christ. It was Father Goreh's letter that proved that the faith which I professed (I mean the Brahmo faith) was not taught by our Veda as I thought, but it was the Christian faith which was brought before me by my friends disguised under the name of Brahmo religion. Well, I thought if Christ is the source of this sublime faith, why should not I confess Him openly to be my Lord and my Divine teacher?[31]

Phrased in these terms, 'heresy' is at once a condition of Christian conversion as well as of its subversion. The form and content of *The Letters and Correspondence of Pandita Ramabai* have particular salience in relation to the dual, contradictory function of heresy. Originally compiled by Sister Geraldine of the Community of St Mary the Virgin as vital source material for writing the history of conversion in India, the epistolary exchange between Ramabai and other sisters of the order was preserved in the hopes that it would contribute one day to the writing of her biography.[32] But Sister Geraldine's proposed biography was not necessarily intended in the spirit of hagiography, nor was it meant to record the inspiring story of a great Indian woman who had witnessed and received God's truth and then returned to India to translate Christian truth into social service, Indeed, most missionary accounts of Christian conversions among natives are written as celebrations of achievement—that is, the acquisition of one more soul for the proselytizing enterprise. Pandita Ramabai's story was an exception to the principle of missionary biographies, for Sister Geraldine had a much more cautionary tale in mind when she decided to preserve Ramabai's often volatile letters. She believed her subject, Pandita Ramabai, had historical importance as an imperfect, erring sinner whose quarrels with certain doctrinal aspects of Christianity constituted an allegorical tale of warning to true believers.

If Ramabai is relegated to the ranks of a heretic by the very people who seek her conversion, their refusal to accept her conversion as a final event condemns as heretical the spiritual questioning they would have otherwise welcomed as a definitive step towards conversion. Thus, as long as Ramabai continued to probe into the varieties of Christian belief found in English sects, her receiving of Christian grace was deferred indefinitely and she remained disqualified from being accepted as a true Christian convert. From the missionaries' perspective, conversion is the affirmation of a given set of propositions. For Pandita Ramabai, on the other hand, conversion is a form of self-fashioning, the right to 'have a voice in choosing my own religion'.[33] Ramabai keeps drawing attention to her 'own free will: by it we are to decide for ourselves what we are to do, and fulfill our intended work'.[34] When Ramabai claims the right of free will and choice, she conjoins a theological point with a political and cultural one. She is making the argument, contrary to the missionaries' wish or liking, that Indians have to make their own country, and that the free will, independent conscience, and judgement demonstrated in their religious choices strengthen the kind of moral society Indians must make for themselves. Ramabai recognizes that the missionaries' attempt to restrict her thinking about religious questions is also a form of colonial control, and it is a central feature of her own critique that she makes independent conscience a matter of national reconstruction.

The narrative organization of *Letters and Correspondence* suggests that not only did Ramabai's questioning epitomize wilful pride but, more importantly, it also elucidates why she failed to achieve real conversion and hence justified the missionaries' refusal to acknowledge her baptism. Sister Geraldine writes:

> I have found the most interesting and edifying biographies to be those where the faults of the person under review are not withheld. Shadows shew up the light and help to give true proportion. Secondary lives which are brought onto the stage are often brought into high light and become an inspiration by a truthful narration. A life with all the faults suppressed is dazzling, but tends to depress. Where the opposite plan is followed, that life simply told is bracing and heartening.[35]

The extraordinary point of this passage is that the containment of Ramabai's heresy is possible only by presenting her conversion as a failure. Such an objective goes completely against the customary rationale of missionary writing, which was driven by a compulsion to record successes not only in order to commemorate the certain spread of Christianity but also to satisfy those who were subsidizing missionary efforts abroad. But in this particular case, the recounting of Ramabai's life story as a rough passage through a variety of theological quarrels and controversial arguments—none of which, by the way, was satisfactorily resolved—is seen to offer a more valuable lesson if her conversion is understood *as never having occurred at all*. Ramabai's conversion, presented by the missionaries as incomplete, irresolute, and endlessly deferred, takes place on so many different sites, so many different levels of meaning, that the multiplicity of its occurrence—the distended repetition of her conversion as performative gesture—is taken as definitive proof by missionaries of its lack of credibility. The conflict between Geraldine and Ramabai was most pronounced on the issue of baptism. When Geraldine insisted that Ramabai could not assume her baptism implied full conversion to Christianity, in the absence of her complete acceptance of church tenets, Ramabai was forced to re-enact her conversion by other intellectual means, which took her through a cycle of religious introspection, dialogue and disputation.

The Unitarian Heresy, or Sectarian Options

Pandita Ramabai's correspondence with the missionaries is noteworthy in another respect. The religious controversies and intellectual debates of the nineteenth century are rehearsed not in the Oxford classroom as in John Henry Newman's *Loss and Gain*, but in an often heated exchange between English missionaries and their Indian Christian initiate—an exchange that is consciously framed by the reality of colonial relationships. Two historical positions—that of colonial subject and religious dissenter—dramatically collapse into a single one in the missionaries' representation of Ramabai's questioning. The blurring of Ramabai's colonized status with the position of those coming out of a dissenting religious tradition in England produces a description of colonial acculturation as a process not significantly different from the containment of English religious dissent. Ramabai's refusal to accept the main tenets of the Anglican church put her firmly in the subject position of England's hated Dissenters. Her rejection of the Thirty-Nine Articles, coupled with an insistence on her own five articles of faith, aligns her unmistakably with several dissenting groups falling outside the Anglican fold. In asserting her faith on the grounds of direct scriptural interpretation unmediated by institutional authority, Ramabai affiliates herself to a tradition of protest that claims the autonomy of religious subjectivity from church intervention:

> I shall tell you my Articles of Faith which I am so far able to draw from the Scripture, as my limited knowledge of the Word of God enables [me to do]. I have of late, as you know, after realising the sublime truths of Christ's teaching, become one of the least of his disciples, and believe in Him as the Messiah of God, and therefore am bound to receive every word which falls from His lips as the command of God which comes to me through His meditation. I am baptized according to His direction in the name of the Father, of the Son and of the Holy Ghost; and, therefore, I call myself a Christian, though I do not know if after hearing my creed my fellow Christians would call me so.[36]

In this last line, Ramabai enters the unambiguous ground of heresy by calling her faith 'my creed' and setting aside the doctrinal creeds considered pivotal to Anglican worship. Though she may declare herself a Christian, she does so in defiantly subjective terms, marking the distance between herself and a community of Anglican believers by her claims to the sanctity of private interpretation. Rewriting the Thirty-Nine Articles of the English church into her own five articles of faith, Ramabai denied the terms of membership by which alone, at one time, she would have been accepted as a subject of both England and Christianity. As instruments of enforcing allegiance to the Church of England, the Thirty-Nine Articles also historically established the terms of inclusion in the English nation. This fact did not escape Ramabai, who read as emotional blackmail the sisters' condition that she had to subscribe to the Thirty-Nine Articles if she were to remain attached to St Mary's Home in Wantage. The drama being played out between Ramabai and the sisters turned Wantage into a microcosm of England itself.

Ramabai's increasing attraction to Unitarianism accompanied her inquiry into sectarian differences. Her Unitarian sympathies came from a range of popular religious literature that missionaries denounced as distortions of Christian doctrine. Their indictment of mass-based pamphlet literature as sources of heretical thinking is suggestive of the deep sectarian divide in English society, just as Ramabai's intellectual resistance to religious authority allies her, as a colonial subject, with the English masses' disaffection from a rule that represented only landed and clerical interests. Indeed, Unitarian heresy becomes, for Ramabai, the means of contesting colonial authority. Her reaction against Trinitarianism stems from her perception that it is the very foundation of Englishness; axiomatically, anti-Trinitarianism lends itself to strong expressions of anti-colonialism.

The major obstacle in Ramabai's acceptance of the missionaries' faith was that pillar of Trinitarianism, the Athanasian Creed. No issue caused greater bitterness between the missionaries and Ramabai than the doctrine of the Trinity, and when Ramabai virtually ordered the sisters not to teach her daughter 'anything about the mysterious Trinity, and about the deity of our Saviour, until you quite convince me that these doctrines are according to the Bible',[37] she pushed them to the point where they were no longer willing to humour her claims to individual interpretation ('She is altogether off the lines,' complained an exasperated Geraldine).[38] In reality Ramabai's primary objection against praying to Christ, and to the Holy Ghost, as a person separate from the godhead had less to do with a close, sustained reading of anti-Trinitarian literature than with a deep-seated reluctance to accept Christ as a metonym for the godhead in its entirety, a reluctance that she attributed to her own dissatisfaction with a religion like Hinduism where godhead is dispersed among different icons. When she asserts that 'I am not commanded by Christ (in the New Testament) to address my prayers either to Himself or to the Holy Ghost alone',[39] her statement has shock value because not only does it deny that Christ partakes of the divinity of God but it also implies that the claim to being the son of God is a declaration of faith that can be made by others in totally non-blasphemous ways, as long as God is recognized as the only true divinity. In other words, the importance of Christ lies in his being the messenger of hope, divine mercy and salvation, rather than in any specific identification with God or in having attributes that are interchangeable with God's.

To a large extent there was a certain literalness in Ramabai's understanding of the Trinity, since she appeared to believe it referred to three separate aspects of divinity, whereas the crucial historical issue that failed to engage her in any sustained way was whether Christ the Son was of similar substance (*homoiousios*) as God the Father, or of the same substance (*homoousios*). This was, of course, the fundamental conflict that had led, in AD 325, to the adoption of the Athanasian Creed by Constantine to resolve the dispute. Not only did the creed assert that Christ is identical with God and, together with the Holy Ghost, constitutes the Trinity, but it emphasized that the Trinity comprises three aspects of a single, *uncreated* unity, with God the Father being the one underived or unbegotten principle. Because the godhead is uncreated, Christ the Son is not considered to have been begotten in human fashion but rather is an image of the godhead. 'To be begotten', therefore, simply means completely to share in the entire nature of God the Father.

To insist otherwise, as did the fourth-century bishop of Antioch, Arius, who asserted that 'the Son is an unrelated and an independent being totally separated from, and different from the substance or nature of the Father',[40] was to invite public condemnation as a heretic, and Ramabai was sufficiently well acquainted with church history to know the dangers of recapitulating the Arian heresy even in nineteenth-century England. With a religious history still haunted by the hangings and public prosecutions of anti-Trinitarians, England was not yet a place for the open expression of Unitarian feeling. The Athanasian Creed pronounced Arianism a heresy and condemned those who were guilty of professing it. As late as 1695 a Scottish student Thomas Aikenhead was hanged for declaring the Trinity an absurdity and Christianity an illusion. Such events occurred despite the fact that a leading religious figure like Archbishop John Tillotson (1630–1694) complained about the Athanasian Creed (albeit privately): 'I wish we were well rid of it.'[41] Nor were institutions of higher learning exempt. William Whiston (1667–1752), who succeeded Isaac Newton to the chair of mathematics at Cambridge, lost his professorship because of his Arianism.

Even efforts at compromise aroused parliamentary disapproval, and those who tried to accommodate Arianism to Anglican doctrine suffered the consequences. David Lawton provides an absorbing history of some of these developments which culminated in the radical Unitarianism of such figures as the great scientist Joseph Priestley and William Frend. Frend was dismissed from Cambridge for his disavowal of the Athanasian Creed and for putatively authoring an influential pamphlet, *An address to the members of the Church of England and to Protestant Trinitarians in general, exhorting them to turn from the false worship of three persons to the worship of One True God* (1788). Lawton's conclusion that 'enforcement of orthodoxy against Unitarianism extended into the highest ranks of Church and University—and continued to do so into the nineteenth century' reveals that there was virtually no space in public life to discuss Unitarianism without repeating an offence against both English Christianity and the English state.[42] For the close identification of Trinitarianism with English nationhood was certainly not lost sight of even by an intrepid inquirer like Pandita Ramabai, who in her sporadic attacks on Anglican church doctrine quickly discovered that impugning the Trinity was tantamount to inveighing against the English Crown itself.

Ramabai's attraction to a Unitarian conception of divinity sprang from what she perceived as its clearcut demarcation of the divine from the human. In the absence of such necessary distinctions in its own religious system, Hinduism was reduced to a mindless pantheism, and Ramabai turned to Unitarianism because it offered an ideal expression of a religious faith in which the divine could be steadily contemplated as a pure entity. When Ramabai is faulted for saying human beings are not perfect, she defends herself by saying that perfection implies an absence of distinction between humans and God: the virtue of Unitarianism, in her opinion, was that it preserved this distinction. The Wantage missionaries were correct to conclude that Ramabai's dissatisfaction with pantheistic expressions of worship drew her compulsively to the Brahmo

Samaj, a reformist branch of Hinduism that resisted the facile blurring of human and divine features.

But as in so many other instances, where Ramabai's 'heresy' produced an ambivalence in the missionaries' attitudes to her intellectual probings, the sisters were simultaneously aware that Ramabai's resistance to Trinitarianism had a positive aspect, because her rejection of godhead in three figures reinforced her rejection of the polytheism of Hinduism and its blurring of human and divine. A letter by Dorothea Beale, principal of Cheltenham Ladies College, to Canon William Butler reflects the missionaries' ambivalence: 'She will never perhaps think exactly as we do, but if she did, she would not so well be a teacher for India. I am now beginning to see why she does not so readily accept sacramental teaching as we do. She is afraid of its being confused by native thought with their own pantheism. She sees dangers, which would not occur to us.'[43]

Though Ramabai may not have engaged directly with the historical debate on the substance of godhead, she did engage quite conspicuously with two related issues: the possibilities of perfection and the Incarnation. Her seemingly innocuous discussions with Sister Geraldine about the impossibility of human perfection led her to make some of her strongest statements about Christ as an independent being totally distinct from the substance of God the Father, and thus to reveal her own developing position as a Unitarian. Ramabai's argument may be summarized as follows: proceeding from the dictionary definition of perfection as 'not defective, completed, unblemished, possessing every moral excellence', she maintained that if human beings are describable in these terms, they would have foregone the progressive condition of souls and become not merely transfixed in time but God himself, since only God can be outside time, Since this is theologically impossible, the maximum state to which human beings can aspire is to be *like* God but not *as* God. Therefore, the real translation of Christ's 'Be ye perfect', is to strive for perfection and approximate God, but remain substantially distinct from God and therefore imperfect. Trying to be perfect *like* God and *becoming perfect* are thus two totally separate arguments, the first signifying a paradox of necessary imperfection and the second a theological cul-de-sac:

> If we understand 'Be ye perfect,' etc., literally and in its fullest sense, then 'As the Father' also must be taken literally and full[y] which I know according to Christian teaching cannot be. For if we were to become *like* or *as* or equally perfect with the Father, we should undoubtedly be so many supreme Gods, as the Vedantists say. There would not be any difference between us and the Father in perfection. Such a thing is an impossibility to me at least. I do not at the same time say that we shall not be perfect like the Father in a certain degree, but I object to saying that we shall be as perfect (not defective) as the Father is.[44]

Ramabai had less to say about the Incarnation, but her chief difficulty lay in reconciling immaculate conception with the doctrine of the Trinity: three beings are either separate from each other or they are one, but they cannot be both. Similarly, one is either born the way that human beings are, or one is uncreated; one cannot have both a human birth and be uncreated at the same time. To her mind, the entire idea of God emptying himself of omnipotence and omniscience in order to undergo human birth as Christ and suffer human travails is simply incompatible with the perfection and oneness of godhead.

The subject of the Incarnation roused Ramabai to new heights of theological argumentativeness. Whereas she was incredulous about the Trinity because the concept

of three deities made Christianity no different from Hinduism, discussions of the
Incarnation left her much more defensive about Hinduism. One might even say she was
perverse in her defence, since her reason for wishing to leave Hinduism was precisely its
free mixing of human and divine attributes. Earlier, she had expressed great doubts in
believing that the boundless and pure essence of godhead could ever be limited or mixed
with the impurities of the lower human nature, though it may be everywhere and remain
boundless and pure in every limited thing.[45] Her dissatisfaction with Hinduism sprang
from its erratic combinations of divine and human elements. But Christianity fared
no better in her analysis, and she mercilessly lampooned some of its more salient
contradictions. For instance, if the traditional Christian objection to Hinduism lay in
the latter's conception of God as alternatively incarnate (that is, many persons) *and*
One, Christianity itself could not claim to be exempt from the same tendency. 'If Christian teachers laugh at the Hindoos because they want to reconcile these two opposite
natures, on what ground, may I ask, they can establish their doctrine . . . that Jesus
Christ although omnipotent and omniscient emptied himself for a time of his
qualities[?]'[46] Needless to say, her conclusion that no religion could base its theology on
the Incarnation did not win much favour with the missionary sisters.

To Ramabai, the intermixture of human and divine was not merely a problem of
substance; it had as much to do with the capacity to distinguish good from evil. In fact,
Ramabai disparaged discussions of the Trinity in terms of substance alone by showing
how foolish Hinduism had been made to appear because substance overtakes morality,
as when incarnation is described as air filling up different rooms, 'so the three persons
being one fill three persons, yet they are one [like] air, and that at last these different
vessels or bodies will be broken up and the whole essence of God will be again united.'[47]
If Hinduism was pilloried for treating deity as substance, neither could Trinitarianism
be exempt from the same charge, and Ramabai mercilessly applied what appeared to the
sisters as cold logic to dismantle their arguments.

Similarly, if human birth is irreconcilable with unchanging essence, so too is the
narration of national history with the scheme of spiritual redemption. Indisputably, no
point of doctrine in Christianity has created more problems for narrative than the
Incarnation, which symbolizes the uneven, discontinuous relationship between human
history and scriptural revelation. When Ramabai asks, 'How could Christ be called the
offspring of David if He had not a human father', her question not only voices scepticism about the coexistence of opposites in the figure of Christ, but it also interrogates
the construction of universal religion as a counterpart to national hagiography.[48]
Ramabai's insistence on the exceptionalism of human birth also emphasizes the parti-
cularism of national history, and resists all attempts to accept the birth of Christ as
simultaneously signalling the rise of a new nation.

Despite the missionaries' obvious outrage at Ramabai's persistent questions, it is
partly out of a sense that she would be useful to her people only when she was able to
discuss Christianity dispassionately as one among many other religious systems that led
Dorothy Beale to advise Sister Geraldine that

> she must study Christianity as a philosophy. She cannot receive it merely as an historical
> revelation, it must also commend itself to her conscience. *We say* (who are brought up as
> Christians),—'Such things *were* and they reveal to us such and such truths.' She *can* only

say, 'Such and such things are metaphysical necessities, therefore I am ready to receive evidence.' And it was thus that St. Paul often spoke to the Greek-thinking converts. 'It was *necessary*, is common in his mouth; and so our Lord spoke to His disciples.'[49]

The sisters rationalize Ramabai's resistance to the Trinity as in fact a healthy sign of her determination to distinguish all aspects of Hinduism from her faith. Yet, although the missionaries recognized that Ramabai's Unitarianism was logically the only way she could justify leaving Hinduism, the fact remained that it brought her simultaneously to the brink of heresy. The sisters were caught in a position where they wished Ramabai at once to think and *not* think like themselves.

Ramabai's objections to praying in the name of Jesus Christ were not only on the grounds that Trinitarian worship blurred the divide between human and divine. Her reluctance must also be linked to her acute awareness that the ascription of full deity to Christ meant the exclusion of Jews from the community of Christ. Her opposition to the exclusionary character of Trinitarianism mounted with Sister Geraldine's declaration that 'the Apostles distinguished the faithful from Infidels and Jews in that the former called on the name of the Lord Jesus Christ'.[50] 'In the name of Christ' functions, for Ramabai, as a cue for a politics of exclusion that England had come to symbolize. Although Ramabai's own probings into the fabric of English social life led her to recognize the plurality of England—that there existed, besides Anglican believers, a whole host of other religious communities including Jews, Dissenters, Methodists, Wesleyans, and Nonconformists—she was also made fully aware that such central pillars of the Anglican church as the Athanasian Creed and swearing by the Thirty-Nine Articles historically denied an inclusive role to these other groups. Under the cloak of heresy, non-Anglican groups had for long been deprived of citizenship rights.

Early in Sister Geraldine's text we are told that Ramabai was 'dangerously inflated by her getting hold of points of controversy from her non-Conformist friends and dragging them clumsily and offensively into her letters'.[51] These friends are not named, but elsewhere Geraldine reveals that Ramabai's reading includes a great deal of 'popular religious literature' from which she derived ideas deemed to be distortions of Christian doctrine, though it was also the case that some of these ideas were no more palatable to Ramabai than they were to the missionaries. At other times, the sisters would not even countenance the fact that Ramabai's inquiry extended into some of the leading heresies of English history, and they obstinately concluded that her questions must come 'from a *native* source'.[52] This directly contradicts their earlier perception that she had derived 'heretical' ideas from English popular pamphlet literature. Significantly, Ramabai's reading indicates her interest in a comparative perspective between and within religions, particularly in those books that compare 'Heathen philosophy' with Christianity. We learn, for instance, that she had bought *History of Different Sects in India* 'by an Indian gentleman and also Max Müller's "Biographical Essay" '.[53]

Ramabai's intellectual interest in, if not close identification with, a mass-based religious ideology contained in English popular pamphlet literature curiously links her spiritual probings with the religious dissensions of English working-class radicalism. We do not know the full extent of Ramabai's acquaintance with English Nonconformity, especially in its lower-class expression, but her marked interest in the forms of religious controversy that were most specifically coming from the English working classes is not easily reconcilable with standard interpretations of Ramabai as an elitist, upper-caste Brahmin woman who had little interest in or contact with lower-class movements in India.[54] How then does one explain the uneven pattern of her class consciousness? Was her inability to connect with movements across class and caste in India—with non-elite women, shudras, and other low-caste groups—a product of her own Sanskritic, Dharmashastric background, a background that she was never able to surmount despite her Christian conversion? By the same token, did her conversion to Christianity open up a transnational space of identification that was impossible within the more narrowly defined caste structure of India? Could Ramabai, a high-caste Brahmin woman, indeed find unlikely points of contact with English working-class radicalism through her conversion?

A starting point for answering these questions is the course of English sectarianism as a whole and its relation to Ramabai's discovery of English Nonconformity. The decline of the established churches by the middle of the nineteenth century saw a new polarization developing in English religious life. On the one hand, there was renewed interest in established religion among the upper classes, particularly among conservatives who sought to remobilize the well-entrenched system of established churches to preserve a paternalistic, hierarchical society. On the other hand, the conservatism that favoured maintaining the status quo was countered by movements for political reform, which saw in the proliferation of new religious sects and ideologies the opportunity for conveying new ideas of political change. The dissenting churches were among the most significant institutions in nineteenth-century British society, partly because they revived the hopes of those who believed the collapse of the French monarchy and the weakened power of the papacy augured a new era of equality and social justice.

Theological controversy may have deepened the divide within the established church, but it also opened up a much more heterogeneous set of religious ideas. For instance, the 1790s saw a great acceleration in the growth of Nonconformist religion. In a society where theological controversy provoked widespread engagement, the range of religious options to choose from was reflected in a bewildering array of descriptive labels, which signified hairsplittingly different doctrines and believers such as Calvinist, Arminian, Socinian, Anabaptist, Baptist, Paedobaptist and the like. These tags of religious identification were seen by many in England as reflecting fundamental choices, and the definitions played an important part in the way the key players saw themselves and others. As a number of historians of English religion have pointed out, the structure of English society was such that sectarian identity influenced most areas of life; even those least interested in religion found that there were occasions when such an identity was forced upon them.[55]

If it was customary in nineteenth-century English discourse to place colonial subjects in the same frame of reference that included England's working classes, it is equally the case that resistance to the rule of empire by colonized peoples evoked comparisons to another oppositional group internal to England: the heterogeneous group of religious dissenters, atheists and sectaries. The effect of such comparisons was to revive memories of an odious history of rank divisiveness in England's past. The bloody battles between Catholics and Protestants, and the subsequent fracturing of these two main groups and the proliferation of various subsects, remained too vividly etched in the English national consciousness for the questionings of a young native convert like Pandita Ramabai to go unnoticed. For her spiritual probings had the effect of recalling England's highly divisive past and threatening the return of the suppressed memory of fissures in English religious history. The sisters' grave apprehensions about Ramabai's questioning are due in part to the fact that she was beginning to learn about sectarian differences in English history, for these differences provide the various subject-positions from which Ramabai launches her critique of Anglicanism. At various points in their often virulent correspondence the Wantage sisters describe Ramabai successively as a Wesleyan, a Nonconformist, an Anabaptist, and an English Dissenter. Interpellated in these terms, Ramabai is identified with sectarian tendencies in England and charged with the crime of repeating, through her questioning, the violent schisms that tore England apart in earlier times.

Not only did the English missionaries seek to present a unified version of Christianity but they also fiercely resisted Ramabai's inquiry into sectarian differences—an inquiry that culminated in her realization that she had a choice in the precise form of the Christianity she embraced. Ironically, Ramabai's recognition of the splintered, sectarian history of English Christianity brought her to the insight that the existence of religious differences creates the option of choosing a particular idea of religion in which to believe. Ramabai commented disparagingly that 'missionaries who want to convert the Hindoos to their own religion would do well to take care not to call themselves the only inheritors of truth, and all others "the so-called false philosophers", for the Hindoos as a rule will not be content to look or hear only one side'.[56] Such a sense of choice radically transformed her prospective identity as a convert into that of a heretic.

This leads one to surmise that Ramabai's modernity derives less from her repudiation of Hindu tradition than from her embrace of an ideology of free will and choice. Ramabai's understanding of religious choice as a byproduct of English sectarianism suggests a line of thought that allows one to rethink the conventional polarization between tradition and modernity. As the details of Ramabai's conversion emerge more precisely, we learn that the proliferation of sects in English religious history impressed itself on her imagination in intellectually enabling ways. As Ramabai engaged in an animated exchange with her English sponsors, she began to see that there existed a fractured Christianity which the missionaries, for their part, were trying to present as an undivided religion identical with Anglican England. Hence, their unusual description of the Anglican church as Catholic Christianity, 'the holy, apostolic Christianity', which Ramabai learned was a misnomer only long after she had parted company with the missionaries. Remarked an amused but also bemused Ramabai in 1886, 'The Roman Catholics say the Protestant interpretation (including the English Church) of the word "Catholic" is purely imaginary'; she then taunted Geraldine by sarcastically pointing out that 'she had no right to call the Dissenters heretics, because she herself belonged to a Church which is but a Dissenting sect of the Roman Catholic'.[57]

Recent scholars have drawn attention to the crucial role of choice in distinguishing conditions of modernity from those of premodernity. Christopher Queen describes the exercise of individual choice based on reason, careful deliberation and historical consciousness as defining characteristics of modernity. If modernity comprises a complex range of ideas, philosophies and systems, the ability to process them calls for not only reason to make the requisite discriminations between them but also the skill to evaluate the quality of their respective demands on one's attention. Such evaluation is itself a form of choice, but the important point is that choice is possible only when the heterogeneity of belief-systems is made visible. Such acts of conscious selection account for new types of conversion narratives, which reflect the individual subject's greater access to a range of traditions, ideas and doctrines.[58] In this context, the more empowering aspects of English sectarianism for a young convert like Ramabai take on new meaning, for religious choice is as much a part of the logic of modernity as an increasingly differentiated individual subjectivity. If Ramabai is repeatedly accused of indiscriminately exercising reason in areas where faith took precedence, in her defence it would have to be said that the varieties of Christianity practised historically in England required that she respond not with faith but with reason—that is, with the mental acuity to respond to minute distinctions between creeds, as well as the judgement to assess their relative importance within their respective branches of Christianity.

As Ramabai progressively moves towards defining her idea of religion from the sectarian options offered by English Christianity, her own status as a convert undergoes radical change. Sister Geraldine's description of English dissent emphasizes the dilution of religious truth as a product of rank sectarianism. In her earnest yet anxious correspondence with Ramabai she attempts to persuade the impressionable young Indian convert that the Anglican church represents a healthy syncretism, in sharp contrast to the dogmatism of individual sects:

> Since [Wesleyanism] sprang into existence it had split up into 80 different sects drifting farther away from the Truth [which] shewed that their original separation from the Church was in itself a wrong act. This led to a conversation on dissent generally . . . *that all dissent was the undue stretching-out of one doctrine so as to hide or overshadow the other doctrines of the Christian Faith.* I said that in the Church's teaching, a perfect harmony was kept between all the dogmas of the Christian Faith: each had its due value given and helped to form a perfect texture; whereas in dissent an undue importance being given to one doctrine, the symmetry of the whole was marred.[59]

Geraldine's account of Anglicanism is nothing short of an aesthetic description of religious utility. If dissent signifies the attenuation of truth by competing hegemonies, which assert the dominance of one doctrine above all others, then Anglican orthodoxy represents that essential syncretism by which all creeds are kept in perfect aesthetic balance. Anglicanism does so not by manifesting a plurality of difference but by merging into oneness. Not entirely dissimilar to the Arnoldian idea of culture as a containment of disparate forces by filtering the 'best that is thought and known', Geraldine's aestheticized religious ideal explains why sectarianism is as disruptive to the perfect balance represented by Anglican England as working-class anarchy is to English culture.

Silence and Heresy

'The silence of a thousand years has been broken, and the reader of this unpretending little volume catches the first utterances of the unfamiliar voice. Throbbing with woe, they are revealed in the following pages to intelligent, educated, happy American women.'[60] These are the words of Rachel Bodley, dean of the Women's Medical College in Philadelphia, as she introduced Pandita Ramabai to the Western world. These resonant words open Bodley's preface to Pandita Ramabai's hugely successful book, *The*

High-Caste Hindu Woman (1888), and establish the terms for the evaluation of Indian women's emancipation as emergence into 'utterance'.

If Ramabai is known at all in the West, it is precisely because she heralded a new, yet unknown voice whose calm, dispassionate presentation of a patriarchal religion from a female point of view ruptured the Orientalist celebration of Eastern philosophy as a repository of sublime mysteries. Rachel Bodley's account locates the hitherto suppressed narrative of the Hindu woman within a continuum of silence that it was Ramabai's particular achievement to disrupt. If Ramabai is remembered as a Hindu social reformer of great note, her outspokenness about the conditions of women's oppression stands out above all other characterizations of her social activism. Her access to public forums such as the print media and the lecture platform allowed her to make the necessary interventions that gained a 'hearing' for her 'voice'. Thus, according to Bodley's rhetorical stance, it stands to reason that if silence is oppression, then speech is liberation.

Yet the fearless Ramabai also confessed that she 'was obliged to keep silence', especially on the subject of church doctrine.[61] This is a strange admission, given that *The Letters and Correspondence of Pandita Ramabai* leaves no doubt in any reader's mind that Ramabai was not one to suppress her scepticism about received notions of religious faith, nor refuse engagement in the most forthright manner with ideas that she found unacceptable. Indeed, thus far I have been arguing just the reverse: that Ramabai declined to accept Christian faith as a given, especially on other people's terms, and was willing to carry on her quarrels with received notions right up to the highest authorities in the Anglican church.

Why then did she resolve on numerous occasions to 'hold my tongue . . . and not say one single word' but 'read the Bible by myself, and follow the teaching of Christ?'[62] Is her withdrawal into silence a surrender to the impossibility of free intellectual debate on questions of religious worship? Or rather does her preferred choice of following Christ's teachings reflect a growing Pauline inclination to replace scriptural exegesis with the practice of private faith? But does that then suggest Ramabai's retreat into spiritual isolation, producing a rhetoric of self-fashioning of the sort that characterizes John Henry Newman's final conversion as an intensely private experience, contrary to the worldliness of his engagement with belief? As we observed earlier about Newman's conversion, his antipathy to large-scale dissemination of convictions arrived at through a laborious process of intellectual dissent grew out of a sense that the compulsion to proselytize masked an intellectual anxiety about the durability of hard-won convictions. Hence his willingness to slip into silence, or what he calls a 'state of repose . . . a tranquil enjoyment of ceritude.'[63] Does Ramabai's retreat into silence signify a comparable withdrawal into the self-enclosed world of private experience?

First, the pattern of Ramabai's silences reveals a curious feature. She claims that she ceases to argue further on doctrinal issues whenever she feels the futility of doing so, especially when she is misunderstood by the missionaries or accused of being difficult and proud: 'I see I cannot make you understand what I mean, nor can you make me believe in all your doctrines exactly as you believe in them.'[64] Ramabai is told in no uncertain terms that her heresy must remain unspoken, or otherwise it will result in the sisters' severing of their relation to her ('I feel my duties as your teacher are now at an end,' cautions Sister Geraldine ominously).[65] Yet while Ramabai recedes into silence on crucial theological points, she continues her resistance to missionaries on other fronts.

Disarmed by the charge of sinful pride in her theological quarrels with the missionaries, who equate her speech with wilfulness and thus effectively muffle her probings into religious questions, Ramabai's alternative method of expressing her disagreement with official interpretation is to 'talk back' to the sisters, angrily challenging them in their control of her and in the matter of her daughter's religious up-bringing. As an expression of colonial insubordination, the petulance and shrillness of her retorts displace blasphemy as an offence against religious doctrine and sentiment. Even when she is evidently impugning prevailing creeds, her 'heresy' takes the form of a stern tongue-lashing:

> Am I to submit to this kind of teaching? Am I to submit to the teaching of the clergy like Canon Butler, who denies that I have a voice in choosing my own religion, or to you who say that my conscience is no conscience at all and who say that outside your Church no truth can be bound, and if I tolerate with all the bodies of Christian people, I cannot be truthful? . . You or rather some of the clergy of your church think that they could make many converts to their faith in India by telling them the Anglican Church only teaches the true religion, but I think it otherwise.[66]

This passage nicely illustrates the thin line separating heresy—as an offence against orthodox doctrine—from rank verbal assault ranging from sheer impertinence to outright insubordination. The most striking quality of Ramabai's alternating silence and speech is her uncanny ability to mix intellectual interrogation with insolence, as she strategically blurs the boundaries between the two and shifts the focus of her transgression from heresy to effrontery. In the above passage, for instance, it is significant that nowhere does she attack points of doctrine; there is no engagement with ideas—only retort, condescension and retaliation. Similarly, ordering Sister Geraldine to desist from teaching her daughter Manorama the rudiments of Trinitarian belief, including the Athanasian Creed and the Thirty-Nine Articles, Ramabai's rebuke is more noticeable for its sharply reprimanding tone than for an analytical objection to Trinitarianism. If Ramabai is disarmed by the charge of pride, she in turn immobilizes the missionaries by the grating vehemence of her response.

Because the severity of Ramabai's tone conveys the uneven quality of a relationship presumed to be built on pedagogical trust but now exposed as paternalistic in fact, the missionaries are unable to reduce her recalcitrant posture to pride alone. Indeed, Ramabai's tone creates a context for her challenge of church doctrine—a context that includes the colonial conversion of subject peoples, the imposition of a religious creed which is interchangeable with imperialist hegemony, and the whole structure of unequal relationships that these presuppose. Her 'heresy' is transformed from a repudiation of specific points of doctrine into a sharp questioning of the rationale of colonial expropriation, culminating in an unequivocal denunciation of the arbitrary imposition of one people's will on others.

The missionaries' attempt to control Ramabai by curbing her speech is consistent with what Gyan Prakash has described as a general colonial attempt to normalize what cannot be named or recognized—in this case, her intellectual independence and spiritual integrity.[67] Ramabai was fully aware of the terror and fear that filled the missionaries in the face of her transgression's unnameability. That is why she could scornfully rebuke them for making 'the word "pride" almost meaningless by applying it to everything that you see in me'.[68] And there was a certain truth in her accusation, for vastly conflicting kinds of verbal behaviour—be it a lack of communication or persistent questioning—were all attributed to the same cause; pride assumed an explanatory power that far exceeded the behaviour that it putatively described. Apparently for missionaries and colonial officers alike, it was much easier to deal with their native subjects' outright rebellion and even 'heathenish' superstition than with Indians' rewriting of Christianity to suit their own purposes. What were administrators and missionaries to do when subjects claimed belief as entitling them to independent judgement? As an unmanageable part of colonial rule, belief was resistant to the space that was sought for it in programmes of governance and reform. Indeed, colonial manipulations were actually far more successful in creating a space for English culture than in regulating belief. The successful introduction of English literature is a case in point.[69]

Yet it is also the case that Ramabai oftens turns to silence as a form of resistance to doctrinal coercion. Silence in such instances is preparatory to the private interpretation that made her so subversive in missionaries' eyes. The missionaries in their turn read this as evidence of her 'alienation from her friends'—in other words, as conclusive proof of her ever-present, errant pride distancing her further and further from divine mercy. And so the circle of accusation continues. Given that it was unlikely Ramabai would easily change her mind about central doctrinal points, how could she be brought to a situation where she would refrain from uttering views that the church declared to be heresies, yet at the same time not withdraw into a silence that had equally heretical outcomes?

Indeed, the missionaries' dilemma centred around the complex, even contradictory function of silence. In her refusal to speak, Ramabai was as transgressive as when she committed herself to speech. For as Dorothea Beale, principal of Cheltenham Ladies College where Ramabai was a student and instructor, confides in a private letter to Sister Geraldine, 'If she does not find someone to whom she can speak freely, she will be silent, and might easily pass into Unitarianism.'[70] The relation between silence and heresy is clearly more complex than can be understood by descriptions of heresy hunting as a matter of policing by silencing alone. As the last-quoted remark makes clear, complete suppression of speech is no more effective in stemming the tide towards heterodoxy than the threat of punishment or ostracism from community. Though curbs may be effectively placed on speech to prevent unacceptable utterances, the ferment from which those utterances are produced remains unchecked. Therefore, speech must be allowed, but only in such ways that its influence will be confined to a carefully circumscribed space and not extend beyond it.

It is of no small significance that the limited space offered to Ramabai for voicing her religious doubts is that of an enlightened but enclosed community of women. The sisters' repeated declaration that Ramabai could not speak to a man about certain religious subjects—'there are some subjects that she could only discuss with a woman'—offers the construction of a feminist community as a counterpoint to existing barriers in social interaction between men and women.[71] Sister Geraldine's assurance that 'to a woman she can speak on the Incarnation as she could not to a man' discovers in the confessor relationship not only a practice for maintaining institutional authority but also a convention for forging sisterly bonds.[72] The conditions for the possibility of speech have a gendered aspect that merges with the boundaries of acceptable theological doctrine. For, of course, the missionaries' refashioning of community is not aimed at establishing sisterhood but, instead, at containing heresy. The feminist bonding offered by the Wantage order leaves intact the structure of patriarchal authority derived from church tradition, even as it encourages the new convert to enact her heresies on a stage especially constructed for her via feminism. The difference, of course, is that on this particular stage Ramabai's heresies will be restrained and rendered harmless, even though they are articulated freely as sisterly communication.

Yet here too the missionaries failed to meet their objectives entirely. Though the sisters assumed that the inhibitions a woman might be expected to feel about discussing the virgin birth would be naturally applicable to Ramabai, a Hindu widow, they were not prepared for her obstinate refusal to avoid questions about immaculate conception, nor did they have a ready answer to her blunt remark that 'as far as we know of the history of mankind told in the Scripture, and from other sources, as well as by our experience, we know that no man except the first couple was ever born without the natural course'.[73] Amid these scattered remarks is a refusal by Ramabai to accept a community of women as her sole interlocutors in theological debate.

Nowhere is this refusal more apparent than in her translation of 'conversion' into the sphere of gender relations. Of her many actions that so chagrined her mentors, none was as aggravating as her insistence on teaching English to both men and women. Other teachers attached to the Wantage order were known to instruct men at the Working Men's College, so her request was not an unusual one. Yet the alarm bells that it set off exposed the Orientalist assumptions about Hindu women that still guided missionary policy. In her caustic response to Sister Geraldine's disapproving letters, Ramabai reminds her that in the course of their numerous pilgrimages she and her brother habitually addressed communities of male scholars, as a result of which she earned the title of Saraswati, or goddess of learning.

> It surprises me very much to think that neither my father nor my husband objected [to] my mother's or my teaching young men while some English people are doing so. You can call some of my countrywomen 'hedged' but you cannot apply this adjective to Marathi Brahmin women. You have yourself seen that Marathi ladies are neither hedged nor kept behind thick curtains. . . . Can I confine my work only to women in India and have nothing to do with men?[74]

When reprimanded that it was indelicate of her—a Hindu widow—to teach men or visit 'gentlemen friends', especially given her own orthodox background, Ramabai rebuts with one of the most sustained anti-Orientalist diatribes in nineteenth-century letters. Simultaneously, she punctures almost all the cherished notions of women's reform held by English missionaries and claims a more privileged status as a Hindu woman by virtue of exposure to indigenous reform movements (like the Brahmo Samaj). Is this backsliding or sheer perversity? That question worries the missionaries, and Ramabai's determination to set her own agenda for women's reform coalesces into the 'objectives': 'Unless I begin to have a regular and pure intercourse with men, I shall in vain hope and try to help my countrywomen.'[75] For the feminist community proposed by Sister Geraldine is akin to the secluded *purdahnasheen*, zenana-style arrangement from which Ramabai and other Indian women had determined to emerge. By the time Geraldine perceives that the source of Ramabai's vehemence is a retrograde feature of caste society missionaries had long sought to remedy, Geraldine realizes she has no choice but to permit the transgressions that her attempt at forging sisterly bonds sought to contain.

I see now why she makes this a matter of principle. I think we must remember that God seems to have anointed her with power to throw down the pernicious caste restrictions and those barriers which wrongly separate men and women. In this she has worked with all whom God set over her—father, mother, brother, husband. She would feel herself disloyal to their memory, who approved of her (a young girl) speaking in mixed assemblies if she gave in to any rules which said a woman should not teach boys. . . . It seems to me a matter in which we ought not to bind her conscience.[76]

Producing inevitable conflict and ambivalence in the Wantage sisters' dealings with Ramabai is their representation of England as at once a desirable symbol of modernity and a source of corruption. Although the learning contained in Western knowledge has the power to dispel Hindu superstition, the sisters fear that it also fosters a superciliousness taking the form of either self-estrangement or a false sense of independence.[77] Either way, separation from earlier patterns of understanding and behaviour complements the alienation brought about by Ramabai's loosening of ties to family and community. If the missionaries object to the self-sufficiency of Ramabai's posture, they cannot help concluding that English education contributed in no small way to it. Ramabai recognizes the inherent contradiction in such a representation and, in her counterattack, forces the missionaries to peer into the mirror of modernity as the source of human depravity, displacing biblical explanations of depravity as the result of original sin. When challenged by the sisters who trace Ramabai's and other colonized Indians' arrogance to the detrimental effects of Western education, Ramabai turns the customary missionary explanations of human pride and sinfulness adroitly against them: 'I believe it is not learning or wisdom that makes people either proud or idle. It is their own nature that makes them so.'[78] Ironically, Sister Geraldine's ponderous words on Ramabai's proud nature return to haunt the nervous missionary, and it is Ramabai who, in deflecting them back towards her, has the decisive word on the subject.

Notes

1. A.B. Shah, ed., introduction to *The Letters and Correspondence of Pandita Ramabai* (Bombay: Maharashtra State Board for Literature and Culture, 1977), p. xi. Hereafter cited as *Correspondence*.
2. Letter from Pandita Ramabai, Poona, to Sister Geraldine, C.S.M.V., Wantage, 11 December 1893, in *Correspondence*.
3. In *Home and Harem: Nation, Gender, Empire, and the Cultures of Travel* (Durham: Duke University Press, 1966), Inderpal Grewal points out the difficulties of positioning Ramabai within the critiques of Hindu patriarchy, since this discourse was also deployed by English missionaries to achieve their own aim of Christian conversion (p. 180). Arguing that there were no 'neutral spaces' for articulating the problems and oppressions of Hindu women, Grewal maintains that Ramabai's genius lay in appropriating the rhetoric of the colonial state and missionaries to construct her own independent agency. Much the same is argued by Antoinette Burton in *Burdens of History: British Feminists, Indian Women, and Imperial Culture, 1885–1915* (Chapel Hill: University of North Carolina Press, 1994): resistance to the imperialist gestures of British women, she maintains, spurred Ramabai to an acute self-consciousness (p. 32). Teresa Hubel, in *Whose India? The Independence Struggle in British and Indian Fiction and History* (Durham: Duke University Press, 1996), also conjoins Ramabai's critique of imperialism and Hindu patriarchy. My own argument has a considerably different focus, for my suggestion is that Ramabai's agency is constitutive of her developing religious sensibility, and not a mere strategy appropriated from her colonial mentors. Her critiques of colonialism not only aimed

to dismantle Hindu patriarchy but also served to create her own ideal religious system in which her critical sensibility remained intact.

4. Pandita Ramabai, *The High-Caste Hindu Woman* (Philadelphia: Press of the J.B. Rogers Printing, 1988), p. 103. See also Meera Kosambi, 'Women, Emancipation, and Equality: Pandita Ramabai's Contribution to Women's Cause', *Economic and Political Weekly*, 29 October 1988: WS38–WS49, for a thorough treatment of Ramabai's social activism.

5. Quoted in S.M. Adhav, *Pandita Ramabai* (Madras: Christian Literature Society, 1979), p. 15. It is interesting that four decades earlier, in 1841, John Henry Newman made the argument that a completely Protestant document like the Thirty-Nine Articles still made room for the English clergy to accept their vocation on the authority of the Church of Rome. In denying the exclusionary intents of the articles, Newman made the claim that the interpretive possibilities of the document allowed for its being brought in harmony with the Book of Common Prayer. 'The Protestant Confession was drawn up with the purpose of including Catholics; and Catholics now will not be excluded. What was an economy in the reformers, is a protection to us. What would have been a perplexity to us then, is a perplexity to Protestants now. We could not then have found fault with their words; they cannot now repudiate our meaning.' John Henry Newman, 'Remarks on Certain Passages in the Thirty-Nine Articles', in *Religion in Victorian Britain: Sources*, vol. 3, edited by James R. Moore (Manchester: Manchester University Press, 1988), p. 13.

6. Letter from Pandita Ramabai to Sister Geraldine, 22 September 1885, in *Correspondence*, p. 88.

7. Letter from Sister Geraldine to Pandita Ramabai, October 1885, in *Correspondence*, p. 104.

8. E.P. Thompson, *Witness against the Beast: William Blake and the Moral Law* (Cambridge: Cambridge University Press, 1993), p. 10.

9. Letter from Sister Geraldine to Pandita Ramabai, October 1885, in *Correspondence*, p. 103.

10. Letter from Sister Geraldine to Pandita Ramabai, in answer to objections she made to the Catholic faith, 5 October 1885, in *Correspondence*, p. 91.

11. Letter from Pandita Ramabai to Sister Geraldine, 12 May 1885, in *Correspondence*, p. 61.

12. Letter from Pandita Ramabai to Canon Butler, 3 July 1885, in *Correspondence*, p. 74.

13. See letter from Sister Geraldine, in Wantage, to Pandita Ramabai, in Poona, 14 December 1896, in *Correspondence*, p. 339: 'It is that I *hold* the Faith which the Church has taught for nearly nineteen centuries, and *you choose* for yourself a spurious production: that *I have been willing to learn from the Church*, and you are unwilling to "hear the Church". And our Lord says of such: "If any man neglect to hear the Church, let him be unto thee as a heathen man and a publican." ' Emphasis in original.

14. Letter from the Rev. Mother, C.S.M.V. to an Exterior Sister, C.S.M.V., 1 November 1883, in *Correspondence*, p. 20.

15. Letter from Sister Geraldine, Wantage, to Pandita Ramabai, Cheltenham, 10 May 1883, in *Correspondence*, p. 53.

16. Letter from Pandita Ramabai, Cheltenham, to Sister Geraldine, Wantage, 12 May 1885, in *Correspondence*, p. 59.

17. Letter from Dorothea Beale, Cheltenham, to Sister Geraldine, Wantage, 8 May 1885, in *Correspondence*, p. 49.

18. Pandita Ramabai, *My Testimony* (1907: 10th ed. Kedgaon: Ramabai Mukti Mission, 1977), p. 17; quoted in Meera Kosambi, 'Indian Response to Christianity. Church and Colonialism: Case of Pandita Ramabai', *Economic and Political Weekly*, 24 October 1992, p. WS-62.

19. Ibid.

20. Letter from the Rev. Mother, C.S.M.V., to an Exterior Sister, C.S.M.V., 1 November 1883, in *Correspondence*, p. 19.

21. Ram Bapat, 'Pandita Ramabai: Faith and Reason in the Shadow of the East and West', in *Representing Hinduism: The Construction of Religious Tradition and National Identity*, edited by Vasudha Dalmia and H. von Stietencron (Delhi: Sage Publications, 1995), p. 226.

22. Pandita Ramabai, *My Testimony*, pp. 18–20; quoted in ibid., p. 227.

23. Bapat, 'Pandita Ramabai', p. 228.
24. Ramabai, *My Testimony*; quoted in Bapat, p. 227.
25. Bapat, 'Pandita Ramabai', p. 227.
26. Letter from Dorothea Beale to the Bishop of Bombay in England, 22 May 1884, in *Correspondence*, p. 42.
27. Letter from Sister Geraldine, London, to Dorothea Beale, Cheltenham, January 1886, in *Correspondence*, p. 114.
28. Letter from Pandita Ramabai, Cheltenham, to Sister Geraldine, Wantage, 12 May 1885, in *Correspondence*, p. 59.
29. Letter from Sister Geraldine, Wantage, to Pandita Ramabai, Cheltenham, 19 May 1885, in *Correspondence*, p. 53.
30. Letter from Pandita Ramabai, U.S.A., to Dorothea Beale, Cheltenham, 22 May 1887, in *Correspondence*, p. 176. Emphasis added.
31. Letter from Pandita Ramabai, Cheltenham, to Canon Butler, Wantage, 3 July 1885, in *Correspondence*, p. 74. A Sanskrit and Marathi scholar, Father Nehemiah Goreh (Nilakanta Shastri) was, like Ramabai, a Chitpavan Brahmin who converted to Christianity. Ramabai had occasion to know him in Poona in the years prior to her departure for England. She often claimed that he was one of the few people to whom she could confide her religious doubts and questions; while in England, she frequently corresponded with him for clarification about points of Christian doctrine.
32. Sister Geraldine, 'Apologia Pro Opere' (1917), in *Correspondence*, p. 3.
33. Letter from Pandita Ramabai, Cheltenham, to Sister Geraldine, Wantage, 7 November 1885, in *Correspondence*, p. 112.
34. Letter from Pandita Ramabai to Sister Geraldine, July 1884, in *Correspondence*, p. 25.
35. Sister Geraldine, 'Apologia Pro Opere', in *Correspondence*, p. 4.
36. Letter from Pandita Ramabai to Dorothea Beale, 21 June 1885, in *Correspondence*, p. 157.
37. Letter from Pandita Ramabai to Sister Geraldine, 20 September 1885, in *Correspondence* p. 86.
38. Letter from Sister Geraldine to the Dean of Lincoln, 1 July 1885, in *Correspondence*, p. 71.
39. Letter from Pandita Ramabai to Sister Geraldine, 20 September 1885, in *Correspondence*, p. 87.
40. Shah, introduction to *Correspondence*, p. xxxiii.
41. David Lawton, *Blasphemy* (Philadelphia: University of Pennsylvania Press, 1993), p. 126.
42. Ibid.
43. Letter from Dorothea Beale to the Rev. Canon William Butler, Wantage, July 1885, in *Correspondence*, p. 78.
44. Letter from Pandita Ramabai to Sister Geraldine, June 1885, in *Correspondence*, p. 70.
45. Letter from Pandita Ramabai to Dorothea Beale, 1 September 1885, in *Correspondence*, p. 136.
46. Letter from Pandita Ramabai to Dorothea Beale, 30 June 1885, in *Correspondence*, p. 128.
47. Ibid.
48. Letter from Pandita Ramabai to Dorothea Beale, 29 November 1885, in *Correspondence*, p. 160.
49. Letter from Dorothea Beale to Sister Geraldine—Proposal for Ramabai to leave at midsummer, 22 April 1885, in *Correspondence*, p. 32. Emphasis in original.
50. Letter from Sister Geraldine to Pandita Ramabai, October 1855, in *Correspondence*, p. 96.
51. Sister Geraldine, 'Apologia Pro Opera', in *Correspondence*, p. 4.
52. Letter from Dorothea Beale to the Rev. Canon William Butler, Wantage, July 1885, in *Correspondence*, p. 79. Emphasis in original.
53. Letter from Pandita Ramabai to Sister Geraldine, 25 March 1885, in *Correspondence*, p. 37. Ramabai came to know Max Müller quite well when she was in England, and was invited to visit his home at Oxford, where he was then a professor of comparative philology. Though he admired her vast learning in Sanskrit and Hinduism, he deplored her Christian conversion, writing in an 1895 letter from Oxford: 'What I feared when Ramabai became a Christian, has happened: She has impaired her power of doing useful work among her countrymen. Her native friends do not quite trust her, her European friends do not always remember what they owe to

her. In all essentials, Ramabai had been a Christian even while she was still a Brahmin; and when she openly professed herself a Christian, it was because she felt the necessity of belonging to some communion, to be one with her friends. . . . I did not persuade Ramabai to become a Christian, because I know she *was* a Christian in heart, which is far better than a Christian by profession'. Quoted in Adhav, *Pandita Ramabai*, p. 12.

54. Bapat, 'Pandita Ramabai', p. 227.

55. Hugh McLeod, *Religion and the Working Class in Nineteenth-Century Britain* (London: Macmillan, 1984), p. 36.

56. Letter of Pandita Ramabai to Dorothea Beale, February–March 1886, in *Correspondence*, p. 170.

57. Ibid.

58. See, for instance, Christopher Queen, 'Ambedkar, Modernity, and the Hermeneutics of Buddhist Liberation', in *Dr Ambedkar, Buddhism and Social Change*, edited by A.K. Narain and D.C. Ahir (Delhi: B.R. Publishing, 1994).

59. Letter from Sister Geraldine, Bath, to Pandita Ramabai, October 1885, in *Correspondence*, p. 102. Emphasis added.

60. Rachel Bodley, introduction to *The High-Caste Hindu Woman*, p. i.

61. Letter from Pandita Ramabai, Cheltenham, to Canon Butler, Wantage, 3 July 1885, in *Correspondence*, p. 74.

62. Ibid. p. 76.

63. John Henry Newman, *An Essay in Aid of a Grammar of Assent* (Notre Dame: University of Notre Dame Press, 1979), p. 166.

64. Letter from Pandita Ramabai to Sister Geraldine, 15 October 1885, p. 107.

65. Letter from Sister Geraldine, at Bath, to Pandita Ramabai, October 1885, in *Correspondence*, p. 106.

66. Letter from Pandita Ramabai to Sister Geraldine, 7 November 1885, in *Correspondence*, p. 112.

67. Gyan Prakash, introduction to *After Colonialism: Imperial Histories and Post-colonial Displacements* (Princeton: Princeton University Press, 1995), p. 6.

68. Letter from Pandita Ramabai to Sister Geraldine, 15 October 1885, in *Correspondence*, p. 108.

69. See my *Masks of Conquest: Literary Study and British Rule in India* (New York: Columbia University Press, 1989).

70. Letter from Dorothea Beale, Penshurst, to Sister Geraldine, 22 April 1885, in *Correspondence*, p. 32.

71. Letter from Dorothea Beale, Cheltenham, to Sister Geraldine, April 1885, in *Correspondence*, p. 33.

72. Letter from Dorothea Beale, Penshurst, to Sister Geraldine, April 1885, in *Correspondence*, p. 32.

73. Letter from Pandita Ramabai to Dorothy Beale, 29 November 1885, in *Correspondence*, p. 159.

74. Letter from Pandita Ramabai to Sister Geraldine, 12 May 1885, in *Correspondence*, pp. 60–1.

75. Ibid.

76. Letter from Dorothea Beale, Cheltenham, to Sister Geraldine, Wantage, 8 May 1885, in *Correspondence*, p. 49.

77. British administrators themselves feared that the introduction of English education created self-alienation and false independence in the colonized population. See my *Masks of Conquest*, pp. 142–65.

78. Letter from Pandita Ramabai, Cheltenham, to Sister Geraldine, Wantage, July 1884, in *Correspondence*, p. 25.

9

The Daughters of Aryavarta*

Madhu Kishwar

The nineteenth-century social reform movements were the first organized, all-India response to the challenges posed by colonial rule. They were initiated by the urban educated elite who, although they were a small proportion of the population, made extensive use of modern means of communication and thus came to acquire a widespread social, political and ideological hegemony. In this paper, I will focus on the hegemony this elite acquired in defining the 'women's question' in large parts of north India.

While focusing on the women's reform movement in Punjab, led by the Arya Samaj, I will address the question of why the women's issue came to be one of the central issues for reformers; why women's education came to occupy such an important place in the social reform movement; and the state of women's education in Punjab before the Arya Samaj started its reform activity. I will also deal with the question of women's own response to the process of social change. I have tried to show that women were not mere passive recipients of welfare activity, as most of the available historical literature suggests they were, but that their participation in the questioning process gave rise to self-generated activity by individual pioneers and by women's organizations.

Dayanand's call to purge Hinduism of distortions by restoring its Vedic purity and to defend it from attack by colonial Christianizing forces received a ready response from the educated elite which emerged from the ranks of small businessmen, traders and money-lenders situated in urban and semi-urban areas. This elite adapted his teachings to their own needs and aspirations.

The Arya Samaj movement was, on the one hand, an attempt by the educated elite to reform Hinduism and, on the other, to defend itself from ideological onslaught by the colonial rulers. Through this movement, the elite tried to evolve new forms of organization to promote its own interests.

The Arya Samaj was not meant as a radical challenge to the existing structures of society. Even while it represented an assertion of indigenous culture, it picked up for reform precisely those issues which British rulers had pointed to as evidence of the degenerate state of Indian society. Operating within the parameters of the given social structure, the Arya Samaj sought to reform only those features which they thought acted as obstacles in the way of the economic and social advancement of the educated elite.

*From *Indian Economic and Social History Review*, vol. 23, 1986, pp. 151–86.

Nowhere is this more evident than in its programme concerning caste discrimination and the low status of women—the twin foundations of Hindu society.

The First Phase

Since Dayanand Saraswati acted as the intellectual mentor of the Arya Samaj, an evaluation of his ideas on the question of women's status in society provides interesting insights into the nature of the reform movement undertaken by his followers and the educational institutions developed by them. Revivalism, based on the authority of the Vedas as interpreted by Dayanand, was the salient feature of and the prime sanction behind the movement. The depressed condition of women was also seen in the context of the presumed degeneration of Hindu society because of its departure from Vedic ideals.

However, Dayanand, in his writings, does not seem concerned with women as individuals. He recognizes women only in their familial roles as wives and mothers.[1] Since marriage was seen as the key institution of society, women were seen as essential acquisitions for men. However, even though Dayanand tried to argue in favour of relatively more humane treatment of women, his views on the importance of monogamous marriage show clearly the conservative social functions he wanted it to serve: (*a*) hierarchical relations which teach one group to serve another; (*b*) imposition of sexual restraint on women in order to ensure that they produce 'healthy' legitimate children for their husbands; (*c*) preservation of private property which can be inherited only by rightful successors:

> If the institution of marriage did not exist, all amenities of domestic life will come to an end. None will serve another. Downright adultery and illicit connections will increase, all men and women will be afflicted with disease, physically and mentally weakened, and will consequently die young. . . . No one will have a title to succeed to another's property, nor will any person be able to retain possession of anything for any great length of time.[2]

However, in the sphere of religion, unlike Manu, Dayanand's interpretation of the Vedic tradition upheld the right of all individuals, including those from the most oppressed groups in Hindu society—women and Shudras—to enter into direct communion with god. It was from this premise that Dayanand went on to champion the cause of women's education: 'All men and women (i.e., the whole mankind) have a right to study.'[3] An ignorant wife could not participate as an equal partner with her husband in social and religious duties as women in the Vedic age did. Other reasons advanced in favour of women's education included: 'If the husband be well-educated and the wife ignorant or vice versa, there will be a constant state of warfare in the house.'[4]

Moreover, he felt that without education, women could not distinguish right from wrong, behave themselves agreeably towards their husbands and relatives, beget children properly, train, nurture and bring them up well, do or see domestic duties done as they ought to be done.[5] He advocated compulsory education for all boys and girls.

Dayanand believed that men and women were created to unite in wedlock and propagate the human species. He advocated certain reforms in marriage customs which became an integral part of the Arya Samaj creed. Dayanand envisaged an ideal marriage as one in which both parties freely exercised their choice: 'The best form of marriage is that by choice (*swayamvara*), after the education of the contracting parties is finished and their *brahmacharya* . . . periods completed'.[6]

Marriage and procreation were seen as the primary duties of every woman, but an ill-matched marriage was worse than no marriage at all.[7] Women were to exercise their choice in marriage, not only because Dayanand advocated some form of individual freedom for women but also because 'when people choose their partners for life themselves . . . the children born of such a union are also of a superior order.'[8]

Remarriage for the twice-born was totally ruled out, except in the case of virgin widows and men who had had no sexual experience[9] because if remarriage was freely allowed, 'on the death of one party, the other will take away the property of his or her deceased consort, when he or she marries again. This will give rise to family disputes.'[10] Moreover, 'if a widow remarries, many a noble family will be blotted out of existence, and its property destroyed (by constant alienation)'.[11] He felt that 'remarriage involves loss of true conjugal love and infraction of duty towards the departed husband or wife'.[12]

However, widowed men or women without children could enter the *niyoga* form of alliance for the sole purpose of begetting children. They were to meet only in the 'season of women', 'once a month'.[13] The institution of niyoga would help counter evils like prostitution wherein men of 'noble' families were 'spoilt' by harlots and fallen women.[14]

Adultery and prostitution were condemned on the grounds that

> whoever wastes this invaluable fluid [spermatic fluid] in illicit intercourse with other people's wives, prostitutes, or lewd men, is the greatest fool, because even a farmer or a gardener, ignorant though he be, does not sow the seed in a field or a garden that is not his own but belongs to another man.[15]

However, this whole scheme of rules of conduct had to pay due regard to and be attuned to the expected frailties of men: 'If a man be not able to control his passions while his wife is pregnant, he may contract *niyoga* with (a widow) and beget offspring on her, but let him never misconduct himself with a prostitute or commit adultery.'[16]

Even when formally granting men and women the right to choose marriage partners, very strict rules about male and female segregation were advocated, making nonsense of their formal freedom.

> The boys' school should be at least 3 miles distant from that of the girls'. The tutors and other employees, such as servants, should, in the boys' school, be all of the male sex, and in the girls' school, of the female sex. Not even a child of 5 years of the opposite sex should be allowed to enter the school.[17]

A life of absolute celibacy and austerity had to be lived till adulthood, so as to avoid any excitation of passions and senses before marriage and to preserve the vital energy of the body. Dayanand's suggestion was that 'the king [should] encourage the practice of *brahmacharya*. Let him put a stop to prostitution and the custom of plurality of wives.'[18]

The basic message of Dayanand's reform movement was that 'women must not be ill treated' because they are the custodians of the family and the repositories of its honour. But there was absolutely nothing new in this message. Manu had said the same thing, yet the problem had remained. In fact, it may have become more acute with time. Why then was this message suddenly being resurrected with such vigour?

The answer is provided if one looks at the low status of upper-caste Hindu women, whose life condition the Arya Samaj tried to uplift, as well as at the dynamics of social change that Punjab underwent as a result of its integration into the colonial system. That the urgency of the women's question felt by the Samajists was not just a matter of a new-found spirit of 'liberal humanism' or sudden 'enlightenment' of the Hindu male reformer becomes obvious when we take note of the contemporary situation to which they were responding.

In Punjab, in 1881, 24.8 per cent of women over 15 years of age in all communities were widows. The figure for Hindus and Sikhs was 25.8 per cent.[19] In 1901, 1,363 out of every 10,000 females of all ages in Punjab were widows (as against 623 widowers per 10,000 men).[20] The phenomenon of child widowhood and ban on widow remarriage was almost exclusively confined to certain upper castes and classes. The 1901 Census observes: 'the higher their [the castes'] social position, the lower is the age of betrothal and marriage.'[21]

To the reformers, the dangerous repercussions of the oppressive institution of compulsory widowhood seemed uncomfortably apparent:

> In such cases, their situation becomes one of utter helplessness, and the result is, as well it might be, that they generally yield to temptation, and many of them become women of abandoned character, and thus swell the ranks of prostitutes, leaving thereby an indelible blot on the honour of those who even claim any relationship whatever with them.[22]

Even though the evidence put together by the reformers of a large increase in the number of urban higher-caste widows who became prostitutes is scanty and difficult to draw definite conclusions from, they seem to have taken whatever information they had as a warning signal of danger to all women of upper caste and class status as well as to widows. For example, on 13 May 1900, *The Indian Social Reformer* reported that between 1893 and 1897, the average number of convicts imprisoned in British India for the offence of 'causing miscarriage, exposing children and concealment of birth of child' was 15 in Madras, 38 in Bombay, 48 in Bengal, 116 in the North Western Provinces and Oudh, 32 in Punjab and 12 in the Central Provinces.[23] These are not large numbers but *The Indian Social Reformer* drew its own conclusions, saying that for every one such case 'that is brought to light . . . there may be many thousands behind the veil. . . . Even taking into account the most utilitarian ideas, the need of widow marriages is the more observable and felt by witnessing these gruesome cases.'[24] The 'gruesome case' referred to here was that of the murder of a 25-year-old widow and her newborn child.

In the reformers' view, there was an increasing incidence of abandonment of widows by their families, leading to a large increase of vice in the cities. The reformers were deeply perturbed by the increase of open prostitution in the new large towns. Among well-off families, *nautch* girls were an integral feature of entertainment at all festive occasions. Men of this class traditionally resorted to prostitutes, as a way of life and a mark of status. However, the newspapers of the times, especially those that became vehicles of the reform movement, were full of self-righteous outcries against this 'evil'.

The reformers thought that upper-caste widows were becoming more vulnerable because the undivided family, which was supposed to shelter helpless women, was on the decline. They conveniently forgot that the worst forms of exploitation of women usually happened within the family, and were perpetrated by the women's male relatives.

Unlike most low-caste women, many upper-caste deserted wives who were forced to earn their own living could neither seek nor get any employment outside the house and generally employed themselves in spinning cotton and grinding corn.[25]

The few occupations available to upper-caste women were especially threatened by colonial intrusion. For instance, the destruction of the handicraft industry due to the large-scale flooding of the Indian market with foreign mill-made cloth had a severely adverse effect on women.[26]

Whatever little employment was available to women was available mostly to lower-caste women because they had fewer restrictions on their mobility and suffered from fewer ritual caste taboos regarding the kind of work they were allowed to do. In certain ways, the upper-caste *pardanashin* women, if widowed or abandoned by their families, were rendered even more vulnerable than lower-caste women. The 1901 Punjab Census reported:

> . . . women are only employed in relatively large numbers, in the indefinite and disreputable occupations. Out of all females in these provinces, only 13,09,182 or only 10.6 are actual workers and their employments are practically confined to personal and household services, the preparation of food and drink, light and firing, dress and general labour including earth-work—in other words, to menial occupations. . . . In other words, women when employed at all, or allowed to earn a living must work at the most degrading and roughest occupation.[27]

Trained only for a life-time of dependence, both mental and physical, enclosed in a world whose limits were exceedingly narrow, the upper-caste widow or deserted wife was helpless if maltreated. The only options available were prostitution, conversion to Christianity (and thereby finding of shelter in a Christian mission) or going to a pilgrimage centre to survive on charity. The first two options do not seem to have been frequently chosen. But even stray cases evoked a near-hysterical response because even the threat of prostitution or conversion posed a serious challenge to those who had an interest in preserving the traditional family as an institution. Rejection and social ostracism of such women was not enough. This form of defiance had somehow to be stopped.

The famine of 1896–97 seems to have further aggravated the plight of pardanashin widows and this was also commented upon by the 1901 Punjab Census. The vernacular papers were full of reports about missionaries taking advantage of the situation and trapping women into Christianity. For instance, the *Chaudhvin Sadi* of August 1896, from Rawalpindi, complained that great injustice had been done to one Abdul Rahman in Peshawar district when his wife, Babboo Jan, was lured by a missionary lady. Apparently, the woman had complained that her husband severely maltreated her because she could not bear a child.[28]

During the famine years, reports of the sale of women and children became frequent. *Rahbar-i-Hind* of 19 November 1896 sounded the alarm by reporting that missionaries had purchased some Indian children for five annas each for the purpose of conversion.[29] *Siraj-ul-Akbar* of December 1896 reported that people had been reduced to such straits by the famine that parents were beginning to sell girls to a missionary lady for one seer of oats per child.[30] The *Punjab Samachar* from Lahore, of 9 January 1897, concluded that 'the prevalence of the famine, on the one hand, and the poverty of the people, on the other, are helping the missionaries in their work, and if this state of things continues, all indigent people will embrace Christianity before long'.[31] Most papers at this time reported an increase in criminal offences in connection with women, as a result of the famine. The plight of pardanashin women, especially widows, who could not seek work at relief works was stated to be particularly vulnerable, and demands were made that the government make special arrangements to help this class of sufferers.[32]

The warnings continued for many years. As late as 1918, one of the reformers said: 'One of the greatest evils today is the alarming increase in the number of prostitutes . . . in each quarter of every big city . . . we must devise some means to put a stop to further recruitment of our wives and widows.'[33]

The institution of child marriage also made education virtually impossible for upper-caste women. In a fast-changing world, purdah and illiteracy ensured the virtual isolation of these women from the reality of their husbands and sons who were adapting to the demands of colonial structures. This was slowly but definitely creating for the men a wide schism between the private world of the home and family and the increasingly Westernized public world of employment and politics. Thus, the institution of the family was experiencing new stresses. One way of absorbing the stress was to expose women to a 'feminine' version of the education that men were receiving.

The Decline of Indigenous Education

The Education Commission of 1884 found that there were 1,029 girls' schools under government inspection in 1865–66. They declined to 317 in 1881–82.[34] Indigenous schools were dying out with the destruction of the traditional elite which patronized them. The government was taking little initiative to fill the vacuum. Colonial administrators noted with regret that 'if there is any one class of natives who might be considered as practically excluded from the benefits of Government primary schools for girls, it is the higher class who keep their women in strict purdah . . .'[35]

In the Punjab of the pre-annexation days, different communities maintained their respective schools. Very little information exists about the exact nature of education in Punjab just before British annexation. According to the *Punjab Education Commission Report*, boys received secular and religious education and also some vocational training, as, for instance, at the pathshalas of the trading community, which laid special emphasis on mathematics and account keeping.

But, for girls, the *Punjab Education Report* goes on to say that learning was confined to the reading of religious texts. Among the Muslims and Sikhs, the imperative to read the sacred texts made female literacy socially acceptable. Among the Hindus of the upper castes, girls were taught in the privacy of their own homes. However, very rarely were they taught to write, for this was considered an accomplishment at which only the superior class of courtesans were supposed to be adept. The few who could write hesitated to admit the fact.[36]

The British system of education had been introduced for men with a clear purpose in mind. It aimed at creating a new social base for British rule and to produce a sub-elite which could man the colonial administrative structure. The reasons for extending education to women were not as clear even to the colonial rulers when they opened government schools for girls. However, on one point both the rulers and the reformers were in absolute agreement. Education for girls was not meant to equip them for professions or for government service; the introduction of schools for girls was an attempt to transplant into Indian soil the Victorian ideal of the woman as 'housewife', as the presiding deity of home and hearth, whose business in life was to create for her husband a pleasurable haven when he returned home from each day's tiring business in the harsh, competitive outside world.

This was the ideal posed before Indian women as a part of the effort to 'civilize' them. However, even the creation of this strange hybrid required funds and energy. Not much of either could be spared for Indian women. Therefore, female education always remained secondary to male education. Considering how pitifully small was the amount the British spent on men's education, it is no wonder that government schools for girls came to be no more than a token effort. It was the missionaries who took a major initiative in fostering the ideology of the Victorian housewife, by aiming to demonstrate to families that girls who had been to mission schools became superior housewives and mothers.[37]

After annexation, the first initiative for female education in Punjab seems to have originated from Sir Robert Montgomery who, during his tenure as lieutenant governor, held a Grand Educational Durbar at Lahore in February 1862. He 'impressed upon the European officers and native gentlemen present the importance which he attached to the education of women, and invited their co-operation'.[38] He entrusted the cause of female education to the leaders of different communities. Committees were set up to oversee the female schools. The involvement of the community leaders was supposed to lend a certain respectability to the idea of female education. Major Birch, Deputy Commissioner, speaking about Amritsar in his report for 1869–70, remarked that there were 96 girls' schools, containing 2,300 pupils, 'whose attendance was secured solely by the influence of the gentry'.[39]

But the administration of girls' schools by British-appointed 'community leaders' led to corruption and mismanagement of finances, with the result that many schools existed only in name.[40] In 1869–70, a general survey of schools revealed many such anomalies, and resulted in the reduction of the total number of schools from 2,539 in 1868 to 2,084 in 1869–70.[41] The total number of female pupils in female government schools and aided schools at the close of the academic year 1868–69 was 17,458. By the end of the academic year 1869–70, it had fallen to 13,208, that is, by about 24 per cent.[42] The Education Department tried to justify the decline by asserting that the remaining schools would be better managed[43] and it was decided that grants should not be given to any schools not open to inspection. Yet, a few years later, the lieutenant governor observed that 'a certain amount of instruction was given to a considerable number of girls, but that little real progress was reported'.[44] At the turn of the century, the picture was still one of decline, with the brunt being borne by girls' institutions: 'The decrease in institutions was on the side of both males and females, being in somewhat greater proportion in the case of the latter; whilst the fall in scholars was confined exclusively to the males.'[45]

The half-hearted efforts of the Education Department were being supplemented by vigorous missionary activity. For instance, at Hoshiarpur Mr Perkins, the Deputy Commissioner, 'fearing to offend the natives, he never insisted on the schools being regularly visited, but left the management to a Native Committee'.[46] The schools, 'after lingering . . . for some months, were closed at last as utterly useless', after which the wife of a native missionary opened a school and enrolled 120 girls within a short time.[47] The process is an interesting one, whereby the traditional schools run by different religious communities were supplanted by supposedly 'secular' government schools. Then, the neglect of the latter made way for the overtly Christian mission schools.

The support to the mission schools was not only indirect—by leaving the field open for them. It also took the form of direct financial aid. Thus, in the year 1869–70, the average grant-in-aid spent per student in mission schools was Rs 8.3 while the average amount spent for each non-mission school student was Rs 1.9.[48] In 1884, the Report of the Provincial Committee of the Education Commission clearly stated: 'With the exception of schools for Europeans and Eurasians, and a very few under Native management, grants-in-aid, in the strict sense of the term, are drawn only by the missionary societies.'[49] From 1869 onwards, only those institutions which complied with government rules received aid, and indigenous schools were excluded. In 1869, there was a correspondence between the Government of India and the Government of the Punjab respecting the grants awarded under this article, and the Government of India decided eventually that 'Grants-in-aid from imperial funds are not admissible to purely vernacular primary schools'.[50]

Even though the Education Department tried to make-believe that 'a great effort was [being] made for the extension of female education',[51] the mechanics of grants distribution often discriminated against women's institutions: 'Municipal and district committees are not likely to give fair grants to aided female schools unless bound to do it.'[52] The officials giving evidence before the Commission also asserted that the grants given to girls' schools were on 'a larger scale and on less onerous terms than schools for boys'.[53] The Lahore Arya Samaj, in its testimony, clarified the meaning of this ambiguous phrase: 'The grants to girls' schools are not given on less onerous terms. The same conditions are required of both the boys' and the girls' schools. There is only this little difference, that while inspection is enforced in boys' schools, it is not enforced in girls' schools.'[54] The Samaj demanded that all schools be open to inspection.[55]

In other words, the special concession made by the Education Department in favour of girls' schools was the old one of allowing them to wither away, under the pretext that the community would object to inspection. That this was not likely to have been the case is clear from the report of a lady who inspected the girls' schools in the Jullundur district as early as 1861–62: 'My visits and the little presents I made them seemed to create a great excitement, and immediately after my departure some 30 or 40 girls enrolled themselves as scholars.'[56] The decision taken regarding the need for inspection in 1869–70 was obviously not being implemented.

Even when inspection began to be carried out, the casual attitude to female education was evident. The convenience of the inspectors rather than of the students seemed to be the determining factor: 'Schools should be established in localities convenient for superintendence, and in groups.'[57] The Inspector of the Lahore circle complained that because the girls in villages could not be collected for examination at one central spot (as the boys could), the Assistant Inspector was 'detained in each district much longer than would be necessary for the examination of the boys' schools' while his wife, the Inspectress, visited each female school separately.[58] The Director of Public Instruction said, 'it will be sufficient that she [the inspectress] should be in the District long enough to enable the Assistant Inspector to examine the boys' schools'.[59] Thus, the subordinate role and status of the wives of colonial administrators joining their husbands in the 'civilizing mission' reinforced the subordinate status of women's education in India.

Moreover, the infrastructure provided for government girls' schools was not conducive to a healthy development of any kind, physical or mental. The atmosphere prevailing in the schools was an extension of the confinement which girls, especially those of the upper castes, suffered at home, and the lack of space and fresh air in which those of the poorer classes lived. The Lahore Inspector noted in 1909–10: 'At present little girls have to sit for hours in dark and ill-ventilated so-called classrooms which cannot have a wholesome effect on their health.'[60] Government-aided mission institutions provided a much better atmosphere.[61]

Physical education, too, was totally neglected in government schools. Once again, the blame for this was sought to be placed on the parents who, it was said, would think 'drill or any kind of rhythmic and regular exercise rather too much like the posturing of dancing girls'.[62] However, mission schools and later, even the Arya Samaj schools, succeeded in imparting physical education. The government was not willing to admit the fact that the question of giving physical training could hardly arise when the schools' quarters were so cramped.

The neglect and lack of concern visible in government schools was in sharp contrast to the situation in mission schools, which served as more direct instruments of cultural and ideological domination. They provided better facilities, with physical education and singing as an integral part of the curriculum. To begin with, the curriculum of government girls' schools was the same as that of boys' schools, supposedly 'secular' and 'modern'. The contradiction of providing the same course of study for both boys and girls lay in the fact that the curriculum was geared towards clerical employment. The colonial structure was not capable of providing jobs even to the small percentage of educated men. There were, especially in Punjab, scarcely any employment avenues for educated women nor was the government keen to promote any.

The quality of instruction at government schools was so poor that, at best, they succeeded in imparting the barest literacy. The state of affairs in normal schools, which trained teachers, was so bad that the students were taught hardly anything more than they would have to teach the children. Therefore, there was no question of anything more than bare literacy percolating down to girls' schools. The teachers worked for miserably low salaries. In a 1899–1900, four out of five female teachers in government schools were found to be 'unqualified' and many of them to be 'quite inefficient'.[63] Arithmetic could not be taught in many of the schools because of the teachers' ignorance of the subject.[64] Mr Briggs, whose wife superintended the girls' schools in Dera Ghazi Khan district, observed: 'The teachers are nearly all of them ignorant of all subjects taught in schools save a little reading.'[65] In this respect, mission institutions were scarcely better. In the Ludhiana Mission Orphanage school, 'their acquaintance with arithmetic is as yet of an elementary nature, though quite sufficient for domestic purposes'.[66] The dominant opinion came to be that 'in all girls' schools . . . actual cooking and housekeeping should be given an importance above any book learning'.[67]

Domestic economy was the fancy name given to the science and art of household drudgery. A certain minimum efficiency and organization was necessary, even to teach this. But most government schools were in a state of listlessness with the poor, low-paid teachers applying the only method they knew—and by which they themselves had been trained in the normal schools, if trained at all—that of learning by rote. Thus developed the ironical situation described by the Inspectress of Schools in her report for the year 1910–11, long after the reform effort had entered the field and made significant changes, while government schools still stagnated:

> [Domestic economy] is not taught practically in most of the day schools, and though the text books are memorised, the girls do not appear to make any use of their knowledge in daily life. For instance, they read of the necessity of boiling milk and filtering water and keeping the air in a room fresh by opening the windows and doors frequently, yet even the teachers do not trouble to take any of these precautions in their school rooms.[68]

Mission schools, however, were performing this job more efficiently.

The education introduced by the colonial rulers was clearly not meant to expand horizons for women but to narrow them: 'In a country of female seclusion it is hardly worthwhile for girls to learn by heart the countries, cities, mountains, etc., of the world. Only such instruction should be imparted to girls as may help them in becoming good housewives. Moral education should have the first place.'[69] This orientation produced very negative consequences and left a very harmful legacy, especially considering the fact that seclusion affected only a very small proportion of the total population. It was virtually unknown among the poor 'low' castes. Significantly, it was these 'low' caste girls who were at this time flocking to government and mission schools while the upper castes deliberately avoided sending their daughters to them.

Ignoring the real needs of the 'low' caste women from poor families, most of whom were compelled to earn a living, they were to be trained according to the model of a Victorian housewife, even though they came from castes and classes wherein women could not be merely housewives and mothers. Hazi Ghulam Shah, Member, Education Commission, reported on the situation up to the 1880s: 'Only girls from the lower and middle classes are sent to these schools.'[70] Khan Ahmad Shah, Extra Assistant Commissioner, Hoshiarpur, corroborated this evidence.[71] Miss Mary Boyd of the SPC Mission, Delhi, confirmed that the caste base of the mission institutions was no different from that of government institutions.[72]

Thus, it was women of the 'lower' classes who were taking to education, just as were men of the 'upper' classes, in the hope of employment. Yet, the Education Department kept attributing the unsatisfactory state of female education to the paucity of female teachers. In 1869–70, most of the ills of female education were ascribed to 'the impossibility of obtaining suitable teachers'.[73] The Amritsar Female Education Committee anticipated that 'all objections to married girls going to the schools will be removed when female teachers are appointed to them'.[74] They put great hope in their training schools: 'The point on which the success of the whole system rests is the normal school which was commenced by Mrs Rodger in June 1869, when 40 women were admitted.' It seemed to be making 'very creditable progress'.[75] Yet, by 1899–1900, the situation seemed to them to be just as bad.[76]

The few female teachers who were available found much less favour with the upper castes than did even the male teachers, provided the men were not too young. The reason for this attitude was: 'No respectable native women have as yet taken to teaching as a means of obtaining a livelihood.'[77] The word 'respectable' invariably connotes the upper castes and classes.

It is significant that not only were most students in government and mission female schools from the lower castes but so were the majority of men and women in normal schools who were training to be primary school teachers. Primary school teaching was a low-status occupation for men because of 'so miserable a pittance' given by the government by way of a salary.[78] The three government schools at Lahore, Ambala and Rawalpindi were reported to be 'attended, as a rule, by a very inferior class of men [because of] . . . the low salaries of teachers of vernacular schools, and the insufficiency of the stipends allowed to pupils at the normal schools'.[79] In 1869–70, the salary of a village school teacher was fixed at Rs 10 a month instead of Rs 5 as previously, in the hope of obtaining a 'better class of men'.[80] But this was done by reducing the number of schools, throwing many teachers out of jobs, without being of much benefit to the rest, due to 'the great and sudden rise in the cost of all the necessaries of life, as a man on Rs 10 a month is now scarcely better off than one on Rs 7 was five years ago'.[81] During 1889–90, 46 out of 316 stipends lapsed in the normal schools, among many other reasons, 'owing mainly to the unpopularity of educational service in the primary schools, because less than the minimum salaries prescribed are frequently given by the Boards'.[82]

Since so few women teachers were available, men teachers were employed in female schools. But W.M. Holroyd of the Punjab Education Department admitted: 'Frequently an incompetent old man is employed when no female teacher is available. . . . If [salaries] were on the same scale as those provided for boys' schools, all other difficulties might perhaps be surmounted.'[83] That is, female teachers were paid even lower salaries than male teachers in boys' schools.

The Punjab Education Report of 1869–70 also noted that there was a predominance of Muslim women of low castes in female schools. 'No less than 2,793, or about four-fifths of the pupils in these schools, are Muhammadans, and 2,087 girls are learning Urdu.'[84] Muslim women of higher classes were also training at the normal schools but they belonged to aristocratic families in a state of decline. These women were often the sole supporters of their families. A breakdown of the list of women in the female normal schools of the Delhi mission, who were desirous of obtaining employment, was given in the Punjab Education Report, 1869–70. All the women were said to be from 'well connected' families.[85] It was mainly lower-caste women, and those upper-caste women who had no means of support, who were taking to education at this time, even though the education imparted in these schools had little relevance to their life conditions. They turned to these institutions for the same reasons that they accepted the charity of the missionaries. These were among the very few ways in which women could earn a meagre livelihood.

Female education was becoming an explosive issue for several reasons.

The upper classes look upon indiscriminate extension of education with disfavour. They consider education as their sole birthright and privilege, and any extension of it to the lower classes as destroying that distinction which they formerly enjoyed. They say also that education unfits the lower classes for their position and occupation in life, and makes them discontented.[86]

A lower-caste woman who acquired a modern education and moved into a 'respectable' profession came to represent a threat to both the caste and the sex hierarchies.

The lower-caste woman was even less acceptable as a teacher than was the European woman.[87] The upper-caste men would rather have European women teachers than women of their families.

G.W. Leitner, the orientalist, was even more forthright on this issue:

> The female education given by us was avoided by the more respectable, because it too closely resembled that enjoyed by a class, which, if not criminal, to which our system is now reducing it, was not reputable, although under the caste system which prevents society being gangrened, it confined vice and made it hereditary, if not respectable.[88]

For centuries, sexual exploitation, in varied forms, of lower-caste women had been the privilege of upper-caste men. Prostitutes were mostly lower-caste women. The performing arts and even the art of writing were practised only by these 'fallen women'.

The content of female education was suspect because of the danger of Christianization, and became even more so when the teacher was a low-caste woman convert. An added reason for branding her 'immoral' was that government schools, with their male teachers and inspectors, were associated with a relatively freer mixing of the sexes which was more prevalent among the lower castes but taboo among the upper castes. The colonial administrator was eager to placate this sentiment. The Assistant Commissioner of Hoshiarpur, Sardar Gurdayal Singh, argued before the Education Commission against the idea of having mixed schools: '. . . the girls who come to school are generally of poor classes. . . . No Natives, except perhaps of the lowest rank in society, will send their daughters to the same school with boys.'[89] This attitude of contempt towards a freer mixing of the sexes among the lower castes persisted even after the social reformers entered the field of female education in Punjab.

Secular or Religious Education for Girls?

The growing contradiction between the kind of education provided by government schools and their purported intention to produce educated housewives was time and again pointed out in the course of the debate on whether women's education should be secular or religious. The upper castes were averse to giving their daughters the same education as their sons. Miss Greenfield, in her evidence before the Education Commission, noted: 'The people ask, "Are our daughters to become Munshis and do "naukari" that they should learn Urdu?'[90]

Upper-caste opinion on the right kind of education for women was summed up by Khan Ahmad Shah, Extra Assistant Commissioner, Hoshiarpur:

> With the exception of a few books especially compiled for girls, the course of instruction is the same as that followed in primary schools. Such instruction is not liked by the people, and the existing schools are not popular among the respectable classes. . . . In fact, to render these schools really useful and popular, religious instruction is indispensable. Neither would it be so impracticable, as in the case of boys, as there are separate schools for Christian, Muhammadan and Hindu girls.[91]

Orientalists like Leitner also agreed that women's education should be essentially religious. Leitner's reasons for holding this view were linked to the interests of colonialism. But the logic was not very different from that of the others operating in the field of female education.[92] Leitner felt convinced that it was the women in the joint family who were the bulwark of religion, fear of god and fear of authority. Though the nationalist ideas of the educated youth might be tolerated by his female relatives at home, the moment he challenged the supremacy of religion or god, Leitner felt he would be 'slapped on the mouth with his mother's slipper'.[93] Therefore, Leitner went on, to educate girls in the same manner as boys would be ruinous. Hence, it was better to have girls instructed in indigenous religious schools, by Pandits and Mullas or to let them pick up a smattering of education at home, so that religious dogmatism should continue to be the dominant colour of women's mental world.

The same idea was reiterated by the Punjabi elite for not very different reasons. Lala Mulraj, Extra Assistant Commissioner, said:

> As to the girls' schools for Hindus and Muhammadans maintained by the Missionaries, perhaps they are doing more harm than good to the country by trying to shake the faith of the girls in their religion, which is so intimately connected with morality, and by teaching them to sing Christian songs in the vernacular. If the primary girls' schools maintained by the Government and the Missionaries were closed, it would make a great saving of resources and be productive of no harm. Female education, at least among the Hindus, can be left alone.[94]

This tussle between the Punjabi elite, on the one hand, and the government and the missionaries, on the other, triggered off the effort of the Arya Samaj for reform in women's status, with women's education as a central theme.

Strengthening of the patriarchal family was an important motivation behind the reforms suggested. The evils of child marriage, the brutal life that came with compulsory widowhood, prostitution (especially when its tentacles began to reach the women of upper-caste homes) and the increasing estrangement between husband and wife due to the spread of colonial education, were all posing a threat to the stability of the patriarchal family of the upper castes and classes. Hence the question of reforms in the status of women from these sections of society became one of the central questions in the movement to reform Hindu society.

The Arya Samaj Response

The Samajists began their campaign by advocating the adoption of pure and simple Vedic rites instead of the elaborate, expensive rituals of orthodox Hinduism at the time of marriage. A major step in marriage reform was taken with the advocacy of widow remarriage.

The Amritsar Samaj led the drive by propagandizing in favour of widow remarriage and offering assistance whenever such a marriage was arranged.[95] Each event was conducted in a grand public manner with the maximum possible publicity.[96] For instance:

> The opponents of the Arya Samaj . . . will be greatly surprised to hear that another widow marriage has been celebrated under the auspices of the Umritsar Arya Samaj, on the 10th September 1885. This is the second widow marriage which has taken place at Umritsar through the efforts of the local Arya Samaj. In the present case the pair belonged to the Arora caste, one of the high castes of the Punjab. . . . Impressive songs suited for the occasion were first sung. . . . Great sensation prevailed.[97]

The campaign was carried on with great ingenuity. Pamphleteering was the most common method. Often dramatic in style, the literature presented Samaj ideology in numerous forms—lectures, dialogues, moral tales, poetry—offering didactic entertainment to the literate Hindu.[98] Munshi Jiwan Das in his tract *Sadah-i-Haq* (The Plain Truth), Pandit Lekh Ram in *Risala-i-Nawid-i-Begwan* (A Treatise Containing Glad News For Widows), Atma Ram in *Masala-i-Niyog* and Munshi Chatar Bihari Lal in *Risala-i-Dharm Mitra* stated the Samaj arguments in favour of widow remarriage. But it was very rarely that the arguments presented were as bold as in one of the articles in *Arya Patrika* which argued that nature had created men and women equal; therefore, if an old widower could marry a 10-year-old girl, it was necessary to allow a 60-year-old widow to marry a 10-year-old boy. The author argued that he had no doubt that if this were possible, there could be no dearth of old women wishing to marry young boys.[99] But this was a stray voice. By and large, it was the remarriage of 'virgin' and child widows which gained the approval of the Samajists. Marriages of mature widows, especially those with children, were very rare, although one such marriage was reported as early as 17 February 1894, in the *Tribune*.

As a result of the sustained campaigning, remarriage of child widows gained slight acceptance by the early twentieth century, as shown, for example, by the fact that every single issue of *Saddharma Pracharak* for 1907 and 1908 carried more than one advertisement on behalf of men desirous of marrying young widows, and of widows willing to remarry. *The Vedic Magazine* reported that between 1895 and 1901, a total of 400 such marriages were conducted by the Arya Samaj.[100] And yet, practice lagged behind precept.

It is also noteworthy that the Samaj concentrated on marriage as the most desirable way of integrating widows into society, even while they hesitated to marry widows. Thus, on the one hand, they sought to neutralize the threat to the family that these unattached women represented while, on the other, they never raised the issue of maltreatment of wives. Marriage was assumed to be the aim of woman's life and the panacea for all ills besetting her. The vision of a single, independent woman did not figure prominently in Arya Samaj ideology.

Issues, such as widow remarriage and ban on child marriage, required mainly propaganda work which entailed the condemnation of social evils prevalent in the community. Much of the constructive effort for the betterment of women came to centre around the question of women's education because through it the reformers could concretely demonstrate their vision of women's role in a reformed society. When the Arya Samajists took up the cause of female education, the upper-caste women were their main focus. The financial support came from the commercial and trading classes. The lists of subscribers and donors printed in Samaj journals testify to this. The curricula in Samaj schools catered to the perceptions of men regarding the education required by women of their castes and classes. There was a heavy dose of religion and domestic economy together with general education. The course was geared not towards employment, but towards the production of a 'modernized' educated housewife.

The Arya Samaj efforts gradually made female education more 'respectable'. A certain level of education became a desired qualification in the middle-class marriage market. With the growth of this trend, attendance at government schools also began to alter in terms of caste and class composition. The content of education in these schools also began to change along the lines laid down by Samaj schools. The Education Department encouraged this trend, and lower-caste girls were channellized into mission schools set up especially for low-caste students. These schools, as the Education Reports show, came into existence around the turn of the century.

The Arya Samaj played a crucial role in bringing about this shift in the class and caste base of women's education, linked to a corresponding shift in its content.

Arya Samaj Opens Schools for
Girls—and Splits

The first initiative, it seems, was taken by the Amritsar Samaj, but it met with only indifferent success. Not only was public opinion luke-warm but actual financial support was also lacking. Various innovative measures were adopted. For instance, the Amritsar Samaj, through its appeals, managed to persuade 'all the pleaders at present practising in Umritsar . . . to pay out of their daily income a donation of two annas a day . . . which comes up to two or three rupees a day'.[101] As early as 1885, the Amritsar Samaj announced the establishment of two girls' schools in the city and a third one to be started at Kutra Dula.[102]

During the 1880s, the Amritsar Samaj remained in the forefront of this activity. The Lahore Samaj, which had a larger financial base, remained on the whole indifferent, though it did run a not very successful girls' school.[103] By 1889, the Ferozepur Samaj had also managed to organize a fairly successful girls' school. The following year, the Jullundur Samaj made another attempt after having failed the first time. In 1890, a Kanya Pathshala was established at Jullundur.

An incident related in the autobiography of Lala Munshi Ram throws light on why the Jullundur Samaj took up women's education as a priority issue.[104] One day, when Lala Munshi Ram came home, his daughter, Ved Kumari, came running to him, reciting a stanza she had learnt at the mission school: '*Ek bar Isa Isa bol, tera kya lagega mol? Isa mera Ram Ramayya, Isa mera Krishna Kanhayya*' (Try saying Jesus, Jesus, once, it will cost you nothing; Jesus is my Ram, Jesus is my Krishna). Munshi Ram was duly alarmed, especially when told by his daughter that Hindu girls were taught to despise the Shastras. There and then, he decided that Hindus would have to undertake the education of women if they wanted to preserve their culture and religion. They would have to fight the insidious influence of Christianity invading their homes through the backdoor.

On 26 December 1886, a resolution was passed in the Antrang Sabha of the Jullundur Samaj that 'a zenana school be opened for which an expenditure of one rupee per month would be sanctioned.'[105] But the same year's report of the Arya Samaj mentions that the zenana school run by the Samaj was in bad shape because a good teacher was not available.[106] Lala Devraj's mother, Kahan Devi, took charge of it and for some time, classes were held in her house under the instruction of one Mai Ladi who had earlier been working in the mission school. But after a while, the Samaj stopped the paltry grant of Re 1. Smt Kahan Devi for some time continued personally to finance the venture, but the school had to be closed down very soon for lack of students.[107]

Another attempt, made in 1888–89, proved equally disappointing. However, the third attempt made in 1890–91 proved more successful. One male and one female teacher were appointed. The school had an estimated expenditure of Rs 10 per month.

The 1892 Arya Samaj Annual Report mentioned with satisfaction the progress of the school and expressed confidence that one day it would become a Mahavidyalaya. There were already 55 girls in the school which still taught only up to the primary class. With growth came financial problems but Lala Devraj devised ingenious methods of dealing with these. Apart from the *raddi* fund and the *atta* fund—techniques already in use by the DAV fund raisers—Devraj took to begging in the streets of Jullundur and neighbouring small towns.[108]

The real turning point, however, came with the proposal of Lala Dev Raj and Lala Munshi Ram to start a high school for girls—a Kanya Mahavidyalaya—at a projected cost of Rs 250,000. It was to have a girls' hostel and a *vidhwa ashram*. But as soon as a public announcement of the project was made, with an appeal for funds, a storm of protest was raised—surprisingly, by none other than the DAV wing of the Arya Samaj. This became the starting point for a prolonged and bitter controversy between the two wings of the Arya Samaj (the 'Mahatmas' and the 'college party') as to the necessity for starting a high school for girls at that particular juncture.

The debate was sparked off by Lala Lajpat Rai who, in a lengthy article in the January 1894 number of the Dayanand Anglo Vedic College *Samachar*, argued that it was 'premature, from a practical point of view, to think of giving high education to girls'.[109] A series of letters appeared in the *Tribune* of 1894, on this subject. The opponents of higher education for girls insisted that the establishment of such an institution would be at the cost of elementary education for girls and would divert resources from the much more important task of ensuring the success of DAV institutions for boys. It was also argued that since government efforts for girls' education had not made much headway, the experiment was doomed to failure. The DAV wing dismissed the relevance of similar, even higher institutions in Bombay and Calcutta.[110] Lala Lajpat Rai was convinced that the spread of education amongst women had no important inducements behind it.[111]

The loopholes in the DAV group's arguments are obvious. First, when the government had taken measures to limit the spread of higher education among Indian men on the grounds that primary education needed to be first consolidated, it was Lala Lajpat Rai himself and others of his thinking who opposed this argument. Second, when they pointed to the failures of government efforts as an index of the impracticability of female education at higher levels, they assumed that the government had put all its resources at the disposal of women's education. As we have seen, this was far from being the case. The Lahore Arya Samaj, which opposed higher education for women when undertaken by the Jullundur Samaj, had itself, in its evidence before the Education Commission, 1883, pointed out that insufficient attention was paid by the government to the education of girls. Third, they harped on the need to destroy prejudice as a prerequisite for initiating higher education among girls, but combating these prejudices was possible only in the process of struggle for women's education.

On the other hand, the champions of women's education rightly argued that the issue could not be dealt with as a problem of 'economics' and 'statistics' alone,[112] but only in the long-term perspective of its impact on future generations. In fact, '. . . want of proper teachers, and want of schools in proper quarters, and the absence of any real improvement that these schools effect in their students are the causes of the present undesirable situation'.[113] They argued further that '. . . to deny high education to our women is to deny them, as a class, any education whatsoever'; because primary education was dependent on the availability of trained women teachers.[114]

To the argument that women could not utilize education to take up jobs as men did, none of the sections of the Arya Samaj had any answer nor did they desire to pose the question seriously. This is because even the champions of higher education for women advocated it primarily as a means to bridge the mental gap between husbands and wives, mothers and sons. Moreover, they argued that ignorant women had a 'negative influence' as wives and mothers.[115]

Female education was considered the most effective way of countering the subversive activity of the missionaries. A more practical point was that unless higher education was given to women, there would be no primary school teachers for girls. Conservative opinion regarded this problem as almost insoluble. They felt that girls should not have male teachers and that the government would not be able to induce respectable Hindu and Muslim women to study in female normal schools. In their view, with Christian women as teachers, girls' schools were likely to do more harm than good. Under such circumstances, they found it difficult to suggest the best method of providing teachers for girls' schools. The Samajists discovered 'the best method' which would also solve another grave social problem:

> Few well-to-do, even easily circumstanced parents, guardians or husbands will care to allow their girls and wives to engage in service after their marriage; but there is a class of females— at present a pest on the society, *source* of untold suffering and crime all around—who can be nicely utilised for the purpose; I mean the Hindu widows (emphasis added).

It was not possible to find '. . . purer and healthier—from a moral point of view— assylum [*sic*] for the Hindu widows, than the circle presided over by men of spotless character like Lalas Munshi Ram and Dev Raj of Jullundur'.[116]

But the fear persisted that higher education would lead to a particularly condemnable phenomenon—'overculture'—among women, which would become not only 'the cause of domestic aberration' but also of the 'annihilation of the race itself' because the effect of education would be 'physical deterioration' among women.[117]

The proponents of the women's cause admitted that higher education for girls was not an unmixed blessing, but they assured their opponents that nobody was 'seriously thinking of turning out ladies mistresses of arts'.[118] They tried to convince their opponents that 'the character of girls' education should be different from that of boys in many essential respects. . . . The education we give our girls should not unsex them.'[119]

It is obvious from this debate that neither of the two sections of the Arya Samaj addressed itself to the task of emancipating women. On the contrary, women's roles within the family as wives, daughters and mothers were re-emphasized and extended to conform with the requirements of the family in a changing situation. Women had to be able to adjust to the new style of life being adopted by men, had to come out of seclusion and act as hostesses. They had to supervise the education of children in addition to feeding them. They had to be 'managers' of the family's internal existence, which was becoming increasingly complex with the changing tempo of life in large cities. Here, there was no difference between the different sections of reformers. Even those, like Lajpat Rai, who actively opposed any effort for women's higher education, could, in the same breath, declare that '. . . the nature of the duties imposed on a wife and mother in the Hindu scriptures and books of law, makes a fairly good education an absolute necessity for a wife and a mother'.[120] But

With all the sorrow and pain that an educated Hindu feels for the present position of Indian womanhood, he would not have his daughters and sisters go out into the world in search of employment as the girls in Europe do, not to speak of other excesses to which they are all liable by virtue of their conditions of life. . . .[121]

This unwillingness to question the legitimacy of certain institutional forms of women's oppression defined the narrow limits of Arya Samaj activity. They wanted women 'enlightened' but 'dependent'; they wanted to give them 'dignity' but not 'freedom'. The contradiction was not resolvable. They could not envisage any significant change in the social role of women although a number of outstanding women were appearing all over India as professionals. The names of Anandibai Joshi, Rukmabai, Pandita Ramabai, Cornelia Sorabjee, and their achievements, were well known among the educated in Punjab because contemporary newspapers gave frequent coverage to their activities.

Stunted Ideology

It is indeed ironical that the initiative for founding institutions for the higher education of women came from the more orthodox Gurukul wing while the so-called 'progressive' college party, headed by Lala Lajpat Rai, Lala Hansraj, Lala Lal Chand, vociferously opposed it. However, the dichotomy was only skin deep. The two groups were agreed that the main purpose of women's education was to produce good Arya wives and mothers.

One of the decisive factors in the greater concern for women's education of the Gurukul party was perhaps that after its break with the DAV wing, this section concentrated on reform of religious ritual and marriage customs according to the Samaj version of Vedic tenets. The college party, on the other hand, concentrated most of its energy on evolving a new concept of national education for men, which could equip Punjabi Hindus to compete successfully in jobs and professions. Therefore, unlike the DAV wing, the Gurukul wing faced more directly the problem of 'unenlightened' women in the family acting as obstacles in the reform campaign.[122]

The Gurukul wing needed *updeshikas* who could directly deal with women's resistance, without the mediation of men—just as the zenana missionaries had been doing. Updeshikas could not be produced unless women were equipped with learning.

However, the Arya Samaj ideology remained limited in analysing the nature and causes of the downtrodden status of women of even their own class. The myth of the golden Vedic age when women supposedly were accorded a high status provided a necessary refuge from missionary attacks. Even when they admitted deterioration in the status of women, they attributed it solely to the corruption of Hindu society by Arabic, Islamic, Greek, Buddhistic and other alien influences. 'The first stroke was directed against the personal freedom of the women by the introduction of *Purdah*.'[123] This was the farthest the Samajists went by the way of providing a 'historical' explanation for the oppression of women—as though the problem began and ended with purdah, and as though women's oppression was unique to the Islamic world.

Dayanand had set the tradition for the Arya Samaj of an eclectic interpretation of the Vedas. They could be interpreted to mean almost anything that the reformer felt was most suited to his purpose. Whatever was unsuitable could be dismissed as an aberration or a later corruption. 'The Hindu scriptures and the Hindu law as administered and understood in India, before Buddha (500 BC) assign a very high position to women in the social economy of the nation.'[124] The code of Manu was affirmed even by the most enlightened Samajists like Lajpat Rai as the 'best known code of Hindu law'. If there were certain points in it which caused embarrassment by their blatant contempt for women, they could easily be explained away: '. . . the code of Manu as known to us today, is not the code which was known as such to the pre-Buddhist Aryas (Hindus) . . . it is a manual of decadent Hinduism.'[125] However, it was felt that in spite of its corruptions '. . . even the present code assigns a very high position to women and exhibits an extraordinary solicitude for their safety, for their welfare, for their purity, and for their honour'.[126] Both males and females had to be subordinated to the male head of the family, because 'the family is *patriarchal*, and not *matriarchal*' (emphasis in original), but in all other respects, the legal position of women in the joint family was much 'better than that of men'. Even if

> she has no voice in the management of the family property, nor in its disposal, nor at the time of partition, but her right to be maintained according to the rank and position of the family out of the family property is secured against all claims, internal or external.

In denying her property rights, '. . . the principle is to keep the mother function free of all anxieties and pecuniary cares. Every woman is a mother in *embryo*. That is her supreme function in life. That is her social mission' (emphasis in original).[127]

The ancient authority was resurrected, not only to condemn the present unhappy state, but also to define the limits up to which the 'present' could go in the direction of change. It provided an alibi for halting whenever necessary. However, though the dominant ideology did not envisage a role for women outside the home, the fact of participation in the movement did open the way for Samaj women to enlarge their sphere of activity.

Women's Own Initiatives

Various Stri Samajes came into being all over Punjab under the auspices of the Arya Samaj during this period. These provided valuable support for the Kanya Mahavidyalaya (KMV) experiment during its crucial early years.

The Ludhiana Stri Samaj was particularly active. It supported a Vedic female school and an ashram for widows.[128] It held regular meetings and performed the devotional ceremonies just as the regular Samaj did.

Hariana, in district Hoshiarpur, was one of the most turbulent centres of agitation. At one lecture on 'Nari Dharma' given by Mai Bhagwati, more than a thousand women were present.[129] Women *pracharikas* were few and far between, yet even in the predominantly Muslim district of Dera Ghazi Khan, a woman addressed a meeting of women in a private house. She said: '. . . a woman should have no guru but the husband and implicit obedience to him was the first duty of a woman.'[130]

Most surprising, a woman updeshika, Pandita Surender Bala, of the Jullundur Samaj, spoke at a mixed gathering of about 800 women and 500 men in Phagwara, on the subject of female education. The *Tribune* remarked on this event, saying 'nearly the whole population of the town must have been there'.[131] The Jullundur Stri Samaj was established in 1891, and met weekly at the Kanya Mahavidyalaya.[132]

Even though the KMV management was predominantly controlled by men, the success of the venture became more and more dependent on the active involvement of the female staff and students. For instance, girls and female teachers went on a number of fund-collecting tours, both in the province and outside. In 1908, Savitri Devi toured with Devraj to Karachi. Both gave a number of lectures on women's education and collected Rs 2,000.[133] In 1916, Kumari Lajjyawati travelled all over the United Provinces and Calcutta with Lala Devraj, and collected Rs 15,000.[134] In 1917, she vowed to collect rupees one lakh, and toured India, Burma and Africa to fulfil her vow.[135]

Mai Bhagwati and Guru Bibi Devi were two of the most indispensable workers in the early days of the KMV. Mai Bhagwati was one of the initiators of the movement in Punjab. Devraj called her

> the inspiring spirit behind this great venture, at a time when we have only Rs 8 as our capital. . . . now the times have changed . . . but [she] started work at a time when great social stigma was attached to a woman who dared to go around unveiled. Hariana for us is holy as Hardwar.[136]

Mai Bhagwati was born into the eminent Mehta family of Doaba, Jullundur, and was married while she was still a child. Even though she excelled in household duties, she was more inclined towards educating herself. At the age of 14, in the face of stiff opposition from her family, she started learning to write from a Pandit in Hariana. Only her mother stood by her. She lived with her in-laws till the age of 26 but, in spite of her best efforts, did not find domestic harmony. Her husband's family abused her for her learning and often threw her books into the fire. So, at 26, she returned to her village and started studying independently, because even her own brothers ostracized her. She continued her studies and opened a Putri Pathshala in her own house.[137]

She was among the first women who went from place to place, carrying the Samaj message. The impact she had is obvious from the following *Tribune* report which, by its very exaggeration, gives an interesting insight into how the possibility of women extending their activity outside homes, however marginally, filled men with consternation: 'Of late, a correspondent says, it has become difficult to get well-cooked dishes at any house in Hariana, and few people stop at Hariana, for fear of indigestion on their way to other places.'[138]

Mai Bhagwati also had the distinction of being the Editor of *Sahayak*, the first Hindi magazine devoted to the cause of women's education to come out of Punjab. It was a sister publication of *The Regenerator of Arya Varta*. Its specific aim was to 'propagate the idea of women's education and call upon men to uplift the condition of women'. She was so respected for her learning within Arya circles that with her name as Editor, the title invariably used was Fellow of the Arya Samaj.[139]

She taught at the KMV too and Devraj gratefully refers to her support when he is tracing the history of the KMV. Her popularity is evidenced by press reports of her death and funeral:

> We do not know if Mother Bhagwati's name is much known outside boundaries of this Province, yet she has, in her own line, done more to further the cause of social progress in this country, on strictly national lines, than perhaps most of those recognised reformers whose names are constantly before the public. It is our melancholy duty today to announce

her untimely death, which took place at Hariana . . . on the night of the 21st instant. Thousands of her townsmen of all classes mournfully followed her bier to the burning ground. Every member of her sex in Hariana, contributed one *thuthee* and *chanathee* each towards her *mrittyak havan*, the *hom* performed in connection with funeral obsequies. She had close relations with the Arya Samaj, which loses in her the most potent instrument it relied on in the work of raising Indian womanhood to the position assigned to her by the *Shastras*. She was broad in her sympathies, and. . . . in these days of sectional feeling and *biraderi* spirit, for her liberal views and broad-mindedness in this respect she should serve as a model.[140]

Savitri was another woman who worked with single-minded devotion for the KMV. She came there as a child widow and studied even though her family was opposed to the idea. She had only Devraj's support. Poems in *Jalvid Sakha*, the organ of the KMV, testify to her zeal. In 'Savitri Stotra', every stanza ends with the refrain 'Savitri, Savitri'. Though the virtues for which she is extolled in this poem are the traditional 'womanly' ones of patience, selflessness and cheerful devotion, they acquire a new meaning because they are not placed at the disposal of the husband and in-laws, as were the qualities of the mythological Savitri, but are devoted to the cause of women's education.[141] The use of a religious genre of poetry—the *bhajan*—to create a new symbol, a child widow who is to inspire future generations of women, is interesting,

Savitri was the first Acharya of the KMV and the moving spirit behind the foundation of the Vidhwa Ashram or Widows' Home in 1907. She devoted most of her time and energy during the last years of her short life to this Vidhwa Ashram. She also travelled all over the country, mobilizing support and resources for the KMV.

Most of these women were impelled into the movement by force of personal circumstance. All of them were unusual women insofar as they attempted to break away from the traditional roles sought to be imposed on them. The Arya Samaj provided them with a refuge. Lajjyawati remained unmarried and saw the KMV through, as it were, three eras. As an exceptionally bright little girl, she was inspired by Lala Devraj to undertake the work of spreading the KMV message far and wide. She was a powerful speaker even as a child, and devoted her life to the KMV which she later took under her wing. She remained its principal until a few years ago. The meticulous care which was a feature of Devraj's way of running the institution was carried on by her. She is one of the very few to have lived through the transition, when the KMV was opening new horizons to girls like herself, encouraging them to travel, to be independent and fearless, to the present time, when such pioneers are themselves caught up in running these institutions which have been transformed into very stultifying and repressive centres of education, wherein women are subjected to severe restrictions which often exceed those found in conservative homes.

Pandita Surender Bala was another outstanding woman, one of the most versatile of the Samaj pracharikas, and an excellent singer of bhajans. She was very successful in addressing public meetings in many different places, spreading the message of women's reform. However, despite her notable contribution, she was treated somewhat like an outcast within the Arya Samaj fold. She was not considered respectable enough, since she lived with one of the prominent Samaj reformers to whom she was not married. Had he not been so influential within the Arya Samaj she would have been, in all likelihood, thrown out of the Samaj.[142] However, his place in the movement does not seem to have been affected by the relationship.

Devraj's wife and his mother played an important role in the day-to-day functioning of the institution. Valuable help came from various other women workers and students in editing the *Panchal Pandita*, the organ of the KMV from 1897, and in devising the KMV syllabus.

In this situation Devraj's ideas of what women could and should do underwent a definite change, as his justification of his decision to introduce English at the KMV shows. The success of the experiment of introducing education among girls and bringing away girls from their homes to study collectively had a logic of its own. The attempt to prove that women could be 'equals' in certain, if not in all, respects, had unforeseen consequences. Once the movement forward had begun, it became increasingly difficult to draw the line 'thus far and no further', particularly since there had never been any definite consensus among the Samajists as to where that line should be drawn.

The KMV became a centre of gravity for educational efforts in the entire province. The *Panchal Pandita* became an instrument to carry the message far and wide. It was a 'monthly magazine of 16 pages Hindi and 4 pages English . . . solely devoted to the interests of Indian women' started by the founders of KMV in 1897.[143] It took the information about the experiments being conducted at the KMV to different Samajes, almost all of which opened pathshalas. By 1918, more than 104 pathshalas followed the syllabus laid down by the KMV. Even some government schools included the books devised by the KMV in their syllabus, as well as the *Panchal Pandita*.[144] It was thus well on the way to fulfilling the objectives with which it was launched: 'Of furnishing good reading matter to our sisters, cultivating their mental faculties by . . . widening their interests by giving them a view of the world outside the closed zenanas, and of infusing in them liberal sympathies and elevating ideas.'[145]

While the schools at Bhadod, Ludhiana and Kartarpur were opened as branch schools of the KMV, there were many other Samaj schools which had a loosely affiliative character, insofar as the KMV *pracharaks* acted as catalysts for their formation. It was common for the KMV students and teachers to visit Samajes far and near, taking with them the message of women's education. The issues of *Panchal Pandita* are full of news of KMV girls going out and delivering lectures that inspired other Samajes to follow the KMV model.

The KMV's role as a nucleus of educational activity in Punjab and North India is nowhere more apparent than in its initiative in producing literature for women, most of which was written by Devraj. Some of these books were translated into Marathi, Telugu, Gujarati and other languages. The Punjab and Central Provinces governments recommended these books for their schools. In 1904, it meant a break-through, and Devraj got an award of Rs 200 for his contribution in the field of children's literature. The print orders give an idea of the popularity these books enjoyed and the role they played—*Pahli Pathawali*: 70,500 copies; *Doosri Pathawali*: 43,500; *Akshar Dipika*: 4,000 (27th edition); *Patra Kaumudi*: 20,500 (11th edition); *Katha Vidhi*: 72,500 (16th edition); *Balodyan Sangeet*: 34,000.[146] The KMV ran a Sahitya Bhandar for the distribution of such literature. Moreover, the KMV was able to play a central role in the spread of women's education because, right from the start, it had addressed itself to the task of training teachers. By 1910, the KMV had produced 50 *adhyapikas*, female teachers, who were working in different schools all over the province.[147] By 1913–14, they numbered 86.[148] Devraj's message to all his students was that 'each one of the girls should become a Pathshala by herself so that not a single girl in the country should be left illiterate'.[149] Girl students, when they went home for the summer vacation, not only collected funds for the KMV but were also encouraged to take a pledge that they would educate at least two persons.[150] Many students came back to do some honorary teaching at KMV.[151]

The Issues Left Untouched

However, it is significant that education in the KMV was not oriented towards providing employment or preparing the girls for it. Teaching was viewed more as a mission than a job so the shortage of female teachers mentioned in the Education Department Reports persisted as late as the second decade of the twentieth century.

Education in the KMV became an added qualification for girls in the urban middle-class marriage market. The issues of *Saddharma Pracharak* carried advertisements regularly which listed KMV education as a desirable qualification for young brides.

Though women's education did become the central question of the movement, it was envisaged only as a means to an end.

> The aim of all education besides booklearning, is to build up character and efficiency. . . .
> This is particularly so in the case of girls who have to adapt themselves to the environments into which their marriages carry them. She is a householder first and everything else afterwards. . . . She must not only live but also believe and think like her husband before she can be happy. She must realise the future of her children and must sympathise with the system of education which is to bring them up as bread earners in the modern world.[152]

This was the justification offered as late as 1935–6 when the KMV decided to introduce university examinations for its students. The literature produced by the KMV bears ample testimony to the narrow range of issues taken up. Dayanand had taken for granted that 'nature' had determined different roles and positions for men and women in social organization. These were not seen as social creations. The later Samajists used this as a major ideological weapon to contain and halt women's emancipation.

In its handling of women's issues, the Arya Samaj left certain crucial areas untouched. In the various discussions of the husband–wife relation, the emphasis is on 'love', 'tolerance', 'faithfulness'. The wife is expected to embody these virtues, and win her husband's heart with her charms and accomplishments. But the question of control over income is never raised; the underlying implication is that although the couple should discuss household affairs together, the husband will have the last word.

It is surely significant that even while expressing horror at the maltreatment of widows, the question of what a wife should do, if mal-treated, was not raised. Therefore, neither in theory nor in practice did they question the power imbalance that is structured into the husband–wife relation in the existing family system.

The question of women's own choice in marriage is tentatively raised through stories but such marriages are never allowed to take place in defiance of the parents' wishes.

The ideological stand on the question is pitifully clear in the item in *Jalvid Sakha* of November 1932:

> Mrs Sushila Devi, by the grace of God has done well in both the Vidyalaya tenth class exam and the Punjab University Matriculation exam. She was married this July. Though she was very anxious and eager to study further, she had to bow before the wish of her pujya [worthy to be worshipped] parents.[153]

Issues such as prostitution were not even touched, except by way of self-righteous indignation against prostitutes for 'polluting society'. The question of women's employment figured only marginally on the agenda of 'reform' even though increasing destitution was taken note of. Remarriage of child widows to save them from misery and a life of 'sin' seemed a more attractive alternative than equipping them to stand on their own feet (which was seen as a distinct threat to society).

Niyoga, advocated by Dayanand, was quietly dropped and widows who were not virgins were advised to devote themselves to social service. Extreme sexual repression and austerity were advocated for them—in the KMV widows' homes the girls were not even supposed to rest their head on a pillow. The *Panchal Pandita* carried articles which preached that widows should not live like married women but should practise self-control and determine to spend their lives in *vidya* and *dharm prachar*.[154] Not only was the question of remarriage avoided but even sati was glorified, as in the story of Ratnadevi, a queen from ancient times who burnt herself on her husband's pyre. There was also a laudatory mention of 'a real sati in Kanpur' in the *Panchal Pandita* of May 1906. Thus, the heavily patriarchal ideology tainted even the zeal for reform. All the institutions sponsored by the Arya Samaj bear its mark.

The curriculum of the KMV maintained the emphasis on subjects of 'feminine interest' until the government, after independence, put pressure on it to make the curriculum conform to the general university curriculum whereby men and women are prepared for the same stultifying examinations.

Unfortunately, the key purpose which the pioneers sought to achieve through female education left its indelible mark on the educational policy and the character of most women's educational institutions.

To Sum Up

The Arya Samaj helped remove some of the prejudices against women's education among the urban middle classes. It also fought against the more blatant forms of women's exploitation. Women's status was somewhat altered within the family. While the Arya Samaj did not address itself to the question of the emancipation of women, it created certain preconditions for the alleviation of some aspects of their oppression. Yet why did it fail to develop further?

The life histories of the Samaj women clearly reveal that women were not passive recipients of reform. Right from the beginning, they took the initiative themselves and the women's organizations and institutions that sprang up in the period were a reflection of a certain activity and unrest amongst women. But from all the literature I have so far been able to go through on the subject, it is very clear that the trend of women's thinking on the question of their own status does not reveal the development of an independent self-view. This is also true of the women's organizations and institutions that mushroomed in and around the Arya Samaj.

The Samaj movement was led and initiated by men who kept the activity of women's institutions under strict control and tutelage. For instance, around 1889, when the Stri Samaj was being founded in Jullundur, it was decided that it would be allowed to come into existence only if it accepted the jurisdiction of the Purush Samaj (men's Samaj) over it.[155]

Women, therefore, joined the movement as subordinate partners—an extension of the wifely role of helpmate—and Stri Samajes tended to play a subsidiary role. In fact, the Arya Samaj women's movement was so well contained that no subversive woman of the Pandita Ramabai variety could ever emerge out of it. Even when women were allowed to speak for themselves, they spoke the language of men and their thinking remained within the parameters carefully defined for them by the patriarchal worldview. This is amply evidenced by the famous bhajans of Mai Bhagwati, which she wrote to 'purify' the minds of women, and the short stories in *Julvid Sakha*, all of which are designed to inculcate the virtue of *pativrata*; the women who is unfaithful to her husband is usually depicted as dying an untimely death in the throes of remorse. So also, the essays written by Savitridevi in the *Panchal Pandita* advocate complete austerity as a sort of end in itself, and sub-limation of all desires into Samaj activity.[156]

In some ways it can be said that the Arya Samaj movement was intended to 'reform' women rather than to reform the social conditions which oppressed them. Women were to be educated into becoming more suitable wives and mothers for the new, educated men. The conditions of seclusion under which these upper-caste women lived meant that, for the most part, they lived in a world of their own. Since they had very limited contact even with their own husbands, in some ways, they had been pretty much left to themselves to devise their own inner forms of life within the repressive culture of the zenana. In the process, their thinking had become inaccessible to men. But now, this extreme form of seclusion was creating its own problems because the needs of men seemed to have suddenly changed, making it necessary for women to change their lives and attitudes to adapt to men's requirements.

There is a remarkable continuity of anachronism in Arya Samaj ideology, starting from Dayanand for whom the rationale of women's existence was the mother function, to present-day eminent Arya Samajists, several of whom I interviewed. Even today, they feel that the movement played a very positive role in attempting to produce 'good Hindu mothers'. The conceptual framework, rooted in a strong patriarchal tradition, contained in itself the seeds of obscurantism which came to characterize the movement after its first flush of reform activity.

Therefore, it was not by accident that a movement, which pioneered the struggle for the rights of women in the North, became the arch champion of social conservatism, as soon as it began reaping the fruits of its own struggle. After the first generation of prominent Arya Samajists, succeeding generations were not only unwilling to carry the movement forward and build on the foundations laid by the first generation, but even tended to disown and recoil from the by-products of the very logic of their own reform movement.

Notes

1. *Light Of Truth* (or an English translation of *Satyarth Prakash* of Swami Dayanand Saraswati, by Chirangiva Bharadwaj), (Lahore, Kaviraj Satya Vrata Bharadwaj, 3rd edition, 1927), p. 98.
2. Ibid., pp. 126–7.
3. Ibid., p. 73.
4. Ibid., p. 74.
5. Ibid., p. 75.
6. Ibid., p. 81.
7. Ibid., p. 83.
8. Ibid.
9. Ibid., p. 117.
10. Ibid.
11. Ibid.
12. Ibid.
13. Ibid., p. 121.
14. Ibid., pp. 120–1.
15. Ibid., p. 126.
16. Ibid., p. 127.
17. Ibid., p. 29.
18. Ibid., p. 189.
19. *Census of India*, Punjab, 1901, para 40, chapter 4, p. 219.
20. Ibid., para 39, Chapter 4, p. 218.
21. Ibid., para 44, Chapter 8, p. 334.
22. *Arya Patrika*, 1 August 1885, p. 6.
23. *The Indian Social Reformer*, 13 May 1900, Editorial, 'In League Against The Widows', p. 290.
24. Ibid., 'Dekhani Notes', p. 294.
25. *Census of India*, Punjab, 1881, para 749, Chapter 8, p. 389.
26. *Appendix to Education Commission Report, Report by the Punjab Provincial Committee and Memorials Addressed to the Education Commission* (Calcutta, Superintendent of Government Printing, 1884), Evidence of the Rev. F.H. Baring (Batala), p. 159.
27. *Census of India*, Punjab, 1901, para 7, Chapter 9, p. 366.
28. *Punjab Native Newspaper Reports*, received up to 12 September 1896, vol. 9, no. 37, p. 519.
29. Ibid., received up to 28 November 1896, vol. 9, no. 46, p. 675.
30. Ibid., received up to 19 December 1896, vol. 9, no. 51, p. 723.
31. Ibid., received up to 23 January 1897, vol. 10, no. 4, p. 56.
32. *Punjab Native Newspaper Reports*, received up to 28 November 1896, vol. 9, no. 46, p. 671. See also vol. 9, no. 51, received up to 19 December 1896, p. 721, and vol. 10, no. 6, received up to 6 February 1897, p. 83.
33. Ram Chandra, 'The Problem of Fallen Women in India,' *The Vedic Magazine*, vol. 11, no. 10, May 1918, pp. 549–53.
34. *Appendix to Education Commission Report* (Punjab, 1884), op. cit., pp. 28–9.
35. Evidence of Miss Rose Greenfield, *Appendix to Education Commission Report* (1884), op. cit., p. 227.
36. G.W. Leitner, *History of Indigenous Education in the Punjab Since Annexation* (Calcutta, 1882), pp. 98, 104.
37. See Minna G. Cowan, citing documents from the World Mission Conference Report, *The Education of Women in India*, 1912.
38. *Appendix to the Education Commission Report* (1884), op. cit., p. 10.
39. *Report on Popular Education in the Punjab and its Dependencies for the Year 1869–70*, by Captain W.M. Holroyd, Director of Public Instruction, Punjab (Lahore, 1870), Lahore Circle Report, p. 31.

40. For one example, see ibid., Ambala Circle Report, p. 15.
41. Ibid., Director's Report, p. 4.
42. Ibid., p. 3.
43. Ibid., Section IV, p. 31.
44. *Appendix to the Education Commission Report* (1884), op. cit., p. 25.
45. *Report on Public Instruction in the Punjab and its Dependencies* (Lahore, 1900), Chapter 1, p. 3.
46. *Report on Popular Education in the Punjab* (1869–70), op. cit., Report of Inspector, Lahore Circle, p. 17.
47. Ibid., p. 17.
48. *Appendix to the Report on Popular Education in the Punjab* (1869–70), pp. xxx–xxxi. In this table we also find that the 24 mission schools for females received a total of Rs 5,286 for 637 students on the rolls at the close of the year 1869–70. In comparison, 405 non-mission schools with a total of 8,951 students on the rolls for the same period received Rs 17,311. The average grant-in-aid for a mission school was thus Rs 220, while the average grant-in-aid for the other schools was Rs 43.
49. *Appendix to the Education Commission Report* (1884), op. cit., p. 71.
50. Ibid., pp. 71–2.
51. Ibid., p. 8.
52. Ibid., p. 159, in 'Evidence of the Rev. F.H. Baring', pp. 156–61.
53. Ibid., p. 381, in 'Evidence of Dr. G.W. Leitner', pp. 352–402.
54. Ibid., p. 481, in 'Answer of the Lahore Arya Samaj to the Questions Suggested by the Education Commission', pp. 466–85. See also pp. 197, 464.
55. Ibid., p. 473.
56. G.W. Leitner, op. cit., Appendix VI, p. 18.
57. *Report on Popular Education in the Punjab* (1869–70), op. cit., Report of Inspector, Ambala Circle, p. 30.
58. Ibid., Section 1, p. 7.
59. Ibid.
60. *Report on Public Instruction in the Punjab and its Dependencies 1909–10* (Lahore, 1910), p. 18.
61. *Report on Popular Education in the Punjab* (1869–70), op. cit., Report of Inspector, Ambala Circle, p. 44.
62. *Report on Public Instruction in the Punjab and its Dependencies 1908–1909* (Lahore, 1909), p. 18.
63. *Report on Popular Instruction in the Punjab for the Year 1899–1900*, op. cit., p. 61.
64. *Report on Popular Education in the Punjab* (1869–70), op. cit., Report of Inspector, Lahore Circle, p. 30.
65. Ibid., Report of Inspector, Multan Circle, p. 11.
66. Ibid., Report of Inspector, Ambala Circle, p. 43.
67. *Report on Public Instruction in the Punjab for the Year 1894–95* (Lahore, 1895), p. 80.
68. *Report on Education in the Punjab for 1910–11* (Lahore, Government Press, 1911), pp. 7–8.
69. *Appendix to the Education Commission Report* (1884), op. cit., Evidence of Khan Ahmad Shah, Extra Assistant Commissioner, Hoshiarpur, p. 126.
70. Ibid., p. 115.
71. Ibid., Evidence of Khan Ahmad Shah, op. cit., p. 126.
72. Ibid., Evidence of Miss Mary R. Boyd, Zenana Missionary, SPG Mission, Delhi, p. 183.
73. *Report on Popular Education in the Punjab* (1869–70), p. 1.
74. Ibid., Report of Inspector, Lahore Circle, p. 31.
75. Ibid., p. 31.
76. *Report on Public Instruction in the Punjab for the Year 1899–1900*, op. cit., p. 61.
77. *Appendix to Education Commission Report* (1884), op. cit., Statement of Delhi Literary Society, p. 529.

78. *Report on Popular Education in the Punjab* (1869–70), op. cit., p. 1.

79. Ibid., Section VI, p. 39.

80. Ibid., Report of the Inspector, Lahore Circle, p. 1.

81. Ibid., p. 1.

82. *Report on Public Instruction in the Punjab* (1899–1900), op. cit., pp. 57–8.

83. *Appendix to Education Commission Report* (1884), op. cit., Evidence of W.R.M. Holroyd, Director of Public Instruction, Punjab, p. 254.

84. *Report on Popular Education in the Punjab* (1869–70), op. cit., Section IV, p. 31.

85. Ibid., Report of Inspector, Ambala Circle, pp. 47–8.

86. *Appendix to Education Commission Report* (1884), op. cit., in Evidence of Rev. K.C. Chatterjee, Punjab, p. 529.

87. Ibid., Statement of Delhi Literary Society, p. 529.

88. G.W. Leitner, op. cit., pp. 108–9.

89. *Appendix to the Education Commission Report* (1884), op. cit., Evidence of Sardar Gurdayal Singh, Assistant Commissioner, Hoshiarpur, p. 238.

90. *Appendix to the Education Commission Report* (1884), op. cit., Evidence of Miss Rose Greenfield (Ludhiana), p. 227.

91. Ibid., Evidence of Khan Ahmad Shah, op. cit., p. 126.

92. G.W. Leitner, op. cit., p. 42.

93. Ibid., p. 42.

94. *Appendix to the Education Commission Report* (1884), op. cit., Evidence of Lala Mulraj, Officiating Extra Assistant Commissioner, Gujrat (Punjab), p. 325.

95. Kenneth W. Jones, *Arya Dharm, Hindu Consciousness in 19th Century Punjab* (Berkeley, University of California Press), p. 101.

96. Ibid., p. 101.

97. *Arya Patrika*, 12 September 1885, pp. 6–7.

98. *Arya Dharm*, op. cit., p. 102.

99. *Arya Patrika*, 8 August 1885, p. 3.

100. 'Child Widows in India', *Vedic Magazine*, vol. 8, no. 6, Margshish, 1971, p. 462.

101. *Arya Patrika*, 12 September 1885, p. 4.

102. Ibid., 3 October 1885, p. 4.

103. *Arya Dharm*, op. cit., p. 104.

104. Cited in Satyadev Vidyalankar, *Lala Devraj* (Jalandhar City, Kanya Mahavidyalaya Prabandh Kritra Sabha, 3rd edition), (1st edition 1937), pp. 111–12.

105. *Lala Devraj*, op. cit., p. 112.

106. Ibid., p. 112.

107. Ibid.

108. *Tribune*, 16 March 1892, p. 4 and 23 April 1892, p. 4. See also *Lala Devraj*, op. cit., pp. 128–9.

109. *Tribune*, 24 March 1894, Letter of Sundar Das Suri, pp. 4–5.

110. Ibid., p. 5.

111. Ibid., 28 March 1894, Letter to the Editor by Lala Lajpat Rai, p. 5.

112. *Tribune*, 11 April 1894, Letter to the Editor by Sundar Das Suri, p. 5.

113. Ibid., 7 April 1894, Letter by Lala Harkishen Lal, p. 4.

114. Ibid., 14 April 1894, Letter by Bulaki Ram, p. 5.

115. Ibid., 7 April 1894, Letter by Lala Harkishen Lal, p. 4.

116. Ibid., 25 April 1894, Letter by Ralla Ram, pp. 4–5.

117. Ibid., 21 April 1894, Letter by Sheonarain citing Herbert Spencer, p. 5.

118. Ibid., 26 May 1894, Letter by Shiv Dayal, p. 5.

119. Ibid., 11 April 1894, Letter by Sundar Das Suri, p. 5.

120. Ibid., 18 March 1915. Lala Lajpat Rai, 'The Position of Indian Women', II, p. 5.

121. Ibid., p. 5.

122. Ibid., 9 May 1894, Letter by Lala Harkishen Lal, p. 5.
123. Ibid., 18 March 1915, Lala Lajpat Rai, 'The Position of Indian Women', II, p. 5.
124. Ibid., 7 March 1915, ibid., I, p. 3.
125. Ibid., p. 3.
126. Ibid.
127. Ibid.
128. *Arya Dharm*, op. cit., p. 107, citing *Tribune*, 24 October 1891, p. 4.
129. *Tribune*, 13 January 1892, p. 5.
130. Ibid.
131. Ibid., 17 June 1893, p. 3.
132. *Lala Devraj*, op. cit., p. 91.
133. Ibid., pp. 29–30.
134. Ibid., p. 130.
135. Ibid.
136. Ibid., p. 98.
137. 'Jeevan Charitra Mai Bhagwati Ji', *Panchal Pandita*, April 1902, pp. 17–19.
138. *Tribune*, 13 July 1892, p. 3.
139. *Panchal Pandita*, May 1902, pp. 9–10.
140. *Tribune*, 25 July 1899, Editorial, p. 3.
141. *Jalvid Sakha*, November 1933, p. 3.
142. From personal conversations with Acharya Lajjyawati at the KMV, Jalandhar, 1978.
143. From the advertisement for the *Panchal Pandita* on the inside cover of every issue of the magazine. The same advertisement also used often to appear in *Tribune* during these years.
144. *Panchal Pandita*, November 1905, p. 4.
145. Ibid., June 1900, p. 22.
146. *Lala Devraj*, op. cit., p. 198.
147. *Panchal Pandita*, May 1910, p. 24.
148. *Lala Devraj*, op. cit., p. 155.
149. Ibid., p. 180.
150. *Panchal Pandita*, September 1906, p. 23.
151. Ibid., p. 24.
152. *Vidyalaya Vindication* (Jullundur, 1933), p. 19.
153. *Jalvid Sakha*, November 1932, pp. 10–11.
154. See, for example 'Vidhwayen', *Panchal Pandita*, July 1903, p. 21. See also 'Vidhwa Dharm,' *Panchal Pandita*, December 1901, pp. 7–8.
155. *Lala Devraj*, op. cit., p. 111.
156. See, for example, Savitri, 'Indriya Daman', *Panchal Pandita*, 15 October 1901, pp. 13–21.

10

Viresalingam and the Ideology of Social Change in Andhra*

JOHN AND KAREN LEONARD

We argue here that religious polemic sanctioning social change became part of regional ideology in coastal Andhra during the early twentieth century. The Telugu language and communication through the vernacular were powerful shapers of that message. In Andhra, Indian nationalism had an anti-priest, anti-orthodox, anti-ritual and anti-authoritarian stance which was unusual. Nationalist ideology was modelled on Bengal's Brahmo Samaj in its commitment to religious and social reform and its neutrality to Christianity. One powerful personality, Viresalingam (1848–1919), shaped much of the thought and social reform activity of coastal Andhra as well as that region's cultural identity. Speakers of Telugu and Tamil, almost equal in number, were combined under British rule in the Madras Presidency, and both cultures flourished in the capital city of Madras. However, because of Viresalingam's work, the area's two vernacular cultures proved quite distinct.

The emphasis on regional cultural traditions, characteristic of nationalism in coastal Andhra, ultimately proved to be more significant on an all-India level than the stress on Sanskritic cultural traditions, which was part of social reform and then nationalism in Madras. The demands for recognition of Andhra's identity irritated the leaders of the Indian National Congress from 1913 to 1920 and the leaders of the Indian Union from 1946 to 1952, confronting the national leadership with what it considered to be a threat to the national integrity of India. The leaders eventually gave way in both cases and accepted the Andhra demands: in 1920, for the local Congress organizations based on linguistic boundaries and, in 1952, for the creation of an Andhra state. These concessions signified the recognition of a political pluralism which has since become accepted and extended throughout India.

The Coastal Andhra Region

The cultural centre of coastal Andhra was the city of Rajahmundry located in the Northern Circars[1] that stretches along the Bay of Bengal to the northeast of Madras. This area formed by the deltas of the Krishna and Godavari rivers was the traditional centre of

*From Kenneth W. Jones, ed., *Religious Controversy in British India: Dialogues in South Asian Languages* (Albany, NY: State University of New York, 1992), pp. 151–77.

Telugu culture. Rajahmundry was a religious centre, the most auspicious one on the Godavari River. Traditionally, every Hindu pilgrim from coastal Andhra to Banares had to stop on his return trip at Rajahmundry. The Brahmans in the town were noted for their 'great sense of devotion to sacrifices and rituals',[2] and an important element of regional Hinduism in the Circars was the Sankaracharya, or religious authority, one of several spiritual heirs of Sankara, founder of the Smarta Brahman sect. The Sankaracharyas were influential public figures respected by most Hindus, although their legal jurisdiction was limited to Smartas. Coastal Andhra Smartas owed allegiance to the Sankaracharya whose *math* (centre of learning and preaching) was at Virupaksha. He occasionally came on tour to Rajahmundry, which was famed for its learned as well as its religious Brahmans. Since the eleventh century, Rajahmundry had been the centre of the Telugu literary world.[3]

In 1769, the British assumed direct administration of the Northern Circars. They made Rajahmundry the headquarters of Godavari District; although the Collector shifted to Kakinada in 1859, other government institutions were not transferred.[4] In 1875, Rajahmundry had a District and Session Judge's Court, a Sub-Collector's office and a Tahsildar's office, a Provincial School and a Telegraph Office, the Superintendent of Police's office and two (central and district) jails.[5] Government service became a major source of employment. Several *zamindars* abandoned their family estates to live in the town. Missionaries and local Hindu merchants began schools. Rajahmundry retained its reputation as a sacred centre, and Brahmans continued to perform rituals and sacrifices, but the character of the town was irrevocably altered, not only by the addition of new institutions but by social and cultural changes which flowed from Madras, capital of the Presidency. Madras was a city of 406,000 in 1881, while Rajahmundry's population was 25,000.[6]

In Madras Presidency, as elsewhere in India, the educational system constructed by the British had a certain complementarity with the indigenous system of education, especially at the lower levels. The government's first actions were concentrated at the collegiate level, and after their unquestioned success, provincial and then lower schools were added. Education up to the second form, or through the fourth class, was in the regional languages, and neighbourhood schools performed this function. Christian missionaries established alternative schools, and these were more widespread, if less coordinated. In many towns, the missionary system was the only one, and Hindu parents sent their children despite fears of conversion, because of the incentives to acquire education. To provide what the government would not, and to avoid Christian religious instruction, Indians began to establish private schools in the various district towns. Most of these schools began as acts of charity by individuals, but then upper-caste, Western-educated urban Hindus formed committees and established Hindu secondary schools.

The chief beneficiaries of English education throughout Madras Presidency were Brahmans, traditionally the literate group. By 1891, for every non-Brahman who knew English there were eight Brahmans who did, although Brahmans composed only 3 per cent of the population.[7] The first institutions of higher education were in Madras, so Tamil Brahmans dominated the Civil Service. Telugu Brahmans played a subsidiary role in the public life of most of the Madras Presidency,[8] and until 1877 their closest college was in Madras. College classes for the first two years of the college curriculum began in Rajahmundry's Provincial School only in 1873, and in 1877 the Provincial School became the Rajahmundry Government High School and College. This was the only school in the Telugu-speaking area to offer a baccalaureate programme, beginning some three decades after Madras. The Rajahmundry College did not entirely replace the Madras colleges for the northern districts, but by 1880–1 over 13 times as many Godavari District students obtained a collegiate education in Rajahmundry as were enrolled in Madras colleges.[9]

Christianity was represented in Rajahmundry by the time Viresalingam was growing up; although less so than in other areas of South India. Government schools and private schools set up by Indians, many of them government approved and subsidized, dominated Western education in Rajahmundry. In 1881, mission education accounted for only 7 per cent of the boys and 12 per cent of the girls in Rajahmundry schools.[10] The only missionaries in Rajahmundry were the American Lutherans, most of whose activities were conducted outside the town. Lutheran missionaries had started several schools in Rajahmundry, including a girls' school, which catered chiefly to Christian converts from the Mala, or untouchable, caste. The mission suffered from manpower and financial limitations and concentrated on evangelism, not education.[11] Some of the missionaries who served in Rajahmundry were allies of Viresalingam and some were rivals, but they played relatively minor roles in social reform and politics. They did not set the context or shape the ideology of social and political reform in important ways in coastal Andhra.

The introduction of the printing press and the consequent modification of the South Indian scripts in the early nineteenth century radically altered the conditions of creation, transmission and distribution of literature. This technological innovation was for a long time limited to Madras, which in 1875 had 48 presses and produced 616 books in English and the South Indian regional languages. Coastal Andhra in 1875 had only about eight presses and produced 31 books, and most of the presses in coastal Andhra were owned and operated by the British administration, European merchants or missionaries. Godavari District had three presses but published only two books or pamphlets in 1875.[12] This imbalance was evident also in books printed in the regional languages: in 1876 Tamil books outnumbered Telugu books 2.5 to 1.[13]

Viresalingam and His Work

The social reform movement and the rise of regional consciousness in coastal Andhra began with the activities of Kandukuri Viresalingam, and his character was indelibly stamped upon it. The reforms which he initiated were continued by his followers, and his ideas were adopted by the next generation. His central place in the formation of Andhra's modern identity was recognized by those who followed:

> Mr Viresalingam conveyed to his generation in a multitude of forms the consciousness of the power of these changing causes [from] contact with Western culture and Christianity. We are led to conclude that, if he was not the original centre and first cause of them all, he had, however, laid the foundation for many of them in a sound and secure manner. He was, as it were, the initial principle of change throughout the whole course of the Telugu advance in recent times.[14]

Viresalingam, the central figure in Andhra social reform and nationalism, was a Telugu Niyogi, or secular, Brahman whose family had migrated from Kandukur in the

Nellore District to the Godavari delta area. Born in 1848, he grew up in one of only two double-storeyed houses in the old section of Rajahmundry. This large house indicated the high status of Viresalingam's grandfather. *Diwan* to a local zamindar, his position had enabled him to support many relatives, donate land to learned scholars and celebrate marriages with great pomp. Viresalingam's grandfather had spent rather than saved his money, however, and since Viresalingam's father and uncle had not obtained the same high position,[15] the house symbolized to the young Viresalingam the contrast between past and present achievements.

This sense of current decline was further enhanced by domestic troubles.[16] His father had died when Viresalingam was four, and his uncle was the sole support of the joint family. Viresalingam's mother and his uncle's wife quarrelled constantly, making a strong impression on Viresalingam that was reflected in his writing on the beneficial effects of education on women.[17] Viresalingam was married at 13 to a 10-year-old girl from a nearby village; he later educated her and drew her into his social reform activities. Continued quarrelling in the home led the uncle to partition the joint family, leaving a 15-year-old Viresalingam with his bride and widowed mother in the spacious Rajahmundry house.

Viresalingam's memories of his early religious training were not very strong. Aside from his initiation as a Brahman at age six, he recalled only the ardour of his religious devotion[18] that persisted throughout his life, despite changes in his specific beliefs. His early education was typical of boys heading for government employment. He learned the rudiments of Telugu and even memorized some Sanskrit verses in *pyal*, or neighbourhood schools. He learned to read and write classical Telugu and at age 10 was apprenticed to a relative who worked as a clerk in a government office.[19] Before he went to the office he was tutored in Sanskrit, and at night his uncle instructed him in English and arithmetic. Viresalingam persuaded his mother to let him resume studying full time, and at 11 or 12 he entered the government school at Rajahmundry. His proficiency in Telugu won him prizes that paid the school tuition.[20] Marked by his classmates as a scholar, he composed poems of exceptional virtuosity in 1868–69, one of which became a text for the Bachelor of Arts examination in Telugu. He also tutored the English principal of his school in Telugu and contributed articles to the Telugu journal that the principal established.[21] Viresalingam completed his schooling in 1870.[22]

Education in a Western-style school changed Viresalingam's ideas, those on religion first of all. Keshav Chandra Sen, the Bengali religious reformer and Brahmo Samaj leader, visited Madras in 1864. Three years later Viresalingam's curiosity led him to read Sen's speeches. That same year, a new secondary school teacher, Atmuri Lakshminarasimham, encouraged students to meet and discuss Brahmo Samaj doctrines opposing caste and idolatry and advocating education, particularly for women. The group of five or six met either at the teacher's home or at Viresalingam's,[23] and Viresalingam's earliest writings show the influence of Brahmo Samaj tenets.[24]

After his schooling, Viresalingam took teaching jobs, qualified for various government posts,[25] and, finally, chose a publishing career. Viresalingam began a monthly journal, *Viveka Vardhani*, in 1874.[26] Depending upon the press for a living was precarious, but the government adopted several of his Telugu books as school texts, which earned him substantial sums. The independent life of a publisher and author attracted him.[27] But pressure from his family, friends and relatives to take a regular job coincided with an offer from the Rajahmundry Provincial School, which he joined in 1876 as an assistant teacher of Telugu. He remained there for the next 21 years.[28] Viresalingam's autobiography gave his motives for returning to teaching: he wanted a job which would be independent and not compromise his strict moral values. Thus he ceased looking for government or legal positions, both of which required actions that he considered repugnant and demeaning.[29]

Viresalingam's search for an independent profession rested upon his stubbornness and his inability to compromise in personal relations, which offended many and drove away all but the most devoted of his friends. He recalled an incident as he walked with a group of friends:

> While I was the only one who favoured the river path, the others preferred the market road. They all set off down that road, looking back to see if I would follow them. Then I started along the river bank and reached home. The same thing happened the next day. We disagreed about which way to go, and so I began to take the river path. Then they followed me, saying that whatever I think I follow it adamantly without caring for what others say.[30]

Viresalingam's aggressive, independent ways had certain advantages, evident in his initial reform efforts in Rajahmundry, but those same ways repeatedly deprived him of close allies and drove him from Rajahmundry to Madras and then back again at the end of his life.[31] Yet the impact of his activities and his ideas spread beyond Rajahmundry and decisively shaped the development of Telugu culture.

Viresalingam's initial impact on regional and Hindu self-consciousness among Telugu intellectuals came through journalism. His venture with *Viveka Vardhani* in 1874 was a continuation of the tradition of mixing literature, items of public interest, essays on religion and social comment, but he also reported on the news. *Viveka Vardhani's* English section had a variety of editors and reported news prominently, while much of the commentary was in the Telugu section that Viresalingam edited. He consistently criticized the government and he made his journal the leading advocate of social reform in coastal Andhra. He did so partly by attacking the policies of the leading Telugu scholar at Presidency College, Madras, Kokkonda Venkataratnam, and indulging in polemics with him on nearly every conceivable topic. These were polemics by scholars and for scholars, written in classical Telugu.[32]

Viresalingam's early literary works conformed to scholarly traditions and were lauded for their virtuosity. He wrote poetry, and he specialized in *achcha* Telugu, or non-Sanskritic Telugu. This was a technical feat, since it restricted the writer's choice of vocabulary and made adhering to the rules for composition more difficult. In 1875, he received a silver trophy at a meeting of Telugu scholars in Madras for his literary achievements. Thus he came to know the elite among Telugu scholars, those who published books, held important positions and presented their views to the government.[33] At 27 Viresalingam was honoured by this group for excelling at the traditional tasks of Telugu scholars: making translations and writing grammars. Through his journal, however, he would realize his true literary potential and be fêted for quite different achievements: innovative literary forms and, through them, the expression of new social and religious reform ideas.

Religious reform via the Brahmo Samaj had made an impression on the young Viresalingam. The Brahmo movement was making an impact in Madras and coastal Andhra, although the nature of that impact differed substantially in the two places. The non-Brahman character of the Brahmo Samaj in Madras was established early. Although a Telugu Brahman revived and led the group from 1878, its reputation as a centre of anti-Brahman feeling grew.[34] The South India Brahmo Samaj leadership and membership had little in common with the majority of the educated elite in Madras, the Tamil Brahmans, and the movement all but disappeared from Tamil Nadu's intellectual history.[35]

In the Telugu-speaking region, however, Brahmo Samaj ideas became part of Telugu literary and political culture. In Rajahmundry, Viresalingam and a few friends met together sporadically for prayer meetings based on the model of the Brahmo Samaj of Calcutta, and in 1878 they formed the Rajahmundry Prarthana Samaj. This society was at first secret, and members sang hymns and heard lectures in Viresalingam's home. After a year, apprehensions eased. The association moved to the Maharajah of Vizianagaram's Girls' School and invited the public to join.[36] Of the eight active members, five were Niyogi Brahmans, two were Vaidiki Brahmans and one was a non-Brahman Telaga. By occupation, five were teachers, one was a lawyer and one a government clerk.[37] Since most of the reformers were teachers, they could recruit students and keep the association going. This was the first religious reform organization in coastal Andhra that lasted for any length of time, and it served as a base from which other associations were formed.

The 1870s in coastal Andhra saw little evidence of debate over social conditions and little social reform activity. Machilipatnam, the district headquarters of Krishna District, had an outstanding journal, *Purusartha Pradayini*, but no social reform activities; in 1879 local leaders were still trying to begin an association and reading room.[38] In Kakinada, the Cocanada Literary Association was founded in 1878 and was politically oriented from its beginnings, but the Kakinada journal was not effectively tied to the association and did not campaign for the issues it discussed.[39] Elsewhere in coastal Andhra there were sporadic meetings of students and local Brahman officials to debate changing specific customs but these discussions did not produce tangible results.[40] Even in Rajahmundry, early reform activities produced few results, but journalistic activity, public meetings, organized voluntary associations and some leaders among the educated elite forged the conditions in which a social reform campaign could be waged.

Through his journal *Viveka Vardhani*, Viresalingam was developing an ideology of social reform and actively seeking an issue for a reform campaign. In the journal, he introduced himself to the public with a poem:

> I am a Brahman who learned a foreign language and passed an examination in that language.
> I have an interest in the Telugu language, and I want to aid the development of the country.
> I have some talent for writing poetry.
> I write particularly about moral questions which are universal, in an easy style, without using difficult compounds, so that everyone may understand.
> I also use foreign words.[41]

In the first line, Viresalingam identified himself as a member of the educated elite, while in the third he implied that he was a scholar in Telugu. Then he went on to state his concern for writing prose, and writing it so that people could understand it—he wanted to write in spoken, not classical, Telugu. He linked the development of Telugu with that of the country. Elsewhere, he stated that his journal had two aims: the improvement of the Telugu language and the improvement of the country.[42]

Viresalingam wanted to develop Telugu not only by modifying the language but also by using it to reform society. Language reform was to be carried out by simplifying Telugu to increase peoples' comprehension of it. He conceived of language as a means to combat the evil conditions in society and to propagate the moral standards essential for the country's progress. These journalistic goals represented a conscious break with tradition in Telugu usage.

The documentation of his intellectual odyssey is somewhat limited, but Viresalingam distinguished three periods when discussing the evolution of his journal, *Viveka Vardhani*.[43] The first two periods fell before the first widow marriage he performed in December 1881, and the last followed that crucial event. The first period was brief, from 1874 to 1876. He wrote about social conditions that affronted him—the corruption of officials, the role of prostitutes in public life, the degraded position of women and the widespread ignorance of the masses. If there was a focus to his writings then, it was on the problem of cultural contact between India and the West and the reasons for the decline of ancient Indian civilization. Viresalingam idealized the past and contrasted it with the current degraded state of society. He was especially concerned with the role of the Brahmans, keepers of the texts and traditions.

Viresalingam's explanation for the decline of ancient India became more complex with time and touched directly on the Brahmans as preservers of India's civilizational values. How he explained this decline varied with the opposition that faced Viresalingam at any one time in his career. At first, he blamed the Muslims for the destruction of ancient India's greatness: they had shattered political unity and subjugated Indians. Loss of political independence removed morality from law and order; suspicion and mutual distrust became endemic. Brahmans were humiliated and had to take up professions like low-level civil service jobs, and some were even reduced to begging. The prevailing fact in political life was oppression, and the dominant emotion in social life was fear: Indian civilization had lost its confidence and power.[44] This attribution of the decline to external forces came as Viresalingam was just beginning to write about social reform and was still committed to the role of a scholar and teacher. Opposition to his ideas was slight and came chiefly from scholars; he had undertaken no significant reform activities.

Then came a transitional period. Scholars sharpened their attacks after Viresalingam defied orthodox burial customs and began to criticize Brahmans, and a perceptible shift occurred in his account of the decline of ancient India. Increasingly Viresalingam blamed scholars for the deterioration of knowledge and standards of morality.[45] However, this internal factor, evident in his speeches and lectures during 1875–6, still played only a subordinate role in Viresalingam's thinking.

As Viresalingam attacked current practices and beliefs, he began to attribute malpractices to scholars, pseudoscholars or teachers, basing his argument on the place of knowledge in a country's civilization. At first arguing that Muslim rule had forced Brahmans to abandon their honourable professions of preserving knowledge and had encouraged various corruptions,[46] Viresalingam began to trace the deterioration of knowledge to two new causes: one was the preference of scholars for revelation, rather than observation and inference, as a source of knowledge; the other was the scholars' concern for form rather than meaning, for Sanskrit and poetry rather than for the regional languages and prose.[47] He traced these two causes to ancient Indian civilization prior to the coming of the Muslims and saw them as precluding the rise of a scientific tradition in India. They were also the principal evils of the present day that needed to be rectified. Thus he focused on internal causes for India's decline—on scholars and their faults.[48]

During these years Viresalingam used his journal to experiment with new literary forms, farcical one-act plays about social conditions and stories illustrating moral principles specifically for women. These innovative forms set his journal off from its competitors and were significant in the development of Telugu literature. Their content was as notable as their form. Many of his one-act plays satirized Brahmans, highlighting the evils and absurdities of contemporary society. He developed social stereotypes of 'the orthodox'. Viresalingam used his farces to pillory his enemies; since his attempts at disguising the personalities he portrayed were ineffective, a target of his writing could easily find himself with a new nickname, that of a character in one of Viresalingam's plays. These farces were the first instance in modern times when the Telugu spoken dialect was employed for dramatic purposes. Viresalingam used the spoken dialect for *all* his characters, Brahmans and untouchables alike (the conventions in Sanskrit drama allowed only a few low-born characters to use spoken dialects).[49]

As Viresalingam was increasingly criticized by his fellow scholars during 1875–6, his responses in his journal pointed to ancient scholars seduced by the lure of power and wealth, confused by the urge to acquire prestige and misled into fabricating stories that the mass of illiterates believed. He began to question the later accretions to Hindu traditions, such as the *itihasa* and the *puranas*; to note the purity of thought in *Smrti* and the Vedas, including the Upanishads; and to claim inclusion of gross superstitions in *Smrti*, the *dharmasastras*, the *itihasa* and the *puranas*. Since *Smrti* was often used to confute him, it was natural that he should try to discredit it. He argued that contemporary Indians were merely continuing the prostitution of education and the adoption of debased jobs initiated by the ancient Indian scholars. Contemporary scholars seldom studied the Vedas or even the *dharmasastras*, so spurious customs based on later texts had crept in and lowered the standards of scholarship and morality.[50]

Viresalingam based his ideas about progress on the cyclical ages of Hindu cosmology, postulating that since the literal descriptions of the darkest of the four ages fit the present, contemporary society was in the last age and anything that succeeded it was bound to be better. Rejecting the inevitability of the destruction of the world, he argued that steady improvement would culminate in a future golden age, thus assimilating the Western idea of progress to traditional Hindu beliefs and making it part of his conception of societal development.[51] To justify cultural borrowing from the West, he argued that the West had first borrowed from India—mathematics, via Greece—and thus India was responsible for achievements derived from mathematics.[52] Furthermore, mutual cultural borrowing involved no subordination of one civilization to another. The leading ideas in Viresalingam's programme of regeneration were in fact indigenous scholarly ones: the ameliorative power of knowledge and the intrinsic strength of a unified people. He believed that education would instil morality in the leaders of society and create a climate of opinion favourable to reform. This education would be both moral and practical, since knowledge concerning the sciences and humanities had to be tempered with a knowledge of moral principles.[53]

Education was one remedy for India, and unity—of race, religion and caste—was the other. In his speeches and writings, Viresalingam appealed to his audience to promote unity, not just at the philosophical level of Vedantic speculation, but at a social level. He advocated the formation of debating clubs, caste organizations, trade unions, almost any kind of organization which would bind men together. These associations would be like building blocks, in themselves small and useless, but together indispensable.[54] These essentially scholarly ideas reflected his initial activities, rectifying abuses that afflicted Brahmans and combating specific corrupt practices of officials in Rajahmundry.

Viresalingam's first reform efforts had been personal and idiosyncratic. He refused to call in Brahmans for rites connected with the removal of a beehive from a roof beam in his house, although it was customary to employ them to do so;[55] and he joined Basavarazu Gavarrazu, a friend, in defying Brahman burial customs when Gavarrazu's son died. The two of them buried the corpse themselves, hoping to encourage secular Brahmans to participate in funeral processions and discourage ideas about pollution.[56] He wrote against Brahman marriage customs such as bride-price, child marriage of girls and marriages restricted by sect and kinship,[57] but he found it difficult to promote changes in these even among his friends. Girls' education was a popular reform—Viresalingam had founded a girls' school in 1874 when teaching in a nearby small town and, in 1881, he began another in Rajahmundry. Finally, in 1874, Viresalingam turned his attention to the controversial issue of widow marriage.

The Widow Marriage Campaign

That Telugu-speaking reformers took the lead on the widow marriage issue in the Presidency seems indisputable. In Madras, the Hindu Widow Re-Marriage Association had been formed in 1874 but served only briefly as a forum for voicing the arguments for widow marriage before it languished. Its leaders were Brahmans but not Tamil Brahmans, and it used English, not a regional language, for its meetings. The Tamil Brahman establishment was more concerned in the 1870s with educational policy, questions of management (by government or private institutions), and the role of Indian languages (including Sanskrit). The fear that Western education would lead to secularism was strong. After Viresalingam formed the Rajahmundry Widow Marriage Association in 1879, the Madras Hindu Widow Re-Marriage Association became active again. The Rajahmundry and Madras reformers cooperated in limited ways over the next two decades.[58]

When Viresalingam began to plan a widow marriage campaign in the Telugu-speaking Circars, he spent over a year meeting with various people and scholars to discuss the question of widow marriages.[59] Because of the scholars' reluctance to agree with his textual interpretations, Viresalingam became convinced of their unwillingness to cope with change, and he began to attack them as agents and even the sources of religious authority. In the spring of 1881, he challenged his religious superior, the Sankaracharya from Virupaksha, when he came to Rajahmundry. In his journal Viresalingam attacked the Sankaracharya, claiming that he was coercing donations from people by threatening excommunication. He also denigrated the Sankaracharya's personal disciple and presumptive heir. At a March meeting, Viresalingam presented a petition signed by 30 Niyogi Brahmans asking for the Sankaracharya's approval of widow marriages. Viresalingam spoke in favour of widow marriages and another pandit spoke for the opposition.

Later in the meeting the audience was informed that the Sankaracharya would sanction widow marriage only if the majority of caste Hindus in Rajahmundry approved. This meant, of course, that local custom would prevail; it cut off the debate and silenced Viresalingam. Since the Sankaracharya left the meeting without commenting on the validity of Viresalingam's interpretation, Viresalingam believed he was still free to persuade other Hindus of the correctness of his argument.[60]

This confrontation was the first of several clashes between Viresalingam and the Sankaracharya. Viresalingam continued to criticize or subvert religious authority in pursuit of his reform goals. Viresalingam was a Smarta and under the Sankaracharya's religious authority, but Brahmans from different sects joined in the appeal for approval of widow marriages. Thus the confrontation illustrated the more general religious role of the Sankaracharya and also the interest in the widow marriage issue; it cut across sectarian boundaries and united reformers of different sectarian backgrounds.

Formed in 1879, the Rajahmundry Widow Marriage Association[61] held its first widow marriage in 1881, when a secret executive committee and, in effect, a new association were formed. The Prarthana Samaj had been dominated by teachers; in this new association, there were as many officials as teachers on the executive committee.[62] Many members were students from the Rajahmundry Government College. The teachers recruited students directly from their classes for social reform activities and also served as role models for their students, who were in many cases living away from home for the first time. Viresalingam in particular was admired, since he was recognized as the foremost Telugu scholar of his age, and students remembered that he advocated social reform in his classes. He concentrated especially on exposing and ridiculing the ideas and practices of orthodox Hindus, creating in the classroom the same social stereotypes that he wrote about in his journal.[63] As the widow marriage campaign aroused controversy, students formed bodyguards for Viresalingam and other leaders in danger of physical attack from their orthodox opponents.[64] After the first marriage in 1881, students went out to villages, found widows and arranged to bring them to Rajahmundry; some became bridegrooms themselves despite threats and beatings from their parents.[65] The intense excitement and enthusiasm of the 1881–4 widow marriage campaign, when 10 marriages of widows were celebrated, deeply marked the young men who participated.[66] Some 30 more widow marriages had been celebrated in Andhra by 1919, making this the most intensive campaign in all of India.

From the time of Viresalingam's first speech on widow marriage in 1879 it took almost two years to find a widow who would remarry and a bridegroom for her. In December 1881, the first widow marriage was performed. It took the help of British officials to conduct it: to secure the bridegroom's leave from his job, depute a police detachment of Muslims and Christians from Madras, and threaten to arrest orthodox Hindu leaders if there were overt disturbances.[67] The orthodox had persuaded Brahman cooks, water carriers and priests not to carry out their customary duties, but the reformers countered the threatened boycott by paying more for all the services.[68] Four days after the highly publicized wedding, another widow was brought by her mother to Rajahmundry and married; this event was even grander, since many British officials joined the procession and many more people came to watch it.[69]

Both the reformers and their opponents organized themselves for these controversial events. The Widow Marriage Association left the publicity to Viresalingam, whose journal made him the most effective spokesman, but the other leaders secured support from officials in the district towns. In Kakinada, Godavari District headquarters, a local merchant, Paida Ramakrishnayya, offered to donate thousands of rupees once the marriages began, and he kept his promise.[70] The opponents organized too. Before the first widow marriage, the orthodox opposition was led by Vaidiki or priestly Brahman scholars;[71] then an association against widow marriages was formed in Rajahmundry led by Western-educated men, indicating a shift in the leadership of the orthodox opposition. Although scholars still had an important place, Western-educated men holding government positions became the leaders. Similarly, their tactics shifted. Until this time, orthodox opponents would enforce traditional sanctions, withdraw essential domestic and religious services, and refuse to contract marriage relationships or fulfil kinship obligations. But now they asked the Sankaracharya to make the reformers outcastes. When the Sankaracharya complied, it was the Municipal Council President of Rajahmundry who convened a meeting to announce the expulsion of the reformers from their castes.[72] Some 30 people who attended the wedding meals were expelled, their readmission to caste dependent upon formal, public acknowledgement of the Sankaracharya's authority and a ceremony of penance.[73] Among the reformers outcasted by the Sankaracharya were non-Smartas, indicating his more general authority among Hindus.

This counterattack was very effective, and only Viresalingam and one friend, Basavarazu Gavarrazu, ultimately resisted submission to the Sankaracharya. Viresalingam had his own well; he and his wife had no children and, as a Telugu Brahman pandit, he performed the marriages himself. The worst blow to the reformers was the loss of their chief patron, the Kakinada merchant, who performed penance and swore not to give any more money to the reformers.[74] Viresalingam was bitter about the failure of the educated elite to support the reform campaign and withstand social pressure. From this experience, he concluded that education had to be extended to women and the masses; once educated, they would not be intimidated by those opposed to social change. Enthusiasm for reform in Rajahmundry declined noticeably, and it was harder to find brides and bridegrooms. Violence used by both sides during the months after the first two widow marriages—college students fought with the young disciples of priests—resulted in the filing of lawsuits by both sides, although only the priests' disciples were convicted.[75]

Another lawsuit filed as a consequence of the first widow marriage was far more significant. One of the non-Smartas outcasted by the Sankaracharya, Atmuri Lakshminarasimham, filed a court case against him. The initial decision, against the reformers, was appealed to the Madras High Court in August 1882, and this caused misgivings among orthodox and reformers alike. (The two most prominent social reformers in Madras denied any association with the appeal.[76]) Viresalingam's closest follower, Basavarazu Gavarrazu, filed the appeal, and its outcome was surprising. The Madras High Court upheld the lower court decision with respect to Sankaracharya's ecclesiastical powers—he could expel people from caste—but decided *against* Sankaracharya because of the way he had notified reformers of his action. He had sent them postcards through the mail, and this violated the laws against defamation! They fined him Rs 200.[77]

The real question here was whether or not the government had the legal power to pass judgement on a duly constituted source of Hindu religious authority. Advocates of reform in Rajahmundry supported the initial court case, although some were ambivalent about it, and they did not oppose the appeal. They were disappointed in the decision, fearing it would diminish support for social reform.[78] In Madras, the response was different. Just as they had opposed the appeal itself, without exception the Madras social reformers condemned the court's decision to fine Sankaracharya.[79] In Rajahmundry, widow marriages continued—four took place between the time of the appeal and the High Court decision seven months later, and four more took place before internal dissension led to the decline of the movement in 1884. By the time of the High Court decision, the reformers no longer needed police protection.[80]

These 10 widow marriages had an impact far beyond their numbers. Most of the child widows were from the Brahman castes,[81] but the Rajahmundry widow marriages included two Komati (merchant) couples. There were more secular Brahmans than priestly ones among the eight Brahman couples, but every Brahman sect and branch was represented in these couples, and the tenth marriage was an intersect Brahman marriage. The Rajahmundry Widow Marriage Association sponsored all 10 marriages and all save one were held in Rajahmundry; that one was held by Rajahmundry reformers in Madras.[82] This small group displayed remarkable diversity and involved a wide range of the educated elite and their families in controversy over the reform.

After 1884 serious dissension among the reformers caused the movement to lose momentum, although 30 more widow marriages were performed before Viresalingam's death in 1919. What is significant here is that the dissension no longer concerned whether or not widow marriages were religiously sanctioned or were a useful reform. The dissension was over how to support the married couples (many bridegrooms lost their jobs and the Widow Marriage Association provided them housing, allowances and sometimes employment),[83] and, after 1886, over the provisions of the will of Paida Ramakrishnayya. He had honoured his pledge to the Sankaracharya not to give money directly to the Rajahmundry reformers, but he had channelled money to them through the social reform leaders in Madras, and upon his death he left a trust fund containing Rs 10,000 for the widow marriage movement. This was to be administered by Atmuri Lakshminarasimham, the teacher who had first propounded Brahmo Samaj doctrines to Viresalingam. He was now a judicial official and the filer of the court case against Sankaracharya. Viresalingam's unfortunate tendency to alienate his closest allies inspired him to attack Lakshminarasimham in a farce just at this time, so that disagreements among the reformers and bridegrooms produced factions within the association. Lakshminarasimham refused to use the trust fund for new couples, preferring to keep it for those already married.[84] There had already been rivalry among the leaders—before 1881, three of them, including Viresalingam and Lakshminarasimham, had founded competing girls' schools in Rajahmundry—but it did not interfere with the widow marriage campaign until the mid-1880s.

The widow marriage campaign in Andhra showed the impact of direct, positive action; its symbolic achievements were many. The direct challenge to religious authority, in this case that of the Sankaracharya, appealed to college students and helped keep Hindu revivalism out of the social reform movement in coastal Andhra. An antipathy to religious authority appeared in later reform movements initiated by Viresalingam's students.[85] The widow marriage movement had offered direct, positive action with tremendous potential for dramatization, maximum publicity and controversy.

Despite the setback to the widow marriage campaign, reform activities proceeded. The dissension and the loss of old members through death (especially Basavarazu Gavarrazu in 1888) and dispute coincided with the initial experiments by the British in local government and with the emergence of nationalism throughout India. Thus the energies of the educated elite were drawn into new fields. There was, however, continuity in some areas. Religious reform remained an attractive alternative and was less threatening to orthodox Hindus; girls' education proceeded to grow and Telugu literary activities featured both innovations and controversy.

The vital relationships between social reform, religious reform and literary activity were recognized by contemporary social reformers. Attacks on orthodox customs and views were conducted through the widow marriage campaign, religious reform associations and literary activity. The widow marriage campaign gave an impetus to innovations in Telugu literature; it continued under Viresalingam's leadership. In 1883, he began *Sati Hita Bodhini*, a journal written for women, and he used this genre to inculcate his ideas on social reform. This type of writing was developed by his former pupils to become almost a separate field of Telugu prose.[86]

Literature as a means of reform became a cultural tradition in coastal Andhra, and literary activity became a suitable alternative field of endeavour for many social reformers. Telugu journalism was also pressed into the service of social reformers. Most significant, journal debate during the 1880s in coastal Andhra was carried on in Telugu and not in English—there was no English-language newspaper for coastal Andhra until 1921, when the Congress leader T. Prakasam published one from Madras.[87] *The Hindu*, published in English from Madras from 1878, reported little on coastal Andhra, and this neglect was, in a sense, fortunate for Telugu journalism, for the important issues of the day were discussed and analysed only through the Telugu journals. This strengthened Telugu journalism and forced the educated elite to use Telugu and solve the problems inherent in transforming the regional language. The negative aspects of this situation were that people in other parts of India were unaware of what was happening in coastal Andhra and that parochialism was encouraged among Telugu-speaking people. But by the 1890s, educated men and women in Andhra were committed to the use of Telugu as a serious medium of expression in journalism and literature, and they were engaged in transforming the regional language and its culture.[88]

Social reform proved to be the chief determinant of the direction of cultural change in the Telugu language and literature. The modification of the Telugu script for printing, the initial efforts at prose composition, and the introduction of new literary forms had occurred by the mid-nineteenth century, developed by Telugu scholars who tried to control the changes. The transition to a new phase of culture occurred in the late 1870s, when Viresalingam began employing innovative literary forms in his social reform publicity. The cultural change wrought by the social reform campaign also led to a shift in the men and institutions associated with the development of Telugu literature.

Scholars in Telugu began to be superseded by the educated elite as effective communicators, and consequently the structure of the Telugu literary culture was altered. The main motivation for this modernization of Telugu was the hope that it would bridge the gulf which the educated elite felt between themselves and those who did not know English. Viresalingam's concern with the masses developed after his disillusionment with the educated elite—he emphasized the moral benefits of education for women and the masses so that they would not hold back the educated elite and could themselves participate directly in reform efforts.[89] This modernization was also an attempt to bridge the gulf between urban and rural people, and, to some extent, between Brahman and non-Brahman.

If social reform activity accelerated cultural change, it also accelerated the process of political development in the area. Because social reform was the first organized activity initiated by the educated elite in coastal Andhra, it had a significance which transcended its success or failure in the performance of widow marriages. The educated elite started journals, organized associations, recruited supporters and planned campaigns around the idea of social innovation. The leaders of social reform recruited members and attracted sympathizers. Reform activity was an experience for students and others that accustomed them to nontraditional groups and activities. Social reform was also an arena of political activity. The centrality of the Rajahmundry Government College in the educational life of the Circars and the central position of Viresalingam in both social reform and literary activities gave a strong initial base for the widow marriage campaign and heightened its impact. But Viresalingam's stubbornness and controversial personal relations ensured that other reformers split off from him and built associations and institutions of their own. Thus reform efforts did not proceed under the direction of just one man, but through the rivalry of several major figures and the allegiance to them of many others. These shifting alignments broadened the arena for reform ideas and activities. Viresalingam's associations and institutions may have depended upon personal and financial support which sometimes proved elusive, but his ideas decisively shaped social and political concepts in coastal Andhra.

Viresalingam's Thought

Viresalingam's responses to the questions posed by Westernization changed over the years. Before 1876, he had conceived of the problems largely as arising from a confrontation between India and the West. Attributing the rise of the West chiefly to unity and a scientific tradition he harnessed these achievements to his conception of progress for India. In that period Viresalingam had been unsure about which cultural tradition or group he should favour to bring about the changes he desired in society. The second period, from 1876 to 1881, when he was actively engaged in the widow marriage campaign, was a transitional one for him in which he worked out tentative answers to these questions. From 1881 to 1888, when the first two marriages had been successfully performed, Viresalingam fully developed the ideas that he had begun to formulate during the transitional period, a period that coincided with the decline of the social reform movement and an increase of political activity at the local and national levels. Viresalingam's solutions were his ultimate intellectual response to problems that he had encountered in the early 1870s. His followers adopted many of his ideas, but faced with different tasks, they used his thought to meet the situations facing them in the late 1880s.

Viresalingam's social reform experience during the transitional period decisively shaped his intellectual development. His initiation of the widow marriage campaign in 1879 shifted his attention from assessing the reasons for India's decline to determining practical means of achieving its regeneration. Viresalingam's concerns about India's relationship to the West receded in importance as he was confronted with the immediate problems posed by Indian society. His narrowed view relegated the West to a category of 'other countries'[90] where the issues of child marriage, bride price, and prohibition of widow marriage did not exist. Viresalingam invoked 'other countries' in his arguments only to show that the situation in India was not a universal one. While stating that the elimination of undesirable social conditions was a universal goal, he was reluctant to point to the West as the specific model for India's future. He did not mind taking Western knowledge of natural science as a model for India, because he argued that Western science had originated with ideas borrowed from India.[91] It would have been difficult, however, for him to apply this same argument of cultural borrowing in the areas of social structure and social relationships. Hence he tried not to associate desirable social conditions explicitly with contemporary Western society. The development of universal goals absorbed his attention from 1880 onwards.[92]

Viresalingam's understanding of progress recurred throughout his writings in the phrase 'the development of the country'.[93] He used the word *development* to designate those activities that used rational means to improve Indian social conditions and, in the process, freed individuals from the control of traditional authorities to allow the realization of individual potential. By country he meant a local area, for he spoke of the many countries within the Madras Presidency. He did not intend it to stand for a nation or a geopolitical unit, either; he related progress to the improvement of social conditions and social classes. His 'country' is best understood as synonymous with *society*.

Believing that education was the key development activity, Viresalingam expanded his ideas about who should be educated, though he did not change his ideas about its content. His view of education was a very broad and complex one, for he approached it from a metaphysical point of view and linked it implicitly with his ideas on religion. Thus he equated education with the particular knowledge that allowed one to perceive truths about the nature of the world. The existence of divinity was one such truth.[94] This knowledge was to be derived from observation and critical reflection; Viresalingam applied these criteria to his proofs of the existence of divinity as well as to more mundane matters.[95] He placed a new emphasis on science, especially Western science based on an empirical tradition of observation and experimentation, which he grasped as being similar to his own ideas about knowledge. In the 1880s, he began to translate scientific treatises on subjects like biology, physics and astronomy into Telugu. He valued science because it was a systematic method of investigating phenomena that gave a consistent, 'true' picture of the nature of the world, unlike the accounts of creation that he read in the Hindu epic literature.[96] Science was a tool with which Viresalingam could expose superstition and ridicule the basis of existing customs. He hoped to use scientific explanations to refute the arguments of traditional scholars and win the allegiance of the educated elite for social reform.

Morality was the second major element in Viresalingam's ideas on education. He believed that science and morality were different aspects of the truth—each represented a way of perceiving divinity and each confirmed the existence and benevolence of divinity.[97] Viresalingam deprecated the contemporary equation of Western education with material advantages, because he connected education with religious training. It was chiefly the moral benefits of education that he wanted to confer on women and the masses.[98] He advocated moral teaching of a nondenominational nature that would stress the truths common to all religions: the existence of God, God's benevolence and kindness, and the individual's need to adopt appropriate moral behaviour, based on reason, in order to please God.[99]

At first Viresalingam believed the purpose of education was to create an elite group—emancipated from the inhibiting bonds of custom and tradition—to lead society to a higher level through social reform. This was his view before he tried to gain the support of the educated elite for the widow marriage campaign in 1881.[100] When he first encouraged the education of women, he was concerned only with upper-caste women, particularly those related to members of the educated elite. When this elite failed to support the widow marriage campaign and other reforms, Viresalingam understood that education for an elite group was not sufficient, because pressure from the rest of society could intimidate the few educated men and prevent them from achieving reforms. Therefore, he considered the extension of educational opportunities to the lowest levels of society as a step necessary to emancipating the educated elite.[101] He had already advocated teaching science (hygiene) and morality to high-caste women; these were now to be taught in a simplified form to the masses.[102]

With the inclusion of the masses in Viresalingam's educational goals, his concept of the elite changed, although his belief in its potential to improve the country was always a consistent strand in his thought. Even before 1876, he had praised the educated, but his essays on their role in society had conveyed a quality of ambivalence, since at that time the educated elite in coastal Andhra was small in numbers and still adhered to the lifestyle of the political elite. In that early period, Viresalingam had looked to the traditional scholars as possible promoters of change, but, from 1879 to 1881, his belief in that group's capacity to accomplish this work waned rapidly, and he turned to the educated elite as more appropriate agents of change. His hopes for support from the educated reached a high point in October 1881, when he declared that only Western-educated men should continue to write books in the regional language, since the works of traditional scholars were of no benefit to society.[103] When many of them refused to participate in social reform activities, and some even showed a reluctance to promote education, Viresalingam began to be disillusioned with them.[104] By 1884, his disenchantment was complete, but Viresalingam still believed that if change was to come it must be led by the educated, and he continually urged their commitment to social reform while he criticized them for adopting political reform exclusively.[105]

Viresalingam now envisaged a new mission for the Western-educated elite: constrained from participation in active social reform, they were to be the main instruments in the implementation of universal education. In an essay written in June 1883, he listed the tasks for the educated elite. Only one, the abolition of child marriage, was concerned with social reform; the other tasks focused on the development of education and its consequences for society.[106] After Viresalingam's redefinition of 'progress' to include the improvement of the social conditions of the masses, he began to argue for universal education.[107] He argued, as he had before, that scientific and moral training should be adapted especially for women's education and would prepare them to accept changes in society.[108] Viresalingam went on to argue that the effect of education on the masses would be the same: it would drive out superstition, inculcate morality and provide a receptive climate for social reforms. He did not expect all people to become educated, but he hoped a majority would eventually take advantage of educational opportunities and move from ignorance and poverty to a middle rank in society, a social stratum then rather sparsely occupied by the educated elite.[109] In his view, the masses occupied the lowest level of society, not for economic reasons, but because of their lack of education.

Viresalingam set several tasks for Western-educated men. He anticipated that women and the masses would not take advantage of education initially unless they were under some social pressure to do so. Therefore, the first task for educated men was to send their daughters to school and educate their wives. Next, these literate men must work to dispel the current belief that the *dharmasastras* prohibited the education of Sudras. When this was accomplished, Viresalingam wanted members of the elite to enter the villages and persuade rural people to become educated. Finally, his programme for the elite included the writing of Telugu books on science and morality for the masses. The educated elite was still to be the active agent of change in society, though Viresalingam expected help from the government in providing educational facilities.[110]

Viresalingam had called on the government school system to implement his ideas,[111] but his expectations of government assistance were actually not very great. He had difficulty obtaining approval for his girls' school, and he knew that the municipalities and the Department of Public Instruction in Madras were reluctant to expand government-managed educational facilities. Furthermore, while science classes were relatively easy to introduce or strengthen in the government schools, morality instruction (in the form of nondenominational religious doctrines) was not so easily inserted into the curriculum. Viresalingam wrote repeatedly in his journal, *Viveka Vardhani*, on this theme of introducing moral training into the school curriculum, but the opposition was great, so he considered other ways to inculcate morality in students. In his assessment, the most effective alternative was to utilize Telugu literature.[112]

Viresalingam's identification of the regional language with a Telugu culture was shared but slightly by different segments of the population in 1882. By 1884, his belief in universal education and a Telugu medium of instruction implied linking together the different levels of culture among Telugu-speaking people. This new and broader goal became included in the meaning of his phrase 'the development of the country'.[113] Thus Viresalingam's concept of Telugu as a tool in the service of the educated elite had changed drastically; he now saw it as a vehicle for the transformation of the masses. The interaction between his views on reform and his ideas concerning the people who should benefit from reform eventually led him to consider changes in the Telugu language and literature that he had not anticipated in 1874, innovations that led to the fuller development of the new cultural tradition of literature as a means of reform and eventually to a new and broader culture itself.

From 1880 to 1888 there was a clear progression in Viresalingam's thinking about Indian society. Viresalingam's earlier use of metaphor, though frequent, lacked a consistent pattern. When he discussed the masses his metaphors invariably represented them as being at a low level of development—such as a child.[114] Then, with the introduction of local self-government in 1884 and the organization of the Indian National Congress in 1885, Viresalingam's images of them emphasized their 'youth'. He envisioned society as an organism and saw its parts in anthropomorphic terms. He did not revert to the hierarchical ranking of *varnas* or castes and their approximation to parts of the body, an image featured in the Rig Veda, for he focused on the activities of society. He made his ideas explicit in the following way: social and political reform were both growths of society and, since society was organic in nature, the two had to develop evenly. Coordinated growth was healthy, while uneven growth was a sign of disease. He stated that, in political terms, Indian society was progressing from childhood to adolescence. The Government of India was the mother who would grant measures of independence as soon as the adolescent proved capable of exercising it. Viresalingam disavowed his earlier reliance on the educated elite by concluding that one segment of society should not be allowed to forge ahead of other segments, such as women or the masses.[115] This even development of all sections of society was another way in which Viresalingam expressed his idea that the unity of society was essential for progress.

Viresalingam's concept of society as an organic entity initially led him to distrust political reformers. He never quite lost this feeling, even though he came to laud the founding of the Indian National Congress. Local politicians attempted to argue that social reform was not a necessary accompaniment to progress and that contemporary customs were either admirable or impossible to change; Viresalingam reacted sharply to such assertions. He consistently criticized local political reformers for deserting social issues; yet, on another level, he praised the Indian National Congress for its work in promoting the unity of India.[116]

Ultimately, Viresalingam's thinking about the development of Indian society stemmed from two problems. The first was India's low position *vis-à-vis* the West; this led him to consider largely abstract ways to elevate a country's status. The second problem was the failure of the Western-educated elite to actively support social reform— social pressures exerted by the rest of Indian society meant that educated men were actually being used to enforce conformity to existing social practices. Thus leadership at an elite level obviously was not sufficient to change society; followers also had to be receptive to change, for all levels of the population had to progress together. Viresalingam's recognition of the power of uneducated people to subvert the implementation of socially desirable goals made him realize the magnitude of their power and the need to harness it for progress. This led him to campaign for mass education and the broadening need of the regional language and its literature. He began to equate the development of Telugu culture with the progress of the masses. Earlier he had identified the development of Telugu with progress of the country and its status; by this time he was concerned about the status of the masses as well as that of the country.[117] Viresalingam never made the final, direct equation—the identification of the people with the country—because he still believed in the leadership of an elite, the inherent inertia of the masses and the wisdom of the British administration in India.[118] Yet his intellectual development, in retrospect, represents a far-reaching attempt to build nationalist consciousness on a cultural base.

One can trace in Viresalingam's intellectual odyssey the interaction of his perceptions and actual social reform experiences through time. Viresalingam began his intellectual inquiry into the origins of the decay of Indian society when he was a young teacher in a village school. His early concern for education made him stress teaching as the key to change, although he was uncertain about exactly what to change at that time. His position as a Telugu scholar inclined him towards that language as the medium of cultural change, and his position as a member of the educated elite and as a Brahman stressed the role of an elite in guiding the country's destiny. But his experience in the widow marriage campaign modified these early ideas and led him to consider mass education as a necessary prerequisite for the inauguration of social reform. Mass education could be conducted only through Telugu, and this made him consider the further expansion of Telugu as the opener for a cultural change much greater than the one he had conceived originally. Beginning as an imitator of the traditional Telugu scholars, he ended his career as a great popularizer and prophet of cultural change for the masses.[119]

Conclusion

The relationship of social reform, literary, and political activity to regional identity forged by Viresalingam decisively shaped the character of the Indian nationalist movement there and contrasted with the lack of such a relationship in Madras. From 1879 to 1913, the educated elite established organizations at three levels—local, district and regional—and social and religious reform associations stemming from Rajahmundry and Viresalingam's widow marriage campaign were fundamental to development of these groups all over coastal Andhra. Subsequent stages of political development focused on the creation of political contacts and consciousness at the district and regional levels. In 1892, the first conference at the district level was held in Krishna District,[120] and a few delegates came from other districts too.[121] Within three years leaders initiated meetings in other districts, and social conferences were held in conjunction with these district meetings.[122] In 1905, conferences drew attendees from all of coastal Andhra.[123] Some of these gatherings were explicitly political in nature and some, like the Andhra Theistic Conference, were not. From these supra-local conferences came the impetus to inaugurate a political movement in order to secure the recognition of Andhra's separate identity.[124]

The continuing relevance of key social reform ideas to political activity in coastal Andhra, both on the regional level and eventually in the nationalist movement, was unusual, for social reform ideas became increasingly irrelevant in shaping the development of nationalism in other regions of India. But the nationalists in coastal Andhra retained the idea of attaining social modernity, social progress, with its emphasis on the educated elite as the catalyst and the Telugu language and cultural traditions as the means. Modernity was now conceived of as a series of regional political communities within the Indian nation, where law and an Indian government would be the instruments creating new social conditions. Viresalingam's rooting of the idea of progress in the regional culture and his sustained attack on Sanskritic traditions destroyed the intellectual basis for any type of Sanskritic revivalism in Andhra. Viresalingam's first attacks were on the priestly Brahmans, and then he included traditional scholars. For many years his newspaper, the leading one in Andhra, vilified priests, scholars and aspects of ancient Aryan civilization. Thus succeeding generations grew up with a declining status of priests and traditional scholars; consequently, they accepted the futility of using Sanskritic traditions to build a modern identity.

In Madras, Christians and non-Brahmans attacked Brahmans; in coastal Andhra, Western-educated Brahmans, led by Viresalingam, attacked 'the orthodox'. Discrediting the image of the orthodox Brahman was central to the evolving ideology of social change and national progress. The 'new Brahman' conscience in Andhra questioned traditional religious authority as the social reformers sought to transform their regional culture through the modification of Telugu, the expansion of education and social and religious reform activities. Despite his history of alienating even allies in the implementation of his ideas, Viresalingam was an ideological thinker and polemicist whose ideas decisively shaped the regional culture and nationalist ideology in Andhra. He criticized the existing structure of social and political authority and provided a vision of indigenously generated social change and national progress. He reconceived of both individuals and their collective identity in coastal Andhra, insisting that educated men confront the failure of priestly Brahmans and scholars to uphold Indian society, that they commit themselves to new goals and form new associations, that they assume responsibilities for the condition of women and the masses in Andhra society. Later leaders went far beyond Viresalingam in questioning British political authority in India. Nonetheless, his emphasis on regional cultural traditions had far-reaching political implications, and his widow marriage campaign gave future leaders a direct and overwhelmingly political experience in bringing about social change.

Bibliographic Essay

The reconstruction of the social reform movement in coastal Andhra during the period 1874–91 required a synthesis of two very different types of sources: biographies and autobiographies in Telugu, and English-language newspapers. Neither type of source was sufficient by itself because events in Andhra had few connections with events of an all-India importance. Not until 1907, when Bipin Chandra Pal toured South India protesting the partition of Bengal, did Andhras participate noticeably in events whose significance transcended the regional boundaries. This isolation meant that the history of coastal Andhra during this period of social reform was not fully understood in Madras. The English-language newspapers in Madras mentioned some of the highlights of the social reform movement and thus provided a rough chronology of events in the region, a chronology which could then be linked with major events in Madras and the rest of India. Yet this chronology was at best only an outline.

For a full understanding of social reform and its significance in Andhra, the Telugu sources were crucial. Most valuable were Kandukuri Viresalingam's autobiography and collected works. For the period preceding the widow marriage campaign his autobiography was indispensable. Newspaper reports were very brief at that time, and it would be virtually impossible to describe that early social reform activity without Viresalingam's account. Once the widow marriage campaign began, the two main sources were Viresalingam's 1885 report to the Association, 'Rajahmahendravara Stri Punar Vivaha Caritramu', which he included in his collected works, and an English account by Viresalingam's ex-student, D.V. Prakasa Row. Reminiscences of Viresalingam's students and followers, especially those of Rayasam Venkata Sivudu, Valluri Suryanarayana Rau and Cilakamarti Lakshminarasimham, filled out the narrative. The opposition to social reform had to be glimpsed mainly through the eyes of the reformers themselves, for the only biography of an opposition leader, that of Vedamu Venkataraya Sastri, mentions a few relevant facts only briefly and omits any discussion of other opposition leaders or connections with them. The decline of the social reform movement in Rajahmundry coincided with the school careers of three future prominent Andhra political leaders, K. Venkatappayya, T. Prakasam and A. Kaleswara Rao, and their autobiographies furnished revealing accounts of the social reformers' participation in reform activities.

During the decades of the 1870s and 1880s the English-language newspapers relied on correspondents in coastal Andhra for news of that region. The correspondents for the British-owned newspapers were probably Europeans, since most of their news concerned the activities of British officials and missionaries. Even Indian-owned newspapers like *The Hindu* did not pay much attention to events in coastal Andhra, for reports from there were irregular and brief even at the best of times.

Other types of sources, such as records of the Madras government or missionary reports, were of little use for this topic. The general policy of the Government of India was to refrain from undertaking social reform, and, except in individual instances, the Government of Madras did nothing to encourage social reform. This lack of interest was evident in those few cases (such as the circulation of Mr Malabari's Notes) when the government was compelled to act. Also, British administration at the local level did not pay much attention to the social reformers or include information about them in the reports to higher levels of government, since the social reformers' actions did not impinge directly upon the administration.

The lack of missionary reports for this period was disappointing. Neither the missionary college at Rajahmundry nor its affiliate in Guntur had preserved records from the nineteenth century. The most valuable missionary sources for this study were the journals published in North America. Missionary records usually dealt with the business of managing the mission, whereas the letters of some missionaries to journals provided a few insights into social reform and Viresalingam's life. Even the archives of the Lutheran Theological Seminary in Philadelphia have preserved only statements regarding itineraries and travelling expenses of missionaries and disputes within the mission. The Lutheran Theological Seminary at Gettysburg has an extensive collection of records and manuscripts for the Lutheran mission in Guntur. The journals of women missionaries were valuable for descriptions of social reform activities and missionary attitudes towards these. These Canadian Baptists had their Telugu Mission headquarters in Kakinada; archives are in McMaster University, Hamilton, Ontario. Although none of their records or journals illuminates any of Viresalingam's actions, there are a few letters in the *Canadian Missionary Link* dealing with Paida Ramakrishnayya. Another journal, *Among the Telugus*, first appeared in 1900 and is valuable for material on social conditions in Kakinada.

Sectarian histories of missionary activity in coastal Andhra, moreover, are uniform in their concentration on those activities which contributed to the growth of Christianity. Although the missionaries in coastal Andhra were pioneers in promoting education, and, interestingly enough, admired and utilized Viresalingam's writings on monotheism and the restrictive aspects of the caste system, they wrote little about Indian society except as it affected their work.

The diaries of Viresalingam, 1897–1916, are in the possession of Y. Venkat Rao, Rajahmundry, who picked them up one day when he noticed a pile of waste paper outside the Viresalingam Theistic High School. There were probably earlier diaries, but even so, their value is limited. Viresalingam recorded the events he considered important but did not comment on them. Most entries deal with the prices of food in the local market and would be valuable for an economic historian. Other financial entries were of value in tracing his supporters for his various projects.

Notes

*When John died in 1985, an outline for this article was on his desk. I have relied heavily on his two unpublished manuscripts to complete it. I am indebted to Professors G.N. Reddy and K.V. Narayana Rao of Sri Venkateshwara University (the former was John's Telugu professor) and Professor Charlotte Furth of the University of Southern California and Professor Montgomery Furth of The University of California, Los Angeles, for their helpful readings of the manuscript.

1. The other two are Rayalaseema, a slightly less populated dry area north-west of Madras (most of the present Nellore District), and Telangana, separately administered as part of the Nizam's Dominions until 1948 and of Hyderabad State until 1956.

2. Cilukurvi Virabhadra Rau, *Rajamendra Pura Caritra* (Rajahmundry: 1915), pp. 33–4); F.R. Hemingway, *Godavari* (Madras: Madras District Gazetteer, 1915), 1, p. 247; Digavalli Venkata Siva Rau, ed., *Kasi Yatra Caritra*, 3rd ed. (Bezwada, 1941), pp. 344–5.

3. K.A. Nilakanta Sastry, *A History of South India*, 3rd ed. (Madras: Oxford University Press, 1966), p. 406.

4. Henry Morris, *A Descriptive and Historical Account of the Godavary District in the Presidency of Madras* (London: Madras District Manual, 1878), pp. 244, 303–4.

5. Morris, *Godavary District*, p. 22.

6. For comparisons between Rajahmundry and Madras, see John G. Leonard, Urban Government Under the Raj', *Modern Asian Studies* 7, no. 2 (April 1973), pp. 227–51 and Susan J. Lewandowski, 'Urban Growth and Municipal Development in the Colonial City of Madras, 1860–1900', *Journal of Asian Studies* 34, no. 2 (February 1975), pp. 341–60.

7. Government of India, *Census of India*, 1891–2 (Madras, 1893), vol. 13, p. 181.

8. This was a precipitating cause of the Andhra movement—only in the Circars region did Telugus outnumber Tamils in government positions. See John G. Leonard, 'Politics and Social Change in South India: A Study of the Andhra Movement', *Journal of Commonwealth Political Studies* 5, no. 1 (March 1967), pp. 60–77.

9. Government of India, Indian Education Commission, *Report of the Madras Provincial Committee* (Calcutta, 1884), p. 38; Government of Madras, *Report on Public Instruction in the Madras Presidency for 1880–1881* (Madras, 1881), pp. 65–7.

10. Government of Madras, *Madras Financial Proceedings*, no. 58 (10 January 1884), India Office Library.

11. Morris, *Godavary District*, p. 24; Martin Luther Dolbeer, Jr., *A History of Lutheranism in the Andhra Desh, 1842–1920* (New York: Board of the Foreign Missions of the United Lutheran Church in America, 1959), p. 14; Martin Luther Dolbeer, Sr., *The Andhra Evangelical Lutheran Church: A Brief History* (Rajahmundry: Department of Religious Education, Andhra Evangelical Church, 1951), pp. 27–30.

12. Government of Madras, *Report on Public Instruction in the Madras Presidency for 1876–77* (Madras, 1877), p. 135.

13. Government of Madras, *Report on Public Instruction for 1876–77*, p. 136. This ratio is best understood with the help of data drawn from later sources: it seems to approximate the proportion of Tamils to Telugus in Madras City, which was 2.7 to 1; see Government of India, *Census of India*, 1891–2 (Madras, 1893), vol. 14, pp. 137, 139. The ratio of Tamils to Telugus in Madras Presidency was 1.1 to 1; see Government of India, *Census of India*, 1911, vol. 12, pt. 2 (Madras, 1912), p. 140 for details.

14. J. Gurunatham, *Viresalingam, the Founder of Telugu Public Life* (Rajahmundry: S. Gunnesworao Bros., 1911), pp. 165–6.

15. Tanguturi Prakasam, *Na Jivita Yatra* (Rajahmundry: Kalahastri Tamma Rao and Sons, 1957), p. 48; Kandukuri Viresalingam, *Surya Caritramu* (Rajahmundry: Hitakarini Samaj, 1954), vol. 1, pp. 1–2, 8–9, 17; A. Ramapati Rao, 'Jivitamunandali Konni Mukhya Ghattamulu', in

Yuga Purusudu Viresalingam (Hyderabad, n.d.), p. 223. Viresalingam's father and uncle were revenue officials for the Government of Madras.

16. The following information about family life comes from Viresalingam's recollections in *Caritramu*, vol. 1, p. 18 *passim*, pp. 30–4, and about his wife, pp. 10–11 (but he gives no details of their early years together).

17. Kandukuri Viresalingam, 'Stri Vidya', *Viveka Vardhani* (hereafter abbreviated *VV*), February 1875 in *Kandukuri Viresalingam Kavikrta Granthamulu* (hereafter abbreviated *KVKG*), 8 (Rajahmundry, 1951–2), pp. 330–2.

18. Smarta Brahmans are followers of Sankara (*c.* 788–820), believers in monistic or Advaita Vedanta who are supposed to conform to Smrti traditions. Viresalingam expressed devotion by repeating the Gayatri from one hundred to one thousand times each day and visiting the river Godavari and the various Saivite and Vaishnavite temples for prayer. His only recollections of specific practices were of fasting on Shivaratri (fast day of the God Shiva) and of putting the three horizontal stripes of Shiva on his chest, upper arms and face while he was praying: Viresalingam, *Caritramu*, vol. 1, pp. 19, 56.

19. Viresalingam, *Caritramu*, vol. 1, pp. 15, 17. For *pyal* schools, see *The Foreign Missionary* (Philadelphia), 10, no. 2 (February 1889), p. 11, and 'South Indian Pyal Schools', *Christian Mission Intelligencer* 10, n.s. (September 1874), pp. 287–8.

20. Viresalingam, *Caritramu*, vol. 2, p. 138.

21. A. Rampati Rau, 'Pantulu Gari Grantha Racana Mudranamula Vivaramulu' (A Bibliography of Viresalingam's Writings), in *Yuga Purusudu Viresalingam*, p. 206; Viresalingam, *Caritramu*, vol. 2, p. 146.

22. Viresalingam first stated that he passed the Matriculation examination in 1871 but later gave 1870 as the date: Viresalingam, *Caritramu*, vol. 1, p. 66 and vol. 2, p. 146. Although his claim was accepted by his biographers (*The Hindu*, 19 January 1893; Gurunatham, *Viresalingam*, pp. 26–7; V.R. Narla, *Veeresalingam* [New Delhi: Sahitya Akademi, 1968], p. 18), examination of several contemporary sources does not show his name in the lists of students who passed the Matriculation; see Government of Madras, *Godavary District Gazette*, 1869–1871; Government of Madras, *Fort St. George Gazette*, 1869–1871; *Madras Times*, 1870.

23. Viresalingam, *Caritramu*, vol. 1, p. 60. At this time Keshav Chandra Sen had broken with the older Brahmo Samaj members led by Devendranath Tagore and had organized his own association; in contrast to Tagore's stress on the gradual changing of Hinduism, Sen emphasized the necessity of more drastic uprooting of old customs. S. Natarajan, *A Century of Social Reform in India* (Bombay: Asia Publishing House, 1959), pp. 48–9; The Brahmo Samaj, 'Jesus Christ: Europe and Asia' (a lecture given on 5 May 1877), *Keshub Chunder Sen's Lectures in India*, 3rd ed. (Calcutta, 1899), pp. 30–1.

24. Kandukuri Viresalingam, 'Satyamu', *VV*, November 1874, in *KVKG*, vol. 8, pp. 313–20.

25. He began in 1871 as an assistant teacher in the Rajahmundry Provincial School, then passed a government examination qualifying him to practise in the lower courts. In 1872 he accepted a job as headmaster of a village school. That same year he passed a translator's examination in English and Telugu, but he continued to teach and in 1874 became headmaster of a school in Dowleshwaram, a large village near his Rajahmundry home. He lived in the village but walked to town frequently to participate in the activities of the Provincial School Club. In 1875 he passed an English precis writing examination that qualified him for a sub-magistrate's position. Viresalingam, *Caritramu*, vol. 1, pp. 66–77.

26. He first had his journal published in Madras and then persuaded six men to finance the purchase of a press which was set up in his Rajahmundry home. After a quarrel with the Dowleshwaram school management, he left them in 1875 and began a printing business in Rajahmundry. A rupture with his partners followed and he bought them out, using funds from his books. Viresalingam, *Caritramu*, vol. 1, pp. 88, 92–5, 99.

27. Viresalingam, *Caritramu*, vol. 1, pp. 88, 94.

28. Viresalingam, *Caritramu*, vol. 1, p. 99.

29. Viresalingam, *Caritramu*, vol. 1, pp. 77, 92. Viresalingam refused a government job when one was offered to him: Viresalingam, *Caritramu*, vol. 1, p. 13. He attacked government service as the 'meanest' of jobs: Kandukuri Viresalingam, 'Aikamatyamu', *VV*, July 1875 in *KVKG* vol. 8, p. 366.

30. Viresalingam, *Caritramu*, vol. 1, p. 59.

31. For details of Viresalingam's life and career, especially his later career, which cannot be covered here in outline, see John G. Leonard, 'Kandukuri Viresalingam, 1848–1919: A Biography of an Indian Social Reformer' (Ph.D. diss., University of Wisconsin, 1970).

32. Members of the educated elite in the 1870s had difficulty following some of these essays: Nidudavolu Venkata Rau, *Andhra Vacana Vangmayamu* (Madras, 1954), p. 147; G.V. Sitapati, 'Telugu', in Nagendra, ed., *Indian Literature* (Agra: Lakshmi Narain Agarwal, 1959), pp. 53–5, 63–5; Rayasam Venkata Sivudu, *Sri Viresalinga Samsmrti* (Guntur: R.V. Sivudu, 1931); Konda Venkatappayya, *Sviya Caritra*, vol. 1 (Vijayawada: Andhra Rastra Hindi Pracara Sangham, 1952–55), I, p. 60. Classical Telugu, or the poetic dialect, differed from spoken Telugu and had a highly Sanskritized vocabulary and syntax. Poetry was the only approved form of literary creation until the last part of the nineteenth century, with grammar and rhetoric recognized as subsections of poetry. Prose was used for business or government purposes in the spoken dialect and was considered 'village' or crude Telugu. Not only did poetry have a particular structure and dialect, it was also confined to particular subject matter, much of it erotic in nature. This posed a problem to scholars looking for texts for classroom use in the new educational systems. The initial formulation of a solution to this problem for educators in Telugu had come from one of Viresalingam's scholarly predecessors, Cinnaya Suri (1809–62). This non-Brahman became head of the Department of Telugu at Madras Presidency College and standardized many of the rules for classical Telugu as applied to prose.

33. A. Ramapati Rau, 'Viresalingamu Pantulu Savimarsa Parisilanamu' (Ph.D. diss., Osmania University, 1964), pp. 37–8; A. Ramapati Rau, 'Mukhya Ghattamulu', in *Yuga Purusudu*, p. 223.

34. Following the visit of the famous Bengali Brahmo Samaj leader, Keshav Chandra Sen, a Brahman in Madras started a Veda Samaj in 1864; many members were non-Brahmans, however. The founder was Rajagopalacharlu; his friend, Subbarayalu Chetty, a non-Brahman, seems to have been the principal leader. The Veda Samaj limited its activities to preaching, although it started a Tamil journal, *Tattvabodhini*, to propagate the view of the association's leaders. Sridharulu Naidu, a non-Brahman in charge of the association from 1867 until 1874, changed the name to the Southern India Brahmo Samaj and framed regulations more in keeping with Brahmo traditions in Calcutta: Sivanatha Sastri, *History of the Brahmo Samaj*, vol. 2 (Calcutta: R. Chatterjee, 1912), pp. 456–65. After Naidu's death in 1874 the association was dormant until 1878 when a Telugu Brahman, Mannava Buccayya, teacher at a girls' school in Madras, revived it and associated it with the Sadharan Brahmo Samaj in Calcutta. Viresalingam, *Caritramu*, vol. 1, pp. 93–4. For its anti-Brahman character, see Sivudu, *Samsmrti*, p. 38; *The Madras Mail*, 24 November 1881, p. 3.

35. According to R. Srinivasan, the Brahmo movement 'has been wholly forgotten by the Tamils'. He was unable to find books or pamphlets on it in Madras libraries, Brahmo characters in Tamil novels, or more than one Tamil Brahman in the Madras chapter of the Southern Indian Brahmo Samaj. In contrast, he noted the prominence of Telugus in it and the involvement of Telugu zamindars in funding it and of Telugu school teachers in popularizing Brahmo and reformist ideals in Andhra. Citing a 1912 source, he listed six samajs in the Tamil region and 20 in the Telugu-speaking region. (The Madras Presidency had 17,038,000 Tamil speakers and 15,782,000 Telugu speakers in 1911 [*Census of India*, 1911, vol. 12, pt. 2 (Madras, 1912), p. 140].) Finally, he remarked on the appearance of missionaries in Tamil novels in the proselytizing roles given to Brahmos in Bengali literature (and, we add, Telugu literature) of that period: R. Srinivasan, 'The Brahmo Samaj in Tamilnadu', *Journal of the University of Bombay*, arts nos. 44–5 (1975–76), pp. 80–1, 213–25.

36. Viresalingam, *Caritramu*, vol. 1, pp. 138–9; Sastri, *Brahmo Samaj*, vol. 2, pp. 494–5. Despite its name, this association was not derived from the Prarthana Samaj movement in western India.

37. One's occupation was unknown. Viresalingam, *Caritramu*, vol. 1, pp. 135, 159.

38. *The Madras Mail*, 27 October 1880, p. 2.

39. *The Hindu* (Madras), 19 November 1885, and 1 December 1884, p. 5.

40. *The Madras Standard*, 17 November 1879, p. 3, and 13 June 1881, p. 3.

41. Viresalingam, *Caritramu*, vol. 1, p. 79.

42. Viresalingam, *Caritramu*, vol. 1, pp. 79–80.

43. Viresalingam contributed several early articles to journals in Masulipatnam and Madras, but his earliest surviving writings are from *VV*, the articles which he reprinted in the volumes of his collected works: Viresalingam, *KVKG*, vol. 8, pp. 31–47.

44. Viresalingam, *VV*, February 1875, in *KVKG*, vol. 8, p. 335.

45. Although Viresalingam attacked contemporary 'false' scholars as early as January 1875, he began criticizing ancient Indian scholars in April 1875, and he accentuated this criticism in October 1875 and July 1876. See the following articles by him: *VV*, January 1875, in *KVKG*, vol. 8, pp. 325–9; *VV*, April 1875, in *KVKG*, vol. 8, pp. 347–8; 'Brahmanavicaramu', *VV*, October 1875, in *KVKG*, vol. 8, pp. 400–1; 'Brahmanulunu, vari vrttulunu', *VV*, July 1876, in *KVKG*, vol. 8, p. 431.

46. Viresalingam, *VV*, January 1875, in *KVKG*, vol. 8, p. 326; Viresalingam, *VV*, July 1875, in *KVKG*, vol. 8, pp. 36–8; Viresalingam, 'Pramanavicaramu', *VV*, October 1875, in *KVKG*, vol. 8, pp. 392–404.

47. Viresalingam, *VV*, April 1875, in *KVKG*, vol. 8, pp. 348–9.

48. Viresalingam, *VV*, July 1876 in *KVKG*, vol. 8, pp. 428–38.

49. The one-act farce 'Brahma Vivahamu' he published in his journal's supplement, *Hasya Sanjivani*, in July 1876 and he republished this in 1878 as a separate piece. It ridiculed the logic used to justify Brahman marriage customs: Ramapati Rau, 'Pantulu Gari Grantha Racana', in *Yuga Purusudu*, p. 207; Viresalingam, 'Brahma Vivahamu', in *KVKG*, vol. 2, pp. 1–67. He developed the farces to attack social evils: Viresalingam, *Caritramu*, vol. 1, p. 140. His use of colloquial speech offended critics: letter of G.V. Appa Rao, 2 June 1912, as quoted in Vedamu Venkataraya Sastri, *Vedamu Venkataraya Sastrulavari Jivita Caritra Sangrahamu* (Madras, 1949), p. 121. In Madras, however, attacks on Brahmans were deprecated by social reformers: *Athenaeum and Daily News*, 3 June 1874.

50. Viresalingam, *VV*, July 1876, in *KVKG*, vol. 8, pp. 428–38.

51. Viresalingam, *VV*, January 1875, in *KVKG*, vol. 7, p. 329; Viresalingam, *VV*, April 1875, in *KVKG*, vol. 8, pp. 347–9; Viresalingam, *VV*, July 1875, in *KVKG*, vol. 8, p. 364; Viresalingam, 'Aikamatyamu', in *KVKG*, vol. 7, pp. 8, 9.

52. Viresalingam, *VV*, July 1876, in *KVKG*, vol. 8, pp. 431–9.

53. Viresalingam, *VV*, April 1875, in *KVKG*, vol. 8, pp. 343–9.

54. Viresalingam, *VV*, July 1875, in *KVKG*, vol. 8, pp. 363–71; Viresalingam, 'Aikamatyamu', in *KVKG*, vol. 8, pp. 4–13.

55. Viresalingam, *Caritramu*, vol. 1, p. 69.

56. Viresalingam, *Caritramu*, vol. 1, pp. 143–5. Burial rather than cremation prevailed among Telugu Brahman Virashaivites of the Aradhya sect.

57. Viresalingam, *Caritramu*, vol. 1, pp. 140–3.

58. A detailed comparison of the Andhra and Madras social reform movements is in John G. Leonard, 'Viresalingam and the Making of Modern Andhra: Social Reform in Rajahmundry and Madras, 1874–1891' (MS, 1968). A summary appears in Karen I. Leonard and John G. Leonard, 'Social Reform and Women's Participation in Political Culture: Andhra and Madras', in Gail Minault, ed., *The Extended Family: Women and Political Participation in India and Pakistan* (Columbia, Mo.: South Asia Books, 1981), pp. 19–45.

59. Viresalingam, *Caritramu*, vol. 1, pp. 152–8, 277. Kandukuri Viresalingam, 'Rajahamahendravara Stri Punar Vivaha Caritramu', in *KVKG*, vol. 7, pp. 6–8. The latter was an unofficial report presented to the Rajahmundry Widow Marriage Association by Viresalingam on 9 June 1885. It contained a description of the widow marriage campaign and Viresalingam included it in his collected works. Hereafter it will be cited as 'Vivaha Caritramu'. For an example of an orthodox Hindu argument, see Vedamu Venkataraya Sastri, *Stri Punar Vivaha Durvada Nirvapanamu*, 2nd ed. (Madras, 1924).

60. Viresalingam, *Caritramu*, vol. 1, pp. 163–6; *Indian Law Review* 6 (Madras Ser.): pp. 382–3.

61. Viresalingam, *Caritramu*, vol. 1, p. 159; Viresalingam, 'Vivaha Caritramu', in *KVKG*, vol. 7, pp. 11–12.

62. Viresalingam, *Caritramu*, vol. 1, pp. 159, 161–2. D.V. Prakasa Row, 'The Widow Marriage Movement in Madras', *Kayastha Samachar* (Allahabad), vol. 7, no. 6 (1903), p. 540.

63. Sivudu, *Samsmrti*, pp. 2–4, 135–43; Subba Rao, *Memories*, pp. 19–25; *Sundara Rao*, pp. 3–13; C. Cilakamarti Laksminarasimham, *Sviya Caritramu* (Vishakapatnam, 1957), p. 51; Valluri Suryanarayana Rau, *Suryanarayaniyamu* (Kovvuru, 1936), p. 165.

64. Viresalingam, *Caritramu*, vol. 1, pp. 166–8, 170, 252–4; Venkatappayya, *Caritra*, vol. 1, p. 36.

65. Suryanarayana Rau, *Suryanarayaniyamu*, pp. 166–7; Viresalingam, *Caritramu*, vol. 1, pp. 158–62, 171; Viresalingam, 'Vivaha Caritramu', in *KVKG*, vol. 7. p. 11; Prakasa Row, 'Widow Marriage', p. 540.

66. Suryanarayana Rau, *Suryanarayaniyamu*, pp. 166–7.

67. A Deputy Tahsildar found a mother willing to have her widowed daughter remarried and Viresalingam sent a college student to go to the village and bring the girl in the night to his home. Then Viresalingam found a bridegroom, a young man who had been educated for many years in his house, was enthused about widow marriages and was of the right sect. Viresalingam, *Caritramu*, vol. 1, pp. 158–9, 181–4, 188; Viresalingam, 'Vivaha Caritramu', in *KVKG*, vol. 7, p. 17; Prakasa Row, 'Widow Marriage', p. 542.

68. Intimidation from the orthodox Hindu side resulted in Viresalingam's cook and family priest ceasing their services, and many reformers did not attend the wedding because of such threats: Viresalingam, *Caritramu*, vol. 1, pp. 189, 191; Viresalingam, 'Vivaha Caritramu', in *KVKG*, vol. 7, pp. 20–2.

69. Viresalingam, *Caritramu*, vol. 1, pp. 190, 196; Viresalingam, 'Vivaha Caritramu', in *KVKG*, vol. 7, p. 23; Prakasa Row, *Kayastha Samachar* 7, no. 4 (1903): pp. 294–6.

70. Viresalingam, *Caritramu*, vol. 1, pp. 160–1; Viresalingam, 'Vivaha Caritramu', in *KVKG*, vol. 7, p. 11; Prakasa Row, *Kayastha Samachar* 8, no. 5 (1903): p. 413.

71. Venkataraya Sastri, *Vedamu Venkataraya Sastrulavari Jivita Caritra Sangrahamu*, pp. 36–7; Viresalingam, *Caritramu*, vol. 1, pp. 152–8.

72. Viresalingam, *Caritramu*, vol. 1, pp. 172, 184–5, 187, 197–9; Viresalingam, 'Vivaha Caritramu', in *KVKG*, vol. 7, p. 12; Prakasa Row, 'Widow Marriage', p. 542; Venkatappayya, *Caritra*, vol. 1, p. 61.

73. Viresalingam, *Caritramu*, vol. 1, pp. 197–9, 281–2; Viresalingam, 'Vivaha Caritramu', in *KVKG*, vol. 7, pp. 18–20, 23–4, 25; Prakasa Row, *Kayastha Samachar* 8, no. 4 (1903): pp. 296–7.

74. Prakasa Row, *Kayastha Samachar* 8, no. 4 (1903): pp. 298–301, 294; Viresalingam, *Caritramu*, vol. 1, pp. 204–9.

75. Viresalingam, *Caritramu*, vol. 1, pp. 215–19, 230, 242, 246; Viresalingam, 'Vivaha Caritramu', in *KVKG*, vol. 7, p. 31; Prakasam, *Yatra*, p. 89; Venkatappayya, *Caritra*, vol. 1, p. 36; Prakasa Row, *Kayastha Samachar* 8, no. 4 (1903): pp. 299–301.

76. *The Madras Mail*, 12 September 1882, p. 3.

77. *Indian Law Review* 6 (Madras Ser.): pp. 381–96; Viresalingam, *Caritramu*, vol. 1, p. 235; Prakasa Row, *Kayastha Samachar* 8, no. 4 (1903): p. 298.

78. *Hindu Desabhimani* in *Madras Native Newspaper Reports*, October 1882; *Vizag Observer*, no. 20, and *Purusharthapradayini*, nos. 4, 5 and 6, in *Madras Native Newspaper Reports*, July 1883.

79. *The Madras Standard*, 27 April 1883, p. 3; *The Madras Mail*, 25 April 1883, p. 2, and 26 April 1883, p. 3.

80. Viresalingam, *Caritramu*, vol. 1, pp. 196–266; Prakasa Row, *Kayastha Samachar* 8, no. 5 (1903): p. 414.

81. Five per cent of Hindu girls in Madras Presidency, but 11 per cent of Brahman girls, married before the age of 10; and 3.3 per cent of Brahman girls 10 to 14 were widowed, compared to less than 1 per cent of all girls 10 to 14. The marriage percentages before the age of 10 are from 1881: *Imperial Census of 1881* (Presidency of Madras) (Madras: Government of India, 1883), vol. 1, pp. 70–3, and the widow percentages from 1891: *Census of India*, 1891 (Presidency of Madras) (Madras: Government of India, 1893), XIII, pp. 146–7.

82. Gurunatham, *Viresalingam*, p. 101; Viresalingam, 'Vivaha Caritramu', in *KVKG*, vol. 8, pp. 41–2.

83. Viresalingam had given many of the bridegrooms allowances in their college days to permit them to continue their educations, and the marriages themselves usually cost more than they ordinarily would have for boys of that status—thus expectations were raised but the benefits after marriage were not very great. Viresalingam mentioned only a few bridegrooms who were dissatisfied but the situation was obviously more serious. The old reform association was dissolved, and a new one was constituted specifically to exclude some bridegrooms and to counter the demands of the married couples. Viresalingam, *Caritramu*, vol. 1, pp. 278–9; Gurunatham, *Viresalingam*, pp. 115–17.

84. Viresalingam, *Caritramu*, vol. 1, pp. 325–75; Gurunatham, *Viresalingam*, pp. 104–12; Prakasa Row, *Kayastha Samachar* (Allahabad) 8, no. 5 (1903): pp. 415–17. For the satire Viresalingam published, see Kandukuri Viresalingam, 'Dambhacarya Vilasanamu', *VV*, 13 March 1886, and Ramapati Rau, 'Grantha Racana', in *Yuga Purusudu*, p. 211. Lakshminarasimham's initial reaction was to burn *Viveka Vardhani* at a public demonstration, although he later apologized for this outburst; see Viresalingam, *Caritramu*, vol. 1, pp. 347–54.

85. *The Indian Social Reformer* 16 (1905): pp. 548, 560.

86. Gurunatham, *Viresalingam*, pp. 180–1. In the 1880s, journals were still the main outlet for Telugu authors, and Viresalingam published scholarly works on Telugu poetry in his journal until he was forced to discontinue it in 1890 because of competing journals and government pressure. Then he and his friend Nyapati Subba Rao started a monthly journal which Viresalingam edited, *Cintamani*. From 1891 on this journal featured novels published serially, and although a few novels had been published just prior to this time (including one by Viresalingam), Telugu novels really originated with this journal's encouragement (Venkata Rau, *Andhra Vacana*, pp. 139–41). Telugu journals founded in 1885 in Madras competed with *Viveka Vardhani* in its last years: *Andhra Prakasika* was closely allied with the Madras Mahajana Sabha, a political association formed in 1884, and the Brahmo Samaj leader in Madras, Mannava Buccayya, began *Hindu Jana Samskaram*, which represented the interests of social reform in Madras. Other specialized journals began in 1885 and 1891. The type of men who edited these journals changed for most Telugu journals from 1885 to 1891, a change coinciding with the decline of social reform. The new editors were not Western-educated Telugu scholars but members of the educated elite who practised journalism as a profession. Educated as lawyers or teachers, these men were more attuned to the new currents in politics than the older editors. The Madras Mahajana Sabha got publicity for its efforts from the English-language *The Hindu*, but *Andhra Prakasika* (Telugu) and *Swadesamitra* (Tamil) became regional-language journals allied with the Sabha: *The Hindu*, 21 January 1885, p. 5; *The Madras Mail*, 18 September 1885, p. 4. *Andhra Prakasika* soon outstripped *Viveka Vardhani* and the *Andhra Bhasha Sajivani* in circulation, but it concentrated solely on political issues. Buccayya was a friend of Viresalingam, and his *Hindu Jana Samskaram* combined political and social comment and

equalled *Viveka Vardhani's* circulation: *Madras Native Newspaper Reports*, January to December 1885 (Madras Record Office). The literary journal *Amrta Granthamali* of Nellore began in 1885 and the Rajahmundry Prarthana Samaj journal *Satya Samvardhani* began in 1891: *Amudrta Grandha Cintamani* (Nellore), no. 9 (1887); Sivudu, *Samsmrti*, p. 31. For the new editors, *The Hindu*, 8 April 1895, p. 4; Sivudu, *Samsmrti*, p. 31.

87. Prakasam, *Yatra*, p. 252.

88. Much later, in the beginning of the twentieth century, this process stimulated an interest in a political guarantee—an Andhra state—for the continuation of the Telugu cultural revival. See John G. Leonard, 'Andhra Movement', *Journal of Commonwealth Political Studies* 5, no. 1 (March 1967), pp. 60–77.

89. Viresalingam, *VV*, July 1880, in *KVKG*, vol. 8, p. 485; Kandukuri Viresalingam, 'Desabhimanamu', *VV*, July 1881, in *KVKG*, vol. 8, p. 555; Kandukuri Viresalingam, 'Sangha Duracara Nivaranamunaku Stri Vidya Yavasyakamu', *VV*, March 1885, in *KVKG*, vol. 8, pp. 639–40.

90. Kandukuri Viresalingam, 'Stri Punar Vivaha Visayakopanyasamu', in *KVKG*, vol. 7, pp. 13, 48.

91. Viresalingam, 'Stri Punar . . .', in *KVKG*, vol. 7, pp. 5, 48, 56.

92. Kandukuri Viresalingam, 'Desabhimanamu', *VV*, July 1880, in *KVKG*, vol. 8, pp. 482–3.

93. Viresalingam, 'Desabhimariamu', *VV*, July 1880, in *KVKG*, vol. 8, p. 482.

94. Viresalingam, 'Stri Punar . . .', in *KVKG*, vol. 7, pp. 6–16.

95. Kandukuri Viresalingam, 'Hindu Matamulu', in *KVKG*, vol. 7, p. 3.

96. Kandukuri Viresalingam, 'Kalamu Yokka Viluva', *VV*, March 1880, in *KVKG*, vol. 8, p. 460; Kandukuri Viresalingam, 'Vaidyulu', *VV*, February 1881, in *KVKG*, vol. 8, p. 510; Viresalingam, *VV*, October 1881, in *KVKG*, vol. 8, p. 562.

97. Kandukuri Viresalingam, 'Isvara Datta Pustakamulu', in *KVKG*, vol. 7, p. 22; Viresalingam, 'Stri Punar . . .', in *KVKG*, vol. 7, pp. 6, 11.

98. Viresalingam used the phrase 'common folk' or 'ordinary people' (*samanya janulu*) which has a vulgar connotation in Telugu. Our use of 'the masses' expresses the social distance which Viresalingam felt separated him from the masses of illiterate people.

99. Kandukuri Viresalingam, 'Rajakiya Pathasalalu', *VV*, March 1881, in *KVKG*, vol. 8, p. 526; Kandukuri Viresalingam, 'Kulina Brahmana Vivahamulu', *VV*, August 1885, in *KVKG*, vol. 8, p. 647; Viresalingam, *VV*, July 1880, in *KVKG*, p. 489.

100. Viresalingam, *VV*, July 1880, in *KVKG*, vol. 8, p. 485; Kandukuri Viresalingam, 'Desabhimanamu', *VV*, July 1881, in *KVKG*, vol. 8, p. 555.

101. Kandukuri Viresalingam, 'Sangha Duracara Nivaranamunaku Stri Vidya Yavasyakamu', *VV*, March 1885, in *KVKG*, vol. 8, pp. 639–40.

102. Viresalingam, 'Isvara Datta Pustakamulu', in *KVKG*, vol. 7, p. 22.

103. Kandukuri Viresalingam, 'Desa Bhasalu', *VV*, October 1881, in *KVKG*, vol. 8, pp. 556–66.

104. Kandukuri Viresalingam, 'Desabhivrddhi', *VV*, January 1883, in *KVKG*, vol. 8, p. 597.

105. Kandukuri Viresalingam, 'Patupaduta', *VV*, November 1884, in *KVKG*, vol. 8, p. 633.

106. Kandukuri Viresalingam, 'Vidyadhikula Yokka Krtyamulu', *VV*, June 1883, in *KVKG*, vol. 8, p. 607.

107. Viresalingam, *VV*, October 1881, in *KVKG*, vol. 8, p. 566.

108. Kandukuri Viresalingam, 'Vidyadhikula Yokka Krtyamulu', *VV*, March 1882, in *KVKG*, vol. 8, pp. 577–8; Kandukuri Viresalinga, 'Andhra Bhasabhivrddhi', *VV*, June 1882, in *KVKG*, vol. 8, pp. 580–1.

109. Viresalingam, *VV*, November 1886, in *KVKG*, vol. 8, p. 667; *The Hindu*, 12 January 1885, p. 6.

110. Viresalingam, *VV*, March 1882, in *KVKG*, vol. 8, pp. 577–8; Kandukuri Viresalingam, 'Desa Bhasa', *VV*, November 1886, in *KVKG*, vol. 8, p. 670.

111. Viresalingam, *VV*, June 1882, in *KVKG*, vol. 8, pp. 580–1; Viresalingam, 'Vidyadhikula Yokka Krtyamulu', *VV*, March 1882, in *KVKG*, vol. 8, pp. 577–8; Viresalingam, *VV*, January 1883, in *KVKG*, vol. 8, p. 600.

112. Kandukuri Viresalingam, 'Stri Vidyabhyasamu', *VV*, February 1884, in *KVKG*, vol. 8, p. 624; Viresalingam, *VV*, November 1886, in *KVKG*, vol. 8, p. 667.

113. Viresalingam, *VV*, June 1882, in *KVKG*, vol. 8, p. 667.

114. Viresalingam, *VV*, November 1884, in *KVKG*, vol. 8, p. 633; Viresalingam, *VV*, November 1886, in *KVKG*, vol. 8, p. 667.

115. Viresalingam, *VV*, July 1881, in *KVKG*, vol. 8, p. 554; Kandukuri Viresalingam, 'Janmantaramu', in *KVKG*, vol. 7, pp. 9–10

116. Viresalingam, *VV*, March 1882, in *KVKG*, vol. 8, p. 577; *The Hindu*, 12 January 1885, p. 6; Kandukuri Viresalingam, 'Desiya Mahasabhalu, Dani Yuddesamulunu', in *KVKG*, vol. 8, pp. 1–6.

117. Viresalingam, *VV*, November 1884, in *KVKG*, vol. 8, p. 633; Kandukuri Viresalingam, 'Kulacara, Matacara Samskaranamu', *VV*, April 1887, in *KVKG*, vol. 8, pp. 674–7; Viresalingam, 'Desiya Mahasabha . . .', in *KVKG*, vol. 8, pp. 21–46.

118. Viresalingam, *VV*, November 1886, in *KVKG*, vol. 8, p. 667.

119. Viresalingam, 'Desiya Mahasabha. . .', in *KVKG*, vol. 8, pp. 8–17.

120. Viresalingam, *VV*, November 1886, in *KVKG*, vol. 8, p. 667.

121. *The Hindu*, 15 July 1893, p. 3; Government of Madras, *General Index to Proceedings, Government of Madras*, 1894 (Madras, 1893), p. 339.

122. Cilakamarti Lakshminarasimhan gives an amusing description of the educated elite travelling from one district conference to another: *Caritramu*, pp. 127, 165–75.

123. *The Hindu*, 3 July 1895, p. 6; *The Madras Times*, 10 June 1895, p. 4; for a description of how social reform issues were treated in the different conferences, see Viresalingam, *Caritramu*, vol. 2, pp. 56–8.

124. *The Hindu Weekly Edition*, 11 April 1907, pp. 9–10; *The Indian Social Reformer*, 15 (1905), pp. 436–7.

11

Conjugality and Hindu Nationalism

Resisting Colonial Reason and the Death of a Child-Wife*

TANIKA SARKAR

At the risk of provoking startled disbelief, I propose to place ideas about Hindu conjugality at the very heart of militant nationalism in Bengal.[1] Historians have seen the centrality of debates around colonial laws relating to women and marriage in the discourse of liberal reformers. Thus far, however, they have not located these themes within early Hindu nationalism.

I will examine three interlocking themes in this chapter. First, I believe that in the last four decades of the nineteenth century a fairly distinct political formation had emerged, which could loosely be called revivalist-nationalist. This was a mixed group of newspaper proprietors, orthodox urban estate-holders of considerable civic importance within Calcutta, and pandits as well as modern intellectuals whom they patronized. Such people used an explicitly nationalist rhetoric against any form of colonial intervention within the Hindu domestic sphere. Their rhetoric marked them off from the broader category of revivalist thinkers who did not necessarily oppose reformism in the name of resisting colonial knowledge. At the same rime, the revivalist-nationalist group's commitment to an unreformed Hindu way of life separated them from liberal nationalists of the Indian Association and Indian National Congress variety. Needless to say, the groups spoken of here were not *irrevocably* distinct or mutually exclusive. Yet, despite the overlaps, there was clearly a distinctive political formation of nationalists who contributed to the emerging nationalism a highly militant agitational rhetoric and mobilizing techniques that were built around a defence of Hindu patriarchy.

The second theme involves exploring why the revivalist-nationalists chose to tie their nationalism to issues of conjugality, which they defined as a system of non-consensual, indissoluble, infant marriage.

And, finally, in relation to the third theme, we need to dwell upon the arguments they fabricated. We find that the age of consent issue forced a decisive break in their discourse. It made it imperative for revivalist-nationalists to shift to an entirely different terrain of arguments and images, moving from the realm of reason and pleasure to

*From Tanika Sarkar, *Hindu Wife, Hindu Nation: Community, Religion and Cultural Nationalism* (Delhi: Permanent Black, 2001), pp. 191–225.

that of discipline and pain. My elaboration of these themes is intended to widen the context of early nationalist agitations and provide them with an unfamiliar genealogy.

A few words are necessary to explain why, in the present juncture of cultural studies on colonial India, it is important to retrieve this specific history of revivalist-nationalism, and to work with a concept of nationalism that incorporates this history. Edward Said's *Orientalism* has fathered a received wisdom on colonial studies that has proved to be as narrow and frozen in its scope as it has been powerful in its impact. Said's work proceeds from a conviction about the totalizing nature of a Western power-knowledge which gives to the entire Orient a single image with absolute certainty. Writings of the Subaltern Studies pandits and of a group of feminists, largely located in first-world academia, have come to identify this singular structure of colonial knowledge as the originary moment for all possible kinds of power and disciplinary formations. Going hand in hand with 'Orientalism', this concept is seen by such academics to reserve for itself the whole range of hegemonic capabilities. This unproblematic and unhistoricized 'transfer of power' to structures of colonial knowledge has three major consequences: first, it constructs a monolithic, unstratified colonized subject who is powerless and without an effective or operative history of his/her own. The only history that she is capable of generating is 'derivative'. As a result, the colonized subject is absolved of all complicity and culpability in the makings of structures of exploitation over the last two hundred years of Indian colonial history: the subject's only culpability lies in the surrender to colonial knowledge. As a result, the lone political agenda for a historiography of this period shrinks into native contestations of colonial knowledge—since all power supposedly flows from this single source. Every species of contestation, by the same token, is taken to be equally valid. Today, with the triumphalist growth of aggressively communal and/or fundamentalist identity politics in our country, such a position comes close to indigenism. In fact it comes close to being intellectually Fascist in its authoritarian insistence on the purity of indigenous epistemological and autarkic conditions.

The Saidian magic formula has weird implications for the feminist agenda as well. The assumption that colonialism had wiped out all past histories of patriarchal domination, replacing them neatly and exclusively with Western forms of gender relations, has naturally led on to an exclusive identification of patriarchy in modern India with the project of liberal reform. While liberalism is made to stand in as the only vehicle of patriarchal ideology (since it is complicit with Western knowledge), its opponents—the revivalists and the orthodoxy—are vested with a rebellious, even emancipatory agenda, since they prevented colonisation of the domestic ideology. And since, for such academics, colonized knowledge is regarded as the exclusive source of all power, all that contests it is supposed to possess an emancipatory possibility for women. By easy degrees, then, we reach the position that while opposition to widow immolation was complicit with the colonial silencing of non-colonized voices and, consequently, was an exercise of power, the practice of widow immolation itself was a contestatory act outside the realm of power relations since it was not sanctioned by colonialism. In a country where people will still gather in their lakhs to watch and celebrate the burning of a teenaged girl as sati, such cultural studies are grim with political implications.

It is apparent that colonial structures of power compromised with—and indeed learnt much from—indigenous patriarchy and upper-caste norms and practices which, in certain areas of life, retained considerable hegemony. This indubitable fact opens out a new context against which to revaluate liberal reform. Above all, we need to remember that other sources of hegemony, far from becoming extinct, were reactivated under colonialism and opposed the liberal-rationalist agenda with considerable vigour and success. The historian cannot view the colonial past as an unproblematic arena within which all power was on one side and all protest on the other. It is necessary to take into account a multi-faceted nationalism (and not simply its liberal variant), all aspects of which were complicit with power and domination even when they critiqued Western knowledge and challenged colonial power.

II

A summary of controversial legislative activity pertaining to Hindu marriage in the late nineteenth century will help map our discursive field. The Native Marriage Act III of 1872 was, for its times, an extremely radical package which prohibited polygamy, legalized divorce and laid down a fairly high minimum age of marriage. It also ruled out caste or religious barriers to marriage. Predictably, the proposed bill raised a storm of controversy. Its jurisdiction was eventually narrowed down to such people as would declare themselves to be not Hindus, not Christians, not Jains, not Buddhists and not Sikhs. In short, its scope came to cover the Brahmos alone, whose initiative had led to its inception in the first place.[2]

Furious debates around the bill opened up and problematized crucial areas of Hindu conjugality—in particular the system of non-consensual, indissoluble infant marriage whose ties were considered to remain binding upon women even after the death of their husbands. This polemic hardened in 1887 when Rukma Bai, an educated girl from the lowly carpenter caste, refused to live with her uneducated, consumptive husband, claiming that since the marriage was contracted in her infancy it could be repudiated by her decision as an adult. She was threatened with imprisonment under Act XV of 1877 for non-restitution of conjugal rights. The threat was removed only after considerable reformist agitation and the personal intervention of Victoria.[3] The issue foregrounded very forcefully the problems of consent and indissolubility within Hindu marriage.[4]

In 1891 the Parsi reformer Malabari's campaign bore fruit in the Criminal Law Amendment Act 10 which revised Section 375 of the Penal Code of 1860, and raised the minimum age of consent for married and unmarried girls from 10 to 12.[5] Under the earlier penal code regulation a husband could legally cohabit with a wife who was 10 years old. The revivalist Hindu intelligentsia of Bengal now claimed that the new act violated a fundamental ritual observance in the life-cycle of the Hindu householder—that is, the 'garbhadhan' ceremony, or the obligatory cohabitation between husband and wife which was meant to take place immediately after the wife reached puberty. Since puberty, in the hot climate of Bengal, was quite likely to occur before she was 12, the new legislation meant that the ritual would no longer remain compulsory. If the wife reached puberty before attaining the age of consent, then obviously garbhadhan could not be performed. This in turn implied that the 'pinda', or ancestral offerings, served up by the sons of such marriages would become impure and that generations of ancestors would be starved of it. The argument provided the central ground for a highly organized mass campaign in Bengal. The first open mass-level anti-government protest in Calcutta and the official prosecution of a leading newspaper were its direct consequences.[6]

This summary might be taken to suggest, Cambridge School fashion,[7] that nationalist initiative was actually a mere reflex action, following mechanically upon the legal initiatives of the colonial state. This was far from being the case. Not only was colonial initiative itself generally a belated and forced surrender to Indian reformist pressure, Hindu revivalist reaction against both was ultimately constituted by a new political compulsion: it was coterminous with a recently acquired notion of the colonized self which arose out of the 1857 uprising, the post-Mutiny reprisals, Lyttonian discriminatory policies in the 1870s, and the Ilbert Bill racist agitations in the 1880s. These experiences collectively modified and cast into agonizing doubt the earlier choice of loyalism that the Bengali intelligentsia had made, fairly unambiguously, in 1857. Our understanding of responses to colonial legislation can make only very limited and distorted sense unless they are located within this larger context.

Whereas early-nineteenth-century male liberal reformers had been deeply self-critical about the bondage of women within the household,[8] the satirized literary self-representation of the Bengali 'baboo' of later decades recounted a very different order of lapses for himself: his was a self that had lost its autonomy and now willingly hugged its chains. Rethinking about the burden of complicity with colonialism hammered out a reoriented self-critique as well as a heightened perception about the meaning of subjection. It is no accident that even the economic critiques of drain, deindustrialization and poverty would come to be developed by the post-1860s generations.

With a gradual dissolution of faith in the progressive potential of colonialism, a dissolution that accompanied political self-doubt and the failure of indigenous economic enterprises,[9] there was also a disenchantment with the magical possibilities of Western education. Earlier reformers had been led to look hopefully at the public sphere as an arena for the test of manhood, of genuine self-improvement. But now, with activities shrinking into parasitic petty landlordism and tenure-holdings, or to mechanical chores within an oppressive and marginalized clerical existence, the *bhadralok* household increasingly resembled a solitary sphere of autonomy, a site of formal knowledge where—and only where—education would yield practical, manipulable, controllable results. The Permanent Settlement had generated a class of parasitic landlords with fixed revenue obligation whose passivity was reinforced by uninhibited control over their peasants' rent. The gap between a fixed sum of revenue and flexible rent procurement in a period of rising agricultural prices cushioned an existence of fairly comfortable tenure holding. The Rent Acts of 1859 and 1885, however, breached that security. Organized tenant resistance of the late nineteenth century led to heightened anxieties and uncertainties among the landed gentry. The household, consequently, became doubly precious and important as the only zone where autonomy and self-rule could be preserved.[10]

In the massive corpus of household management manuals that came to occupy a dominant place in the total volume of printed vernacular prose literature of these years, the household was likened to an enterprise to be administered, an army to be led, a state to be governed[11]—all metaphors rather poignantly derived from activities that excluded colonized Bengalis. Unlike Victorian middle-class situations, then, the family was not a refuge after work for the man. It was their real place of work. Whether in the Kalighat bazaar paintings[12] or in the Bengali fiction of the nineteenth century, workplace situations remain shadowy, unsubstantial, mostly absent. Domestic relations alone constitute the axis around which plots are generated, in sharp contrast with, for example, Dickensian novels.[13]

The new nationalist worldview, then, reimaged the family as a contrast to and a critique of alien rule. This was done primarily by contrasting two different versions of subjection—that of the colonized Hindu male in the world outside, and that of the apparently subordinated Hindu wife at home. The forced surrender and real dispossession of the former was counterposed to the allegedly loving, willed surrender and ultimate self-fulfilment of the latter.[14] It was in the interests of this intended contrast that conjugality was constituted as the centre of gravity around which the discursive field on the family organized itself. All other relations, even the mother–child one (which would come to take its place as a pivotal point in later nationalist discourse) remained subordinated to it up to the end of the nineteenth century. It was the relationship between the husband and wife that mediated and rephrased, within revivalist-nationalism, the political theme of domination and subordination, of subjection and resistance as the lyrical or existential problem of love, of equal but different ways of loving.

The household generally, and conjugality specifically, came to mean the last independent space left to the colonized Hindu. This was a conviction that was both shaped and reinforced by some of the premises of colonial law. English legislators and judges postulated a basic division within the legal domain: British and Anglo-Indian law had a 'territorial' scope and ruled over the 'public' world of land relations, criminal law, laws of contract, and evidence. On the other hand, there were Hindu and Muslim laws which were defined as 'personal', covering persons rather than areas, and ruling over the more intimate areas of human existence—family relationships, family property and religious life.[15] Early nationalists chose to read this as a gap between on the one hand the *territory* or the *land* colonized by an alien law, and on the other the *person*, still ruled by one's own faith. This was a distinction that the Queen's Proclamation of 1859, promising absolute non-interference in religious matters, did much to bolster.[16] Even in subjected India, therefore, there could exist an interior space that was as yet putatively inviolate.

Far from trying to hegemonize this sphere and absolutize its control, colonial rule, especially in the post-1857 decades, tried to keep its distance from it, thus indirectly adding to the nationalist conviction. The earlier zeal for textualization and codification of traditional laws was gradually replaced by a recognition of the importance of unwritten and varied custom, of the inadvisability of legislation on such matters, and of urging judicial deference, even obedience, to local Hindu opinion.[17] Towards the end of the century, a strong body of Hindu lawyers and judges came to be formed whose conformity to Hindu practices (Hindutva) was often taken to be of decisive importance in judicial decision-making, even though their professional training was in Western jurisprudence, not in Hindu law.[18] There was, moreover, an implicit grey zone of unwritten law whose force was nevertheless quite substantial within law courts.[19] Take a Serampore court case of 1873, for instance, where a Hindu widow was suing her brothers-in-law for defrauding her of her share in her husband's property by falsely charging her with 'unchastity'. Her lawyer referred frequently to notions of kinship obligations, ritual expectations from a Hindu widow and moral norms and practices of high-caste women.[20] Clearly, these arguments were thought to possess value in convincing the judge and the jury, even though overtly they had little legal significance. Far from laughing peculiarly Hindu susceptibilities out of court, English judges, even the Privy

Council, seriously rationalized them. Referring to the existence of a Hindu idol as a legal person in a different law suit, an English judge commented: 'Nothing impossible or absurd in it . . . after all an idol is as much of a person as a corporation.'[21] Legal as well as ritual niceties about the proper disposition of idols were seriously debated, and sacred objects were brought into courts of law after due ritual purification of the space.[22] The introduction of a limited jury system between the 1860s and the 1880s in Bengal further strengthened the voice of local Hindu notables, and, consequently, of local usages and norms. An official recommendation of 1890 curtailed the powers of the jury in many directions but left the powers of settling marriage disputes intact in their hands.[23]

Nor did colonial legislators and judges form a unified, internally coherent body of opinion on proper Hindu norms and practices which they would then try to freeze. A substantial debate developed over a proposal in 1873 to transfer the cognisance of cases connected with marriage offences, especially adultery, from criminal to civil courts. While Simson, the Dacca commissioner, recommended the repeal of penal provisions against adultery, Reynolds, the magistrate of Mymensingh strongly demurred: 'I have always observed with great aversion the practice of the English law in giving damages in cases of adultery and seduction, and wanted it to remain a criminal offence.'[24] About cases of forfeiture of property rights by 'unchaste widows', there was a clear division between the high courts of Allahabad on the one hand and those of Bombay, Madras and Calcutta on the other.[25] The divisions reflected the absence of any monolithic or absolute consensus about the excellence of English legal practice as a model for Indian life.

These decades had in England seen profound changes in women's rights *vis-à-vis* property holding, marriage, divorce, and the rights of prostitutes to physical privacy,[26] Englishmen in India were divided about the direction of these changes and a significant section felt disturbed by the limited, though real, gains made by contemporary English feminists. They turned with relief to the so-called relative stability and strictness of Hindu rules. The Hindu joint-family system, whose collective aspects supposedly fully submerged and subordinated individual rights and interests, was generally described with warm appreciation.[27] Found here was a system of relatively unquestioned patriarchal absolutism which promised a more comfortable state of affairs than what emerged after bitter struggles with Victorian feminism at home.

The colonial experience, in its own way, mediated and reoriented debates on conjugal legislation in England. There were important controversies: the best known being between John Stuart Mill and James Fitzjames Stephen on the issue of consensus *vs* force and authority as the valid basis for social and human relations. Stephen, drawing on his military-bureaucratic apprenticeship in India, questioned Mill's premise of complementarity and the notion of the companionate marriage.[28]

There was no stable legal or judicial model that could, therefore, be imported into India. Prior to the Judicature Act of 1873 there were four separate systems of courts in England, each applying its own form of law, and these were often in conflict with each other.[29] In any case, the prolonged primacy of case-law and common-law procedures with-in England itself made English judges in India agree with Indian legal and nationalist opinion that customs, usages and precedents were far more valid sources of law than legislation.[30]

A general consensus about the differentiated nature of colonial law, then, postulated a fissure within the system wherein Hindus could insert their claims for a sectoral yet complete autonomy, for a pure space. The specific and concrete embodiment of this purity seemed to lie more within the body of the Hindu woman rather than the man—a conviction shaped, no doubt, by the growing self-doubt of the post-1857 Hindu male. Increasingly, irony and satire, a kind of black humour, became the dominant form of educated middle-class literary self-representation. There was an obsessive insistence on the physical manifestation of this weakness. The feeble Bengali male physique became a metaphor for a larger condition. Simultaneously, it was a site of the critique of the ravaging effects of colonial rule. 'The term Bengali is a synonym for a creature afflicted with inflammation of the liver, enlargement of the spleen, acidity or headache.'[31] Or, 'Their bones are weak, their muscles are flabby, their nerves toneless.'[32] Or, 'Bengal is ruined. There is not a single really healthy man in it. The digestive powers have been affected and we can eat but a little. Wherever one goes one sees a diseased people.'[33] Through the grind of Western education, office routine[34] and enforced urbanization, with the loss of traditional sports and martial activities, the male Bengali body was supposedly marked, maimed and completely worn down by colonialism. It was the visible site of surrender and loss, of defeat and alien discipline.

The woman's body, on the other hand, was still held to be pure and unmarked, loyal, and subservient to the discipline of shastras alone. It was not a free body by any means, but one ruled by 'our' scriptures, 'our' custom. The difference with the male body bestowed on it a redemptive, healing strength for the community as a whole. An interesting change now takes place in the representation of Hindu women in the new nationalist discourse. Whereas for liberal reformers she had been the archetypal victim figure, for nationalists she had become a repository of power, the Kali rampant, a figure of range and strength.[35]

What were the precise sources of grace for Hindu women? A unique capacity for bearing pain was one. So was the discipline exercised upon her body by the iron laws of absolute chastity, extending beyond the death of the husband, through an indissoluble, non-consensual infant form of marriage, through austere widowhood, and through her proven capacity for self-immolation. All these together imprinted an inexorable disciplinary regimen upon her person that contained and defined her from infancy to death.

Such discipline was not entirely confined to the normative or conceptual sphere. Bengal, with the exception of the Central Provinces and Berar, and Bihar and Orissa, had the highest rate of infant marriages—a custom that cut across caste and community lines and did not markedly decrease even after the Act of 1891.[36] Before it was banned, Bengal had also been, as we know, the heartland of the practice of sati. The Hindu woman's demonstrated capacity for accepting pain thus became the last hope of greatness for a doomed people. As we saw, Bankimchandra linked sati with national regeneration:

> I can see the funeral pyre burning, the chaste wife sitting at the heart of the blazing flames, clasping the feet of her husband lovingly to her breasts. Slowly the fire spreads, destroying one part of her body and entering another. Her face is joyful. . . . The flames burn higher, life departs and the body is burnt to ashes. . . . When I think that only some time back our

women could die like this, then new hope rises up in me, then I have faith that we, too, have the seeds of greatness within us. Women of Bengal: You are the true jewels of this country.[37]

Bankim had plenty of reservations on other aspects of Hindu conjugality,[38] but he seemed to identify with it at its most violent point of termination, through a highly sensualized spectacle of pain and death, a barely disguised parallel between the actual flames destroying a female body and the consuming fires of desire.

III

There were two equally strong compulsions and possibilities in the construction of Hindu womanhood—love and pain—which produced deep anxieties within early nationalism.

The accent on love had, from the beginning, underlined acute discomfort about mutuality and equality. Pandit Sasadhar Tarkachuramani, the doyen of Hindu orthodoxy, argued that a higher form of love distinguished Western from Hindu marriages. While the former seeks social stability and order through control over sexual morality, the latter apparently aspires only towards 'the unification of two souls'. 'Mere temporal happiness, and the begetting of children are very minor and subordinate considerations in Hindu marriage.'[39] The revivalist-nationalist segment of the vernacular press, polemical tracts and manuals translated the notion of marriage of souls as mutual love lasting practically from cradle to funeral pyre. This uniquely Hindu way of loving supposedly anchored the woman's absolute and lifelong chastity.[40] Yet the very emphasis on love, so necessary as a critique of alien oppression and misunderstandings of the Hindu order, was a double-edged weapon: once it was raised, sooner or later the question of the mutuality of such love was bound to arise. Was it equally binding on both partners? If not, and since Hindu males were allowed to be polygamous, could its jurisdiction on women be anything more than prescriptive? Particularly if marriage was imposed on her at birth, without the question of her consent or choice?

Nothing in the Hindu shastras would confirm the possibility of mutually mono-gamous ties. To redeem this absence there appeared, for the first time in the history of Hindu marriage, a wave of polemical literature that valorized, indeed insisted on, male monogamy: 'We find tracts that advise widowers never to remarry.'[41] Manuals advocating self-immolation for the adult widow now simultaneously advise that child widows should be remarried; they have no obligation towards a husband whom they have not, as yet, come to love.[42] Not just sacred texts but custom too now allows a wide spectrum of castes to make a second marriage possible for men if the first wife is barren or bore no sons.[43] Yet in the absence of a shastric or custom-based injunction against polygamy, and given the reluctance among Hindu revivalist-nationalists to invite reformist legis-lation, male chastity was fated to remain normative rather than obligatory, while the woman's chastity was not a function of choice or willed consent. This was a compromise that became fundamentally difficult to sustain.

Through much of the 1880s we find a studied silence on this uncomfortable equa-tion within the Hindu marriage and a self-mesmerizing repetition of its innately aesthetic qualities. The infant-marriage ritual is drenched in a warm, suffusing glow. 'People in this country take a great *pleasure* in infant-marriage. The *little bit* of a woman, the infant bride, clad in red silk, her back turned towards her boy husband. . . . The drums are beating, and men, women and children are running in order to glimpse that face . . . from time to time she breaks forth into *little* ravishing smiles. She looks like a *little lovely doll*' (italics mine).[44] The key words are little, lovely, ravishing, pleasure, infant and doll.[45] They are inserted at regular intervals to make the general account of festivities draw its warmth from this single major source—the delight-giving and delighted infant bride. The community of 'men, women and children' that forms for the occasion is bonded together by a deeply sensuous experience, by great visual pleasure, by happiness. The radiant picture of innocent celebration is rounded off through the cleverly casual insertion of the phrase 'boy husband'. Yet infant marriage was prescriptive only for the girl. The groom of the 'lovely doll' could be, and frequently was, a mature, even elderly man, possibly much-married already. A strategic and organizing silence lies at the heart of this image of desire and pleasure.

Even if the quality of Hindu love was assumed to be 'higher', Hindu marriage was still placed firmly within mainstream developments in the universal history of marriages which had supposedly trodden a uniform path from the 'captive' stage to fairly permanent, often sacramental, systems. Consent-based alternatives, whether in ancient Indian or in class-based modern Western traditions, were dismissed as aberrations or minor variations.[46] A long editorial, significantly entitled 'The Bogus Science', questioned the sources and authenticity of reformist knowledge: the nature of their evidence, of deduction, of arrangement of proof.[47] A powerful eugenics-based argument against infant marriage (infant marriages produce weak progeny) was countered by a climatic view of history:[48] irrespective of the age of the parents, a tropical climate was in any case bound to produce weak children: reformers were thereby accused of casuistry or weak logic. And since the penal code had earlier laid down 10 as the minimum age of consent, how would raising it to 12 ensure genuine consent? 'A girl of fourteen or sixteen is not capable of legally signing a note of hand for 5 rupees and she is, *ipso facto*, a great deal more incompetent to give her consent to defile her person at twelve.'[49] It was also considered more than a little dishonest to place such importance on the woman's consent in this one matter since, within post-marital offences, 'in the case of the wife the point does not turn on consent, for, if that had been the case, there would have been no such offence as adultery in the Penal Code'.[50] A high premium was thus placed on the rule of rationality in the defence of Hindu marriage.

Hindu rationality was represented as more supportive than reformist or colonial projects. Given the physical and economic weakness of women, an indissoluble marriage tie had to be her only security. This contention conveniently overlooked the fact that, in a polygamous world, indissolubility was binding, in effect, on women alone. A clear-eyed kulin brahmin widow had remarked: 'People say that the seven ties that bind the Hindu wife to the husband do not snap as they do with Christians or Muslims. This is not true. According to Hindu law, the wife cannot leave the husband but the husband may leave her whenever he wants to.'[51] It was also maintained that consent was immaterial since parents were better equipped to handle the vital question of security than an immature girl.[52] Security also largely depended upon perfect integration with the husband's family, so the sooner the process began, the better it was for the girl.[53]

Hindu marriage, in the rather defensive discourse of the 1880s, then, was more pleasurable and more beautiful, kinder and safer, more rational, and guaranteed by a sounder system of knowledge. In any case, it was essentially a part of universal deve-lopments in the history of civilizations: differences in marriage systems between the Hindu and the non-Hindu were played down, if not obliterated.

The Rukma Bai episode of 1887 made it imperative at last to rewrite this narrative of love and pleasure in the language of force. The earlier lyricism in relation to such 'love' had already been ruptured from time to time to underline and recuperate the basic fact of non-consensuality. At a meeting convened at the palace of the Shova Bazar Raj, Rajendralal Mitra had insisted: 'in it [Hindu marriage] there is no selection, no self-choice, no consent on the part of the bride. She is an article of gift, she is given away even as a cow or any other chattel.' Approving laughter greeted his exposition and he went on: 'There is in Hinduism not the remotest idea of choice and whoever changed any small part of it was no Hindu.'[54] Rukma Bai's action violently foregrounded the sexual double standards and made a mockery of the notion of the loving heart of Hindu conjugality. A lot of the debate centred around the vexed question of whether a woman could sue for separation from an adulterous husband. 'Among the Hindus, unchastity on the part of the husband is certainly a culpable offence but they set much higher value upon female chastity': its erosion would lead to the loss of family honour, growth of half-castes and the destruction of ancestral rites.[55] Bare, stark bones that formed the basic foundation of Hindu marriage now began to surface, threatening to blow the edifice of love away. 'A good Hindu wife should always serve her husband as God even if that husband is illiterate, devoid of good qualities and attached to other women. And it is the duty of the government to make Hindu women conform to the injunctions of the Shastras.'[56] The basis of conjugality now openly shifts to prescription.

Rukma Bai had forced a choice upon her community—between the woman's right to free will and the future of the pristine essence of Hindu marriage: the two could no longer be wedded together as a perfect whole. Revivalist-nationalists had to treat the two as separate, conflicting units, and indicate their own partisanship.

That came forth in no time at all. 'It is very strange that the whole of Hindu society will suffer for the sake of a very ordinary woman.'[57] Or, 'kindness to the female sex can-not be a good plea in favour of the proposed alteration.'[58] Interestingly, the episode had shown up another fault in the image of the Hindu community. Rukma Bai belonged to the carpenter caste, where divorce had been customary. Whose custom must colonial law recognize now? Was Hinduism a heterogeneous, indeed, self-divided, self-contradictory formation, or was it a unified monolithic one? The revivalist-nationalist answer, once again, was unambiguous. 'The Brahmin caste occupies the highest position and all laws and ordinances have been formed with special reference to that. All the other castes conduct themselves after the fashion of the Brahminical castes.'[59] Or, 'it is true that divorce obtains among some low-caste people and the government should be really doing an important duty as a ruler if it should make laws fixing and negotiating the uncertain and unsettled marriage customs of the people.'[60]

The debate prised open the imagined community along lines of caste and gender and delineated the specific contours of the revivalist-nationalist agenda. This could no longer base its hegemonic claims on its supposed leadership of the struggle of a whole subjected people for autonomy and self-rule in their 'private' lives. Its nationalism became more precisely defined now as the rule of brahmanical patriarchy. Its rationality was based on the forced and absolute domination of upper-caste male standards, not universal reason leading towards freedom and self-determination for the dispossessed. If it aspired to detach Hindus from colonized reason and lead them to self-rule, it would only do so by substituting for it a brahmanical, patriarchal reason based on scripture-cum-custom, both of which were disciplinary and oppressive for the ruled subjects—as was the colonial regime in the sphere of political economy. The contestation of colonization was no simple escape from or refusal of power: nor had colonialism equally and entirely disempowered all Indians. Resistance was an agenda itself irrevocably tied to schemes for domination, an exercise of power that was nearly as absolute as that which it resisted.

IV

Curiously, one possibility within Hindu marriage had not occurred to reformists or to Bengali Hindu militants—the possibility of the sexual abuse of infant wives. There had been, from time to time, the occasional stray report. The *Dacca Prakash* of June 1875 reported that an 'elderly' man had beaten his child-wife to death when she refused to go to bed with him. Neighbours had tried to cover it up as suicide but the murder charge was eventually proved. The jury, however, let off the husband with a light sentence.[61] The *Education Gazette* of May 1873 had reported a similar incident when the 'mature' husband of a girl of 11 'dragged her out by the hair and beat her till he killed her' for similar reasons. He was let off with a light sentence as well.[62] Reporting remained sporadic and the accounts were not picked up and woven into any general discussion about Hindu marriage as yet. The controversy over the right age of consent continued to hinge on eugenics, morality, child rearing and family interests.

In 1890 Phulmonee, a girl of 10 or 11, was raped to death by her husband Hari Maiti, a man of 35. Under existing penal code provisions, however, he was not guilty of rape since Phulmonee had been well within the statutory age limit of 10. The event, however, added enormous weight and urgency to Malabari's campaign for raising the age of consent from 10 to 12. The reformist press began to systematically collect and publish accounts of similar incidents from all over the country. Forty-four women doctors brought out long lists of cases where child-wives had been maimed or killed because of rape.[63] From the possible effects of child marriage on the health of future generations, the debate shifted to the life and safety of Hindu wives.

Phulmonee was the daughter of the late Kunj Behari Maitee, a man from the 'Oriya Kyast' caste, who had been a 'Bazar Sircar' at Bow Bazar Market. It was a well-paid job and it seems that, by claiming 'Oriya Kyast' status, the family was aspiring to a superior caste position in consonance with their economic viability: Maitees were otherwise categorised as a low Sudra group. The family frequently referred to its specific caste practices in court with some pride. They said that while they adhered to child marriage, they forbade cohabitation before the girl's menstruation and that, in this respect, Phulmonee had not come of age. Their version was that the newly married couple had been kept apart according to caste rules, and that Hari, on a visit to his in-laws, had stolen into Phulmonee's room and had forced himself upon her, thereby causing her death. Hari Maiti, however, insisted that since their marriage she had spent at least a fortnight at his house and they had slept together all the time. He made no mention of caste rules against pre-menstrual cohabitation. It seems, then, that caste customs remained loose and flexible, and that each family would allow considerable manipulation within them.

Even though Hari Maiti had insisted that on the last night they had not had intercourse, medical opinion was unanimous that the girl had died of violent sexual penetration. If the court accepted that Hari was right and that Phulmonee had slept with him earlier, then it could go a long way to show that since nothing untoward had happened earlier, on the fatal night in question Hari would not have had any reason to suspect that more vigorous penetration might lead to violent consequences. He would, in fact, have been able to seem convinced that intercourse was perfectly safe. The English judge, Wilson, clearly indicated that he chose to accept Hari's version, thus exonerating him from the charge of culpable homicide. The charge of rape, in any case, was not permissible since the penal code provisions ruled out the existence of rape by the husband if the wife was above the age of 11. The judge was equally opposed to any extension of the strict letter of the law, in this case to devise exemplary punishment for a particularly horrible death: 'Neither judges nor juries have any right to do for themselves what the law has not done.'

The judge built up his case on the hypothetical argument that the couple had slept together earlier. He chose to ignore the version given by the women in the girl's family—of Radhamonee, Bhondamonee and Sonamonee, the mother, aunt and grandmother of the girl.

> I think it is my duty to say that I think there exists hardly such solid and satisfactory ground as would make it safe to say that this man must have had knowledge that he was likely to cause the death of the girl . . . You will, of course, in these, as in all matters, give the benefit of any doubt in favour of the prisoner.
>
> The weight of concern is, very blatantly, on the exoneration of the man rather than on the fate of the woman. The law itself was shaped so as to preserve custom as well as the male right to the enjoyment of an infantile female body.

What needs to be particularly noted here is that, throughout the trial, the judge was saying nothing about a husband who insisted on sleeping with a child, or about the custom which allowed him to do so with impunity. Above all, he was not making any judgmental comparison between the ways of husbands, Eastern or Western. In fact, he bent over backwards to exonerate the system of marriage that had made this death possible: 'Under no system of law with which Courts have had to do in this country, whether Hindu or Mohammedan, or that formed under British rule, has it ever been the law that a husband has the absolute right to enjoy the person of his wife without regard to the question of safety to her.'[64]

Both the Hindu husband and the Hindu marriage system are generously exempted from blame and criticism. There is, in fact, an assertion about a continuity in the spirit of the law from the time of the Hindu kingdoms to that of British rule. A significant body of English medical opinion confirmed the clean bill of health that the colonial judiciary had advanced to the Hindu marriage system. Even in a strictly private communication, meant for colonial officialdom alone, the secretary to the Public Health Society wrote to the Government of Bengal:

The council direct me to lay special stress upon the point . . . that they base no charge against the native community.

They reverently cited the work on Hindu law by Sir Thomas Strange to evoke, in near-mystical terms, the supreme importance of his marriage rules to the Hindu, and the inadvisability of external interference with them.

The council admit that our native fellow subjects must be allowed the fullest possible freedom in deciding when their children should be ceremonially married. That, in the constitution of Hindu society, is a matter with which no Government could meddle and no Government ought to meddle.

They proceeded to review the considerable medico-legal data on sexual injuries inflicted on child wives and concluded that, whatever the weight of evidence on the matter, the system of infant marriage must continue unabated. The age of commencing cohabitation could be raised *only if Hindus themselves expressed a great desire for change* (emphasis mine).

Contrary to received wisdom, then, there is hardly here a vision of remaking the Hindu as a pale image of his master, nor of designs of total change and reform. Macaulay's notorious plan of recasting the native as a brown sahib was not necessarily uniformly dominant for the entire spectrum of colonial rule. Even when dominant, it had to make crucial negotiations with other imperatives and value preferences and, above all, with the everlasting calculations of political expediency. If, at the time of Macaulay, the Anglicist vision of a Westernized middle class had appeared as the strongest reservoir of loyalism, soon enough other alternatives emerged and were partially accommodated, modifying the earlier formula and crucially mitigating its reformist thrust. Our moment of the 1890s comes after a long spell of middle-class agitation over demands on constitutional rights, of Indianization of the services, of security against racial discrimination and abuse. It comes after the outburst of white racism over the Ilbert Bill issue, when the educated middle class was temporarily vested with the possibility of standing in a position of judicial authority over Europeans. Empowering the Indian through Westernization, consequently, came to be envisaged as the most threatening menace to colonial racial structures.[65] It was a moment when the slightest concession to Indian liberal reformism would be made most unwillingly and only in the belief that it represented a majority opinion.

The new legislation was conceived after the reformist agitation had convinced the authorities that the 'great majority' was ready for change.[66] After the Phulmonee episode, revivalist-nationalists were maintaining a somewhat embarrassed silence; this was broken only after the proposed bill came along. During the interval the reformist voice alone was audible. Since this, for the moment, looked like the majority demand, political expediency coincided temporarily with reformist impulse and the government committed itself to raising the age of consent. At the same time, official opinion in Bengal did not extend the terms of the specific reform to larger plans for invasive change. On the contrary, it displayed a keenness to learn from the codes of Hindu patriarchy. Did a recognition that they were confronted with the most absolute form of patriarchal domination evoke a measure of unconscious respect and fellow feeling among the usually conservative, male English authorities, rather than the instinct for reform? As the secretary to the Public Health Society put it: 'The history of British rule and the workings of British courts in India manifest a distinct tenderness towards . . . the customs and religious observances of the Indian people.'[67]

There was still the mangled body of 'that unhappy child, Phulmonee Dassee', a girl of 10 or 11, sexually used by a man whom she had known only a few weeks, 29 years her senior, a man who had already been married (aunt Bhondamonee's evidence in court). There was the deposition of her mother Radhamonee: 'I saw my daughter lying on the cot, weltering in blood. Her cloth and the bed cloth and Hari's cloth were wet with blood.'[68] There was unanimous medical opinion that Hari had caused the death of a girl whose body was still immature and could not sustain penetration. She died after 13 hours of acute pain and continuous bleeding, The dry medical terminology somehow accentuates the horror more than words of censure:

> A clot, measuring 3 inches by one-and-a-half inches in the vagina . . . longitudinal tear one and three quarters long by one inch broad at the upper end of the vagina . . . a haematoma three inches in diameter in the cellular tissue of the pelvis. Vagina, uterus and ovaries small and undeveloped. No sign of ovulation.[69]

Phulmonee's was by no means an isolated case. Dr Chever's investigations of 1856 mentioned at least 14 cases of premenstrual cohabitation that had come to his notice, and the subsequent finding incorporated in Dr McLeod's report on child marriage amply corroborated his data.[70] We may presume that only such cases as would have needed police intervention or urgent medical attention entered the records. These were, then, cases of serious damage that resulted from premature sexual activity. An Indian doctor reported in court that 13 per cent of the maternity cases that he had handled involved mothers below the age of 13. The defence lawyer threw a challenge at the court: cohabiting with a pre-pubertal wife might not have shastric sanction, yet so deep-rooted was the custom that he wondered how many men present in court were not in some way complicit with the practice.[71]

The divisional commissioners of Dacca, Noakhali, Chittagong and Burdwan deposed that child marriage was widely prevalent among all castes, barring the tribals, in their divisions. The commissioner of Rajshahi division found that only in Jalpaiguri district 'Mlechhes and other aboriginal tribes do not favour child marriage . . . amongst the Muhammadans and Rajbungshis, females being useful in field work, are not generally married until they are more advanced in age'. On the whole, the practice was more common among lower castes. The average age of marriage for upper-caste girls was slowly moving up to 12 or 13 due to the relatively large spread of the new liberal education among them, and, ironically, to the growing pressures of dowry which forced parents to keep daughters unmarried till they could put together an adequate amount of dowry.[72] In fact, the compulsion to delay marriage till the dowry could be collected would have found a convenient ally in the new liberalism. Among the lower castes, on the other hand, emulation of brahmanical orthodoxy rather than of liberal values would be a more assured way of claiming pure ritual status. Wherever infant marriage prevailed, there was no way of ensuring that cohabitation would be delayed till the onset of puberty.

While both scriptural and customary injunctions were too strongly weighted in favour of early marriage to allow a raising of the age of marriage for girls, certain parts of the shastras did prescribe against pre-pubertal cohabitation among married couples. Nobinchandra Sen, poet and district magistrate of Chittagong, suggested that this injunction could be reinforced with legislation. Official opinion tried to distinguish between two distinct levels in marriage; the wedding ceremony itself was interpreted as a sort of a betrothal, after which girls remained in their parents' homes. It was only after the onset of puberty that they went through a 'second marriage' and went off to live with their husbands. A group of medical reformers' (Indian as well as European doctors who advocated changes in marriage rules on strictly medical grounds) as well as administrators advised legislation to ban marital cohabitation, before the performance of the second marriage. They hoped that there was sufficient shastric as well as customary sanction behind the practice.[73]

It was soon clear, however, that too much was being made of the 'second marriage'. It was not generally taken to constitute a distinct separate stage within marriage as a whole. While there was widespread recognition that girls should begin regular cohabitation only after they attained puberty, the custom was customarily violated. Once the marriage had been performed, domestic (especially female) pressure pulled the wife into the husband's family. In any case, it was difficult to decide exactly at what age girls attained puberty or make sure that no girl was sent off to her husband any earlier. Viable legislation would have to spell out a definite age at which puberty started rather than indicate a general physical condition.

The definition of puberty proved to be the stumbling block. According to custom, it was equated with the onset of regular menstruation. And here, revivalist-nationalists were treading delicate ground. While they wanted to oppose the proposed age of 12, they could not push the age too far back, since they had not opposed the earlier penal code ban on marital cohabitation before the girl was 10. If they now chose to construe the earlier ban as an oppressive intrusion which had already interfered with Hindu marriage practices, then they could no longer sustain their present agitational rhetoric to the effect that the current intervention was the first fundamental violation of Hindu conjugality, and therefore spelt the beginning of the end of the only free space left to the Hindu. Without this sense of a new, momentous beginning of doom, the pitch of the highly apocalyptic rhetoric would fall flat. If the new legislation were to be seen as merely a part of a long-drawn-out process, then opposition to it could hardly invest itself with a life-or-death mission. They therefore insisted that 'true puberty' only occurred between the of ages of 10 and 12. Even if menstruation occurred earlier, it was a fluke and not a regular flow. The earlier penal code regulation had not therefore interfered with the garbhadhan ceremony. Since, in the hot climate of Bengal, menarche was sure to start between 10 and 12, further raising the age of consent would constitute the first real breach in ritual practice.

Reformers argued that puberty sets in properly only after 12. In this, they used a different notion of puberty. While revivalist-nationalists unequivocally equated puberty with menarche, medical reformers argued that puberty was a prolonged process and menarche was the sign of its commencement, not of its culmination. The beginning of menstruation did not indicate the girl's 'sexual maturity'—which meant that her physical organs were developed enough to sustain sexual penetration without serious pain or damage. Until that capability had been attained, they argued, the notion of her consent was meaningless.

It is remarkable how all strands of opinion—colonial, revivalist-nationalist, medical-reformer—agreed on a definition of consent that pegged consent to a purely physical capability, divorced entirely from free choice of partner, from sexual, emotional or mental compatibility. Consent was put into a biological category, a stage when the female body was ready to accept sexual penetration without serious harm. The only problem lay in establishing when this stage was reached.

It would be simplistic, however, to conclude that there was complete identity of patriarchal values between reformers and revivalists. Whatever their broader views, reformers always had to struggle along with a minimalist programme since nothing else would have the remotest chance of acceptability either with the legislative authorities or in Hindu society. We only have to remind ourselves about the explosive protests that this legislation provoked. Reformist campaigning for legislation was more a consciousness-raising device, a foregrounding of issues of domestic ideology than pinning effective hopes of real social change to acts. Nor was the minimalist programme of insisting on the woman's physical safety an insignificant matter, under the circumstances. Revivalist-nationalists on the other hand, grounded their agenda on the most violently authoritarian regime of patriarchal absolutism. Their insistence upon self-rule in the domestic sphere coincided with their insistence that the Hindu girl should sacrifice her physical safety, and even her life if necessary, to defend the community's claim to autonomy.

As the reformist campaign gathered momentum and as the government, by the end of 1890, seemed committed to Malabari's proposals, Hindu militants were faced with two options. They could accept a radical reorientation of their earlier emphasis: that is, they could admit of a basic problem within present marriage practices and then separate them from past, supposedly authentic, norms. This way, they could still maintain their distance from reformers by insisting on reform from within in place of alien legislation from outside. While this would have amounted to an honourable face-saving device, it would still have implied an assault on the totality and inviolability of what had so far been exalted as the essential core of the system. Worse still, it would have amounted to a surrender to missionary, reformist and rationalist critiques of Hindu conjugality. On the other hand, it could come to terms with the phenomenon of violence and build its own counter-campaign around its presence. If difference was found to lie not in superior rationality, greater humanism, pleasure or love, but rather in pain and coercion, then these constituents of difference should be admitted and celebrated.

V

The Age of Consent Bill could have reasonably been faulted on many counts. It was an unbelievably messy and impractical measure. The reporting and verification of violations were generally impossible in familial situations. Even if the girl—provided she survived—and her parents were willing to depose against the husband, neighbours, whose evidence was crucial in such cases, usually protected the man. Proving the girl's age was fairly impossible in a country where births, even today, are not often registered. Medical examination was often inconclusive. Where matters did eventually reach the court, the jury and British judges, fearful of offending custom, rarely took a firm stand. In 1891 the mother of a young girl had pressed for legal action in such a case and the girl herself gave very definite evidence in court. On the basis of a dental examination the English magistrate, however, could not be absolutely certain that she was not over 12. The husband was consequently discharged.[74] Unnerved by the massive anti-bill agitations, the government hastened to undermine the scope of the act. Five days after its enactment. Lord

Lansdowne sent circulars instructing that enquiries should be held by 'native Magistrates' alone, and in any case of doubt prosecution should be postponed.[75]

The nationalist press referred to these problems from time to time but used them as auxiliary arguments rather than as central ones. Certain other kinds of political criticism found a stronger resonance. There was a powerfully articulated fear about the extension of police intrusion right into the heart of the Hindu household.[76] There was also strong opposition on the grounds that an unreformed and unrepresentative legislature should not legislate on such controversial matters[77]—a criticism that sought to link the anti-Bill agitation with (Moderate) Congress-type constitutional demands. These protests too remained rather marginal to the true core of the Hindu revivalist-nationalist debate, which was carried on by hardliners like the newspapers *Bangabashi, Dainik O Samachar Chandrika* and *The Amrita Bazar Patrika*.

Hindu nationalists started on a very familiar note that had been struck on all sorts of issues since the 1870s: a foreign government was irrevocably alien and immune to the meaning of Hindu practices. And where knowledge does not exist, there power must not be exercised. A somewhat long illustration from the *Dainik O Samachar Chandrika* sums up a number of typical statements on the matter.

> That a woman should, from her childhood, remain near her husband, and think of her husband and should not even think of or see the face of another man . . . are injunctions of the Hindu Shastras, the significance whereof is understood only by 'sattvik' [pure] people like the Hindus. The English look to the purity of the body. But in Hindu opinion she alone is chaste and pure who has never even thought of one who is not her husband. No one who does not see with a Hindu's eye will be able to understand the secret meaning of Hindu practices and observances. . . . According to the Hindu the childhood of a girl is to be determined by reference to her first menses and not to her age . . .[78]

The first point made here is a methodological one that disputes the attempt to comprehend any foreign system of meaning through one's own cognitive categories (and immediately proceeds to do so itself by generalizing on English attitudes about the body and the soul). The meaning of Hindu female childhood is then made different through a different arrangement of medical, sexual, moral and behavioural conditions. While revivalist-nationalists do not, as yet, insist on complete autonomy in the actual formulation and application of personal laws, they do claim the sole and ultimate right to determine their general field of operations. The claim is justified by breaking up and dispersing the sources of Hindu conjugality among numerous and ever-shifting points of location. Some could be based on written texts, some located in oral traditions, yet others in ritual practice, and—most problematic of all—a whole lot could be simply embedded in an undefinable, amorphous, diffused Hindu way of life, accessible to Hindu instincts alone. The intention is to disperse the sources of Hindu law and custom beyond codified texts, however authoritative or authentic those might be. Even an ancient authority like Manu, who advocated 16 as the upper limit of marriage age for girls, was dismissed as someone who wrote for the colder northern regions—where puberty came later. Charak and Susruta were dismissed even more summarily as near-Buddhists who had scant regard for true Hindu values. The process of wide dispersal renders Hindu customs opaque and infinitely flexible, to the point of being eternally elusive to colonial authorities.

The crucial emphasis lay in the reiteration that the proposed law was the first of its kind to breach and violate the fundamentals of Hinduism. The argument could only be clinched by derecognizing the importance of earlier colonial interventions in Hindu domestic practices. Sati, it was argued, was never a compulsory ritual obligation and its abolition therefore merely scratched the surface of Hindu existence. The Widow Remarriage Act had a highly restricted scope, simply declaring children born of a second marriage to be legal heirs to their fathers' properties.[79] Reformers replied that the new bill was no unprecedented revision of custom either, since the penal code had already banned cohabitation for girls before the age of 10. Since girls could attain puberty before that age, the sanctity of the garbhadhan ceremony had already been threatened. Hindu revivalist-nationalists retaliated with a reference to the elusive sources of Hindu custom and a notion of the Hindu 'normalizing' order which could be grasped by pure-born Hindus alone: 'It seems they [the reformers] do not know the meaning of *Adya Rim* [real menses]. Mere flow of blood is no sign of *Adya Ritu*. A girl never menstruates before she is ten and even if she does the event must be considered unnatural.'[80] This took care of the 1860 Penal Code provision against cohabiting with a girl under 10. An 'authentic' Hindu girl, according to revivalists, does not reach puberty before she is 10. The earlier ban had therefore not really tampered with Hindu practices. Were the ceiling to be extended to 12, a serious interference would occur. The meaning of physicality itself is constituted differently and uniform biological symptoms do not point to a universal bodily developmental scheme, since Hindus alone know what stands for the normal and the abnormal in the body's growth.

The insistence that the English were about to commit a primal sin against Hinduism, that an unprecedented attack was going to be mounted on the last pure space left to a conquered people, was necessary to relocate the beginnings of true colonisation here and now—so that a new chronology of resistance could also begin from this moment, redeeming the earlier choice of loyalism. 'The Indians have felt for the last two centuries that India is no longer theirs, that it has passed into the hands of the Yavanas. But the Indians have, up to this time, found solace in the thought that though their country is not theirs, their religion is theirs.'[81]

Or, even more forcefully and explicitly, 'No, no, a hundred battles like that of Plassey, Assay, Multan could not in terribleness of effect compare with the step Lord Lansdowne has taken.'[82] With the possibility of protest in the near future, apocalyptic descriptions of subjection became common: 'The day has at length arrived when dogs and jackals, hares and goats will have it all their way. India is going to be converted into a most unholy hell, swarming with hell worms and hell insects. . . . The Hindu family is ruined.'[83]

It was this language of resistance and repudiation that gave the Age of Consent controversy such wide resonance among the Bengali middle class. The *Bangabashi*, in particular, formulated a rhetoric in these years with phenomenal success,[84] becoming in the process the leading Bengali daily, changing over from its weekly status, and pulling a whole lot of erstwhile reformist papers into its orbit for some time. Even Vidyasagar, the ideal-typical reformer figure, criticized the bill.[85]

The response of a fairly pro-reform journal, the *Bengalee*, epitomizes the way in which the new agitational mood reacted on a potentially reform-minded, yet largely nationalist, intelligentsia. It had supported the bill quite staunchly up to the end of

January 1891, after which there seemed to occur an abrupt change of line. In February, after reporting on 'an enormous mass protest meeting, the largest that had ever been held', it started to find problems with the legislation—albeit more of a constitutional kind, with reflections upon the unrepresentative nature of the legislature.[86] In March it covered yet another mammoth protest meeting and then redefined the grounds of its own opposition. 'It is no longer the language of appeal which opponents of the Bill address to the rulers of the land. . . . However much we may differ from the opponents of the measure, we cannot but respect such sentiments.'[87]

We therefore turn to the 'language' of the opponents, to the *Bangabashi*. Here was a radical leap from mendicant appeals, from oblique and qualified criticism and from guilt and shame-ridden self-satirization, here was the birth of a powerful, self-confident nationalist rhetoric. 'Who would have thought that a dead body would rise up again? Whoever thought that millions of corpses would again become instinct with life?'[88] There was an exhilarating sense of release in the naming of the enemy.

> The Englishman now stands before us in all his grim and naked hideousness. What a grim appearance. How dreadful the attitude . . . The demons of the cremation ground are laughing a wild, weird laugh. Is this the form of our Ruling power? Brahmaraksharh, Terror of the Universe; Englishmen . . . do you gnash your teeth, frown with your red eyes, laugh and yell, flinging aside your matted locks . . . and keeping time to the clang of the sword and bayonet . . . do you engage yourselves in a wild dance . . . and we . . . the twenty crores of Indians shall lose our fear and open our forty crores of eyes.[89]

Very confidently, almost gleefully, every former trapping of rationalization was peeled away from the core message. Admittedly, sanction for infant marriage came from Raghunandan alone, who was a late and local authority. It might well lead to other deaths.[90] It did, in all likelihood, weaken future progeny and lead to racial degeneration; but 'the Hindu prizes his religion above his life and short-lived children'.[91] Hindu shastras undoubtedly imposed harsh suffering on women: 'This discipline is the pride and glory of chaste women and it prevails only in Hindu society.'[92] There were yet other practices that might bring on her death.

> Fasting on *Ekadashi* [fortnightly fasting—without even a drink of water—to which widows are meant to ritually adhere] is a cruel custom and many weak-bodied widows very nearly die of observing it . . . it is prescribed only in a small 'tatwa' of Raghunandan. Is it to be banned, too, for this reason, and the guardian of the widow arraigned in front of the High Court and pronounced guilty by the Baboo jurors?[93]

There would be other Phulmonees who would die similar violent deaths through infant marriage. Yet:

> the performance of the garbhadhan ceremony is obligatory upon all. Garbhadhan must be after first menstruation. It means the first cohabitation enjoined by the shastras. It is the injunction of the Hindu shastras that married girls must cohabit with their husbands on the first appearance of their menses and all Hindus must implicitly obey the injunction. And he is not a true Hindu who does not obey it . . . If one girl in a lakh or even a crore menstruates before the age of twelve it must be admitted that by raising the age of consent the ruler will be interfering with the religion of the Hindus. But everyone knows

that hundreds of girls menstruate before the age of twelve. And garbhas [wombs] of hundreds of girls will be tainted and impure. And the thousands of children who will be born
of those impure garbhas will become impure and lose their rights to offer 'pindas' [ances-
tral offerings].[94]

Even in translation the power of the voice comes through. The repetitive short
sentences joined by 'ands', the frequency of the word 'must', the use of vast and yet vaster
numbers to build up inexorably towards a sense of infinite doom—all add up to an
incantatory, mandatory, apocalyptic mode of speech that is the typical vehicle for a
fundamentalist millenarianism. All external reasoning has been chipped away, just the
bare mandate is repeated and emphasized through threats and warnings. This is an
immensely powerful, dignified voice, aeons away from timid mendicancy or morbid
self-doubt. This is the proud voice of the community legislating on itself total defiance
of foreign rule and alien rationalism. It speaks the authoritative word in the appropriately
authoritarian voice. The Hindu woman's body is the site of a struggle that for the first
time declares war on the very fundamentals of an alien power-knowledge system. Yet it
is not merely a displaced site for other arguments but remains, at this moment, the heart
of the struggle. Bengali Hindu revivalist-nationalism, at this formative moment, begins
its career by defining itself as the realm of unfreedom.

This contestation of alien reformism and rationalism, this defence of community
custom, represses the pain of women whose protest was drowned to make way for a
putative consensus. It is no longer possible to resurrect the protest of Phulmonee and
of many, many other battered child-wives who died or nearly died as a result of marital
rape. We have, however, several instances when cases were lodged at the initiative of the
girl's mother, sometimes forcing the hand of the male guardians—for those times a rare
demonstration of the woman's protest action. We also have a court deposition left by a
young girl who was severely wounded and violated by her elderly husband.

> I cannot say how old I am. I have not reached puberty. I was sleeping when my husband
> seized my hand. . . . I cried out. He stopped my mouth. I was insensible owing to his
> outrage on me. My husband violated me against my will. . . . When I cried out he kicked
> me in the abdomen. My husband does not support me. He rebukes and beats me. I cannot
> live with him.

The husband was discharged by the British magistrate. The girl was restored
to him.[95]

Notes

1. I use the term 'militant nationalism' in a somewhat unconventional sense here: not as a part of
a definite and continuous historical trend but as a moment of absolute and violent criticism of
foreign rule that was developed by a group of Hindus in the late 1880s and early 1890s, largely over Hindu marriage controversies. Certain newspapers, especially the *Bangabashi*, took the
lead in mobilizing protest, organizing mass rallies, and provoking official prosecution. That
particular group, however, soon withdrew from the scene of confrontation. In the Swadeshi
Movement of 1905–8, the *Bangabashi* would remain quiescent, even loyal to the authorities.
I owe this piece of information to Sumit Sarkar. For an excellent study of the newspaper, see
Amiya Sen, 'Hindu Revivalism in Bengal' (Ph.D. thesis, Delhi University, 1980).

2. Charles H. Heimsath, *Indian Nationalism and Hindu Social Reform* (Princeton: Princeton University Press, 1977), pp. 91–4; Ajit Kumar Chakraborti, *Maharshi Debendranath Tagore* (Allahabad, 1916; Calcutta, 1971), pp. 406–35.

3. The act of 1877 was a colonial intervention to tighten up the marriage bond which the Hindu orthodoxy strongly defended on the grounds that it coincided with and reinforced the true essence of Hindu conjugality.

4. See Dagmar Engels, 'The Limits of Gender Ideology: Bengali Women, the Colonial State, and the Private Sphere, 1890–1930', *Women Studies, International Forum*, vol. 12, 1989.

5. Heimsath, pp. 147–5.

6. See extracts from *Bangabashi* and *Dainik O Samachar Chandrika* between 1889 and 1891 in *RNP*.

7. For this version of Cambridge historiography on Indian nationalism, see J. Gallagher, A. Seal and G. Johnson, *Locality, Province and Nation* (Cambridge, 1973).

8. I have discussed this in 'Hindu Household and Conjugality in Nineteenth-Century Bengal', paper read at the Women's Studies' Centre, Jadavpur University, Calcutta, 1989.

9. N.K. Sinha, *Economic History of Bengal* (Calcutta, n.d.), vol. I.

10. See my Introduction within the present volume [*Hindu Wife, Hindu Nation*].

11. See for instance Prasad Das Goswami, *Amader Samaj* (Serampore, 1896); Ishanchandra Basu, *Stri Diger Prati Upadesh* (Calcutta, n.d.); Kamakhya Charan Bannerji, *Stri Shiksha* (Dacca, 1901); Monomohan Basu, *Hindur Achar Vyavadhar* (Calcutta, 1872); Chandranath Basu, *Grahasthya Path* (Calcutta, 1887); Bhubaneswar Misra, *Hindu Vivaha Samalochan* (Calcutta, 1875); Tarakhnath Biswas, *Bangiya Mahila* (Calcutta, 1886); Anubicacharan Gupta, *Grihastha Jivan* (Calcutta, 1887); Narayan Roy, *Bangamahila* (Calcutta, n.d.); Chandrakumar Bhattacharya, *Bangavivaha* (Calcutta, 1881); Pratapchandra Majumdar, *Stri Charitra* (Calcutta, n.d.); Purnachandra Gupta, *Bangali Bau* (Calcutta, 1885); and many others.

12. See the preponderance of this theme in the collection of W.C. Archer, *Bazaar Paintings of Calcutta* (London, 1953).

13. See, for instance, plots in the novels of Bankimchandra, *Bankim Rachanabali*, vol. I.

14. Prasad Das Goswami, op. cit.

15. See, for instance, Sir William Markby, Fellow, Balliol College and erstwhile judge in Calcutta High Court, *Hindu and Mohammadan Law* (1906; reprinted Delhi, 1977), pp. 2–3.

16. See frequent reference to the Queen's Proclamation in the agitational writings in the nationalist press, *RNP*, 1887–91.

17. Markby, op. cit., for a convergence of the views of this Orientalist scholar-cum-colonial judge with Hindu legal opinion; and c.f. Sripati Roy, *Customs and Customary Law in British India*, Tagore Law Lectures, 1908–9 (reprinted Delhi, 1986), pp. 2–6.

18. See J.D.M. Derrett, *Religion, Law and the State in India* (London, 1968).

19. For a clarification of the notion of unwritten law, see Robert M. Ireland, 'The Libertine Must Die: Sexual Dishonour and the Unwritten Law in the 19th Century United States', *Journal of Social History*, Fall 1989.

20. *The Bengalee*, 7 March 1873.

21. Markby, op. cit., p. 100.

22. This relates to a case involving the disposition of a Shalgram-shila in the case of Surendranath Bannerjee *vs* the chief justice and judges of the High Court at Fort William, July 1883. See an account in Subrata Choudhary, 'Ten Celebrated Cases Tried by the Calcutta High Court', in *High Court at Calcutta, Centenary Souvenir 1862–1962* (Calcutta, 1962).

23. Sharmila Bannerjee, *Studies in the Administrative History of Bengal, 1880–1989* (New Delhi, 1978), pp. 151–5.

24. Cited in *The Bengalee*, 26 April 1873.

25. See extracts from *Murshidabad Patrika, Dacca Prakash* and the *Education Gazette* in April 1875, *RNP*.

26. See Phillipa Levine, *Victorian Feminism, 1850–1900* (London, 1987), pp. 128–43. Also see Holcombe, *Wives and Property—Reform of the Married Women's Property Law in 19th Century England* (Oxford, 1983).
27. Markby, op. cit., p. 100.
28. Mendus and Rendall (eds), *Sexuality and Subordination, Interdisciplinary Studies of Genders in the 19th Century* (London: RKP, 1989), p. 133.
29. See also Holcombe, 'Victorian Wives and Property: Reform of the Married Women's Property Law, 1857–82', in Martha Vicinus, *A Widening Sphere: Changing Roles of Victorian Women* (London: Methuen, 1977).
30. Markby and Sripati Roy, op. cit.
31. *The Amrita Bazar Patrika*, 4 February 1873.
32. *The Hindoo Patriot*, 16 August 1887.
33. *The Amrita Bazar Patrika*, 28 January 1875, *RNP* Bengal, 1875.
34. See Sumit Sarkar, 'The Kalki-Avatar of Bikrampur: A Village Scandal in Early Twentieth-Century Bengal', in Ranajit Guha (ed.), *Subaltern Studies VI* (Delhi, 1989).
35. See 'Nationalist Iconography' in this volume [*Hindu Wife, Hindu Nation*].
36. *Report of the Age of Consent Committee, 1928–29*, Government of Bengal (Calcutta, 1929). For some statistical observations on this matter, see pp. 65–6.
37. *Kamalkanter Daptar*, op. cit.
38. Tanika Sarkar, 'Bankimchandra and the Impossibility of a Political Agenda' in this volume [*Hindu Wife, Hindu Nation*].
39. *Bangabashi*, 9 July 1887, *RNP*, 1887. For a critical discussion of such views see Rabindranath Tagore, *Hindu Vivaha* (*c.* 1887). Rabindranath himself, in this extremely convoluted logical exercise, grants a practical purpose to infant marriage purely for better breeding purposes but, in the process, Hindu conjugality is denied all effective or spiritual pretensions. *Rabindranath Rachanabali*, vol. 12 (Calcutta, *c.* 1942).
40. Chandrakanta Basu, *Hindu Patni and Hindu Vivaha Bayas O Uddeshya*, cited in *Hindu Vivaha*, op. cit., also by the same author, *Hinduttva*, op. cit.
41. See for instance Prasad Das Goswami, op. cit., Bhubaneshwar Misra, op. cit., Kalimoy Ghatok, *Ami* (Calcutta, 1885).
42. Monomohan Basu, op. cit.
43. Ibid.
44. *Sulabh Samachar O Kushadahe*, 22 July 1887, *RNP*, 1887.
45. Far from invariably evoking a sense of superiority and disgust among Englishmen, the spectacle would very often arouse similar sentiments. Compare a description of a marriage procession by an English tourist with our earlier account: 'It was the prettiest sight in the world to see those gorgeously dressed babies . . . passerbys smiled and blessed the little husband and the tiny wife'; John Law, *Glimpses of Hidden India* (Calcutta, *c.* 1905).
46. *The Hindoo Patriot*, 25 July 1887.
47. Ibid., 16 August 1887.
48. Ibid., 12 September 1887.
49. Ibid., 1 August 1887.
50. *Surabhi O Patrika*, 16 January 1887, *RNP*, 1887.
51. Nistarini Devi, *Sekaler Katha*, first published serially in *Bharatbarsha* between 1913 and 1914. Jana and Sanyal (eds), *Atmakatha* (Calcutta, 1982), p. 11.
52. Chandrakanta Basu, op. cit.
53. *The Hindoo Patriot*, 19 September 1887.
54. Cited in *The Hindoo Patriot*, ibid.
55. *Dainik O Samachar Chandrika*, 22 June 1857.
56. *Bardhawan Sanjivani*, 5 July 1887, *RNP*, 1887.
57. *Dhumketu*, 4 July 1887, *RNP*, 1887.
58. *Sambad Prabhakar*, 30 June 1887, *RNP*, 1887.

59. *Bangabashi*, 25 June 1887, *RNP*, 1887.
60. *Nabibibhaker Sadharani*, 18 July 1887, *RNP*, 1887.
61. *Dacca Prakash*, 8 June 1875, *RNP*, 1875.
62. *Education Gazette*, 11 May 1873, *RNP*, 1873.
63. Heimsath, op. cit.
64. Bengal Government Judicial JC/171, Proceedings 96–102, 1892, Nos 101–2. File JC/17–25. Honourable Justice Wilson's charge to jury in the case Empress *vs* Main Mohan Maitee, Calcutta High Court. Report sent by Arcar, Clerk of the Crown, High Court, Calcutta, to Officiating Chief Secretary 90B, no. 6292-Calcutta, 8 September 1890.
65. See Mrinalini Sinha, *Colonial Masculinity: The 'Manly Englishman' and the 'Effeminate Bengali' in the Late Nineteenth Century* (Manchester: Manchester University Press, 1995), pp. 33–69.
66. Bengal Government Judicial NF JC/17/, Proceedings 104–17, June 1893. From Simmons honorary secretary, Public Health Society of India to chief secretary, Government of Bengal, Calcutta, 1 September 1890.
67. Ibid., C.C. Stevens; officiating chief secretary 908, to secretary, home department, Government of India, Darjeeling, 8 November 1890.
68. Letter from Simmons, op. cit.
69. Bengal Government Judicial, J C/17/, op. cit.
70. Ibid.
71. *McLeod's Medical Report on Child Wives*, Bengal Government Judicial, ibid.
72. Ibid.
73. Ibid.
74. *The Bengalee*, 21 March 1891.
75. *Dagmar Engels*, op. cit.
76. *Surabhi O Patrika*, 16 January 1891, *RNP*, 1891.
77. *The Bengalee*, 21 March 1891.
78. *Dainik O Samachar Chandrika*, 14 January 1891, *RNP*, 1891.
79. *Nabayug*, 15 January 1891, *RNP*, 1891.
80. *Dainik O Samachar Chandrika*, 15 April 1896, *RNP*, 1896.
81. *Nabayug*, op. cit.
82. *Bangabashi*, 21 March 1891, *RNP*, 1891.
83. Ibid.
84. See Amiya Sen, op. cit.
85. Mentioned in *The Bengalee*, 7 March 1891.
86. *The Bengalee*, 28 February 1891.
87. Ibid., 21 March 1891.
88. *Bangabashi*, 28 March 1891.
89. Ibid.
90. *Dainik O Samachar Chandrika*, 15 January 1891.
91. *Bangabashi*, 25 December 1890.
92. *Dainik O Samachar Chandrika*, 14 January 1891.
93. Ibid., 11 January 1891.
94. Ibid.
95. *The Bengalee*, 25 July 1891.

12

Rebellious Wives
and Dysfunctional Marriages

Indian Women's Discourses and Participation in the Debates over Restitution of Conjugal Rights and the Child Marriage Controversy in the 1880s and 1890s*

PADMA ANAGOL

Introduction

Ahistoric landmark in the social legislation of nineteenth-century British India was the Age of Consent Act of 1891, the culmination of the long-drawn debates on restitution of conjugal rights, divorce and child marriage of the 1880s.[1] On 19 March 1891, the Indian Penal Code and the Code of Criminal Procedure were amended so that the Age of Consent for girls was raised from 10 to 12 years making sexual intercourse with unmarried and married girls below 12 years rape and punishable by 10 years' imprisonment or transportation for life. According to the well-known reformer and historian of nineteenth-century India, S. Natarajan, this Act was the last measure of reform in India effected by influencing British public opinion, the first measure of reform by which Indian public opinion was aroused, the first time Indian leaders harnessed the potential of the Indian masses, and the first time that politics and reaction were successfully linked.[2] It is, therefore, little wonder that the Age of Consent controversy has become a major case study for social and cultural historians of India.

The historiography on the Age of Consent is impressive. Over a period of 50 years a vast body of scholarly literature has become available on this subject. American cultural historians of the 1960s were eager to point out the importance of social legislation for the emergence of nationalism in modern India. Charles Heimsath, for example, argued that the real importance of the Bill was in terms of the nationalist movement and the popular support won for Hindu orthodoxy; these strands are being reinvestigated and reconfirmed in greater detail by the latest scholarly works which use post-colonial and

*Revised and extended version of Padma Anagol, 'The Age of Consent Act (1891) Reconsidered: Women's Perspectives and Participation in the Child Marriage Controversy in India', *South Asia Research*, vol. 12, no. ii (November 1992): pp. 100–19. The author is grateful to Sage Publications for permission to reprint some sections of the article.

poststructuralist theories.[3] However, the works most pertinent to this study are those that have resulted from the second wave of feminism in the 1970s. This saw a new shift in several disciplines, accentuating the absence of gender as a category in previous scholarship and showing a determination to remedy this through a new treatment of old issues.[4]

Later studies analysed how the category of woman was manipulated as a sign in the cultural contest for legitimation between the colonizer and the colonized, and are valuable additions to modern Indian social history.[5] However, the conspicuous irony about these analyses emanating from 'gender studies' is the scant attention paid to women's perceptions and participation.[6] It is hard to believe that a social reform movement and the by-products of colonialism such as education, access to legal and administrative institutions, new opportunities of travel and the vernacular and English print technology would not have been accessed by women. And this observation throws doubt on the conclusions of post-colonial studies which seem eager to obscure women's agency lest the study of the latter disrupt their preferred programme of homogenizing imperial policies as a relentless and brutal exercise of power over the colonized. Sumit Sarkar has rightly pointed out that the very notion that colonial rule might have provided some good for men or women is masked by Saidian scholarship's insistence on the malevolent nature of imperialism besides repeating the crime of objectifying women by employing them as a site over which to debate the nature of colonial power.[7] Some current studies have shown how there was more reaction than reformist zeal amongst Bengali men during the passing of the Act. Discussing Bengal's reaction over the debates opened by the Phulmonee Dassee case, Tanika Sarkar has demonstrated how Bengali men had effectively forced the creation of a 'state within a state' by insisting that the household space remain a zone of autonomy and self-rule for the Hindu male.[8] If official voices, and reformist and reactionary male discourses are analysed it begs the question: why not women's voices? Surely it is pertinent to ask how did women act or react to a Bill that was meant for their welfare? How did they counter the rising tide of reaction expressed by their menfolk against their empowerment?[9] Was there a movement of self-assertion building in certain parts of India among women which could have threatened Indian men into reacting against the onslaught on their hold of patriarchal practices?

This study attempts to answer some of these questions. It addresses the problem of the invisibility of women in Indian history by charting the growth of feminist consciousness among the *bhaginivarg* (sisterhood) in Maharashtra on the issue of marital reforms. More significantly, the oppositional discourse created by women is contrasted with that of the dominant male discourses, highlighting the differences between them. In the first section of this article the focus is on the origins of consciousness among women on the issue of child marriage in contrast to the discourse of the state and Indian men. The popular participation of women in the agitation against child marriage and their lobbying techniques for legislation to raise the Age of Consent are the focus of the discussion in the second section.

Birth of Indian Feminism: Nineteenth-century Maharashtra

Indian feminism grew out of the women's movements of the late nineteenth century, reaching full maturity in the early twentieth century. Indian women's subjectivities were forged within the context of colonialism; and they had a choice now, of selecting from a wide array of discourses on tradition and modernity. The rise of feminism in India was made possible through a combination of factors: the presence of a colonial economy, the opportunities thrown up by the social reform movement which allowed for a requestioning of Hinduism and presented new choices of religion such as Christianity and the hope of forming new sects and cults, and the new web of modernizing impulses, which inter-acted with the contending circumstances and criteria of sex, race, status, class, caste and religion.[10] In western India women chose and applied gendered critiques to the older religion and some embraced conversion to other religions such as Christianity as a way of expressing their discontent with Hinduism's misogynist view of womanhood whilst others remained within it. Christian feminists had made a clean break with the Indian past by rejecting Hinduism on the basis of a gendered approach to religion. They had fruitfully applied the 'welfare' and 'mission' rhetoric of Christianity to assert themselves in breaking with traditional roles and legitimating their entry into public professional roles. Their refusal to belong to any one church as well as their rejection of clerical media-tion along with funding from non-Indian sources had given them autonomy to create a unique brand of Indian feminism and also provide leadership to the women's move-ment.[11] However, Christian feminist leaders were able to sustain women's interests only as long as the active phase of the reform movement lasted. Their alignment to mission Christianity, which at this time equated Christianity with civilizing values and modern-izing impulses with the West, meant that they denounced nationalism and its growth. Eventually, it had two effects; firstly, it prevented them from effectively countering the nationalist ideologies of the early twentieth century with new strategies for enrolling women into their movement that had hitherto promised emancipation with conversion. Secondly, it paved the way for the leadership of Ramabai Ranade who in due course marginalized Christian feminists with a takeover of the women's movement.

Although Hindu women questioned Hinduism and Hindu customs and rituals, unlike their Christian counterparts, they did not reject it. This meant working within the structures of Hindu society and its limitations.[12] Several Hindu feminist leaders overcame the hindrances of working within Hindu society through a strategy of assimi-lation and accommodation. Separate female institution-building programmes by women were to prove to be the vehicle for the movement of Hindu women's embracing of modernity and in the development of the Maharashtrian women's movement. First, it enabled women to mobilize in pursuit of the goal of their own welfare. Secondly, it contributed immensely to the transformation of women's public roles. This was made possible by the astute leadership of the far-sighted women who founded these organiz-ations. Their feminism, which embodied the ability to 'assimilate and accommodate', kept the larger Hindu society's criticism of their programmes to a minimal level.

By the early half of the 1870s, around 50 to 70 women were gathering in the hall of the Prarthana Samaj every Saturday to listen to lectures given by prominent reformers. However, not only did they listen but they also learnt the art of oratory in their own right, leading to the formation of the Striyancha Sabha (Women's Society), in the 1880s.[13] This organization conducted weekly meetings for women only, where educated women would read essays, give public lectures and impart instruction in various subjects to other women. The content of the lectures and essays reveals an overriding desire to com-bat popular prejudices against female education in Maharashtra,[14] whilst simultaneously making women understand the advantages of learning. By the 1880s, as the movement grew stronger, women in other areas, such as the towns of Dhulia, Poona, Nasik and Solapur, were forming similar groups, and the process of women instructing their fellow women gathered pace. While the women read the glories of ancient Hindu literature, they also read Western literary, philosophical and explicitly feminist texts that dealt with the position of women with Kashibai Kanitkar, Rakhmabai, Anandibai Joshi and Ramabai Ranade revealing their admiration for and the influence on them of the writings of George Eliot, Jane Austen and Mill's *Subjection of Women*. The rise of new women's institutions emboldened by the new feminist strategies of accommodation and assimilation saw to the mushrooming of Stri Sabhas in various towns.[15]

These women's networks were further strengthened by the transformation of older social events and ceremonies that predated the feminist movement such as the women's ritual known as *halad-kunkum* held mainly in western and southern India, and other social gatherings, such as *kirtans*, where learned men and women delivered sermons from religious books or from ancient myths usually accompanied by musical instruments. These rituals and ceremonies provided a framework, which the women's movement could build on to bring their new message about the need for female education, women's rights to property and inheritance, the evils of child marriage and enforced widowhood to a wider audience too. Female reformers, like Annapurnabai and Ramabai Ranade, now expanded the participants' horizons even further by incorporating educational schemes within them, such as readings, lectures and essay contests.[16]

Greater political capacities began to be expressed by women and this period saw the establishment of the first independent women's organization, the Arya Mahila Samaj,[17] which specifically highlighted women's needs and aspirations. The Arya Mahila Samaj was Pandita Ramabai's brainchild but women like Ramabai Ranade and Kashibai Kanitkar worked hard to popularize it among Hindu women. Furthermore, not only did they carry out door-to-door canvassing in order to persuade women to attend the group's meetings, but also, when Pandita Ramabai departed for England in 1883, they became President of its Poona and its Bombay branches respectively.

Certainly, the issues surrounding *samajik sudharana* (social reform) aroused many shades of opinion amongst women, necessitating an outlet for the expression of their views. An ideal medium for them to communicate with one another was through the mode of print periodicals, which provided a place where they could discuss their problems in 'Letters to the Editor', armed with the knowledge that their identity would be protected and thus solicit solutions from the journal's readers on a variety of gender-related social reform issues. Journals, such as those produced by the 'Women's Press' in Maharashtra, conducted by and for women in the Marathi language, allowed for the evelopment of the notion of bhaginivarg within a larger women's collective.[18] By providing a space where women could freely discuss the issue of social reform and its implications on every aspect of women's lives, including education, domestic economy, religious and national identities, urban versus rural life, the conduct of religious rituals and widowhood, as Susie Tharu and K. Lalita have previously asserted, the 'women's periodicals' were a key instrument in the transformation and progress of the women's movement in India.[19] Indeed, such was the importance of the issue to many of its female readership, that many of the women's journals devoted whole issues to the subject. Even a superficial survey of the Marathi literary scene reveals the enthusiastic entry of women in appreciable numbers: many of them welcoming the 'condition of women' as a moot question posed within the social reform movement, which they adapted and wrote about in their literary ventures. Writing had thus given women the opportunity to *recast themselves* as modern women, rather than being *recast by men*, thus preparing themselves for the rapid changes brought by the colonial world.

The period of the Maharashtrian women's renaissance was between 1860 and 1920 and their writing demonstrates a strong Western influence, as they utilized genres such as essay writing, novels and short stories to disseminate their message of reform. The massive growth in publication during this period gave them new ways of expressing themselves and communicating that had never been open to them before. A strong business sense is not only demonstrated by their awareness of what the market wanted but also reflects their awareness of the value of the work they were producing; indeed, many promising women writers including the 'isolated' Tarabai Shinde held the copyrights to their own works, indicating a much higher level of alertness in business and public ventures.[20] In this area of publishing at least, women were able to assert themselves in a way that would have been unthinkable in the past. Although very different forms, the campaigning journalism of the women's press, the domestic science treatises and the school textbooks are notable, therefore, in demonstrating an increased self-confidence in building a distinct women's identity.

Although more traditional Indian genres, such as the ballad and religious poetry (Bhakti hymns), continued to exist, the new forms allowed women to create 'resistance' literature, in the form of treatises and tracts which used inversion techniques and role reversals to explore gender relations, aimed at suggesting a different, more egalitarian world. Maharashtrian women resorted to a rich vocabulary in the Marathi language to express ideas that are now considered feminist terms and enrich the Indian feminist lexicon with concepts and terms such as the following: bhaginivarg (sisterhood); *strihak* (women's rights); *strivarg* (womankind or womanhood); *strianubhav* (women's experience); *bandhivasan* (bondage); *dasyatva* (slavery); *mokaleek* (independence or freedom); *strijati* (female sex); *purushjati* (male sex); *purusharth* (manliness and masculinity).[21] These phrases occur regularly in the colloquial and formal texts written by Maharashtrian women and the most significant of the magazines within the broader women's press of the time, *Arya Bhagini*, literally uses the concept of *bhagini* (sisters) in its title—a telling sign of the times. The invention of this feminist lexicon reveals the nature of the advanced state of late nineteenth-century feminist thought and speaks volumes regarding the realization of 'selfhood' and the formation of women's subjectivities in western India. An instance of the maturity of the feminist movement in late nineteenth-century India is provided by women's public participation in the Age of Consent debates of the late 1880s and early 1890 to which we will turn shortly.

Dysfunctional Marriages and Women's Recourse to Law Courts

Women's self-authorization programmes were not restricted to writing alone, in fact they spilled over in the public sphere whereby they accessed knowledge of state procedures such as 'petitioning' and law courts in claiming their rights to property, livelihood, remarriage, mobility and custody of children.[22] Analysis of court records proves that the women's movement of the late nineteenth century was advanced enough when we see them utilizing the instruments of colonial economy, especially their recourse to the law courts for restitution of conjugal rights, divorce, separation, maintenance and remarriage.

The problems of dysfunctional marriages had been attended to by women throughout the nineteenth century through recourse to the law courts in the Bombay Presidency. The history of suits for the restitution of conjugal rights in India reveals that women were ready to use British law as a resource to improve their position and assert their rights in marriage. In a pattern, which would be further developed in the late nineteenth century, it also reveals that Indian male recognition of the empowering nature of colonial law for women was quickly followed by successful attempts to check its effectiveness by lobbying the colonial authorities. Restitution of conjugal rights was the only relief offered by British law to all Indian communities in cases of marital disharmony, whether they were Hindus, Muslims, Parsis or any other religious community;[23] suits for the restitution of conjugal rights were unknown in pre-colonial India. Scripture-based Hindu law did not sanction it, although customary laws did incorporate less formal ways of dealing with marital disputes. The concept of restitution of conjugal rights was, in fact, an importation from English Ecclesiastical law. Blackstone's summary of this legal suit in Britain allowed suits for the restitution of conjugal rights to be brought whenever either the husband or the wife was 'guilty of injury or subtraction, or lives separate from the other without any sufficient reason in which case they will be compelled to live together again'.[24] Although the law governing the restitution of conjugal rights was grafted onto the existing Indian Penal Code in the nineteenth century with little modification,[25] the form that it subsequently took in this period was wholly controlled and shaped by Indian interpretations of marital rights and obligations.

For Indian Parsis and Muslims, marriage was regarded as a contract; for Hindus, however, it was a religious union, although it was not a sacrament according to Ecclesiastical law as the Christian tradition defined it, because Hindu men continued to take second and third wives. Furthermore, these ties were not forged between consenting adults as arranged marriages, especially in the period under study; they were often agreements between families, not agreements between the couple themselves. Indeed, the notion of consent often did not arise, as the spouses were usually betrothed as children if not infants. Importing the concept of restitution of conjugal rights and applying it to Hindus was therefore entirely inappropriate; as lawyers and judges continually pointed out during this period, suits for the restitution of conjugal rights did not formally constitute part of any of the major religions in India, despite the fact that all of them did make reference to the broad duties involved in cohabitation and duties. In cases of severe disagreements between couples, the most common practice was for the wife to voluntarily flee to her natal family or be driven to seek their help by the husband. In the 150 case studies conducted for this study, separation had normally already taken place before the cases came up in court, with women often recounting their tales of gratitude to members of their extended families for care and maintenance.[26]

In the mid-nineteenth century, Indian law recognized two kinds of matrimonial suits for the purpose of obtaining conjugal rights. The first was for Restitution of Conjugal Rights (Act XV of 1877, Schedule 11, Article 35), available to both parties, that is, husband and wife. But the second was restricted to the husband claiming the society of his wife, namely recovering his wife from a person harbouring her with ill-intent (Act XV of 1877, Schedule 11, Article 34). Sections 259 and 260 of the Code of Civil Procedure of 1882 provided comprehensive regulations for the execution of decrees of both suits. Section 260 of the revised Code of 1877 provided that if a spouse refused to comply with a decree given in a suit of restitution of conjugal rights then he or she could be dealt with by imprisonment or attachment of property, or both. These decrees interfered extensively with customary law and, in the later nineteenth century, were arbitrarily used against women. Formerly, women could seek the help of the extended family in cases of violence against them by husbands but the wording of Section 259 meant that the extended family could not interfere, especially if the person 'harbouring' her was a distant relative; for example, an uncle instead of a 'parent'. Section 260 also worked against women with a little property in the form of *stridhana*. However, it is a testimony to women's resilience and determination that they increasingly resorted to the first form of suit, restitution of conjugal rights, knowing full well that the husband would rather agree to a maintenance grant than give up the privilege of making polygamous arrangements.

The origin and history of ecclesiastical jurisdiction reveals clearly that suits for restitution of conjugal rights had been entertained from the first introduction of English law in India. Matrimonial disputes amongst the various settlers of Bombay had been frequently brought and uniformly heard in the Supreme Court of Bombay (from 1823 to 1856) and prior to this, the Mayor's Courts (until 1823) that preceded the Supreme Courts. The Recorder's Court of Bombay lists a total of eight cases heard from 1800 to 1856; two involved the Armenian community, five were of Parsis and one concerned a Muslim couple. It is a point worth noting that seven out of the total of eight cases for the restitution of conjugal rights were brought by the wives against their husbands.[27] The wives demanded that the husbands should take them back and treat them with 'conjugal kindness'; if they refused, alimony should be provided to them. In six of a total of seven cases heard in the Recorder's Court of Bombay between 1800 and 1856, the court granted alimony to the wives. This inventory of facts crystallizes the manner in which the British courts were upholding the right of the Indian wife for a maintenance grant in the case of a failed marriage and were holding men to their marital duties. This situation was not to the liking of Indian patriarchs and soon the winds of change were to blow with the rise of Indian lawyers speaking on behalf of their male clients who wished to engage in polygamous relations or keep mistresses without their rebellious wives getting any kind of maintenance from them.

In 1856, the Privy Council was to hear the most celebrated case in the history of the restitution of conjugal rights. This was Ardaseer Cursetjee v. Perozeboye, a dispute between a Parsi couple from Bombay. Ardaseer's astute Indian lawyer brought a suit challenging Ecclesiastical jurisdiction over Indians.[28] The set of arguments proposed by the Bar in London reveals a great sensitivity towards safeguarding the rights of Indian women. A point in case is the set of arguments used in defence of the wife, Perozeboye, by Charles Jackson. He argued against exercising Ecclesiastical jurisdiction over Hindus, Muslims and Parsis and for suits to reinstate conjugal rights amongst Indians to be refused. However, he also argued that women should have access to legal remedy in cases of gross marital neglect by husbands by adapting the law of alimony. He further demonstrated that wives and husbands could not be forced to cohabit as the notion was anomalous to Asian marriage laws; furthermore, it was only Christian marriages that treated the woman as part of the man (Canon law considered a man and his wife as one person), thus meaning that the case could only be dealt with by Ecclesiastical courts and not by the civil courts. In India, no such principle existed in either Islamic, Hindu or Zoroastrian laws, meaning, he argued, that in such instances 'Native married women are *femme soles* and the Supreme Court at Calcutta treat them so'.[29] According to this reasoning, Ardaseer was guilty on three counts, of having forcibly evicted his wife from the house, refusing to take her back and having failed to maintain her—all these facts of abandonment and cruelty meant that there was nothing 'to prevent his wife from bringing an action against her husband for damages, or a suit for a maintenance past and present'.[30]

The force and conviction of these arguments was enshrined in the final judgement given by the Right Hon. Lushington of the Privy Council who upheld Jackson's argument that the courts in India, on the Ecclesiastical side, should not entertain such suits, but that the British state was obliged to provide legal remedies to subjects in suits arising in matrimonial matters; Perozeboye was therefore directed to apply for adequate relief in a civil court against her husband. Two facts emerge forcefully in this history of the legislation on the restitution of conjugal rights that were to have far-reaching implications and consequences. Early nineteenth-century cases show that suits for restitution were brought by wives against neglectful and cruel husbands in the hope that, if they were not taken back, at least the court would grant them maintenance rights. In the precedent created by the Ardaseer case, we also find that British legal experts were reluctant to apply Ecclesiastical laws to the Indian situation; moreover, the gendered arguments also reveal their anxiety to create safeguards for the protection for married Indian women. Since marriage in India was deemed more a contract than a sacrament, wives were encouraged to apply on the Equity side of Ecclesiastical Courts for maintenance and alimony from uncaring husbands. After this groundbreaking case, in which the Privy Council ruled that Ecclesiastical law could not be strictly applied to non-Christian suits for restitution of conjugal rights, these cases increasingly came to be entertained on the civil side of the courts in India. The early history of conjugal relations, especially case law as it emerges in modern India, demonstrates that it is difficult to sustain the view that 'English law was an instrument of oppression'.[31]

Instead, the argument here is that, in the late nineteenth century, English law as interpreted by Indian legal scholars and reformers becomes a tool for oppressing women and was a creation of Indian male agents with little assistance from their British counterparts who were mostly pressurized by the 'trial' of Indian newspapers into consenting to Indian orthodox opinion. Firstly, the Privy Council judgement that Indian marriages were more contractual than sacramental in character was turned on its head by Indian legal experts, who argued the reverse; that Hindu unions were religious and hence sacraments and it was actually Christian ones which were more contractual in nature. Following this new definition of Hindu marriages, the Privy Council's understanding and ruling of Indian wives' status as *feme soles* was overturned by conservative Indians who redefined the position of Indian wives as *feme covert* and bound the Hindu woman in the person of the Hindu male (i.e., her husband). Secondly, the early law enshrined in Privy Council rulings had instituted restitution of conjugal rights as a marital remedy to 'protect' the 'rights' of wives. By subverting the emphasis onto 'duties' of wives in the later nineteenth century, Indian elites overturned the implications of this legal remedy especially in the Rakhmabai case. Originally acting as a force for the empowerment of Indian women, British law was manipulated by Indian male elites who successfully contrived to turn it into a source of women's oppression.

In the nineteenth century, considerable obstacles stood in the way of women attempting to redress marital injustices. Ill-treated and abandoned wives fortunate enough to have the support of parents or the extended family looked to the civil courts to intervene and resolve marital disputes. As divorce was disallowed under the British interpretation of Hindu law, women resorted to the strategy of seeking the dissolution of their marriages on technical points of law. For example, a suit by a Hindu mother, as the guardian of her infant daughter, in favour of a declaration that the alleged marriage of the daughter with the defendant was null and void, was held to be a suit of a civil nature and was adjudicated upon.[32] Similarly, there were attempts to set aside marriages which had already taken place, on various grounds, for reasons such as the bride having been given away by her mother and not her father or by her stepmother when her paternal grandmother was alive, or having been married to a person belonging to a different caste, or her husband marrying a second wife, having previously agreed that if such a marriage occurred, the first marriage should be considered dissolved.[33] Non-Brahmin wives also sought divorce, but due to the operation of the colonial reinterpretation of Hindu law, it was increasingly difficult for women to exercise this option.

If we judge by statistics alone, the cases which annually came before the civil courts in the Bombay Presidency (including subordinate, district and high courts) between 1881 and 1885 consisted of 727 suits for enforcing decrees for the restitution of conjugal rights and 81 suits for the dissolution of marriages. The latter were usually between Christian husbands and wives, while the former involved Hindus and Muslims. Not all of these suits were by deserted wives seeking legal remedies to their dysfunctional marriages. Guardians and parents of young girl-wives brought quite a few of these cases to the court in their anxiety to protect them; presumably they followed the technical route described in the previous paragraph.

Given the factors that militated against women seeking legal redress, it is surprising that so many cases came to court. Achieving a remedy through civil courts was not a popular method, especially for women who had very few resources or did not know that Act XV, Schedule II, of 1877 provided an unwilling wife the option of serving six months' imprisonment in a civil jail instead of acquiescing to her conjugal duties. Mahipatram Rupram, a district judge, recorded that *vakils* (pleaders) never provided this vital information to female clients, despite the fact that they were forfeiting at least one source of income.[34] Furthermore, Rupram shows how it was only the wide publicity given to the Dadaji *vs.* Rakhmabai case in the vernacular newspapers that alerted the public in the remoter parts of Maharashtra to the fact that a wife could actually choose imprisonment in preference to the company of her husband. The anxiety of Indian male lawyers to restrict women's access to knowledge that could potentially have empowered them speaks volumes of their fear of women undertaking independent action. It is also an indicator of their desire to maintain the status quo that privileged men by containing the legitimate claims of rebellious wives in a society where the traditional power networks were being eroded as the colonial courts grew in influence. A by-product of this was the empowerment of women, who increasingly sought the British law courts which were determined to uphold the popular perception that the Raj stood for the 'rule of law' and justice. It was precisely the Maharashtrian women's acts of assertion that led to a backlash from the indigenous male population.

An interesting trend in the assertive acts of women is that many female clients preferred to use the criminal courts, as they were less expensive and more effective than the civil courts. Maharashtrian wives were also aware of the fact that, even if they applied for restitution of conjugal rights and won the case, the civil courts could not, in a practical sense, enforce their decree. By practising polygamy, a husband could always informally defy court orders by taking new wives and ignoring or maltreating his previous wife.[35] In their replies to the government regarding changing the laws that governed suits over the restitution of conjugal right and separation, Mahipatram Rupram and M.G. Ranade pointed out that even illiterate women knew they could obtain payments as alimony from their husbands by applying to a magistrate;[36] moreover, many of these applications were likely to be successful. Between 1881 and 1885, a total of 2,874 wives brought cases against their husbands before the criminal courts of the Bombay Presidency, demanding redress in the form of maintenance payments for the ill-treatment they had suffered. Without doubt, one can say that 2,874 cases in four years reflects on the dysfunctionality of Indian marriage arrangements.

Not all of the suits quoted above were brought by adult wives; some of the cases were lodged by the parents of neglected child-wives. The statistics were compiled by M.G. Ranade, a celebrated social reformer and seasoned legal expert, who argued that 'the large majority of the cases under chapter thirty-six are undoubtedly due to the neglect of marital duties by husbands towards their wives'.[37] He uncovered considerable evidence of women's dissatisfaction with contemporary marriage laws; moreover, he recognized that they were not inclined to see the status quo continue, especially when they perceived the Raj as a good government that looked after its subjects irrespective of gender. Ranade's close observations and his everyday interactions in the courts led him to become a prominent advocate of divorce, although he stood alone and unsupported by his fellow-reformers.

Given indigenous and colonialist constructions of the Indian woman as passive, even a few isolated cases of women resorting to the courts would be highly significant. Yet the statistics on matrimonial disputes are considerably higher. If we combine civil and criminal cases, thousands of women every year sought legal redress to improve the quality of their domestic lives in the Bombay Presidency. Contemporary Indian men were quick to realize the subversive nature and veiled implications of the assertive acts of women. When we understand the constraints on women actually bringing a case to court, it is clear that Indian women were resisting a system of marriage that perpetuated maladjusted conjugal unions; in other words, what we witness during this period amounts to a great rebellion of wives against ill-treatment or abandonment. By signalling autonomy and self-determination, women's actions led to the resident patriarchs of nineteenth-century India formulating a formidable and negative response persuading us to seek explanations within Indian societal structures rather than viewing it as simply a tussle between metropolitan claims of unreserved masculinity versus Bengali effeminacy as some scholars have suggested.[38] The significance of this wives' rebellion needs to be understood if we are to properly assess the nature of debates set off by the Rakhmabai and Age of Consent controversy.

Counter Discourses of Women on Child Marriage

If Indian wives were quietly exercising their rights in the courts to maintenance and alimony in cases where there was gross neglect of conjugal duties by husbands, as a result of the national publicity over what became known as the 'Rakhmabai case', the 1880s were to bring changes in the marital remedies available to warring couples. For good reasons, the Rakhmabai case became one of the most publicized legal disputes of the later nineteenth century, and it was to have far-reaching consequences. Out of the contentious debates over the restitution of conjugal rights and divorce in the Rakhmabai case, there arose the greatest social reform issue of the nineteenth century, the child marriage controversy.

Unlike Indian men, who were aroused on a mass scale by the publication of 'Notes on infant marriage and enforced widowhood' in August 1884 by Behramji Malabari, a Parsi journalist and reformer from Bombay, the first signs of the bhaginivarg or women's collective coming together is discernible during the Rakhmabai-Dadaji episode. Rakhmabai, a product of the emerging women's movement in Maharashtra, was the daughter of Jayantibai and Janardhan Pandurang. She became an heiress to a modest fortune from her natural father, Janardhan Pandurang, on the remarriage of her mother, Jayantibai, to Dr Sakharam Arjun, an eminent surgeon and well-known reformer of Bombay.[39] In 1884 Dadaji Bhikaji filed a suit for the restitution of conjugal rights in the Bombay High Court. He was married when he was 20 to Rakhmabai, who was then 11 years old. The marriage was not consummated as Rakhmabai reached puberty in her mother's home at a much later age, by which time the marriage had broken down irrevocably. Dadaji's contention was that his in-laws coveted Rakhmabai's inheritance and had therefore contrived to keep the spouses apart.[40] Considering the facts that her stepfather and mother had independent means of income and were wealthy and that Dadaji himself had not bothered to claim marital rights for over 15 years, neither of his contentions were convincing. Rakhmabai's narrative of events differed dramatically from her husband's. She claimed that it was Dadaji's inability to earn an honest livelihood, his immoral lifestyle, his refusal to educate himself and his ill-health (he was in the intermediary stage of tuberculosis) which prevented her from living with him.[41]

She also explained the various occasions on which her acute aversion towards him had been formed:

> He abused my relatives including my mother in language, which was shameful. He set at defiance the efforts made by my father and grandfather to educate him and took to ways which a woman's lips cannot utter. Mr Dadajee went through every course of dissipation till my aversion for him was firmly settled.[42]

Significantly, Rakhmabai did not stress the factor of incompatibility which other Maharashtrian women were utilizing as an instrument in negotiating more rational marital arrangements, but instead placed her emphasis on complaints that an average traditional Hindu family could relate to, such as the life-chances of a bridegroom and his economic prospects. She pointed out that even a caste panchayat would agree, on the basis of textual precepts, that a man had to provide for his wife in order to claim her person because Hindu marriages were *contractual* in nature as the arrangement had been made between the family elders rather than by her as a child-bride or Dadaji as a young groom. An interesting shift in the male debates on Hindu tradition was the highly selective process of picking up those points of objection from Rakhmabai's statements that diverted the debate from the *duties of a husband* to that of the *duties of a wife* and inverting her statement that her marriage was more *contractual* in character than *sacramental*.[43] The case took four years for a final resolution through two legal suits.[44] In the second suit the ambivalence in the judicial discourse was evident when, accommodating the massive reaction that had been expressed in the media, the court ruled that Rakhmabai would have to face imprisonment if she refused to fulfil her wifely duties.[45] Rakhmabai chose imprisonment rather than live with her husband.[46] Her defiant act was publicized by the astute nationalist B.G. Tilak and other conservatives as showing the evil consequences of an English education, and was coupled with the sensational cry of 'Hinduism in danger'.[47]

The case of Rakhmabai was intricately interwoven with the Age of Consent debates. The question of the consummation of marriage was of material importance to the restitution of conjugal rights. The ecclesiastical laws in English courts did not, as a rule, order a wife to go back to her husband when the marriage had never been consummated. However, in the case of Rakhmabai, this was overruled by citing the custom of infant marriage in India whereby the girl-bride remained in her natal home until puberty when she was handed over to her husband's family in fulfilment of her marital obligations.[48] In this sense the second verdict was the state's recognition of the cultural laws that governed Hindus, but the colonial government's retraction was read by feminists as a devious alliance between the imperial state and the Indian male. Expressing her disappointment, Pandita Ramabai wrote, 'They (the government) have promised to please the males of country at the cost of women's rights.'[49] On the other hand, Rakhmabai's defiance of the court order was understood by Maharashtrian orthodoxy as an educated women's refusal to abide by the time-honoured Hindu tradition of remaining under her husband's protection.[50]

Between June and September 1885, Rakhmabai published a series of letters in the *Times of India*, on the subjects of infant marriage and enforced widowhood, under the pseudonym of 'The Hindu Lady'.[51] Her letters sparked a major conflagration among all sections of Maharashtrian society and were discussed minutely in the newspapers (including the women's press) right up to the end of 1885. Following the controversial Dadaji *vs.* Rakhamabai case, the Government of India considered amending Section 260 of Article 14 of the Code of Civil Procedure of 1882 in so far as its provisions related to the execution of decrees for the restitution of conjugal rights and divorce. Leading Indian judges and administrators were requested to give their opinions, while no woman, however prominent was consulted on an issue that so directly concerned women's well-being.[52] Nevertheless, Maharashtrian women voiced their opinions through their own press, through literary writings and letters in the Anglo-Indian press, and by enlisting the support of British feminists. Rakhmabai followed closely the reaction to Malabari's 'Notes', which prompted her to express not only her own personal views but also the perspectives of the bhaginivarg or the women's organizations she was part of at the time. While acknowledgeing the gratitude of Indian women to Malabari for his exertions, she constructed a gendered critique of child marriage startlingly different from that of Malabari.

In her first letter Rakhmabai wrote that child marriage had ruined her life:

> I am one of those unfortunate Hindu women, whose hard lot it is to suffer the unnameable miseries entailed by the custom of early marriage. This wicked practice has destroyed the happiness of my life.[53]

Her observations were also drawn from the lives of female friends, thus formulating general propositions based on the combined experiences of women. She began her analysis with the statement that the institution of child marriage cut across caste and class considerations and adversely affected all age and sex groups, but 'women', she concluded, were its 'greatest victims'.[54]

Infant marriage, according to women, was the most persistent obstacle to the psychological development of the female sex, stultifying a women's personality through the denial of higher education. The issue of female literacy preoccupied the attention of Maharashtrian women throughout the second half of the nineteenth century. The need for and nature of education, and the obstacles to its achievement were such an integral part of women's consciousness that it ended in splitting them into two groups— traditionalists and moderates—according to the ideology they professed.[55] However, the relevant strand for discussion here is: why was child marriage viewed as the greatest hurdle in the mental development of the female sex? Women believed that the structure of Indian marital relationships based on clan, caste and kin cramped the physical space and liberty of expression of women.

Giving graphic details of the lifestyle of a girl before and after marriage, Rakhmabai drew an accurate picture of how the imposition of a code of behaviour, forms of women's speech and a strictly regimented life, robbed the girl-wife of all incentive to develop individuality. In her opinion, control through the hierarchical relationships of the in-laws' home aimed, 'to make the girl as docile as a beast and as submissive as a slave'.[56] If the girl was married at the age of seven or eight the domestic code actively cajoled her to please rather than displease, to agree rather than disagree and divest her speech and thinking processes from the use of argument and dialogue. Writing about how she became aware of *stri-sudharana* (improvement in the position of women), a prominent feminist leader from Amravati, Yashodabai Joshi, recalls the oppressive atmosphere of her in-laws' home which she refers to as 'just plain slavery'.[57] The control exercised by in-laws was so absolute that without their permission not even a pre-pubescent girl-wife residing at her parent's home could go to school.

This belief reverberates in numerous letters to the editors of women's magazines, besides the memoirs and semi-fictional writings of women written during the late nineteenth century.[58] Contrasting the picture of a girl-wife with that of a boy-husband, Rakhmabai further noted that child-marriages 'do not entail on men half the difficulties which they entail upon women'.[59] According to her, men enjoyed full marital and physical freedom, and religion and custom did not interfere in any way with their liberty. In her opinion:

Marriage does not interpose any insuperable obstacles in the course of their studies. They marry not only a second wife, on the death of the first, but have the right of marrying any number of wives at one and the same time, or any time they please. If married early, they are not called upon to go and submit to the tender mercies of a mother-in-law; nor is any restraint put upon their actions because of their marriage. But the case for women is the very reverse of this.[60]

Men, she argued, protected the interests of a male child, whether it was over the right to education or remarriage, and actively connived in prohibiting the mental development of women. Unlike the modernizing discourses of liberal men who argued that the education of women would gradually lead to the abolition of child marriage, women argued, to the contrary, that it was precisely the institution of child marriage which placed obstacles in the way of female literacy.

If we turn to the male liberal discourse on the Age of Consent issue, a totally different picture emerges. In the 'Notes' circulated by Malabari, he constructs a powerful picture of Indian society, characterized by incapacitated adults, sickly children, over-population, and acute poverty leading to epidemics. The consequences of child marriage in his view were:

The breaking down of constitutions and the ushering in of disease. The giving up of studies on the part of the boy-husband, the birth of sickly children, the necessity of feeding too many mouths, poverty and dependence. . . .[61]

He insisted that the state had to address the question of child marriage on the purely economic grounds of 'over-population in poverty'. Eugenics and public health were powerful strands of argument in such indigenous discourse as seen in attempts to reform cultural practices. Management of the nation's health was an integral part of liberal discourse on child marriage as early as the 1890s, and the 1920s debates over the Age of Consent simply re-opened debates built on this strong tradition, contrary to what some scholars have suggested in their works.[62] M.G. Ranade, an influential reformer and a feminist, preferred to argue for legislation mainly on the grounds of checking the reproduction of a weak race and hence the economic ruin of India. He argued that early marriage led to premature consummation and resulted in the physical deterioration of the race; it diverted the attention of youths from their studies, checked enterprise and filled the country with weaklings bred of over-population.[63] He also argued for state interference on the ground that Indians were incapable of self-help due to their bondage to the past.

What is of significance to the discussion here is the singular absence in the indigenous male discourse of a gendered critique for the raising of the Age of Consent. It could be argued that elites of progressive opinion used public health arguments as a tactical move especially in cases such as M.G. Ranade, a sympathizer and friend of the women's movement in Maharashtra, in order to manoeuvre the state into overcoming its promise of non-interference in domestic matters. However, opinions expressed by liberals on other vital questions of women's education used the same 'rejuvenation of the race' theories. Dr Kirtikar, President of the Pathare Prabhu Reform Society, for example, argued in several lectures that the only reason why a woman was entitled to education was because she was the 'mother of the Indian race', and hence had to have a good knowledge of health and hygiene in order to raise strong and healthy children.[64]

The failure to admit gender inequalities is blatantly exposed by another trend in Indian liberal discourse. Liberals and conservatives alike argued that women themselves were active proponents of the institution of child marriage and opposed all reform. An Inamdar of Dharwar, Tirmal Rao Venkatesh, skilfully drew a picture of the origins of infant marriage as a recent phenomenon, owing entirely to the 'whims of females, belonging to rich families, who not only put up, but compel their male members to bring about infant marriages', simply as he put it, for the sake of enjoying the fun and pleasure of going through the ceremonies attendant upon such marriages.[65] However, it was the non-interventionists or 'reform from within' group, who successfully framed women as the chief culprits. The gist of their arguments was that women in India were conservative by nature, that they imbibed the claptrap of Hindu tradition more effectively than men, first in their parents' and subsequently in their in-laws' home, and that by the time they reached middle age they personified orthodoxy itself. Therefore, legislation would make no difference and child marriage would only disappear with modernization.[66] It would be no exaggeration to conclude here that women were fighting a dual battle—one was to stem the anti-legislationist arguments of their own menfolk and the other was to convince the state of the need for such social legislation.

In contrast to this discourse stood women's own views. They agreed that many women did block reforms but, by studying the conservative attitudes of women, they concluded that centuries of conditioning brought on by man-made shastras could not be wiped out in a few years. Reform-minded women were consistent in their opinion that Hindu men jealously guarded their rights through the connivance of Brahmanical priests. As Krupabai put it: 'Men treated women as mere appendices to their own great selves'; an educated bride was also by no means welcome to a man because, 'The fact of his wife being in any way above him will be gall wormwood to his inflated, self-satisfied nature.'[67] This male conspiracy, she contended, led to the situation where:

a majority of our women resort to the most pernicious habit of gossiping about their neighbours, and quarrelling among themselves. Poor souls! They are not to be blamed; they know of no higher mode of existence; there is nothing to occupy their minds, no interest is taken in them: they are treated as toys and humoured with gilded trinkets or any such trifles.[68]

How did women react to this situation? Krupabai maintained that women are born and brought up to think themselves inferior, and they finally learnt to extract pleasure from housekeeping and dressing up.[69] Even though women were inured to their pitiful existence, she argued for the abolition of infant marriages altogether as the only way women could in practice share men's freedom and rights.[70] Rakhmabai summed up this view when she wrote: 'Reduced to this state of degradation by the dictum of the shastras, looked down upon for ages by men, we have naturally come to look down upon ourselves.'[71]

Women, therefore, pleaded that state intervention was not just desirable but essential. They believed that abolition of child-marriage would enable them to take advantage of higher education and that this would restore a necessary sense of dignity and pride in women's ability to plead their own cause.

A significant trend in the women's literature of the time entailed a proposed restructuring of the institution of marriage. Thus arose an analysis of 'why' and 'how' the Hindu marriage system maintained such absurd customs as infant and child-marriage. The reasons proposed by them were radically different from those of Indian men. There was no engagement with shastric injunctions on the primacy of the marriage consummation ceremony or *garbhadana* (literally, 'gift of the womb') which characterized the arguments of the indigenous male sections. Instead, they traced child marriage to the financial considerations of the boy's parents, the anxiety of the girl child's parents due to the low status accorded to the female sex, and the psychological need for a woman to be a mother-in-law in order to gain access to power in a Hindu joint family.

Taking up the issue of monetary transactions during marriages, they condemned the system of *hunda* (dowry) as the main reason why parents of male children succumbed to the institution of child marriage. Parents of female children constantly worried about them and were in the habit of sounding out the marriage negotiator who was either the family priest or a close relative. The latter found a suitable groom; the prospects of finding a better groom were relatively dependent on the size of the dowry. The anxiety of parents about a girl remaining unmarried led them to marry her off early or, if poor, they would wed their daughters to widowers, forcing them to become second or third wives to elderly men.[72] Women empathized with a girl child's status within a household which led them to view women who promoted child marriage with a degree of tolerance. Many women held the opinion that a girl-wife did not enter her husband's house to be the sole mistress but as the lowest in the hierarchy of family members and occupied the humblest position. The only way a woman could exercise any power was to bear sons and arrange their marriages as soon as possible in order to reach the exalted status of the mother-in-law.[73] Moving away from the utilization of the shastras in their arguments for the abolition of infant marriages and raising the Age of Consent was the single most radical stand taken by women during the Age of Consent controversy and whilst it marks the maturity of their feminism it also stands starkly in contrast to male discourses which fell back on the use of shastras whether the males in question were reformist or reactionaries in their perceptions of this question.

Another strand in women's arguments was their insistence that raising the age of marriage for girls alone would not be effective in practice: the age of consent for boys had to be raised too. This argument centred round the inability of a young husband to face the wrath of the conservative members of his family even as he bravely encouraged the education of his girl-wife. Personal narratives and the biographical and semi-fictional writings of women discusses the economic dependence of youthful husbands on their extended family and how these ties effectively prevented them from protecting their wives' efforts to educate themselves.[74] Autobiographical accounts of women who participated in the Age of Consent agitation clearly reflect how women were left to their own devices in countering the opposition of in-laws without the support of their husbands. Ramabai Ranade recalled in an autobiography which became a classic of Marathi literature, how- about 14 widowed aunts, cousins, and a sister-in-law, along with her step-mother-in-law in the vanguard, formed an orthodox camp within the household to torment her when she persisted in educating herself.[75] Their allegations that she was neglecting her household duties were unjustified as she rose at dawn in order to make time for her education. It was the unanimous view of women writing on this subject that, in the face of such formidable circumstances, only a very few courageous young women would continue to educate themselves. If, instead, girls were married after the age of 14, they would benefit from the extra time within their parents' home and their chances of a higher education would be greatly increased.

The indifference of Indian men to the suffering the female sex endured on account of child-marriage was angrily noted by women. Writing in Marathi journals, women expressed their shock and disgust at the cowardice of men in facing reality. Their studied discourtesy and contempt for 'reformers' correspondingly forms an important factor in women's implicit belief in the efficacy of the colonial government. After the replies of leading men to Malabari's proposals had been published, women wrote at length expressing their annoyance, not at the 'opinions of the old-fashioned, credulous and religious older generation', which they felt were comprehensible, but at the opinions of young learned men who aped modern ideas only as far as dress and diet were concerned while they were actually worse than conservative people in their views.[76] The reference here was to the 'reform from within' group who opposed legislation. Among women a special phrase had been coined for hypocritical reformers—*Potepurte sikhalele lok* (literally, those who gain a Western education not for self-improvement but merely to look after their stomachs).[77] 'Sati', argued one woman, would never have been abolished, left to the Indians, but was the greatest favour done by the British government, saving thousands of lives of women from the agonies of the fire.[78] She, and others like her, urged the government to show the same firmness of conviction over the Age of Consent issue.

When we consider whether or not male reformers advocated state intervention it is enlightening to allude to Tarabai Shinde's emphatic invective: to her all social reform societies were 'fake' and the work of male reformers as much use as a 'spare tit on a goat'.[79] It is remarkable that although considered a pioneer of women's rights in western India, even the modernizing Malabari did not support social legislation at first. In the 'Notes' circulated in 1884, Malabari did not invoke the aid of the legislature on the issue of child marriage except in a benign form. He proposed a system of incentives and disincentives to be offered by the government that would include suggestions such as 'no married [male] student shall be eligible to go up for University examinations, five years hence', and the public sector 'may prefer the unmarried to the married, all other qualifications being equal'.[80] Given the absence of divorce, women argued that there were many extenuating reasons explaining why wives deserted their husbands, or committed suicide or homicide. Even though, with good reason, women hesitated about writing explicitly on the subject of divorce, the statistical analysis of the previous section reveals that many abandoned or neglected wives sought separation and maintenance for themselves and their children. In marked contrast to Malabari's proposals, Rakhmabai recommended divorce as the primary means of resolving domestic tensions within a marriage that had broken down irrevocably.[81] At the height of conservative reaction from indigenous quarters, Indian women advocated some radical measures that represented a potential revolution in Indian conjugal affairs. Indian women's valorization of the achievements of colonial benevolence should not be read as a simplistic admiration for an alien government but stemmed from their observations that their own menfolk held in the thraldom of the Indian past would not move forward to share the benefits of British rule with the members of the other sex.

A solidarity between Hindu, Christian and Jewish Indian women is discernible over the Rakhmabai case and the Age of Consent controversy. These episodes also provided the first instances when British feminists successfully allied with Indian women. The uniting ground was the realization that it was the rights of women that were at the heart of the debate, rather than a tussle between traditionalists and reformists, native and English masculinity, and Western and Eastern religion as the rhetoric used by the Indian men seemed to imply. Maharashtrian women enlisted the support of British feminists both for guidance as well as to mobilize strength for propaganda purposes. It has been argued that in the nineteenth century European medical men were effectively performing the function of maintaining the image of the physical and moral superiority of the ruling race.[82] Their counterparts, the imperial medical women, were also, in effect, performing a similar function. Much of the medical evidence cited by Indian women in support of the agitation came from European female doctors who gave lectures on eugenic theories of weak and sterile populations issuing from the Indian race due to the ill effects of child marriage.[83] At Rakhmabai's request, Dr Edith Pechey-Phipson, a prominent doctor in charge of several hospitals in Bombay and one of the celebrated pioneers of the medical education campaign for women in Britain, assumed leadership of this movement and along with a few influential Indian women they formed 'The Hindu Lady Fund' to raise Rs 5,000 for costs incurred by Rakhmabai over the second suit.[84] Pandita Ramabai launched a scathing attack on the government's inertia, through letters and articles in influential newspapers while the Indian National Association publicized her case in England. Rakhmabai struck up a longstanding friendship with British feminists who eventually helped her to leave India in March 1889 to pursue a medical education in London.[85] Indian women's reliance on imperial feminists significantly reflects their loss of faith in Indian men.

Conjugal Incompatibility and Child Marriage

One of the prime concerns of women in their programme of restructuring Hindu marriage relations arose from their analysis of the unhappiness of Indian wives within the system of arranged marriages and the absence of choice of partners. They linked wives' discontent to the prevalent institution of child marriage. Malabari had made a fleeting reference in his 'Notes' to unhappy unions in Indian marriages due to child marriage, though he did not go on to argue that the government should intervene on this ground. The replies of eminent men whose opinion was solicited to his 'Notes' were silent on this issue, except for the well-known reformer R.G. Bhandarkar, who insisted that there were no 'ill-assorted marriages' in India.[86] Liberal discourse did not wish to publicly acknowledge the existence of unhappiness in child marriages.

We should turn for a moment to the women's views to see whether they considered incompatibility and ill-treatment to be the main effects of child marriage and, if so, what remedies they proposed. Among women there was a unanimity of opinion about child and arranged marriages creating tensions between couples. There was no genuine affection between a husband and wife in India, wrote a woman to *Arya Bhagini*, because both were too young to know the meaning of love and merely accepted a mechanical imposition of the duties and obligations on them.[87] Gulabbai recalled what a farce her whole marriage was to her:

When I was 11 years old I was married to my husband who was then 13 years of age. When they sent me to my in-laws, I remember crying my heart out the whole day. He used to go to school and to me it appeared he was making merry the whole day and when he returned home he was immersed in play with his friends. We started to live together with the fact thrown upon us that 'he is a husband and I am a wife', there was nothing beyond this. . . . What happiness can one see in such a relationship.[88]

Many women wrote about the bewilderment that a young girl experienced with the onset of puberty and the sudden enforcement of sexual duties. The mental immaturity of the girl-wife, they argued, built up resentment within her and allowed conjugal strife to set in.[89] Incompatibility was usually a result of child marriage, wrote Girijabai in a compilation of her essays and lectures. The girl-wife's immaturity created a barrier to communication between them and her husband (who was usually older than her) could not rationally convince her of anything that he considered important. For this reason alone she stood for restraining girls below 14 and men below 20 from marrying.[90]

If a union of minds was unlikely in this set-up then what was the solution? Instead of child marriage, women showed a strong preference for adult marriages and choice of partners rather than arranged marriages. They attributed domestic strife to the discontent and unhappiness of young wives, and came up with the radical suggestion that choosing a spouse should not be men's prerogative alone but that women should be consulted too.[91] This was the main reason why *swayamvar* (the ceremony by which a woman chose her spouse in an open competition between male suitors and supposed to have been in vogue in ancient India) was enthusiastically proposed, rather than as a cultural defence, as was the case with revivalist and nationalist discourse. The 'golden age' theories were utilised in more skilful and complex ways in women's emancipatory programmes than has been understood by contemporary scholarship.[92]

The Marathi journal *Masik Manoranjan* interviewed various prominent Maharashtrian women activists who had participated in the Age of Consent agitation. Among these, it is worth discussing the views of Kashibai Kanitkar who was an important member of the Arya Mahila Samaj and a highly regarded author in the Marathi literary scene of the late nineteenth century. She is reported to have said that 99 per cent of marriages were unhappy ones, but that the degree of unhappiness could be considerably reduced by raising the Age of Consent. According to her if human beings were married at a very young age they would later on say, 'I was deceived, I was cheated', and rebel against the marriage bond.[93] Her opinion was that no girl should be below 14 and no boy below 20 at the time of marriage, and that both sexes should have the freedom to choose their partners so that in the event of a breakdown in their marriage, 'they will not point fingers at others but at themselves'.[94] Her argument was that the responsibility in such a vital issue as marriage should be shouldered by adults alone rather than by children.

Women were acutely aware of the romantic notion of Indian womanhood propagated by Orientalist and revivalist discourse, but contested it strongly. The *Subodh Patrika*, the official organ of the Prarthana Samaj, reported the views of the famous Indologist, Max Müller, on the issue of child-marriage. At the height of the agitation, he had idealized Indian marriages, believing that love and affection were generated in infant marriages through the mere fact of the child-spouses growing up together in one home. Thus he implicitly endorsed the idea that domestic harmony reigned in arranged marriages. The growing women's collective, the bhaginivarg, took him to task by writing to the women's press disputing his findings. The editor of the women's magazine *Arya Bhagini* criticized him for his lack of firsthand experience of India and his excessive reliance on a textual knowledge of the East thus:

> Max Muller saheb is living in a foreign country and will do so forever. He has no first-hand knowledge of an average Indian nor of the behaviour and conduct of our men. Therefore the statements made by the saheb are not uniformly applicable to everyone of us. Among cases of child marriage only around four or five couples out of a hundred live in a state of mutual love and harmony. And around ninety couples do not experience this state of love and affection; instead there is constant bickering and quarrelling in the home.[95]

The analysis of child-marriage led women to believe that it was the cause of domestic unrest and of misery to child wives, and so they called for the regulation of conjugal relations through raising the age of consent.

Public Participation of Women: Meetings and Memorials

The first memorial proposed by women from the Bombay Presidency was done through the collaboration of British feminists in Bombay and London. In the middle of 1890 the work of a Women's Committee supporting the Age of Consent Bill in Bombay was reported in leading newspapers. This Committee consisted of influential English and Maharashtrian women.[96] Their counterpart in London was Millicent Fawcett who lobbied through the Indian National Association for legislative action by the government as an 'act of conscience'.[97] The Women's Committee decided to send a memorial addressed to the Queen with 2,000 signatures of Maharashtrian women. The signatories' social position and caste were to be indicated, too, but in order to protect their interests, their identity was to remain confidential and was not to be revealed to the press.[98]

The memorial pleaded for 'the necessity for legislation in the interests of child-wives and other female minors'. The remedy they sought was that 'the criminal law in India may be so altered as to protect at least girls under fourteen from their husbands as well as from strangers'.[99] The petitioners pointed out the absurdities and anomalies in the criminal law of 1860 which fixed the Age of Consent for British girls at 12 and for Indian girls at 10. They argued that in India girls did not normally attain maturity before 14, basing their contention on the medical evidence produced by European women doctors in India. Impressive statistics were harnessed as evidence for the grievous consequences of early consummation, which resulted in child retardation and maternal mortality.[100] They pointed to the anomaly in the law whereby a girl of 18 could not validly consent to grievous harm to her person, but she could to rape. Also a girl under 12 could not validly consent to the removal of jewels from her person, but she could to 'the theft of her honour'.[101] Finally, they argued that the Queen's 'keen maternal interests' in her subjects should influence her to take action to redeem the status of her weakest subjects—the women of India—and make the law in India conform to the English law.

Between the despatch of the first memorial (December 1890) and the deliberations of the Viceregal Council on the Bill (March 1891) a great deal of activity was reported among Indian women. At least eight women's meetings are reported to have been held in western India and one in Bengal to consider aspects of the Bill and to pass resolutions and write new petitions. Mrs Ghosal of Calcutta, under the pseudonym of 'Srimati' (Mrs) informed the *Statesman* that at a private meeting of middle-aged Hindu ladies, a unanimous verdict was passed in favour of Sir Andrew Scoble's Age of Consent Bill. She said, 'Trustful of the government, the ladies hail any legislation that aims at an amelioration of the nameless doom to which among others, the married girlhood of India are subjected'.[102] The average attendance at these meetings varied between 75 and 250 women. The gatherings were always in urban centres like Pune, Bombay, Amravati and Ahmadabad, and consisted entirely of educated, middle-class women. It seems likely that the women were galvanized into action due to the massive reaction to the Bill.

An innovation in male agitational techniques as a result of the reaction to the Bill was the holding of public meetings of gigantic proportions by men organized on a caste or professional basis. Unscrupulous methods were used to recruit large numbers both for meetings and petitions.[103] While women successfully adopted the new form of constitutional agitation of holding public discussions, they condemned the methods of their male opponents. An important item on women's agenda was to inform the government of the unscrupulous practices used by the anti-legislationists. Orthodox Hindus in Maharashtra did apparently feel the women's meetings to be a threat. Tilak, the leader of the opposition, writing in the *Kesari* and *Mahratta*, registered the unity of women over the Bill, but tried to dismiss their memorials as ineffectual.[104] Some sensational vernacular papers, representing reactionary views, reported that anti-legislationist groups intended to break the influence of liberal women by organizing their wives and sisters to hold counter-meetings.[105] However, no reports of such subversive meetings by women are recorded and this merely suggests the fears of orthodoxy in the face of a united feminist collective.

If the opposition in Maharashatra felt the threat posed by women's public participation, the reverse was true too. The unprecedented traditionalist group's agitation against the Bill prompted women from differing faiths to unite on an issue which they increasingly saw as a gendered one. Typically, in one such meeting, the speaker, while arguing a case for firm commitment and unity among women said, 'The question concerns our most vital interests rather than those of *men*.'[106] Likewise, a woman writing under the authority of a 'mother of several children' said that allowing a husband or stranger to have sexual intercourse with a pre-pubescent girl was an outrageous act. She added:

> Women as a sex, were subject to and underwent far more excruciating pains and miseries and risks of the worst kind happening in child-bearing and child-birth, than man, the opposite sex, had ever conception of . . .[107]

Therefore, she cautioned against listening to the views of men as they were not a reliable index of what women went through, and advised a severe punishment for men indulging in premature cohabitation. Women thus turned the age of consent controversy into a sex-specific case where the experience of women was privileged over the textual interpretations offered by men.

Two kinds of public participation were evident among women. They joined either as members of caste- or religious-affiliated women's bodies or under the umbrella of secular women's organizations.[108] The proceedings of the women's meetings, as well as their petitioning, revealed no further collaboration with British feminists during the passage of the Act. However, there is no indication of disagreement between them. One obvious explanation for this is that the leadership of these organizations was entirely controlled by Indian women; another is that the firmness and confidence exhibited by them made outside help superfluous.[109]

The difference between the first memorial drafted with the help of British feminists and addressed to the Queen and the later petitions gives a clue to the unique aspects of the objectives and participation of Indian women under the supervision of their own feminist leaders. In the first memorial under the guidance of British women, the proposed minimum age of consent for girls was 14 years. By February 1891, when no response had been received to their memorial, women leaders like Rakhmabai Modak and Dhaklibai Sukthankar thought that the reason for the non-response to their first memorial was that 14 years appeared too high an age limit to the imperial government and hence all of their subsequent petitions proposed 12 years as the minimum age.[110] A second difference can be discerned in the construction of arguments for raising the age of consent. While the first memorial concentrated on the anomalies of the Penal Code, the later petitions personalized the issue as one concerning the strijati. The 514 petitioners from the Arya Mahila Samaj argued that while representations against the Bill were by male oppositionists, as far as women were concerned, 'the feeling in favour of the Age of Consent Bill among the female classes is indeed very general wherever the object of the Bill is correctly understood'.[111] Thus not only did the issue concern the strijati alone, but it also had the full consent of the women of Maharashtra. The tone of the later petitions was also marked by a caution which is missing in the first memorial. While some petitions requested guarantees against the misuse of the criminal process (by vesting it exclusively in magistrates), others asked for a less severe punishment in the case of husbands found guilty of breaching the Act.[112]

Finally, the question that arises from this study is why and how was agency uniquely vested in Maharashtrian women? The question is especially pertinent as the existing historiography explicitly or implicitly denies such agency to Bengali women of the same period. Several external factors contributed to the development of women's consciousness in Maharashtra. The social reform movement took a different course there from that in Bengal. In Bombay the social reform movement was more circumspect and less revolutionary. Under the guidance of the Prarthana Samajists, it was eager to change public opinion and developed practical ways of relating their convictions and practices to the existing social structure and thus found a readier public acceptance. In Bengal it was fiery and did not therefore establish a popular base as seen in the Brahmos who, no doubt, created an integrated new philosophy of life but separated themselves from society at large.[113] The specific case of the Age of Consent debate is a good illustration. In Bengal the debate hinged on the control of female sexuality and Bengali women's sexual nature.[114] On the west coast in the hands of B.G. Tilak, the debate became a nationalist issue. Even for reformers like K.T. Telang the aim was to show that social reform must precede political reform. Scholars like Bhandarkar, who cited scriptural sanction for the postponement of the garbhadana, sought to eventually prove that such a delay in holding a religious ceremony was granted in the texts and therefore implied no 'loss of religion' to the ordinary scripture-abiding Hindu and no 'danger to Hinduism' as far as the larger society was concerned. The lines on which the debate was conducted through indigenous male discourse necessarily sharpened the differences for women. Clarity marked the debate by women on the Age of Consent as they realized that it was a gender issue rather than a national or religious one.

Yet another important difference was the slow but sure building of a regional discourse within Maharashtra during this period. There is evidence of anxiety in the way Maharashtrians painstakingly distinguished themselves from Bengalis. After the publicizing of the Phulmonee case, when a Bengali husband killed his pre-pubescent wife in the act of intercourse, Bengal was reported as being a culturally backward region of India in the vernacular newspapers of western India. Even the progressive groups in western India cited the speeches of R.C. Mitter or Sir Stuart Bayley and believed the many allegations made about Bengali women's sexuality. Their rationale was that in a region like Bengal, where purdah was rife, and women were not allowed to look at men other than their close blood relations, it was only natural that Bengali women were full of sexual thoughts and craved the company of their husbands before puberty.[115] On the other side of the coin they represented Maharashtrian women as purdah-free and upheld the region's cultural practices which made consummation of marriage before puberty an exception.[116] The tone and colour of the debates in Maharashtra at once freed women from defending their sexuality and simultaneously set up an agenda on which they could participate on equal terms. This is epitomized in the arguments used by female petitioners who agreed that consummation of marriage before the girl reached the age of 12 was indeed rare in Maharashtra but who also argued that the government had to recognize the existence of the practice in other regions of India and make provisions against it.[117]

Conclusions

In significant ways women's perceptions and their participation in the child marriage debates of the 1890s challenged the social reformist ideology and practice of the nineteenth century. Their position in the debates was an expression of the tensions between their new-found aspirations for education, individuality, and desire for a change in conjugal relations on the one hand and the unchanging balance of power within home, family and society on the other. In their personal lives women attempted to translate the public debates about the role and position of women into practice at home where these relations were actually played out, and here they encountered insuperable obstacles. This led them to move their personal anxieties into a public arena with the child marriage debates.

The Age of Consent debates gave them the opportunity to bring into public prominence their frustration in translating social reform ideals into the domestic sphere. It was precisely their attempt to change their role and position in the domestic realm which enabled them to create a gendered critique of child marriage and armed with the knowledge of the true nature of Indian gender inequality as a creation of indigenous conditions they were equally clear about the *potential* of colonial power to rectify it. Women's discourses on marriage and marital reforms show that they were concerned with gender oppression rather than with colonial oppression and hoped to tap into the possibility of invoking state aid in ending their misery and pain. Their articulation of the cumulative experiences of women allowed them to contextualize their problems, thus enabling them to counter the dominant, male discourse which relied on textual interpretations of the shastras. Women's enduring contribution to the social reform movement and the women's movement of the late nineteenth century therefore is their insistence of the use of a *context-over-text* argument in the way they approached the Age of Consent issue.

The maturity of the Maharashtrian women's movement becomes clearly demonstrable in the Age of Consent controversy. Their attack on the shastras is the most important marker in their progression towards feminism, binding them into a community of women with common interests. The utilization of their women's collective, the bhaginivarg, in marshalling the arguments of gender-specific issues via the women's press is yet another milestone in their progress towards sexual equality. The third and equally important achievement was their insistence on strianubhav (women's experience) as a primary category of analysis of women's subordination rather than a harking back to an imagined past. The bhaginivarg had developed a clearly feminist perspective by relating to the everyday misery of belonging to the strijati, be it a child-wife or widow. The construction of a critique on the 'condition of the strijati' based on either their own personal experiences or the everyday existence of their *bhagini* (sisters) bonded Hindu, Jewish, Christian women together. Another remarkable feature of nineteenth-century Indian feminism was that women's discourse on social reform was based on humanitarian ideals, rather than the arguments used by male social reformers who constantly sought the sanction of the shastras for it. The differences in the arguments proposed by male reformers from those of their female counterparts also high-lights the inescapable conclusion that it would be an affront to call Hindu women reformers' function a 'mediating role' in late nineteenth-century and early twentieth-century Maharashtra. Far from it, their constant contestations of men's role in holding women back as well as their separate women's organizations reveal an independent and assertive role in which men played a minimal part.

Some contemporary scholars have argued that simply because the government had not consulted women's opinions on the restitution of conjugal rights or the Age of Consent it is perfectly all right to dismiss women's voices as being beyond the terms of the debate. Such an argument is unsustainable. By studying the viewpoints and public participation of women in social debates such as the Age of Consent we are now in a position to observe subaltern perceptions of the Raj. One of the richest insights into how the colonial state was viewed by subordinated groups is provided through a study of women's assertion and resistance. Fear, submission and deference—the more readily associated reactions of Indian women towards their menfolk—are missing when it comes to their attitudes to the state. Whilst claiming recognition of their rights, women appeal to the state as the supreme arbiter of justice. Women's adulation of the Raj and their firm belief in the state's will to do good can be read as a sign of how the state was utilized as a tool to counteract patriarchal injustices. The Raj is seen as a humanitarian resource and the final arbiter—wherein the state is registered as the sovereign authority, far more so than the patriarchal head of the household. Women had used the opportunities supplied by colonialism by signing petitions, lobbying sympathetic male officials, joining secular and religious organizations and organizing meetings and rallies.

The greatest impact women's crusades in the late nineteenth century had can be discerned in their persuasion of the government to legislate in favour of women. Highlighting
of the insensitivity of men and the double standards embedded within men's thinking
on sexuality caused an outrage that stimulated the movement well into the twentieth
century for legal reform, for the case of women doctors and for women's suffrage.

What this chapter offers is an argument to look at women's counter-discourses over
the question of marriage reform against the backdrop of their actions in their movements of self-assertion through their recourse to the colonial courts in the crucial
decades prior and leading up to the 1890s—that is, the centrality of women's extensive
resorting to and accessing of the British law courts for the resolution of their dysfunctional marriages, their seeking of alimony and maintenance and divorce on technical
points in the courts. By concentrating on women's agency and contrasting it with the
Indian male reformist and revivalist discourse it should be clear that if the Hindu
patriarchal system felt it was under siege during the child marriage controversy, it was
because of the real threat posed by the actions of their own women-folk rather than the
unreserved expression of English masculinity over the native one. The oppositional
discourse of the female subject in creating her own identity and initiating her own desires
via the law courts and subsequently in her creation of the bhaginivarg and their successful lobbying with the government had led to Tilak's attempt to shore up patriarchy.
Male hostility to women's public participation as seen over the Age of Consent agitation
also explains why Tilak's nationalist programme had such ready appeal in Maharashtra.

Maharashtrian women's participation in the popular agitation over the Age of Consent debates of 1891 effectively takes Indian women's popular protests back into the
nineteenth century.[118] Women's organized protest during the passage of the Bill was an
instance of the process through which they overcame religious, caste and class distinctions.
The realization that the Age of Consent was an issue relating to the well-being of the
strijati united them. Women's groups in the reformist era did not possess a clear-cut
ideology or managerial skills like the women's organizations of the 1930s. However, it
was precisely their non-adherence to nationalist and political reformist ideologies which
gave them the necessary space and freedom to unite on a gender-specific basis.[119] This
also provides a case study for the differences in women's responses in various British
colonies such as Kenya over the clitoridectomy issue.[120] In India female pressure groups
gave their opinions unsolicited and tried to persuade the government by their lobbying
techniques even though the sexual politics of the colonial government prevented consultation with women. It would be an affront to our foremothers' words and actions if
scholarship left unrecognized their contribution towards raising the Age of Consent.

Notes

1. The Age of Consent refers to the age at which the law recognized that an individual was
   eligible to give consent to sexual intercourse.
2. S. Natarajan, *A Century of Social Reform in India* (London, 1959), pp. 82–3.
3. C.H. Heimsath, 'The Origin and Enactment of the Indian Age of Consent Bill, 1891',
   Journal of Asian Studies, 21:4, 1962, pp. 491–504.
4. In 1982, Meredith Borthwick argued that the Age of Consent Bill provided a case-study in
   which Bengali women came to public prominence as symbolic objects rather than as a group
   speaking on their own behalf. See her article, 'The *Bhadramahila* and Changing Conjugal

Relations in Bengal', in M. Allen and S.N. Mukherjee (eds), *Women in India and Nepal* (Canberra, 1982), p. 116.

5. Dagmar Engels drew attention to the opposition between two gender systems in which the male control of female sexuality in Bengal was threatened by the dominant ideology of Victorian sexual values: 'The Age of Consent Act of 1891: Colonial Ideology in Bengal', *South Asia Research*, 3:2, 1985, pp. 107–34. Most recently Mrinalini Sinha has argued that the evaluation of Bengali masculinity was a crucial element in the rationalization of empire: 'The Age of Consent Act: The Ideal of Masculinity and Colonial Ideology in Nineteenth-Century Bengal', in T.K. Stewart (ed.), *Shaping Bengali Worlds, Public and Private* (Michigan, 1989), pp. 99–127.

6. Two exceptions are the works of Geraldine Forbes and Barbara Ramusack who have studied women's participation for a later period (the Sarda Act, 1929). See Forbes, 'Women and Modernity: The Issue of Child-Marriage in India', *Women Studies International Quarterly*, 2, 1979, pp. 407–19; Ramusack 'Women's Organisations and Social Change: The Age of Marriage Issue in India', in N. Black and A.C. Cottrell (eds), *Women and World Change: Equity Issues in Development* (London, 1981), pp. 198–216. However, both these works assume that Indian women's participation in child marriage agitations began only with the Child Marriage Restraint Act of 1929.

7. Sumit Sarkar, 'Orientalism Revisited: Saidian Frameworks in the Writing of Modern Indian History', *Oxford Literary Review*, 16, 1994, p. 220.

8. Tanika Sarkar, 'Rhetoric against Age of Consent: Resisting Colonial Reason and Death of a Child-wife', *Economic and Political Weekly*, 28:36, 4 September 1993, pp. 1869–71 and 1874.

9. The now familiar argument about a 'lack of sources' does not hold good here as there is ample evidence to the contrary. Many newspapers, both English and vernacular, carried reports of women's meetings, letters, articles and details of their memorials. The major source for earlier studies has been the 'Legislative Council Proceedings', which contain women's petitions as well as speeches by Indian members of the Legislature, listing the numerous activities of women in support of the Bill. See Krishnaji Lakshman Nulkar's speech in *Extract from the Abstract of the Proceedings of the Council of the Governor-General of India*, 19 March 1891. Appendix A24 (hereafter cited as *Proceedings*).

10. Padma Anagol, *The Emergence of Feminism in India, 1850–1920* (Ashgate, 2005).

11. For more details see ibid., especially Chapter 2 titled 'Discriminating Converts: Christian Women's Discourse and Work'.

12. For details see ibid., especially Chapter 3 titled 'Beyond Kitchen and Kid: Hindu Women's Discourse and Work'.

13. *Subodh Patrika*, a Marathi weekly and the literary mouthpiece of the Prarthana Samaj regularly reported the proceedings every week from the 1880s onwards.

14. See Gangutai Bhandhari's speech, *Subodh Patrika*, 6 February 1881, p. 163; Durgabai Joshi's essay, *Subodh Patrika*, 13 February 1881, pp. 167 and 171.

15. Ramabai Ranade's Hindu Ladies Social Club, Yashodabai Joshi's Vanita Samaj in Amravati, Girijabai Kelkar's Bhagini Mandal in Jalgaon and the pioneering Shri Saraswati Mandir of Solapur are instances of this awakening. See Chapters 2 and 3 in Anagol, *The Emergence of Feminism in India, 1850–1920*.

16. Sarojini Vaidya, *Shrimati Kashibai Kanitkar: Atmacharitra ani charitra* (Mrs Kashibai Kanitkar: Autobiography and Biography) (Bombay, 1979); see p. 14 for *halad-kunkum* and pp. 89 and 177 for *kirtans* and its new use. Also Ramabai Ranade, *Himself: The Autobiography of a Hindu Lady*, trans. Katherine Gates (New York, 1938), p. 116.

17. Pandita Ramabai had brought various women's groups under the umbrella organization of the Arya Mahila Samaj.

18. I have identified 10 Marathi journals run by *kartris* or 'women-editors' that collectively encompass the women's press of the late nineteenth and early twentieth centuries. The periodicals were meant for an audience of women and came from different parts of Maharashtra. They

are: *Arya Bhagini*, edited by Anandibai and Manakbai Lad; *Saubhagya Sambhar*, edited by Sarubai Goa from Kolhapur; *Swadesh Bhagini*, edited by Tarabai Navalkar from Bombay; *Subhodini*, by Godubai Shinde from Nipani; *Strisaundarya Latika*, by Mrs Penkar from Bombay; *Bhamini Prakash*, by Chimabai Kadam from Poona; *Maharashtra Mahila*, by Manorama Mitra of Bombay; *Grihini Ratnamala* by Sitabai Sawant in Bombay; *Striyanchi Maithrini* by A.A. Abbott, a female missionary; and finally *Simanthini* for which I have no details. The runs vary greatly but their life-span approximately begins in the late 1870s and ends around the 1920s.

19. *Women Writing in India*, vol. 1 (New York, 1991), pp. 167–9.

20. This information is culled from Catalogue of Books printed in the Bombay Presidency starting from the Quarter Ending 30 September 1867 to Quarter Ending 31 December 1896.

21. For an analysis of feminist vocabulary in nineteenth-century Maharashtra, see Anagol, *The Emergence of Feminism in India, 1850–1920*.

22. For details, see ibid., especially Chapter 4 titled 'Women's Assertion and Resistance'.

23. Paras Diwan, *Law of Marriage and Divorce* (Allahabad, 1991), p. 283.

24. Cited in Rakhmabai, *Indian Law Reports* (hereafter *ILR*), 10 Bom., 312, 1885.

25. 'The Indian Divorce Act, 1869', Section VII, Clause 32, reproduced in Diwan, *Law of Marriage*, p. 749.

26. For more details, see Chapter 6 titled 'Women as Agents: Contesting Discourses on Marriage and Marital Rights', in Anagol, *The Emergence of Feminism in India, 1850–1920*.

27. The eighth was a warring Muslim couple disputing the validity of the marriage. These statistics are compiled from E.F. Moore, *Reports of Cases Heard and Determined by the Judicial Committee and the Lords of Her Majesty's Privy Council on Appeal from the Supreme and Sudder Dewanny Courts in the East Indies* (Bangalore, 1858), Hereafter *Moore's Indian Appeals*.

28. 'Ardaseer Cursetjee v. Perozeboye, 12 and 14 April 1856', ibid., vol. 6.

29. '*Femme sole*' is better understood in relation to its sister concept the '*femme covert*'. In nineteenth-century English law the wife was regarded as the 'property of her husband' because the doctrine of coverture declared that the legal personality of the woman was merged in her husband's after marriage. A '*femme covert*' often referred to a married woman who could not alienate her property including that which had come to her before marriage, nor sign contracts, or make a will without the consent of her husband. However, a degree of autonomy was embedded in the term '*femme sole*' which was defined as: 'A wife with a separate estate could deal with *that* [sic] property as if she were unmarried, or what the law called a *feme sole*.' This quote and information is from Mary L. Shanley, *Feminism, Marriage and the Law in Victorian England* (Princeton, 1989), pp. 25–6.

30. Ibid., p. 372.

31. Amongst a host of scholars, see in particular Sudhir Chandra, *Enslaved Daughters: Colonialism, Law and Women's Rights* (New Delhi, 1998).

32. See the letter of Dayaram Gidumal, Acting Assistant Judge, Ahmedabad, to the Secretary to Government, 15 September 1887, 'Proposed amendment'.

33. Ibid., p. 173.

34. See his confidential letter dated 6 August 1887, 'Proposed amendment'.

35. See the reply of Tirmal Rao Venkatesh Inamdar, retired Judge, Court of Small Causes, Dharwar, 14 August 1887, in 'Proposed amendment'.

36. See their replies in 'Proposed amendment'. Ibid.

37. Reply by Rao Bahadur Mahadev Govind Ranade, to the Chief Secretary to Government, 19 September 1887, 'Proposed amendment'.

38. Mrinalini Sinha, 'Potent Protests: The Age of Consent Controversy, 1891', in *Colonial Masculinity: The 'Manly Englishman' and the 'Effeminate Bengali' in the Late Nineteenth Century* (Manchester, 1995), pp. 138–80.

39. Jayantibai lost claims to her first husband's property as the Widow Remarriage Act of 1856 disallowed remarried widows from inheriting their previous husband's property. See Lucy

Carroll, 'Law, Custom and Statutory Social Reform: The Hindu Widows' Remarriage Act of 1856', *Indian Economic and Social History Review*, 20:4, 1983, pp. 363–88.

40. 'An Exposition of Some of the Facts of the Case of Dadaji vs. Rakhmabai', *Law Tracts* (Bombay, 1887), pp. 1–13.
41. 'Rukhmabai's Reply to Dadajee's "Exposition" ', reprinted from the *Bombay Gazette*, 29 June 1887, *Law Tracts*, Bombay, 1987.
42. Ibid., p. 3.
43. The emphasis is mine.
44. There was a third legal suit, too—a libel action by Dadaji against the *Bombay Gazette*, which had investigated the lifestyle of Dadaji and his uncle and validated Rakhmabai's version. On 5 July 1888, the Bombay High Court dismissed Dadaji's claims on sufficient evidence that he had suppressed information. Realizing that he would lose any further suits, he negotiated an out-of-court settlement with Rakhmabai whereby she paid him Rs 2,000 (a large fortune for the 1880s) on the assurance that he would take no further legal action against her. This version of events, from a Marathi biography of Rakhmabai and based on new information, is the more credible because Dadaji's sudden interest in claiming his marital rights from Rakhmabai followed the news of her sole inheritance to a considerable estate from her natural father. The eventual resolution of the case also indicates the monetary considerations in marital disputes. See Mohini Varde, *Dr. Rakhmabai: Ek Arth* (The Saga of Dr Rakhmabai) (Bombay, 1982), pp. 85–92.
45. In 'Dadaji Bhikaji v. Rakmabai', *ILR*, 10 Bom. 301,1886, pp. 572–9.
46. Rakhmabai spent a day in prison according to her own testimony to a friend. In Varde, *Dr Rakhmabai*, p. 62.
47. '*Hindudharmavar ghav ghalnaren navin trikut*' (The New Confederacy of Three in Assaulting Hinduism'), *Kesari* (Marathi), 20 September 1887, p. 2
48. *ILR*, 10 Bom. 301, p. 575
49. Letter to Dorothea Beale, 22 May 1887, in A.B. Shah (ed.), *Letters and Correspondence of Pandita Ramabai* (Bombay, 1977), p. 175.
50. Rumours abounded among conservative groups that women were being encouraged to defy their guardians by male reformers so that attendance at the female schools run by Pandita Ramabai would increase significantly, *Hindu Punch*, 12 February 1891, reported in the Bombay Native Newspaper Reports (hereafter *NNR*), 14 February 1891.
51. It was a common feature among women during this period to use pseudonyms, probably prompted by fear of the awesome reaction in Maharashtra against the abolition of child marriage. However, the pseudonyms indicated their gender and were validated by citing their marital status or class. It was a clever strategy to say, for example, 'from a mother of three children', thus privileging their experience over that of men. It at once gave them a superior position to quote the evil consequences of child marriage on women as opposed to men.
52. This pattern was repeated in the Age of Consent controversy too.
53. 'A Hindu Lady', 'Infant Marriage and Enforced Widowhood', *Times of India*, 26 June 1885, p. 4.
54. 'Infant Marriage', p. 4.
55. See Chapter 3 in Anagol, *The Emergence of Feminism in India, 1850–1920*.
56. 'Infant Marriage', p. 4.
57. Yashodabai Joshi, *Amchi Jivanpravas* (The Journey of Our Life Together), (Pune, 1965), p. 18.
58. Champubai Madhavrao Nadkarni, Letter to Editor, *Arya Bhagini* (Marathi), 28 July 1891; Dhakbai Trimbhakran Desai, Letter to Editor, ibid., 1 November 1891; also opinions of Ahalyabai Morevale, Krishnabai and Lanibai Dhurandar, ibid., January 1893.
59. 'Infant Marriage', p. 4.
60. Ibid.

61. B. Malabari, 'Notes on Infant-Marriage and Enforced Widowhood', p. 3, in Government of India, Home Department, *Selections from the Records*, Serial No. 3, V/23/49/22.

62. See M. Michel, 'The Sarda Act, Political Strategy and Trends in Discourse in the Child-Marriage Debate in India during the 1920s', unpublished M.A. dissertation (Hannover, 1989), p. 121.

63. M.G. Ranade, 12 February 1885, *Selections from Records*, p. 92.

64. Dr K.R. Kirtikar, *An Address on the Occasion of the Second Anniversary of the Saddaharma Samaj of Thane*, 20 July 1883.

65. Letter, 30 December 1884, *Selections from Records*, p. 55.

66. See the reports and letters of Pandurang Balibhadra, Narayan Bhikaji, Deputy Collector, Nasik; Dr Bhikajee Amroot Chobhe, Assistant Surgeon, Pune, in *Selections from Records*, pp. 49, 63–5, 143.

67. K. Satthianadhan, 'Female Education', in *Miscellaneous Writings of Krupabai Satthianadhan* (Madras, 1896), p. 19.

68. Ibid., p. 21

69. Ibid., p. 27.

70. K. Satthianadhan. 'Hindu Social Customs', in *Miscellaneous Writings*, pp. 25–31.

71. 'Infant Marriage'.

72. See articles by Anandibai Lad on 'Lagnyachi chali' (Marriage Traditions), and 'Laukar lagna kamyachi chal' (The Custom of Child-Marriage), in *Arya Bhagini*, March 1886.

73. Pandita Rambai, *The High-Caste Hindu Woman* (London, 1888), especially chapters 2 and 3.

74. S.M. Nikambe, *Ratanbai: A Sketch of a Bombay High Caste Hindu Young Wife* (London, 1895).

75. R. Ranade, *Amchya Ayushyathil kahi atavani* (A Few Reminiscences of Our Life) (Bombay, 1963), pp. 42–68.

76. See 'Samajik sudharana' (Social Reform), *Arya Bhagini*, June 1891, p. 51.

77. 'Gaud Saraswat Brahman Stri' (pseudonym) (A Gaud Saraswat Brahman Lady), 'Letter to the woman-editor', *Arya Bhagini*, p. 52.

78. 'Eka susiksit stri kadun' (By an Educated Lady), 'Gulabbai ani Sevatibai yancha bodhapar samvad' (Instructive Debates Between Gulabbai and Sevatibai), *Arya Bhagini*, July 1891, pp. 60–1.

79. Tarabai Shinde, *Stripurushtulana* (Women and Men: A Comparison), 2nd edn, ed. S.J. Malshe [1st edn, 1882] (Bombay, 1975), p. 18.

80. Malabari, 'Infant Marriage in India, Paper 1', in *Infant Marriage and Enforced Widowhood*, p. 2.

81. Rakhmabai, 'Infant Marriage', p. 4.

82. D. Arnold, 'Medical Priorities and Practices in Nineteenth-Century British India', *South Asia Research*, 5:2, 1985, pp. 167–83.

83. Dr E. Pechey-Phipson, *Address to the Hindus of Bombay on the subject of Child Marriage*, Bombay, 11 October 1890, *IOL Tracts 799*.

84. British and Indian women included Mrs Greton Gary, Dr Edith Pechey-Phipson, Mrs Lyttleton, Mrs Portman, Lady Cowasjee Jehangir, Mrs Bhaunagari; From Varde, *Dr. Rakhmabai*, p. 64. See details as reported in *Jame-Jamshed*, in *NNR*, 16 March 1887.

85. See Varde, *Dr. Rakhmabai*, pp. 97–114, for details.

86. R.G. Bhandarkar, 24 February 1885, *Selections from Records*, pp. 133–4.

87. 'Eka susiksit stri kadun' (By an Educated Lady), 'Gulabbai ani Sevatibai yancha bodhapar samvad' (Instructive Debates between Gulabbai and Sevatibai), *Arya Bhagini*, pp. 52–3.

88. Ibid.

89. Kashibai, the female biographer of Anandibai Joshi, records the fearful delusions of the nine-year-old Anandibai who refused to enter her husband's bedroom for days because she thought there was a tiger there! K. Kanitkar, *Sou. Da. Anandibai Josi yance caritra* (Biography of Mrs Dr Anandibai Joshi) (Pune, 1888), p. 2. Gangutai recalled her intense repulsion at the term *naura* (husband) due to a childhood experience of sexual assault. G. Patwardhan, *Chakoribaher:*

Ek atmakatan (Beyond the Courtyard: An Autobiography), (Pune, 1974), pp. 2–3.

90. G. Kelkar, 'Tarunpide va samajik sudharana' (The Younger Generation and Social Reform), in *Grihini Bhushan, Bhag Dusra, Puspahar* (Guide-Books for Women, Part Two, A Garland of Flowers) (Jalgaon, 1921), pp. 72–84.

91. Anandibai Lad, 'Laukar lagna karnyachi chal', *Arya Bhagini*, p. 5; and K. Satthianadhan, 'Female Education', *Miscellaneous Writings*, pp. 16–17.

92. It is, therefore, simplistic to state that all women who rejected the 'Golden Age' theory (the orientalist notion of a supposedly glorious ancient Indian past) became feminists and those who did not remained in the traditional mould, as has been argued by Uma Chakravarti, 'Whatever Happened to the Vedic Dasi? Orientalism, Nationlism and a Script for the Past', in K. Sangari and S. Vaid (eds), *Recasting Women: Essays in Colonial History* (New Delhi, 1989), pp. 27–87.

93. Quoted in S. Vaidya, *Srimati Kasibai Kanitkar: Atmachiritra ani charitra* (Mrs Kashibai Kanitkar: Autobiography and Biography), (Bombay, 1979), p. 23.

94. Ibid., pp. 231–2.

95. 'Eka susiksit stri kadun, 'Gulabbai ani Sevatibai bodhpar samvad', *Arya Bhagini*, September 1981, pp. 78–9.

96. Lady Reay and Dr Pechey-Phipson were the British representatives; the Indian women were Rakhmabai Modak, Pandita Ramabai and Dr Rakhmabai.

97. *Induprakash*, 22 December 1890, p. 3.

98. The memorial itself was published in verbatim in all the leading newspapers: *Maratha*, 14 December 1890, and *Induprakash*, 6 October 1890.

99. Memorial of 1,600 women of India to Queen Victoria, sent by W. Lee Warner, Secretary to the Government of Bombay, 30 December 1890, in 'Papers Relative to the Bill to Amend the Indian Penal Code and the Code of Criminal Procedure, 1882', *Proceedings*, April 1891, Appendix N.

100. The memoralists also suggested the likelihood of a sterile population resulting from child-marriage: see Memorial of Lady Doctors in India, signed by Monelle Mansell and 49 others, 22 September 1890, *Proceedings*, Appendix A15.

101. Memorial of 1,600 women of India, *Proceedings*.

102. *Induprakash*, 16 February 1891, p. 3.

103. The most publicized of these demonstrations were the Tulsi Bagh and Madhav Bagh meetings in Bombay. Leaflets carried such sensational messages as 'Violate your religion or suffer trans-portation for life'; 'Government interferes in domestic delicate matters'. On the basis of such slogans the anti-legislationsits were able to collect 10,000 signatures in a day. *Gujarati, NNR*, 21 February 1891 and *Vartahar, NNR*, 21 February 1891.

104. *Kesari*, 24 February 1891, *NNR*, 28 February 1891; *Mahratta*, 30 November 1890, *NNR*, 6 December 1890.

105. *Pune Vaibhav*, 7 December 1890, in *NNR*, 13 December 1890. Other vernacular newspapers which condemned women's meetings and participation were *Jagad-hitechchu, Vartahar* and *Hindu Punch*, reported in *NNR*, 7 March 1891.

106. 'Correspondence, Poona News', *Induprakash*, 2 March 1891, p. 4.

107. *Induprakash*, 8 December 1890.

108. Examples of the first kind are Zoroastrian Women's Club, the Bene-Israelite Women's Organisation, Nitiprasarak Mandal and the Native Christian Women's Society. Among the second type were the Arya Mahila Samaj of Bombay and the Aryan Ladies' Association.

109. The new-found confidence was expressed by some women in dropping their pseudonyms during this agitation, like Rakhmabai and Krupabai.

110. Petition from the Aryan Ladies' Association, Pune, by 65 Hindu and 23 Bene-Israel women, *Proceedings*. Also petition of certain Parsi and Native Christian women, Pune, 23 February 1891, to the Governor-General of India, signed by 128 Parsi and 83 Native Christian women, in *Proceedings*, Appendix A12.

111. A petition from Dhaklibai Sukthankar, Secretary, Arya Mahila Samaj, Bombay, 4 March 1891, to K.L. Nulkar accompanied by a 'Memorial of 514 Native Ladies', of Bombay and Pune, *Proceedings*, Appendix A18.
112. A memorial adopted by 60 high-caste Hindu women from Ahmadabad. Reported in *Times of India*, 25 February 1891, p. 5.
113. Other details of these variations are to be found in Heimsath, *Indian Nationalism and Hindu Social Reform*, pp. 14, 86–7, 104–8.
114. See Engels, 'The Age of Consent Act', pp. 122–4.
115. *Sudharak*, in *NNR*, 24 January 1891; *Subodh Patrika, NNR*, 21 February 1891; *Indian Spectator, NNR*, 14 February 1891.
116. This was common ground, shared by both pro- and anti-legislationists, in Maharashtra.
117. Petition from Secretary, Arya Mahila Samaj, Bombay, *Proceedings*.
118. Contrary to the assumption of historians who have suggested that it was not until the passing of the Sarda Act of 1929. Cf. Forbes, 'Women and Modernity', p. 413, and Ramusack, 'Women's Organisations and Social Change', p. 203.
119. Adherence to nationalist ideals and allegiance to nationalist leaders probably shackled women's organization to a lukewarm ideology of women's emancipation, where they were neither feminists nor suffragists. The stand-point of the All India Women's Conference in the child marriage issue of 1929 is discussed in Forbes, 'Women and Modernity', pp. 414–15.
120. For a refreshing analysis, see S. Pedersen, 'National Bodies, Unspeakable Acts: The Sexual Politics of Colonial Policy-Making', *Journal of Modern History*, 63:4, 1990, pp. 647–80.

13

Punjab and the North-West*

Kenneth Jones

Transitional Movements among the Sikhs

The Nirankaris

Baba Dayal Das (1783–1855) founded the Nirankaris, a movement of purification and return. Dayal Das was born into a Malhotra Khatri family in Peshawar and raised as a pious, religiously oriented boy, but beyond this we know little of his early life. After his parents died, Dayal Das moved to Rawalpindi where he opened an apothecary shop. Apparently disenchanted with contemporary religion, Dayal Das concluded that Sikhism was decadent, filled with falsehood, superstition and error. Sometime during the decade of the 1840s, he called for the return of Sikhism to its origins and emphasized the worship of God as *nirankar* (formless). Such an approach meant a rejection of idols, rituals associated with idolatry, and the Brahman priests who conducted these rituals.[1] A repudiation of Brahman priests meant also a rejection of those Sikhs allied with them. Dayal Das quickly ran into opposition from the established religious authorities; consequently, the movement progressed in secret until the British gained control of the Punjab.

The Nirankaris focused more on deficiencies in religious practice than on a critique of theology. The appropriate path to God was through worship based on meditation rather than complex ritual. Dayal Das urged his disciples to meet each morning for daily worship in their *dharmshalas*. He stressed the importance and authority of Guru Nanak and of the Adi Granth (the source of all authority and knowledge). His disciples were 'to worship the formless God, to obey the *shabad* of the guru [in the Adi Granth], to clean the shoes and feet of the congregation [as an act of humility], to serve one's parents, to avoid bad habits, and to earn one's livelihood through work'.[2] In accordance with Sikh tradition, Dayal Das taught a religious code for the householder, that is, an individual who retained his familial and social ties and had not withdrawn into the role of a mendicant.

In addition Dayal Das taught that women should not be treated as unclean at childbirth; disciples should not use astrology or horoscopes in setting the time for ceremonies; the dowry should not be displayed at marriages; neither lighted lamps nor blessed sweets, *prasad*, should be placed in rivers; and no one should feed Brahmans as

*From *Socio-Religious Reform Movements in British India* (*The New Cambridge History of India*) (Cambridge: Cambridge University Press, 1989), pp. 87–95, 103–6, 109–15.

payment for conducting rituals. Eating meat, drinking liquor, lying, cheating, using false weights—all were forbidden. Each should follow a strict moral code and use only the proper life-cycle rituals as taught by Dayal Das. The new ceremonies included those of birth, naming of a child, a shortened marriage ceremony that had at its core a circumambulation of the Adi Granth, and a death-rite requiring that the body be immersed in a river or cremated. All ceremonies eliminated the services of a Brahman priest.

Slowly the Nirankaris attracted new members. Because of persecution, Dayal Das purchased land on the edge of Rawalpindi where he constructed a dharmshala, which became a centre of worship and was known as the Nirankari Darbar. Baba Dayal Das died on 30 January 1855 before he could bring organization and cohesion to this movement. The Nirankaris of Rawalpindi placed his body in the Lei River at a spot where he used to meditate. Later it was known as Dayalsar and considered sacred by the Nirankaris. Before his death Dayal Das named his son, Baba Darbara Singh (1814–70), to succeed him.

Darbara Singh, born under the name of Mul Rai, was an energetic and persuasive leader who was determined to cut all ties with Hinduism. A year after he had replaced his father, Darbara Singh began to issue *hukamnamas* (statements describing both doctrine and approved rituals). He toured the Rawalpindi area and while travelling preached, converted and married his followers according to their own rites. In 1861 he visited Amritsar and asked permission to perform the Nirankari marriage ceremony at the Golden Temple. This request was rejected; however, he conducted such a service in Amritsar on 17 April 1861.[3] In 15 years Darbara Singh opened 40 new subcentres as the number of disciples continued to grow: under him the Nirankaris had their most rapid period of expansion. He died on 13 February 1870, and his younger brother, Rattan Chand, succeeded him.

Rattan Chand established new centres and appointed *biredars* (leaders) for each congregation or *sangat*. The biredars oversaw these groups and were charged with reciting the hukamnamas every 15 days. Thus they provided a tie between the head of the Nirankari movement and its members. Rattan Chand developed Dayalsar into a religious hub as new *biras* (congregations) were added to the surrounding towns and villages. In 1903 he wrote a will leaving all property of the association to his successor, and before his death on 3 January 1909 he named his son, Baba Gurdit Singh, to fill that office. Gurdit Singh headed the movement until his death on 26 April 1947.

The historical impact of the Nirankaris remains a matter of some debate, since even the most basic information is open to question. The census of 1891 stated that there were over 60,000 Sikhs in this movement. John Webster considers these figures exaggerated, and those of the 1921 census as too low with the more realistic estimate of around 5,000 members.[4] Drawing on Sikh tradition, the Nirankaris focused on Guru Nanak, on Sikhism before the establishment of the Khalsa by Guru Gobind Singh at Anandpur, and the militarization of the faith. In this they pursued a path open to both orthodox, keshadhtiris, Sikhs and to the non-baptized ranks of the *sahajdharis*, but drew members mainly from the urban non-Jat section of the Sikh community. The Nirankaris stressed proper religious practice, issued hukamnamas to define its concepts of what was correct, and built a series of worship centres staffed by their own priests. They did not clash with or oppose the British, but grew in part through the establishment of British rule in the

Punjab since that freed them from the restriction of the Sikh government. The Nirankaris thus became a permanent subsection of the Sikh religion and in doing so helped
to clarify the lines dividing Sikhs from Hindus. Their dependence on Guru Nanak and
early Sikhism for their model of 'pure' religion separated them from another transitional
movement, the Namdharis.

The Namdharis

Baba Ram Singh (1816–85) founded this transitional movement. He was born into a
poor carpenter's family in the village of Bhaini Arayian in Ludhiana district. Little is
known about Ram Singh's early life. Apparently he received no formal education and
was married at the age of seven. Later his wife was addressed as 'Mata' or mother by members of the Namdhari movement.[5] In 1836, when Ram Singh was 20, he joined the army
of Ranjit Singh and served until 1845. While a soldier he demonstrated a deep commitment to religion and began to attract his own following. In 1841, he met Balak Singh
of Hazru in Campbellpur district and became his disciple. Balak Singh urged his listen-
ers to live a simple life and to reject all ritual except for repeating God's name. Those who
accepted Balak Singh's leadership saw him as a reincarnation of Guru Gobind Singh.
Before his death, Balak Singh chose Ram Singh as his successor.

In 1855 Ram Singh returned to Bhaini, where he reopened the family's shop and
lived there until his exile in 1872. Gradually disciples flocked to Bhaini where Ram
Singh ran a free kitchen and preached his ideas of a purified Sikhism. In 1857, he formally inaugurated the Namdhari movement with a set of rituals modelled after Guru
Gobind Singh's founding of the Khalsa. Ram Singh used a recitation of *gurbani* (hymns
from the Granth Sahib), *ardas* (the Sikh prayer), a flag, and baptism for entry into the
new community. Each of the baptized Sikhs was required to wear the five symbols with
the exception of the *kirpan* (sword) no longer allowed by the British government. Instead of the sword, Ram Singh required them to keep a *lathi* (a bamboo stave). In addition the Namdharis wore white clothes with a white turban and carried a rosary to
further set them apart from all others.

Ram Singh demanded that his adherents abandon the worship of gods, goddesses,
idols, graves, tombs, trees and snakes. Popular saints were rejected along with the rituals
conducted by Brahman priests and the authority of the hereditary custodians of the Sikh
gurdwaras (centres of worship). He also condemned the claims to special status by the
Sodhis and Bedis, descendants of the Sikh gurus. The Namdharis were told to abstain
from 'drinking, stealing, adultery, falsehood, slandering, back-biting and cheating'.[6]
The consumption of beef was strictly forbidden, since protection of cattle remained one
of the Namdharis' most ardently held values. Proper behaviour was enforced by pan-
chayats (village courts), which dispensed the appropriate punishment for a particular
transgression. Ram Singh condemned beggary and thus the role of mendicants. His was
a householder's religious path that stressed hard work, cleanliness and a moral life.

The Namdharis granted women a degree of equality. They too were initiated
through baptism, allowed to remarry when widowed; dowries were rejected, and child
marriage forbidden. For men, there was an emphasis on strength and martial qualities
drawn from the teachings of Guru Gobind Singh and, no doubt, from Ram Singh's

years as a soldier. As he articulated his ideas, the movement grew and the village of Bhaini became a point of pilgrimage later known as Bhaini Sahib. In time Namdhari worship acquired a new dimension. Hymns were accompanied with shouts of joy (*kuks*), as the worshipper slipped into a state of ecstasy. This form of worship resulted in the Namdharis being referred to as *kukas* (shouters). Many outside the Namdhari community saw them as peculiar and extreme, but they considered themselves as bearers of the only true Sikhism.[7]

Ram Singh attracted many of his disciples from the peasant and untouchable castes and transformed them into a disciplined community. Sangats were organized in any village that had a group of Namdharis. Each sangat had its own place of worship, a *granthi* (scripture-reciter), and a free kitchen. The granthi taught Gurmukhi and the Sikh scriptures to both children and adults. Sangats were grouped together and administered by *subas* (governors), *naib subas* (assistant-governors) and *jathedars* (group leaders), whose primary function was to collect funds and remit them to the headquarters at Bhaini. The Namdharis also maintained a system of preachers to spread their message and their own postal runners to ensure communications within the community. Among the Namdharis, prophetic letters appeared that described a reincarnation of Guru Gobind Singh in the person of Ram Singh, and predicted the re-establishment of the Sikh kingdom.[8]

The Punjab government became sufficiently uneasy with the Namdharis that on 28 June 1863 they interned Ram Singh in his village where he was held until the end of 1866. By 1863, the Namdharis were estimated to have between 40,000 to 60,000 members and approximately 100,000 by 1871.[9] The impressive growth of this movement as well as its militant ideology led the Punjab government to keep them under close surveillance and to prohibit Namdhari missionaries from preaching to Sikh troops of the British-Indian army. The period from 1867 to 1870 remained quiet as the Namdharis continued to make converts. Yet some type of conflict with the government seemed almost inevitable. When Ram Singh visited Amritsar in 1867, he arrived with nearly 3,500 followers, converted 2,000 and conducted himself as a prince. He travelled with an escort of soldiers, held court daily and exchanged gifts with local rulers. The clash, when it finally exploded, was not over Ram Singh's acquisition of secular status, but the issue of cow protection.

Under Ranjit Singh the slaughter of cattle had been outlawed, but the British lifted this ban. Cattle once more became a source of meat for the British and for Punjabi Muslims. The latter also publicly sacrificed cattle on the Islamic festival of 'Id. Both Hindus and Sikhs objected to this and found offensive the presence of slaughter-houses and meat shops. The Namdharis were pledged to protect cattle and to end their slaughter. In 1871 two incidents occurred as Namdharis put their beliefs into practice. On the night of 15 June, a small band attacked a Muslim slaughter-house in Amritsar. One month later a second attack took place in Raikot, Ludhiana District. The British arrested those involved and hung eight of them; however, this did not quiet matters. Another band marched on the small Muslim state of Malerkotla in January 1872. They intended to seize weapons and possibly begin an uprising against the government. To this threat the British reacted with speed and viciousness. The Deputy Commissioner of Ludhiana, Mr L. Cowan, rushed to Malerkotla, arrested the Namdharis, and on 17–18 July executed 65 of them.

In the aftermath a mixed military and police force raided Bhaini and arrested Ram Singh; he was exiled to Burma where he died in 1885. The government stationed a police post in the village of Bhaini where they remained until 1922. With the removal of Ram Singh, his younger brother, Baba Budh Singh, became head of the Namdharis. During the remainder of the nineteenth century studies of Namdhari attempts to find allies against the British in Nepal, Kashmir and Russia illustrated their enduring hostility toward the British government. Pilgrims continued to reach Bhaini, but the movement was effectively curtailed. The census of 1891 counted 10,541 Namdharis and in 1901 the number had risen to only 13,788.[10]

The teachings of Ram Singh and his guru, Balak Singh, promised a return to purified Sikhism, not of Guru Nanak, but of Guru Gobind Singh. Both leadership and membership came from the Jat peasant class of Punjab, the same segment of society that had supported Guru Gobind Singh and his version of Sikhism. They shared with the Nirankaris the belief that Sikhism was decadent and degenerate and they too sought to return it to past purity. The Namdhari vision of a restructured Sikhism, however, called for a total reshaping of the Sikh community into a militant, religious-political dominion that threatened established religious authority and brought them into direct conflict with the British-Indian government. With their ecstatic devotionalism, a millennial vision of the future, a tightly organized religious community that contained elements of a parallel government they, like the Tariqah-i-Muhammadis, struck against British political dominance and in return were suppressed. Neither Namdharis nor Nirankaris, both transitional movements, were concerned with adjusting to the cultural influences of the colonial milieu, a world that had only begun to penetrate the Punjab.

The Creation of the Colonial Milieu

Once again we must look to Delhi and Ludhiana for sources of imported knowledge, technology, and the beginnings of cultural interaction in the North-West. After the annexation of 1849 and the uprising of 1857, Lahore became the premier city of the North-West; the centre of provincial administration as well as a place of social, educational, and religious ferment. Students travelled to Lahore from throughout the province. There they received an education, participated in the culture of Lahore and then disseminated it throughout the North-West when they departed for jobs in other cities and towns.

The conquest of the Punjab generated a sudden need for educated Indians to staff government offices and the institutions erected by Christian missionaries. Brahmans and Kayasthas were recruited from Bengal and from the North-Western Provinces. Their arrival created an elite situated below the English rulers, but above Punjabis who lacked an English education or an understanding of the new colonial world. Bengalis provided three models for emulation: one as orthodox Hindus, a second as converts to Christianity, and a third as members of the Brahmo Samaj. Of the three types, the Brahmos were the most outspoken, aggressive and articulate. In 1863 a few Bengalis and Punjabis founded the Lahore Brahmo Samaj. Much of the dynamics of this society derived from the leadership of Babu Novin Chandra Roy, a Bengali employed as paymaster of the North-Western Railway offices in Lahore. He wrote extensively as an advocate of socially radical Brahmoism, fought for increased use of Hindi, and succeeded in recruiting new members among Bengalis and Punjabis. The Lahore Brahmo Samaj was aided by visits from leading Bengali Brahmos. Keshab Chandra Sen spoke in Lahore in 1867 and 1873, Debendranath Tagore in 1867, 1872 and 1874, and Protap Chandra Majumdar in 1871.[11]

Islamic influences also reached Punjab and the North-West from the Gangetic plain and particularly from Delhi. The career of 'Abdul-Minan Wazirabadi illustrates the diffusion of Islamic ideas. He was born in Jhelum, travelled first to Bhopal and then to Delhi for his education. In Delhi he studied under Nazir Husain and when he returned to the Punjab, he brought the ideology of Ahl-i-Hadith with him, becoming one of this movement's most effective exponents.[12] Another prominent supporter of Ahl-i-Hadith in Punjab was Maulawi Muhammad Husain of Batala (Gurdaspur district), who began publishing the newspaper *Ishaat-i-Sunnah*.[13] At an extreme of movements of return, the Lahore Ahl-i-Qur'an, founded by 'Abd' Ullah Chakralawi, rejected orthodox Islam as well as all movements such as the Ahl-i-Hadith that accepted forms of authority other than the Qur'an. Chakralawi and his few followers clashed with all other Muslim groups, remaining as they did on one end of a continuum of advocates for religious and social change.

New types of Islamic organization began to appear in the years after the Mutiny. In 1866 the Anjuman-i-Himayat-i-Islam (the Society for the Defence of Islam) was founded in Lahore by Muhammad Shafi and Shah Din, both followers of Sayyid Ahmad Khan. This society opened schools that included western education and required the study of English. They emphasized female education, loyalty to the British-Indian government, and opposed the Indian National Congress. This organization was not limited to Lahore. The parent association established branches throughout the subcontinent.[14] Three years later the Anjuman-i-Islamiyah (the Islamic Society) was organized in Lahore to teach Muslim youth the principles of Islam and elements of western knowledge. Thus, influences from Muslim movements outside of the North-West flowed into that area and beyond through societies and organizations created in the North-West. The largest of the Hindu acculturative socio-religious movements, the Arya Samaj, also demonstrated the inward and outward flow of ideas and organizations. . . .

The Dev Samaj

As with many of the first Aryas in Lahore, the career of Pandit Shiv Narayan Agnihotri as a religious leader grew from his involvement with the Lahore Brahmo Samaj. Pandit Agnihotri was born into a family of Kanauji Brahmans on 20 December 1850.[15] At the age of 16 Agnihotri enrolled in the Thomson College of Engineering at Roorkee. As a student he was introduced to Vedanta through the teachings of Shiv Dayal Singh who, in 1871, formally initiated Agnihotri and his wife as his own disciples. Two years later Agnihotri left Roorkee for Lahore where he accepted a position as drawing master in the Government School.

After settling in Lahore, Pandit Agnihotri was attracted to the Brahmo Samaj through the influence of his guru and of Munshi Kanhyalal Alakhdhari. He joined the Samaj in 1873 and quickly became a major figure in that organization. The Pandit was a dramatic speaker, prolific writer, and a successful journalist. While a member of the Brahmo Samaj, he spoke and wrote in favour of marriage reform and vegetarianism. He expounded the rationalistic and eclectic Brahmo doctrine. Gradually he committed more of his time to the Samaj and, in 1875, Agnihotri became an honorary missionary of the Samaj.[16] Five years later, he travelled to Calcutta where he was ordained as one of the first missionaries of the newly established Sadharan Brahmo Samaj.

Pandit Agnihotri met Swami Dayananda in 1877 and, although many of their ideas were compatible, they clashed with each other on a personal basis. Afterwards Agnihotri repeatedly attacked Dayananda and the Arya Samaj. Writing in Hindi, Urdu and English, Agnihotri borrowed criticism from European scholars to reject Dayananda's interpretation of the Vedas. Aryas replied with a stream of tracts condemning Agnihotri, first as a Brahmo, and later as leader of his own religious movement. Pandit Agnihotri became increasingly involved in the work of the Brahmo Samaj. He took a modified Brahmo form of *sanyas* on 20 December 1882 and changed his name to Satyananda Agnihotri. As a full-time practitioner of religion, Agnihotri left his post as drawing master, but still retained his married life. Friction developed within the Brahmo Samaj and doubts in the Pandit's own mind so that in 1886 he resigned from the Punjab Brahmo Samaj.

On 16 February 1887 Agnihotri founded the Dev Samaj (Divine Society). At first this organization was considered an extension of the Brahmo Samaj, but it soon began to deviate from their doctrines. Agnihotri rejected Brahmo rationalism and taught instead that only the guru, in the person of Agnihotri, could provide a path of eternal bliss. At the upper end of an evolutionary ladder, he possessed the 'Complete Higher Life', a stage of being beyond the dangers of degeneracy and disintegration. A soul moved up this ladder of life or down it. Degeneracy could be achieved by anyone, but progress upward required the guidance of an enlightened soul, and in this world the only guide was Pandit Agnihotri. In 1892 he initiated the dual worship of himself and God. Three years later, the worship of God was dispensed with, leaving the guru as the sole point of attention for members of the Samaj.

The Dev Samaj held regular services consisting of hymns, a sermon and readings from the *Deva Shastra. Murti puja* (idol worship) was combined with these other types of worship. Agnihotri or his portrait replaced the traditional idol. In its patterns of worship and its ideology, the Dev Samaj fused traditional concepts with demands for radical social change. It taught a code of honesty in public and private. The Dev Samajis were forbidden to lie, steal, cheat, accept bribes or gamble. They should take neither liquor nor drugs and were expected to be strict vegetarians. Adultery, polygamy and 'unnatural crimes' were outlawed and each member was expected to follow a useful life—that is, to work and live as a householder. All levels of membership looked to Agnihotri, known later as Dev Bhagwan Atma, for guidance in their lives and in their search for fulfilment.

The Dev Samaj demanded that its members abandon all caste restraints; they were expected to practise intercaste dining and intercaste marriage. Pandit Agnihotri also wished to restructure the role of women. He attempted to eliminate child marriage by setting the age of marriage at 20 for boys and 16 for girls. Agnihotri discouraged excessive dowries, the seclusion of women, and their traditional mourning rites. He taught that widow marriage was acceptable and married a widow himself after the death of his first wife. The Dev Samaj encouraged the education of women and opened a coeducational school in Moga (Ferozepore district) on 29 October 1899.[17]

The emphasis on a stern moral standard plus considerable social radicalism appealed to educated Punjabi Hindus, 'graduates, magistrates, doctors, pleaders, moneylenders, landlords and Government servants', who comprised the membership of the Dev Samaj.[18] The Dev Samajis were almost totally educated men and even contained a large percentage of literate women. This, and their position in society, gave the movement far greater influence than sheer numbers would allow. This acculturative socio-religious movement was always an elite organization drawing its membership from the highly educated upper-caste Hindus of Punjab. Centred on a guru, the Dev Samaj produced a mixture of religious tradition and radical social change, especially in the role of women. The Samaj peaked in 1921 when it had 3,597 members. After the death of Pandit Agnihotri the Dev Samaj declined, but it did not disappear. It continued to practise the Vigyan Mulak Dharma (Science Grounded Religion).[19] The radicalism of the Dev Samaj, Brahmo Samaj, and Arya Samaj, the attacks by individual critics, such as Kanhyalal Alakhdhari, and the criticisms of the Christian missionaries stirred orthodox Hindus to defend their religion from all who opposed it. . . .

Acculturative Movements among the Sikhs

The Singh Sabhas

A series of events led to the founding of the first Singh Sabha at Amritsar. The Sikh community had been shaken by Namdhari unrest, the speeches of Shraddha Ram and Christian conversions. In the beginning of 1873, several Sikh students at Amritsar Mission School announced that they intended to become Christians. This incident stirred a small group of prominent Sikhs to form the Singh Sabha of Amritsar, which held its first meeting on 1 October 1873. Among those who helped to establish the Sabha were Sir Khem Singh Bedi, Thakur Singh Sandhawalia, Kanwar Bikram Singh of Kapurthala and Giani Gian Singh. Sandhawalia became its president and Giani Gian Singh its secretary. The Sabha intended to restore Sikhism to its past purity, to publish historical religious books, magazines and journals, to propagate knowledge using Punjabi, to return Sikh apostates to their original faith, and to involve highly placed Englishmen in the educational programme of the Sikhs.[20]

The Singh Sabha was directed by an Executive Committee consisting of the president and secretary plus a few members. As the Sabha expanded, new officers were appointed, a vice-president, assistant secretary, a *giani* (scholar of the Sikh scriptures), an *updeshak* (preacher), a treasurer and a librarian. They were elected each year and could be reelected. Members had to be Sikhs with a strong belief in the teachings of the gurus. They paid a monthly subscription and were asked to pledge themselves to serve the community and to be loyal to Sikhism. All the original members were baptized Sikhs, although no requirement for this was written into the constitution of the Sabha.[21] They met every two weeks, and held anniversary celebrations and special meetings on festival days or in response to specific challenges by other religious groups. The Sabha soon began to issue *hurmatas* (records) of its decisions, each of which was the result of a majority vote. The Sabha also kept records of its income and expenditures, and produced annual reports.

The Singh Sabha represented the leaders of the Sikh community. It was joined by members of the landed gentry, the aristocracy and various types of temple servants: *pujaris* who conducted rituals, granthis who recited the Sikh scriptures, *mahants* who administered the gurdwaras, gianis and descendants of the gurus.[22] The Sabha prepared a calendar that listed the correct dates of the births and deaths of the ten gurus. They embarked on the preparation of a definitive text of the Dassam Granth; however, this task proved so demanding that a separate organization, the Gurmat Granth Pracharak Sabha, was founded to finish it. The Singh Sabha published numerous tracts and books and in 1894 organized the Khalsa Tract Society to popularize Punjabi, the Gurmukhi script, and to issue monthly tracts on the Sikh religion.[23] Soon the Singh Sabha of Amritsar was emulated by a new organization that also proved to be a competitor for leadership within the Sikh community.

The Lahore Singh Sabha held its first meeting on 2 November 1879. This new society was led by Professor Gurmukh Singh (1849–98) and Bhai Ditt Singh (1853–1901). Gurmukh Singh drew others into the Lahore Sabha through his personality, his extensive writings and his efforts in the field of journalism.[24] This new Singh Sabha announced goals similar to those of the Amritsar society. They also wanted to return Sikhism to its past purity by expunging all elements of non-Sikh origin. The Lahore Sabha intended to publish literature on Sikhism and authentic texts of the various Sikh scriptures. They wished to impart 'modern' knowledge through the vehicle of Punjabi, and published journals and newspapers to achieve these ends. The first president of this Sabha was Diwan Buta Singh, and Bhai Gurmukh Singh served as its secretary. The Lahore Singh Sabha formed an Educational Committee to encourage Sikh learning and also invited sympathetic Englishmen to join in the Committee's project. Another of the early acts of this Sabha was to affiliate with the Singh Sabha of Amritsar.

Differences between the Lahore and Amritsar societies quickly surfaced. The Lahore Sabha was more democratic and accepted members from all castes including untouchables. Their programme of purifying Sikhism directly opposed the vested interests of the Amritsar Sabha. The career of Bhai Ditt Singh illustrates the type of friction that erupted between the two organizations. Ditt Singh, himself of low-caste status, wished to remove the 'evils of caste' and 'guru-dom' from the Sikh community. Because he was an effective writer, he became the main propagandist for the Lahore Sabha. His publications chided high-caste Sikhs for denigrating converts, especially from the lower castes; Ditt Singh also attacked the hereditary priests and claimants to special status as descendants of the gurus. His tract, *Sudan Natak* (A Dream Drama), ridiculed the religious establishment and resulted in a court case, the first of many that grew from his writings.[25] The Lahore Sabha soon confronted considerable opposition within the Sikh community, and, was banned from meeting in many local gurdwaras. Consequently, the Singh Sabhas found it necessary to erect their own gurdwaras served by priests who accepted the Singh Sabha ideology.

The Lahore Sabha expanded with local branches in many of the Punjab towns. The Amritsar Sabha developed its own societies, but its growth was far slower than the Lahore society. In 1880 a General Sabha was established in Amritsar to provide a central organization for all Singh Sabhas. On 11 April 1883 this was renamed the Khalsa Diwan, Amritsar. It included 36 to 37 different Singh Sabhas as well as the Lahore association. The officers reflected an attempt to bring all groups together to heal the differences between them. Raja Bikram Singh of Faridkot accepted the title of patron, Baba Khem

Singh Bedi was president, Man Singh officer-in-charge of the Golden Temple, Bhai Ganesh Singh and Bhai Gurmukh Singh the joint secretaries. This effort at unity lasted but a short time. In 1886 the Lahore Singh Sabha created its own Khalsa Diwan (Sikh Council). Only the Sabhas of Faridkot, Amritsar and Rawalpindi allied with the original Diwan; the rest turned to the Lahore leadership and to its radical ideology of social and religious change.[26]

The Lahore Khalsa Diwan received assistance from the Maharaja of Nabha as its patron, while Sir Attar Singh served as its president and Bhai Gurmukh Singh as its secretary. At first they had good relations with the Arya Samaj. Several young Sikhs joined the Aryas, seeing in it many of the same ideals that motivated members of the Singh Sabha. The two organizations appeared to be moving along parallel paths. Dayananda criticized Sikhism, but the Aryas had not emphasized this until the occasion Pandit Guru Datta attacked Sikhism and labelled Guru Nanak 'a great fraud'. Other Aryas, including Pandit Lekh Ram and Lala Murli Dhar, joined this denigration of Sikhism. As a result, three young, educated Sikhs, Bhai Jawahir Singh, Bhai Ditt Singh Giani and Bhai Maya Singh, departed the Samaj for the Lahore Singh Sabha. They became staunch defenders of Sikhism against all external criticism, especially from the Aryas. Arya–Sikh relations ranged from vicious tract-wars to cooperation in the area of *shuddhi*, but as the two movements matured they tended to draw further and further apart.

The Singh Sabhas continued to expand, new branches were founded that, at times, created their own distinct ideas and programmes. The Bhasur Singh Sabha became a hub of Sikh militancy under the leadership of Bhai Teja Singh. Members of this Sabha were required to wear the five symbols of orthodoxy, to accept strict religious discipline, and if they did not do so, were expelled. Its members were treated as equals regardless of their class or caste origins. The Bhasur Singh Sabha was aggressive in its missionary zeal and extreme in its ideology. In time it developed into the Panch Khalsa Diwan and competed with other Khalsa Diwans. Not all deviation or enthusiasm by local Singh Sabhas proved as controversial. Under the leadership of Bhai Takht Singh (1860–1937), the Ferozepore Singh Sabha opened a girls' high school and hostel when the education of women was still unacceptable to many Sikhs. Other Sabhas connected with the Lahore Diwan built orphanages, opened schools for all classes and castes, and produced a stream of literature, tracts, journals and newspapers.[27]

Although strong differences in membership, ideology and programmes divided the Amritsar and Lahore Diwans, they did cooperate in establishing a Sikh college. Representatives of both Khalsa Diwans met in Lahore to draw up plans for the proposed college. A hukamnama was issued from the Golden Temple that requested each Sikh to give a tenth of his income for the college project. Sympathetic Englishmen organized a committee in London to raise funds and donations were requested from the Sikh ruling families. This institution became a degree-granting college in 1899 and the foremost success of Sikh efforts in higher education.

During the 1890s, Sikhs in both wings of the Singh Sabha movement became increasingly concerned with the question of Sikh identity; were they or were they not part of the Hindu community? Competition with Hindu movements had done much to fuel this discussion. Western scholars, involved in translations of different Sikh scriptures, added further stimulus to controversy surrounding the role and meaning of

Sikhism. In 1898, the Sikh philanthropist, Sardar Dayal Singh Majithia, died leaving his wealth to the Dayal Singh Trust. His widow contested his will with the result that an English court had to decide whether the deceased was a Sikh or a Hindu. Throughout 1898, 1899 and 1900, the lawsuit and the question of Sikh identity were argued in public meetings, in the press and through numerous publications. The more radical Sikhs claimed that Sikhism was separate from Hinduism, while others maintained it was a subdivision of Hinduism. The Arya Samaj added more fuel to this debate.

Sikh leaders of the Rahtia community, untouchable weavers from the Jullundur Doab, demanded that the Singh Sabhas remove their social and religious liabilities. Sikhism rejected caste, they maintained, and so this error of ignorance and Hindu influence should be extinguished. Since the Singh Sabha leaders did not respond to their pleas, they turned to Lala Munshi Ram of the Arya Samaj. He welcomed them and, on 3 June 1900, the Samaj conducted a public ceremony of shuddhi in the city of Lahore for 200 Rahtias. The Aryas gave each of them a sacred thread signifying his pure status, shaved their beards and hair, and introduced them to the proper rituals of worship. In short, the Rahtias were transformed into clean-caste Hindus. The Sikhs, who witnessed this spectacle, became enraged, seeing it as sacrilege and a threat to their community. In the following months Aryas continued to purify members of the Rahtia caste and Sikh leaders pulled further away from the Hindu community. In 1905 Sikh reformers struck back as they succeeded in 'cleansing' the Golden Temple of Brahman priests, idols and Hindu rituals. This action strengthened the argument that Sikhs were separate from the Hindu religion, an idea which gained wider and wider acceptance among educated Sikhs during the twentieth century.[28]

Meanwhile leadership within the Sikh community shifted. The Lahore Singh Sabha lost many of its prominent members. Sir Attar Singh died in 1896, Bhai Gurmukh Singh in 1898 and Bhai Ditt Singh in 1901. Attention moved to a new organization, the Chief Khalsa Diwan founded in Amritsar, where it first met on 30 October 1902. A constitution and an elaborate structure of organization were adopted and, in 1904, the society was registered with the government. Sikh leaders again attempted to unite the diverse organizations within their community under one umbrella. Yet only 29 of the 150 Singh Sabhas then in existence agreed to join the Chief Khalsa Diwan. Membership was limited to baptized Sikhs and the organization depended on individual subscriptions for financial support. The Chief Khalsa Diwan failed to transcend internal divisions among the Sikhs, divisions that surfaced in the decade after World War I.

Initially Sikhs had responded to the loss of political domination much as had the Muslims of north India, but they differed in the models of Sikhism used for their socio-religious movements. The Singh Sabhas sought an adjustment to British control, but the two wings differed in their membership within the Sikh class and caste structures. These differences were manifest in the competing ideologies each group articulated. The Lahore Singh Sabha spoke for a rising educated elite and the Amritsar Sabha, while calling for changes in religion, rejected any fundamental restructuring of authority within the community. It paralleled many of the orthodox defensive movements of the Hindus and of Islam which drew upon the strengths of pre-British elites and members of the religious establishment. The Amritsar Singh Sabha wanted only limited adjustment of British culture. Both wings realized the need to gain a command of western knowledge if Sikhs were to compete successfully with Hindu and Muslim Punjabis, but here again they differed on the extent of this education and who should receive it. In the development of their ideas the two branches of the Singh Sabhas helped to redefine the 'true' Sikhism and to draw lines between it and the other religious communities in Punjab. In the twentieth century the Singh Sabhas were overwhelmed by other organizations. In the first decade they were supplanted by the Khalsa Diwans and then in the 1920s by the struggle for control over the Sikh place of worship. Paralleling the Arya Samaj and Singh Sabhas, a socio-religious movement among Punjabi Muslims also added to this general process of self-definition that characterized so much of the nineteenth century. . . .

Notes

1. There is some disagreement on just when Baba Dayal Das began to preach and draw to him disciples. See John C.B. Webster, *The Nirankari Sikhs* (Delhi, Macmillan Company, 1979), p. 10; information from this section will be from Webster or it will be cited specifically.
2. Ibid., p. 14.
3. Man Singh Nirankari, 'The Nirankaris', *Panjab Past and Present* (April 1973), pp. 5–6.
4. See Nirankari, 'The Nirankaris', pp. 6–7, 10; and Webster, *The Nirankari Sikhs*, p. 16.
5. Fauja Singh Bajwa, *The Kuka Movement: An Important Phase in Punjab's Role in India's Struggle for Freedom* (Delhi, Motilal Banarsidass, 1965), pp. 5–6; this is the basic source used for the Namdharis and any other sources will be cited.
6. Ibid., pp. 24–5.
7. Khushwant Singh, *A History of the Sikhs* (Princeton University Press, 1966), vol. 2, pp. 128–9.
8. Ibid., p. 130.
9. Estimates of size vary; Bajwa claims between 300,000 and 400,000 by the end of the 1860s, but the lower, 100,000 figure is given in G.S. Chhabra, *Advanced History of the Punjab* (Ludhiana, 1962), p. 370.
10. Chhabra, *Advanced History*, p. 379.
11. Kenneth W. Jones, *Arya Dharm, Hindu Consciousness in 19th-Century Punjab* (Berkeley, University of California Press, 1976), p. 16; and Sivanatha Sastri, *History of the Brahmo Samaj* (Calcutta, R. Chatterjee, 1911), vol. 1, p. 395.
12. Barbara Daly Metcalf, *Islamic Revival in British India: Deoband, 1860–1900* (Princeton University Press, 1982), p. 292.
13. Spencer Lavan, *The Ahmadiyah Movement, a History and Perspective* (Delhi, Manohar Book Service, 1974), p. 10.
14. J.N. Farquhar, *Modern Religious Movements in India* (New York, Macmillan, 1919), pp. 347–8; Lavan, *Ahmadiyah Movement*, p. 10.
15. P.V. Kanal, *Bhagwan Dev Atma* (Lahore, Dev Samaj Book Depot, 1941), p. 51. J.N. Farquhar states that Agnihotri was born in 1850, but gives no source for this information. The remaining dates in Kanal's work are uncontested and so it has been used as the standard biography for this section. Other sources will be cited.
16. Farquhar, *Modern Religious Movements*, p. 173.
17. Kanal, *Bhagwan Dev Atma*, pp. 345–6; and Census, 1911, *Punjab Report*, p. 139.
18. Census, 1911, *Punjab Report*, p. 139.
19. Census, 1931, *Punjab Report*, p. 301.
20. Harbans Singh, 'Origins of the Singh Sabha', *Panjab Past and Present* (April 1973), pp. 28–9.
21. Gurdarshan Singh, 'Origin and Development of the Singh Sabha Movement, Constitutional Aspects', *Panjab Past and Present* (April 1973), p. 46.

22. See Teja Singh, 'The Singh Sabha Movement', *Panjab Past and Present* (April 1973), pp. 31–2; and N.G. Barrier, *The Sikhs and Their Literature* (Delhi, Manohar Book Service, 1970), p. xxiv.
23. Teja Singh, 'Singh Sabha Movement', p. 32.
24. Barrier, *Sikhs and Their Literature*, p. xxvi; and Chhabra, *Advanced History*, pp. 382–3.
25. Barrier, *Sikhs and Their Literature*, p. xxvi.
26. Gurdarshan Singh, 'Origin and Development', pp. 48–9.
27. For a discussion of Sikh papers, books and tracts, see Barrier, *Sikhs and Their Literature*.
28. Kenneth W. Jones, 'Ham Hindu Nahin: Arya–Sikh Relation 1877–90', *Journal of Asian Studies*, no. 3 (May 1973), pp. 468–75.

14

Muslim Women and the Control of
Property in North India*

Gregory C. Kozlowski

Whether or not women control wealth and partake of the prestige which goes with it depends very much on where and when they live. By occupation, region, ethnicity and history, the peoples of the Muslim world are as diverse as any on the globe. That they have not, to date, created a single distinctly 'Islamic' system which solves to everyone's satisfaction the complex issues arising from the acquisition, distribution and transmission of wealth is a reflection of the internal variety of Muslims.[1] Defining the nature of property, selecting the individuals who possess it and sorting out the distinctions of status which necessarily accompany ownership are issues as perplexing for Muslims as for the rest of humanity.[2]

The Holy *Qur'an* contains many verses which deal with women's rights to property. Its fourth chapter, known as 'The Women', asserts that women are entitled to inherit a portion of a parent's or husband's wealth. Whether a legacy or earned by her own efforts, material goods, once acquired, are supposed to remain in a woman's control. At least in theory, neither marriage nor any other bond gives males a claim to them while the woman lives. But sacred books usually set standards which mortals have trouble living up to. Merely reading the Holy *Qur'an* does not supply us with a detailed historical or ethnographic account of how Muslims behave when faced with the crucial problem of who should receive how much of what. Local conditions always have a way of limiting compliance with scriptural injunctions. Some Muslims ignore all or part of what the Holy Book and the *shari'ah*, the systemization of Islam's moral imperatives, command on the subject of a female's rights to property. Some societies deny women the full exercise of their Quranic privileges. In a few others, women are able to enjoy somewhat more than the standards of the faith grant them.[3]

Building sociological generalizations about Muslim women and property can be difficult as microscopic examination of a relatively circumscribed period or region reveals tremendous variation in the ways women acquire or lose property and its social perquisites. This essay describes some aspects of the processes by which Muslim women in North India succeeded or failed to obtain material goods and the influence they brought during the era of Mughal ascendancy, which lasted from the early sixteenth to the middle of the eighteenth centuries. There follows a more detailed discussion of the

*From *Indian Economic and Social History Review*, vol. 24, no. 2 (1987), pp. 163–81.

changes introduced by the British whose rise to economic and political supremacy began about the same time as the Mughal decline and reached its height at the end of the nineteenth century. With regard to Muslim women and property, the major distinction between the two regimes lies in their differing definitions of wealth as well as the different administrative establishments which enforced those norms.

While the Mughals ruled, most wealth was generated by control of the land's produce or from commerce. Land in itself was not the measure of wealth. What mattered more was command over the surplus crop or better still the cash it generated.[4] In the Mughal period, 'owning' land did not define social dominance, but ruling and exacting tribute from the people living on it did. Merchants were concerned with fairly liquid forms of wealth: cash and trade goods, but the legal and revenue administrations of the British gradually made the ownership of land the chief determinant of wealth. Land became a form of private property and social status was linked to its possession. The Anglo-Indian courts enforced the doctrine that land was something which individuals owned.

Whether based on control of cash or real estate, there were certain aspects of the social structure of property relations which changes in the law or its administrative machinery could not alter. During both the Mughal and the British periods, women tried to assert their legitimate ownership claims. When they did, they dealt with similar restraints. The wealth of a woman's parents was one. Daughters in wealthy families were advantaged, in poor families bereft. The number and sex of siblings imposed further limits. When it came to inheritance, males had clear preference, but a woman without brothers was more likely to succeed to a substantial portion of her parents' estate. The expectation that women would marry was universal. Within marriage, a woman's relationship to property depended partly on the amount of wealth that came with her, partly upon the generosity or parsimony of her husband's family. Rich women sometimes married poor men and therefore exercised greater authority over joint holdings. If the situation was reversed, however, a woman seeking a share of property considered part of her husband's estate was likely to face the opposition of her spouse's kin. When applied to the preceding list of qualifications, the adjectives 'Muslim' or 'Indian' provide no greater analytical precision. Women in Europe and America had to face similar constraints.[5]

Although women living in British India had to contend with restrictions like those of their Mughalera grandmothers, the presence of alien laws and institutions added new opportunities at the same time as they eliminated a number of old ones. Because the Anglo-Indian courts tended to apply a text-book version of Islamic social dogmas, their decisions appeared to strengthen the inheritance rights of women. The courts' judgements usually forced a partition of estates according to the portions prescribed in the Holy *Qur'an* and authorities on shari'ah. Though women received a share, it was smaller than the one males obtained. In this respect, the British-Indian courts preserved and even encouraged inequality. A woman's right to her 'bridal gift' (*mehr*) provided an example of the courts' arriving at the opposite extreme.[6] Prior to the establishment of British rule, mehr was mostly a part of matrimonial ritual. It was a contractual obligation, a symbol of the bridegroom's status, but not a sum of money which anyone expected to be paid in full. British courts extended the prerogatives of Muslim women by permitting them control of a husband's property until payment of the mehr.

In other cases, however, the courts' rulings worked to deny women access to property. Anglo-Indian courts recognized the customary laws of a number of North Indian castes, most of which prohibited female inheritance. The courts also ruled against using a pious endowment (*waqf*) as a device to avoid the partition of an estate. Especially in the absence of male heirs, waqfs had been used to deliver control of an undivided estate to the founder's wives and daughters. Like the courts, the political arm of the raj pursued no consistent policy with regard to the property rights of women. To a favoured few, it granted exemptions from both the Muslim and Hindu inheritance systems. For example, it constructed a special code of regulations for the *ta'alluqdars* of Avadh which featured a system of male primogeniture.[7]

The impact of the Anglo-Indian courts and administration on questions relating to women's control of property was uneven. Sometimes the courts confirmed those rights, sometimes enhanced and sometimes denied them. The British left in place an uncertainty about women's rights which was not new, a deeper ambiguity not linked to colonialism. Even the imposition of a bureaucratic system which was both imperial and alien could not eliminate a perennial strain between the customary behaviour of Muslim peoples and the written norms of their faith.

Women and Property in the Mughal Age

The Mughals were among the last in a long line of Muslim invaders. For over 500 years, India was a frontier for the rest of the Muslim world. Like any frontier, it attracted people looking for wealth. The Mughals made theirs, but also became rulers of an empire which contained the descendants of previous migrants and conquerors. Both Sunni and Shiah sects were present. Turks, Afghans, Arabs, Iranis and Abyssinians were part of the ethnic mix. The Mughals themselves were a hybrid people. The progeny of the Turko-Mongol state-builders Jenghiz Khan and Timur, the Mughals' court culture had been shaped in the Persianized cities of Central Asia. Though they possessed great authority and shared the faith of their predecessors, the Mughals did not homogenize the various social groups they encountered.[8]

These invaders and immigrants pursued many different occupations. Most were soldiers, others were clerks and litterateurs, still others religious specialists or merchants. In time, indigenous groups embraced the faith of Islam, but their conversion did not make them abandon their previous employment or discard all their pre-Islamic ways. For example, the Khojahs, a merchant caste which followed the cult of Vishnu, came under the influence of the Ismaili branch of the Shi'i sect. Though they gradually accepted all the tenets of that sect, they maintained their old customs with regard to the disposition of property.[9]

Scores of wandering Sufi saints converted the Jats who became the dominant agricultural caste in the Panjab. When it came to the transmission of property, Muslim Jats behaved like their Hindu and Sikh caste-fellows well into the nineteenth century.[10] Jat custom sought to prevent any division of agricultural holding by inheritance. Women were excluded as heirs and Jats sometimes practised female infanticide or polyandry in order to guard against the partition of homesteads.[11] Quranic revelations abhorred such conduct, but they seem to have had little influence over the way Jats behaved.

Low status groups, like the Julahas, a weaver caste living throughout North India, were Islamicized. Even castes considered ritually permanently impure by Hindus, notably the Chamars (scavengers and leatherworkers), were admitted.[12] Whether or not women controlled property was not a burning issue for those who lived at the bottom of society. There, deprivation oppressed male and female alike. Women who were not crushed by burdens of labour and indigence did have the chance to gain control of property.

In the era of Mughal dominance, the character of the state had much to do with defining the nature of the wealth available. Like all pre-modern states, that of the Mughals relied for its existence on control of agricultural surpluses. It tried to extract from cultivators as much as possible of everything not required for survival. The Mughals took advantage of an active economy in which a great deal of silver circulated. They were able to force cultivators to convert surpluses into cash to meet state revenue demands. By the late sixteenth century, they managed to collect most of their tribute in cash.[13]

For the imperial house and the state service elite, therefore, cash was the most common and most coveted form of wealth. Some of it was converted into luxury goods such as jewellery, precious stones, carpets and furniture. It paid for the well-appointed households enjoyed by the privileged. In all things, the imperial style set the standard for the rest of affluent society. Families connected by employment or treaty to the Mughal state, even those with more modest resources, did their best to imitate the court.

The elite's relationship to the land expressed an emphasis on moveable forms of wealth. The official/noble calculated the value of his appointment by the amount of cash which could be extracted from the district the emperor assigned him, not by acreage. Rank in the Mughal system was expressed by a number which represented the number of troopers he was expected to support from his grant. The outfitting and maintenance of those soldiers required cash. In its emphasis on the value of the land's produce, the Mughal state reflected the cultivators' own concerns. For them, their courtyard or village grain heap was most important, not the size of the plots they farmed.[14]

Apart from Mughal officials, local 'big men'[15] had authority over and a share in agricultural surpluses. Several avenues led to influence in a given locality. Some big men were successful adventurers. Others were religious figures, or members of a forceful clan, or the descendants of officials of defunct states. Whatever the source of their prominence, those 'big men' did not think of themselves as 'landowners'. Their self-estimate was expressed in the choice of titles by which they identified themselves. From the Sanskritic traditions came 'Raja,' 'Maharaja' and their many permutations, all having the meaning of 'one who rules'. Even petty strongmen used them. A number of Perso-Arabic terms conveyed a similar meaning: 'ra'is', 'malik', and 'nawab', all implied that those who claimed them were lords of men, not owners of land. Members of local elites thought of themselves as 'little kings'. Likewise, the word used to describe their holdings, riasat (a word that British officials consistently translated as 'estate'), was by etymology and usage more evocative of 'state' than 'estate'.[16] Although rajas and nawabs had a political-economic base independent of the Mughal emperors, they gained prestige by emulating imperial court style. It was a confirmation of their claim to regal status.

The importance of trade in Mughal times reinforced the cultural and political definition of wealth as something consisting of moveable property. Moreover, no clear class boundary separated political-military leaders and merchants. Emperors and nobles had no aversion to trade. Men and women of the imperial household invested in and profited by mercantile enterprise. Those who derived their wealth primarily from commerce were frequently allied to the state and like the state nobility or local gentry played the same cultural game of 'ape the emperor'.[17]

No matter how wealth was gained, everyone seemed to share the expectation that wealth was not simply a matter of having. It involved *spending*. One efficacious way of spending was the building and supporting of religious shrines such as mosques, the tombs of saints, or special halls known as *imambarahs* used in the ceremonial mourning of the martyrdom of the Prophet's grandson, Imam Husain. A closely connected activity was the sponsoring of the festivals held in and around these holy sites. Both local and imperial nobles gave money to religious specialists, beggars and their own dependants. Frequent benefactions were providing shrouds for the poor and meals, for example, on feast days, at weddings or funerals, as well as digging wells and building caravanserais. In giving her or his gift, a donor did more than express personal piety; she or he dispensed wealth to announce social primacy. Everyone knew that those who offered the gifts assumed a superior place in society. By accepting them, ordinary people acknowledged the leading status of the donor. Patrons received this popular respect and regarded it as a confirmation of their pre-eminence.[18]

Although Muslim women rarely acted as rulers, they came close to exercising significant social authority through the distribution of largesse. This activity proved that some women controlled wealth and spent it as they wished. Wives, daughters and close relations of the Mughal emperors issued their own decrees, under their own seals, They built mosques, tombs and other religious buildings. They gave stipends to their servants or to favourite scholars, saints and litterateurs. Their names were publicly associated with particular institutions or individuals. Ordinary people gave female patrons the same sort of respect which males received.[19] As noted above, less wealthy but socially ambitious families tended to imitate imperial style. For example, women in families which were only modestly wealthy maintained, from their own funds or with money their husbands gave as household expenses, a floating population of widows and spinsters who were called 'connections' (*rishtahdar*).[20]

Women's involvement with charity and support of the faith raises the question of the public role of women. The life of Muslim women, according to some commentators, is lived in dichotomy between private and public spheres.[21] Women may enjoy considerable authority in the home, but have no public role. However, women who acted as patrons clearly did have a public persona and enjoyed the same social prestige which male benefactors received.

Mughal administrative documents give some evidence that women of middling economic station gained control of their wealth through imperial grants. The *A'in-i Akbari* and *Akbarnamah*, which provide an idealized description of the emperor Akbar's reign, report that four types of people deserved support:

1. seekers of true knowledge;
2. devout persons who abandoned this world;
3. the destitute;
4. nobles whose 'ignorance' preventing their taking gainful employment.[22]

Each of those groups might include women, but imperial decrees indicate that women usually received a share of the empire's revenue when they were heirs of a male who belonged to one of the four categories mentioned above. For example, wives and daughters of religious scholars often received a portion of their husband's or father's assignment after their male relative's death. The imperial treasury (*diwan*) often reduced by a fourth, third or half the income directed toward a female. However, given that respectable women had few ways of earning their livelihood, that steady portion was preferable to beggary.[23]

Books written to guide Muslim rulers stressed that a sultan or emperor should appoint religious scholars (*qazis*) to enforce the rules of the Islamic code of conscience (shari'ah). Texts like the *A'in*, noted above, fell within the 'mirror of princes' genre, therefore its claim that Akbar did maintain a highly organized system of shari'ah courts was probably something of a pious boast. Appointments as qazi were often awarded on the basis of the incumbent's personal connections with influential nobles. More important, the personal character of Mughal rule meant that many different officials, not just qazis, shared authority in matters touching the distribution and control of property. For example, all government grants, such as those made to the widows or daughters of religious scholars (when one would expect the shari'ah to be most closely observed) came under the authority of the various imperial or provincial treasurers (*diwans*), not qazis. In the Mughal empire, as in most so-called Muslim states, the *Qur'an* and shari'ah did not always inform governmental practice.

Lack of juristic rigour may have worked to the benefit of some women. At least, no universal ban excluded women from possessing and distributing wealth. Surviving Mughal administrative and literary works seemed to accept without comment the idea that women could exercise all the privileges of ownership. Unlike the highly organized shari'ah courts of the Ottoman empire, those of Mughal India either did not keep detailed records of their proceedings, or those records have perished. Without that crucial documentary evidence, the degree to which the *Qur'an's* regulations on inheritance were enforced must remain a matter of speculation. Mughal society's emphasis on moveable wealth could have made it easier to carry out the kind of minute subdivision of estates recommended by the Holy Book, a process which guaranteed women a portion of close relatives' property. That some women of upper and middling status controlled wealth was certain. On the other hand, males might have pressured women to renounce 'voluntarily' their inheritance rights.[24]

In the eighteenth century, almost every aspect of the social order began to disintegrate. As the Mughal empire collapsed, several mutually hostile successor states, including that of the British, emerged. As the armies marched and counter-marched across northern and central India, they threatened the livelihood of rich and poor alike. As the conflict increased, male and female suffered together.

Standard histories of the period paid little attention to the ways in which the wars of succession affected the material condition of women. Only a few poets left some hint of the special torments which these conflicts imposed on females. For example, one of Mirzah Rafi ud-din Sawda's 'Laments' for the city of Delhi (*Sherashob*) presents an incident whose touching detail must reflect the author's witnessing of one woman's struggle. He writes of a high-born woman who left her home to find a few coins to buy food. Her clumsy attempts to walk in a veil indicated that her status had kept her in the sanctuary of a harem. Too proud to beg, she tried to sell a rosary, claiming that it was made from the sacred earth of Karbala. The Shi'i Muslims, who should have revered the rosary, ignored her. Only a passing Sunni Muslim took interest and his only object was to start a theological wrangle over the errors of the Shi'i sect. Unable to preserve her dignity, the woman ran back to her house to starve in silence and seclusion.[25]

British rule brought comparative calm. It also brought a system of new laws, new definitions of property and power, new statutes, institutions and procedures for claiming one's rights. Muslims, male and female, had to adapt to a new order of economic, social and political dominance.

The Property Rights of Muslim Women under British Rule

India's British rulers, no less than the Mughal kings preceding them, depended on a tax or tribute levied on any agricultural surplus.[26] In securing that revenue, however, the British were at a distinct disadvantage. They were few in number and almost completely ignorant of local arrangements of wealth and power. For example, Robert Clive won the right to collect tribute from the district surrounding Fort William and, eventually, the appointment as treasurer of the Mughal province of Bengal, but he was never able to discover an absolutely stable method of collecting the cash.

Clive wanted to intrude as little as possible in the existing administration. He thought that Mughal officials would remain in their places, bringing in the money as in former times. By exercising minimal control over the Mughal system, Clive hoped to keep British costs in running the provincial government low. The Company would then accumulate a hoard of silver rupees with which to purchase trade goods. This indirect approach failed to create that store of cash; much of the revenue disappeared before it came within British reach.

After the failure of Clive's effort to turn a profit through the previous administration, the Company tried to make use of tax-farms. Letting out revenue collection to the highest bidder brought on a different set of disasters. Tax-gatherers pressed the peasants too hard. By 1770, cultivators were fleeing British territory or dying of starvation.

To guarantee the flow of cash, British administrators began to take a larger role in the collection of revenue. They tried to specify the identities of those Indians responsible for the payment of levies on crops. At one time or another, depending on the currently popular theory of political economy, the British fixed that responsibility on 'landed aristocrats,' or 'cultivators,' or 'village brotherhoods'. Despite the many regional variations, the cumulative effect of administrative action was to shift the focus of the revenue-collecting process. Previously, officials, local gentry, even the cultivators themselves, sought control over a portion of the produce of the land or the coin into which it was converted. Under the various British systems, the land itself became most important. An individual's tax burden was established on the basis of how much land she or he 'possessed', rather than on how much was produced or what the crop earned at sale.

On the question of property, the laws of England had attained a great deal of specificity by the eighteenth century. Land was, with certain exceptions, defined as 'private property'. The implications of that idea may be seen in an analogy based on a more readily imagined piece of private property: a watch. If someone 'owns' a watch, she or he may dispose of it in any way. The owner may sell it, pawn it, or leave it to heirs.

The owner even has the right to destroy it. In India, the British began to apply similar absolute notions to land. Once possession was fixed, the person holding land was, in theory, free to pursue his or her own inclinations. That entailed some risks. A spendthrift might mortgage land and then lose it to repay the debt. Indeed, as early as the 1790s, officials were concerned about the great number of land transfers which occurred. It was a problem which administrators brought up again and again throughout the raj.

From the early days of their rule, the British recognized that Muslims had a body of regulations governing almost every aspect of life. The Indian government periodically restated its intention to apply those rules which were officially known as 'Muhammadan law'. In attempting to use Muslim law Anglo-Indian judges faced some difficulty in determining just what that law was. Muslims themselves disagreed about its content. Moreover, the judges themselves were usually ignorant of the general character and specific injunctions of what Muslims called 'shari'ah'.[27] For over 70 years, Charles Hamilton's translation of the *Hedaya*, a twelfth-century guide for qazis, published in 1791, was the only major text available in English. The translation had several flaws. Not only was Hamilton biased and ill-informed, he also had a tendency to run together the translation with his own footnotes and commentary.[28] The *Hedaya* itself was only one of many texts which Muslim scholars in India relied on. Its official acceptance by the Anglo-Indian courts gave it greater authority than Muslim scholars had ever granted it.

Whatever the technical and linguistic faults of the translation, the *Hedaya* exhibited some of the limits of shari'ah as a code governing the acquisition, control and inheritance of property, especially land. As most other texts in the genre, *Hedaya* concerned itself primarily with ritual matters such as the proper way of performing the five daily prayers or the Meccan pilgrimage. When discussing the material dimensions of life, its opinions were most applicable to contracts and other commercial transactions involving cash or moveable goods. Thus, the shari'ah, as it was understood in India, suited the pre-British system in which coin was the economic foundation of the affluent. The shari'ah's lack of interest in the land as wealth gave the British more leeway in establishing their own system of property rights.

During the period of British hegemony, Muslim scholars (*ulama*) did little to fill the gap between the shari'ah's concerns and the economic necessities of the British empire. Some individuals who happened to be Muslims did enter the Anglo-Indian juridical bureaucracy. However, few of them came from families which maintained a tradition of learning in shari'ah. Since they took their training in government law schools, often in England itself, they wrote judgements in a fashion similar to their British colleagues.

In the nineteenth century, most of the 'traditional' religious scholars tried to stay as clear of the imperial government as possible. The scholars of the theological school at Deoband asked their followers to avoid the Anglo-Indian courts entirely. That their adherents mostly ignored this request indicated that the ulama of Deoband lacked great influence in the practical aspects of life. Though people sent several thousand requests for opinions on matters of prayer and ritual purity, they took inheritance or other disputes involving land to the British courts.[29]

Religious thinkers representing all shades of opinion called for the strict enforcement of women's Quranic rights. However, few of them offered any advice on how females might assert those rights. The heroine of one of Nazir Ahmad's novels, an educated and spirited lady, acquires some spare cash by being frugal in the household budget. Significantly, she uses the extra money to help the poor and to further the education of girls. While Nazir Ahmad may represent the group known in Urdu as the 'followers of the new light', even so staunchly 'orthodox' a scholar as Mawlana Ashraf Ali Thanwi made similar appeals for female economic rights. Like Nazir Ahmad, he did not seem to have a realistic understanding of the obstacles women faced. In 1902, Mawlana Ashraf published a book which was to serve as a guide for the lives of Muslim women. Its Urdu title is *Bihesht-i Zewar*, literally, 'The Ornament of Paradise'. It is a combination of a religious encyclopaedia and a bride's handbook. It became very popular and was often given to women as a wedding present. As with other works on shari'ah, most of its sections dealt with basic beliefs and practices. It did, however, include a section of advice on household management. As with Nazir Ahmad's novels, the conduct of worldly affairs was discussed wholly in terms of domestic economy. While women may have wanted to assert their rights to houses and fields, the novelist and the scholar drew most of their examples from the weighing of chickpeas or flour and the purchase of jewellery; simple transactions, when compared to the convolutions of land tenure or inheritance disputes.[30]

Given the ulama's comparative lack of effective involvement in issues of women's property rights, the British courts could (and did) exercise considerable discretion in formulating their judgements. As noted above, the *Qur'an* contained revelations which ordered the division of an individual's estate. The text itself specified certain heirs and the portions each received. In the event of a parent's death, for example, a daughter's share was half that of her brother. When the courts applied this principle, a woman who pressed for her inheritance obtained at least a portion. But many groups in North India did not strictly follow Quranic writ. Khojahs and Muslim Jats completely excluded female heirs. Other Muslims recognized women's inheritance rights only when comparative affluence made it convenient to do so.

Faced with conflicts between code and customary conduct, the courts often took a highly 'orthodox' position, assuming that Muslims ought to follow strictly their scripture and sacred law. British judges ruled against practices they thought contrary to the *Qur'an*.[31] Even so, their application of Quranic standards was not consistent. In other cases, the courts upheld the inheritance practices of Jats and Khojahs. Judges supported those decisions not on the basis of Muslim precept, but by referring to a maxim of Roman law: '*usus et conventio vincunt legem*' (usage and custom supersede the written law). As with most legal dicta, judges were free to follow or ignore whatever wisdom they offered. Since the Anglo-Indian courts did not consistently enforce either the written law or traditional practice, 'custom' became a kind of camouflage for the use of judicial preference.[32] Therefore, custom could sometimes be invoked to abrogate rights which the *Qur'an* demanded.

Provincial administrators also had a hand in denying women their scriptural claims to property. Among officials the belief that political concerns outweighed considerations of abstract justice was widespread. Some believed that any division in the agricultural holdings of politically significant groups would disrupt the stability on which British rule rested. Thus, the government tolerated the exclusion of female heirs so long as it pacified the pillars of the imperial social and economic order.[33]

Muslims who were among the ta'alluqdars of Avadh had a special exemption from Quranic rules of inheritance. Ta'alluqdar was an official designation which survived British absorption of the kingdom of Avadh. Clan chiefs, military adventurers and the former ruler's courtiers all claimed the title. During the Revolt of 1857, coincidentally a period when the British were trying to displace them, several of the ta'alluqdars gave qualified support to the rebels. The British were impressed by the potential power of these magnates and sought to win the loyalty of the greatest of them by giving them ownership of the lands which in the days of Avadh's independence had been their tax-farms. Having thereby established over 260 estates, the British government made certain by law that these properties would not be lost. The special code governing *ta'alluq-dari* succession bound both Muslims and non-Muslims to accept male primogeniture as the basis of inheritance. Females received, at best, a cash allowance, never their Quranic rights.[34]

The official solicitude of judges and administrators was reserved for individuals and groups considered politically important. Most Muslims taking disputes over property to the Anglo-Indian courts faced the possibility that their cases would be decided on an 'orthodox' version of their faith's commandments, even if their families' customary practice was not quite so strict. Judicial records showed that many women realized the advantages of taking their complaints to imperial courts. They were able to challenge family custom and gain possession of a part of an estate's lands instead of just a stipend. The hope of potential gain somewhat offset the expenditure of time and money which a court case required.

Muslim women who initiated a law suit contended with the impediment created by the common custom of limiting the movements of respectable ladies. Though some women were able to appear in court, many had to conduct their cases through male agents. The number of males permitted contact with purdah-observing women was limited to her own or her husband's closest kin or, more rarely, to some intimate friend of the family. The closeness of the personal ties between women and their male representatives may have helped to ensure the honesty of go-betweens. Still, male relatives and friends sometimes abused their trust and used litigation for their own benefit.[35]

Taking evidence from secluded women provided only one example of the procedural difficulties which purdah created. A special delegation from the court had to be sent to the women's home. As she sat behind a screen, she extended her hand outside the barrier. Someone in the delegation who knew the woman well came forward to attest that the hand and voice belonged to the lady involved in the case. The court's officers interrogated her or took a deposition while she was hidden from their gaze. Judges quickly realized the potential for fraud in this indirect procedure. Some British judges compensated for the possibility by patronizing purdah-observing women. In one case, a judge ruled that secluded ladies must be assumed to be ignorant of the nature of any document they signed, even if they could read and write.[36] Women themselves must have found the entire system equally troublesome.

The British-Indian legal system did reward tenacity. Provided that she did not belong to one of the juridically or administratively exempt groups, a woman could expect that strict Quranic standards would be applied when considering her property rights. But the triumphs gained by the skilful application of legal force could be short-lived. When possession of land became the measure of wealth, a woman who won a division of her parent's or husband's estate inadvertently diminished the material foundation of whatever social status she had. If succeeding generations continued the process of division, a family which once enjoyed wealth and status could begin to lose both.

Rulings of the Anglo-Indian courts on Muslim endowments were examples of how a rigorous application of scriptural standards restricted non-Quranic means of women gaining control of their parents' estates. The Arabic word translated as 'endowment' was waqf, plural: awqaf. Awqaf often provided the economic base for mosques, schools and other religious institutions.[37] They also gave individuals more choice in selecting heirs and disposing of the income from property than the rules of shari'ah. Thus, if a man had only daughters, by the *Qur'an* dictates, their share did not significantly increase. Distant male kin took what would have been the son's portion. Shari'ah did not grant testamentary powers similar to those of the Euro-American legal traditions. According to the Holy Book, a bequest must not include more than one-third of an estate. Moreover the 'will' had to be made in favour of 'strangers': people who were not heirs under Quranic regulations. Turning one's property into a waqf made it possible to have some choice in matters of inheritance. An individual could direct that an endowment's income be given only to daughters, precluding the possibility of having the wealth divided up among male cousins. Also, the founder of the endowment could name daughters as custodians (*mutawallis*) leaving them in effective control of an undivided estate.[38]

As the British established property rights in land, the courts began applying the strictest rules of inheritance. Muslim landholders began using endowments as a method of settling family property. As early as the 1830s, Muslims who faced the prospect of having their estates divided and forcing their daughters to take a smaller share while letting some of the property leave the control of the immediate family, started creating awqaf.[39] For women, endowments were something of a two-edged sword which could cut off male cousins, but, if they had brothers, it could also be used to cut off daughters. Endowments sometimes specifically excluded women from control of an estate. Still, a significant number of awqaf created in the nineteenth century benefited daughters, occasionally to the exclusion of sons who were wastrels or incapable of managing property.[40]

In the 1870s, two sorts of dissatisfaction led to legal challenges of endowments which were family property settlements. Relatives who felt cheated by the terms of an endowment were one source.[41] Creditors whose efforts to seize a debtor's property were frustrated by the claim that a waqf was immune from sequestration, provided the second.

Judges of the Indian courts and Law Lords of the Privy Council spent almost 20 years considering the issue of Muslim endowments. A few decisions of the Indian bench upheld awqaf whose income went primarily to founders' immediate kin.[42] Most decisions went against the practice. In 1894, the Privy Council issued a definitive verdict in the matter.[43] It decided that to be 'orthodox' a waqf must have a wholly 'charitable' and 'religious' purpose. Since imperial courts followed the rule of precedent, the decision put an end to the practice of bequeathing control of property to women and other relatives through the establishment of a waqf.

Contrary to the opinion of the Privy Council, awqaf were seldom merely a device for enriching a family. Almost all deeds of endowment carried some provision for the support of religious institutions, ceremonies and the distribution of public charity. Such patronage was firmly embedded in a society in which such largesse was an essential part of social prominence. Though probably not intended, the Privy Council's and courts' decisions restricted one of the few chances that Muslim women had to gain and hold a public honour.

In one instance, the Anglo-Indian courts did enhance the property rights of women, namely in the payment of a bridal gift. For Muslims, marriage is a contractual rather than sacramental act. In the wedding ceremony, the marriage bond is established when the couple signs a written covenant. In consideration for the wife's side of the bargain, the offering of her person, the husband promises a gift of money known as mehr. A very small portion of that promised sum is paid at the time of the wedding. The rest is due in event of a husband's death or of divorce.[44] Even in Mughal times, marriage established an alliance between two family groups. As a quasi-political arrangement, marriage raised questions of status which focused themselves on the amount of mehr promised. An inflation of the promised sum was an indication of prestige. Though tens of thousands of rupees were pledged, in practice, no one expected that the whole amount would ever be paid. Indeed, the husband and his family expected that the wife would eventually renounce her claim.[45] However, the literalist bent of the British courts meant that judges usually ordered that the money promised be paid.

Once aware of the potential gain which scrupulous application of shari'ah presented, some widows initiated suits to obtain full payment of their bridal gifts. The bitterness with which their husbands' families opposed such demands indicated that this was an unprecedented and unwelcome assertion of women's rights. A husband's relations often resorted to the charge that a supposed widow, no matter how many children she might have borne him, was a prostitute or mistress. Since the widow had only to produce a marriage contract or witnesses to its signing, such accusations were fairly easy to refute. Most were able to do so and Anglo-Indian courts ruled in the widow's favour, granting them control over their husband's estate until the mehr was paid. Because such great sums had been pledged, the courts gave women what was in effect lifetime control of the property.[46]

Women usually gained property by inheriting it from fathers or husbands. Some got possession through deeds of endowment or suits for the payment of bridal gifts. A few Muslim women were more independent and acquired wealth through their own efforts. Dancing girls, singers and courtesans were indirect recipients of male-controlled property. Although the scriptural tradition of Islam asserted a puritanical moral code and recommended segregation of the sexes, courtesans had a special place in North Indian society. Most of the cities had neighbourhoods in which entertainers or prostitutes (the distinction was by no means absolute) lived and worked. The 'Hira Mandi' (literally 'The Diamond Market') in Lahore and the 'Chawks' of Delhi and Lucknow were only three of the most famous pleasure districts in the region. Those whose talents as dancers, singers or poets added to the prospect of carnal delight were at the centre of high fashion. Even males whose interests were artistic rather than sexual provided such women with substantial gifts of money, clothing and jewellery.[47] Respectable women were able to invite courtesans to visit them in their homes. In addition, their trade did not prevent Muslim courtesans from acquiring a reputation for exceptional piety. They sponsored religious festivals, wrote religious poetry themselves or sustained poets who did, and hosted ceremonies in their own houses.[48] A systematic study of these genuinely independent women remains to be done. Therefore, the writer and reader are left with generalizations. Women on the less affluent side of the profession probably led brief and miserable lives. Only a few were able to keep the wealth they received and invest it in land or houses. Since the social order accepted their relative independence from males, they were able to leave their estates to whomever and for whatever purpose they pleased. When courtesans' estates were the subject of legal disputes, it was usually due to squabbling among their chosen heirs.

The number of law suits in which Muslim women participated shows that some of them adapted quickly to the intricacies of the Anglo-Indian law of property. Their use of the courts proved that women knew how to make the judicial machinery work to secure their rights. Their awareness of the potential advantages of legal warfare did not mean that such women were in the vanguard of a feminist crusade. Their concerns and motives, as expressed in the course of litigation, were firmly rooted in the family and neighbourhood and expressed in the language of the Mughal era. Even wealthy courtesans had to operate in a world in which males occupied a favoured niche. A few courtroom victories could not change that. If wealthy and assertive women had a place in that society, its dimensions were fairly narrow and tightly wrapped in the threads of kinship and community. When women sought relief from the British courts, it was usually to preserve a social order in which their personal role was ambiguous.[49] The courts did little to alter that uncertainty. If improvement in the status and rights of women was a mark of 'modern' society,[50] then neither the administrative nor the legal arms of Anglo-Indian government were the engines of modernization. What they gave to women with one hand, they often took away with the other. As in the Mughal period, a woman of a wealthy family who was aware and protective of her prerogatives was more likely to retain or expand them, but her efforts were restricted by the amount of wealth available, the number of claimants to it and a persistent uncertainty about the rights she possessed.

Notes

Acknowledgements: The author thanks Drs Gail Minault and Joan Erdman for supplying helpful corrections on the style and substance of this paper. Any errors are, of course, his own. Research on this paper was made possible, in part, by a grant from the American Institute of Indian Studies.

1. For a hint of the variety which marks the social arrangements of Muslim societies, see D.F. Eickelman, *The Middle East: An Anthropological Approach*, New Jersey, Prentice-Hall, 1981; as these specifically relate to women in West and Southwest Asia, L. Beck and N. Keddie eds., *Women in the Muslim World*, Cambridge, Mass., 1978; E. Fernea and B. Bezirgan eds., *Middle Eastern Women Speak*, Austin, Texas, 1977; for a review of these and other recent publications, see D. Waines, 'Through a Veil Darkly: The Study of Women in Muslim Societies', in *Comparative Studies in Society and History*, 24 (1982), pp. 642–59; on Muslim women in the subcontinent, see H. Papanek, 'Purdah: Separate Worlds and Symbolic Shelter', ibid., 15 (1973), pp. 289–325; G. Minault ed., *The Extended Family: Women and Political Participation in India and Pakistan*, Columbia, Missouri, 1981; and H. Papanek and G. Minault eds., *Separate World: Studies of Purdah in South Asia*, Delhi, 1982.

2. V. Kiernan, 'Private Property in History', in J. Goody et al. eds., *Family and Inheritance: Rural Society in Western Europe, 1200–1800*, Cambridge, 1976, pp. 328–60.

3. Many studies of the Holy *Qur'an* and shari'ah take a reified approach to women's rights, for example, J. Espositi, *Women in Muslim Family Law*, Syracuse, 1982. However, when wrenched from their social and historical contexts, studies of law tell little about the actual lives of Muslims; see G. Kozlowski, *Muslim Endowments and Society in British India*, Cambridge,

1985, pp. 5–7, 98–106, 123–31. In what sense can we speak of an 'Islamic law' before the advent of European imperialism? See J. Nielsen, '*Mazalim* and *Dar'al-'Adl* under the Early Mamluks', in *Muslim World*, LXVI/2 (1976), pp. 114–32; for examples of denial of women's rights, see the works cited in note 1; for an example of a time and place in which women apparently enjoyed greater control of property, see R. Jennings, 'Women in Early Seventeenth Century Ottoman Judicial Records: The *Sharia* Courts of Anatolian Kayseri', *Journal of the Economic and Social History of the Orient*, XVIII/1 (1975), pp. 53–113; and his 'Loans and Credit in Early Seventeenth Century Ottoman Judicial Records: The *Sharia* courts of Anatolian Kayseri', ibid., XVI/2–3 (1973), pp. 168–216.

4. W. Neale, *Economic Change in Rural India*, New Haven, 1962, pp. 5–7, 20–37; on the material base of Mughalera elites, see I. Habib, *The Agrarian System of Mughal India*, Bombay, 1963; and appropriate articles in R. Frykenburg ed., *Land Control and Social Structure in Indian History*, Madison, 1969. Recently Dharma Kumar has attempted to refute Marxist scholars who deny that private property in land existed in South Asia, 'Private Property in Asia? The Case of Medieval South India', *Comparative Studies in Society and History*, 27/2 (1985), pp. 340–66; however, nothing that Kumar writes really demonstrates that the individuals involved were not primarily concerned with the produce of the land rather than the land itself.

5. D. Herlihy, 'Land, Family and Women in Continental Europe, 701–1200,' in *Women in Medieval Society*, S. Stuart ed., Philadelphia, 1976, pp. 13–47; also, in the same volume, S. Walker, 'Widow and Ward: The Feudal Law of Child Custody in Medieval England', pp. 159–72; also, H. Habakkuk, 'Family Structure and Economic Change in Nineteenth Century Europe', *The Journal of Economic History*, XV/1 (1955), pp. 1–12; many of the articles in *Family and Inheritance* deal with issues of women's rights of inheritance.

6. *Murtazai Bibi vs. Jumna Bibi (and others)*, Indian Law Reports, Allahabad Series (hereafter, *All*), XII, 264–65 and unpublished papers related to the case from the Appellate Side Record Room of the Allahabad High Court (hereafter, *AA*).

7. T. Metcalf, *Land, Landlords and the British Raj*, Berkeley, 1979, pp. 200*ff*.

8. For a basic introduction to Indo-Muslim history, see S. Ikram, *Muslim Civilization in India*, New York, 1964.

9. On the Khojahs, see C. Dobbin, *Urban Leadership in Western India*, Oxford, 1972, pp. 113–21; and J. Hollister, *The* Shi'a *of India*, 1979 (reprint), New Delhi, pp. 378–412.

10. C. Tupper, *Punjab Customary Law*, 4 vols, Calcutta, 1881.

11. D. Ibbetson, *Punjab Castes*, 1974 (reprint) Delhi, pp. 97–163.

12. For a survey of the various officially designated groups, see F. Robinson, *Separatism Among Indian Muslims*, Cambridge, 1974, pp. 10–32.

13. I. Habib, 'Potentialities of Capitalistic Development in the Economy of Mughal India', *The Journal of Economic History*, XXXIX/1, pp. 32–78.

14. Neale, *Economic Change in Rural India*, pp. 5–7; on Mughal government see, M. Ali, *The Mughal Nobility Under Aurangzeb*, Bombay, 1966; and S. Blake, 'The Patrimonial-Bureaucratic Empire of the Mughals', *Journal of Asian Studies*, XXXIX/1 (1979), pp. 77–94.

15. This is a literal translation of the widely used Hindustani phrase, '*Bara Adami*', often applied to neighbourhood and village notables.

16. On this terminology, see Kozlowski, *Muslim Endowments*, pp. 47–8.

17. On merchants, commerce and their relation to the Mughal state, see M. Pearson, 'Political Participation in Mughal India', *Indian Economic and Social History Review*, IX, 2, (1972), pp. 113–21 and S. Chandra, 'Aspects of the Growth of a Money Economy in India during the Seventeenth Century', ibid., III/4 (1966), pp. 321–31.

18. J. Calmard, 'Le Patronage des Ta'ziyeh: Elements pour une Etude Globale', in P. Chelkowski ed., *Ta'ziyeh: Ritual and Drama in Iran*, New York, 1979, pp. 121–30.

19. *Edicts of the Mughal Harem*, trans. S. Tirmizi, Delhi, 1979; also, Mrs Meer Hasan Ali, *Observations on the Mussulmans of India*, Delhi (reprint), 1973, I, pp. 66*ff*.: one of the most famous examples of female patronage is the tomb of the Emperor Humayun (d. 1556) in Delhi. His

widow, known to posterity as 'Hajji Begum', directed the building of the tomb and paid for it with her own funds. Legend has it that the tomb served as a school for women. Humayun's sister, Gul Badan Begum, wrote a chronicle for part of her brother's reign: *Humayun-Nama*, trans. A Beveridge, Lahore (reprint), 1974, which incidentally provides some information about the lives of women in the royal household.

20. J. Malihabadi, *Yadon ki Barat*, Karachi, p. 30; and *Mujibunnissa (and others) vs. Abdul Rahim and Abdul Aziz, Cases On Appeals to the Privy Council*, unpublished documents submitted in support of suits before the Privy Council, bound in numbered volumes and stored in the library of Lincoln's Inn (hereafter *LI*), vol. 441, p. 610.

21. Eickelman, *The Middle East*, pp. 141–57, reviews the work of a number of scholars writing on women in that region's societies; also G. Minault, 'Introduction', in *The Extended Family*, pp. 3–18.

22. S. Moosvi, '*Suyurghal* Statistics in the *Ain-i Akbari*', *Indian Historical Review*, II/2 (1976), pp. 282–98, p. 284.

23. Z. Malik, 'Documents of *Madad-i Ma'ash* Grants during the Reign of Muhammad Shah, 1719–1748', *Indo-Iranica*, XXVI/2+3 (1973), pp. 97–123; and S. Rashid, '*Madad-i Ma'ash* Grants under the Mughals', *Journal of the Pakistan Historical Society*, 9 (1961), pp. 90–108.

24. *Mussumat Khanum Jan vs. Mussumat Jan Bibi, Sadr Diwani Adalat Reports, Calcutta*, IV, pp. 210*ff.*; also, *Shamsudin vs. Abdul Hosein, Bombay Law Reporter* VIII, pp. 252–68 and C. Vreede-de Stuers, *Parda*, Assen, Netherlands, 1968, pp. 13–15.

25. M. Barker et al. eds., *Naqsh-i Dilpazir: An Anthology of Classical Urdu Poetry*, Ithaca, 1977, pp. 113–14, 139–40; see also R. Russell and K. Islam, *Three Mughal Poets*, London, Allen and Unwin, 1969, pp. 37–68.

26. For scholars' debate over whether Mughal revenue should be considered 'tax', 'rent', or 'tribute', see appropriate articles in *Land Control and Social Structure in Indian History*; also E. Stokes, *The English Utilitarians and India*, Oxford, 1959.

27. Kozlowski, *Muslim Endowments*, pp. 116–31.

28. Burhan ud-din al-Maghinani, *Al-Hidayah* (*Hedaya*), trans. C. Hamilton, reprint of Grady's 1870 edition, Lahore, 1975; for complaints about *Hedaya's* accuracy, see Amir Ali, *Mahommedan Law*, Calcutta, 1892, vol. I, pp. 244–56; despite the complaints, Hamilton's translation is still used as a textbook in Indian and Pakistani law schools: bad books never die, they are enshrined in syllabi.

29. B. Metcalf, *Islamic Revival in British India: Deoband, 1860–1900*, Princeton, 1982, pp. 146–56.

30. Mawlana A.A. Thanwi, *Bihesht-i-Zewar*, Delhi, pp. 331*ff.*; on Nazir Ahmad and Mawlana Thanwi, see C.M. Naim, 'Prize-winning *Adab*', in B. Metcalf ed., *Moral Conduct and Authority*, Berkeley, 1984, pp. 290–313 and, in the same volume, B. Metcalf, 'Islamic Reform and Islamic Women', pp. 184–95.

31. *Cassamally Jairajbhai vs. Sir Currimbhoy Ibrahim, Indian Law Reports, Bombay Series* (hereafter, *Bom.*), XXXVI, pp. 241*ff.*

32. Ibid., and W. McCormack, 'Caste and the British Administration of Hindu Law', *Journal of Asian and African Studies*, I/1 (1966), pp. 27–34; also, M. Galanter, 'Changing Legal Conceptions of Caste', in M. Singer and B. Cohn eds., *Structure and Change in Indian Society*, Chicago, 1968, pp. 299–336.

33. For example, D. Gilmartin, 'Kinship, Women and Politics in Twentieth Century Punjab', in *The Extended Family*, pp. 151–73.

34. T. Metcalf, *Land, Landlords and the British Raj*; for a fictionalized account of a woman's life in a ta'alluqdari household during the 1930s and 1940s, see A. Hosain, *Sunlight on a Broken Column*, New Delhi, 1979.

35. *Mazhar Husain Khan vs. Abdul Hadi Khan, All.* XXXIII, pp. 400*ff.*, and *AA*; also C. Vreede-de Stuers, *Parda*, pp. 49–50.

36. *Sajjid Husain (and others) vs. Nawab Ali Khan, Oudh Law Reporter*, IV, pp. 1*ff.*

37. For the notion that endowments are charitable and religious trusts is oversimplified, see Kozlowski, *Muslim Endowments*, pp. 60–2.

38. Ibid., pp. 53–9.

39. The waqf in question was founded by Qamr ud-din in 1838 for his two wives and four daughters, see *Phate Saheb Bibi (and others) vs. Damodar Premji*, Bom. III, pp. 79*ff*; *Nizam Ghulam (and others) vs. Abdul Gafur (and others)*, Bom. XIII, p. 638; *LI*, vol. 367, pp. 731*ff*.

40. *Abdul Rajak vs. Bai Junbabai*, Bombay Law Reporter, XIV, pp. 295*ff*; also, *Agha Ali Khan (and others) vs. Altaf Hasan Khan (and others)*, All. XIV, pp. 430*ff*.

41. *Murtazai Bibi vs. Jumna Bibi*, All. XII, pp. 265*ff*; see also Sheik Ahsanullah's case cited in note 43.

42. *Fatima Bibi vs. The Advocate General of Bombay*, Bom. VI, pp. 42*ff*; and *Deoki Prasad (and others) vs. Inaitullah*, All. XIV, pp. 375*ff*.

43. *Sheik Mahomed Ahsanulla Chowdhry vs. Amarchand Kundu (and others)*, Indian Law Reports, Calcutta Series, XVII, pp. 498*ff*; also, *Meer Mahomed Israil Khan vs. Shastri Chura Chose (and others)*, ibid., XIX, pp. 412*ff*; and *Bikani Mia vs. Shuk Lal Poddar*, ibid., XX, pp. 116*ff*.

44. *Hamina Bibi vs. Zubaida Bibi*, All. XXXIII, pp. 182*ff*.

45. C. Vreedede Stuers, *Parda*, pp. 13–15.

46. *Syeda Bibi (and another) vs. Mughal Jan (and others)*, All. XXIV, pp. 231*ff*, also, Murtazai Bibi's case cited in note 41.

47. A. Sharar, *Lucknow: The Last Phase of an Oriental Culture (Gazashtah Lucknow)*, trans. E. Harcourt and F. Husain, London, 1975, pp. 34–5, 80–1, 145–7; for a fictionalised account of the life of an independent woman, see Mirza Mohammed Hadi Ruswa, *The Courtesan of Lucknow (Umrao Jan Ada)*, trans. K. Singh, Delhi, 1970.

48. *Biba Jan vs. Kalb Husain (and others)*, All. XXXI, pp. 136*ff*.

49. D. Lelyveld, *Aligarh's First Generation*, Princeton, 1978, pp. 35–56.

50. M. Galanter, 'Modernization of Law', in M. Weiner ed., *Modernization*, New York, 1966, pp. 153–65.

15

Prize-Winning *Adab*

A Study of Five Urdu Books Written in Response to the Allahabad Government Gazette Notification*

C.M. Naim

The officers of the British East India Company had started taking interest in the education of Indians even in the eighteenth century, but it was not until 1813 that a clear mandate in that regard was announced. That year, for the first time, a clause was inserted in the East India Company Act, declaring that 'it shall be lawful for the Governor-General in Council to direct that . . . a sum of not less than one lac of rupees (Rs. 100,000) in each year shall be set apart and applied to the revival and improvement of literature, and the encouragement of the learned natives of India, and for the introduction and promotion of a knowledge of the sciences among the inhabitants of the British territories in India'.[1] Although 10 years went by before any action was taken, the next four decades saw the rapid development of an educational system that included both private and government institutions, catering to the traditional literary classes of both Hindus and Muslims. A major controversy developed, during this initial period, on the question of the medium of instruction. A group of so-called 'Orientalists' wanted to continue with the traditional medium of classical languages (Arabic, Persian and Sanskrit), whereas another group of 'Anglicists' wished to use English. Eventually, the 'Orientalists' lost to the 'Anglicists' at the level of higher instruction. At the levels of primary and secondary education, they lost to regional vernaculars that, in turn, remained inferior in status to English.

In 1854, the Education Despatch from the Board of Control in London further directed the East India Company to expand its efforts, leading, among other things, to the establishment of regional departments of public instruction and the institution of universities in the Presidency towns of Calcutta, Madras, and Bombay. The despatch emphasized the 'importance of encouraging the study of the vernaculars as the only possible medium for mass education. . . . [It] further advocated the promotion of female education and Muslim education, the opening of schools and colleges for imparting technical instruction, and insisted on a policy of perfect religious neutrality'.[2] In

*From C.M. Naim, *Urdu Texts and Contexts* (Delhi: Permanent Black, 2004), pp. 120–50.

North India, the effects of these policies were felt with the extension of the British authority over Delhi and the North-Western Provinces after 1803, over the Punjab after 1849, and over Oudh after 1856. The abortive revolt of 1857 did not significantly slow down the process; the policies of the Company were affirmed and continued by the Crown.

The decline of 'Oriental' learning, the increasing awareness on the part of literate people of the range of scientific knowledge available in English, and the need to provide school texts in regional vernaculars, led a number of individuals and associations to produce translations as well as original works in Urdu in the realm of what was seen as *'ilm* (knowledge; science), as opposed to *shi'r* and *dastan* (poetry and tales). It is interesting to note that just when the teachers and students at the famous Delhi College (for the instruction of the natives) were engaged in translating into Urdu books on analytical geometry, optics, and galvanism, Goldsmith's *History of England*, selections from Plutarch's *Lives* and Abercrombie's *Mental Philosophy*,[3] the traditional *munshis* at the equally famous College of Fort William (for the instruction of British officers) were busy putting into simple Urdu the *Gulistan* of Sa'di, the *Tale of the Four Dervishes*, the *Tale of Amir Hamza, Singhasan Battisi, Shakuntala* of Kalidasa and a selection of stories from the *Arabian Nights*,[4] the books that the British thought were necessary to learn 'the language and the manners of the people of Hindostan'. The aim of the people at Delhi was to promote 'ilm in India through the medium of the vernaculars, whereas John Gilchrist of Fort William desired to 'form such a body of useful and entertaining literature in (Hindustani), as will ultimately raise it to that estimation among the natives, which it would many years ago have attained among an enlightened and energetic people'.[5] The work at Fort William dwelt upon the achievements of the past; the work at Delhi College was concerned with the needs of the present and the future.

The two aims were not necessarily in conflict—the syllabi of courses at Delhi reflected that fact—but as the motives behind education became increasingly utilitarian and the nature of education itself came to be defined by the British, a dichotomy between literature (now referred to as *adab*) and science (now referred to as 'ilm) began to be felt by many of the newly educated Muslims. It was at this time that the lieutenant-governor of the North-West Provinces, Sir William Muir, issued his momentous call for useful books in the vernacular. Its text follows.

Allahabad Government Gazette, Notification No. 791A, dated the 20th August 1868.

It is hereby announced that, with the view of encouraging authorship in the language of the North-Western Provinces, the Hon'ble the Lieutenant-Governor is pleased to make it known that rewards will be given for the production of useful works in the *vernacular, of approved design and style, in any branch of science or literature.*

For this end, the writing may be original composition, or it may be a compilation, or it may be even a translation from books in any other language. Theological treatises will not be received, nor treatises containing anything obnoxious to morality. There is no other condition either as to the subject or treatment. The theme may belong to history, biography, or travel, science, art, or philosophy; it may be a work of fact or of fiction, and may be composed either in prose or verse. In short, the only condition is that the book shall subserve some useful purpose, either of instruction, entertainment, or mental discipline; that it shall be written in one or other of the current dialects, Oordoo or Hindee, and that there shall be excellence both in the style and treatment.

Neither is there any restriction as to the author, whether in respect of birth, place of education, or residence.

The reward will, as a rule, in each case be one thousand rupees; but it may be more, or it may be less, according to the merits of the work.

The Lieutenant-Governor will be prepared to give at least five such prizes in the coming year.

Books suitable for the women of India will be especially acceptable, and well rewarded.

The Government will ordinarily be prepared to aid in the publication of any meritorious work by subscribing for a number of copies. Such assistance will be exclusive of and in addition to the rewards now promised.[6]

Altaf Husain Hali, the great poet and biographer of Sir Sayyid Ahmad Khan, describes this announcement as one 'for which Hindustan will always be grateful'. He continues, 'Though the awards stopped after a few years, the effect of the announcement itself was like a current of electricity. It galvanized all the people who possessed, to whatever degree, the talent to compose and compile in the vernacular, but did not know how to put it to good use.'[7] It is difficult for us to establish the accuracy of Hali's judgment—we do not have access to any list of either the applicants or the winners—but there is no denying the announcement's significance from another perspective. Within the heartland of Urdu, it was the first and perhaps the most widely disseminated declaration of official support for 'useful' literature in general and for books for women in particular. It also established the fact that the Government of India was the new patron of learning, that the patronized learning was to be put to use for the general good as conceived by it, and that it had the power not only to approve certain ideas through rewards and disapprove others through neglect, but also to disseminate the approved ones through the educational system—the books so favoured being purchased for libraries and prescribed for various examinations.

It is our purpose in this study to examine five Urdu books that won different prizes under the terms of this announcement. One of the five fell into oblivion rather quickly; another fared better, and went into at least three printings; the remaining three, all by one author, have stayed in print since they first appeared, two of them having been a part of the syllabi of instruction for many generations of Urdu speakers. We shall try to identify the reasons for their appeal, or non-appeal, to their British patrons and native readers. In that process we shall also compare them with such classics of adab as *Gulistan*, *Akhlaq i nasiri*, and *Qabus nama*.

We shall begin by looking at the book that gained the least success: *Nata'ij al-ma'ani* by Mirza Mahmud Beg Rahat, published at Agra in 1874.[8] Rahat was a Mughal from Delhi. He began his professional life as a soldier in Skinner's Regiment, later joined the service of Akbar Shah II (d. 1837) as the '*amil* of a village, and finally became a confidant and courtier of Nawwab Jahangir Muhammad Khan of Bhopal (d. 1844). After the Nawwab's death, Rahat returned to Delhi to live a life of retirement, but the Mutiny of 1857 forced him to leave home again in search of patronage. We know that he went to Patiala and wrote a book of poems, some of them praising the local rulers, but apparently did not get what he desired. He died sometime before 1881.

While in Patiala, Rahat took his book of poems to a publisher, who agreed to publish it but advised him to abstain from such efforts and instead write a book 'in prose . . . in the clear language of everyday speech, with contents beneficial to the general public', which could then be submitted to the authorities as per the Gazette Notification no. 791A. 'For then,' the publisher friend continued, 'the patronage of these ocean-hearted pearl-throwers and the munificence of these pearl-raining clouds in the sky of generosity, will remove that dust of unhappiness which the unappreciativeness of the people of this age has cast on the mirror of your disposition.'[9] Rahat was quick to respond and very soon put together a book, containing some events that had happened to him as well as some stories that he had heard. He called it *Nata'ij al-ma'ani* [Conclusions (full of) intrinsic qualities].

The book consists of 67 stories arranged into five chapters, preceded by the traditional benedictory sections, including one honouring Queen Victoria, and followed by a short, prayerful conclusion. According to Rahat, the first chapter has stories dealing with the *'adl* (justice) of the rulers, the second, the *sakhawa* (generosity) of the wealthy, the third, the *shuja'a* (bravery) of the soldiers, the fourth, the *chalaki* (cunning) of officials and retainers (*ahl i kar*) and thieves, and the fifth contains entertaining tales that 'earlier wits have told before nobles and kings'. At the end of most stories Rahat has added a *qit'a* of two couplets to point out the moral or 'conclusion' that is to be drawn from that tale. The stories are all quite entertaining, several of them describing events that happened to the author himself, but their edifying nature is often a bit dubious. His concluding couplets, therefore, often appear forced, and are of generally poor quality. That is somewhat surprising, inasmuch as Rahat was the disciple of no less a poet than Mu'min, and wrote better verse elsewhere. The prose of the stories exhibits some literary pretension, but not to an excessive degree. The language is closer to the prose of the storytellers of Fort William than to that of the dastan-narrators of Lucknow. In that sense it is relatively simple and colloquial. Nevertheless, it is still the language of a learned man, who could not help but write as if for other men of worldly knowledge and experience.

The book did receive some reward, as is indicated in a publisher's note at the end, but perhaps only a nominal one, because no sum is indicated. No copies of the book were bought by the government, nor was it ever prescribed for any examination. The author, apparently, uses the *Gulistan* of Sa'di as his model, arranging his stories into chapters and adding aphoristic couplets at the end of each story. He writes with approval of such virtues as justice, generosity, bravery, presence of mind, sweetness of discourse and the like—all well-known themes of adab—but his scope remains limited. He is neither comprehensive nor sharply focused. His tales convince us that he must have been an excellent courtier, but by the same token he is not the kind of edifying author that the new educators would have approved of. He does not talk of useful new sciences; rather, he suggests a life in which the wisdom of age and experience counts for more. Even the Englishmen who appear in his tales appear as rulers and soldiers, in no way different from the Indian protagonists. The milieu of baronial courts and the celebratory tone in which it is—quite successfully—depicted by Rahat had little appeal for earnest English civil servants and eager Indian wage earners.

The next book to be discussed is *'Aql o shu'ir* (Intellect and Sagacity) by Maulawi Sayyid Nizam ad-Din, son of Maulawi Sayyid Amir 'Ali, probably of Lucknow, published in Lucknow in 1873 by the famous Newal Kishore Press.[10] According to an inscription on its title page, it was awarded a prize of Rs 300, and 300 copies were bought by the government for its Department of Public Instruction. Another inscription, in

English, runs: 'Aql-o-Shu'ur, For Indian Girls, Boys, Ladies and Gentlemen.' Encyclopedic in conception, it is an amazing cornucopia of both fact and fiction. Some idea of the ambition behind it, and the style of its execution, can be had from this excerpt from its preface.

> Nizam, of humble name and little fame, begs to submit to his alert readers, the keen seekers of knowledge, that for a long time this recluse of the house of despair remained hidden behind seclusion's veil, and despite possessing a tongue of flame, cared little for fame, choosing to be mute like a candle. . . . The anguished heart shed many a tear, and the sickened soul was gripped with fear, lest the gale of ignorance extinguish the lamp of learning, plunging into darkness the heavens a-turning. A storm of indiscrimination raged on all sides; the barge of discernment sank out of sight. No one cared, none gave a hoot, to listen to men of merit, to give ear to their suit. I wept for my talent, so fine yet so battered; I cried out this verse as my hopes lay shattered.
>
> Whom can I show my mind, so gallant?
> This age, alas, has no patron of talent.
>
> But Allah be praised, the notice issued by the English Government, so firm and determined, instigated me to add glory to my name, and gave me an occasion to indulge in expression, and for sooth obtain fame. Verily, the Nawwab Lieutenant-Governor Bahadur acted like a messiah . . . Consequently, hoping for a reward, and bearing in my heart a desire for the general good, I began this book. . . . The name of this treatise, full of merits, is 'Aql o shu'ur. Its every phrase has a benefit, hidden, and its every chapter has a purpose, given. Without a doubt, it is an elixir for those who are parched for learning, and without any reservation it can be taught to ladies and children. The author has divided it into an Introduction, ten Chapters, and a Conclusion. The Introduction is called *Tajalli i nur* (Lights and Splendour), the Chapters are called '*Uqul i 'ashara* (The Ten Intellects) and the Conclusion is titled *Jauhar i fard* (The Singular Substance). The meaning of Knowledge and Ignorance, the nature of Reason, single letters and compound phrases, the counsels of the wise and the advice of the learned, the rules of morphology and syntax, logic and ethics, rhetoric and prosody, refinements of speech and elegance of expression, Geography and History, Arithmetic and Geometry, Physics and Chemistry and Astronomy, marvels of the world and the world of fantasy, the history of the Freemasons, the secrets of mesmerism and electricity, the wonders of the steam-engine and telegraphy, electroplating, compass, thermometer, photography, the art of calligraphy and drawing, letter-writing, horsemanship, swordsmanship, gymnastics and wrestling, disputation and debate, etc.—all of these subjects, subtly and carefully, have been transferred from the tablet of my heart to the surface of these pages.[11]

The above list is merely a summary of the contents. To enhance the fascinating quality of the book, the enterprising author has provided numerous line drawings, probably of his own making, to illustrate the text.

The text is cast in the form of a tale, whose characters carry allegorical names. In the Land of Freedom, in the city called the Abode of Learning, ruled a king, whose name was Embodied Intellect. He had a son, Cherisher of Wisdom. When the prince reached the age of six, the king asked his five ministers to suggest some plan of education for him, and eventually accepted the advice of his fifth minister—a genie—called Word-Fathoming Sagacity. The minister then flew off to the region of Qaf to bring an old friend of his named Sage of the Age. It took this sage five years to instruct the prince in all branches of learning, and the king evaluated his progress in a public examination at the end of every six months. Thus each of the ten chapters is in two parts: in the first, the sage covers a range of topics as he instructs the prince; in the second, the prince ranges over a number of related—and not so related—subjects as he answers his examiners. At the end the king abdicates in favour of his son, the sage returns to his mountain peak, and we all live happily every after.

The book must have gained some popularity, for it went through at least three printings, the third in 1914. But it could not possibly have been a prescribed textbook in schools; its sales must have been to libraries and individual men, and they were boosted by the fact that the government bought 300 copies for its own institutions. It does not have much in it to appeal to women and girls, who are, in fact, never mentioned in the text after the inscription in English on the title page. It is primarily a book for adult males, for the 'gentlemen' of the author's time, and it is easy to see its appeal for them.

First, in language and style it is not unlike the dastans that were extremely popular in that area at that time. Its narrative structure is that of a tale; its prose is flowery and rhyming, interspersed with verses in Persian and Urdu; and it makes use of many elements of the supernatural. Even its long lists of the names of flowers, foods, countries and so on, are like those that the traditional storytellers were fond of reeling off at any opportunity. It is a quest story—a quest for knowledge, in this case—and its prince-hero undergoes tests—not trials by fire, in this case, but public examinations, much like interviews for jobs.

Secondly, it contains basic information on a great many 'wonders' of Western civilization, such as the railway, telegraph and photography, not to mention the Freemasons.

Thirdly, it does not denigrate the traditional branches of learning, such as prosody, letter-writing and astrology. In fact, it delineates them in much detail.

Fourthly, it also purports to be a guide of a more practical nature, explaining to its readers how to do electroplating, make electric cells, take photographs, and survey land, activities not quite providing the *hunar* (skill) that a prince may need to possess to earn a living, but practical nevertheless. In spirit, of course, this is like what the princely author of *Qabus nama* had in mind when he taught his son how to be a musician, an astrologer or even a merchant.

Fifthly, it is indeed the first book of its kind in Urdu: a compendium of 'useful information' for ordinary curious persons. If nothing else, it provides them with such exciting, though rudimentary, facts on a vast array of subjects as would add to their self-esteem and self-assurance in the company of the better educated.

Finally, even while celebrating the glories of '*aql* (intellect)—each of its chapters is called an 'aql—it does not question any of the social or religious constructs of its time. Religion, society, science—they appear in a state of peaceful coexistence in this book. It does not challenge any of its readers' beliefs, nor even their superstitions. The 'ilm (knowledge; science) of *tilismat* (supernatural mysteries) is as seriously dealt with as are the '*ulum* of physics and astronomy. Its worldview is traditional: theistic and hierarchical. Although its author carefully avoids making any overt mention of religion—there is hardly any quotation from the Qur'an or *hadith*—he takes the supreme authority of God as given. He is careful to tell us that there are two types of 'aql: '*aql i ma'ad* (the 'aql of the hereafter), whose fruit shall be received after death, and '*aql i ma'ash* (the 'aql of living), which is useful in this world. That he devotes his book entirely to the latter is, no doubt, due to his narrow interpretation of the condition in the Gazette Notification against 'theological treatises'. Likewise, though he declares that all classes of men should pursue 'ilm, his book deals only with the 'ulum of the gentry. It contains, for example, no mention of such 'hand-soiling' occupations as agriculture and trade. Its ethics are similarly traditional. The author has incorporated in it material from numerous earlier books of adab, and constantly appeals to the authority of the past to underscore the validity of his remarks.

It must therefore have appeared as a near-perfect book to many of its gentlemen readers of that time who, secure in their religious beliefs and confident of their social habits, but curious about Western technical achievements, must have found it as much comforting as it was informative. As for the British, if they were not totally beguiled by its scientific airs, they were still right in giving some reward to a pioneering enterprise of such magnitude. Needless to say, as education spread and literary tastes changed, as the 'wonders' became commonplace and the traditional 'ulum lost their value in the job market, the same qualities eventually made it quite irrelevant to the new gentry. What the new *sharif* folk wanted was provided to them by Nadhir Ahmad, three of whose many award-winning books will be considered below.

Nadhir Ahmad (1830–1912) was a man of remarkable talent. Born in a family of *maulawis* and *muftis* of Bijnore, he studied Persian, Arabic and other traditional subjects, first with his father, then later under other maulawis in Bijnore and Delhi. A chance encounter led to a scholarship to study at Delhi College, where he joined the Arabic class, studying calculus, trigonometry, algebra, geography and natural philosophy, along with Arabic literature. That course of study lasted eight years. Because of the objection of his father, he did not study English at that time, but made up for it later. He began his professional career as a maulawi of Arabic, but soon moved on to be a deputy inspector of schools in the Department of Public Instruction. Later, by displaying his genius in translating the Indian penal code into Urdu, he was nominated to the Revenue Service and became a deputy collector in the North-West Provinces. Still later, he rose to high administrative positions in Hyderabad state. Throughout his life, along with his professional work, he continued to write and translate. In the annals of Urdu literature he is deservedly given a very high position, not only for writing the first 'novel' in Urdu, but also for writing some of the most influential books in that language.[12]

The three books under consideration are his first three novels: *Mir'at al-'arus* (The Mirror of the Bride), first published in 1869, *Banat an-na'sh* (The Daughters of the Bier), first published in 1872, and *Tauba an-nasuh* (The Repentance of Nasuh), first published in 1874.[13] Together they formed for him 'a syllabus for the instruction of women: *Mir'at al-'arus* for teaching household arts (*umur i khanadari*), *Banat an-na'sh* for teaching useful facts (*ma'lumat i dururi*), and *Tauba an-nasuh* for teaching piety (*khuda parasti*)'.[14]

Mir'at al-'arus was begun in 1865–66 as a reader for his daughter and was completed in 1867–68. The book became very popular among the female relatives of the author. He even gave a copy of it to his daughter as part of her dowry. Later, it was submitted in competition, and in 1869, the first year of the awards, won for the author not only the full prize of Rs 1000 but also a watch as a personal token of appreciation from the lieutenant-governor. The government purchased 2,000 copies of the book for its institutions and recommended its inclusion in school syllabi.

Banat an-na'sh followed in 1872 and won the prize of Rs 500. The author called it the second part of *Mir'at*, but it was not a sequel.[15] It merely expanded upon some events that were briefly mentioned in the first book. In its preface, Nadhir Ahmad said: '*Mir'at* was intended to teach ethics (*akhlaq*) and good housekeeping (*khanadari*). This book does the same, but only secondarily, its primary concern is with scientific knowledge (*ma'lumat i 'ilmi*). Now remains the topic of religious piety (*dindari*). If time allows . . . that too, God willing, shall be presented next year.'[16]

He kept his word and presented for competition in 1873 his masterpiece, *Tauba an-nasuh*. It won him the first prize again, came out in 1874, and has not been out of print since. Matthew Kempson, the director of public instruction at that time, liked it so much that he translated it into English and published it in London in 1884.

Both *Mir'at* and *Tauba* have been a permanent part of the syllabi of Urdu schools from their first publication. *Mir'at* has had many imitators, and its main motif of two sisters, one good and the other bad, has been used in innumerable novels and stories aimed at the female audience. It has been translated into several Indian languages, and an English version came out in London in 1903. *Tauba*, a superior and more complex book, has had no imitators, but it was itself an imitation of Daniel Defoe's *The Family Instructor*, part I. Nadhir Ahmad felt no need to acknowledge that fact, nor did his English admirers. They were right. Borrowing the bare plot from Defoe, Nadhir Ahmad made it his own by developing better, more believable characters and by creating a compelling air of authenticity through accuracy of description and naturalness of dialogue. By any measure, his book is a far superior work of creative imagination than Defoe's.

Mir'at, in the days of its greatest popularity, was simply known as the story of Akbari and Asghari. These are two sisters living in Delhi: Akbari, the elder, married to a man named Muhammad 'Aqil, and Asghari, the younger, still living with her mother but engaged to be married to 'Aqil's younger brother, Muhammad Kamil. The fathers in both families live on their jobs, away from Delhi. Akbari is illiterate, ill-tempered and absolutely without any talent. Soon after her marriage she demands a house of her own, but once installed, quickly manages to make a mess of it. Asghari, on the other hand, is literate, sweet-tempered and multitalented. Before her marriage she runs her mother's house, and after her marriage, transforms the life in her husband's quarters. She first rids the house of a thieving maid, then slyly gets her husband to mend his ways and obtain a job. She starts a school for girls in her house, brings Akbari and 'Aqil back into the fold, and carefully arranges the marriage of her sister-in-law into a wealthy family.

Nadhir Ahmad never explains just why the two sisters turned out to be so different from each other. He seems, however, to imply that while Akbari had taken after her mother, who remains nameless in the book, Asghari was like her father, appropriately named Durandesh Khan (Farsighted) and may have received proper instruction from him at an early age. They also correspond with each other, a fact that forcefully brings out the importance of literacy. Asghari's innate good nature, some proper upbringing, and a degree of education have made her a paragon of virtues. Just as her calmness never gives way to hysteria, so does her sharp mind never fail to come to her rescue. The most outstanding thing about her is her practical bent of mind (*hikma i 'amali*). She is a remarkably practical person and a meticulous planner. She dominates the book. Her own father and brother are only marginal characters, whereas the three male members of her husband's family have much to say and do in the book, yet all three of them are totally inept and impractical compared with her. She leads them and they follow. She is also shrewd enough to know when to be direct and when subtle. She is always right, and this does begin to annoy us. Because she is always serious and never invites us to laugh with her, we may catch ourselves inclined to laugh at her. That we do not quite do so is only a proof of Nadhir Ahmad's success in impressing us with his ideal sharif woman. Asghari was Nadhir Ahmad's beloved heroine, and he had to write a second book, *Banat*, to tell us all that he had wanted to tell about her.

Banat is ostensibly the story of Husn Ara, a spoiled girl from a rich family, who is sent to Asghari for instruction. It presents Asghari as the ideal teacher. To underscore that role she is generally referred to as *ustaniji* (lady teacher). An equally important role is also played by a protégée of hers, her sister-in-law Mahmuda. Together they inculcate good values and habits in Husn Ara, and also expand her knowledge in terms of facts of geography, history, and general science. They also teach her and the other girls in Asghari's *maktab* how to cook, sew and manage household budgets. The facts are conveyed through stories and interpolated comments; the skills are taught through playing with dolls and through small projects. *Banat* apparently presents Nadhir Ahmad's ideal of a school for girls: run by an individual or two, catering to a small number of students (carefully selected for their aptitude), and self-supporting. The teacher receives no salary—as a sharif lady, Asghari could not be expected to charge a fee. The girls do handicrafts, which are sold to raise funds for school expenses. As for the syllabus of this ideal school, Nadhir Ahmad gives a detailed description of it at the end of *Banat*, when he describes what Husn Ara had learned in her approximately three years there.

> When Husn Ara joined the *maktab* she was a little over ten years old. As her thirteenth year ended, the family in Jhajjar began to press for marriage. In the meantime, Husn Ara had learnt to read the Qur'an, and, since she regularly read two sections every day, knew it as if by heart. As for Urdu, she could read and write with no difficulty. Even her handwriting was fair. Urdu translation of the Qur'an, *Kanz al-musalla, Qiyama nama, Rah i najat, Wafat nama*, the story of the King of Rum, the story of the *Sipahizada*, the miracle of the King of Yemen, *Risala i maulud sharif, Mashariq al-anwar*—these were the religious books that she had read. In addition she had studied the fundamentals of arithmetic up to the fractions, the geography and history of India, *Chand pand, Muntakhab al-hikaya*, and *Mir'at al-'arus* [all by Nadhir Ahmad]. She could read Urdu newspapers. In addition to reading and writing, she had learned all the arts (*hunar*) that a woman needs to manage a household. She had also learned as many useful facts (*ma'lumat i mufida*) as would be sufficient to add comfort and pleasure to the rest of her life. But what she had learned from books was only a thousandth part of what she had learned from Asghari and the other students.[17]

Banat begins with the arrival of Husn Ara at the maktab and ends with her departure, but it is not a chronicle of her educational progress. It is mainly concerned with the early days: how Asghari and Mahmuda slowly induced her to give up her bad habits and gave her a taste of the fruits of education. These are the titles of some of the chapters: Husn Ara's contempt for the other girls and how Mahmuda cured her of it; Mahmuda makes Husn Ara understand that those who are rich are also the needier; Husn Ara begins to get up early; the meaning of true generosity; some fun with arithmetic; air pressure; magnetism; the need for civilization; some description of the English people; the geography of Arabia and the ways of the Bedouins.

Compared with *Mir'at, Banat* is dull and didactic. It has no story to hold our attention. All through it, Nadhir Ahmad, the deputy inspector of schools, is in the forefront; Nadhir Ahmad, the novelist, displays himself only in some of the conversations where his command of the subtleties of feminine speech becomes evident. It was rightly given a lesser award. Moreover, it has not been as popular, though it too has remained in print.

Two major concerns inspire most of Nadhir Ahmad's fiction: the uplift of sharif women and the proper upbringing of sharif children. Together they form the foundation of what is critically important for him: the family. For him, the enrichment and fulfilment of the lives of individuals can take place only within the context of a family, within which each member has his or her share of responsibilities, that share determining the individual's worth. The uplift of an entire society, according to him, can come about only if its constituent members—the individual families—are first brought to a state of enlightenment. (Nadhir Ahmad, of course, assumes society to be hierarchical, and focuses his attention on sharif families.)

Sir Sayyid, the great educationist-reformer and a senior contemporary of Nadhir Ahmad, in order to transform his Muslim compatriots, wanted to duplicate in Aligarh the corridors of Oxford and Cambridge—and perhaps also the cricket fields of Eton and Harrow. Nadhir Ahmad, for the same purpose, sought to change the life in the courtyards and kitchens of ordinary homes, and frequently presented glimpses of English domesticity for the edification of his readers. What first-hand experience he had of it is not clear, probably very little and even that misunderstood, such as his understanding of the 'royal powers' of Queen Victoria, who is often mentioned in exaggerated terms in his novels. In *Banat* there is a long section describing the virtuous and happy life of an English family that bears no resemblance to reality. These people, however, serve a useful purpose in his scheme, just as does the English lady doctor in another novel. They provide strong, intelligent and practical women as models for emulation.

Four of Nadhir Ahmad's seven novels are concerned with the problems of women. *Mir'at* and *Banat* deal with the difficulties caused by their lack of proper education, an area wherein, according to Nadhir Ahmad, they were themselves mostly to be blamed. The other two books are concerned with the pain and suffering that their male-dominated society inflicts on them, by allowing men to have a second wife (*Muhsinat*, or *Fasana i mubtala*, 1885), and by not allowing widows to remarry (*Ayyama*, 1891). In each of these four novels, Nadhir Ahmad presents at least one major female character who impresses us by being different from the prevalent image and self-image of Muslim women. These creations of Nadhir Ahmad are amazingly dynamic people, possessing sharp and practical minds. In each instance, they are more competent, stronger, and more effective than almost all the male characters. Even the best of the men tend merely to preach. They have power and wield it, but we get the impression that if pressed to answer, these men may not be able to justify the authority and superiority they claim.

Nadhir Ahmad holds that 'the cart of life cannot move an inch unless it has one wheel of man and another wheel of woman'. He writes,

> No doubt God created woman a bit weaker than man, but He gave her hands and feet, ears and eyes, wit (*'aql*), understanding (*samajh*) and memory (*yad*) equal to any man. The boys make use of these gifts and become *'alim, hafij, hakim*, craftsmen, artisans, experts in every art and craft. The girls waste their time in playing with dolls and listening to stories, and remain devoid of *hunar* (talent; art). However, those women who recognized the value of

time and put it to good use became famous in the world just like men. For example, Nurjahan Begum, Zeb an-nisa' Begum, or, as in our days, Nawwab Sikandar Begum and Queen Victoria, who have run, not just some small household, but an entire country, even the world.[18]

He reminds women of the popular opinions held about them: women are faulty of intellect (*naqisat al-'aql*); women are crafty and sly; they are obstinate and fickle; if women (*zan*) had deserved any better they would have been called *ma-zan* (don't beat!) instead of *zan* (beat!). Seeing no hope for their relief from the seclusion of parda, which would allow them knowledge through experience, he concludes that the only way for women to improve themselves is through education. 'Education has more importance for women than for men.'[19]

In giving such importance to women, in allowing them the inherent capacity to be coequal with men in almost all matters, and in laying such emphasis on women's education, Nadhir Ahmad was going against the prevalent views. The greatest Muslim educator of that time, Sir Sayyid, wrote hardly anything concerning women and was in fact not in favour of 'wasting' any national effort on their education. The education of husbands and sons was of far greater importance to him. He believed that the benefits of education would eventually filter down through them to women. We are not suggesting that Nadhir Ahmad's was a lone voice—there were many others who expressed sorrow at the plight of women—but it was certainly the most radical and far-reaching. The radical nature of Nadhir Ahmad's ideas becomes clear when we compare them, on the one hand, with the views on women in such popular classics of adab as the *Qabus nama* (eleventh century) and the *Akhlaq i nasiri* (thirteenth century), and, on the other, with the opinions of Maulana Ashraf 'Ali Thanawi, a younger contemporary and one of the most influential Muslims of twentieth-century India.

The two medieval classics[20] are, of course, directed towards men. They pay attention to women only insofar as men need wives to perpetuate their line and look after domestic chores; problems also arise because men sire daughters as well as sons. Although these treatises allow that women can be chaste and kind, thrifty and efficient, and adorned with wit and honesty—for these are the qualities to be preferred in a wife—the underlying attitude is somewhat misogynistic. Although women can be the best of friends, they can also be the worst of enemies (*Qabus*). Women cannot be trusted, so one should not share one's secrets with them, nor should one consult them in every matter (*Akhlaq*). You should not marry a wealthy woman, for she will look down upon you, nor a beautiful woman, for she will be faithless, nor a non-virgin, for she will tend to compare you with other men all the time (*Qabus* and *Akhlaq*). Do not give yourself into the hands of your wife: though she may be a paragon of virtue and beauty (*Qabus*). Do not fall in love with your wife, but if you do, hide it from her (*Akhlaq*).

As for daughters, according to *Qabus*, they are better not born, but if born, they should be either by the side of a husband or in the lap of a grave. Their education is to be limited to domestic chores and the rites of religion. Interestingly, whereas the earlier book, *Qabus*, is not against women being taught how to read, the later one, *Akhlaq*, is bluntly against it. As for learning how to write, that is forbidden by both. Writing is perhaps seen as a more active and dynamic expression of the self and the intellect than mere reading, and women are not considered to have either in a positive sense. It is significant that in both the books the first instruction concerning sons is that they should be given good names. This does not obtain in the case of daughters.

Maulana Ashraf 'Ali Thanawi's *Bihishti zewar* is directed towards Muslim women, and may be the first book of its kind in Islamic adab literature.[21] First published in 1905, it was written at a time when female education was rapidly making progress in India, and Muslim women themselves were playing an active role in that process. Whereas Nadhir Ahmad had intended his novels to be useful to all women, Thanawi is concerned with the needs of Muslim women alone. According to Thanawi, women, through their actions, affect not only their children, but also their husbands; thus what they do or do not do affects society as a whole. He then reasons:

> Poor faith (*bad i'tiqadi*) gives birth to bad ethics (*bad akhlaqi*), bad ethics produce bad actions (*bad a'mali*), bad actions lead to bad interaction with others (*bad mu'amalagi*), which is the root of all evil in the society. Since the opposite of something is its antidote, it is evident that the cure in this case is the knowledge of religion ('*ilm i din*).[22]

Accordingly, his syllabus for women includes the Qur'an (vocalizing of the Arabic, and understanding of the Urdu translation), rules of *fiqh* insofar as they concern women, and some essentials of domestic bookkeeping, health care, cooking and other such things. No history or geography for him, nor the wonders of the heavens. According to him, women should be taught how to read, for that will improve their language, strengthen their faith and make them better homemakers. As for the art of writing, it has its uses too, such as keeping of accounts and communicating through letters, but it should be taught only to those who are not bold (*bebak*) by nature. Otherwise it may be harmful. 'After all,' he concludes, 'writing should not be more dear to you than your honour (*abru*).'[23]

Thanawi is against the newly opened *zanana* (all female) schools and the books that were taught there. He strongly disapproves of the newly emerging 'feminine' literature, including the four novels of Nadhir Ahmad mentioned above. Near the end of *Bihishti zewar*, he lists the names of some 'harmful' books and includes the four novels. He then adds: 'These four books contain some discourses that teach discernment (*tamiz*) and proficiency (*saliqa*), but they also contain discourses that weaken faith (*din*).'[24] Inasmuch as Thanawi does not elaborate further, we can only speculate about the objections he may have raised. The obvious ones would be: (1) Nadhir Ahmad's equating of Islam with other religions; (2) his praise of the Christian English at the cost of Muslim Indians; (3) his making fun of certain types of maulawis. But we will not be far wrong, perhaps, if we add to that list (4) his depiction in the two later novels of the sensual aspects of marital ties and the emotional needs of women; and (5) his portrayal of highly capable and dynamic women, who tower over the men around them.

As noted earlier, Nadhir Ahmad is concerned with Muslim women's lot as a whole, and not merely with the corruption of their religion. He believes in the efficacy of education as a given universal, and feels no need to anchor his espousal of it in the Qur'an and hadith, as does Thanawi. Nadhir Ahmad sees women as victims of their own lack of initiative as well as of the unmitigated authority of men, and champions their cause. He perhaps feels very close to them; he portrays them well in his novels. He feels no need to improve their language; in fact, it is his command of their idiom that makes his dialogues ring so true. With reference to women, Nadhir Ahmad displays an attitude and opinions that must have appeared radical to the orthodox of his time. It would be wrong, however, to think of him as one who took his religion lightly. On the contrary, Nadhir Ahmad stresses again and again that religion—any religion—has to be at the core of a person's being, to generate for him or her the values to live by. Within the context of Islam, that is Thanawi's belief too. It is no surprise, then, to find him giving full approval to Nadhir Ahmad's third novel, *Tauba an-nasuh*: he lists it among the books it would be beneficial for women to read.[25]

In his preface to *Tauba*, Nadhir Ahmad declares:

> In this book we discuss that duty of mankind which is called 'the upbringing of children'. . . . [which] does not amount merely to giving them nourishment so that they grow big, or teaching them some profession so that they can earn a living, or arranging their marriages, 'but also includes the polishing of their morals (*akhlaq*), the improvement of their dispositions (*mizaj*), the reform of their habits ('*adat*), and the correction of their ideas and beliefs (*khayalat aur mu'taqidat*).

Further:

> My intention was to prove to people the importance of instruction in good ways and fine morals, and do so without underscoring religion (*bila takhsis-i madhhab*). But to separate goodness (*neki*) from religion would be like trying to separate the soul from the body, the fragrance from the flower, the light from the sun.

He then goes on to stress that though his book was not without religious discourses, it contained nothing that could hurt the religious sentiments of other communities. 'Thus, though the story is about a Muslim family, even the Hindus, by changing a few words, can benefit from it.'[26]

Tauba is about Nasuh, a sharif Muslim of Delhi, and his attempts to reform the ways and manners of his family members by inculcating in them a deep respect for their religion, its rituals as well as its ethics. Nasuh takes on this task after himself going through a radical transformation under traumatic circumstances. In a cholera epidemic, Nasuh loses his father and another relative; soon afterward he, too, falls ill. On his sickbed, he is filled with self-pity at having to die when he still has so many things to take care of in this world. As the doctor's medicine puts him to sleep, Nasuh has a dream: he sees himself as if present in the *kachahri* (court of justice) of God. There he encounters his deceased father, who tells him of the exactitude and severity of God's judgment, and the need to inspire one's acts on Earth with the true sense of piety in order to fully discharge the individual and social responsibilities laid down upon mankind by his Creator. Recovering from the illness, Nasuh launches his campaign. He finds a willing ally in his wife, Fahmida, who had already had a poignant and instructive encounter with their younger daughter, Hamida. The older daughter, Na'ima, however, does not take to religion easily. She goes off to stay with an aunt, whose religious household eventually has the desired effect on her. Of the sons, the younger two, 'Alim and Salim, accept Nasuh's programme readily, because they had already found influencing factors outside their own family: in one case, a book of moral principles given by a Christian missionary, and in the other, the company of a poor but pious schoolmate. It is the eldest son, Kalim, who proves to be the most obstinate. He challenges the authority of his father and the importance of religion in one's life. He runs away from home, has several misadventures and returns repentant, but dying. With his death ends the book.

It is not our purpose here to provide a critique of *Tauba* as a novel; we are concerned only with the didactic aspirations of the book. To that extent, it will suffice to look closely at only one major theme: the tussle between the reforming old-new and the recalcitrant young-old, represented by the father and the son respectively. Nasuh is older in age, and exercises his traditional authority as the father; his emphasis on religion can also be called old-fashioned. But his reforming efforts are directed at such cherished cultural values as he had himself lived by until that eventful dream. These same values, however, are obstinately held onto by Kalim, his father's son in more ways, perhaps, than the author realizes.[27] In fact, Kalim sees no reason for change. He is already living by the values a person of his background and position—that is, a sharif young man—is expected to have, with the full knowledge and, therefore, tacit approval of his father. He is popular as a poet. He is ranked high among the players of chess, backgammon, cards and other games. His pigeons are among the best in the city, and none can beat him in a kite-flying match. He is well-read, and he can write well. As he tells his mother, 'Just as there are other sons of respected and sharif families, so am I one. If I am not better than all, I certainly am not worse than any.'[28] He regards his father's demands as unfair, and leaves home to seek his fortune on the strength of the talents he possesses and cherishes. He leaves British India and goes to a small native state, and when his poetry does not get him far, he becomes a soldier, only to be mortally wounded in his first skirmish.[29] In contrast to him, his 're-formed' younger brothers do very well indeed: one gets a job in the Education Department, the other becomes a practitioner of *yunani* medicine.

Kalim is by no means an uneducated person; on the contrary, he is well read in Persian and Urdu classics. We are told that he is popular in the city as a poet. In his conversation, Kalim is shown as constantly quoting poetry. He thinks poetry adds force to his arguments, and marks him as an educated man. In a clear sense he lives up to his name. But Nadhir Ahmad has only contempt for that kind of 'education'; he regards it as useless for this world and harmful for the other. In his authorial voice, he says: 'Kalim was cursed with poetry' (*Kalim par sha'iri ki phitkar thi*).[30]

As for the books that Kalim had read and collected, Nadhir Ahmad has Nasuh destroy them in what may be one of the most horrifying scenes in Urdu novels. After Kalim has left the house, Nasuh inspects his rooms, and finds a large cabinet full of books in Urdu and Persian. They consist of 'false tales, foolish discourses, obscene ideas, vulgar subjects, all far removed from decency and goodness'.[31] And so he has the full cabinet dragged outside and burnt to ashes. What Lord Macaulay had only hinted at in his famous Minute, Nadhir Ahmad has Nasuh put into action. That conflagration symbolizes, more than anything else, the rejection of the 'old' by the 'new', of literary excellence in favour of social usefulness, of 'metaphor' in favour of 'realism'. It must have left an indelible mark on the minds of many generations, for nearly 70 years went by before anyone found fault with Nasuh and saw Kalim as a victim of circumstances, as a 'strange mixture of good and evil'.

In his preface to *Tauba*, Nadhir Ahmad quotes the following verse (33:72) from the Qur'an:

Lo! We offered the trust unto the heavens and the earth and the hills, but they shrank from bearing it and were afraid of it. And man assumed it. Lo! he hath proved a tyrant and a fool.[32]

In a footnote, Nadhir Ahmad explains 'trust' to mean 'aql, variously translated as intellect or reason. It is the loss of this 'aql that has led, according to Nadhir Ahmad, to the dreadful state in which the Muslims of India find themselves. The rise of the British, conversely, is due to their making full use of their 'aql. In *Banat*, Asghari tells her girls: 'The British are embodiments of 'aql, otherwise they couldn't have come here, thousands of miles from their home, and become kings.'[33] Nadhir Ahmad is nonetheless devoutly religious, having come to his faith after a period of anguish and doubt in his youth.[34] Faced with the question of reconciling religion with reason, he shows his characteristic inclination to be practical: he ignores it, at least in these three prize-winning books.[35] Consequently, these books are readily acceptable to the average Indian Muslim, who can easily see that he requires 'aql, to succeed in this world, and religion, to redeem him in the hereafter. If religion leads to good habits, which in turn lead to success here, so much the better for religion. In fact it may appear that success and rewards are of decisive importance in Nadhir Ahmad's vision. He wants his readers to receive their due reward in this earth as well as in heaven. After all, he makes a point of letting us know the heights of success his 'good' people do reach.

> In Khanum's Bazar there stands a huge mansion built by Asghari. In fact, the neighbourhood is named after her. That lofty mosque in Jauhari Bazar that has a well and a tank was built by her too, as was the entire colony of Tamizgunj. In Maulawi Hayat's mosque, twenty travellers are fed daily through her generosity. She also built that *sara'i* for travellers in Qutb Sabib. It was she who distributed 500 copies of the Qur'an in one day in the mosque of Fatehpuri, and it is from her house that 1,000 blankets are given to the poor every winter.[36]

Compared with the achievements of Asghari, the heroine of the 'aql books, the success of Nasuh's 'good' children is not especially outstanding, but nevertheless, success it is.

> Before it all happened, 'Alim was having a hard time passing even the Entrance examination, Now, however, he passed his B.A. One excellent job after another was offered to him, but he, due to his good nature, chose the Department of Education, so he could be of benefit to his compatriots. The other son, Salim, when he grew up, became a *tabib* of such eminence that even now the finest tabib of Delhi practise medicine using his prescriptions, As for Hamida, that saint-from-birth, she memorized the Qur'an and studied the hadith. Indeed, all the interest in education that you see among women of the city, is entirely due to Bi Hamida.[37]

What is also noteworthy here is a certain apparent split or separation. 'Aql, guide to the steam-engine, telegraph, and efficient households, is extolled in *Mir'at* and *Banat*. There is no mention in them of the need to say one's prayers regularly. The prayers are highlighted in *Tauba* which, in its turn, stays away from the wonders of modern science. The Qur'an, the Word of God, and Nature, the Work of God, are pragmatically kept separate. Unlike his great contemporary Sir Sayyid, Nadhir Ahmad feels no need to demonstrate a tight fit between the two, at least not in these three books, his most popular ones. Here the natural world and the world of the supernatural seem to exist in perfect harmony, neither enroaching upon the territory of the other—a reassuring concept for the average Muslim then, as it is now.

The medieval classics display a more holistic attitude. Beginning with the concept of the Oneness of God, they extend it to perceive unity within all phenomena. They develop a concept of '*ishq* ('love') to describe what they perceive as an interrelationship between all beings as well as between their multifarious expressions of themselves. Such 'ishq finds no mention in these novels of Nadhir Ahmad, nor, for that matter, in Thanawi's book. (It appears again later in the writings of Muhammad Iqbal, 1877–1938.) Similarly, the earlier books, written for the nobility, came out of societies where the temporal authority was a part of the community of believers: the world belongs to God, and the country and command belong to the king, but the king himself can be said to be a 'slave of Allah'. Nadhir Ahmad, on the other hand, writes for the emerging middle- and lower-middle classes of wage-earners in a society where, not too long ago, the cry of the town crier used to be: 'The world (*khalq*) belongs to God, the country (*mulk*) to the King, and the command (*hukm*) to the Company Bahadur.'

To conclude, these novels of Nadhir Ahmad are just the right kind of success stories that the Muslims of India needed to hear in the trying years after the failure of the Mutiny and the dissolution of all symbols of their temporal power. Separating the world of God from the world of Caesar—in effect though not, perhaps, in intention—and suggestive of an Islamic version of the Protestant ethic of success, these novels are precisely the kind of adab that both the rulers and the ruled seem to have desired at that particular time in history. This explains their success.

Notes

1. Quoted in Y.B. Mathur, *Women's Education in India, 1813–1966* (New York: 1973), p. 4.
2. Ibid., p. 7.
3. 'Abd al-Haqq, *Marhum dihli kalij* (Delhi: 1945), pp. 141–3.
4. M. Atique Siddiqi, *Origins of Modern Hindustani Literature* (Aligarh: 1963), pp. 159–60.
5. Gilchrist to College Council, quoted in ibid., p. 127.
6. *Allahabad Government Gazette* (India Office Records V/II/1248), pp. 349–50. Emphasis added. The author is grateful to Miss Maureen Patterson of the University of Chicago for her help in obtaining a copy of the notice.
7. Altaf Husain Hali, *Hayat i javed* (Lahore: 1965), p. 323. Hali also suggests that the initial impulse for instituting such awards may have come from Sir Sayyid, who broached the subject in an address presented to Sir William Muir on behalf of the Scientific Society at Aligarh, on 9 May 1868.
8. Mahmud Beg Rahat, *Nata'ij al-ma'ani*, ed. Gauhar Naushahi (Lahore: 1967). The biographical and bibliographical information presented here is based upon Professor Naushahi's valuable introduction.
9. Ibid., p. 28. The printed text has two errors: '1891-A' for 791-A and 'August 1864' for August 1868. The source of the errors is not clear.
10. Sayyid Nizam ad-Din, *'Aql o shu'ur*, 3rd ed. (Lucknow: 1914).
11. Ibid., pp. 3–4.
12. A number of books have appeared in Urdu on Nadhir Ahmad and his various novels, but by far the best and most comprehensive is by Professor Iftikhar Ahmad Siddiqi of the University Oriental College, Lahore: Iftikhar Ahmad Siddiqi, *Maulawi Nadhir Ahmad Dihlawi: ahwal o athar* (Lahore: 1971). It is an invaluable source of insights into the social, religious and literary issues that were of concern to the Muslims of India in the nineteenth century. In English, one can consult with much benefit Muhammad Sadiq, *A History of Urdu Literature* (London:

1964), pp. 316–25, and Shaista Akhtar Banu Suhrawardy, *A Critical Survey of the Development of the Urdu Novel and Short Story* (London: 1945), pp. 41–65.

13. The following editions of these novels have been used in this study: *Mir'at al-'arus* (Karachi: Sultan Hasan & Sons, 1963), *Banat an-na'sh* (Lucknow: Tej Kumar Press, 1967), and *Taubat an-nasuh* (Lahore: Majlis-i Taraqqi-yi Adab, 1964); this carefully edited edition also has an introduction by Professor I.A. Siddiqi.

14. Nadhir Ahmad, in his preface to *Fasana i mubtala*, ed. Sadiq ar-rahman Qidwai (New Delhi: 1971), p. 9. There is some internal evidence to suggest that the series was planned.

15. According to Muhammad Sadiq (*A History of Urdu Literature*, p. 323), *Banat* is based on the *History of Sandford and Merton* by Thomas Day, 'a pedagogic [story] that came in the wake of Rousseau's *Emile*.' This fact was never acknowledged by Nadhir Ahmad or his English patrons. One is also hard put to understand the significance of the title of the book, which refers to a constellation of stars (Ursa Major) and literally means 'the daughters of the bier'.

16. *Banat*, p. 2.

17. Ibid., p. 228.

18. *Mir'at*, p. 15.

19. Ibid., p. 25.

20. Kaikaus ibn Iskandar, *Qabus nama*, ed. Sa'id Nafisi (Tehran: 1342 Shamsi), pp. 95–9; Nasir ad-Din Muhammad at-Tusi, *Akhlaq i nasiri* (Lahore: 1952), pp. 212–21.

21. Muhammad Ashraf 'Ali Thanawi, *Bihisht zewar* (Lahore: n.d.). The edition used here is popularly known as the *Taj bihishti zewar*, after its publishers, Taj Company Ltd., Lahore. It is based on the definitive edition published by Maulana Shabbir 'Ali in 1925, but differs in pagination and some arrangement of the text. It is perhaps the best-printed edition.

22. *Bihishti zewar*, sec. 1, p. 3.

23. Ibid., p. 80.

24. Ibid., sec. 10, p. 54.

25. Ibid., sec 10, p. 53. I am indebted to Professor Barbara Metcalf for bringing Thanawi's comments to my attention.

26. *Tauba*, pp. 5–8.

27. Kalim's obstinacy in his ways is identical with Nasuh's rigidity in his reforming zeal. Both require some traumatic experience to bring about a change in them.

28. *Tauba*, pp. 179–80.

29. Kalim goes to Daulatabad, ready with a panegyric, but when he arrives there, he finds that the English have already curbed the powers of its wastrel ruler and set up an administrative council manned by pious and competent people. Kalim decides to become a soldier, a foolish decision made out of vanity, which, according to Nadhir Ahmad, is 'another accursed habit of poets'.

30. *Tauba*, pp. 265, 326.

31. Ibid., p. 253. Nadhir Ahmad's opinion of classical Urdu literature, particularly poetry, was not different from that of his contemporary Hali, who described it in his *Musaddas* as being 'worse in stench than a latrine'.

32. Muhammad Marmaduke Pickthall, *The Meaning of the Glorious Qur'an*, (Mecca: 1977), p. 450.

33. *Banat*, p. 198.

34. Ram Chandra, Nadhir Ahmad's favourite teacher at Delhi College, a Hindu, had converted to Christianity in 1852, and Nadhir Ahmad very nearly followed suit. Siddiqi, *Maulawi Nadhir Ahmad Dihlawi*, pp. 66–8.

35. Later in his life, Nadhir Ahmad translated the Qur'an into Urdu and also wrote a more formal adab book, *al-Huquq wa al-fara'id* (in three parts). The former became quite popular for a while, but the latter never caught on. Unfortunately, neither was available to me at the time of this writing.

36. *Mir'at*, p. 77.

37. *Tauba*, pp. 347–8.

16

Sayyid Mumtaz 'Ali and *Tahzib un-Niswan*

Women's Rights in Islam and Women's Journalism in Urdu*

GAIL MINAULT

Historians have often explained religious and social reform in India in the nineteenth century as the result of the Western impact upon the minds of men. Others have recognized that this was entirely too simple an explanation for the intellectual and social changes that took place in India and other places that fell under foreign colonial rule. The equation of Westernization and modernization has given way to a search for the indigenous sources of social change. Recognizing the modernity of tradition is one thing; however, understanding the intellectual processes that produced indigenously generated change is another. With that purpose, we seek to analyse the thought and activities of individuals who were both religious reformers and vernacular[1] publicists. Each of these vernacular-using reformers was involved in religious controversy: with Christian missionaries, with members of other Indian religions, with members of their own faith, or all of the above. Each derived his arguments from within his own tradition, though none was reluctant to use organizational forms and printing technology derived from the West. When such a reformer did adopt an idea, he did so through a process of translation, borrowing what was congruent with his own cultural assumptions and transforming it into his own terms. In analysing the origins and style of the arguments used by these reformers, we seek a greater understanding of the relationship between religious revival and social innovation in nineteenth-century India, the complex alchemy of change from within as well as impact from without.

Sayyid Mumtaz 'Ali: Early Life and Intellectual Background[2]

Sayyid Mumtaz 'Ali (1860–1935) is an excellent example of a vernacular-using reformer. His education included training in the Islamic classical languages and English, but he thought and wrote in Urdu, developing a clear and persuasive style. He was involved in religious debate early in life and later published polemical works of religious controversy; however, Mumtaz 'Ali was best known for his pioneering role in Urdu journalism for women. In 1898, he founded the weekly newspaper *Tahzib un-Niswan* (roughly translated: The Women's Reformer) in Lahore together with his second wife, Muhammadi

Begam. *Tahzib un-Niswan* was not the first Urdu periodical for women, but it was the first to survive,[3] and it changed the lives of thousands of purdah-observing women over the years by giving them a window on the world beyond the narrow walls of their *zananas*.[4] *Tahzib* contained new ideas on housekeeping and childrearing, featured and encouraged creative writing by women, discussed women's legal rights in Islam and the necessity for the mothers of the next generation to be educated, and invited letters from its readers to the editor, Muhammadi Begam, who as a woman understood their problems. *Tahzib un-Niswan* was an important element in the broader movement for women's education among Indian Muslims in the late nineteenth and early twentieth centuries. Mumtaz 'Ali, as its founder and manager, would thus appear to be a typical Westernizing reformer, perhaps with an advanced education in English and only a rudimentary knowledge of Islamic doctrine.

Such, however, was very far from the case, for Mumtaz 'Ali had a thorough vernacular education and training in the classical Islamic curriculum. Further, his family was closely associated with the reformist intellectual tradition of Shah Waliu'llah of Delhi. His father, Sayyid Zulfiqar 'Ali, came from a landed family in Saharanpur District, north of Delhi. The family burial ground is in the small town of Deoband, the location of the principal Islamic madrassah (theological school) of northern India, founded in 1867.[5] Sayyid Zulfiqar 'Ali had studied in Delhi in the years before the 1857 revolt with Maulana Mamluk 'Ali Nanautawi, a leading disciple of Shah Waliu'llah's successors. One of his fellow students was Zulfiqar 'Ali from Deoband, who became one of the founders of the Deoband madrassah and father of Mahmud ul-Hasan Deobandi, later known to his religious followers as the Shaikh ul-Hind. Sayyid Mumtaz 'Ali and Mahmud ul-Hasan were also friends and contemporaries who studied together at Deoband under Mamluk 'Ali's successors, Maulanas Muhammad Yaqub and Muhammad Qasim Nanautawi. Mumtaz 'Ali did not complete his education at Deoband, but retained his connection to the tradition of Islamic reform institutionalized at the Deoband madrassah. It was a connection both intellectual and familial. Mumtaz 'Ali was not related by blood to the leaders of the Deoband school, but he shared the 'familial' link of *ustad–shagird* (teacher–disciple) relations through at least two generations.

Mumtaz 'Ali's education began at an Arabic *maktab* in Deoband and continued in the Punjab, where his father was in government service. As they transferred from place to place, his education in the Qur'an, Arabic grammar, Persian literature, *fiqh* (Islamic jurisprudence) and *mantiq* (logic) proceeded until, at the age of 13, he returned to study at Deoband, where he studied the Islamic sciences, with an emphasis on the Qur'an and *hadith* (the prophetic tradition), at the madrassah. He attended the Deoband school for only a year or two before rejoining his father in the Punjab. He was then tutored in English at home, passed his middle exams within two years, and in 1876 joined Lahore Government High School. In 1884, in spite of the fact that he was a bright student, Mumtaz 'Ali failed his Bachelor's examinations; he never repeated the attempt. The reasons for his failure are not altogether clear, but seem to be connected to his religious preoccupations during this period.

Lahore in the 1870s and 1880s was a hotbed of religious controversy. Christian missionaries and Muslim divines debated openly in the bazaars of the old city before huge crowds. Mumtaz 'Ali and his school friends not only enjoyed the spectacle, but also were caught up in discussing religious issues. In addition, the Arya Samaj emerged in this period, with its aggressive proselytizing style, and made religious disputation a three-way contest. *Munazara*, religious debate, was obviously the most exciting game in town.[6] Mumtaz 'Ali, feeling that the local Muslim spokesmen had not adequately answered the Christian missionaries' debating points, devoured works of munazara by the leading Muslim divines, including Maulana Rahmatullah Kairanwi[7] and Maulana Sayyid Abul Mansur Dehlawi.[8] Furthermore, he tried to familiarize himself with the tenets of Christianity in order to formulate better arguments to refute the missionaries; but this led his classmates to worry that he might become a Christian. Sometime in the late 1870s, in conversation with one of his teachers, Babu Chandranath Mitter, Mumtaz 'Ali expressed his dissatisfaction with Muslim debating abilities.[9] Mitter introduced him to some of the writings of Sir Sayyid Ahmad Khan, the founder of Aligarh College, and urged him to write to Sir Sayyid about his religious doubts and concerns.

Sir Sayyid, given his duties at Aligarh and as a member of the Viceroy's Council in Calcutta, was an extremely busy man, but he was touched by the young man's sensitivity and intelligence. He invited Mumtaz 'Ali to visit him in Calcutta in December 1879. Mumtaz 'Ali stayed in Calcutta for about a month, meeting Sir Sayyid frequently. They discussed religious ideas, especially in the context of Sir Sayyid's ongoing commentary on the Qur'an. Mumtaz 'Ali found his doubts answered and his faith in Islam reconfirmed.[10] He also gained new confidence in his own ability to debate religious questions. Even after failing his Bachelor of Arts examinations and taking a job as a translator in the Lahore High Court, Mumtaz 'Ali continued his disputational activities. He published a pamphlet refuting the Ahl-i-Hadith leader, Maulana Muhammad Husain Batalwi's attacks on Sir Sayyid. It is significant that about this same time, his contemporary at Deoband, Mahmud ul-Hasan, was also involved in a published debate with Batalwi over the interpretation of Islamic law, with the Deobandi employing a combination of Hanafi jurisprudence, the Qur'an, and hadith, while the Ahl-i-Hadith spokesman relied almost exclusively on a literal reading of prophetic tradition.[11] Mumtaz 'Ali, in his later work on women's rights in Islamic law, utilized a variety of sources for legal interpretation such as those used by the Deobandis. Nevertheless, like Sir Sayyid, he felt free to criticize hadith when it was self-contradictory, or when it conflicted with the Qur'an.[12]

Mumtaz 'Ali's relationship with the Aligarh leader lasted until the end of Sir Sayyid's life. From time to time, he visited Aligarh to ask Sir Sayyid's advice, though Mumtaz 'Ali did not always take it. On one occasion, he showed Sir Sayyid the manuscript of his work in defence of women's rights in Islamic law, *Huquq un-Niswan*. As he began to read it, Sir Sayyid looked shocked. He then turned to the second page and his face turned red. As he read the third, his hands started to tremble. Finally, he tore up the manuscript and threw it into the wastepaper basket. Fortunately, at that moment a servant arrived to announce lunch, and as Sir Sayyid left his office, Mumtaz 'Ali snatched his mutilated manuscript from the trash. He waited until after Sir Sayyid's death in 1898, however, to publish *Huquq un-Niswan*.[13]

On another occasion, Mumtaz 'Ali wrote to Sir Sayyid asking his advice concerning a name for his proposed journal for women. Early in 1898, he sent Sir Sayyid a list of possible names, asking for his preference. Sir Sayyid replied grumpily, noting that

Mumtaz 'Ali had not asked his advice on whether to start the journal or not, but he offered his views anyway. Sir Sayyid warned Mumtaz 'Ali that if he started a publication for women, he would only earn public condemnation and would ultimately fail. On the other hand, Sir Sayyid said that if he persisted in this folly, he should name it *Tahzib un-Niswan*, in direct reference to his own social reform journal, *Tahzib ul-Akhlaq*. Finally, it seemed, Sir Sayyid admired Mumtaz 'Ali's courage, if not his chosen cause. A few weeks after receiving the old man's letter, news reached Mumtaz 'Ali of Sir Sayyid's death. He started publishing *Tahzib un-Niswan* three months later.[14]

Mumtaz 'Ali thus balanced the intellectual heritage of Deoband and an acquaintance with the leader of Aligarh. Both Deoband and Aligarh had their intellectual roots in the Waliu'llahi reform movement of Delhi. Religious disputation (munazara) with representatives of other religions, both in print and on the public platform, became a Deobandi speciality.[15] The leaders of both Deoband and Aligarh were involved in another form of religious debate as well: with members of their own faith. Sir Sayyid's modernist commentary on the Qur'an did not ultimately carry his community. The Deobandi techniques of religious reform were, however, effective in bringing about a greater awareness of Muslim identity and a more general application of Islamic tenets to everyday life.[16] In their desire to improve the knowledge of Islamic law in the Muslim community in general, and to promote the observance of the injunctions of Islam in the personal lives of Muslims, the Deoband *'ulama* founded a department of Islamic legal rulings, which issued *fatawa*[17] in response to queries from Muslims all over India. In addition, the Deobandis wanted to combat the observance of traditional customs that they felt were un-Islamic. For that reason, they showed some interest in the education of women, at least to the extent of improving their knowledge of Islam, since women were the prime practitioners of a host of rituals that the reformers abominated.[18] Mumtaz 'Ali combined all these influences in his career of religious and social reform. While a young man in Lahore he was motivated by his experience of religious disputation. He derived many of his techniques and arguments from the example of his Deobandi mentors, but Sir Sayyid's avuncular interest gave him the courage of his convictions.

Mumtaz 'Ali's *Huquq un-Niswan*, which so irritated Sir Sayyid, showed the influence of munazara in its style, and in content it was a logical extension of a number of concerns of the Deoband *'ulama*. His treatment of women's rights in Islam and concern for women's education, however, are considerably more advanced in spirit than either his Deobandi mentors or Sir Sayyid.[19] The question thus arises how Mumtaz 'Ali became interested in the status of women in Muslim law and society and made this his special cause. His intellectual background raised certain issues and gave him a method of expressing his views, but personal factors doubtless played a role in the development of his attitudes toward women's rights.

First of all, Mumtaz 'Ali's contact with Christian missionaries in debate raised issues of cultural pride and defence. The missionaries criticized Islam (and other Indian religions) for the low status they gave to women and blamed these religions for the lack of education among Indian women. Mumtaz 'Ali knew that the position of women in Islamic law was theoretically much higher than their current status was in fact. The cause of this discrepancy between the legal position of Muslim women and the actual facts of their lives in India, he felt, must be adherence to false customs. Answering the missionaries with theoretical arguments, therefore, was not enough. Changing Muslim practice had to be the highest priority. Women's adherence to custom had to be combated, but so too—and especially—did the views of men who felt that keeping women in ignorance was part of their religion. To attain these aims, he wrote *Huquq un-Niswan*.

Other reasons for Mumtaz 'Ali's concern about women's status were more personal. He testified that, as he was growing up, he felt special sympathy for his sisters. He lost his mother at 13, and his elder sisters may have played an important role in his upbringing, though this is conjectural. Although an educated man himself, he apparently chose as his wife a woman who was uneducated, a point deduced from the fact that he tried to teach her to read and write.[20] She bore him two children, Wahida and Sayyid Hamid 'Ali, and died in 1895. At 35, Mumtaz 'Ali found himself a widower with two small children to raise. His personal loss may have helped focus his considerable controversialist skills on the question of male–female relations in Muslim society and led him to write, or at least to complete, *Huquq un-Niswan*. Sir Sayyid's rough treatment of the manuscript may have convinced him that he would have to publish it himself. The chronology of this period is uncertain, but sometime before his wife's death, he left his government job to devote himself to writing and publishing. Then, perhaps during his bereavement, he became the proprietor of the Rifah-i-Am, a press in Lahore, and started a publishing firm, Dar ul-Isha'iat-i-Punjab.

Mumtaz 'Ali's bereavement and his fledgling publication projects intensified his sense of the importance of women, not only as nurturers of the young, but also as companions to their husbands. This domestic ideal, including the desire for companionship in marriage, was not usually found among Indian Muslims of that day. Domesticity was, however, a Victorian ideal that Mumtaz 'Ali had acquired either through personal contacts or through reading.[21] Most probably, he had come into contact with Victorian views of womanhood in translated books, through reading Urdu works that reflected 'the angel in the house' in the mirror of North Indian Muslim culture. Mumtaz 'Ali had read the novels of Deputy Nazir Ahmad and admired them.[22] Nazir Ahmad's didactic novel, *Mirat ul-'Arus*, first published in 1869, provided the model for the ideal Muslim woman. Its heroine, Asghari, is a paragon: she was educated, a capable manager, a companion to her husband and a goad to his career, but she never violated social norms. She observed strict purdah and always gave her elders and in-laws their due respect.[23] Mumtaz 'Ali needed an Asghari. The woman he found, Muhammadi Begam (1878?–1908) was perhaps as close to that ideal as real life could afford him.

Muhammadi Begam was the daughter of Maulwi Ahmad Shafi who, like Mumtaz 'Ali's father, was an official in the Punjab government service. The families of Sayyid Zulfiqar 'Ali and Ahmad Shafi were acquainted, and they may have been related. The unpublished biography of Muhammadi Begam mentions that when she was tiny, she used to visit 'Judge Sahib' Zulfiqar 'Ali's house to see his daughters, who were on sisterly terms with her mother.[24] It is clear that the women of the two families were close, if not directly related. When Muhammadi was three, her mother died, and thereafter she visited Judge Sahib's house more frequently. Her father later remarried a woman who was apparently her mother's sister, and who came from Deoband.

Muhammadi, like many girls with numerous brothers, grew up preferring boys' games to playing with dolls. She also studied with her brothers, memorizing the Qur'an and learning to read Urdu. When her sister married in 1886 and moved away, Muhammadi learned to write letters in order to remain in touch. She became a good seamstress, making and embroidering clothes for her younger brothers and her sister's children.

When Muhammadi was thirteen, her stepmother spent considerable time in Deoband for a family wedding, and so she kept house, cooked, did the household accounts, and wrote daily to her sister and stepmother. Even as a teenager, therefore, Muhammadi Begam became used to managing a large household and caring for the younger children. Also during this period, she read Urdu newspapers and books and started studying English grammar. Her education, conducted at home, was somewhat haphazard and was related mainly to practical matters. Yet, she mastered academic subjects relatively easily when she found it necessary.[25]

Mumtaz 'Ali was interested in marrying a woman with some education to be a mother to his children and a companion for himself, but, above all, a partner in his publishing projects. He thus turned to the family of Maulwi Ahmad Shafi and to their remaining unmarried daughter, still quite young but already accomplished. He and Muhammadi Begam were married in November 1897, when he was 37 and she was about 19. When Muhammadi came to Lahore, she took over responsibility for his household[26] and for his children, who apparently adored her.[27] In addition, she continued her studies: Mumtaz 'Ali taught her Arabic and Persian; an English woman came to teach her English; a Hindu woman, Hindi; and a neighbourhood boy, mathematics. As if this were not enough, she enthusiastically supported her husband's plans to start an Urdu newspaper for women.[28] Together, they began publishing *Tahzib un-Niswan* in July 1898. Mumtaz 'Ali's treatise on women's rights in Islamic law, *Huquq un-Niswan*, was published in the same year.

Huquq un-Niswan: Women's Right in Islam

Huquq un-Niswan thus emerged from Mumtaz 'Ali's training in Islamic law, experience of religious debate, sense of cultural pride when faced with an external challenge, acute awareness of the need for internal reform, personal anguish of bereavement, and desire for an educated wife. His treatment of women's rights in Islam was not only surprising for its time, but seems enlightened even by today's standards. At the outset, Mumtaz 'Ali stated that people will probably attack him for blindly following the English,[29] but that is not the case. Anyone who knew the *shari'at* and who followed the example of the Prophet and his family must be prepared to reject ignorant customs. He thus placed himself firmly within the framework of Deobandi reform, seeking to revalidate Islamic law and the prophetic example in Muslim daily life, and to eradicate customary accretions that were superstitious, wasteful of human potential and resources or otherwise ill informed and un-Islamic. Deoband sought to equip the modern Muslim with a re-formulation of the fundamentals of his faith,[30] Mumtaz 'Ali wished to equip Muslim women with a reaffirmation of their equality with men as human souls and with a re-formulation of the fundamentals of their rights in Islamic law. Without such a reformulation, Mumtaz 'Ali feared for the health of the Muslim family and the Muslim community as a whole. He stated that keeping women in ignorance and isolation was not a requirement of Islam, and to say that it was betrayed a lack of understanding of religion as well as a fundamental mistrust of women, which was destructive of family life, of human love and of all that the Prophet stood for in a dynamic, just, human society.[31]

In a brief presentation, one can only give the main lines of Mumtaz 'Ali's argument in *Huquq un-Niswan*, characterize his style and comment upon the significance of the work for Islamic reform. Reading through the work, one is impressed by its careful organization, its logical step-by-step argument and its rationality in dealing with a subject that was close to people's intimate lives and emotions. In style, it was like a debate, setting out the various arguments that his opponents might use, and knocking them down one by one. Its language was simple and straightforward. In all his works, Mumtaz 'Ali took care to write clearly and to define words, especially those from Arabic, that might offer difficulty to his readers. Throughout this work, he quoted copiously from the Qur'an and hadith to support his arguments, but he was always careful to translate and interpret these passages as he went along. He had two primary reasons for writing: first, to convince men that women should be recognized as equal human beings and given their rights; second, to communicate with women, who might not know any of the abstruse terminology.[32]

Huquq un-Niswan was divided into five parts: (1) the various reasons why people say that men are superior to women, (2) women's education, (3) purdah, (4) marriage customs, and (5) relations between husband and wife. The first section, an examination of the reasons why men were considered superior to women, was quite a *tour de force*. It involved Qur'anic and hadith commentary, discussion of points of Islamic law and basic psychological assumptions. It was rigorous, logical, and convincing. Of course, whether Mumtaz 'Ali persuaded his opponents that women are not inherently inferior to men was open to question, since, as he admitted, the opposing arguments were falsely considered an intrinsic part of religion and hence were hard to shake by rational argument. Nevertheless, Mumtaz 'Ali would have been a formidable opponent in debate.

He began his discussion by pointing out that although men and women had different physiques and thus fulfilled different biological functions, they were nevertheless both human beings, and hence equal in God's sight. All arguments for male superiority derived either from this biological difference, or else from ignorance of the true message of Islam. He listed the arguments for keeping half the human race in bondage as follows: (1) God gave men greater physical strength, thus in matters where strength was important, including the capacity to rule, men were superior; (2) men's intellectual powers were also superior to those of women; (3) men were superior in religious matters, for God had sent only male prophets, not prophetesses; (4) verses of the Qur'an were frequently cited in support of male domination over women; (5) God first created man and then created woman to serve him; (6) in the Qur'an, it is stated that the testimony of two women was equal to that of one man, and in the inheritance of property, a daughter's share was only half that of a son, hence women were inferior in these respects; (7) men may have as many as four wives at once, thus clearly, God gave men more powers; (8) even in the afterlife, women had an inferior position, for God granted that men will be kept company by beautiful women (*houris*), but women were to be chaste in paradise.

Mumtaz 'Ali then considered each of these arguments in turn, in order to determine whether they were based on reason and thus truthful, or whether they were irrational and thus falsehood. First, no one can deny that men have greater physical strength, but one must also realize that this did not automatically give men the right to dominate women.

Men could cut down trees or cut people's throats; they were naturally suited to jobs that require strength. But did the ability to do such things bestow on men greater nobility or true superiority as compared to women? A donkey could carry more on its back than a man, but did that mean donkeys were superior to men? As for who had the right to rule, physical strength was not the only capacity that counted. Perhaps, in the dark ages, it was correct to say that 'might makes right'. But with the advance of civilization and the founding of kingdoms with laws and other institutions of government, it was more important for the ruler to have understanding and compassion in order to enjoy the confidence of the ruled. Hence the right to rule belonged not to the strong, but to the wise. Further, when women have been called upon to rule, as in the case of the current Queen-Empress, Victoria, they have ruled with great skill, wisdom and justice.

The second argument, that of greater intellectual capacity, was also without basis. 'Man', in the sense of 'human', was higher in intellectual capacity than other animals, but men and women were of the same species and thus must be compared to other animals as one. There was no necessary connection between greater physical strength and greater rationality or intellectual power. Any differentiation between the brain powers of the two genders must be something that society has attributed to them, not that God had granted. Indeed, if the intelligence of women were less than that of men, the human race would rapidly become stupid, for intelligence would be transmitted in lesser degree to each succeeding generation.

As for the religious reason, that there had never been a woman prophet, Mumtaz 'Ali dismissed it by saying that the extant names of the prophets in the scriptures were all men, but there were thousands of prophets whose names had not survived, and who was to say that there were no prophetesses among them? On the more serious question of the greater spiritual strength of men, he pointed out that one cannot compare all men to all women in spiritual matters. Just as some men are more spiritual than most women, so too were some women more spiritual than most men. He gave as examples Hazrat Amina and Hazrat Fatima, the mother and daughter of the Prophet Muhammad, and Rab'ia of Basra, the mystic poet.

The main reason to put men in authority over women, however, was contained in these frequently cited verses of the Qur'an:

> Men are the managers of the affairs of women for that God has preferred in bounty one of them over another, and for that they have expended of their property. Righteous women are therefore obedient.[33]

Mumtaz 'Ali disagreed with the usual male supremacist interpretation of these verses. Analysing the original Arabic, he states that it was by no means clear who had different qualities from whom. It may have meant that some human beings have higher qualities (bounty) than others, but not necessarily men over women. Probably sensing that this was not a very strong argument, Mumtaz 'Ali then presented the view that this verse dealt with areas where men did have greater authority (business and property management), but did not mention areas where women were more competent (responsibility for children, servants, the household). Hence, one could not generalize from this verse that women should be subordinate to men in all things.

The argument that Adam was created first and Eve second and that this proved his superiority was unworthy of serious consideration, said Mumtaz 'Ali. One could as easily argue that God did not want women to be alone, so for her protection and happiness, He created man first. In the matter of court witnesses, where two women's testimony was equal to that of one man, Mumtaz 'Ali pointed out that this verse in the Qur'an referred specifically to business matters, in which women may have less experience. But their lack of experience was a product of social conditions, not an inherent defect. In testimony over marriage, divorce, adultery—matters where women were just as experienced as men—the Qur'an made no distinction. Mumtaz 'Ali went on to cite hadith in support of his argument that there were cases in which one woman's testimony could be decisive. For example: in the case where a woman served as wet nurse to a boy and girl who later married, only she would be in a position to confirm that the marriage was incestuous in Islamic law. Hence, to say that a woman's testimony was unequal to that of a man was a misreading of Islamic law and deprives half of humankind of legal rights.

In matters of inheritance, it was true that a daughter inherited only half the share that a son received. But one could argue that a daughter may take a dowry from her paternal home at the time of marriage, and, in addition, she was entitled to *mahr* (dower) from her husband, so an unequal portion in inheritance was only just to her male siblings. This provision, however, in no way implied unequal rights to property, and it certainly should not be used to argue that the daughter was inferior to the son.

Mumtaz 'Ali also subjected the polygamy argument, that a man may take four wives at once, to intense scrutiny. He argued that the Arabic text permits four wives, but, once again, it was not clear whether it means one at a time, or as many as four simultaneously. He tended to favour the first interpretation, that a man, if widowed or divorced, may remarry up to four times. On the other hand, Mumtaz 'Ali also argued that if a man wished to remarry while still married to his first wife, he must seek her permission. He cited hadith to support this contention, which seemed to go against his first interpretation given above. He also noted that various schools of Islamic law permitted stipulations in marriage contracts forbidding polygamous remarriage, or making divorce automatic in the event of a husband's remarrying. This ruling confirmed the necessity for the husband to obtain his wife's permission before remarriage. Mumtaz 'Ali's position on the polygamy issue, while somewhat inconsistent, nevertheless made a point concerning male and female status: men could not simply do as they pleased without consulting the women involved, and hence women were not mere chattels, but full partners in a contractual agreement, marriage. Thus, the polygamy argument was no proof of male superiority.

Finally, concerning the houris of paradise, Mumtaz 'Ali argued that, although in the Qur'anic verse all the pronouns that referred to 'the believer' were masculine, stating that 'he' will find a spouse in heaven, the true meaning of the verse is that when 'one' goes to paradise, he/she will find his/her spouse there. If this grammatical analysis had not convinced the reader, Mumtaz 'Ali went on to point out that, in any case, believers who enter paradise will have changed their essence, and to the soul, all distinctions of gender were meaningless.

Having disposed of these arguments, Mumtaz 'Ali maintained that the intellectual superiority of men had in no way been proven, and in fact, experience showed that girls, if given the chance, were often quicker and more diligent students than boys. He noted that some boys went to school and derived very little benefit from it, whereas their sisters, without any formal education, might learn to read and write through perseverance. As for moral strength, he maintained that here, too, women had the edge. He gave as an example the plight of widows in India. In spite of the fact that the Qur'an granted widows the right to remarry, Muslims as well as Hindus considered this a great scandal. On the other hand, widowers readily remarried. Women therefore were expected to show greater self-sacrifice in this matter, as in so many others. Was that not evidence of their greater moral fibre?

This analysis of the first section of *Huquq un-Niswan* gives some indication of Mumtaz 'Ali's method. He combined Qur'anic and hadith commentary with logical argumentation and a certain amount of sociological acumen, the whole conveyed in a straightforward Urdu style. His position was clearly reformist, even revolutionary, in the context of his times. He showed that the distinctions made between men and women that were justified on religious grounds were, in fact, the products of social custom. If these distinctions were subjected to the cold scrutiny of reason, well bolstered by a knowledge of the religious sciences, the fallacy and injustice of male supremacy became clear.

Mumtaz 'Ali continued in this vein through the succeeding sections of the work. It is not possible to summarize the entire work here;[34] it is sufficient to note that, however revolutionary *Huquq un-Niswan* was, it had little effect. Part of the reason for that was simply its controversialist format. Religious debate between religions, or even between sects of a given religion, may have excited public interest, especially when the arguments were brief and formulaic and convinced the members of a particular faith that their beliefs were the best. A long, carefully reasoned work such as this, one that asked every Muslim to reexamine his basic beliefs and to change his intimate behaviour, was a different matter. *Huquq un-Niswan* may have caused a few ripples when it was published, but they quickly dispersed. Its original printing of 1,000 copies was never repeated. It was undoubtedly too far in advance of its times. Given the current debate over Muslim personal law reform, however, it should now be reprinted.

Tahzib un-Niswan: Women's Journalism in Urdu

If *Huquq un-Niswan* had few repercussions, *Tahzib un-Niswan* had a rather different fate. When Mumtaz 'Ali and Muhammadi Begam began publishing *Tahzib*, they mailed it out gratis to names on the civil list, hoping to enlist subscriptions. Their prospective subscribers responded by returning the paper to sender, with obscenities scrawled on the label. Somebody plastered a poster on the outer gateway of Mumtaz 'Ali's house, accusing him of promoting prostitution. It was hardly an auspicious beginning to a publishing venture. After three or four months, the journal had only 60 or 70 subscribers. But the couple persisted, and gradually the number of subscribers increased. After four years, *Tahzib* had some 300 to 400 subscribers. The weekly started out with eight pages, then grew to 10, and finally to 16 pages. Both Mumtaz 'Ali and Muhammadi Begam wrote for it, and they solicited articles from friends, relatives and literary acquaintances. Mumtaz 'Ali emphasized that Muhammadi Begam was the editor; he was only the financial manager. She exercised full editorial control over the choice of articles and subjects covered. By emphasizing that a woman was in charge, he hoped to encourage women to contribute. It worked. Over the years, the proportion of articles and letters written by women increased to a majority.[35]

Muhammadi Begam worked very hard to make the weekly a success. She rose early to pray, to take care of the children, the food and the house. She worked late into the night to bring out the journal, personally writing a great deal of the material, editing and answering letters, often not getting to sleep until after 1 a.m. It was no surprise that their first child, a daughter, was stillborn. Mumtaz 'Ali and Muhammadi Begam later became the parents of a son, Sayyid Imtiyaz 'Ali, born in October 1900. Muhammadi Begam was thus wife, mother, companion in life's work, and was educated and an accomplished homemaker. She proved that it was possible for a woman to 'have it all', even in Indian Muslim middle-class society at the turn of the century. But as her sisters elsewhere have more recently discovered, 'having it all' could be hard work. Her health was seriously affected. Unlike Asghari, her fictional counterpart, Muhammadi Begam was mortal. Mumtaz 'Ali became a widower for the second time in November 1908.[36]

Before her death, however, Muhammadi Begam helped to make Urdu journalism for women not only acceptable, but successful. She wrote voluminously: journal articles, novels, books of etiquette, housekeeping manuals and cookbooks. Her novels included *Safiya Begam*, a didactic tale about the evils of marrying off a daughter without her consent, and *Sharif Beti*, a story about a woman starting school at home, patterned, in part, after Nazir Ahmad's *Mirat ul-'Arus*.[37] *Khanadari* was a manual of modern housekeeping, covering such topics as household cleanliness, the proper purchasing and preparation of food, the need to keep drinking water pure, the use of ice, the rules of nutrition and child care, the care of clothing and bedding, hospitality to guests, the preparation of *pan*, among other subjects.[38] *Adab-i-Mulaqat* was an etiquette book dealing with social gatherings, how to offer hospitality at such 'modern' functions as tea parties, and what to do when visiting. This was especially useful information for purdah-observing women who were just beginning to socialize with women beyond their immediate family circle and who were unsure of how to behave.[39]

The content of Muhammadi Begam's writings reflected the content of *Tahzib un-Niswan* during its first 10 years under her editorship. The bulk of the articles in *Tahzib* were aimed at the purdah-observing woman at home, focusing on her need for broadened horizons through the medium of this publication and the communication with the outside world it provided. Articles discussed education, housekeeping and child care, gave recipes, advice to the daughter-in-law on how to get along with her mother-in-law, and tips on etiquette. A constant theme was the reform and simplification of custom, the need to eliminate wasteful expenditure on rituals and ornaments.[40] Mumtaz 'Ali's ideas in favour of women's education and women's rights in Islamic law also appeared in *Tahzib* and achieved much greater circulation through that medium than they ever did in *Huquq un-Niswan*.[41]

Tahzib classified itself as a newspaper, so it also carried numerous short articles and news items, notices of women's meetings and of fund-raising drives for schools, summaries of speeches to reform organizations, as well as poetry and creative writing. Longer pieces were serialized over several issues. The weekly format made possible a great deal of give-and-take between the journal and its readers, and among the readers. An article appeared, and a week or two later, a reply. Or several replies surfaced over the next few weeks, offering a variety of views, often in vehement disagreement with the editorial. The style was straightforward and conversational, aimed at the reading level of women educated at home. One especially popular section was 'Mahfil-i-Ta'hzib', which included letters to the editor and replies, but also letters from readers addressed to other readers—*tahzibi bahin*, the sisterly network of *Tahzib's* subscribers—asking for advice on everything from education and child rearing to gardening tips and how to remove difficult stains. *Tahzib* thus struck a balance between popular format and reformist substance. It maintained a simplicity and clarity of style with a content both practical and high minded. Muhammadi Begam set the tone and secured the collaboration of other well-known or fledgling women writers of the time: Zohra and Atiya Fyzee of Bombay,[42] Bint Nazar al-Baqar of Sialkot,[43] Khujista Akhtar Banu Suhrawardy of Calcutta,[44] and the Begam of Bhopal. Atiya Fyzee sent back accounts of her travels in Europe, and they were published in weekly instalments. Nazar al-Baqar wrote short stories and essays and was also active in fund raising for girls' schools. She later became the editor of *Phul* (Flower), a newspaper for children that Mumtaz 'Ali started about 1910 as a companion to *Tahzib*. Mumtaz 'Ali's publishing firm also produced didactic social novels, educational texts and useful works of advice by a number of early women writers of Urdu, thereby encouraging women's creativity in longer format.[45]

Tahzib overcame initial opposition and succeeded because it met a felt social need. Mumtaz 'Ali was not the only educated Indian Muslim male of his time who desired a more enlightened home life, nor was Muhammadi Begam the only literate Muslim woman of her time who lacked a source of news and an outlet for self-expression. Mumtaz 'Ali articulated his religious anguish and psychological strain in a controversialist work, *Huquq un-Niswan*, that made little impression, perhaps because it was too cerebral. But his long-term solution to his individual domestic and professional needs struck a more responsive chord. His partnership with Muhammadi Begam also resulted in a publication that was considerably less controversial. Women writing for other women were somehow less threatening to the men who had to sanction the subscriptions. *Tahzib un-Niswan*, in the long run, was undoubtedly more productive of social change than *Huquq un-Niswan*, for instead of urging men to change their beliefs, it encouraged women to alter their lifestyles.

That *Tahzib un-Niswan* survived Muhammadi Begam's death was a tribute to the magnitude of her accomplishment. Mumtaz 'Ali's daughter, Wahida, became the editor until her marriage in 1913,[46] and then his daughter-in-law, Asaf Jahan,[47] edited it. Later, his son by Muhammadi Begam, Sayyid Imtiyaz 'Ali 'Taj' and his wife, Hijjab (Isma'il),[48] carried on the family enterprise.

The later volumes of *Tahzib* reflected women's advancing level of education and a variety of activities outside their homes. The style, still clear, became somewhat more complex as the vocabulary increased. Notices of meetings grew in number; speeches by women to women's organizations were reported. Groups of women in provincial towns, following the earlier efforts of their sisters in the cities, organized to raise funds for new girls' schools. Articles discussed the necessity of English education for women, and the journal printed the names of women passing their Bachelor's, Master's, and medical degrees with warm congratulations and exhortations to other readers to do likewise. Articles begin to appear on the current political scene, the events of World War I, non-cooperation, *swadeshi* and the controversy between the Muslims and the government over the founding of Aligarh Muslim University. Women started collecting funds for political purposes: the Khilafat movement and Turkish relief. *Tahzibi* sisters wrote travel accounts of sightseeing in India, in Europe (Rome, Paris, and London without a veil), and of the hajj pilgrimage. Literary criticism appeared. And a greater number of younger women contributors began to take issue with the strictures of purdah, with polygamy and with unilateral divorce.[49]

The latter were issues first raised by Mumtaz 'Ali in *Huquq un-Niswan*, now adopted by the readers of *Tahzib* as their own. Mumtaz 'Ali had also advocated a reform of Muslim divorce law, anticipating by some 40 years the Dissolution of the Muslim Marriages Act of 1939.[50] The readers of *Tahzib*, through their membership in women's organizations, were active in urging its enactment, which was a major breakthrough in Muslim women's legal rights. Mumtaz 'Ali, unfortunately, did not live to see that realization of a cause he had long championed. He died in Lahore in June 1935 while working on a multivolume dictionary of the Qur'an, *Tafsil ul-Bayan*. He was buried in Deoband with his ancestors. One may view this as a symbolic return to his roots in the soil of religious controversy and reform.

Conclusion

Mumtaz 'Ali's polemical writings were initially inspired by debates with Christian missionaries and Arya Samaj reformers in the Lahore of his youth. Cultural pride and defence were very much a part of his motivation in taking up religious debate. But as he matured and gradually focused on the status of women as his prime issue, Mumtaz 'Ali increasingly addressed himself to members of his own faith. In so doing, he used Islamic sources and forms of argument to challenge established notions about women which, he maintained, were based on social customs that went against the true spirit of the Islamic message. His openly reformist work, *Huquq un-Niswan*, was not well received, but instead of causing a stir when it was published, it was largely ignored—surely the worst thing that could happen to a message designed to change society. He was not discouraged, however, but persevered in advancing his ideas through the medium of journalism.

Mumtaz 'Ali's career, his partnership with his wife, their efforts to broaden the horizons of Muslim women through their periodical and ultimately to bring about some reform in women's status have not received their due in historical accounts. The reasons for this have to do both with their means of expression and their chosen audience. Mumtaz 'Ali and Muhammadi Begam were vernacular reformers who wrote in Urdu and based their arguments for change on Islamic traditions of controversy and internal reform. Mumtaz 'Ali brought together a number of intellectual antecedents that included the Deoband school with its emphasis on studies of the Qur'an and hadith, Sir Sayyid Ahmad Khan's religious reformism, and the heated debates among spokesmen for different religions that he had witnessed while a student. He was also exposed to some English education and adopted the periodical press as his medium of communication, but his inspiration, the sources of his ideas, and his chosen language of expression were all from within his own culture.

Muhammadi Begam observed purdah all her life, was educated at home, fulfilled her family roles, and was in every way a respectable middle-class Muslim woman. This husband and wife team chose to reform the Muslim home from within by addressing women, a task that was neither easy nor publicly rewarding in their day. And yet the journal they founded, which survived them, spread ideas in favour of women's education, social change, and legal reform, and made a lasting impact upon the lives of educated Urdu-speaking Muslims for several generations. The study of such vernacular reformers provides a deeper understanding of processes of change in traditional societies and avoids the Westernization–modernization equation that has proven too simple an explanation for a complex phenomenon.

Bibliographic Essay

The life and work of Sayyid Mumtaz 'Ali of Lahore was one example of the concern with the status of women among Indian Muslims in the late nineteenth and early twentieth centuries. Women became the focus of a host of writings by men, and later by women, dealing with the education needed for social and religious reform and to combat Muslim backwardness. Many of these writings issued from adherents of the Aligarh movement, but others were written by 'ulama. Muslim thinkers were coming to terms with the new realities of political power in India and the social and cultural challenges of that situation, but they did so in terms of their own traditions of religious controversy.

Motivation behind this concern for women's status was varied. Cultural defence was a primary reaction to the religious representatives of the West, the missionaries. Early Muslim religious polemicists answered Christian arguments by concentrating on theological issues, attacking the doctrine of the Trinity as being counter to monotheism and charging that Christian scriptures had been altered and corrupted. Summaries of these early polemics appear in Avril Powell, 'Maulana Rahmat Allah Kairanwi and Muslim–Christian Controversy in India in the Mid-19th Century', *Journal of the Royal Asiatic Society* (1976): 42–63; and in Barbara Metcalf, *Islamic Revival in British India: Deoband, 1860–1900* (Princeton: 1982), especially chapter 5. Other useful sources for this period include Christian W. Troll, *Sayyid Ahmad Khan: A Reinterpretation of Muslim Theology* (Delhi: Vikas, 1978); Sir William Muir, *The Mohammedan Controversy* (1897; reprint, Allahabad: 1979); and Imdad Sabri, *Asar-i-Rahmat* (Delhi: 1967).

When controversy with the missionaries advanced beyond basic theological questions to social ethics, Muslims had to respond to Christian attacks on purdah, polygamy, and the ease of divorce in Islam. Cultural defence remained a motive in this later confrontation, coupled with pride in Muslim family life and a desire to develop a more individualistic basis for adherence to the tenets of Islam. Deoband and Aligarh both advanced ethical arguments defending the shari'at as a guarantor of women's rights and attacking Christian hypocrisy. Barbara Metcalf's *Islamic Revival in British India* provides a summary of Deoband's role in legal commentary. Other secondary sources include Aziz Ahmad, *Islamic Modernism in India and Pakistan, 1857–1964* (London: 1967); and Sheila McDonough, *Muslim Ethics and Modernity* (Waterloo, Ontario: 1984). Primary sources include Sir Sayyid Ahmad Khan's articles on women in M. Ismail Panipati, ed., *Maqalat-i-Sir Sayyid*, vol. 5 (Lahore: 1961), 186–208; and Mumtaz 'Ali, *Huquq un-Niswan* (Lahore: 1898). Muslim ethical response also included apologetic ones, exemplified by Maulwi Chiragh 'Ali, *Proposed Political, Constitutional, and Legal Reforms in the Ottoman Empire and Other Mohammedan States* (Bombay: 1883); and Sayyid Amir 'Ali, *The Spirit of Islam* (1922; reprint, London: 1965). Both devoted chapters to the status of women in Islam, emphasizing the historical development of views on women's status within Muslim and Christian religious traditions and the importance of the Prophet's message for women in that context.

The Deobandi best known for his writing on women was Maulana Ashraf 'Ali Thanawi, whose *Bihishti Zewar* became the standard guide-book to religious and home life for generations of Muslim brides. Thanawi's work was an integral part of the Deoband school's drive to abolish non-Islamic customs in the home, as a part of their general programme of Islamization in the personal lives of Muslims. It is perennially in print in Urdu, and a partial English translation is Rahm 'Ali al-Hashmi, *Bihishti Zewar: The Requisites of Islam* (Delhi: 1975). Barbara Metcalf is at work on a fuller translation; see her articles: 'Islam and Custom in Nineteenth-Century India', *Contributions to Asian Studies*, 17: 62–78; 'The Making of a Muslim Lady: Maulana Thanawi's *Bihishti Zewar*', in M. Israel and N.K. Wagle, eds., *Islamic Society and Culture* (Delhi: 1983), 17–38; 'Islamic Reform and Islamic Women: Maulana Thanawi's Jewelry of Paradise', in Barbara Daly Metcalf, ed., *Moral Conduct and Authority* (Berkeley and Los Angeles: 1984).

Another study of customs prevalent among women, written as part of the movement of reform, but also with an ethnographer's eye to preserving a record of such customs is Sayyid Ahmad Dehlawi, *Rusum-i-Delhi* (reprint, Rampur: 1965). Sayyid Ahmad Dehlawi also wrote a number of other works for women, including the didactic tale against wasting time, *Rahat Zamani ki Mazedar Kahani* (Delhi: 1910), and a guide to letter-writing style, *Insha-i-Hadi un-Nissa ma Tahrir un-Nissa* (Delhi: 1910). Sayyid Ahmad also started a newspaper for women which did not survive; he is best known as a lexicographer.

Writers who sought to defend Muslim culture through revitalizing family life by means of women's education include Maulwi Nazir Ahmad, whose novels *Mir'at ul-'Arus* (1869) and *Banat un-Na'ash* (1872) became the prototypes for a host of didactic social novels in Urdu. *Mir'at ul-'Arus* is continuously in print and was translated into English as *The Bride's Mirror* by G.E. Ward (London: 1903). Another writer of the same generation, Altaf Husain Hali, wrote *Majalis un-Nissa* (1874), a dialogue in story form advocating women's education. *Majalis* was reprinted in 1971 by Maktaba-i-Jamia (New Delhi) with an introduction by Saleha Abid Husain. I have translated it into English, together with 'Chup ki Dad', one of Hali's poems about women. They have been published as *Voices of Silence* (Delhi: 1986). *Majalis* was adopted as a textbook in vernacular girls' schools for several generations following its original publication and served as a prototype for numerous other edifying works for the education of women. These include *Tahzib un-Niswan wa Tarbiyat un-Niswan* by Shah Jahan Begam of Bhopal (reprint, Lahore: n.d.); *Kitab-i-Niswan* by Pir Enayatuddin Ahmad (Amroha: 1914); *Baqh-i-Niswan* by S. Abdur Rashid Khan (Hyderabad: n.d.); and many more.

Didactic Urdu novels, written with an eye to reforming Muslim family life and improving women's status, were written by Nazir Ahmad's son, Bashiruddin Ahmad, and his nephew, Rashidul Khairi. Bashiruddin's novels include *Iqbal Dulhan* (Delhi: 1914), *Husn-i-Ma'ashirat* (Delhi: 1914), and *Islah-i-Ma-ishat* (Agra: 1917). The prolific production of Rashidul Khairi, who also founded the women's literary magazine *Ismat* in Delhi in 1908, included the tragic trilogy *Subh-i-Zindaqi*, *Shab-i-Zindaqi* and *Sham-i-Zindaqi*, constantly reprinted by Ismat Book Depot in Delhi, and after 1947, in Karachi. Mumtaz 'Ali's wife, Muhammadi Begam, wrote several Urdu novels, as did

Nazar Sajjad Hyder (mother of the contemporary Urdu novelist, Qurratulain Hyder). These latter were entitled *Akhtarunnissa Begam, Ah-i-Matluman* (1918), *Harman Nasib* (1920) and *Jan Bat* (1935). These are only a few of the many early Urdu novels, of varying literary value, but important as sources of social history. A good survey of these often obscure works is contained in Shaista Akhtar Banu Suhrawardy (Begam Ikramullah), *A Critical Survey of the Development of the Urdu Novel and Short Story* (London: 1945).

Many graduates of Aligarh and other Western-style educational institutions were concerned to find educated wives for themselves and for future generations of the emerging Muslim middle class. This group is exemplified by Shaikh Abdullah, the founder of Aligarh Girls' School in 1906 and a tireless propagandist for women's education in his capacity as Secretary of the women's education section of the Muhammadan Educational Conference. The proceedings of this conference and other Muslim social reform organizations, such as the Anjuman-i-Himayat-i-Islam of Lahore and the Anjuman-i-Islam of Bombay, contain debates about women's education and information about the founding of schools. The records of the Muhammadan Educational Conference are available at Aligarh University; the journal of the Anjuman-i-Himayat-i-Islam is in the Research Society of Pakistan in Lahore. A history of the Anjuman was published in Lahore on its fiftieth anniversary in 1938. A useful short history of the Anjuman-i-Islam of Bombay is S. Shahabuddin Desnawi, 'Anjuman-i-Islam—Ek Tahrik', *Ajkal* (October 1981): 15–22, 45.

The most effective medium of communication of new ideas to Muslim women, however, was the Urdu periodical press. Further, these Urdu journals for women, of which *Tahzib un-Niswan* is a prime example, constitute one of the most useful sources for the social history of Indian Muslims during this period. These journals contain articles by both men and women debating the pros and cons of social and religious reform, various types of education for girls, and the abandonment of useless customs. Periodicals also provided women with useful information to improve their homemaking and child-rearing skills, and offered women a forum for the public expression of their own views. In addition to *Tahzib* (founded 1898), *Khatun* established by Shaikh Abdullah in 1904 and *Ismat* founded by Rashidul Khairi in 1908 were the major journals reflecting the spread of women's education and women's increasing self-expression. But there were many others as well: *Mu'allim-i-Niswan*, founded by Muhibb-i-Husain in Hyderabad in the 1890s; *Pardanashin* of Agra; *Zillus-Sultan* of Bhopal, mouthpiece of the Begam of Bhopal; *Sharif Bibi, Zebunnissa* and *Nur Jahan* of Lahore; *An-Nissa, Khadima* and *Safina-i-Niswan* of Hyderabad; *Khatun-i-Mashriq, Niswani Dunya, Anis-i-Niswan, Avaz-i-Niswan* and *Sada-i-Niswan*, all of Delhi; *Saheli* of Amritsar; and *Hayya, Ziya* and *Harim* of Lucknow.

The bibliography on 'the woman question' among Muslims, broadly considered, is thus voluminous, and includes polemical pamphlets, studies of custom, works of educational value and advice for women, didactic novels, the proceedings of reform organizations and journals for women, not to mention biographies, autobiographies and collections of letters. The primary sources, almost without exception, are in Urdu, though some translations and secondary sources have appeared in recent years. I have found these sources by searching libraries with Urdu holdings in India and Pakistan and by searching out families associated with the founding of schools and journals for women. The most complete files of *Tahzib un-Niswan* and *Khatun* are at Aligarh

Muslim University library. *Ismat* can be found at the Ismat Daftar in Karachi and at the Urdu Research Centre in Hyderabad. Occasionally, as with the manuscript biography of Muhammadi Begam (see note 2), private family papers yield a treasure. I have also found pamphlets, educational works, obscure novels and journals by haunting secondhand booksellers in the Urdu bazaars of the subcontinent. To describe all the treasures unearthed, and characters encountered, in the quest for the invisible women of Indo-Muslim history would take far too long. Suffice it to say that women and the family were central to men's preoccupations as they faced the multiple challenges of the encounter with the West and sought to defend and revitalize their culture from within.

Notes

1. The term 'vernacular' is used here in the sense of a modern Indian language, as opposed to classical or ritual languages such as Sanskrit, Arabic, or Persian, or a modern foreign language such as English. Some have objected to the term as a pejorative, implying a spoken dialect rather than a literary language. That is not the implication here. The Indian languages discussed are literary languages of considerable range and subtlety that also have the advantage of being spoken in their respective regions. With the advent of the printing press, these languages became the media of communication between those who were literate and those who had access to the printed word through various forms of community readings or public performances. For a discussion of this phenomenon in rural Bengal, see Rafiuddin Ahmed, *The Bengal Muslims, 1871–1906: A Quest for Identity* (Delhi: Oxford University Press, 1981), pp. 72–105; for a parallel in early modern Europe, see Natalie Zemon Davis, 'Printing and the People', in her *Society and Culture in Early Modern France* (Stanford: Stanford University Press, 1975), pp. 189–226.

2. There is no biography of Mumtaz 'Ali. The following account is pieced together from: Sayyid Mumtaz 'Ali, 'Tahzib un-Niswan', *Tahzib un-Niswan* (hereafter *TN*) 21, Jubilee no. (6 July 1918): 424–33; Abul Athar Hafiz Jalandhari, 'Maulvi Sayyid Mumtaz 'Ali', *TN*, 38 (6, July 1935): 607–17 (originally published in *Makhzan* in 1927, this article was reprinted in *Tahzib un-Niswan* as an obituary); MS biography in Urdu of Muhammadi Begam, Mumtaz 'Ali's second wife, by her sister, Ahmadi Begam (Begam S. Wahid 'Ali), kindly lent to me by Naim and Yasmin Tahir of Lahore; Interviews in Lahore in 1977 with Naim and Yasmin Tahir (S. Mumtaz 'Ali's granddaughter) and Hijjab Imtiyaz 'Ali (daughter-in-law of S. Mumtaz 'Ali). I would like to express my gratitude to the Tahirs, without whose cooperation this research would not have been possible.

3. Sayyid Ahmad Dehlawi started the biweekly *Akhbar un-Nissa* (Women's Newspaper) in Delhi in 1887, but it closed after a very brief run. Another journal for women, the monthly *Mu'allim-i-Niswan* (Women's Guide), edited by Maulvi Muhibb-i-Husain, appeared in Hyderabad in the 1890s but closed in 1901. *Tahzib un-Niswan* ran from 1898 into the 1950s.

4. Purdah and *zanana*: purdah is the custom of veiling and seclusion of women. Zanana is the women's quarters of a household, usually an inner courtyard. For studies dealing with these concepts, see Hanna Papanek and Gail Minault, eds., *Separate Worlds: Studies of* Purdah *in South Asia* (Columbia, Mo.: South Asia Books; Delhi: Chanakya Publications, 1982).

5. For a history of the school and its reformist intellectual tradition, see Barbara D. Metcalf, *Islamic Revival in British India: Deoband, 1860–1900* (Princeton: Princeton University Press, 1982).

6. Rafiuddin Ahmed emphasizes the importance of religious disputations, or *bahas*, as social events in his *Bengal Muslims*, pp. 75–82.

7. The adversary of the missionary, Pfander, in Agra in the 1850s. See A.A. Powell, 'Maulana Rahmat Allah Kairanwi and Muslim-Christian Controversy in India in the Mid-19th Century',

Journal of the Royal Asiatic Society (1976) (hereafter *JRAS*): 42–63; Christian W. Troll, *Sayyid Ahmad Khan: A Reinterpretation of Muslim Theology* (Delhi: Vikas, 1978), pp. 68–70.

8. The leading Muslim spokesman in the Shahjahanpur debates among Christians, Muslims and Arya Samajis in 1875 and 1876. See Metcalf, *Islamic Revival in British India*, pp. 221–30.

9. Babu Chandranath Mitter later became Registrar of Punjab University.

10. It is worthwhile mentioning that Sir Sayyid, too, was a student of Maulana Mamluk 'Ali Nanautawi in pre-Mutiny Delhi, and hence partook of the same Waliu'llahi intellectual tradition as did the Deoband 'ulama. For an intellectual biography of Sir Sayyid that emphasizes his theological contribution, see Troll, *Sayyid Ahmad Khan*.

11. Jalandhari, 'Maulvi Sayyid Mumtaz 'Ali,' *TN* (6 July 1935): 612; Metcalf, *Islamic Revival*, pp. 212–13.

12. Metcalf, *Islamic Revival*, pp. 141–3; Troll, *Sayyid Ahmad Khan*, pp. 140–3; Sayyid Mumtaz 'Ali, *Huquq un-Niswan* (Lahore: Dar ul-Isha'iat-i-Punjab, 1898), pp. 22–30.

13. Jalandhari, 'Maulvi Sayyid Mumtaz 'Ali', *TN* (6 July 1935): 615–16.

14. Mumtaz 'Ali, 'Tahzib un-Niswan', in *TN* (6 July 1918): 425.

15. See Metcalf, *Islamic Revival*, pp. 198–234.

16. Metcalf, *Islamic Revival*, pp. 1–15.

17. *Fatawa*: rulings on points of Islamic law (singular, *fatwa*).

18. Metcalf, *Islamic Revival*, p. 146. Barbara Metcalf, 'Islam and Custom in Nineteenth-Century India: The Reformist Standard of Maulana Thanawi's *Bihishti Zewar*', *Contributions to Asian Studies* 17: 62–78.

19. Sir Sayyid felt that concerns for women's education were premature, given the then current backward state of men's education among Muslims. Mumtaz 'Ali quotes a letter from Sir Sayyid to this effect in *Huquq un-Niswan*, pp. 57–9.

20. Mumtaz 'Ali, 'Tahzib un-Niswan', *TN* (6 July 1918): 425; Jalandhari, 'Maulvi Sayyid Mumtaz 'Ali', *TN* (6 July 1935): 614–15.

21. For the Victorian ideal of domesticity, see Walter E. Houghton, *The Victorian Frame of Mind* (New Haven: Yale University Press, 1957), pp. 341–93.

22. Mumtaz 'Ali, *Huquq un-Niswan*, p. 55.

23. *Mirat ul-'Arus* has been translated into English by G.E. Ward as *The Bride's Mirror* (London: Henry Frowde, 1903); for a quick summary of the plot, see C.M. Naim, 'Prize-Winning *Adab*: A Study of Five Urdu Books Written in Response to the Allahabad Government Gazette Notification', in Barbara Metcalf, ed., *Moral Conduct and Authority: The Place of Adab in South Asian Islam* (Berkeley and Los Angeles: University of California Press, 1984), pp. 290–314; specifically, pp. 301–2.

24. The MS biography uses the term *choti khala* (mother's younger sister) to refer to Zulfiqar 'Ali's daughters, but this may have been a fictive relationship.

25. This account is taken from the MS biography written by her sister, Ahmadi Begam.

26. Though she had many duties, it was a nuclear household, nor had she a mother-in-law, always the biggest trial for any new bride.

27. According to her sister's account, S. Hamid 'Ali was a particularly difficult child who also had a skin condition that required bandaging. He would allow no one but Muhammadi to change his dressings.

28. Mumtaz 'Ali, 'Tahzib un-Niswan', *TN* (6 July 1918): 424.

29. His phrase is *Angrezon ki Taqlid*.

30. Metcalf, *Islamic Revival*, pp. 11–12.

31. Mumtaz 'Ali, *Huquq un-Niswan*, pp. 3–4; the rest of this section summarizes *Huquq un-Niswan*, pp. 3–42.

32. The Urdu word used to describe his style is *salis*: easy, simple, clear, not abstruse. At one point, Mumtaz 'Ali uses the term *maulwiana* to describe difficult Urdu style, as contrasted with the style he wished to achieve. Mumtaz 'Ali, 'Tahzib un-Niswan', *TN* (6 July 1918): 430.

33. This translation is by A.J. Arberry, *The Koran Interpreted*, vol. 1 (New York: Macmillan, 1955), p. 105.

34. For a complete summary of the text, see my article 'Mumtaz 'Ali and *Huquq un-Niswan*: An Advocate of Women's Rights in Islam in the late 19th Century', *Modern Asian Studies*, vol. 24, no. 1 (1990)

35. Mumtaz 'Ali, 'Tahzib un-Niswan', *TN* (6 July 1918): 424–33.

36. Zohra Fyzee, 'Muhammadi Begam', *TN* 33 (14 July 1930): 585–7.

37. Shaista Akhtar Banu Suhrawardy (Begam Ikramullah), *A Critical Survey of the Development of the Urdu Novel and Short Story* (London: Longmans, 1945), pp. 123–30; Muhammadi Begam, *Safia Begam: ya'ni Bachpan ki Mangni ka 'Ibratnak Qissa* (Lahore: Dar ul-Isha'iat-i-Punjab, 1930).

38. Muhammadi Begam, *Khanadari: ya'ni Asa'ish aur Tahzib-o- Kafayat-i-Sh'ari se Rahne-Sahne ke Qa'ide* (Lahore: Dar ul-Isha'iat-i-Punjab, 1933).

39. Muhammadi Begam, *Adab-i-Mulaqat* (Lahore: Dar ul-Isha'iat-i-Punjab, 1935).

40. This too is a refrain in reformist literature for women issuing from Deoband at this time, as Barbara Metcalf's study of Maulana Ashraf 'Ali Thanawi's *Bihishti Zewar* makes clear. Metcalf, 'Islam and Custom in Nineteenth-Century India'; Barbara Metcalf, 'Islamic Reform and Islamic Women: Maulana Thanawi's *Jewelry of Paradise*', in Metcalf, ed., *Moral Conduct and Authority* (Berkeley and Los Angeles: University of California Press, 1984), pp. 184–95.

41. This summary of *Tahzib un-Niswan's* contents is based on reading files of *TN* from before 1908.

42. These sisters were highly educated and visible members of the extended Tyabji clan of Bombay. They were leading advocates of Muslim women's education and of lowering the barriers of purdah.

43. Urdu novelist, later the wife of Sayyid Sajjad Hyder and mother of Qurratulain Hyder, the well-known contemporary Urdu novelist.

44. Educator and member of the politically influential Suhrawardy family of Calcutta.

45. For a good summary of novels by early women writers in Urdu, see Begam Ikramullah's *A Critical Survey of the Development of the Urdu Novel and Short Story* (London: Longmans, Green, 195), pp. 123–65.

46. She married Muhammad Yaqub (later Sir Muhammad Yaqub) of Moradabad. Wahida died in 1917.

47. The wife of S. Hamid 'Ali, Mumtaz 'Ali's son by his first wife.

48. Also an author of Urdu short stories and novels, and the first Muslim woman to obtain a pilot's license.

49. This rapid survey is based on reading files of *TN* from 1914 into the 1940s.

50. Mumtaz 'Ali, *Huquq un-Niswan*, pp. 168–9; John L. Esposito, *Women in Muslim Family Law* (Syracuse, NY: Syracuse University Press, 1982), p. 78.

17

Gender and the Politics of Space

The Movement for Women's Reform, 1857–1900*

FAISAL FATEHALI DEVJI

Introduction

Late-nineteenth-century Muslim India (or rather élite Muslim north India) witnessed the emergence of a powerful new movement concerned with the reform of women's conditions. The reformers concentrated on female education (the basics of which were literacy, home economics and 'orthodox' practices) as a means of both improving the lot of Muslim women and of the community in general. Thus in 1869 Nazir Ahmad published his first novel promoting women's education titled the *Mirat al-arus*; in 1874 Altaf Husayn Hali produced the *Majalis un-Nissa*, a didactic work on the benefits of female education; in 1896 a women's section was created at the Mohammadan Educational Conference; in 1898 Mumtaz Ali began publishing a women's magazine called *Tahzib-e Niswan*; in 1904 Shaikh Abdullah began another women's journal, *Khatun*; in 1905 was published Ashraf Ali Thanawi's monumental female curriculum, the *Bihishti Zewar*; and in 1906 the Aligarh Zenana Madrassa was opened. These actions, of course, did not pass without comment or opposition—both from within and without the ranks of the reformers. Soon, however, opposition to the idea of female education as such was stilled; and the arguments that now raged had to do with the degree of education that was to be imparted to them. Given that educated women were better able to raise children, manage their homes, improve their language, morals and religion (and so perhaps their marital prospects as well), provide intelligent company for their husbands (keeping them away from courtesans), and advance their community in the world, would not too much learning, going to school, and perhaps associating with male teachers and students lead to disobedience, immorality and a rejection of domesticity? Competing versions of restricted curricula, girls schools and home learning provided answers to these doubts.

Now given that the reformist school might have been in some cases a British-derived institution, what did reformist 'education' (*talim*) mean as a concept? Was it too a colonial notion? A European idea of 'female' education? Perhaps we can find out by comparing a few model curricula: Ashraf Ali Thanawi's *Bihishti Zewar*, first published

*From *South Asia*, vol. XIV, no. 1 (1991).

in 1905, embodies an entire female curriculum in itself, from the alphabet to modes of letter writing, polite conversation, recipes, medicines, managing household accounts, sewing and of course, the rules of religion. These latter are so extensive and detailed that mastering them, declared the author, would make women equal to an ordinary *alim* or cleric. Nazir Ahmad similarly instructed women in household affairs but did not emphasize religion to such an extent. He did include in his curriculum, however, subjects such as geography, of which Thanawi disapproved. Shaikh Abdullah's Aligarh Zenana Madrassa taught Urdu, mathematics, Quran, embroidery, cooking, games, Indian history and geography, and after 1914, English.[1] That part of Hali's model curriculum which does not include domestic management is described by the fictive Zubayda Khatun in the *Majalis un-Nissa*:

> By the time I was thirteen, I had studied the *Gulistan* and *Bostan, Akhlaq-e-Muhsini*, and *Iyar-e-Danish* in Persian, and in Arabic the necessary beginning grammar, in arithmetic the common factors and decimal factors and the two parts of Euclid's geometry. I had also studied the geography and history of India, and had practiced both *naskh* and *nasta'liq* calligraphy and could copy couplets in a good hand. At that point, my father began to teach me two lessons a day. In the morning we read *Rimiya-e-Sa'adat* and in the evening *Kalila wa Dimna* in Arabic.[2]

Apart from their natural emphasis on domestic duties and Shaikh Abdullah's later inclusion of English, what is striking about these curricula is that they faithfully reflect the somewhat differing ideals of traditional men's education. Women, in other words, were in all cases being included in the previously masculine (or courtesan) audience of *adab* (morality and etiquette) instruction and literature. Thanawi's curriculum sets out the adab of the religiously inclined person or minor cleric, Nazir Ahmad's and Hali's curricula describe the education of any worldly, well-to-do man, and Shaikh Abdullah's curriculum, with its inclusion of English, prescribes for women the 'conservative' education of a modern man. In fact all these courses of study were meant to do for women what they did for men: promote civilization and Islamization; in short, conversion.

But before inquiring into the historical meaning of women's Islamization, let us try to contextualize it somewhat. Two points come to mind in this regard: one, that the movement for women's reform was not autonomous but part of a more general Islamic 'revivalism' or 'scripturalism'; and two, that it was not universal but confined largely to a group of professionals (the 'service-gentry', as C.A. Bayly would have it) called the *shurafa*. Instead of seeing in revivalism simply a *sharif* reaction to colonialism, however, I conceive of it as a radical shift in an inter-Muslim dialogue—a shift we can identify with the consolidation of the north Indian shurafa as a polity distinguishing itself against both aristocrat and pleb on the basis of 'true' or 'orthodox' Islam. The shurafa, in other words, who did not exist as a community prior to the nineteenth century, created themselves in and through the colonial order as a distinct 'Islamic' or 'revivalist' polity—a self-creation in which their movement of women's reform necessarily participated. And given that their discourse of reform dealt not so much with the nature of women but with the place or space they were supposed to occupy (morally, intellectually and physically) *vis-à-vis* 'outsiders', I shall examine it in terms of a larger sharif struggle over and shift in notions of Muslim space. Let me begin, then, by describing the two major discourses on social and sexual space that were reformed or displaced by the new sharif orthodoxy.

The Legal Discourse

The legal (Shariat) culture of Islam separated society into public-discursive (*am, suhbat* or *jalwat*) and private-non-discursive (*khas* or *khalwat*) realms, privileging the former as the arena of Islam par excellence. The word 'public' here referred neither to a physical space nor to a popular place, but to located action—to a sort of stage composed of the mosque, courts, schools and market, on which certain élite male actors only were allowed to perform strictly regulated scenes in front of a largely non-particular and non-elite audience.

But the relationship between 'public' men or actions and their 'non-public' audience was not one of State and subject. In the first place, the dialogue conducted by public men was technically one involving individuals and not institutions or 'the State'. For Shariat, as is well known, did not recognize the legal status or agency of abstract groups. Secondly, the actors of the public sphere did not dictate to an audience, they represented it—not politically, to be sure, but as a moral collectivity. Thus in legal culture the *faraiz* or obligations incumbent upon all Muslims are divided under two heads: the *farz al-ayn* and the *farz al-kifaya*. The former comprises 'private' or individual duties due from every Muslim, and the latter more 'public' duties (such as congregational prayer, jihad, choosing or nominating a ruler, adjudging disputes, etc.), which could be fulfilled on behalf of *Muslims as builders of a community*, by a few people. By such representation, or even embodiment of the non-public, then, public actors constituted or even created the whole moral community—or, to be more precise, the moral city (whose philosophical archetype is Farabi's *al-Madinat al-Fazilah*). This is why collections of prophetic tradition (*ahadith*) invariably attach great importance to the exclusively moral and regulated character of public action and publicity:

> Narrated Abu Sa'id Al-Khudri: The Prophet said, 'Beware! Avoid sitting on the roads (ways)'. The people said, 'There is no way out of it as these are our sitting places where we have talks'. The Prophet said, 'If you must sit there, then observe the rights of the way'. They asked, 'What are the rights of the way?' He said, 'They are the lowering of your gaze (on seeing what is illegal to look at), refraining from harming people, returning greetings, advocating good and forbidding evil'.[3]
>
> Muhammad b. Hatib al-Jumahi reported the Prophet as saying, 'The distinction between what is lawful and what is unlawful is the song and the tambourine at a wedding.'[4]

This world of free adult men was opposed on the one hand by the ultimately non-discursive (and so in a sense 'private') wilderness, and on the other hand by the domestic realm of the *zaif* (pl. *zuafa*) or 'weak', the space of slaves, youths and women, where rational or responsible discourse neither occurred nor was heard. The private, in other words, was not only the preserve of a clearly defined group of people rather than the particular lair of the woman, it was also 'pagan' when compared to the 'Muslim' public, because it was represented and did not represent, because it had neither stage nor audience—which further meant, of course, that it was relatively unregulated:

> If a man is away or absent from his family for a long time, then on returning home he should not enter his house at night, lest he should find something which might arouse his suspicion as regards his family, or lest he should discover their defects.[5]

Even when in the 'public' realm, the zuafa maintained their non-discursive privacy. They were supposed to walk through such spaces silently and on their margins, neither looking nor looked at. In fact the Shariat's 'tolerant' blindness towards the private did not merely paganize its denizens by default; rather, the zuafa often seem to have been encouraged to participate in non-Shariat forms of Islam (such as certain forms of Sufism and Shi'ism). And this was because they were deemed to pose a threat to or denial of the public Muslim patriarchate—a threat summed up by the charged word *fitna* (social chaos or disruption). The fitna of the zuafa which necessitated their seclusion and rendered what appears to have been a rather insecure Shariat blind, deaf and dumb, was largely expressed in sexual terms. That is to say the chaos posed by the weak consisted in the extraordinarily potent sexual attraction they supposedly exerted—an attraction that 'un-manned' the patriarchate. So the body of the zaif was eroticized to such an extent that the woman, for instance, came to be commonly described as a living sexual organ (*aurat*) which had to be hidden. If a stranger knocked on her door she could not answer him (for the sweetness of her voice induced fitna) but had to clap. If she ventured abroad she was not allowed to move in a way which made her jewellery jingle, for this caused fitna. Even her scent caused chaos. Indeed the woman, while assuredly not the only inhabitant of the private (the typical erotic scenario of the *Thousand and One Nights*, for instance, introduces an unsuspecting adult freeman into a closed space where women, slaves and youths sinfully disport), emerged as its most illustrious captive and model. Thus Al-Hasan b. Dhakwan warns, 'Don't sit with the sons of the rich, for they have features like women, and they are worse temptation than virgins.'[6] Similarly, we are told in Mas'ud al-Qanawi's *Kitab fath al-rahman* that 'the beardless boy is like a woman. He is even worse. It is even more criminal to look at him than to look at a strange woman.'[7] As for the slave, he is sensualized and feminized most illustriously in the literary figures of Yusuf (who deprives Zulaykha and her friends of all self-control) and Ayaz (beloved companion of Mahmud Ghaznavi).

Legal culture, therefore, paganized the zaif by privatizing, sensualizing, and feminizing them. All of which explains the law's almost obsessive concern with maintaining not only a physical, but also a sartorial and behavioural separation between male and female. Indeed it was the concept of a fundamental *similarity or unity* of the sexes that made gender switching or ambiguity possible and so precipitated an almost obsessive or even fetishistic concern with the sartorial and behavioural separation of sexuality. (In law, for instance, the woman was said even to have an inverted penis and to ejaculate.) The woman, then, posed a threat to the patriarchate not because she differed from men, but because she resembled them too closely. We might even go so far as to say that the zuafa had to be paganized precisely in order to *deprive* them of the inherently integrative legal status and agency which they might have claimed and which an early, struggling Islam had in fact extended to them in the plenitude of its radicalism.

I must make it clear, however, that the Shariat's sexual division of social space did not entail a devaluing of sexuality. Indeed the law always glorified licit sexuality and never dichotomized mind/soul and body or the sacral and the carnal.[8] So in his monumental *Ihya Ulum al-Din*, Imam Ghazzali maintains that civilization itself is a result of sexual satiation.[9] How opposed this is to the western tradition from St. Paul to Freud, which identifies potency and creativity with sexual abstention, repression and sublimation! In fact the opposition does not stop here, for it was precisely the sublimated agape (*ishq, hubb, muhabbat*) which Christianity preferred over eros (*mujun*, etc.) that was opposed by Shariat. It was love, described in the literature as an obsession, an illness which attached one from the outside, that constituted the fitna of the zuafa because it destroyed both the free moral agent required by the public sphere and the latter's rational or regulated dialogue as well. This kind of uncontrollable love, which more often than not involved suffering and even death, both resulted from the sexual division of social space and provided its most potent justification. In effect it subordinated the free, adult man to the loved zaif, and so was unreservedly condemned. Thus Ibn al-Jawzi wrote a whole treatise called *Dhamm al-hawa* or The Blame of Love;[10] Ghazzali, in the *Ihya*, describes love as a form of slavery and so advocates that sexual desire should not become attached sentimentally to personalities;[11] and Kai Kaus, in the *Qabus Nama*, advises the reader not to fall in love with his wife, but if he does, not to tell her.

The Mystic Discourse

The Sufis did not reject the legal division of space into Muslim public and pagan private, but rhetorically privileged the latter as the field of a non-discursive mystical experience (love) more true and direct than the dialectical knowledge of the rational public sphere. We might say that in denying the controlled character of the public, Sufism saw in the relatively unregulated private a vision of freedom. Thus the mystics not only tended to locate their shrines and hospices on the peripheries of the moral city, but also directed their discourse towards the publicization of the previously hidden and non-discursive private. In fact the whole vocabulary of Sufism is concerned with revealing the concealed and breaching the barrier that hides it. The images employed in this respect are the unveiling of the woman, the seduction of the youth, and the breakdown of reserve between the wine-bibber and the servant who serves the wine.

The greatest Sufi violation of legal culture, I think, was its constituting the relationship between man and God as one between lover and beloved—its glorification of agape. Indeed the mystics tended to disapprove of eros, going so far as to manufacture an *hadith* claiming 'Whoever loves and remains chaste and dies, dies a martyr'.[12] Sufism, then, appropriated all the negative elements in the legal discourse and placed positive values on them. So God, for instance, was identified as an irrational, unpredictable, pagan woman (or a feminized, zaif man) who held drinking parties (where the wine of mystical knowledge was served) in exclusively private gatherings, and behaved cruelly to her lovers. These in turn joyfully embraced a painful, obsessive, maddening love which finally killed them. This is the world of ghazal poetry, whose themes simultaneously refer to *ishq-e-majazi* (earthly love) and *ishq-e-haqiqi* (true or divine love). In this way the ghazal is critical not only of Shariat theology, but of Shariat society as well.

Let us examine this curious world in greater detail. The lover (*ashiq*) or mystic is disgusted by the arid hypocrisy of Shariat society and wants to attain union with the beloved (*mashuq*) or God, who is usually described as a pagan (*kafir*) or idol (*sanam, but*). To do this he has to endure not only the persecution of legal society, but the alternate indifference and cruelty of his beloved, who often denies him entry to her exclusive wine parties. The lover, then, spends much of his time trying to leave the public world of Islam, in which he is plagued by the ministrations of her sober comforter (*naseh*) and the harangues of the hypocritical divine (*shaykh* or *waiz*), and enter the private mehfil, *bazm* or *majlis* (gathering) of pagan femininity. But the private sphere, while it is extraordinary and precious, is also insecure and emotionally or spiritually exhausts its visitors, who are not infrequently cast out of it. In effect the private cannot be endured for too long—it has to be balanced by the 'normal' public. Thus the Sufi resumes his legal personality (*baqa*) after destroying this legal agency in union with God (*fana*); thus he observes the external rites because the esoteric (*batin*) cannot be maintained apart from the exoteric (*zahir*). As for those lovers and mystics who suffered to the bitter end, they were fated either to wander the wilderness in a state of lover-madness (*junun*) or self-forgetfulness, or to die and gain release. Indeed Sufism is very fond of tragedies (like those of Layla and Majnun or Shirin and Farhad) because they allow one to sympathize with rebels without having to accept victories over the public order. The legal ideal, therefore, proved in the final analysis too strong for many Sufis and their poetic progeny. And in my opinion this was due not only to the fact that Sufism was partially appropriated by Shariat, but also because the mystics, in criticizing the moral city by exalting a private sphere which existed only negatively, in opposition to the public, indirectly acknowledged and presupposed the moral city. In the end, then, mainstream Sufism's critique of Shariat did violence to the zuafa through a kind of voyeurism—a situation in which the zaif was exposed but still remained mutely pagan.

The Orthodox Discourse

The emergent shurafa of the nineteenth century inherited a tradition in which the moral city was given, and the only dispute lay in evaluating the status of the private. In actuality, however, colonialism had crippled the moral city (a process described in Veena Olden-burg's *The Making of Colonial Lucknow*) not only by destroying or ignoring traditional structures of spatial authority (the arena of religion, for instance, was now decreed to be 'private' as opposed to the 'public' state), not only by attempting to insert a 'neutral' space (such as the market, for instance) into the Indian landscape, but also by locating the institutions of public power outside the 'native' city either in the 'civil' or 'military' lines, or in a parallel city such as New Delhi. And it was from the wreckage of this dislocation that the shurafa were able to build their own private polity or political sphere. What they did, in other words, was to abandon the idea of the moral city and abstract from it areas such as the mosque and the school (the courts and market being surrendered to the 'amoral' public sphere of colonialism), areas which were now seen as private, a privacy confirmed by the fact that the mosque and school as sharif fiefs were paired in ortho-dox discourse with the traditionally private areas of the Sufi hospice or shrine and of the domestic realm. We can see this novel pairing in the following couplet by the poet Ghalib Dehlavi:

> *Dayr nahi(n), haram nahi(n), dar nahi(n), asta(n) nahin(n)*
> *Baithe(n) hain(n) rahguzar pe ham, ghayr hame(n) uthae(n) kyu(n)?*

> Neither temple nor mosque, neither door nor threshold
> It is the public road we are sitting on, why should any rival dislodge us?

And if the shurafa created themselves as a polity by fighting over and appropriating as private institutions certain formerly public spaces (these often violent disputes over ritual and educational practice in mosques and schools being 'categorized' usually as 'theological' differences), they imagined themselves in this role primarily through print or print-capitalism, as Benedict Anderson would have it. Print constituted in reformist discourse the space in which a shurafa-as-readership engaged in endless discussion on their private identity. In a sense print displaced 'located action' as the great arena of discourse a discourse that had once been characteristic of the public sphere or moral city. But print, because it 'disenchants' the word into pure medium, cannot really replace the old public as an agora or forum of discourse, for it allows of no dialogue or interaction, stressing, as orthodoxy in general, the imperative, the uniform, and the linear. And this is due not simply to the character of print, but to the sharif appropriation of writing as an instrument of conquest and consolidation. In a word, writing, like orthodoxy, becomes spectacular or declamatory. All of which explains, for example, the lack of calligraphy on modern Muslim architecture (except as pure decoration or historical nostalgia). Previously one 'read' a mosque, for instance, in a participatory way—where the 'meaning' of the words was determined by one's stance and the architectural support of the calligraphy. Now the word has become declamatory and the mosque spectacular: there is no need to combine the two. Indeed we shall see shortly how the spectacular nature of privatized sharif space (the mosque, for example, simply shouts 'Islam') has made it politically so sensitive.

Writing, however, was not the only *medium* which displaced located action as a means of creating the new polity. The formal meeting, too, provided a brand new venue at which the *sharif qawm* (group-nation) was imagined as an objective and abstract entity. The meeting not only prescribed for a polity which existed apart from it, it also came to 'represent' it in this dichotomous, positivist way.

The privatization of the shurafa, then, went further than a shift in spatial values. Not only did they stress a religion of inner belief over (but not at the expense of) one of outward observances—this attitude being a traditional Sufi and not a modern Protestant one—but they also privileged and directed their propaganda towards the country towns (*qasbahs*) where lay many of their family seats and kin networks. For the first time, therefore, the city exports a cultural system to the countryside instead of constituting a cultural magnet attracting both rural emulation and immigration. This change indicates not only the strongly mobilizing character of sharif orthodoxy, it also tells us that the city, the symbolic and administrative centre of both the old regime and the new, was not going to provide the geographical focus of the shurafa. From now on it was the qasbah or town that was to symbolize the arena of Islam even for the city. There is no greater proof of this than the fact that the two pre-eminent institutions of the shurafa, the Dar al-ulum seminary and the Muhammadan Anglo-Oriental College, were established in the towns of Deoband and Aligarh respectively. And the radicality of this establishment resides not merely in its novelty, but in the fact that the power of the shurafa was geographically and symbolically decentred as far as colonial military and administrative foci were concerned. Furthermore, this strategy resembles the old 'self marginalizing' Sufi policy too closely to be coincidental.

Once the moral city had broken down and the 'private' had come to be seen by the shurafa as a sort of 'fortress Islam' in a sea of hostility, then its old pagan image and denizens came to present a formidable problem to the new, orthodox privacy. We might illustrate this problem by quoting another one of Ghalib's couplets:

Khuda ke waste parda na kabe se utha waiz
Kahi(n) aysa na ho. Ya(n) bhi wohi kaffar sanam nikle!

For God's sake do not lift the Ka'aba's veil, o preacher
Lest that same pagan idol appear here as well!

The poet here identifies the cloth covering Islam's holiest shrine with the veil of the Muslim woman, gives a triple meaning to the phrase 'the same pagan idol' (who is therefore not only a woman or the Divine beloved, but also one of the same idols which the Prophet had removed from the Ka'aba), and plays on both meanings of the word *nikle* (meaning to 'appear' and to 'leave').

As the above verse suggests, the zuafa now came to be seen as pagan idols lodged *within* the gates of iconoclastic Islam. Every one of the reformers viewed the woman, for example, as the agent of a sinister, debilitating corruption that attached itself to vulnerable Muslim men *from the inside*, paganizing them and rendering them unable to defend the faith. I submit that such a paranoid situation could only arise once the Muslim man joined the woman in the intimacy of the private; this feeling of masculine vulnerability *vis-à-vis* the marginal feminine could occur only when these men had themselves been marginalized by colonialism.

How was the threat of the zuafa to be neutralized? Most importantly by hegemonically incorporating the youth and the woman into the sharif polity by education or Islamization. Indeed every single reformist tract justifies this incorporation by raising the spectre of a zaif paganization or corruption of Muslim manhood. And so just as the British were proceeding to 'reform' the character and actions of their exotic, irrational Indian subjects through education, these same Indians were engaged in an identical task with their own 'others'. But this Islamization did not necessarily 'free' the zaif in any sense; rather, the Muslim woman and youth now had to be secluded from the world not because they would otherwise disrupt it with fitna, but because *it* would corrupt *them*. As far as the youth is concerned, this novel theme of the pagan public finds its literary *locus classicus* in Nazir Ahmad's *Tawbat un-Nasuh*.

Islamization might not have 'liberated' the zaif, but it did transform his or her character and function. If the Muslim woman, for instance, could no longer be represented as a source of fitna, the Muslim man in the colonial public sphere could. The woman, therefore, had to be secluded from this impure outside world not only to 'save' her from it, but also to render her into a sort of guardian of orthodoxy whose task was to 'save' men from the wickedness of the public. It is only in the nineteenth century, then, that the woman is exalted as a moral influence, a force for good in the immoral city of colonialism. She often becomes, as Bouhdiba remarks in the last chapter of his book *Sexuality in Islam*, a kind of sexual or non-sexual mother figure. In fact reformist literature replaces the aggressive sexual woman with the pathetic or suffering woman-as-mother. The image of a passive, uncomplaining, silently self-sacrificing woman, in other words, was used to justify her education—was used, indeed, as the *object* of her education in didactic works like Hali's *Chup ki Dad* (Homage to the Silent). And while this image might very well have been used in the beginning merely as propaganda (for women's reform), there is no doubt that it soon became the great feminine ideal. The masochism of ghazal poetry, in which the lover willingly provokes and desires the cruelty of his beloved, is transformed here into a sort of reformist sado-masochism in which men are unjust to women only to feel remorseful subsequently. In the hugely popular novels of Rashid ul-Khayri, for example, there is an endless cycle of cruelty, suffering and remorse: the Muslim man flagellating himself on the altar of woman as the symbol of morality and tradition.

In fact once the woman has become a Muslim the (literary) urge to spoil her, to seduce her from herself, becomes almost unbearable, and literary villains (or anti-heroes) from Rashid ul-Khayri onwards take a curious pleasure in deflowering or corrupting *masum* (innocent) women. As the great symbol of sharif Islam, then, the woman becomes a site of desecration and (temporary or ritual) iconoclasm. And need we be reminded that the seduction which accomplishes this desecration constitutes an early new *literary* mode of masculine violence?

Islamization, however, was not only intended to incorporate the woman and the youth into the new sharif polity, it was also meant to free or separate them from the menial-as-zaif. In his monumental *Bihishti Zewar*, for instance, Ashraf Ali Thanawi only follows well-established reformist tradition when he points out that education will release women from all dependency on menials and enable them to *dominate* over their servants. And this by no means is the only separation effected by reform—for the youth, too, is wrenched from the feminine sphere and placed in a new discursive arena: the school. What we see here, in other words, is a programme of 'divide and rule', where the discourse on youth centres about the school (for the importance of the school in sharif discourse see David Lelyveld's *Aligarh's First Generation*),[13] that on women in the domestic, and that on the menial in a space that is ideologically and even physically removed from the above two. What is more, the Islamization of the zuafa and the destruction of their monolithic alterity seems to have resulted in the creation of a specifically Muslim individualism or individuality; that is to say the nineteenth century witnessed the emergence of an abstract Muslim self into the glare of history.

The sharif discourse of reform therefore meant the complete destruction of what had been a relatively unregulated privacy whose very paganness had given the zuafa a kind of protection and identity. In this way the new orthodoxy was rather modern, for it swallowed whole a space which the law had only cultivated a blindness towards, and which Sufism had merely abused voyeuristically. So, for instance, while Shariat shut its ears to the specialized slang (*begamati zaban*) spoken by the woman-as-pagan, and while sufic literature and its progeny delighted in exposing and employing this dialect, orthodoxy made every effort to 'standardize' and destroy it. And if we are to believe the model objections to Islamisation put forward by female characters in the works of the sharif educators only to be refuted, there did exist resistance to this sort of reform. In Altaf Husayn Hali's didactic tract *Majalis un-Nissa*, for example, various female characters put forward objections to reform based, ironically, on traditional legal arguments of fitna. They failed, of course, and yet I firmly believe that this failure constituted a victory of sorts both for Islam and for the zaif—for they are now potentially in a position where they can conduct a dialogue with the very orthodoxy that produced them, as full Muslims. But time is running out, for orthodoxy has not remained stationary. Today's Muslim woman is threatened not so much by the decrepit survivals of her pagan past, but by new theories of genetic inferiority or biological difference. Once the woman had become an abstract Muslim individual, in other words, she was to be distinguished from men non-culturally and non-psychologically for the first time: her uniqueness now very frequently resting on European-derived notions of absolute sexual difference. The classic text in this regard is Maulana Maududi's book, *Parda*.

Conclusion

There occurs in the nineteenth century a fundamental shift in the politics of space. Whereas before the Mutiny, for example, a westernized man like Lutfullah could defend the position of Muslim women to Europeans, using the traditional argument of public fitna and without once mentioning the need for reform or the importance of the private,[14] some decades later Maulana Maududi would not be considered odd for saying, 'The *harim* is the strongest fortress of the Islamic civilization, which was built for the reasons that, if it ever suffered a reverse, it may then take refuge in it.'[15] Indeed it is very probable that such a shift was expressed architecturally by the movement of the domestic or feminine sphere from the peripheries of the main household or as one of its extensions (like the stables), to the centre of the new Muslim home. But this 'privatized' or 'siege' mentality, which led to the wholesale Islamization of the denizens of the old private sphere, was not necessarily a reaction to a real or complete defeat—for it served as the basis of the creation of a new sharif polity. The destruction of the moral city, however, did invest the private citadels of the shurafa with great emotional power—which meant that any defiance of or threat to them by Muslim or non-Muslim, conjured up violent reactions. And in the twentieth century this 'communal' ideology of space seems to have been appropriated by the non-sharif as well. We see its results today not only in tussles over mosques and monuments, but also in the near-hysteria evoked by all discussions of women's issues—for the woman has become the most illustrious symbol of orthodox privacy. Like space, then, the woman has become nothing more than a spectacle (a spectacle who curiously is not seen). She does not speak, she just *is*. The woman as an exclamation of Islam.

Notes

1. Gail Minault, 'Shaikh Abdullah, Begum Abdullah, and Sharif Education for Girls at Aligarh', in Imtiaz Ahmad (ed.), *Modernization and Social Change Among Muslims in India* (New Delhi: Manohar, 1983), p. 229.
2. Altaf Hussain Hali (trans. & ed. G. Minault), *Voices of Silence, English Translations of Majalis un-Nissa and Chup ki Dad* (Delhi: Chanakya Publications, 1986), p. 81.
3. Muhammad ibn Isma'il al-Bukhari (trans. M.M. Khan), *Sahih Al-Bukhari* (Ankara: Hilab Yayinlari, 1972), vol. 3, p. 385.
4. Wali al-Din al-Tibrizi (trans. J. Robson), *Mishkat Al-Masabih* (Lahore, Sh. Muhammad Ashraf, 1963–4), vol. 2, p. 670.
5. Bukhari, vol. 7, p. 123.
6. J.A. Bellamy, 'Sex and Society in Islamic Popular Literature', in Afaf Lutfi al-Sayyid-Marsot (ed.), *Society and the Sexes in Medieval Islam* (Malibu: Undena Publications, 1979), p. 37.
7. A. Bouhdiba (trans. A. Sheridan), *Sexuality in Islam* (London: Routledge and Kegan Paul, 1985), p. 119.
8. Fatima Mernissi, *Beyond the Veil* (New York: John Wiley and Sons, 1975), pp. 1–2.
9. Ibid., p. 13.

10. Bellamy, 'Sex and Society in Islamic Popular Literature', p. 27.
11. Mernissi, *Beyond the Veil*, p. 60.
12. A. Schimmel, 'Eros—Heavenly and not so Heavenly—in Sufi Literature and Life', in Afaf Lutfi al-Sayyid-Marsot (ed.), *Society and the Sexes in Medieval Islam*, p. 133.
13. David Lelyveld, *Aligarh's First Generation* (Princeton: Princeton University Press, 1978).
14. Lutfullah, *Autobiography of Lutfullah: An Indian's Perceptions of the West* (New Delhi: International Writers' Emporium, 1985), pp. 338–40.
15. Mazhar ul-Haq Khan, *Purdah and Polygamy* (New Delhi: Harnam Publications, 1983), pp. 56–7.

18

Women's Question in the Dravidian Movement *c.* 1925–1948*

S. Anandhi

The Suyamariathai Iyakkam (Self Respect Movement) which was launched by Periyar E. V. Ramasamy Naicker in 1926, in an effort to democratize Tamil society, has been the theme of historical research by several non-Marxist and Marxist scholars.[1] In their writings the movement has been characterized in different ways—revivalist, pro-British, secessionist, anti-Brahmin, etc.

A striking feature of the existing studies on the Self Respect Movement is their silence on its consistent struggle against women's oppression and its attempt to dismantle the ubiquitous structure of patriarchy in Tamil society. Although Marxist scholars like N. Ram and Arulalan have briefly dealt with this aspect of the movement,[2] a detailed systematic treatment of the same is yet to be done. This silence is significant because the question of women's emancipation was one of the central themes in the political agenda of the Self Respect Movement,[3] especially during its early phase.

The present paper is a modest attempt to fill this void in the current scholarship on the Self Respect Movement which is a result of writing history from the male point of view.[4] The paper therefore addresses itself to the question of how the movement perceived the women's question and in what manner it tried to resolve it.

Ideas of Periyar

After establishing a break with the Congress in 1924, Periyar[5] began to articulate, rather stridently, his views on such institutions of Tamil society like religion, caste hierarchy and patriarchy. Opposing the reformist zeal of his contemporaries like Gandhi and those of the past like Siddhar and Ramanujam,[6] he called for a total break with the retrograde elements of the Tamil past. Addressing the South Indian Reform Conference in 1928, he said, '. . . I have gradually lost faith in social reform. For one who believes in radical change, self-respect, equality and progress, the alternative (to the present situation) is not mere reform; but radical reconstructive work which would *destroy the traditional structures.*'[7]

This yearning for a total change marked his position on the women's question too. Within the ambience of the Self Respect Movement he was not content with taking up such conventional themes of women's emancipation like widow-remarriage and women's

*From *Social Scientist*, vol. 19, nos 5–6 (May–June 1991), pp. 24–41.

education which, even if successful, did not undermine the existing structure of patriarchy; but he raised questions relating to basic pillars of patriarchy, like the monogamous
family and the norms of chastity prescribed for and enforced upon women. Even while
advocating women's education, his attempt was to direct it against the structure of
patriarchy. He noted, 'The quality of education imparted to woman till now has been
one of training woman to be an efficient house-wife—by designing the curriculum to
include cooking, music, tailoring etc. Thus woman's education has been an advertisement
to acquire a "qualified" husband.' He argued women's education should have the aim
of providing employment for women and thus making them economically independent.[8]

The most important idea he had advanced was about marriage and family which
he identified as the key institutions sustaining patriarchy. Since marriage enabled women to be enslaved as the property of men he insisted that marriage as an institution
should be abolished. Speaking in a women's meeting at Victoria Hall, Madras, in 1948
he attacked the concepts of marriage and family:

> The concept of husband-wife relationship has been one of master-slave relationship. The
> essential philosophy of marriage has been to insist on women's slavery . . . why should
> human beings alone keep such contract of one-man–one-woman relationship . . . until
> women are liberated from such marriages and from men, our country cannot attain in-
> dependence.[9]

Despite his disapproval of marriage as an institution he approved a certain kind of
marriage which transcended the traditional and socially accepted norms for women. He
opposed all ritualistic practices associated with marriages, including the tying of *tali*
around the neck of the bride by the bridegroom which he treated as a symbol of women's
subjection to men. He also opposed arranged marriages and advocated that men and
women should choose their partners at their own free will.[10]

The notion of woman's chastity, which sustained the monogamous family, was
another subject of his criticism. In one of his pamphlets entitled *Penn Yean Adimaiyanal?*
(Why did women become enslaved?), which was initially written as a series of articles
in 1928, he noted: 'The imposition of "pativratha" qualities on women has destroyed
their independence and free-thinking and made them unquestioning slaves—to men—
who are supposed to demonstrate undue faith over chastity.'[11] He also attacked classical
Tamil literary texts such as *Silaparikaram* and *Thirulcural* for preaching chastity as a
necessary quality for women.[12] Instead, he suggested polyandry and divorce as solutions for women's oppression. In speeches delivered at various places in 1935 he argued,
'Divorce is a protective instrument in the hands of many oppressed women. Along with
Divorce Act there should be a provision for compulsory registration of all marriages.'[13]

According to Periyar, while marriage and chastity were key patriarchal institutions,
patriarchy as such was ubiquitous, pervading spheres like language, literature and gender-
based socialization. In his writings about women's oppression and in his speeches at
self-respect marriages he noted with contempt that the Tamil language did not have
words for the male counterpart of adultress and widow.[14] He invented the neologism
for widower, *vidavan* and for male prostitute, *vibacharan* and suggested their use. He
also noted that several words are used in Tamil literature and in daily life in derogation
of women such as *aanmai* (masculinity). He wrote,

Women should not forget that the word *aanmai* itself is used in derogation to women. . . . As long as *aanmai* will exist, women's slavery will only grow. It is definite that the emancipation of women will not materialise till women themselves destroy the philosophy of *aanmai*. . . .[15]

The Tamil language, in his opinion, was 'barbaric', as it did not have 'respectable words for women'.[16] Delivering a speech at Tirupattur in 1946, Periyar strongly criticized Tamil literature for describing women's bodily features at length and ignoring their intellectual faculties. He argued that unless women oppose such a projection of their image in the literature, neither literary traditions nor their own status would change.[17]

Apart from attacking the institutions of patriarchy and condemning its ubiquitous nature, Periyar also underlined its relationship with the control of property.

When people were totally free without property in land, I do not think there were these slavish practices of women's oppression and compulsory marriage contracts. *When there was no concept of accumulating private property . . . there could not have been any compulsion for acquiring heir for the family—property—through child-birth.* Only when the desire for private property came into practice the concept of marriage and imprisoning women to protect the family property also came into practice. Once a woman was made the guardian of man's property, she herself became his property to produce heir for the family . . . women lost their right to worship their gods but only their husbands. The private property which has been the main reason for women's oppression has to be totally destroyed in order to achieve women's liberation.[18]

In the context of Periyar's view that private property, with its need to have inheritors, gave rise to women's subjection in order to produce heirs for property, his advocacy of birth control assumes significance. Arguing that women should have the right to decide to have children, he differentiated his position from the other advocates of birth control by focusing attention on women's choice: 'There is a basic difference between our insistence on birth-control and others' notion of birth-control. . . . They have only thought of family and national welfare through birth-control. But we are only concerned about women's health and women's independence through birth-control.'[19]

Periyar's trenchant criticism of Hinduism was influenced by its role in legitimizing patriarchy.[20] While addressing an audience of women, he reminded them that the *varanashrama dharma* and Hindu religion had treated them only as *dasis* (prostitutes) of gods who, in turn, tested only women's chastity and not that of men. Ridiculing bigamous gods, he said, 'Sisters, you should never perform any rituals to gods who keep two wives and concubines. You must ask the god why he needs two wives and why does he need a marriage every year! How could you worship stones as gods and fall at the feet of Brahmin priests who have legitimised your slavery through religion and rituals?'[21]

Periyar's commitment to the cause of women's emancipation often led him to be critical of his own political comrades. In anguish, he noted, 'The self-proclaimed liberators of women, the Dravidian intellectuals, have kept their daughters, sisters and mothers as mere decorative pieces at home.'[22] He openly condemned the Justice Party ministry, despite his general support to it, for its attitude towards the women's question and its failure to effectively implement the anti-child marriage act. Periyar demanded the resignation of A.P. Patro and other Justice Party ministers from the party as they had failed to enact any legislation to improve the conditions of women.[23] In his personal life too he was self-critical about his inability to practise his preachings and writings on women's liberation. Writing an emotion-laden obituary of his wife, Nagammal, in *Kudi Arasu* (14 May 1933), he noted: 'I am ashamed to state here that I had not practised even one hundredth of what I wrote and preached about women's emancipation at home with Nagammal.'

Periyar's views on the women's question found practical expression in the activities of the Self Respect Movement. The movement, *inter alia*, practised self-respect marriages, organized women's conferences to raise their consciousness and to highlight their problems and involved women in mass agitations.

Activities of the Self Respect Movement

(a) Marriages

One of the important activities of the Self Respect Movement which challenged the traditional Hindu marriages and introduced radical changes in them was the conducting of self-respect marriages. Self-respect marriages were conducted from 1928 onwards among various non-Brahmin castes. These marriages which took place even in the remote villages and were regularly reported in the newspaper of the movement, *Kudi Arasu*, included inter-caste marriages, widow-remarriages and marriages of consent.

The central aim of self-respect marriages was to free the institution of marriage from Hindi rituals which emphasized monogamous familial norms and chastity for women and thus legitimized patriarchy.[24] Accordingly, these marriages were conducted without Brahmin priests and recitation of religious texts. More significantly they did away with the tying of the tali. In keeping with the rationalistic content of the Self Respect Movement, often they were arranged in times which were treated as inauspicious by the Hindu calendar (*Rahu Kalam*). Some of the marriages took place at midnight,[25] which is generally considered to be an inauspicious time. All these challenged and subverted the religious aura that entrapped the institution of marriage.

We shall give below three such marriages to show how the movement refused to treat marriages as a personal affair and converted them into spectacular political events aimed at breaking the traditional norms of patriarchy.

(1) The self-respect marriage between Sivagami, a young widow belonging to an orthodox Hindu family in Thanjavur district, and Sami Chidambaranar, a Tamil scholar and a dedicated activist of the movement, took place in 1930. Though Sivagami had given her full consent to marry Chidambaranar, there was stubborn opposition to the marriage from both the families. This forced Periyar to shift the venue of the marriage from Kumbakonam, the town from which Sivagami hailed, to Erode, Periyar's own native town, well known for trading activities.[26]

The marriage which was presided over by E.V.R. Nagammal did not have any of the rituals of traditional Hindu marriages, including the tying of tali. Speaking at the marriage, Nagammal explained how tali and other rituals associated with Hindu marriages symbolized the slavery of women to men. The couple exchanged rings, took an oath which emphasised friendship and equality between them, and addressed each other as comrades and friends instead of the usual 'husband' and 'wife'. And, as if to highlight the political dimension of the marriage, it was arranged in the venue of the Second Self Respect Conference itself.

In the evening, to propagate the need for widow remarriages and self-respect marriages, the married couple was taken out in a procession in the streets of Erode by the Self Respect Movement activists. People indeed gathered in large numbers along the route of the procession to watch the iconoclastic couple.[27]

(2) The marriage between Kamalambal and Nallasivan which took place in the same year at Nagerkoil near Kanyakumari generated lot of tension among the members of the Saliar caste who are traditional handloom weavers. It was a marriage between a widow and widower, each of them having a child from their previous marriages.[28] The marriage was conducted by Periyar and Nagai Kaliappan[29] in a cinema hall. In the course of the marriage, the bridegroom transferred Rs 5,000 worth of his property to the bride in consonance with the Self Respect Movement's ideal that women should have equal property right as men.

About 2,500 people visited the venue of the marriage to witness the unusual event. While Periyar extolled the virtues of such marriages, A. Ponnambalanar and M. Maragadavalli[30] sang songs of the Self Respect Movement. Pamphlets dealing with the theme of self-respect marriages and the stance of the movement on the man–woman relationship were distributed to the participants.

(3) The self-respect marriage between two activists of the movement, S. Neelavathi and Ramasubramaniam, took place at Pallathur in Ramanathapuram district in 1930. The marriage was attended by about 2,000 male and 500 women activists of the Self Respect Movement. In addition, about 100 local people also participated in it.[31]

Interestingly, as part of the wedding, the audience were allowed and encouraged to ask questions relating to the man–woman relation, marriage, women's emancipation, etc. One of the participants asked Periyar why the Self Respect Movement allowed a second marriage. Periyar's response was that marriages could only be tentative arrangements between men and women and they should not be treated as eternal. He further said that men and women should have equal right to marry anyone of their preference even after having undergone one marriage and divorce should be permitted.[32]

The above three cases which were among the several marriages reported in the pages of *Kudi Arasu* give an idea of how the Self Respect Movement politicized marriages and used them as public events to propagate their views on the women's question. That was why marriage venues were decorated with the symbols and slogans of the movement. For instance, the self-respect marriage venue in a small village near Cuddalore in 1928 had welcome arches bearing slogans like 'Long Live Self Respect Movement' and 'Long Live Vaikkam Veerar'.[33] The walls inside the marriage hall were adorned with huge posters explaining the objectives and activities of the movement.

Invariably, all these marriages, whether they were held at the house of a lowly Marimuthu belonging to the cobbler caste[34] or a political elite like W.P.A. Soundara Pandian,[35] were attended and addressed by activists of the movement—especially by women activists. They spoke on these occasions on themes relating to women's emancipation and demanded legislative protection of women's rights.[36] In an effort to popularize such marriages, Periyar personally attended most of the marriages during the early days of the movement, even if they took place in remote villages.[37]

The movement organized several thousand such marriages in the Tamil areas during its three decades of political career. For instance, between 1929 and 1932 about 8,000 self-respect marriages were conducted.[38] While certain marriages viewed women's liberation as their aim there were still others which were against Brahmin domination as they dispensed with Brahmin priests and sanskritic scriptures. An exasperated Periyar, addressing a marriage party in 1931, objected to calling every anti-priest anti-ritual marriage a self-respect marriage and said that with time, one of the objectives of the movement should be to do away with marriages themselves.[39] Then, freeing marriages from rituals themselves was no doubt a step ahead.

(b) Conferences

Another important aspect of the Self Respect Movement was the conferences it organized. These conferences, which were periodically organized both at the provincial and district levels were characterized by slogan-chanting processions, long speeches aimed at propagating the ideology of the movement and passing of resolutions on various political themes. The Self Respect Movement used these conferences as a regular political site to take up women's issues and to encourage women's political participation.

The first provincial Self Respect Conference was held at Chengleput, near Madras, in 1929.[40] Apart from articulating its views on themes like the Simon Commission, caste oppression and religious institutions, the conference dealt specifically with 'marriage and other rituals'. It demanded that men and women should have the right over property. The Second Provincial Self Respect Conference was held in 1930 at Erode.[41] Within the ambience of this conference, two other conferences were organized: a youth conference and a women's conference. In the context of organizing separate women's conferences, one may note that Periyar passionately believed that women's emancipation would be possible only by the efforts of women. He was critical of man's advocacy of woman's emancipation: 'As of now, men's struggle for women's liberation has only strengthened women's enslavement.'[42] The proceedings of the women's conferences were fully conducted by women activists and it demanded, *inter alia*, compulsory education for girls up to the age of 16, effective and immediate implementation of anti-child marriage and divorce acts, equal property rights for women, implementation of the Devadasi Bill to prevent young girls from being initiated as prostitutes, etc.[43] The fact that there was a separate conference of women did not come in the way of the general conference and the youth conference taking up women's issues. The youth conference, for example, appealed that young men should come forward to marry widows and *devadasis* who were willing to marry.[44]

The practice of having a separate women's conference along with every major self respect conference became a permanent feature of the movement in the subsequent years. The Second Women's Conference held at Virudhunagar in 1931 increased its demands. It also argued that women should not be recruited only for professions like teaching and medicine, but should be inducted even into the army and police; and it called for powers to the local magistrates to identify those temples which encouraged the devadasi system.[45]

While special women's conferences provided an exclusive space for women activists of the Self Respect Movement to articulate themselves on women's issues, their participation in general conferences was also substantial. That is, women were not 'ghettoized' within the movement. Often the much honoured role of delivering the inaugural addresses of conferences fell on the shoulders of women activists. To cite a few instances: in 1931, Indrani Balasubramanian inaugurated the Third Self Respect Conference at

Virudhunagar;[46] in 1932, T.S. Kunchidam inaugurated the Tanjavur District Self Respect Conference;[47] in 1933, S. Neelavathi inaugurated the Third Tanjavur District Self Respect Conference; in 1934, R. Annapurani inaugurated the Tiruchenkod Taluk Adi Dravida Conference;[48] in 1937, Meenambal Sivaraj presided over the Tinnelveli District Third Adi Dravida Conference;[49] and in 1938 the Madurai Self Respect Conference was inaugurated by Rajammal.[50] In the course of the inaugural addresses, these women speakers discussed the various aspects of the women's question. This participation was born of Periyar's efforts to break the culture of silence which influenced the women activists of the movement: he insisted that even the most inarticulate women activists should utter at least a few words in the women's conference.[51] The success of these self-respect conferences in politicizing women can be summarized in the following words of Singaravelu Chettiar:[52]

> Women who have been confined to the kitchen are speaking today from public platforms; they are debating about public issues; they are involved in social work as equals of men: the credit for facilitating all these goes to Periyar.
>
> It is rare to find women in other movements who are as skilled in public oratory as they are in this movement. During the last fifty years, the Indian National Congress could produce only one Sarojini Naidu.
>
> . . . What an ability women belonging to the Self Respect Movement have in organising their own conferences—independently and with true equality. In other movements, women figure only as an adjunct to men's activities; but in our movement, they function as an independent group and involve in—the movement's—activities demonstrating equality with men.[53]

It was the conference of the Progressive Women's Association, held in Madras in 1938, that bestowed the honorific title 'Periyar' (The Great One) on E.V. Ramasamy 'for his unparalleled activism to transform the South Indian Society'.[54] This title became the short-hand for his name all through his life and after.

Some leading women activists were elected to the Central Council of the organizing committee of the Tamil Nadu provincial conference through the conference every year. For instance, at the Third Provincial Conference at Virudhunagar in 1931, Indrani Balasubramanian was elected as council member. When the Samadharma Party conference was held at Erode in 1933, S. Neelavathi and K. Kunchidam were elected as Propaganda Secretaries to establish the Self Respect League in villages. A few other women like R. Annapurani, and Ramamirtham Ammal, were chosen as district and inter-district Samadharma propagandists.[55]

The women members of the Self Respect Movement not only participated in the non-agitational programmes of the movement, such as conferences, but also quite actively in mass agitations. The most significant mass agitation launched by the movement during the period of our study was the anti-Hindi agitation which continued for over two years, from late 1937 to early 1940. The agitation forced the Congress ministry headed by C. Rajagopalachari to reverse its decision to introduce Hindi as a compulsory subject in the school curriculum.

During the initial phase of the agitation, women members of the movement actively participated in processions and meetings. Women clad in sarees with the Tamil flag[56] printed on them and chanting anti-Hindi and pro-Tamil slogans were a distinct feature of these processions and public meetings.[57] The meetings were also addressed by women activists. For instance a huge public meeting organized at the Triplicane beach in Madras on 11 September 1938 to receive a symbolic Tamil army, which marched by foot from Trichinopoly district to Madras propagating the anti-Hindi message, was addressed by not less than four women activists: Ramamirtham Ammaiyar, Narayani Ammaiyar, Va.ba. Thamaraikanni Ammaiyar, Munnagara Azhagiyar.[58] Also, the women activists organized farewell committees to see off their male comrades to prison.[59]

With the agitation gaining strength over time, batches of women activists courted arrest. The first batch of five women consisting of Dr Dharmambal, Ramamirtham Ammaiyar, Malar Mugathammaiyar, Pattammal and Seethammal were arrested on 14 November 1938, in Madras.[60] Wearing sarees printed with the Tamil flag and singing Bharathidasan's evocative song calling for a Tamil army to save the language, they were led in a procession from Kasi Visvanathan Temple in Pethu Nayakkan Pettai to the Hindu Theological School. On the route of the procession they were stopped at various points and garlanded. For picketing the school, they were arrested and imprisoned for six weeks.[61] Though the judge offered them the option of paying a fine of Rs 50 or undergoing 6 weeks imprisonment, they chose the latter.

From then onwards women activists of the movement courted arrest with different intervals, till September 1939 when the last batch of five women were arrested. In total, 73 women were arrested and jailed for their involvement in the anti-Hindi agitation. Significantly, several of them went to jail with their children, 32 children accompanying their mothers to jail.[62] An exasperated member of the Congress ministry commented that women were getting arrested to get milk for their children in the jail! The Madras provincial women's conference held at Vellore in 1938 demanded that the minister concerned take back his comment and offer an unconditional apology.[63] The Self Respect Movement's newspaper *Kudi Arasu* prominently reported the women's involvement in the agitation and published transcripts of the arguments they had in the court and their photographs. And Periyar himself was arrested during the agitation on the charge of inciting women to fill the jails.

In concluding this section, we shall cite an exchange that took place between a woman activist of the Self Respect Movement, arrested for participating in the anti-Hindi agitation, and a prosecuting Inspector in a Madras Court:

> *Prosecuting Inspector*: You are with your small children, prison is painful and your husband will suffer. If you promise you will not do similar things in future (i.e., participating in such agitations), we shall pardon you.
>
> *Woman activist*: . . . We are willing to bear any suffering for the progress of our language, our nation. Our husbands have no right to interfere in this. They are not the ones to do so.[64]

Women Activists and Their Consciousness

A Case Study

The Self Respect Movement, as we have seen, had provided space for and encouraged political activism among women. To explore how far the movement had succeeded in raising the consciousness of women about their own plight, one needs to construct case histories of these women activists. We shall provide below the portrait of an extraordinary woman who began her life as a devadasi,[65] but transformed herself, over the years, to become a front-ranking participant in the Self Respect Movement.

Moovalur Ramamirtham Ammaiyar was born in 1883 in the Isai Vellalar caste, one of the castes from which devadasis were drawn. She was brought up in a devadasi family at the small village of Moovalur in Thanjavur district, and was initiated into the devadasi system at a young age. Writing in *Kudi Arasu* in 1925, she noted, 'I was born in a traditional non-devadasi family . . . My uncle and aunt persuaded my father to force me into prostitution, through the devadasi custom. They also advised not to marry me away, since I would fetch a handsome amount for the family through the profession, given my talents in music and dance. . . . So my parents forced me into this custom. It was during this time, I deeply thought about this custom as evil and read those religious texts which advocated it. I felt that men have forced certain women into this degrading profession to pursue their indiscreet pleasures and for selfish reasons.'[66] This awareness led her to walk out of the despicable devadasi life and marry a musician Suyambu Pillai of her own accord. This marriage created a furore in her community and resulted in her being ostracized.[67]

Ramamirtham Ammaiyar began her political career in the Indian National Congress. As a Congress activist, her full energy was expended in tackling the question of women's position in Tamil society especially that of devadasis. In her words: 'I have been struggling for the past seven or eight years to abolish this *devadasi* custom. I have also organised a conference to reform our women and break the *devadasi* system. Without invitations, I barged into houses, where marriages were held, to advocate simple marriages and to expose the evils of *devadasi* system. I have forced women to keep the promise of discouraging their fellow women from becoming *devadasis*. Some men have been constantly campaigning against my battle against the system. . . . They are threatening . . . that they would smash my skull if I preach in marriages against the *devadasi* system.'[68]

From her writings, it is not clear why she left the Congress to join the Self Respect Movement. However, it is only evident that her break with the Congress which occurred during the mid-1920s was sharp and complete. In 1956, while remembering her involvement in the Self Respect Movement, she wrote, 'once Gandhi had written to me a letter appreciating my efforts towards *devadasi* abolition. I used to worship that letter. After I left the Congress, not only that letter, even Gandhi had got erased from my mind.'[69] One may note here that Ramamirtham Ammaiyar met Gandhi in 1921, during his visit to Mayuram and this meeting gave added fillip to her activism in the Congress.[70]

In the course of her political career in the Self Respect Movement, she acted as a relentless political campaigner against women's slavery. As a full-time activist of the movement, she addressed various conferences of the movement and elaborated how Hinduism and upper-caste men were legitimizing women's slavery.[71] She arranged and addressed several self-respect marriages in different places, and one such significant marriage arranged by Ramamirtham was the widow-remarriage of Sivagami and Chidambaranar, which we have earlier described in some detail.[72] During the anti-Hindi agitation in 1938, she propagated the anti-Hindi message through a *padayatra* from Trichi to Madras and was arrested. This padayatra started on 1 August 1938 from Uraiyur (Trichy), covered around 577 miles and reached Madras after 42 days. During the padayatra about 87 public meetings were addressed by the group.[73]

Significantly, Ramamirtham Ammaiyar authored essays regularly in *Kudi Arasu* on the condition of women. Here one may note that Ramamirtham Ammaiyar had informal education only upto Third Standard. In 1936, she published a voluminous novel in Tamil running into 303 pages, with the title *Tasikalin Mosavalai Allathu Matipettra Mainer* (The Treacherous Net of the Dasis or a Minor Grown Wise).[74] The novel, which did not follow the tradition of Tamil literary style, however, remained an interesting document since 'it is based on personal experiences of the authoress who after all was a professional dasi herself'.[75] It dealt with how two devadasi sisters who were exploited by wealthy men walked out of the profession and organized the Devadasigal Munnetra Sangam (Federation of the Progress of Devadasis) to abolish the system. This semi-autobiographical novel carried a poignant and political preface in which she wrote:

> My strong opinion is that from the ancient time the temple priests, kings and the landlords, . . . in the name of art, had encouraged particular communities to indulge in prostitution.
>   . . . These days more than the Kumbakonam Shastris, Satyamurthy Shastri have been making noise about preserving the Devadasi custom.
>   . . . Our women have been suppressed in all spheres. The legitimisation of the suppression given through religion and *shastras* is evident in the manner in which women have been assigned the role of prostitutes. Through '*Potarrupu Sangam*' I propagated the anti-devadasi message for which among the Devadasi community itself there were opposition. Prominent religious heads, Devadasi agents, reform leaders—everybody openly opposed my stand. . . . Then I decided that it is easy to oppose imperialism and Brahminism but not the Devadasi System.[76]

Another fictional serial that Ramamirtham Ammaiyar wrote in *Dravida Nadu* in 1945, *Damayanthi*, also deals with the question of devadasis. The woman protagonist in the novel breaks out of the devadasi system and becomes a teacher and accuses religious texts of imposing the practice of prostitution on a section of women and questions the rationale of God's carnal desires to have women as dasis. Through the narrative, she also attacked untouchability and the economic exploitation of the poor by the rich.[77]

An irrepressible activist and a writer, Ramamirtham Ammaiyar finally quit the Dravida Kazhagam (which was the new name the Self Respect Movement acquired in 1944) in 1949 to join the Dravida Munnetra Kazhagam founded by C.N. Annadurai along with others. The reason for her quitting the movement was significant: she did not approve of and openly criticized Periyar's decision to marry a 20-year-old woman when he was 60.[78]

The tale of Ramamirtham Ammaiyar was indeed extraordinary. From being a devadasi, she became a foremost champion of the women's cause in Tamil areas. Her commitment to the cause made her disagree with and break away from Periyar despite two decades of comradeship between them. Ramamirtham Ammaiyar does not represent an 'average' woman activist of the Self Respect Movement, but one who marked the outer limit to which a woman activist of the movement could reach out.

The Women's Question: Two Approaches—The Nationalist Movement and the Self Respect Movement

The radical content of the Self Respect Movement's approach to the women's question can be fully understood only when we compare it with other contemporary political movements. The most important political movement which was contemporary to the Self Respect Movement was, of course, the nationalist movement. For lack of space, we

shall present below a synoptic view of how the nationalist movement 'resolved' the women's question, and compare it with the Self Respect Movement.

In a recent paper, Partha Chatterjee has shown that the nationalist movement resolved the women's question by reworking and reaffirming the pre-existing patriarchal
structure. The nationalists, while approving of imitating and incorporating the material
culture of the west, argued that adopting the west in aspects which were spiritual or
anything other than the material sphere of western civilization would threaten the self-
identity of the national culture itself. As an extension of this position, they located home
as the site to retain the 'inner spirituality of indigenous life' and women as the agents
responsible for that. It was advocated that women could meet this responsibility of preserving the spiritual core of the national culture through 'chastity, self-sacrifice, submission, devotion, kindness, patience and the labour of love'. Only within this 'new
patriarchy' did the nationalist movement attempt all its reforms related to women. As
long as women demonstrated these so-called feminine/spiritual qualities, 'they could go
to school, travel in public conveyance, watch public entertainment programmes and in
time even take up employment outside home'.[79]

The nationalist movement mobilized women in the anti-colonial struggle—especially from 1920 onwards—only within the framework of this new patriarchy. The
traditional feminine roles such as nurturing mother, obedient daughter, god-fearing
chaste wife who would never defy the husband were extended to the public realm to
expand women's participation outside.[80] While Abadi Banu Begam had to appear in
public platforms by presenting herself as a mother by invoking her maternal nickname
'Bi Amman',[81] the Calcutta prostitutes' support to the non-cooperation movement
came under fire from the nationalist intelligentsia.[82]

In illustrating how the nationalists in the Tamil-speaking areas addressed the
women's question, one may begin with the views of Thiruvi Kalyanasundaram, an activist in the national movement and a Tamil writer who enjoyed a pan-Tamil appeal despite
his nationalist politics. In one of his earliest and very popular book *Penin Perumai*[83]
('Women's Pride', 1927), he defined femininity as encapsulating patience, endurance,
sacrifice, selflessness, beauty and love, and essentialized femininity as motherhood.
According to him, all women were created to be mothers and they should be worshipped
since they were the pro-creators as well as the transmitters of moral values to the new
generation of children. Opposing the western type of education, he suggested that girls
should be provided with education that would ingrain in them traditional moral and
religious values and train them in such household duties as husking and pounding of
rice, tailoring, etc.

Muthulakshmi Reddy, another nationalist who took up the women's cause through
her activities in the Women's India Association, is much remembered for her campaign
against the devadasi system. Significantly, her opposition to the devadasi system stemmed from her view that it stood in the way of women being chaste wives. Similarly, she
held conservative views on the question of contraception—despite being a medical
practitioner. She did not perceive the link between contraception and women's freedom
and could only advocate—rather reluctantly—the Gandhian ideal of self-control or
brahmacharya as a means of contraception.[84]

Such tendencies were even more acute in the case of other nationalist leaders such
as C. Rajagopalachari and S. Satyamurthy. When Muthulakshmi Reddy initiated the
debate on devadasi abolition, Rajagopalachari, as the President of the Tamil Nadu

Congress Committee refused to take up the issue for discussion.[85] Satyamurthy on the other hand, went to the extent of claiming that the devadasis represented national art and culture and hence the system should be retained and every devadasi should dedicate at least one girl to be a future devadasi.[86] In the same vein, he also vehemently opposed the Child Marriage Restraint Act, on the ground that it would hurt the sentiments of the Hindus.[87]

Thus the nationalists failed to develop a critique of the institution of patriarchy and rather valorized patriarchy as a necessity. It is only too evident that the position of the Self Respect Movement on the women's question was in sharp contrast to that of the nationalist movement. The institutions of patriarchy like family, marriage and chastity, which were defended by the nationalist movement, were called into question by Periyar and his followers. They programmatically attempted to challenge these institutions through means like Self Respect Marriages. In short, while the nationalists preserved patriarchy even while mobilizing women for politics, the Self Respect Movement mobilized them to contest patriarchy.

In saying this, however, we do not imply that the spread of anti-patriarchal consciousness among the followers of the Self Respect Movement was even. It is indeed true that the movement quite clearly exhibited patriarchal consciousness in its functioning, especially during its later phase. One can cite several illustrations towards this: while in the early phase of the movement both men and women were addressed by a single word 'Thozhar' (comrade), with the formation of the Dravida Kazhagam in 1944 women activists were rechristened as 'mothers and sisters'; in the public meetings and conferences during the anti-Hindi agitation, women activists were introduced in terms of the achievements of their fathers and husbands; during the same agitation, women activists themselves likened Tamil language to a chaste woman like Kannagi and called for women's participation to protect the chastity of the Tamil language;[88] and the Dravida Kazhagam's aims and objectives stated in the Trichinopoly conference in 1945 did not have any specific reference to women's issues, but for calling them to participate in the party activities.[89]

These examples go to show that while the Self Respect Movement challenged patriarchy, it failed to create a new anti-patriarchal consciousness even among its own followers. The old regressive ideas carrying patriarchal values were dormant within the movement and asserted themselves when given the opportunity.

Notes

I am grateful to Professor K.N. Panikkar, Biswamoy Pati, Padmini Swaminathan, K. Chandhu, Karunakaran, Meera V. and Anna Chandy for their insightful comments on an earlier draft.

1. The Self Respect Movement is only one phase of the Dravidian Movement and the present paper deals with only this phase. In its subsequent incarnations, it has taken the forms of Dravida Kazhagam, Dravida Munnetra Kazhagam and Anna Dravida Munnetra Kazhagam.

   For some of the non-Marxist studies on the movement, see Robert L. Hardgrave Jr., *The Dravidian Movement*, Bombay, 1965; Eugene Irschick, *The Non-Brahmin Movement and Tamil Separatism, 1916–1929*, California, 1969; Margurite Ross Barnett, *The Politics of Cultural Nationalism in South India*, Princeton, 1976.

   For the Marxist studies, see N. Ram, 'Dravidian Movement in its Pre-independence Phases', *Economic and Political Weekly*, Annual Number, vol. XIV, nos 7 and 8, February 1979;

P. Ramamurthy, *Ariya Mayaiya? Dravida Mayaiya? Viduthalai Porum Dravida Iyakkamum*, Madras, 1987 (in Tamil).

2. N. Ram, op. cit.; Arulalam, 'The Relevance of Periyar: Caste or Class Struggle?', *The Radical Review*, vol. 2, no. 2, May 1971.

3. A brief obituary of Periyar published in *Economic and Political Weekly*, 12 January 1974, succinctly brings out his lifelong commitment to the women's cause: 'He championed the cause of widow-remarriage, of marriages based on consent, and of women's right to divorce and abortion. Pointing out that there was no Tamil word for the male counterpart of an adultress, he fumed, ". . . the word adultress implies man's conception of woman as a slave, a commodity to be sold and hired." Periyar's demand at a conference two years ago that no odium should be attached to a woman who desired a man other than her husband (which the press so avidly vulgarised), as well as Periyar's advocacy of the abolition of marriage as the only way of freeing women from enslavement, were about as radical as the views of any women liberationist.'

4. In the recent past there have been conscious attempts made by historians to write women's history by amassing different kinds of source materials to make women visible in history. For the importance of the need for writing women's history, see Elizabeth Fox-Genovesse, 'Placing Women's History in History', *New Left Review*, no. 133, May–June 1982.

5. E.V. Ramasamy Naicker or Periyar, a Balija Naidu from Erode, began as a merchant, then became a Municipal Council Chairman of Erode, and later a local Congress leader. In 1920 he became an ardent non-cooperationist, propagating khadi and anti-liquor activities. In 1924 he became the leader of Vaikom Satyagraha and was twice arrested. In 1925, after his confrontation with the local Congress leaders at the Conjeevaram conference he openly criticized Congress for not showing interest in the welfare of the non-Brahmins. Finally in 1927 he left the Congress for good and began the Self Respect Movement.

6. Siddhars were iconoclastic mystic poets who represented a movement of revolt against temple worship, casteism and Brahmin priesthood. Their period was AD 10 to 15. Ramanujam was a socio-religious reformer of the twelfth century AD.

7. *Kudi Arasu*, 26 November 1928 (emphasis mine).

8. Ibid., 10 January 1948, 21 September 1946.

9. *Viduthalai*, 11 October 1948.

10. Periyar had delivered numerous speeches and had written extensively in the party newspapers, expressing the above views. To cite only some instances: *Kudi Arasu*, 22 December 1929, 20 September 1931, 29 September 1940, 17 November 1940, 24 November 1945; *Pagutharou*, 1 April 1936, *Pagutharou*, 7 October 1937; *Puratchi*, 17 July 1934.

11. E.V. Ramasamy, *Pen Yean Adimaiyanal?* (Why did women become enslaved?), Erode, 1942, pp. 11–16.

12. Ibid., pp. 16–25.

13. *Kudi Arasu*, 16 July 1935, 26 December 1929; *Viduthalai*, 24 October 1948.

14. *Kudi Arasu*, 26 October 1930, 21 September 1930; E.V. Ramasamy, *Pen Yean Adimaiyanal?* op. cit., p. 48.

15. *Kudi Arasu*, 12 August 1928.

16. Charles Ryerson, *Regionalism and Religion: The Tamil Renaissance and Popular Hinduism*, Madras, 1988, p. 100.

17. *Kudi Arasu*, 21 September 1946.

18. *Viduthalai*, 11 October 1948 (emphasis mine).

19. *Kudi Arasu*, 14 December 1930, 1 March 1931, 6 April 1931, and *Pen Yean Adimaiyanal?* op. cit.

20. *Kudi Arasu*, 22 December 1929.

21. Ibid., 5 July 1948.

22. Ibid., 21 September 1946; see also E.V. Ramasamy, *Pen Yean Adimaiyanal?* op. cit., p. 62; E.V. Ramasamy, *Vazhkai Thunai Nalam*, Madras, 1977, p. 35.

23. *Kudi Arasu*, 23 September 1928, 29 December 1929.

24. We come across one self-respect marriage in which the couples were Muslims. Hajurulla Mohaideen married Kameeja Begam in 1936 without any religious rites and the bride did not wear the customary purdah during the marriage. See *Kudi Arasu*, 16 February 1936.
25. Sami Chidambaranar, *Tamilar Thalaivar* (Leader of the Tamils), Madras, 1983, pp. 118–19.
26. Interview with Sivagami Chidambaranar, Madras, 5 April 1989.
27. *Kudi Arasu*, 11 May 1930.
28. Ibid., 14 September 1930.
29. Nagai Kalliapan was one of the leading propagandists in the movement who travelled to Burma and Malaysia to propagate the movement's ideals among the overseas Tamils.
30. A. Ponnambalanar was a prominent intellectual who wrote frequently in *Kudi Arasu*. M. Maragadavalli was the editor of the journal, *Madhar Maru-manam* (Widow-remarriage), published from Karaikudi during the mid-1930s.
31. S.A.K.K. Raju, *Neelavathi Ramasubramaniam Vazhkai Varalaru* (The Life History of Neelavathi Ramasubramaniam), 1983, pp. 14–57.
32. *Kudi Arasu*, 12 October 1930.
33. *Kudi Arasu*, 23 December 1928. Periyar was called *Vaikom Veerar* because of his leadership in the Vaikom Satyagraha (Temple-entry Movement) in 1924.
34. The self-respect marriage between Marimuthu and Thaiyammal took place on 20 April 1930 at Coimbatore. See *Kudi Arasu*, 27 April 1930.
35. W.P.A. Soundara Pandian, one of the leading activists in the movement during the 1930s, conducted widow-remarriages and inter-caste marriages among the Nadars.
36. For instance see *Kudi Arasu*, 25 December 1932.
37. Sami Chidambaranar, op. cit., p. 323.
38. E. Sa. Viswanathan, *The Political Career of E.V. Ramaswamy Naicker*, Madras, 1983, p. 99.
39. *Kudi Arasu*, 21 June 1931.
40. K. Veeramani (ed.), *Namadu Kurikkol* (Our Objectives), Madras, 1982, pp. 5–12.
41. Ibid., pp. 13 and 16–21.
42. Sami Chidambaranar, op. cit., p. 218.
43. *Kudi Arasu*, 18 May 1930.
44. K. Veeramani (ed.), op. cit., p. 17.
45. Ibid., pp. 25–6; *Kudi Arasu*, 16 August 1931.
46. *Kudi Arasu*, 16 August 1931.
47. Ibid., 26 June 1932.
48. Ibid., 9 April 1933.
49. Ibid., 27 May 1934.
50. Ibid., 7 February 1937.
51. Interview with Rajammal Vasudevan, Darasuram, 21 November 1988.
52. Singaravelu Chettiar, a leading activist of the Self Respect Movement in the 1930s, initiated the Self Respect League and started the Samadharma Party along with Periyar.
53. Singaravelu Chettiar quoted by C.V.K. Amirthavalliar in her speech made at Kuala Lumpur. See *Kudi Arasu*, 20 October 1940.
54. *Kudi Arasu*, 28 December 1938.
55. Under Secretary Safe Secret file, 16 October 1934, Appendix B, Appendix H, pp. 20, 45–8.
56. The Tamil flag carried the symbols of the three ancient kingdoms, i.e. Chera, Chola and Pandias.
57. Sami Chidambaranar, op. cit., p. 179.
58. Illancheliyan, *Tamilar Thodutha Por* (The War Waged by Tamils), Madras, n.d., pp. 118–19.
59. See, for example, *Kudi Arasu*, 18 September 1938.
60. Ibid., 20 November 1938.
61. Illancheliyan, op. cit., pp. 148–9.
62. Ibid., pp. 148–50.
63. *Kudi Arasu*, 28 December 1938.
64. Ibid., 20 November 1938 (emphasis mine).

65. Devadasis were young girls dedicated, by custom, to temples and treated as wedded to God. In practice, these girls, who were often trained in music and dance, were used as concubines by upper-caste men.

66. *Kudi Arasu*, 13 December 1925.

67. Interview with Mr C. Selvaraj (the grandson of Ramamirtham Ammaiyar), Madras, 13 July 1989.

68. *Kudi Arasu*, 13 December 1925.

69. *Murasoli*, Pongal Malar, January 1956, p. 52.

70. Interview with Mr C. Selvaraj, op. cit.

71. For instance see *Kudi Arasu*, 10 September 1933.

72. Interview with Sivagami Chidambaranar, Madras, 5 April 1989.

73. Iryanan, *Suyamariyadai Chudoroligal* (Shining Stars of Self Respect Movement), Madras, p. 60; Illancheliyan, op. cit., pp. 116–20.

74. Moovalur Ramamirtham Ammal, *Tasikalin Mosavalai Allathu Matipettra Mainar* (The treacherous net of the dasis or a minor grown wise), Madras, 1936.

75. Kamil V. Zvelebil, 'A Devadasi as the Author of a Tamil Novel', *Journal of the Institute of Asian Studies*, September 1987, p. 155.

76. Moovalur Ramamirtham Ammal, op. cit., pp. 2–4. S. Satyamurthy was the then minister in the Congress legislature who strongly opposed the legislation against the devadasi system.

77. *Dravida Nadu*, 22 and 29 April 1945, 13 May 1945.

78. Interview with Mr C. Selvaraj, op. cit.

79. Partha Chatterjee, *The Nationalist Resolution of the Women's Question*, Occasional Paper No. 94, Center for Studies in Social Sciences, Calcutta, 1987.

80. For an elaboration of this argument with instances, see Gail Minault, 'The Extended Family as Metaphor and the Expansion of Women's Realm', in Gail Minault (ed.), *The Extended Family, Women and Political Participation in India and Pakistan*, Delhi, 1981.

81. Gail Minault, op. cit., p. 11. Writing about the nationalist movement, Partha Chatterjee notes, 'In fact the image of women as Goddess or mother served to erase her sexuality in the world outside the home' (see Partha Chatterjee, op. cit., p. 20).

82. Sandip Bandyopadhyay, 'The "Fallen" and Non-cooperation', *Manushi*, July–August, 1989.

83. Thiru V. Kalyasundaranar, *Penin Perumai Allathu Vazkai Thunai*, Madras, 1986 (later edition).

84. Barbara N. Ramusack, 'Embattled Advocates: The Debate Over Birth Control in India, 1920–1940', *Journal of Women's History*, vol. 1, no. 2, 1989.

85. Muthulakshmi Reddy papers, Subject file no. 11, part II.

86. Muthulakshmi Reddy's letter to the editor of *Tamilnadu* (a Tamil newspaper) in Reddy papers, Subject file no. 12, part II, p. 79.

87. *Swadesamitran*, 28 November 1928. A leading Congress activist Salem C. Vijayaraghavachariyar got his daughter, who had not yet attained puberty, hurriedly married, before the Child Marriage Restraint Act could be enforced. See C.S. Lakshmi, *The Face Behind the Mask, Women in Tamil Literature*, Delhi, 1984, p. 22.

88. For instance see, V.B. Thamaraikanni's speech at the Madras Tamil Women Conference in 1938. Illancheliyan, op. cit., p. 138.

89. K. Veeramani (ed.), op. cit., pp. 51–64.

19

Multiple Meanings

Changing Conceptions of
Matrilineal Kinship in Nineteenth- and
Twentieth-Century Malabar*

G. Arunima

Introduction

In 1933 the Madras Marumakkathayam (matriliny) Act was passed by the Legislative Council, allowing the division and partition of the matrilineal *taravad* (joint-family). This effectively brought to an end a pattern of kinship and descent, a mode of production centred on the taravad and, above all, a way of life. This article examines why the matrilineal taravad of the Nayars of Malabar was redefined and strengthened in the mid-nineteenth century, yet legally abolished in the twentieth century by the colonial government. It is argued here that the eventual abolition of matriliny came at the end of a long process of transformation of matrilineal principles and practices. Historicising the changes in the taravad allows one not only to explore the realignments of power amongst the Nayars along lines of gender, generation and changing access to property and authority, but also in turn to view this reordering of power relations as responsible for altering the structure of the taravad.

This article is divided into three sections. All deal with the structure of kinship and the nature of the state. While the first is concerned with the precolonial polity in Malabar, the other two examine the changes over the nineteenth and twentieth centuries in the colonial period. It is argued that by focusing on the changes in the taravad, one can trace the changes in matrilineal kinship over a period of time. This in turn involves a reconceptualization of matrilineal kinship—an exercise that examines why there were variations within the system over time. In other words, kinship is not treated like a compendium of rules which can be mechanically applied to understand the ideas, values or customs contained in the social practices of people.

The attempt here is also to counter the essentialist notions inherent within lineage and later descent theories and their influence on an analysis of traditional societies. These have supported the view that in societies such as Africa and India, descent systems of kinship ensured the stability and continuity of society. The households or equivalent corporate structures that were a product of this system, then, are studied as unchanging,

*From *The Indian Economic and Social History Review*, vol. 33, no. 3 (1996), pp. 283–307.

localized and exogamous units, perpetuating the system through unilineal (patrilineal or matrilineal) descent.

The study of matrilineal kinship among the Nayars has traditionally been the preserve of anthropological scholarship.[1] Most of this work was done from the 1950s onwards, and the primary ethnographic material collated by these scholars was often analysed through the filter of an odd assortment, over a long time-span: of secondary historical information like medieval travelogues, gazetteers and censuses. The result was an idealized notion of matrilineal kinship that was unvarying over time as well as across north, coastal and southern Malabar. Thus, essentially, the twentieth-century model of matrilineal kinship is ahistorical; it does not account for changes in patterns of inheritance, marriage, residence or descent, either in the transformative period between the precolonial and the colonial or within the colonial period itself; and finally it does not provide a historically convincing analysis of the abolition of matrilineal inheritance in the twentieth century.

My attempt here is to offer a historical and alternative method for studying matrilineal kinship. By focusing on the changes in three sets of relationships—between men and women; older and younger kin; and landowners and their agricultural dependants—it is argued that the Nayar taravad underwent significant changes in the nineteenth century. Nevertheless, even in the late nineteenth century, kinship amongst the Nayars was matrilineal—albeit a significant variation from its eighteenth- or early-nineteenth-century versions.

My analysis is situated within the framework of the development of Anglo-Indian law. Anglo-Indian law was the product of the attempts of the colonial state to standardize customs all over the subcontinent, and to create a comparative framework for administering the country. As the emergence of the legal system was coeval with processes of revenue settlement, the colonial administration tried to devise laws that dealt with property and propertied groups. In Malabar, the Nayar taravad was a premier land- and property-owning group. The concern of the colonial administration with land and revenue meant that both internal relations of property of the taravad such as inheritance, management and endowments, and the external relations, especially regarding land, such as sales, leases, mortgages or other contracts, would be affected by the new laws.

Anglo-Indian law was, in equal measure, about Brahmanization and anglicization.[2] Integral to the creation of an Anglo-Indian legal system was the utilisation of both texts and customs of the elite and literate groups, who in most instances were Brahmins.[3] Besides, these were part of a legal strategy to standardize Anglo-Indian law—allowing the customs of Nayars to be compared to Nambuthiri Brahmins and those of Malabar to Bengal.[4] Consequently, the Nayar taravad was included within the emergent legal discourse in the mid-nineteenth century in a genealogy of family forms of the joint Hindu family. This meant that all subsequent legal treatments of the taravad constantly referred to its position within this framework, thereby bringing it in line with patrilineal Hindu families in Malabar, and elsewhere. The changes created in Malabar custom due to legal codification were further exacerbated by the vicissitudes of court procedure. By the late nineteenth century, Malabar was the most litigious district in the Madras Presidency,[5] and the changes in the taravad were marked heavily by legal injunctions.

Anglo-Indian law also redefined and standardized property in men and women which affected internal changes in the taravad. Gendering authority implied that certain functions—such as the management and sale of land, maintaining family funds, entering into legal contracts or otherwise representing the family—came to be seen as the preserve of men in the colonial period. Therefore, this article does not only treat women as the bearers of gender, but also explores the process of creating a masculine identity, with distinct rights and privileges.[6] The changing profile of power within the taravad, it is argued, is the key to understanding the transformations in matrilineal kinship, and its eventual abolition.

I. Taravads in the Eighteenth Century: An Overview

Given the state of extant knowledge regarding matrilineal kinship in the eighteenth century, it is difficult to provide a textured ethnography regarding such aspects as the nature of marriage, household formation, inheritance and property relations. Nevertheless, the available information points to a rich diversity of usages. By focusing on the taravad it becomes possible to speculate about the nature of kinship and politics in precolonial Malabar, both in terms of its internal relations and to the state.

The three significant ways in which taravad expansion and consolidation could have occurred in this period were, first, through the fission or fusion of the large, royal taravads, for personal or political reasons; second, through the integration of smaller families, in the wake of increasing commercialization in property and titles to authority, into the emerging nexuses of power; and third, for women to move off and set up new branches, which over time would form a new taravad. A majority of the taravads which were increasing in power at this time, whether royal or merely landowning, also followed matrilineal kinship.[7] The remarkable feature of matrilineal kinship in this period, as witnessed in the emergent taravads, was that it did not display many of the definite rules regarding descent, succession or inheritance which were a century later to be identified by the colonial administration as constituting matrilineal kinship.[8]

'Royal' Households: What was the notion of royalty in eighteenth-century Malabar? It is suggested here that the process of state formation and the emergence of landed house-holds with extra-economic powers probably occurred simultaneously in the period prior to the eighteenth century. There are two interrelated reasons to believe this. First, the caste of Samanthar appears to have evolved out of a differentiation, in status and power, of the Nayars.[9] Second, the customs, or the patterns of kinship and inheritance of the Samanthar[10] and the Nayar were observed to have been similar, even as early as the sixteenth century.[11] Scholars have argued that the kings of Malabar evolved from local powers like the *vazhunnor, desavazhi* and *naduvazhi* and that these positions were later incorporated as administrative functions within the more organized kingdoms such as Calicut. For instance, the Putturam ballads of north Malabar, dated to the period between the twelfth and the fifteenth centuries, have no reference to the Kolathiri or the king of Kolathanad. However, references to vazhunnor and naduvazhis abound.[12] Similarly, the ruler of Kadathanad within medieval European accounts was referred to as Bavanore (vazhunnor). By 1750, the same ruler had adopted the title of raja, with the explicit consent of the Kolathiri.[13] What is significant here is that most of the adminis-trative functionaries like the vazhunnor were usually Nayars[14] suggesting that many of the newly emerging kings were themselves upwardly mobile chieftains and administrators.

Therefore, three processes could have occurred simultaneously in the precolonial period in Malabar. One was the concretization of matrilineal practices among a large section of the agricultural groups such as the Nayars. The second was the differentiation of status and power among them and the emergence of royal or Samanthar castes. This was coterminous with the evolution of a more sharply defined political hierarchy, where local powers, for example, the vazhunnor, appropriated the rights and symbols of authority of kings (apart from adopting such titles) in their own person. A third was how taravad expansion informed the extension of a ruling family's suzerainty over a larger spatial territory. Conversely, a crisis within a large ruling taravad, say a family dispute, would mean the political fragmentation of a kingdom. It is this third aspect that shall be examined here briefly.

Politically, medieval Malabar was characterized by a remarkable degree of decentralization. This was true despite the fact that the kingdoms of Kolathanad and Calicut exercised nominal suzerainty over north and south Malabar respectively.[15] The period between the fourteenth and sixteenth centuries can be seen as the critical phase of state formation in Malabar. Some of the remarkable characteristics of this period were family dissensions, fresh alignments and consequent expansion of territory and power. The Samuthiri's kingdom around Calicut in south Malabar, one of the strongest and most stable, can be seen to have emerged out of several skirmishes, large and small. What is important for the argument here is that many of these represent the transformation of smaller families (like the Eradis of Nediyiruppu) into bigger royal families (the Samuthiris of Calicut) with increasing military success and consequent political power.[16]

It is important to note that the extension of suzerainty of the Samuthiris of Calicut over a large part of south Malabar did not reveal the presence of critical aspects of state apparatus, such as a revenue extracting machinery or a standing army. To an extent, one witnesses the emergence of a bureaucracy and a judicial system under the Samuthiri in Calicut. The state as such was a nebulous and unstable entity. The political stability of the Samuthiri rajas depended to a large extent upon the shifting loyalties of the petty chieftains (the vazhunnor, naduvazhis and desavazhis discussed earlier) and upon the factional fights within their own families, who were prone to forging realignments with competing power groups in the vicinity.[17] Similar factional realignments were taking place within Kolathanad too.

Therefore, it can be argued that the realignments of *tavazhis* or branches[18] or the disruption of existing families through internal disputes could both lead to the formation of new constellations of power. Control over land came not only through internecine power struggles but also through the sale and purchase of land, as well as the symbols of power and administrative authority that went with it. The gains from these operations were consolidated by entering the commercial nexus, both riverine and coastal. The taravad, as an emergent political force in this period, could be seen as a site of administrative, ritual and economic power. Depending on its size and power it would have one or several branches, which may or may not have had a share in the common taravad property. Nevertheless, quite unlike the colonial reinterpretation of the taravad and matrilineal kinship in the nineteenth century, in the eighteenth century most of these attributes were still in a process of being consolidated, and represented greater fluidity.

Taravads and Commercialisation: The expansion of kingdoms, 'royal' households and landowning taravads occurred not only through land colonization, but also through the sale and purchase of land. By the eighteenth century there seems to have been an established trend for the sale of lands and the authority vested in them, which went alongside the ordinary sale and purchase of arable lands. This is evident from both the *attipettolakara-nam* deeds which registered the sale and purchase of *nadus* and *desams* (administrative units) and the *attipetolakaranam* deeds that dealt merely with land or houses. For instance, in the seventeenth century, Puthuvaypa (known as Vypin from the colonial period onwards), an island situated between Cochin and Kodungallur, was sold by the raja of Cochin to Paliath Raman Iravi and his family. The latter, though a branch of the Talapilli rajas, maintained their separate freehold estate. By this sale, everything that was included in the property and all the rights, economic and others, were transferred from the Cochin raja to the Paliath Achan. The roster of items included,

> canals, washing places, roads used by persons, streams, forests with deer . . . *desam, desadhipatyam* (authority over the *desam*) *amsam, sthanam* (title), *ankam* (battle wager), *chunkam* (customs duty) with everything else.[19]

The sale of lands or houses executed through attipetolakaranam deeds on the other hand, would demarcate the exact location of the lands, and would include a detailed description of the property, 'stones, *nux vomica*, thorn-clump, cobras, holes, mounds, treasure, wells, skies, underground, water-course', in order to indicate that the sale re-presented a complete transfer of ownership, and that the property right was exhaustive.[20]

Some of the early-eighteenth-century deeds reveal that such sales transferred rights over markets, rivers and ferries for transporting produce.[21] At other times rights to the taravad, desam and the temple complex, along with ritual and political suzerainty over these were transferred.[22] The new owners became at one stroke both lords and landowners. Not only did they obtain rights to the lands and its produce, but exclusive rights to forests and waters, as well as ritual authority (*urayma*), and the rights to manage the temple in that desam. The rights being transferred through sales, such as these, provided purchasers with a complex of resources, all of which enhanced their ritual, political and economic status. It is significant that these rights were vendible in the eighteenth century.[23] By the nineteenth, the colonial authorities, as a part of their redefinition of the taravad, were to interpret the rights in these properties as both immemorial and impartible.

Taking the two kinds of vendible rights—one in land, and the other in authority—in conjunction, one can see that there were two different, yet coexisting notions of private property in Malabar. This can be one way of investigating the implications of political decentralization in Malabar. Earlier it was argued that even though by the eighteenth century the powerful sections of local Nayar chiefs had appropriated 'royal' status, many definite characteristics of a state (for example, land revenue extraction) could not be identified in Malabar.[24]

If we were to examine this once again in the light of the present discussion of the privatization of rights, this might begin to seem clearer. The right to own and exercise political authority over the territories acquired granted naduvazhis and desavazhis the ability to consolidate their powers as suzerains. However, the existence of *nirattiper* or freehold property sales meant that there could exist a rung of landowners who could possess complete rights over pieces of arable property within the former's territory, without the need to pay tax. As long as there was no single source of power that held the monopoly of force, or, more importantly, of legality, 'the state' in Malabar was akin to a loose confederacy of households. Moreover, the absence of a central power meant not only that a system of revenue payments was non-existent but also that military obligations could not be enforced. The difference that emerged under the British was that the colonial state represented the overarching source of authority which could reinterpret laws in order to suit their military and fiscal needs.

The saleability of rights to title and authority in the eighteenth century did not impede the growing strength of the taravads. In fact the increasing market in titles and territory was consolidating the power of many petty potentates on the interior. Unlike the Samuthiri, many of them showed a great proclivity for entering into treaties with foreign companies, thereby entering into direct trade relations, and ensuring the promise of political recognition in return.

Thus, till the eighteenth century there seem to have been two distinct processes that shaped the evolution of the matrilineal taravad. The first was the combination of familial upheavals and disruptions that led to new political formations among the Samanthar families in the shape of the 'royal' matrilineal taravads all over Malabar. The second was the integration of sections of both Samanthars and Nayars into existing commercial networks and the purchase of titles of lord and landowner, thereby establishing their taravads as the locus of authority in the region.

Women and the Establishment of Taravads: A third aspect regarding the emergence of taravads in the eighteenth century was that by now most new taravads were established by women. It was suggested earlier that there is no concrete historical evidence of the fact that the Nayars or the Samanthar had always followed matrilineal kinship. Here the object is not to explore why a shift occurred from patrilineal to matrilineal kinship in the sixteenth or seventeenth centuries, but to examine extant customs of kinship, residence and inheritance that were in evidence by the eighteenth century, in order to investigate the nature of power relations. A striking difference between the taravads and matrilineages of the eighteenth from their mid-nineteenth-century counterparts was that these could have been set up in a variety of ways. Moreover, similar processes during both periods could have very distinct political implications.

Take, for instance, the common enough strategy of establishing taravads through elopement or marriage.[25] While the eighteenth-century sources suggest that women moving off in this manner did not forfeit their rights in the taravad property, this was definitely not the case by the late nineteenth century. Another way of setting up a new taravad was for women—either just with family retainers, or with their siblings—to move out to one of the granaries in the outlying areas of the property. This was often because the women had access to their own separate revenues and properties in far-flung areas and setting up a new residence on one of these could tantamount to creating a new tavazhi.[26] Contrary to anthropological wisdom, it was not necessary for a woman and her brother, as a unit, to separate from the main family to be able to start a new branch. The critical difference lay in the fact that whether the new taravad was set up by a woman along with her paramour or husband, her brother, or just several retainers, descent would be traced matrilineally through her. Besides, properties like *cherikal* lands and *sthanums* (a particular status within the taravad which could have a monetary value too) demarcated specially for women within a taravad would be inherited unilineally by them.[27]

Nevertheless, while differences on grounds of gender favoured women in the context of residence, descent and, to some extent, property, the situation regarding formal administrative authority in the public sphere differed. Positions within the local administrative hierarchy, like that of vazhunnor, desavazhi, naduvazhi or raja were held mainly by men (the exception being the *Bibi* or the queen of Arackal in Cannanore, belonging to the Arackal taravad who were matrilineal Muslims). In the light of available evidence, it is difficult to evaluate the transformative impact of gendered differences in formal political power of this nature on the relations within the household. It appears that despite formal political power being weighted in favour of men, the nature of authority or property rights within the taravad were not affected significantly.

This is particularly interesting in the case of the *karnavasthanum*—the status of Karnavar that could be seen in some of the larger families. One such were the 'Coyotorical Carnaver' (Koyitara Karnavar) identified by Barbosa, in the sixteenth century, as the governors of the Calicut kingdom. These were probably administrative functionaries who were given the title of Karnavar. There is nothing to suggest yet that the existence of a special *sthanum* of *karnavan* implied that the incumbents to this position were all male, or were the heads, or had greater and undisputed privileges than other members of the taravad. In fact, in 1807, Buchanan noted with special reference to north Malabar that the Nayar taravads were managed by older women and that this right was generally inherited through the female line.[28] Therefore, until the early nineteenth century it could be argued that power differences within the household were more along lines of *generation* than *gender*.

The coexistence of a highly commercialized land market with separate rights to property, especially for women of large taravads, implied that the principle of co-residence could not have been enforced. Similarly, movable properties of an intestate owner were divided equally among the surviving members, irrespective of their sex,[29] unlike court dicta to the converse in the colonial period. Thus, the identifiers of matrilineal kinship according to mid-nineteenth-century colonial jurists and judges, such as co-residence, impartibility and the inalienability of property, were definitely not an essential part of the customary practice in precolonial Malabar.

II. Colonial Redefinitions of the Taravad

With the defeat of Tipu Sultan in 1792, Malabar was officially incorporated into the East India Company's dominions. The legal changes that ensued in the following decades of the Company's and later the Crown's rule had a profound effect on the changes in the matrilineal taravad. It is argued here that Anglo-Indian law and its operation, both procedural (as in case-laws) and textual (as in law books and in high court judgements), redefined the taravad in the nineteenth century. Three broad changes occurred in the first four decades of the nineteenth century. These were the formal identification of a hierarchy of property rights and the legal definition of tenurial statuses; the redefinition of the taravad as an impartible and corporate unit with inalienable rights in land, with the simultaneous selection of a single individual with whom revenue could be settled; and the choice of the eldest male on grounds of age and gender as the individual responsible for managing its economy and making revenue payments. All these changes affected both the internal structure of the taravad and its relation with its external dependants.

Legal Redefinitions: Authority and Property Under Company Rule: In the first four or five decades of the Company's rule there was no clear consensus on how to treat the Nayar taravad or its branches. At the level of the higher courts (provincial, district and *sudr*) there was emerging a tendency to curtail the division of family property.[30] This was often done on grounds of upholding matrilineal law on the basis of Nambudiri Brahmin opinion, *which chose to vest greater rights in the property with the eldest male.*[31] In Malabar, as in Bengal, court officials solicited Brahmin opinion on questions of customary practice in the belief that their origin lay in religious laws. It is interesting that Nambudiri interventions reflected their own customary familial arrangements.

In general it could be said that lower-level courts had not yet begun to follow the precedents set by the sudr court. Court cases demonstrate that both in north and south Malabar it was local usages, and not Nambudiri precepts, that were paramount.[32] Therefore, in the lower courts, if it could be demonstrated that all members of the taravad were aware of, and had consented to, the division, it was considered legally permissible.[33] This was to change by the latter half of the nineteenth century.

Nevertheless, in the early decades of the nineteenth century, even in the absence of a clear legal principle regarding either the treatment of the household or of matrilineal kinship, there was beginning to emerge a distinctive difference in the state's treatment of the taravad. The changes in the structure of authority within the taravad affected the manner in which members within a landholding family could have control over land or capital. Over time, this was reflected in the recognition of the eldest male as the head of the family, invested with incontrovertible rights over the management of the family property. The further recognition of these men as the figures to settle with bolstered their strength.[34]

I would argue that redefining the taravad in relation to its property was tantamount to reinterpreting property itself. Besides, gendering rights and privileges within the taravad had implications for economic and non-economic matters. The investiture of putative rights on men, to headship and to represent the taravad, was akin to a sexual contract[35] between these men and the state. It is argued here that such a sexual contract not only altered power relations within the taravad, by allowing for the evolution of a *patriarchal* figure in the person of the eldest uncle, it also helped to freeze the fluid cultural practices hitherto understood as integral to the Nayar community. For the first time the status of the mother's brother begins to acquire greater political significance, with the mother–child unit being represented as purely domestic or apolitical, transforming the meaning of matrilineal kinship. By the late nineteenth century sexual practices within the matrilineal community would themselves come under severe criticism.

Agrarian Crisis and Legal Intervention: Mid-nineteenth-century changes in agrarian relations further affected power relations within the taravad. Between the 1840s and the 1870s the powers of the Hindu landowners were strengthened by the state's intervention in land rights. The 1840s in Malabar was a period of acute agrarian strife and political unrest, which particularly affected the two southern talukas of Ernad and Walluvanad. It is argued here that while the spate of agrarian violence, or the Moplah outbreaks of the mid-nineteenth century, provided an immediate reason for the judicial redefinition of the taravad, these in turn were a result of the changing economic fortunes of the landed families.

The period between 1825 and 1850 in Malabar had been, unlike the rest of the Presidency, a period of agricultural boom, which allowed the taravads to regain their monetary status to some extent. This allowed the taravads to redeem lands leased to

tenants and cultivators, leading to evictions. Besides, the continuation of revenue collection in this period aggravated the distressed condition of the cultivating populations.
The violence against the feudal lords, bulwarks of the Company's rule, caused panic
amongst the British administrators.[36]

In February 1852, Thomas Lumisden Strange was appointed Special Commissioner
to enquire into the causes of the Mappilla 'outrages'. Strange's intervention in the
agrarian relations of Malabar was the first step providing inalienable rights on lands to
the Hindu proprietors. He argued, on the basis of 'Hindu law', that the landlords of
Malabar could not part with their family estates as their *religious* duty bound them to
it. The fact that landlords always parted with their estates, on mortgages or sales, was
interpreted by Strange as a seasonal relinquishment, and he argued that it would sooner
or later, revert to them.[37] He went on to refine his opinions regarding the property laws
of Malabar and emphasized that the head of the family had exclusive control over the
family and its property.

> Hindus suffer by the idea which has been introduced that a joint share in property involves
> a number of individual shares any of which may be divided off from the estate and forfeited
> to a creditor of the assumed shareholder, *whereas the theory of a Hindu family in Malabar
> is that the head of a family has entire control*, his signature alone can be taken for exigencies
> of the family for due support of the whole, for whom he is responsible.[38] [emphasis added]

There were two implications of his assessment. First, that the Hindu taravads possessed inalienable rights over property; this strengthened not only their claims to a
greater share of the usufruct in relation to their cultivators, but also created the potential
for easy evictions. Second, the investiture of greater rights with the head of the family
over practically all property matters meant the creation of power differences within the
landowning taravad itself.

Co-residence: From the latter half of the 1860s there was an appreciable difference in the
ways in which the courts treated the taravad. Increasingly, it was being represented as an
indivisible and coresidential unit. The implication of this was that from now on, the
courts recognized only those members *who lived together* as part of a taravad. Paradoxically, this meant undermining the power of the larger taravads, as the higher courts
tended to treat each branch of a taravad as a house-and-land unit.[39] These decisions were
challenged by both the household heads and the junior branches. Most karnavans, in
this period of their increasing power, did not welcome separation of the branches from
the main taravad, as they could not dictate terms to them or even hope to control their
assets. Soon a novel strategy was evolved for subverting court orders that forbade the
unity of material interests between the taravad and its branches. This was to establish
formal leases with the branches, or with members of the family who had moved off to
the outlying areas of the estates, and to appoint bailiffs to look after these lands. In other
words, many of the younger members of the taravad, or its branches, were treated as
tenants of the family.[40] Similarly, bailiffs appointed by the family could be its own members—thereby converting a family member into an employee, and providing his maintenance in the form of a salary.[41]

The strategy of leasing lands to members of their own taravads afforded the heads
with many advantages in the latter half of the nineteenth century. Since the head's own

powers were being legally bolstered during this period, this provided a good opportunity for keeping a tight rein over the management of the taravad and the branches. Second, by reducing several members to the status of tenants, the power of the head over the family and agrarian economy grew significantly. Finally, as the improvements made by the members of the family on lands leased to them were not treated as part of the taravad property, it could constitute a part (and often the whole) of their maintenance, reducing the burden on the taravad karnavan to provide them with separate maintenance.[42]

'Patria Potestas' or Reconstituting the Malabar Karnavan: The changed notions of headship from the mid-nineteenth century had critical repercussions for a redefinition of matriliny, especially regarding guardianship, the rights of women to headship, and the rights of younger members within the family.

The creation of the karnavan as a natural, all-powerful figure of authority meant relegating all others within the taravad to the status of dependent kin, accompanied by the assertion that the karnavan was the sole guardian of every member. In a representative dispute of 1872, the courts granted the karnavan the authority to act as the guardian of two children within the taravad, on grounds of *natural right*:

> by the principles of the *laws of Malabar*, the mother herself, while alive and her children too, were under the guardianship of the head of the family, the karnavan. *Their position was precisely analogous to that of a Roman family under patria potestas.* The karnavan is as much the guardian and representative for all purposes of property, of every member within the taravad, as the Roman father or grandfather.[43] [emphasis added]

Such a patriarchal interpretation of the customs of the matrilineal community had its roots in the steady process of transforming Malabar's customary practices which used not only Brahmanical precepts, but also Roman law and laws of equity in equal measure, and otherwise twisted procedure to fit the case. However, the legally bolstered powers of 'natural' headship granted to the karnavan were constantly put to test, and it was in the resolution of legal conflict that many new cultural practices evolved in Malabar.[44]

An example of this was the contested right of women to head taravads. The trouble was not related so much to the actual absence of female heads or *karnavattis*, but that now their authority required external, or judicial, legitimation. Also, the problem was to decide whether the right of headship was inherent in the eldest woman of the family by virtue of her age, or if it was to be granted to her in the absence of any adult males, or if it was simply a standby arrangement till a minor son came of age.

In 1878, Herbert Wigram (the civil judge at the District Court) argued that

> the management of [by] a female, like the management of [by] an Anandravan [nephew] must, in my opinion, always be with the consent of those on whom the law confers the rights of management, i.e., the senior male, and may at any time be resumed.[45]

In other words, while headship by men had come to be seen as normative among the matrilineal Nayars, women who had held comparable rights in an earlier period had to take recourse to courts to prove it. What this also implied was that it was easier to contest the power of a female head than a male's, as the former's rights to the position were made much more conditional, while the latter was seen as a natural right.

By the 1870s and 1880s such gendered asymmetries of power began to become noticeable among the younger kin in taravads too. While younger men could question a karnavan's decision regarding the sale or management of property in an individual capacity,[46] women could do so only if they represented the family.[47] This meant that young men, who possessed putative rights to headship as a gendered right were, in addition, regarded as capable of questioning the legitimate authority of the karnavan as individuals. Thus, here one has access to a very legal understanding of individuality that privileged men in property disputes.

Differences in gendered rights of men and women were not restricted to questions of property alone. These began to be reflected in the changing patterns of residence where women could increasingly move away only after marriage.[48] This was in contrast to both the pre-colonial period and the early years of Company rule, when women could move out, either with a few retainers or with their siblings, in order to create new branches. In the case of property disputes where married women living away from home demanded a partition of property, the resolution was dependent on whether the karnavan approved of the union. Therefore, if it could be proved that a woman's relationship was promiscuous or without the taravad's assent it was tantamount to her forfeiting her right in the family property. Moreover, linking up residence and property issues shows how difficult it would have become for women to move away from the taravad house, or claim their share of taravad property, except when it was with the karnavan's consent.[49]

Meanwhile, men were beginning to move away from the taravad for a variety of reasons—from professional to educational. Besides, they were becoming increasingly successful in property disputes and received their share while living, and working, away from the taravad.[50] In addition, young professional men also had access to self-acquired incomes to support themselves. Therefore, while women's income, mobility and residence patterns were controlled largely by taravad elders, for many young men the burgeoning educational and occupational opportunities of the period provided significant outlets. This naturally had important consequences for the constitution of the late-nineteenth-century matrilineal taravad.

I wish to stress here that it was from the corpus of mid-nineteenth-century legal ideas that the contours of the matrilineal taravad in the post-1860s period were shaped. The main source for this was from the judicial codification and consequent legal proceedings that utilized legal norms and precedents to settle domestic disputes. Family documents and contracts reveal the absorption of ideas of and changes introduced by the British courts in everyday language and practice, and influence in transforming social values and conventions.[51] The literature of the period reflects the concern of the times—laws, litigation and love marriages. The changes in family norms were not imposed and the discourse reveals the contest between different ideas, ideologies and practices for ascendance. It is through this contest that a dominant strain of thought, and over time practice, regarding matriliny and Malabar law emerged which helped to transform the matrilineal taravad.

III. 'Modern Times': The Taravad Curtailed?

Land Legislations and Marital Disputes: By the 1880s the authority of the heads of the households in this period, both within the taravad as the Karnavar and on land as the

janmis, was coming under increasing criticism. Here I wish to emphasize that the taravad that was being attacked at this point was a young creature—a product of 'court-
made law', especially of the 1850s onwards.[52] The attack on the taravad was almost a
logical climax of its strengthening over the past decades. The sources of opposition
against the land-owning taravad were diverse and predictable—from the younger
members of the taravads to the dependant agricultural workers. The only unusual com-
batant was the colonial state itself.

The 1880s witnessed changes in attitudes of cultivators and tenants towards the
taravad as a land-owning force. The mid-century redefinitions of property rights had
secured to the taravads the right to redeem or renew tenures, which affected adversely
the bargaining power of the tenants, cultivators and other dependents. The response was
embodied in such diverse ways as the barrage of property disputes, petitions to the
government to implement tenancy legislation, and in the Mappilla riots of the 1870s.

The agrarian crises of the 1870s put the government into a predicament. Not only
had the rights of *dominium* secured to the taravads by the state created tensions in the
countryside, it had also given landowners immunity against colonial officials in such
critical matters as the exaction of revenue, or failing that in the sale of land. As early as
the 1805 settlement the revenue administrators had recognized the private rights of the
landholders, while at the same time entering either them or their dependent cultivating
tenants as revenue payers. By the latter half of the nineteenth century, this was beginning
to create serious problems for the government. Tenants were becoming economically
weaker and insecure and were beginning to find it difficult to meet revenue claims.
However, this problem was difficult to salvage. Even though the tenants were meant to
be revenue payers the landlords were the owners of the land. This meant that if the state
attempted to take action against a recalcitrant tenant, and put the land up for sale to meet
revenue arrears, the landlord could (and indeed, did) contest the action on the grounds
of ownership. In response to this situation, the state began an attempt to curtail the
powers of the taravad. Legislative measures, such as the Land Registration Act of 1896
and the Compensation for Tenants Act of 1897, were as much a product of state anxiety
for undermining the authority of the taravad, as a response to the agrarian crises of the
preceding years.[53]

It is in this context that one needs to examine the late-nineteenth-century debates
on marriage which formed yet another part of the strategy evolved by the younger
members to redefine and undermine the extant power relations within the taravad. In
1896, the Malabar Marriage Bill of 1887 passed into law. This was in response to the
growing faith in legislation and in the liberal principles of contract among a section of
the educated minority of Malayali men; marriage, as the prime example of contract, was
seen as offering a panacea for the predicament of the taravad, a means of contracting
themselves out of the trammels of the joint family system.[54] They wished to achieve the
status of individuals and it was to this end that they engaged with the colonial state.

The idea of dividing the matrilineal taravad along the lines of *patriviri*-local residence, with concomitant rights to property, was located in the evolutionary social
theories of the late nineteenth century. Theorists, for example, John McLennan and
John Lubbock, who perceived marriage as a natural union, and represented the conjugal,
coresidential unit with common rights over heirs and property as the legitimate domestic unit, were gaining greater popularity in this period. The young professional men who
supported the demand for marriage reform for ensuring the partibility of the taravad

utilized the idea of marriage to gain control over the sexuality and fertility of women. More importantly, the deployment of such a notion of family when taravad relations were already strained spelt the end of matrilineal kinship, even in its highly transformed late-nineteenth-century form. In Malabar, the slow process of social change succeeded in transferring rights over women to new figures of authority within the family—the father/husband. The Marriage Act of 1896 was a failure with respect to its inability to enforce the registration of all matrilineal marriages. However, the scene was set for the seduction of the matrilineal community with the lure of the natural morality of monogamous marriage, conjugal couples and patrilineal descent.

Towards Abolition: c. 1900–1940: The first three decades of the twentieth century witnessed the critical transformation of the taravad that led to its eventual legal abolition in 1933. The demand for marriage, property divisions and tenants' rights had been voiced in a variety of ways—through court rooms, newspapers and in Legislative Council chambers—by the 1890s. The changes in the twentieth century, however, were of a different order and scale. It was not only that matrilineal customs seemed undesirable, but that the immemorial powers of the taravad were no longer legally supported. The three important factors that form the framework within which the legal abolition of the matrilineal taravad took place are the survey and resettlement of Malabar, begun in 1902 and completed in 1936, effectively reducing the taravads to the position of revenue-paying intermediaries; the Tenancy Act of 1930 that strengthened the erstwhile dependants of the taravads by giving them security of tenure; and the Matriliny Act of 1933 that guaranteed the legitimate partition of joint property and provided for individual inheritance. These circumstances, in conjunction, created the conditions under which the taravad was eventually dismantled.

During the same period another issue dominated the politics of the region, which had consequences for the changing attitudes towards matriliny. This was the emergence of caste organizations which voiced the need for community identity—one that was, both in the case of the Nayars and the Nambudiris, centred on issues of marriage, family and tenurial relations. A critical component of the rhetoric of both these caste movements was the attempt to create a *homogeneous community*, defined in opposition to the other. This helped to transform the perceived iniquities of the matrilineal system by offering an alternative source of identity for members of the taravad—that of caste.

Caste: Caste associations of the Nambuthiris and the Nayars were growing in strength in the same period. The process of creating a putative community centred on caste gave the schisms within the agrarian community and land-holding taravads a new direction. Attempts to minimize the differences between the subcastes and strategies to overcome disparities caused by age were among the central aims of the caste organizations.

The main issues that were discussed by the Nambuthiri reformers all the way to the late 1920s were those of taravad reform, education and the relationship between landlord and tenant. According to the rules of patrilineal descent and inheritance, and strict rules of primo-geniture followed by the Nambuthiris, only the eldest son could marry within the community (up to four wives), as well as manage the family property. As all the other members (younger sons and unmarried daughters) could merely have residence and maintenance rights in the family home, and be maintained at a subsistence level, none of them could expect a share of the joint property. Only in the case of the extremely wealthy families was education accessible to more than one son—that too was mainly Vedic learning.

The rhetoric of family reform was couched in highly emotive language:

> the degenerate state of the Nambuthiri community is worse than any other in the world . . . exogamous marriages on the one hand, and life-long dependence of the younger people on the other . . . the sorrowful state of unmarried women, and bickering and strife within families . . . it is impossible to find any family where married life is happy.[55]

The reformers argued that there was nothing more vulgar than the exogamous relations that the younger men had to enter into with Nayar women.[56]

Reforming the structure of the taravad was seen as the only way of ensuring endogamous and monogamous marriages. Thus the community argument gently and subtly diverted the focus of the debate towards the partition of property and the reconstitution of the taravad into nucleated units. It was stressed that while endogamy was essential for all Nambuthiris, it could not be realized until all members of the family could support themselves and their families according to the norms of patriliny.[57] The ideal community was represented as comprising several natural families, each constituted by a man, woman and their children, Such natural ties were to imbue the community with a greater sense of unity and cohesiveness, impossible earlier as caste norms had been divisive, disallowing either the formation of a true sense of community, or the longevity of one. Therefore, all through this period, caste and community sentiments were being used to foster internal reform and reorganization.

Just as the Nambuthiris were attempting to reform the character of the household through appeals to the idea of community, sections of the Nayars were also involved in the same process. The attempt to create a community centred on caste was to immediately effect changes in the structure of the matrilineal taravad. Over time it would help to discredit the practices of the community that the Nayars increasingly considered immoral and retrogressive. The new notions of progress that the Nayars invoked were defined by the need for an identity that would be both patrilineal and broad-based enough to encompass the interests of its different subcastes, with their varied ritual and material statuses. They were, therefore, targeting a wide range of interest groups, from the younger members of the land-holding taravads, non-kin Nayar tenants, and even the poorer sections of the Nayar subcastes—who were mainly cultivators—to menial workers, in the bigger taravads.

The persuasiveness of the caste argument lay in its very inchoate nature which enabled it to represent the putative community as one shorn of all hierarchies and differences. It was asserted repeatedly that drastic reform was essential within the matrilineal community, and this was to begin within the household: 'the practices on the increase in taravads, the suits to get rid of the powers of the karnavar, the demands for maintenance, the attempts towards division—all shows the change in people's hearts, and the move towards patriliny.'[58]

Several Nayar organizations started mushrooming all over Malabar in response to the need for internal organization and caste reform. Endogamy was an important issue among them, as it had been with the Nambuthiris.[59] The other two important aims of the community were to create opportunities for employment for its men, and provide husbands for its women.[60] Various aspects of marriage reform were discussed endlessly in this period, where some called for the abolition of *talikettukalyanam*,[61] or the puberty ritual for girls, while others formed into organizations and collected funds to conduct proper marriage unions themselves.[62]

It was argued increasingly that the colonial state was standing in the way of progress. All that was needed was to 'change laws to accommodate the interests of people who show the desire to move from a matrilineal to a patrilineal system'.[63]

> The only possible way [to achieve a patrilineal system] is individual partitioning and the apportioning of shares . . . with this it can be said that a new path for progress has been discovered in Kerala.[64]

Central to this process of transformation was the creation of a new familial ideology premised on conjugal love. To achieve this a new ideal type of female virtue and womanhood needed to be created, which would gently and without demur, accommodate itself to changing times.

> A perfect wife is the way to perfect marital happiness . . . good behaviour, wealth and status make a woman an asset to the family . . .[65]

Thus slowly the stage was being set for the eventual transformation of the matrilineal community into a patrilineal one. And for this, taravad reform and its substitution by nuclear family units remained essential. The Matriliny Act, enacted in 1933, was designed precisely with this end in mind. With their organizations and rhetoric, the young Nayar men had created the perfect idiom for the transformation of the old order into its new, progressive, form.

Partition: The Tenancy and Matriliny Acts were both passed in the 1930s. The first granted security of tenures to all *kanam* tenants and restricted arbitrary evictions and rack-renting. The latter sealed the demise of the taravad by legitimizing partition into branches, by either male or female member. Three changes proposed under the Matriliny Act were legalizing of *sambandham* marriages, granting the right of adoption, and allowing branches the right to demand partition.[66] Each of these provisions was fundamentally at variance with the system of relationship then extant within the matrilineal community. Marriages and adoption together were to create the natural relationship that endured under the patrilineal system, and the division of property was to sanction the first step towards individual partition.

> It was argued that the Act ought to be permitted, to allow people to lead happier and better lives . . . the movement is a natural one and the expression of legitimate aspirations and progressive ideas.[67]

An interesting twist to this argument was that it favoured the rights of the creditors of Malabar households, as under the present system it was impossible for them to recover their loans. As no member (other than the head) had the right to sell their share, this increased the insecurity of the creditor who could be trapped into lending money, but not receiving timely repayment. The legislation would affect the big, rich and influential taravads adversely, but it was argued that it was inevitable as the agitation would continue till individual partition became the law.

Transforming the Political Economy of Malabar: The changing balance of power between the janmis, tenants and the state was observable not only in the acts of legislation and caste movements of the twentieth century, but also in the transformation of the official discourse in relation to the taravad. With the tenancy legislation of 1930, as well as a completely unstable and unpredictable market situation as a result of the Depression, the future of the big taravads was beginning to look gloomy. Of the greatest importance in the changing relationship between the taravads and state in the post-1930s period was that the latter was able to encroach upon the former's hitherto sacrosanct private rights with impunity, without making even minimal concessions.

MacEwan's report on the settlement and resettlement of the eight talukas in the plains of Malabar district in 1936 formally transformed many of the piecemeal changes that had been effected over the past seven to eight years. Of chief importance in this report were the changes in the terminology and definitions relating to land usages, which formed the quintessence of the changing power relations of the landed taravads and the state, in the latter's favour. The terms private *janmam* and government janmam were dispensed with, to be replaced with *ryotwari* and *inam*, respectively. Simultaneously, the separate assessment rates of *janmabhogam* and *taram* (signifying shares of the janmi and the state, respectively) were abolished, and a consolidated rate of assessment fixed.[68]

Similarly, private lands held by Nambuthiri and Nayar taravad temples were slowly brought within the ambit of state control, by being redesignated as government property.[69] Thus, at least theoretically, all the private janmam rights of the Malabar landowners were destroyed, and they were equated with mere ryotwari holders. Besides, most of these changes were occurring during the greatest economic crisis of the period, the Depression; what was significant was that the government with its renewed efficiency had no trouble in collecting revenue from the people.[70] Thus, MacEwan's resettlement decisively altered the relation of the big taravads with the state and put an end to most of the immemorial private rights of these families.

Conclusion

This article has examined the transformation of matrilineal kinship and inheritance amongst the Nayars of Malabar from the eighteenth to the twentieth centuries. Through focusing on the taravad, it was possible to explore the variety of cultural and legal meanings of matriliny in different historical phases. The changing alignments within the taravad—especially in relation to property, authority, gender and generational power—underlay the changes in kinship. While the ties of reciprocity and interdependence that bound the Nayar taravad to the agrarian economy did not vanish suddenly, its slow and irretrievable transformation resulted in the creation of new identities for women and men, and for the Nayars as a caste in the twentieth century.

The statutory abolition of the matrilineal taravad provided a vent for many resentments against perceived inequities. But the right to exercise an individual claim to erstwhile joint property was only the tip of the iceberg. Legal changes masked beneath its transparent surface a new legal and social morality that was welcomed, and soon became normative among the matrilineal populations. The rhetoric of modernization that had been adopted by the Nayar reformers of the late nineteenth and early twentieth centuries had found its apotheosis in the political idioms of nationalism and communism. In

1976, the Kerala Legislature abolished matriliny. In the process of their incorporation into mainstream politics and in a bid to integrate themselves with the rest of India, the Nayars of Kerala dismantled the last vestiges of barbarism. Hindu laws and patrilineal descent had become almost factual parts of Nayar life and for many among them an impossible dream had been realised.

Notes

1. A representative selection includes essays by E. Kathleen Gough, 'Changing Kinship Usages in the Setting up of Political and Economic Changes among the Nayars of Malabar', *Journal of the Royal Anthropological Institute of Great Britain and Ireland* (hereafter *JRAI*), vol. 89(1), 1959, pp. 23–44 and in D.M. Schneider and E.K. Gough, eds, *Matrilineal Kinship*, pp. 298–304, 384–404; Joan P. Mencher, 'Nayars of South Malabar', in M.F. Nimkoff, ed., *Comparative Family Systems*, Boston, 1965; C.J. Fuller, *The Nayars Today*, Cambridge, 1976; Melinda Moore, 'A New Look at the Nayar Taravad', *Man*, vol. 20(3), 1985, pp. 523–41.

2. J.D.M. Derrett, *Religion, Law and State in India*, London, 1968, has discussed the intricacies of this at great length.

3. A system of using Brahmin pundits to voice opinions on questions of 'law' or give evidence in the Company's courts meant that changes in customary norms would be coloured by Brahmin practices. In Malabar, a lot of the early information during the period of settlement was collected from the members of the big land-holding Nayar, Nambuthiri or Samanthar families.

4. As part of the Regulation for the administration of civil justice in Malabar, the Joint Commissioners recommended that the rules to be followed in the province were to be based on the 'same tendency for Bengal, Bihar and Orissa . . .', *Report of the Joint Commission* from Bengal and Bombay, 1792, Madras, 1862, p. 221. In other words, the Bengal Regulation was taken as the blueprint for Malabar, and only the finer points of difference, which were often to do with tricky questions of 'native' authority, were to be elucidated.

5. By the 1880s, Malabar had the highest number, in the entire Presidency, of suits (both ordinary and small causes) for 'money and moveable property' and 'title and other suits'. The latter, 7,587 in total, constituted a fifth of the total number of cases in the Presidency. *Report of the Civil Administration of Madras Presidency*, 1882, p. 63.

6. Joan Scott discusses the utilization of the category of 'gender' to denote cultural construction of ideas about appropriate roles for men and women. In other words, it refers to the exclusively social origins of subjective identities of men and women—and becomes a 'social category imposed on a sexed body'. See Joan W. Scott, *Gender and the Politics of History*, New York, 1985, especially Chapter 2.

7. While locating any discussion on kinship within the context of a search for its origins is problematic—have the Nayars always been matrilineal?—it is significant to note that there exists a strong argument in favour of a switchover from patriliny to matrilineal kinship among the emerging ruling groups from the sixteenth century onwards. Elankulam Kunjan Pillai, *Studies in Kerala History*, Trivandrum, 1970, pp. 292–323. In the light of this, the question of historicizing kinship, and understanding its 'rules' as a set of strategic transformations becomes more clear.

8. The point that I wish to emphasize here is that there is nothing pre-cultural or inherent about kinship systems. A wide range of anthropologists have been only too conscious of the pitfalls inherent in treating kinship like a set of definite rules determining social relationships., See for instance, B.S. Cohn, 'African Models and Indian Histories', in *An Anthropologist among the Historians and Other Essays*, Delhi, 1987, pp. 200–23; J.F. Collier and S.J. Yanagisako, eds, *Gender and Kinship: Essays Towards a Unified Analysis*, Stanford, 1987; A. Kuper, 'Lineage Theory: A Critical Retrospect', *Annual Review of Anthropology*, 1982, vol. 11, p. 90.

9. This is similar to the argument that the Nayars themselves were not a fixed group of people with definable caste rules in the eighteenth century. Susan Bayly, *Saints, Goddesses and Kings:*

Muslims and Christians in South Indian Society, 1700–1900, Cambridge, 1987, argues that anyone, even non-Malayalee military men, who could bear arms could call themselves 'Nayar' in this period.

10. Two slightly different meanings, depending on the etymology, have been provided for the word Samanthar. Based on the *Veiragya Chandrodayam,* it is suggested that it meant the chief of a district; the later *Keralolpatti* suggests that a son of a Brahman from a Kshatriya mother could be called Samanthar. *Gundert Nikhandu* [Gundert's dictionary], Kottayam, 1962, p. 941.

11. Duarte Barbosa noted that there were similarities in the 'caste and custom' of the Samanthar and the Kshatriyas of Malabar. He was referring to their matrilineal kinship and the system of defining descent in the female line. M.L. Dames, ed., *The Book of Duarte Barbosa: An Account of the Countries Bordering on the Indian Ocean,* London, 1921, vol. II, p. 7. Such customs had been noted among a significant section of the Nayars too. It is significant in the context of Malabar that only a few 'rajas' claimed the status of Kshatriyas. All others, including the Samuthiri, called themselves Samanthar.

12. Chelnat Achyuta Menon quoted in K.S. Mathew, *Society in Medieval Malabar: A Study Based on Vadakkan Pattukal* (Northern ballads), Kottayam, 1979, pp. 20, 69.

13. A. Sreedhara Menon, *A Survey of Kerala History,* Kottayam, 1967.

14. Mathew, *Society in Medieval Malabar,* p. 34.

15. N. Rajendran, *Establishment of British Power in Malabar, 1664 to 1799,* Allahabad, 1979, p. 35; Sreedhara Menon, *A Survey of Kerala History,* p. 172.

16. Sreedhara Menon, *A Survey of Kerala History,* pp. 176–80.

17. See Sreedhara Menon's discussion of the Talapilli rajas. *A Survey of Kerala History,* p. 198.

18. The word tavazhi, by the late nineteenth century had been defined variously as (*a*) relations by the mother's side; (*b*) relations by the wife's side; and (*c*) collateral branches of a family, *Gundert Nikhandu* (Gundert's Dictionary), Kottayam, 1962, p. 436 depending on the etymological source utilized. Interestingly, it probably referred to the variety of extant customs prevalent in Malabar. This highlights the difference between *legal* interpretations and customary usages with the former's tendency to reify one meaning over all others.

19. William Logan, *Malabar Manual* (hereafter *Malabar*), Madras, 1887, Deed 15, 1622, II, appendix XII, xxxii–iii.

20. Ibid., Deed 21, 1677, cxxxvi–vii.

21. Ibid., cxl. Deed 26, 1712.

22. Ibid., cxl–cxli, Deed 27, 1713.

23. C.A. Bayly, *Indian Society and the Making of the British Empire,* Cambridge, 1988, p. 11.

24. It does need to be mentioned here that by the end of the eighteenth century, many of the powerful local potentates had the right to extract customs and similar commercial taxes from the people.

25. In the case of the Nileswaram royal family, a princess from the Samuthiri's family eloped with a prince from Kolathanad to establish her own dynasty. Sreedhara Menon, *A Survey of Kerala History,* p. 181.

26. This was evident especially in the case of Samanthar women, who had special *cherikal* lands set apart for themselves. Dames, *The Book of Duarte Barbosa: An Account of the Countries Bordering on the Indian Ocean,* vol. 2, London, 1921, p. 11. In many of the larger Nayar taravads too this was very common. *Kavalappara Records.*

27. Sthanums, such as Naitear Amma, were reserved for the older women in the Palghat royal taravads and these represented status and power for these women. Francis Buchanan, *A Journey from Madras Through the Countries of Mysore, Canara and Malabar,* London, 1807, vol. II, p. 351.

28. Ibid., p. 513.

29. Ibid., p. 412.

30. Lewis Moore, *Malabar Law and Custom,* Madras, 1900, pp. 6–7.

31. AS 28, 1814, *1 Sudder Decisions,* p. 118.

32. Valia Kava Naitear Amma *v* Kavalappara Valia Nayar, Suit no. 992, 1817, Thekke Pakuthi Zilla Adalat, Vettathnad Thukkidi Munsif's court, *Kavalappara Documents*.

33. AS 203, 1855, Tellicherry, *Zillah Decisions*, p. 15; AS 219, 1856, Calicut, *Zillah Decisions*, p. 19.

34. Olivia Harris, 'Households as Natural Units', in K. Young, C. Walkowitz and R. McCullagh, eds, *Of Marriage and the Market: Women's Subordination in an International Perspective*, London, 1981, pp. 49–66, argues conclusively that in most state formations household heads are made responsible in law for other household members, and that it is usually a male head who negotiates contracts, makes share-cropping arrangements, leases land or other property, and thereby exercises control over the lives of the dependent kin.

35. Carole Pateman, *The Sexual Contract*, Polity, 1988, argues that readings of classic contract theories have tended to repress the 'sexual' aspects of what is actually a sexual–social pact. She argues, on the contrary, that patriarchal right exists throughout civil society. Therefore, modern civil society is the result of a contract between the state and men which *excludes* women on the grounds of 'individuality'. I have utilized Pateman's argument here in two ways. One, her reading of fraternal patriarchy offers one a possibility of analysing patriarchal relations in a context where the locus of attention is not a patrilineal family. Therefore, the specific strengthening of the matrilineal karnavan can be seen as increasing the fraternal patrilineal power of Nayar men as men. Second, within the context of Malabar, the incorporation of the eldest male within the taravad into a contractual sphere of interaction with the state can be seen as a close parallel to the story of the contract theory in western Europe, except that under colonialism even they did not possess complete civil freedom.

36. There were a series of violent attacks on Hindu landowners by their Muslim cultivators, especially in the decades of the 1830s, 1840s and 1850s, culminating in the death of landowners and cultivators alike. Between 1836 and 1854, there were 16 outbreaks against mostly Nayar and Nambudiri janmis, leading to the 'Moplah outbreak' of 1855. Conrad Wood, 'Peasant Revolt: An Interpretation of the Nineteenth and Twentieth Centuries', in Clive Dewey and A.G. Hopkins, eds, *The Imperial Impact: Studies in the Economic History of Africa and India*, London, 1978, p. 138.

37. *Letter*, dated 8 October 1853, from Conolly to Pycroft, containing details of Strange's views on the subject of tenants' rights and family property, 'Correspondence regarding the relations of landlord and tenants', n.p.

38. Ibid., *Letter*, 25 September 1853, Strange to Pycroft.

39. This term was coined by Melinda Moore to signify the impact of British legislation on the Malabar taravad. Melinda Moore, 'A New Look at the Nayar Taravad', pp. 527, 531–7.

40. Kallati Kunju Menon *v* Palat Erracha Menon, *Madras High Court Report* (hereafter *MHCR*), 1862. p. 62.

41. Chemmanathatti Chappunni Nayar *v* Meyene Itiyachi, Appeal No. 64, 1861, in *Judgements of the Sudder Court in Regular and Special Appeals*, n.p.

42. Sundara Ayyar, *Malabar and Aliyasantana Law*, Madras, 1922, p. 185.

43. Thathu Baputty *v* Chakyath Chathu, Civil Miscellaneous Regular Appeal No. 406, 1872, 7 *MHCR*, p. 181.

44. Lucy Carroll, in the context of the Hindu Widow Remarriage Act of 1856, argues that the interpretation of this Act at the three high courts of Calcutta, Bombay and Allahabad utilized three different categories of law—Hindu, customary, and statutory—which over the years succeeded in introducing a pattern of behaviour that would never have been recognized within 'customary' law, and in fact invalidated customs prevalent a few generations ago. See Carroll, 'Law, Custom and Statutory Social Reform: The Hindu Widow Remarriage Act of 1856', *IESHR*, vol. 20(4), 1983, pp. 363–88.

45. AS 434, 1878 quoted in Moore, *Malabar Law and Custom*, pp. 77–8.

46. Padmanatha *v* Govinda, *Indian Law Report* (hereafter *ILR*), 6, 1883.

47. Manika *v* Krishnan, *ILR*, 7, 1884.

48. Of course, in this period virilocal residence did not necessarily imply patri-lineal descent. Women moving off to live with their husbands after marriage were often seen as forming a new tavazhi or branch. By the mid-twentieth century this would be severely disputed.

49. AS 675, *ILR*, 1879. In this particular dispute the woman was forced to forfeit her share of the taravad property because her relationship with her lover was described as 'promiscuous inter-course' by her karnavan, and accepted as such by the court; in AS 59, *ILR*, 1879 the woman was out-casted, and her property not given to her because her relationship with a lower-caste man was deemed to be an alliance without the taravad's assent.

50. Teyan Nair *v* Raghavan Nair, *ILR*, Peru Nair *v* Appu Nair, *ILR*, 2, 1880; Kunhambu *v* Paidal, AS 23, *ILR*, 5, 1882.

51. Apart from family *karars* (contracts) which were being modified so as to utilize procedural elements of case law (like using the laws of limitation) *Eacharattil ms.*, Malayalam language itself began to incorporate the translated equivalents of words such as 'plaintiff', 'defendant', 'court', and so on within its vocabulary. These became a part of common parlance, stories and general folk wisdom fairly soon.

52. C.A. Turner, *Minute on the Draft Bill Relating to Malabar Land Tenures*, Madras, 1885.

53. Peter Robb has argued for a similar trend in the rent law and tenancy debates of eastern India in the same period, where officials were ranged against one another in 'pro-*raiyat*' and 'pro-*zamindar*' positions. This was clearly a time in colonial rule when official policy was avowedly 'pro-*raiyat*'; the motivations of course could be various. Robb, 'Law and Agrarian Society: The Case of Bihar and Nineteenth-century Tenancy', *Modern Asian Studies* (hereafter *MAS*), vol. 22(2), 1988.

54. Extract from the Malabar and Travancore Spectator, 15 August 1895, in Legislative, G.O. No. 118, 8 November 1895, National Archives of India (hereafter NAI).

55. *Mathrubhumi*, 18 December 1923.

56. Ibid.

57. Ibid., 17 May 1924.

58. Ibid., 14 July 1923.

59. Ibid., 11 September 1923.

60. K.P. Kunjunni Menon, 'The Need for a Nayar Samajam', ibid., 14 July 1923.

61. Ibid., 15 May 1924.

62. Ibid.

63. 'Matriliny and the Individual Division of Property', ibid., 19 April 1924.

64. Ibid., 19 April 1924.

65. 'Marital bliss', ibid., 10 November 1923.

66. Department of Revenue, D. Dis. 11888, 14 January 1929, Kerala Regional Archives (hereafter KRA).

67. Ibid.

68. Department of Revenue, R. Dis. 3431/36, 2 April 1936, KRA.

69. Ibid. This was in accordance to the B.P. Misc. No. 1814, 8 October 1920 and section 7, Malabar Land Registration Act, 1896, in B.P. Misc. No. 640, 17 March 1926.

70. C.J. Baker, *An Indian Rural Economy, 1880–1955*, Delhi, 1984, has argued that the main impact of the Depression was to create significant *structural* changes in the economy. It is useful to consider the mid-1930s in Malabar in this context. The Depression can be seen as an important catalyst in transforming the economic relations of the region. With changes in the taravad structure already under way, the division and partition of property acquires a special significance. Not only did these processes speed up, but the structural changes in the economy meant that relations between kin and dependant were evaluated and re-established on a different footing.

20

Women and Gender in the Study of Tribes in India*

Virginius Xaxa

S tudy of groups, which subsequently came to be described as tribal studies, began with the establishment of the Asiatic Society of Bengal in 1784. Since then scholar-administrators have been writing general works on the land and people of different regions. Notable among works with a focus on tribes are Dalton's *Descriptive Ethnology of Bengal* (1872), Risley's *Tribe and Caste of Bengal* (1891), Russell and Hiralal's *Tribes and Castes of Central Provinces of India* (1916) and Thurston's *Castes and Tribes of Southern India* (1906). The need for a census felt by the colonial government and started since 1871 invariably led to a collection of detailed and classified information about people resulting in the identification of certain groups of people as tribes. The criteria used for the purpose were initially ambiguous. However since 1901 a somewhat clearer criterion began to be used. Tribes were identified and described as those who practised animism; later the expression tribal religion was used in its place. Subsequent census enumeration continued with this criterion but other dimensions like geographical isolation and primitive conditions of living were added to it. The latter were never explicitly employed in delineating tribes in the census enumeration. What was explicitly employed was the religion, which was delineated either as animism or tribal religion. Ghurye considered this way of marking off tribes as inadequate and unsatisfactory. He drew attention to the fact that the caste Hindus especially those in the lower rung of hierarchy had in fact elements of animism within their religious practices (Ghurye 1963).

Alongside the census, the British officials also made inventories of tribes in the form of handbooks and monographs. These provide mines of information on different aspects of tribal life. Vidyarthi describes this phase of researches on tribes in India as the formative period, dating from 1874–1919. The other two phases are identified and described by him as constructive (1920–1949) and analytical (1950 onwards). The former is traced to the period when anthropology came to be introduced as a curriculum

*This is a revised and expanded version of the paper presented at a seminar, 'Interrogating Disciplines/Disciplining Gender? Towards a History of Women's Studies in India', organized by the Centre for Women's Development Studies (CWDS), Delhi, in February 2001. I am thankful to Dr Rajni Palriwala for her comments on the earlier draft and to Ms Ritambhara Hebbar for editorial help. I am alone, however, responsible for inadequacies and errors.

in the universities in India and the latter to the adoption of an analytical and action-oriented approach in the study of tribes (Vidyarthi 1982). In the post-independence period, there has been a flood of literature on tribes. These have mainly come from three sources: the Anthropological Survey Of India, University Departments of Sociology and Anthropology and Tribal Research Institutes set up in states having a substantial tribal population. The Tribal Research Institutes were established in the mid-1950s mainly to undertake problem-oriented researches for effective formulation and implementation of developmental programmes in tribal areas.

Tribal Women in Traditional Setting

The ethnographic accounts on tribes in the form of monographs, handbooks or inventories have been the hallmark of the first two phases of tribal studies in India. They provide detailed information on different aspects of life among tribes. These include aspects such as modes of economic activities, systems of marriage, family, kinship, religious practices, technology, arts, artifacts, taboos, customs, traditions, inheritance, succession and so on. It is from these accounts that we get the idea of how women have been situated in tribal societies. These tell us about the division of labour that exists between men and women, the way marriage and divorce is arranged and the place women assume in it, various kinds of restriction and taboos women suffer, rights, privileges and freedom they enjoy and so on.

It is from these accounts that women's position in tribal society has been mainly worked out. Studies on tribal women have not been many nor in depth. Except in some of the works of Elwin (1939), Fürer-Haimendorf (1933) and a few others like Hutton (1921), there has been no explicit discussion on the 'status of women' in tribal society. Even in these works, the assessment of the status of women has been far from uniform. While some say that tribal societies generally assigned high status to women, others opine that women's position in tribal society is the same as in other societies. Writing about the Nagas, Elwin, for example, remarks, 'tribal woman is in herself exactly the same as any other women, with the same position, love and fears, the same devotion to the home, to husband and children, the same faults and the same virtues' (cited in Zehol 1998:1). Yet elsewhere, he refers to Naga women as holding a high and honourable position. They work on equal terms with the men in the fields and make their influence felt in the tribal council. (Elwin 1961: 104). He makes a similar observation with regard to the Baigas when he says that Baiga women enjoy an excellent position in society. They enjoy freedom and authority, play a leading part in marriage ceremonies, and have a reputation for practising witchcraft. Among the Baiga, there is no clear division of labour between men and women (Elwin 1986: 235–6). Fürer-Haimendorf referring to the Nagas writes, 'many women in most civilized parts of India may well envy the women of the Naga Hills, their high status and their free happy life and if you measure the cultural level of the people by the social position and personal freedom of its women you will think twice before looking down on the Nagas as savages' (Fürer-Haimendorf 1933: 101). In a similar vein, Hutton attributes a higher social status to Sema Naga women on the ground that marriages among the Sema Naga are choice-based and a girl is never married against her will. The Sema Naga woman occupies a high position in her husband's house and is treated well (Hutton 1921: 183).

The concern shown towards women in tribal studies is very recent. The earliest such attempt can be traced to the publication brought out by the Indian Anthropological Society in 1978. Attempting to bring out a region-wise survey of tribal women the publication points out that studies of tribal women are practically non-existent; the few that exist are superficial and inadequate.[1] The next serious and concerted effort to give an account of tribal women is seen in the publication of a collection of papers edited by Singh, Vyas and Mann in 1988. Since then there has been a steady rise in the number of studies dealing with tribal women. The journal *Social Change* devoted to its December issue of 1993 a special theme, 'Status of Tribal Women in India'. These recent studies provide a more careful account of the situations of tribal women than the ones presented in the earlier accounts. One can see this in the works of Mann (1996), Chauhan (1990), Zehol (1998) and the journal *Social Change* (1993). The more recent writings also mark a departure from the earlier ones on the status of tribal women. The studies now are increasingly moving in the direction of what in social science literature is described as gender studies. Issues dealt with in these studies have been raised later in the discussion.

The discrepancy in the descriptions about women in tribal society is mainly due to the way that scholars conceive the term 'status'. Broadly one can discern two views. The first refers to women's role in the system, which entails rights and duties. In this, status is linked with one's role in the system. Correspondingly, women's status is analysed and assessed taking into consideration the mutual duties between sexes and the safeguards provided for the protection of each sex against the high-handedness of the other. The other usage of the term status is in the sense of prestige and honour, which may be studied in terms of their legal status and opportunities for participation. In the studies of women, however, such distinction is often overlooked and used almost interchangeably.

Status as 'prestige' and 'honour' can only be studied in relation to values in reference. Tribes have been primarily studied either with reference to the values of enlightenment, that is, freedom, equality and fraternity, or in relation to values prevalent in the dominant society. In short, in studying tribes in relation to the 'other', the values have invariably been either the universal values of enlightenment or the values of the larger society in which freedom is often scorned and hierarchy is much valued. Hardly any attempt has been made to study them in terms of the values prevalent in tribal society.

Women in Changing Tribal Society

Sociologists and social anthropologists have questioned the dichotomous conception of Indian society constructed during the colonial period. The British administrator-scholars conceived tribes as those who not only practised animism/tribal religion as opposed to Hinduism but also lived in complete isolation and without any interaction with the rest of society or civilization. Though the distinction is maintained between 'tribe' and 'civilization' in the writings of the Indian scholars, the two are not treated as isolated but in interaction with each other (Sinha 1958). Consequently tribal society has not been seen as static but in the process of change. Change has been conceived as moving in a number of directions. Of these, the tradition that has been dominant has been one that has focused on change from tribe to caste.

In fact, much of the social anthropological discourse on tribes has been primarily couched in terms of transformation of tribes into castes. Changes occurring in tribal society have invariably been conceived in terms of a tribe moving in the direction of becoming a part of the 'civilization', by getting assimilated into the society the civilization represents. Historians and anthropologists have made such observations not only in the context of the past but also in the context of the present. Kosambi (1975) has referred to tribal elements being fused into the general society. Similarly Bose (1941) makes a reference to tribes being absorbed into Hindu society. The fact that such claims have continued in a large number of anthropological works of the post-independence era points to the persistence of the belief that tribes are being absorbed or assimilated into Hindu society or that tribes are gradually turning into castes. In this journey to absorption or assimilation, tribes are said to be at different levels or stages. These have been reflected in the classifications put forward by social anthropologists for understanding tribal transformation in India. The classification has been couched differently by different scholars. Roy Burman, for example, classifies tribes as those (1) indifferent to Hindu society, (2) negatively oriented, (3) positively oriented and (4) incorporated into Hindu society. Vidyarthi too classifies tribes on somewhat similar lines. He identifies them as those living in (1) forests, (2) rural areas, (3) semi-acculturated, (4) acculturated and (5) assimilated (Roy Burman 1970; Vidyarthi and Rai 1977).

Tribes have not moved only in the direction of Hinduism and the Hindu way of life. Equally important as far as tribes are concerned has been their movement towards Christianity. All these have been considered as significant processes of cultural change within tribal societies. Yet we know little about the way these changes have affected the lives of women in these societies. How have women, whose families have been acculturated to Hinduism, adapted to the ethos of the new religious organization? What has been the extent of continuity and discontinuity? Or what have been their advantages and disadvantages in changed situations? These questions have not been systematically explored in the existing studies.

However, studies on the sanskritization process among tribes do point to some changes. Roy Burman, drawing upon the studies of many scholars made during the 1930s to 1960s, demonstrated how tribes, with sanskritization, are opting for early marriage as a matter of prestige, and discouraging widow remarriage as well as divorce and separation (Roy Burman 1988: 14; Sachchidananda 1988: 80). Mann makes similar observations on the Bhils. The freedom enjoyed by a Bhil woman in the sphere of marriage, premarital sex, divorce, access to decision-making bodies, etc. is gradually being curtailed because of sanskritization. The Bhil woman has been adversely affected in terms of her freedom to select a male and to marry through elopement. Purdah system among Bhil women is again an instance of borrowing from caste Hindus (Mann 1987: 155). Of course, Roy Burman treats much of the divorce and separation in rural tribal India as desertion, which is indicative of the powerlessness of women. In this sense he views sanskritization as a positive influence since it restrains the phenomenon of divorce among them. After all, the upper-caste lifestyle, which those in the lower rung tend to emulate through sanskritization, in principle does not approve of phenomena such as divorce. Interestingly, Roy Burman tends to link age at marriage more with the customary practice of bride price than with sanskritization or distance from it. Citing the case of the Hos of Chotanagpur, he points out that it is not uncommon among them for a girl to wait till her mid-thirties before she can find someone who can pay the bride price and become her partner in life (Roy Burman 1988: 14). With improvement in economic condition or even sanskritization, it is argued that women workers tend to withdraw from outdoor work in agriculture and allied activities. Observations in the existing literature on the inverse relation between sanskritization/rise in social status and withdrawal from manual labour are cited in support of such an argument (Roy Burman 1988: 16). These observations however are succinct, casual and lack analytical rigour. To begin with, it is doubtful if sanskritization is associated with rise in status in the context of tribes.[2] Even if it is as the existing literature suggests, it is not the only basis of rise in status. Education and white-collar employment are equally important. There is no doubt that with sanskritization there has been a tendency to withdraw from manual labour but this cannot be generalized for the whole of the sanskritized population. Such tendency is rather confined to a certain context and stratum. If one takes the case of tribes such as the Santhals, Oraons, Mundas and Hos of eastern India, one finds that the withdrawal from labour is more to do with those who live in a multi-caste village or its vicinity and where they form a small minority. More often than not they are a migrant population. Further, the trend is more to do with well-to-do cultivators than the poor and marginal ones. One finds such a trend even in the case of white-collar employees when they find themselves in a situation where they constitute demographically and ethnically a minority population. In other contexts the withdrawal of women from manual labour has been the exception than the rule. It is a fact that the sanskritization/ Hinduization process has been at work among most of the major tribal groups of eastern India for centuries. The bhagat movements witnessed among most of these groups since the turn of the last century had been an important aid in this process.[3] And yet, the bhagat families in general have shown no withdrawal of women from work in agriculture and other allied activities. On the contrary what one finds is also high participation of women in agricultural activities among the non-tribal population living side with the tribal population in the region. Thus, not only the process of sanskritization but also tribalization has been at work here. This is not only the case in tribal-dominated regions like Jharkhand but seems to be the case elsewhere aw well. At least a careful reading of ethnographic material does suggest this. To illustrate, a study of a population of the Bhils by Mann shows as high as 99.09 per cent of women participation in agricultural activities and 93.64 per cent in livestock-rearing though the population studied had been considerably sanskritized (Mann 1987: 89–90). Rise in status due to a change in occupation has in general again not paved the way for withdrawal from manual labour. Where such households are still tied to land and agriculture, women constitute a major manual labour force. One can see this among the eastern India tribes referred to earlier in the discussion.

Whereas acculturation like sanskritization and Hinduization led to change of a certain kind among tribal women, the change moved in a somewhat different direction in the context of the conversion to Christianity. Christianity opened up the space for tribal women to participate in religious worship side by side with men, a phenomenon that was denied to them in the earlier religious traditions of many tribal societies. In many Protestant denominations, they have been appointed as deaconess, preachers, trustees, etc. They have also been organized into women's groups within churches to carry out social, religious and welfare activities in society (Kelhou 1998: 59–60; Zehol 1998:26–7). Christianity, as practised, made modern education accessible to women in tribal societies. On the other hand, it also introduced a variety of restrictions in the name of ethics and laws of the church, which went against the kind of freedom that they enjoyed in their traditional social set-up. It also set into motion a process of segregation among boys and girls and put a stop to divorce, which was easy to work out under the tribal customary law. Over and above, the gender inequality inherent in the tradition of the Christian churches and denominations reinforced existing inequalities.

Both Hinduization and Christianization thus led to a number of restrictions on the kinds of freedom women enjoyed in the traditional social settings. However in one case, that is, Hinduization, such restriction was a part of the concern for respectability/status; in the other, it was more to do with religious morals and values. An inherent inadequacy of this perspective is that it fails to capture the variety of changes witnessed within tribal societies.

Underlying Assumption

Underlying the accounts on tribes in general lies a basic assumption that tribes are primitive, savage and backward. This is driven home, among other things, through accounts of their modes of making a living, technology, food habits, lifestyle and, more importantly, through representations of their bodies. Tribes were invariably represented as half-clad, clad in only leaves and grass fibres and, at times, naked. In these representations, women had a more prominent place than men. Some ethnographers like Elwin and Fürer-Haimendorf even celebrated such virtues among tribes. Elwin went to the extent of providing detailed narratives of the place of sex in tribal life, sexual life of children, ideas of erotic attractiveness, wooing, and frequency of intercourse, for example, in the case of the Baigas (Elwin 1986: 230–70). That these are governed by certain codes and ethics have been overlooked or under-stressed. Such views held in colonial ethnography have of course undergone change and are no longer entertained in anthropological writings today However, people at large including officials working among tribals, especially at the lower levels, still hold such views. Of course exceptions are not ruled out.

While ethnographers and anthropologists celebrate the status of women in tribal societies in their accounts, people in general look down upon their character, customs and morals. They are invariably treated as inferior and 'low'. A study for example shows that as high as 95 per cent of women respondents from the upper caste considered Bhil women as socially inferior to them (Mann 1987: 105). Now, tribes are so viewed and treated precisely because their values are contrary to the dominant values of the larger society. Mandelbaum puts it this way, 'tribal people generally take direct, unalloyed satisfaction in pleasure of the senses, whether in food, alcoholic, drink, sex or dance. The twice born tend to be ambivalent about such pleasures, they are inclined to defer them or refine them and surround them with elaborate ritual' (Mandelbaum 1970: 583).

The values governing the larger Indian society are however in the process of change. Indeed there has been a paradigm shift with regard to the nature and types of values sought and at work in the post-independence era. The ethos in the era as embodied in the constitution and law is one of freedom, equality and social justice. The latter has also been the prominent rhetoric of the time. With this there has been a shift in the image one had of women in tribal society, especially among the educated and enlightened. The ethnographers, British as well as Indians, were on the whole rooted in the spirit of enlightenment and reason. To them, freedom, equality and fraternity were the bases in the valuation of individuals and groups. They invariably judged the position of women in tribal society in the context of the dominant values of the west, which were contrary to the dominant values of the larger Indian society. Therefore almost all discussions on women in tribal society were pitched against the position of women in a society characterized by the organization of caste.

In recent years, there has been a more pointed discussion on the status of women in tribal society and yet these discussions have also moved in somewhat different directions. Women in tribal society have been portrayed as having a better status than enjoyed by women in a caste type of social organization. Tribal women were shown as having greater freedom with respect to movement outside the home, choice over marriage, divorce and remarriage, access to property and resources, etc. This has been done by and large by examining the literature available in monographs with reference to aspects such as rules of inheritance, right to property, enjoyment of freedom, share in the decision-making process, etc. In short, such a view hinges on the one hand on rights and privileges they enjoy and on the other the kind of role assigned to them by virtue of belonging to a particular gender. Taking these into consideration, tribal women were invariably depicted as having a higher social status than their counterparts in the caste society. These aspects of tribal society are still highlighted and further corroborated by such demographic aspects as sex ratio, female workforce participation and other related issues. Such is the general image that has been portrayed of women in studies on tribal society. Nowhere is this more evident than in the proceedings of the series of seminars that the North-East Regional Centre of the ICSSR carried out on in different parts of the region on the status of women between May 1988 and February 1989.[4] The aspects raised in those seminars have continued to generate interest on those issues but they have been discussed with a somewhat more critical mind than before (Chauhan 1990; Mehrotra 1992, 2004; Manu 1996; Zehol 1998). The economic burden and work load suffered by tribal women as well as their access to education, food and nutrition, modern occupations, political participation especially in the modern context has still not been given the kind of attention it deserves.

Stages of Social Formations

The position of tribal women in the context of all-round socio-economic changes within tribal society has been another area of some concern in the study of women in tribal society. Their position, involvement, participation, restraint, role and activity in various aspects of their lives have been discussed, analysed and interpreted in the context of such wider socio-economic changes. One of the dominant ways of looking at change from this angle is to show changes in the mode of making a living. This is most glaringly reflected in the change from food gathering to food producing or from swidden (slash and burn cultivation) to settled agriculture. Such transformation has also been seen as a shift from communal and collective ownership of land and use of labour to private ownership of land and labour.

Developments such as these have led to critical examinations of the idea of tribal society as an egalitarian one. Forms of inequality in tribal society, in its traditional setting, have been brought under scrutiny. Of these, gender inequality has been highlighted as the most pervasive, irrespective of the stage of their social formation. One of the dimensions which has been highlighted in this context has been the relative position of women and men under different types of social formations such as food gathering and hunting, swidden agriculture, settled agriculture, state formation, etc. (Nathan 1997; Menon 1993). The other way in which the position of men and women has been studied is in the context of different tribal societies without keeping their social formations as the reference point. These have been done with respect to division of labour, forms of property, institution of religion, family and state. Through an examination of these aspects, an attempt has been made to show how the establishment of patriarchy took shape in tribal societies. Studies have shown how in social formations such as food gathering and swidden agriculture, a rigid division of labour was either absent or gender inequality in one was offset by equality in another sphere. The case of the Birhors in Jharkhand, Nathan, for example, shows how the higher importance of men due to their involvement in the public domain, in this case distribution of meat (prestige food) through society, is neutralized by a similar kind of engagement by women through exchange and transaction activities in the market. Similarly among the Khasis of Megha-laya, the higher status of women in society due to rights of ownership held by them over ancestral property is neutralized by men's hold in society over the decision-making process affecting society. It is however not clear if this inequality that Nathan explicates is more to do with shifting cultivation or the institution of matriliny and settled habitation of the population as in the case of the Khasis. Again he primarily traces the monopolization of hierarchy by men to the state formation and the establishment of individual property. Men's control over the ritual and public/political sphere is seen to be a crucial factor in the struggle to exclude women from ownership of land (Nathan 1997). Yet the case of the Khasis with their state-like institution or Jaintias with a full-fledged state institution does not seem to support such an argument (Sen 1985).[5] Women continue to hold ownership over land and the monopolization of hierarchy is still absent among them.

In fact, some of the serious problems women suffer, such as witch-hunting, is traced by scholars to the pattern of landownership in tribal societies. Kelkar and Nathan, for example, argue that it is the life interest of a widow in the entire land of her husband that is a major fetter on the property rights of the husband's male agnates. Following this, they argue that victims of witch-hunting are particularly widows who have life interest in their husbands' land. The life interest of a widow in her husband's land restricts the property rights of the male agnates of the deceased husband, for whom the use of land for accumulation or for consumption has to wait till after the death of the woman. A widow without children is therefore more vulnerable to attack on the pretext of being a witch (Kelkar and Nathan: 263). While there may be some association between the two in some cases, it is difficult to generalize that witch-hunting has primarily to do with ownership of land. Anyone concerned with the study of witchcraft is familiar with the fact that it is too complex a phenomenon to be associated only with property rights. In fact, a number of witch-hunting cases have been reported, from time to time, from the tea gardens of Jalpaiguri district in West Bengal, where the access to property was hardly at the core of the issue (Gupta 1979: 265–7).

The myth of gender equality or higher status in tribal societies has also been brought under scrutiny through examination of such issues as customary law in relation to wo-men. This has been examined in relation to property, marriage, inheritance and so on.

Through discussions such as these it has been shown that women in tribal societies are put at a disadvantage *vis-à-vis* men in their respective societies (Nongbri 1998). It is interesting to note that the very practices that are illustrated as pointers to higher social status in one kind of setting turn out to be an in-built depressor in another setting. Nongbri makes this point in her discussion of bride price. Referring to several tribes in Arunachal Pradesh, she points out how women among them are treated as mere commodities whom men could easily procure through financial settlement through bride price, a custom which was originally intended to compensate the girl's family for the loss of an economically active member. Bride price, as a socially legitimate purchase of a wife, has thus become a convenient justification for men to abuse their wives and treat them as disposable commodities. She writes, 'the system of bride price has proved to be the bane for women and lies at the root of proliferation of polygamous unions as wealthy men can take on a number of wives simply by paying an agreed sum to the girl's family' (Nongbri 1998: 33–4). Unnithan-Kumar in her study of Taivar Girasia, a tribal group of Rajasthan, points out how bride price is viewed not so much as a recognition of a woman's contribution to the household or as a payment for the loss of productive member, but as a compensation to the father of the bride and his agnatic group for the past expenditure on her maintenance, particularly consumption and food. Drawing on this, Unnithan-Kumar argues that bride price (valued in practical terms) is regarded as an important contribution, which women make to production of reproduction. The lack of ownership of property by women is legitimized by the Girasias on the ground that women move on marriage from their natal villages to their affinal villages (Unnithan-Kumar 1997: 205–6).

There are two aspects on which I would like to comment in this context.

(1) It is an established fact that the division of labour in tribal society is based more on sex and age than on rank, hierarchy or occupation. Division of labour has been both fluid and rigid. It is however not clear as to what stage and on what principle the division of labour could be said to have assumed the form of inequality of rank or status between sexes in tribal societies. There is little discussion on how and on what basis the differences especially between sexes came to be graded. Were divisions the mere division of work and labour and therefore devoid of evaluation and gradation, which is intrinsic to the consideration of being high or of low social status? Hence the study of the status of women does pose problems. It is difficult to study them from the perspective of the value inherent in those societies, especially since values in those societies invariably project the idea of collectivity. Equality and sharing therefore turn out to be the overarching value in those societies. Hence rather than talking of high or low social status, it is more pertinent to talk of inequality of gender. In the case of the latter, one can examine the relative position of women and men in relation to their access to equal opportunity, both formal and substantive.

(2) The taboo on women to touch and use the plough in tribal societies has been seen as a way of denying women control over the means of production, that is, land (Nathan 1997; Kishwar 1987: 96). This access to and control over land is however already denied in those societies by the existing customary laws. The Oraon and the Ho women, who are tabooed from holding plough, for example, are already denied access to land by customary laws existing in their societies. The explanation of the denial of women's access to land in terms of taboo thus seems far from adequate. After all even

the Brahmins are tabooed from ploughing. That does not mean denial of their access to land. Even in swidden agriculture, which Boserup describes as a women's farming system, the allocation of plots is made to men in their capacity as the heads of the household though women exercise greater control over the plots after these have been allocated. There has also been tribal land under swidden agriculture that was controlled and distributed by the chiefs, such as among the Mizos, Semas, Konyaks, etc. There is no custom of plough cultivation among these tribes and yet women suffer from lack of access to land even in these communities. This means that even under swidden agriculture there was a relative lack of access and control over land by women. Not only that but a rudimentary form of social differentiation seems to have been at work under swidden agriculture too. It is a different matter that social differentiation is generally associated with the state and private property formation. And yet such formation among the tribes though at work well before the coming of the British was confined to a few pockets or tribes.[6] However, it is the incorporation of tribes into the larger social system under colonial rule and administration that accelerated as well as opened up new vistas of social differentiation among them. The nature of development pursued by the Indian State in the post-independence era has only accelerated and intensified the process at work during the colonial period.

Social Differentiation and Developmental Policy

The process of social differentiation in tribal society has been rooted in forces outside of tribal societies. These included such forces as introduction of private property in land, growth of trade and market, immigration of non-tribes to tribal areas in search of land and employment, spread of modern education, opening up of new occupations, state-sponsored programmes and other similar activities. Accordingly, social differentiation has moved along different lines. They have either lost land and been compelled to take employment as labourers in nearby quarries, coal fields and the emerging towns—as unskilled/semi-skilled workers (Vidyarthi 1970; Banerjee 1981)—or have had to move permanently/temporarily elsewhere for work and employment, such as at plantations that were opened up in Bengal and Assam. There have been others, a minority, that have been able to take advantage of the forces unleashed by the market and benefits extended by the state for tribes. This has led to differentiation among tribes based on such criteria as education, occupation, income, wealth, assets, etc. They have thus become differentiated into such categories as rich, middle and poor besides the landless. This has given rise to a type of class relations that was traditionally absent within tribal societies (Shah 1982; Bose 1984; Pathy 1984) There is however a lack of a gender perspective on the differentiation witnessed by tribal societies over the years. Studies on this aspect are scanty. Hence we have no clear idea as to the kind of relations that have developed or are developing between men and women across the different social categories within tribal society. Of course these are a few studies which provide some insights into this dimension. For example, Punalekar in his study of tribes like Dhodia, Chodhra, Gamit and others in Gujarat points out a division between the well-to-do and the lower strata. This difference in the social and political behaviour is also reflected in the social situation of women of the two categories. Women of the well-off section have come to enjoy certain advantages. The daughters get enrolled in local schools to get pre-primary education.

There is a distinct tendency among these categories to provide them higher education in schools away from the native village. Many of them join professional courses such as teaching and nursing and some even pursue technical courses. They also take advantage of the facilities provided under reservation.[7] Migration to cities for education provides them with opportunities to acquaint themselves with urban ways of living and thinking. Their food habits and dress patterns reflect the influence of the urban way of life. There is also a tendency among them, on the one hand, to emulate the norms and practices of the women of the dominant caste groups and, on the other, to deliberately abdicate or de-emphasize their own traditional customs, rituals and social practices. Also there is a feeling of increasing disregard and even indifference towards women of a lower stratum of their tribe or village.

Additionally, school enrolment is low and the drop-out rate high among tribal women from a lower stratum. They hardly move beyond the primary level. Due to the struggle for survival they are forced to discontinue studies and go out to earn and supplement the family income. They are constrained to work as construction labourers, domestic servants, cart-pullers, scrap collectors, vendors, etc. Yet the hardships they go through and the contribution they make to the family income is hardly recognized by men. In towns the women develop a heightened sense of insecurity and sense of dependence. In fact, often their fathers, husbands or brothers decide about their work and wages. Often women challenge such decisions taken by men if they are taken without their consultation or at lower wage rates (Punalekar 1988: 94–102). Sachchidananda demonstrates how educated Hos in white-collar employment, in recent years, aspire for housebound wives as a mark of higher social status. This ultimately has lowered the status of women (Sachchidananda 1988: 84). One also gets a glimpse of the kind of changes that seem to be emerging especially among the richer section of tribal society from the discussion on bride price. In some of the tribal communities of Arunachal Pradesh, it has been shown how the rich among them have been using the traditional practice of bride price for their own sexual aggrandizement (Nongbri 1998; Mann 1988). A shift from bride price to dowry has also been pointed out among the educated and salaried of some tribes (Misra 1984: 107; Kishwar 1987: 151). Withdrawal of women from activities outside the household has also been reported from tribes in Orissa (Menon 1992: 106). Whereas social differentiation has been one kind of transformation brought about predominantly by the state policies and programmes, the other kind of transformation that has arisen is the increasing disparity between men and women in tribal society, upsetting the hitherto relatively egalitarian arrangement. The state policies and programmes in respect of tribes are broadly of two kinds—protective and developmental. The 'protective' includes constitutional and legislative rights that safeguard the interest of the tribes. Developmental measures include programmes and activities that are initiated for promoting the welfare of tribal people. It is to this aspect of the state agenda that scholars have given the greatest attention.

The fruits of the measures taken under the constitutional provisions have however been far from even. The unevenness is marked across tribes as well as within tribes, especially as regards gender. This is reflected in their representation in education, government and semi-government employment, institutions of governance, etc. The female literacy rate among tribes as per the 1991 census stood at 18.2 per cent as against 29.6 for men. Further, whereas the enrolment ratio for girls has been lower than that for boys, the drop-out the rate has been higher for girls than for boys. As per the All India Education Survey 1986, the enrolment ratio for girls stood at 67.96 as against 111.05 for the boys at the primary level. The corresponding figure for the drop-out rate as per the same report was 78.73 for girls as against 71.57 for boys (Ambasht 1993: 61). In respect of health, most studies tend to suggest poor nutritional status and greater incidence of anaemia among women than men (Basu 1993: 30–1; Menon 1992: 102). Such disparity is visible in white-collar employment as well as in the domain of politics—local, state and national—as one can see from the statistical profile of the tribal population-dominated states of north-eastern India (Govt. of India 2000). Men and women have thus been differentially affected in respect of avenues and opportunities opened up by the state under the constitutional provisions. On the whole women have remained handicapped in almost all these new sectors of social, economic and political life.

Even the measure of autonomy, control or comfort they previously enjoyed in some spheres has now been taken away from them by the state policies and programmes. They have been now constrained to work under more depressing conditions. Fernandes and Menon show how the depletion of natural resources has impacted women. They have been exposed not only to greater hardship and difficulties due to the depletion of resources (land, forest, water) both at the level of the household and the community, but also to greater danger due to the changing nature of work and livelihood. Women now often have to walk long distances to collect wood for fuel and water for household needs. They cannot now easily find fodder for cattle and in certain cases, cannot even meet the daily requirement of food for the family. To cope with such developments and the lack of alternative modes of livelihood tribal men and women have migrated on a large scale to distant places and even to metropolises in search of employment (Fernandes & Menon 1987; Menon 1993: 350). Nongbri has tried to highlight some of the problems a state-sponsored project such as the Supreme Court ban on timber logging has created for the tribal women of the northeast region. She points out how this ban has resulted in an increase in women's already overburdened work responsibilities. It has imposed additional burden on women to meet the economic needs of the family and has also increased their domestic chores manifold. She also points out how it not only threatens women's traditional rights to land and forest, but also enforces their marginalization from the management of natural productive resources (Nongbri 2001: 1898–9).

Conclusion: Emerging Discourse

Tribal communities in India are enormously diverse and heterogeneous. There are wide-ranging differences among them with regard to language, physical characteristics, demographic traits, modes of livelihood and cultural exposure. They are in fact more heterogeneous than the larger Indian population, if caste is excluded from the consideration. The People of India project launched on 2 October 1985 under the auspices of the Anthropological Survey of India enumerated 461 tribal communities, of which 174 have been identified as sub-groups.[8] There is an apparent variation in the traditional treatment and position of women among different tribes. Their roles, activities, participation, rights, privileges, restraints and impositions and so on differ. At the same time, women continue to be governed by customary laws and norms. The data that we have on gender in tribal societies have been sketchy especially in the context of transformations that have been going on in tribal societies in recent years. Given such heterogeneity, it is difficult to generalize on the position of women as a whole across tribal groups in India. What has been observed can at best be described as being illustrative and heuristic.

Despite such heterogeneity, they seem to share one point in common. That is, that they are different from the dominant community of the region. The dominant community has always been seen as alien and as outsiders. Nowhere is this more pronounced than in situations where groups identified as tribes have been in intense competition and conflict with the dominant regional community or even with those from outside the dominant community. In northeast India, such conflict not only resulted in the creation of tribal states but also an exodus of the non-tribal population from the sub-region. Yet such conflict still prevails especially in states or regions where non-tribes still form a significant part of the population (Bhattacharjee 1982; Kumar 1995). In the rest of India, this is reflected much more in Jharkhand than any other region. The outsiders here have invariably been described as exploiters and oppressors and are addressed by terms such as the 'diku'. In Meghalaya also, a very strong term, 'dakhar', is used for outsiders.[9] In a social arrangement such as this, tribal societies have been experiencing a great deal of threat to their identity on account of the nature and type of changes that have been taking place in their societies. There has been a steady erosion of their life support system—land and forest. There has been an increasing pauperization of the majority of tribes. There is a loss of language. There is the danger of tribes becoming a minority in their own land. Given all these, the construction of identity and community has been moving in different kinds of directions. On the one hand, there has been a movement against the influx of outsiders for fear of becoming a minority in their own state or region. On the other, there has been the demand for either an autonomous council or region or state with a view to protect their social, cultural and economic interest. Such articulations are more marked in the eastern and northeastern regions than the other regions of tribal India. In all these, traditions and customary law and therefore even the gender issue play pivotal roles.

This has led to an interesting discussion on gender issues among the intelligentsia of many tribal groups. The issues under discussion have far-reaching consequences on the freedom of women on the one hand and the issue of equality on the other, especially in regard to property rights in land. One of the liveliest discussions has been going on in Jharkhand. The discussion there revolves around three points. One concerns the tribal tradition or, to be more precise, the tribal customary law. As per the customary law, land in many tribal communities is held by the lineage and not by individuals. Individual families have a right of use but cannot transfer it by sale or other means outside the lineage. This being the tribal tradition, the articulation of the demand for a share in ownership of land by women is considered misplaced and against the tribal tradition and ethos. The other two relate to the transfer of tribal land from tribes to non-tribes and the use of the provision of reservation by children born out of inter-tribe marriage. It hardly needs any mention that the latter has emerged out of an encounter of tribes with non-tribes.

One of the marked features of changes in tribal society is the large-scale shifting of the ownership of tribal land from tribes to non-tribes. Several studies point towards the massive land dispossession starting with British rule. This process has got accentuated in post-independence India despite enactment of the Land Transfer Regulation in states with a large tribal population. As in January 1999 the area alienated stood at over 9 lakh acres. The states where this was the most widespread were Andhra Pradesh, undivided Madhya Pradesh, Bihar (now Jharkhand), Gujarat and Orissa. The ways in which tribal land has passed from tribes to non-tribes are mainly through fraud, force, enticement, encroachment and indebtedness (Govt. of India 2001: 119).

One of the ways by which non-tribals are acquiring tribal land is by marrying tribal women. In view of the fact that there is a restriction on the alienation of land from tribes to non-tribes, such methods have become fairly pronounced in areas like Jharkhand. In fact, Singh refers to the large incidence of alienation of tribal land through marriage with tribal women among the Hos of Singhbhum (Singh 1988: 3). Tribal women with such marriages are seen not only as aligning with the dikus but also as conduits of land transfer from tribes to non-tribes. Often after such transactions the non-tribal men desert their tribal wives. This is an emotive issue among tribes in view of the long chain of struggle that they have waged against the alienation of tribal land. Coupled with this is the wider issue of tribal demography. Tribes in their own territory/locality are increasingly losing their numerical ground with far-reaching economic and political implications. In the process, their survival as a group/community seems to be at stake.

Hence anything which tends to jeopardize their land and population is seen with a great deal of indignation. That explains the indignation against women marrying outsiders, especially those who are considered diku. At times of conflict and tension between tribes and non-tribes, social mobilization has been used against such marriage alliances. Sometimes coercion and intimidation have been used against young women in a courtship with men of non-tribal origin. Somewhat related is the issue of reservation. There has been a general tendency among families of mixed (inter-tribe) marriages to take advantage of reservation extended for the tribes. This is indeed problematic. Are children born of a tribal mother and non-tribal father to be considered tribal or non-tribal? The question has two dimensions. One is legal and the other is socio-cultural. After all even 'tribe' as a legal category, in the sense of a scheduled tribe, has a socio-cultural basis. Both these aspects are problematic in the case of families under reference. As per the customary law of the community described as scheduled tribe, the lineage is invariably derived from the father's side, which makes the children's status as tribes problematic. Even if they take their mother's totemic title and seek advantage of the legal provisions for tribes, they are still contravening customary law. And yet one finds children born of such wedlock taking full advantage of the reservation facilities thereby depriving the genuine tribes. Such a phenomenon is fairly widespread in Jharkhand. That partly explains why there is so much resentment of non-tribals marrying tribals.

An equally interesting discourse on tribal society is over the issue of women's property rights, particularly inheritance. A section of tribal society is in favour of property rights in land for women, despite resistance to the same in the name of custom and tradition. In the case of Jharkhand, for example, it is argued that, as per tribal tradition, there is no individual ownership of land. Rather, the tradition there is one of the *khunt-katti* system, in which land is invariably held by a lineage and therefore the property belongs to no one individual. Hence, the question of extending ownership rights in land to women does not arise. However, it may be of interest to note Singh's observation on this aspect. A higher sex ratio among the Ho tribe accounts for a large number of spinsters. A number of them claimed their customary right to maintenance, which was often questioned by their male agnates. Singh, as the commissioner of Chotanagpur, disposed of a large number of cases regarding Ho women's right to maintenance according to custom (Singh 1988: 3). A similar articulation of identity is also evident in a matrilineal society like the Khasis. However, among the Khasis the ethnic identity issue is raised along with the articulation of changes in the system of kinship, viz. kinship role and rules of inheritance (Nongbri 1998, 2000). Resistance to women's property rights is also related to the economics of land size. It is argued that women's entitlement to land rights will lead to further subdivision and fragmentation of already subdivided and fragmented land and will have implications for farm efficiency and viability.

Issues such as these pose the problem of a woman as an individual and citizen on the one hand and as a member of the community on the other. As an individual and as a citizen a woman is entitled to the provisions of human rights as well as of citizenship, which guarantee the individual right to freedom. However, the provision of human rights as well as the Indian constitution also provides for the protection and safeguarding of tribal interest in its capacity as either a minority or an oppressed social group/community. Taking a position either way can only be made at the risk of being accused of ignoring or overlooking the other dimension of the problem. This is sure to be more difficult for non-tribal scholars or activists than for tribals. The problem has to be resolved from within by tribal people themselves.

Notes

1. K.S. Singh, a well-known anthropologist cum historian and former Director-General of the Anthropological Survey of India, has made this observation.

2. Sanskritization is a term coined by the well-known sociologist M.N. Srinivas. The term is used to describe a process whereby the communities lower down the hierarchy emulate the lifestyle of the dominant caste or the caste just above it. By doing so the caste attempts to move up in the ladder of caste hierarchy. The term sanskritization has also been extended to understand the process of social change taking place in tribal society. In my view the extension of the term is inadequate in the tribal context. After all, a higher social status or social mobility is not the overriding concern among them. Further, even with sanskritization they are invariably assigned a low social position. This being the case it seems more appropriate to speak of Hinduization than sanskritization in the tribal context.

3. The core of the bhagat movement is abandonment and exorcism of the minor spirits. It demands adoption of the Hindu rules of ritual purity such as vegetarianism, ritual bath, sacred thread, etc.

4. Eleven regional seminars sponsored by the ICSSR-NERC were held in different parts of northeast India between May 1998 and February 1989. As many as 136 presentations were made in these seminars. Reports of the directors of the regional seminars were discussed at length in a social scientists' meet in Gauhati University between 23 and 25 February 1989. The purpose of this meet was to distil the information and points of view of the vast number of papers and discussants.

5. A full-fledged state developed among the Jaintias well before the coming of the British. No such development took place among the Khasis. However they did have a kind of political system, which was not exactly a state but something close to it. It was a kind of chiefdom.

6. For a good account of state formation in tribal societies, see S. Sinha (ed.), *Tribal Politics and State System in Pre-Colonial Eastern and North-Eastern India*.

7. The benefits of reservation are provided to the members of the scheduled caste and scheduled tribe communities in the domain of politics, government employment and institutions of

higher learning in proportion to the size of their population. Accordingly, 7.5 per cent of seats/jobs have been earmarked for the tribes at the national level. The corresponding figure for the scheduled castes is 15 per cent.

8. Several volumes have been published under the auspice of the project. The publications have been classed into national and state series.

9. The terms used in a pejorative sense have a strong evocative and emotive tone. They are widely employed by the tribes of these regions as a rallying ground for social and political mobilization especially if tribal interest is at stake.

References

Indian Anthropological Society. 1978. *Tribal Women in India. Calcutta.*

Ambasht, N.K. 1993. 'Status of Tribal Women in India: Educational Implications'. *Social Change* 23 (4): 60–5.

Basu, S.K. 1993. 'Health Status of Tribal Women in India'. *Social Change* 23 (4): 19–39.

Bhattacharjee, J.B. (ed.). 1982. *Social Tension in North-East India.* Shillong: North-East Council for Social Science Research.

Bose. N.K. 1941. 'The Hindu Method of Tribal Absorption'. *Science and Society* 7: 188–94.

Bose, P.K. 1984. *Classes and Class Relations among Tribes of Bengal.* Delhi: Ajanta Books International.

Council for Social Development (CBD). 1993. *Social Change* 23 (4) [Special issue on 'Status of Tribal Women in India'].

Chauhan, Abha. 1990. *Tribal Women and Social Change in India.* Etawah: A.C. Brothers.

Dalton, E.T. 1872. *Descriptive Ethnology of Bengal.* Calcutta: Superintendent, Govt. Printing Press.

Elwin, Verrier. 1961. *Nagaland.* Shillong: The Research Dept., Adviser's Secretariat.

———. 1986. *Baigas.* Delhi: Gyan Publication.

Fernandes, Walter & Menon, Geeta. 1987. *Tribal Women and Forest Economy: Deforestation, Exploitation and Social Change.* New Delhi: Indian Social Institute.

Fürer-Haimendorf, Christoph von. 1933. *Naked Nagas.* Calcutta: Thacker, Spink & Co.

Ghurye, G.S. 1963. *The Scheduled Tribes.* Bombay: Popular Prakashan.

Govt. of India (Planning Commission). 2001. *Report of the Steering Committee on Empowering the Scheduled Tribes.* New Delhi: Planning Commission.

———. 2000. *Women in India (A Statistical Profile).* New Delhi: Planning Commission.

Gupta, R.K. 1979. 'Witchcraft Murders in the Duars' in Troisi, J. (ed.), *The Santals: Readings in Tribal Life, Vol. 1: Religion and Magic.* Delhi: Indian Social Institute, pp. 265–75.

Hutton, J.H. 1921. *The Sema Nagas.* Oxford: Oxford University Press.

Kelhou. 1998. 'Women in Angami Society' in Zehol, L. (ed.), *Women in Naga Society.* New Delhi: Regency Publications, pp. 55–61.

Kelkar, G. & Nathan, Dev. 1993. 'Women's Land Rights and Witches' in Miri, M. (ed.), *Continuity and Change in Tribal Society.* Shimla: IIAS, pp. 109–18.

Kishwar, Madhu. 1987. 'Toiling Without Rights'. *Economic and Political Weekly* 22 (3): 95–101; 22 (4): 149–55; 22 (5): 194–9.

Kosambi, D.D. 1975. *The Culture and Civilization in Ancient India in Historical Outline.* Delhi: Vikas Publishing House.

Kumar, B.B. 1995. *Tension and Conflict in North-East India.* New Delhi: Cosmo Publications.

Mandelbaum, D.G. 1970. *Society in India.* Bombay: Popular Prakashan.

Mann, K. 1987. *Tribal Women in a Changing Society.* Delhi: Mittal Publications.

———.1988. 'Bride-Price in Tribal North-East India' in Singh J.P., Vyas, N., Mann, R.S. (ed.), *Tribal Women and Development.* Jaipur: Rawat Publications, pp. 169–78.

———. 1996. *Tribal Women on the Threshold of Twenty First Century.* New Delhi: MD Publication.

Mehrotra, N. 1992. 'Angami Naga Women: Some Reflections on their Status', in Channa, S.M. (ed.), *Nagaland: A Contemporary Ethnography.* New Delhi. Cosmo Publications, pp. 147–80.

———. 2004. 'Situating Tribal Women'. *The Eastern Anthropologist* 57 (1): 61–73.

Menon, G. 1993. 'Tribal Women: The Ignored Sector in the Development Debate' in Miri, M. (ed.), op. cit., pp. 350–3.

———. 1992. 'Socio-Economic Transition and the Tribal Women' in Chaudhuri, B. (ed.), *Tribal Transformation in India*, vol. 1, pp. 88–109.

Misra, P.K. 1984. 'From Bride-Price to Dowry' in Singh, K.S. (ed.), *Economies of the Tribes and their Transformation*. Delhi: Concept Publishing Company, pp. 104–7.

Nathan, Dev. 1997. 'Gender Transformations in Tribes' in Nathan, Dev (ed.), *From Tribe to Caste*. Shimla: IIAS, pp. 247–86.

Nongbri, T. 1998. 'Gender Issues and Tribal Development' in RGICS Paper No. 47 (*Problems in Tribal Society—Some Aspects*).

———. 2000. 'Khasi Women and Matriliny: Transformations in Gender Relations'. *Gender, Technology and Development* 4 (3): 359–95.

———. 2001. 'Timber Ban in North-East India. Effects on Livelihood and Gender'. *Economic and Political Weekly* XXXVI (21): 1893–1900.

Pathy, J. 1984. *Tribal Peasantry: Dynamics of Development*. Delhi: Inter-India Publications.

Punalekar, S.P. 1988. 'Tribal Women and Development Milieu: Social Context and Emerging Contradictions' in Singh, J.P. et al. (eds), op. cit., pp. 98–108.

Risley, H.H. 1891. *The Tribes and Castes of Bengal*. Calcutta: Bengal Secretariat Press.

Roy Burman, B.K. 1994, *Tribes in Perspective*. Delhi: Mittal Publications.

———. 1988. 'Challenges of Development and Tribal Women' in Singh, J.P. et al. (eds), op. cit., pp. 11–27.

———. 1970. *Demographic and Socio-economic Profiles of the Hill Areas of North-east India*. Delhi: Govt. of India, Census Division.

Russell, R.V. and Hiralal, R.B. 1916. *Tribes and Castes of Central Provinces of India*. London: Macmillan & Co.

Sachchidananda. 1988. 'Tribal Women in the Throes of Development' in Singh, J.P. et al. (eds), op.cit., pp. 79–90.

Shah, Ghanshyam. 1982. 'Tribal Issues: Problems and Perspectives' in Chaudhuri, B. (ed.), *Tribal Transformation in India*. vol. 2. Delhi: Inter-India Publications, pp. 113–41.

Sen, S. 1985. *Social and State Formation in Khasi Jaintia Hills*. Delhi: B.R. Publishing Corporation.

Singh, A.K. and Rajyalakshmi, C.1993. 'Status of Tribal Women in India'. *Social Change* 23 (4): 3–18.

Singh, K.S. 1988. 'Tribal Women: An Anthropological Perspective' in Singh, J.P. et al. (eds), op.cit., pp. 3–10.

Sinha, S. 1958. 'Tribal Culture of Peninsular India as a Dimension of Little Tradition in the Study of Indian Civilization: A Preliminary Statement'. *Journal of American Folklore* 71 (281): 504–18.

———. (ed.). 1987. *Tribal Politics and State System in Pre-Colonial Eastern and North-Eastern India*. Calcutta: Centre for Studies in Social Sciences.

Thurston, E. 1906. *Castes and Tribes of Southern India*. Madras: Madras Govt. Press.

Unnithan-Kumar, Maya. 1997. *Identity, Gender and Poverty. New Perspectives on Caste and Tribe in Rajasthan*. Oxford: Berghahn Books.

Vidyarthi, L.P. 1982. 'Research on Tribal Culture of India' in Nayar, P.K.B. (ed.), *Sociology in India (Retrospect and Prospect)*. Delhi: B.R. Publishing Corporation, pp. 351–438.

Vidyarthi, L.P. and Rai, B.K. 1977. *The Tribal Culture of India*. Delhi: Concept Publishing Company.

Zehol, L. 1998. 'The Tangkhul Women Today' in Zehol, L. (ed.), op. cit., pp. 20–9.

21

The Second 'Women's War' and the Emergence of Democratic Government in Manipur*

SAROJ N. ARAMBAM PARRATT AND
JOHN PARRATT

The night has passed,
The whole day has gone,
Lady, tie up your hair,
The hair so dishevelled:
One December 12th has passed,
Another December 12th has come.
Have you forgotten?
Did you believe that your hair could be tied?
Did you believe that this day would ever return?

—(poem by Hijam Irabot)

The story of what V.P. Menon euphemistically termed the 'integration' of the Indian states has still not received the scholarly attention it deserves.[1] The little state of Manipur,[2] situated on India's northeastern border with Myanmar, was one of the last to be incorporated into the Indian union. But remarkably, during the brief twilight period of its re-emergence as an independent state between 1947 and 1949, Manipur conducted the first democratic elections on the subcontinent. That this happened at all was in large measure due to a remarkable popular movement by Meitei women.[3] Beginning as a mass protest against the economic exploitation of the rice supply by Marwari traders, who were aided and abetted by a corrupt king, it developed into the most important single catalyst for the movement for democratic reform, providing a popular platform which underpinned the political activism of the elites who eventually overthrew the old feudal order.

The high social and economic status of women in Meitei society was frequently remarked upon by British colonial officers.[4] Despite the dominance of Hinduism in the plains of Manipur, Meitei women suffered none of the humiliating oppression of their sisters elsewhere on the subcontinent. Above all, the women controlled the food supplies

*From *Modern Asian Studies*, vol. 35, no. 4 (2001), pp. 905–19.

and the markets, and were therefore a dominant economic force. From the beginning of the British period they had showed themselves capable and organized enough to take mass action when occasion demanded. The first *Nupilal* or 'Women's War' in 1904 had effectively forced a former Political Agent to rescind onerous demands he had imposed on the population,[5] and this set in train a tradition of women's political protest which remains to this day.

The Outbreak of the Second *Nupilal*

The agitation began late in 1939 at the main market in the capital Imphal. This was situated at Khwairamband within the British Reserve, and therefore technically under the control of the Political Agent rather than the Maharajah or Durbar. It was a market of very considerable size. According to the Political Agent, Christopher Glimson, over 2,000 women traded there beneath the covered sheds, and double that number in the open air outside.[6] Though there were legally no 'reserved' seats, in practice the regular market women had their own individual places, which were often passed down from mother to daughter, and attempts by outsiders to occupy these places were severely re-buffed. The British officials had never been very successful in imposing order on the women's market. As Sir Robert Reid, the Governor of Assam, remarked, 'Manipuri women are notorious for their independence and their proneness to take direct action to get their own way.' He recalled that when a previous officiating political officer had attempted to introduce stricter regulations on the bazaar it resulted in his 'being sur-rounded by these women and threatened with a ducking in the river unless he withdrew certain orders'.[7]

The bazaar traded in many items, including locally produced fabrics. Most impor-tant of all, however, was the sale of rice. Though there were several rice mills in Manipur, the bulk of the rice consumed in the state was at that time husked by hand by the women, and then sold in the markets. Most of the paddy which was milled was destined for export. Only three mills were owned by Meiteis, so the great bulk of this trade was in the hands of Marwaris. Export contracts were entered into by Marwari traders, in-cluding the supply of the British Army Reserve in Kohima. Permits to export were required, and a cart tax imposed in order to control the export trade. After the British occupation of Manipur in 1891 the Political Agent alone could authorize the export of rice, and the cart tax provided a sizeable revenue for the state. In 1912, however, authorization for export was delegated to a trading company for a fixed payment. Dur-ing the 1920s this change was exploited by the Marwari traders in Manipur, who began to increase the amount of rice exported. This foreign involvement was not a great threat to the women's livelihood in normal times, as there was enough rice to satisfy both local and export demand. In years of poor yield, however, there was the risk that the Marwaris would buy up more rice than could reasonably be spared and that this would be exacer-bated by hoarding. Shortage would force the price up beyond what could reasonably be afforded by the common people, thus seriously threatening the economic well-being of the women and the health of their children. This is what happened towards the end of 1939. A period of excessive rainfall affected growth, and in November the standing grain was further damaged by hail and flooding. Prices escalated, and what little rice was available was largely bought up by the Marwari traders for processing in their own mills.

It was then either immediately exported or hoarded.[8] There is some evidence that the rice yield had in any case been declining steadily since the beginning of the century, and that despite the greater demand because of a growing population very little extra land had been released for cultivation. However that may be, the proportion of the gross amount of rice exported did increase very significantly.[9] Aside from the farming out of the export licence, the introduction of motorized transport also made it possible to maximize the amount that could be shifted during the six-week period permitted for exporting.

Towards the end of 1939 Gimson was thus faced with a serious problem, and with a real possibility of widespread hunger. While technically the responsibility for resolving the situation rested with the Maharajah and the Durbar, it was Gimson and his assistant Sharpe to whom the women turned for help. Christopher Gimson was an experienced officer in the Indian Civil Service. A Cambridge graduate, he had arrived in India in 1911 and had worked for most of his career in Assam. He had been posted to Manipur first in 1918, as President of the State Durbar (a position usually occupied by the Assistant Political Agent), and became Political Agent in 1933. Gimson combined a quiet efficiency with a relaxed approach to his job and a genuine ability to relate to Manipuris at all levels.[10] He seems throughout the Nupilal to have remained friendly and accessible. Gimson's assistant, T.A. Sharpe, however, was inexperienced and hardly qualified to face the demands thrust upon him when he was appointed President of the Manipur State Durbar in August 1939. Though Gimson was later to say that Sharpe 'did well and is personally popular',[11] he was ill equipped to face what proved his baptism by fire. Like Gimson he was a graduate of Emmanuel College, Cambridge, but had come to India only a couple of years before. Reid was later to remark that Sharpe was really too young to have been appointed Assistant Political Agent (he was only 26), but that at the time there was no one more senior available. Clearly the Durbar resented having such a young man as its president, and the Maharajah found it galling to have to take advice from him. As Gimson commented, 'the people do not take much notice of him'.[12]

The situation had been deteriorating for some time before the actual rioting broke out.[13] In some respects the rice issue was the culmination of the many oppressive measures of the misrule of Chura Chand,[14] but it was at the same time the most serious since it struck at the heart of the economic life of the women and the well-being of their families. As early as mid-September a potential problem had been recognized, and the export of rice had been suspended until late November.[15] By the following month the price had risen from Re 1 Annas 12 a maund to Rs 2, and supplies were again running short. Small groups of women then determined to take matters into their own hands and to try to prevent the bullock carts carrying rice from reaching the Marwari storehouses. This they began to do on 7 December.[16] Anti-Marwari feelings were further inflamed by a report of insulting behaviour. Rajani Devi,[17] one of the women's leaders, with some companions had gone on the evening of the 11th to the Marwari shops to try to purchase rice. All the shops were closed, but Juriya Chand Serogi, the son of one of the owners, emerged and taunted the Meitei women that they would that year have to eat broken rice, and that the following year they would be fed on *chengup* mixed with the dust from under his feet.[18] This was an appalling insult, for which the Political Officer later made the father of the accused submit an abject written apology. During the next few days the women took more violent measures. Some carts were seized and others overturned and their loads scattered, and groups of women roamed the streets after dark to try to prevent clandestine deliveries. Some were arrested and briefly jailed. According to the Manipuri State Chronicle the women also persuaded the Meitei mill owners to cease milling rice for export.[19]

In the early hours of 12 December a large number of women gathered and resolved to appeal to the Political Agent to reintroduce the ban on export, and proceeded on his bungalow. Gimson, however, was some 60 miles south of the capital on tour (ironically it was his fifty-third birthday). They then went to Sharpe's office, and subsequently to the Durbar. Sharpe immediately sent the assistant superintendent of police to fetch his superior, and did what he could in the meantime. He gave orders for a complete survey of the rice stocks, and persuaded the Durbar to start an inquiry. He pointed out that a stoppage of exports would require the sanction of the Maharajah and that this was not possible since the ruler had left the country for Nabadwip, to perform *asti* for his late mother.[20] This failed to satisfy the women. By early afternoon over a thousand women had assembled in the market, whence they marched out to put pressure on Sharpe to telegraph the Maharajah.[21] Sharpe agreed and went to the telegraph office, surrounded by the women, who now numbered over 4,000. He successfully despatched his telegram, but it was then found that the Maharajah was not then in Nabadwip. Eventually one of the palace officials, Khaidem Ngonyai, managed to discover his whereabouts and sent a further telegram describing the situation. In the meantime Sharpe attempted to leave the office, but found his way blocked by a solid sea of ladies, who were demanding an immediate answer from the king. Fearing somewhat for the youthful Sharpe's safety, the two senior military officers in Imphal, Major Bullfield and Civil Surgeon Major Cummings, managed to negotiate their way through the crowd to join Sharpe in the telegraph office. However, they too now found their path to freedom blocked. The hostage-taking seems to have been on the whole without violence, and though food was denied the besieged officers a bearer was allowed through with drinks.[22] Time passed and still no reply from Nabadwip came through. Meanwhile back at camp Bullfield's second in command, Captain Stone, was becoming increasingly worried about the fate of his superior officers, and at about 2.30 p.m. led a platoon of soldiers to the telegraph office to find out what was going on. As Mills was later to point out, it was the appearance of the Assam Rifles which caused the crowd to erupt. Some of the soldiers were Kukis and Nepalis, and the sight of hill men and foreigners with fixed bayonets pushing Meitei women aside to make a path for the British officers to escape incensed the bystanders.[23] There was a violent reaction. Many of the women resisted stoutly and a number were severely manhandled. Now the men and children, who had been observers on the fringes of the crowd, joined the fray. The soldiers were pelted with stones, and most of the windows in the telegraph office were smashed. Several women were injured by the soldiers, some seriously,[24] and others were pitched into the cold waters of a nearby pond. It was not until nearly midnight that the British officers left and the compound was cleared.

Gimson got back to the capital at about 3 a.m. on the 13th and immediately tried to negotiate a settlement. The situation was improved at around 1.30 p.m. by the receipt of a telegram from the Maharajah requesting the Political Agent to stop the export of rice with immediate effect. The women now, however, shifted the focus of their protest to the rice mills. In the afternoon a large crowd, mainly composed of women, gathered in the Police Bazaar, which was outside the British Reserve. The crowd swelled to around 10,000, and after an excited meeting decided to march on the rice mills and destroy them. Gimson was forewarned about the demonstration, but decided to take no action to break it up, hoping that the activity would function as a safety valve for the women's frustration. Instead at around 5.30 p.m. he personally went to meet the women's leaders and spent over two hours trying to reason with them. He promised that he would make an order banning the use of mills from operating during the crisis. The three Meitei mill owners swiftly agreed and later on the Marwaris also gave a written undertaking not to work their mills.[25] Fuel for their lorries was also to be denied them.

Next day, however, a rumour began to circulate that one of the Marwaris, in order to get around the ban on the export of raw rice, had soaked and boiled rice to make *chengpak* ('flattened rice') in preparation to send it out of the country. Since his mill was situated at Mantripukhri, a few miles northeast of the British Reserve, it was technically outside Gimson's jurisdiction. The women now determined to carry out their threat of direct action, and set to organizing a march on the mill. Gimson got wind of their plan and drove to Mantripukhri ahead of them. He personally removed the electronic switch to immobilize the mill, and subsequently took the same action with all the mills owned by other Marwaris.[26] He also instructed the Hydro-Electric Board to suspend supplies to them. This effectively prevented the Marwaris getting access to husked rice, since the Meitei women adamantly refused to clean it by hand for them.

By now the conflict had become polarized and increasingly caught up with deeper political motives. Later on the 14th the women regrouped in the Police Bazaar and now, for the first time, the women's movement began to be joined by male political activists. While the most dangerous Meitei revolutionary, Hijam Irabot Singh, was out of the country at the time, the meeting was addressed by one of his colleagues, Kulabidhu Laishram. Passions were further aroused by the report that 18 women had been arrested at Wangjing for rioting. The police seemed determined on confrontation and charged the unarmed crowd repeatedly with lathis. They were eventually dispersed late in the evening. Several arrests were made (including Kulabidhu), a number of people were injured, and it was reported that three women had been killed. Gimson had the Assam Rifles standing by, but was reluctant to commit them.

The Politicization of the Movement

While there were a few men and boys on the fringes of the riot at the telegraph office on 12 December, it is clear that the protest began as a women's movement, and that its focus was on an issue which affected primarily the Meitei women. This was clearly recognized by Gimson in his report on the events of the 12th: 'this was', he commented, 'wholly a women's affair'. He went on to claim that the women were actually resentful and impatient with men who got involved at this stage: 'Men and boys were round the outside (of the protest), but when one of them interrupted a chat between me and one of them (i.e. the women) she rounded on him and the men near him ran away.'[27] Both in its initial stages, and in the demonstrations that continued sporadically for the best part of a year, the bulk of the protesters were women. Though the reimposition of the ban on rice export and the disabling of the mills meant that the 'women's war' had effectively been won, two other contentious issues resulted. The first was the matter of control of the market, the second complaints against the security forces for action taken against the demonstrators.

From 12 December the Khwairamband market had been boycotted by the Meitei women, and most of the trade there had effectively ceased. It is clear the great majority of the women supported this stand, though there is some evidence of coercion. Gimson was puzzled by the continuation of the boycott after the women's original demands had been met, and confessed to Mills that 'no one seems to know what they really want'.[28] But he was witness towards the end of the month (23 January) to what he called 'a grand halabaloo, mostly good tempered banter' between the hard-liners in favour of prolonging the boycott and a minority who wished to get back to normal trading. Some of the latter began to sell in other locations, but this too became a cause of friction. Gimson's main concern seems to have been that, should the supply of market produce continue to be seriously disrupted, this might lead to hunger and further unrest. At the turn of the year he became convinced that the boycott was being sustained more by coercion than persuasion and was unwilling to let it continue unchecked. Rather than take direct action, he gave out publicly that he would reallocate all the seats in the covered sheds at Khwairamband unless they were immediately reoccupied. This began to have the desired effect though it was almost a year before the market was operating at all normally.

The second issue, potentially more damaging to public order, was alleged army and police brutality against the women. The riot outside the telegraph office on 12 December—in which the Assam Rifles became involved—resulted in injuries to a handful of women. Anger at this was not helped by a false rumour which circulated that one of the women taken into hospital after this fracas had died. Gimson investigated the incident several days later, though he failed to appease the women's anger completely. Police violence continued sporadically. In one incident (probably on 18 December) a crowd of women besieged the Police Office demanding the release of several colleagues who had been detained following a disturbance at Wangjing. According to Rajani's eyewitness account of the event, several policemen had their batons taken from them and some new recruits were beaten up and ran away.[29] The climax of this skirmishing came on 28 December. Some of the rice carters were again prevented from selling their loads of rice to the Marwari traders, their goods were scattered on the ground and they were subsequently set upon.[30] The police inspector seems to have aggravated the situation by a verbal attack on the women. A heated argument broke out, leading to a fight during which the inspector personally punched the nearest of the women and kicked a brahmin woman in the forehead.[31] Gimson again found himself besieged by a mass of angry women, this time demanding that the police inspector be charged with assault, and for his own safety he was temporarily sent out of the capital. Relations between the common people and those supposed to uphold law and order had deteriorated to mutual animosity and mistrust. No help could be expected from the Maharajah: when he was not conveniently out of the country on pilgrimage he virtually secluded himself because of the illness of one of his daughters. Those rare occasions when he did agree to meet delegations from his people only reinforced their conviction that he was hand in glove with the Marwari traders and seeking to line his own pocket with their bribes.[32] Nor did they have any more confidence in the Durbar, which (apart from the ineffectual Sharpe) consisted only of the Maharajah's hand-picked henchmen.

Gimson, contemptuous as he was of the officers of state and the inefficient police force, was naturally reluctant to commit the Assam Rifles even within the British Reserve, and law and order elsewhere was not technically within his jurisdiction. Consequently the demonstrations continued for the rest of the year, usually in the Police Bazaar, and the guerrilla warfare between people and police smouldered on, fanned from time to time by the professional political activists. It had become clear that important as the issues of the rice supply, the market boycott, and the inability of the police to keep order were, they were but symptoms of a much deeper malaise. The 'women's war' had succeeded in opening up to public debate issues which had previously been the concern only of the small emergent political elite, namely the incompetence, nepotism and corruption of the rule of Maharajah Chura Chand and the need for wide constitutional reforms.

The Issue of Constitutional Reform

Movements for constitutional reform in the Indian states date from the 1930s and were actively encouraged towards the end of the decade.[33] In Manipur such organized protest may be said to have begun with the neo-traditional Sanamahi movement in the early 1930s,[34] which fiercely attacked the feudalism and brahminism which Chura Chand used to exercise control.[35] The women's war of 1939 effectively shattered what little respect remained for the Maharajah's authority among the common people. Gimson himself clearly read the popular feelings. The correspondence between the PA and his superiors is littered with severe criticisms of Chura Chand's rule and frequently expresses the hope that he would abdicate.[36] Gimson several times urged Chura Chand in writing to act responsibly toward his people, but had to confess that his 'stock has slumped', largely because of the outcasting scandals and his extreme avarice of which his intrigues with the Marwari traders was only one example. 'They cannot believe his promises,' he wrote to Mills, 'and I too have lost all faith.' Though Gimson confessed to personally liking the man he realized Chura Chand was both unpopular and corrupt. Likewise the Durbar, which consisted of the Maharajah's appointees, had lost credibility. Despite this, Gimson himself was not convinced that democratic constitutional reform would improve matters. He personally did not believe that the women's agitation was directed to this end, and with typical colonial disdain pointed out that 'Manipur has no tradition of democracy'.[37] Nonetheless he personally had no objection to proposals for the election of Durbar members and strongly advocated sweeping administrative changes to root out incompetence and corruption in the law courts, police, and land registration. He also proposed that the Maharajah should surrender direct control over the state departments and spend less time outside Manipur. Nor in principle was he averse to the main political party, the Nikhil Manipuri Mahasabha, playing a more active role, though he was damning in his condemnation of the self-seeking of its leaders.[38]

The Meitei revolutionary leaders of course saw things differently. Hijam Irabot Singh,[39] with his socialist anti-feudal agenda, was swift not only to jump on the bandwagon of the women's protest movement but also to seize its controls. At a meeting of the Working Group of the Nikhil Manipuri Mahasabha on the morning of 7 January 1940 Irabot's radical group split away and declared their solidarity with the women's movement. At 2 p.m. that same day he made a dramatic inflammatory speech in which he urged his hearers to avenge the blood of the brahmin woman shed by the state police.[40] He obviously had a wide popular following and was arrested two days later.[41]

The following week, on 14 January, an even more serious confrontation with the military police took place in the Police Bazaar. In this riot (known in local oral tradition as 'the battle of the sticks' because both men and women in the crowd armed themselves with weapons from a handy pile of firewood after the first police lathi charge) several serious injuries did occur and arrests were made.[42] By this time it had become clear to the British that the Indian Congress was fishing in these troubled waters.[43] The Nikhil Manipuri Mahasabha, of which Irabot was a founding member, was certainly influenced by the Indian Congress even though all its leaders were Manipuris. Irabot himself had contacts with Congress as well as with the Communist Party of India. These were powerful and complex currents and cross-currents in the political life of the state, but they owe to the Nupilal of 1939–40 an incalculable debt. For the women's war was the event which above all generated popular political awareness and acted as the main catalyst for the movement which, after a protracted struggle, eventually succeeded in displacing the feudal ancient regime and bringing about democratic elections.[44] Those elections were held in June and July 1948—four years before the first democratic elections in India itself—and by November of that year the little state of Manipur had replaced rule by the Maharajah and his appointed Durbar with a form of 'responsible government' elected on the basis of full adult franchise.

That democratic government was of course swept away when India absorbed the state in 1949. But the tradition of the Nupilal continued to live on. Mass women's protests against atrocities committed by the Indian army in Manipur have taken place from time to time, while the women's groups known as *Meira Paibi*[45] may still be seen patrolling the streets and lanes at night with flaming torches, ready to protect those whom the security forces seek to abuse or detain.

Notes

1. V.P. Menon, *The Story of the Integration of the Indian States* (Bombay, 1961). The most recent detailed study is Ian Copland, *The Princes of India in the Endgame of Empire* (Cambridge, 1997), though it has very few references to Manipur, some of them inaccurate; earlier studies include Vanga Rangaswami's work on southern India, *The Story of Integration: A New Interpretation* (Delhi, 1981).

2. Manipur existed as an independent state until the conflict with the British in 1891. While the British did not formally annex the state they appointed a boy (Chura Chand) as king, and the Political Agent effectively ruled until Chura Chand's coronation in 1907. Thereafter the British continued to retain control over the hill areas and over the 'Reserve' in the heart of the capital, Imphal. On the events of 1891 see John Parratt and Saroj Arambam Parratt, *Queen Empress vs. Tiken-drajit: The Anglo-Manipur Conflict of 1891* (New Delhi, 1992) and on the early British period, see especially Lal Dena, *British Policy Towards Manipur, 1891–1919* (Imphal, 1984).

3. The Meiteis, who comprise around two-thirds of the population of Manipur, live in the valley: the surrounding hill areas are occupied by Naga and Kuki peoples.

4. Among others, by W. McCulloch, *An Account of the Valley of Munnipore and the Hill Tribes* (Calcutta, 1859); R. Brown, *Annual Report on the Munnipore Political Agency* (Calcutta, 1874); and J. Shakespear, 'The Religion of Manipur', in *Folk Lore* 24 (1913), pp. 409–55.

5. The first Nupilal of 1904 began as protest by women against the ruling of the Political Agent that the Meitei men should rebuild colonial officers' bungalows destroyed by suspected arson.

There is some evidence that this movement was manipulated by the princes of the royal house, who were disgruntled at their loss of privileges after 1891.

6. British Library, Oriental & India Office Collection file L/PS/13/1002 (cited below as IOL) Gimson to Reid 21.3.41.

7. IOL, Reid to Gimson 16.12.39: the officer involved was C.G. Crawford, who officiated as Political Agent for six months during 1928.

8. Manipur State Library Archive, File on Women's Agitation 1939–40 (cited below as MSL), Gimson to Mills 13.12.1939.

9. In 1898–9 only 36,436 maunds of rice were exported; by 1925–6 this had risen to 155,014, and in 1938 had escalated to 372,174 maunds. By December 1939, 463,590 maunds had already been exported.

10. There is an oral tradition, preserved in H. Bhuban Singh (*The Merger of Manipur*, Imphal, 1988), that Gimson used to venture out at night into the market, hidden beneath a voluminous shawl, and listen in to what the market women were saying about current affairs; he would then engage them in conversation and try to address their problems. Our meeting with Christopher Gimson in the early 1970s confirms the archival evidence that he combined efficiency with approachability.

11. IOL, Gimson to Reid 20.1.1940.

12. Sharpe was captured and shot by the Japanese in 1944.

13. The role of the Marwari traders in this decline deserves further investigation. There had been an earlier protest against their exploitation of the rice trade as early as July 1920, which had led to a large demonstration and the imprisonment of the leaders. The Marwaris monopolized the import and export trade to the impoverishment of many of the local population, and there is clear evidence that by the 1930s they were bribing the Maharajah for their own advantage. Complaints against them and petitions for their removal were frequent and stretch back to the beginning of the century. They were allowed only within the British Reserve, and even their British protectors were sometimes critical of them. The domination of trade in Manipur by non-Manipuris remains an issue to the present time.

14. It is not the purpose of this paper to expand on these, but among the most serious were: the increasingly oppressive brahmanical regulations, especially the use of outcasting as a means of control and gaining money, the forced labour and forced guard duties, the reintroduction of *amin senkhai* (forced hospitality and portering for the land revenue officers), the law forbidding the collection of *kapok* even from trees within one's own garden, tax on fishing nets even if used for taking fish from one's own pond, and the restriction of certain patterns and colours of *phanek* (the ankle-length skirt worn by Meitei women) to the royal family: see further N. Lokendra Singh, *Unquiet Valley: Society, Economy and Politics in Manipur 1891–1950* (New Delhi, 1998).

15. There is some evidence that this was done as a result of an appeal to the Durbar by Hijam Irabot Singh, the leader of the socialist-communist faction in Meitei politics: on Irabot's role, see Karam Manomohan Singh, *Hijam Irabot Singh and Political Movements in Manipur* (New Delhi, 1989), pp. 101–2. The Maharajah ruled that the export ban should not apply to the Government contract to supply Kohima, and his son Maharajkumar Priyobarta actually opposed the ban when it was discussed in the Durbar. The ban was lifted at the request of the Marwari who had the monopoly of the cart-tax, Kustur Chand Serogi (Manipur State Archives (hereafter MSA), Durbar minute of 9.11.1940 decision to lift the ban from 24.11.1940).

16. MSA unsigned and undated letter to Mills; see also Joykumar Singh, *Social Movements in Manipur 1917–1951* (New Delhi, 1992), pp. 82–4.

17. Rajani Devi's eyewitness account is found in her *Nupilal* (Imphal, 1995).

18. *Chengup* is the powder resulting from several huskings of rice: it is used for feeding pigs and for making beer, both unclean to Hindus.

19. *Cheitharol Kumbaba* (Manipuri State Chronicle) (cited hereafter as *CK*) edited by L. Ibungohal Singh and N. Khelachandra Singh (Imphal, 1987), entry for 11.12.1939.

20. *Asti* is the depositing of the frontal bone in the Ganges.
21. According to the *CK,* Sharpe was pulled down from his car by the women and had to be escorted by Manisana, one of the princes, for his own safety.
22. Oral tradition: it would not be fanciful to attribute the non-violent protest methods as due in part to Gandhian satyagraha which became part of the political agenda in Manipur after the outbreak of war.
23. IOL, Mills to Secretary, Government of India 19.1.40: 'the Manipuris do not take kindly to being pushed about by hillmen.'
24. Gimson's report maintained there were no serious injuries or bayonet wounds. However, around half a dozen women were detained in the hospital after the riot and over 20 others were treated on the spot by Cummins and his medical assistants. Rajani claims there were more injuries than this.
25. IOL, Gimson to Mills 24.12.39.
26. *CK* for 14.12.1939.
27. IOL, Gimson to Mills 24.12.39: a comment on the papers sent to the Registry wryly noted: 'Apparently in Manipur the women do the rioting and the men look on' and again 'the ladies seem to be having high jinks at Imphal' (File P5g/40).
28. MSL, Gimson to Mills 25.1.1939.
29. It is unclear whether the arrest of the Wangjing women was because of an arson attack or because of the destruction of foodstuffs confiscated by the Wangjing constabulary.
30. Gimson reported that the women claimed they had been instructed by the Maharani to stop the carters, which he thought was possibly true: MSL, Gimson to Mills 29.12.1939.
31. For Meitei Hindus this was a particularly heinous act of sacrilege. The police officer, Dhanachandra, was in fact a son-in-law of the Maharajah.
32. MSL, Gimson to Mills 25.12.1939: 'They are saying openly that all he is after is money from the Marwaris.' It is also clear from the Manipuri sources that the king was trying to split the women's movement by bribery.
33. See e.g. the discussion of Ian Copland, *The Princes of India,* pp. 165ff. On the situation in Manipur, see MSL, Gimson to Mills 20.1.1940.
34. See further: Saroj Arambam Parratt and John Parratt, 'Reclaiming the Gods: A Neo-traditional Protest Movement in Manipur', in *Acta Orientalni,* vol. 67 (1999), pp. 241–8.
35. Irabot had in fact made an explicit call for full responsible government as early as 1938 in his presidential address to the Nikhil Manipur Mahasabha. By early 1939 the Durbar was under pressure to submit plans for reform (though the king was very reluctant to do this). In November 1939 the Nikhil Manipuri Mahasabha put forward plans for a legislature with 80% of its members elected by direct adult franchise. The rump of the Nikhil Manipuri Mahasabha which remained after the secession of Irabot's group to form the Praja Sanmeloni, subsequently became the Manipur Congress Party.
36. The British eventually virtually removed him from office into exile, even though they regarded his eldest son and successor, Bodhachandra, as very little better. Reid condemned Bodhachandra unjustifiably as 'the original happy moron' who had a 'feeble mind'. He succeeded Chura Chand in 1941.
37. MSL, Gimson to Mills 20.1.1940.
38. MSL, Gimson to Mills 1.6.1940: 'If it can be turned into constitutional ways it may even be good, but its present leaders are out to make money and I doubt whether most of them have higher ideals than that.'
39. On the career of Hijam Irabot, see especially Karam Manomohan Singh, *Hijam Irabot Singh.* Also, John Parratt and Saroj N. Arambam Parratt, 'Hijam Irabot and the Radical Socialist-democratic Movement in Manipur', *Internationales Asia Forum* (forthcoming).
40. 'We begged for rice and in return received bayonet wounds; for one handful of rice we paid two handfulls of blood . . . Let us take revenge for the spilt blood of the bramini. The women's work is finished, and now has come the time for the men' (MSA, Record of Criminal Case 4,

1940: Manipur State vs. Hijam Irabot Singh). The *CK* commented he was 'imprisoned for making the women go mad'.

41. Gimson reported that around a thousand people congregated daily during the trial which resulted from this speech, threatening that if he were sentenced they would rescue him—though in the event this did not happen when he was jailed: IOL, Gimson to Mills 20.3.1940.

42. For details see Karam Manomohan Singh, *Hijam Irabot Singh*, p. 120. *CK* comments: 'The Mahasabha group (i.e. Irabot's faction) addressed the crowd. The Maharajah gave orders not to assemble but they refused. So the soldiers went in with guns and the crowd was dispersed and ran away. The market was deserted.'

43. Gimson reported that shouts of 'bande mataram' were heard in this riot and opined that, 'it is fairly certain the lead has passed from the women to the Congress group' (Gimson to Mills 14.1.40). The indirect involvement of the Indian Congress within the state from this point has led some present day politicians both within Manipur and India as a whole to misconstrue the original objectives of the Nupilal, and to see it as a revolt against colonial British rule. A particularly striking example of this kind of reinterpretation was evident in the centenary celebrations of the Nupilal in Imphal in 1999. In fact the causes of the Nupilal had very little to do with colonial control, but were explicitly focused on the domination and exploitation of trade by foreign Marwaris and the feudal oppression of the Maharajah and his Durbar.

44. Joykumar Singh, *Social Movements in Manipur*, p. 122, comments bluntly: 'until the outbreak of the "women's agitation" in 1939 the activities of this party (i.e. the Nikhil Manipuri Mahasabha and its derivatives) were not very much significant.'

45. The *Meira Paibi* ('women bearing flaming torches') began in 1979 after a period of particularly vicious abuse of power by the Indian army forces occupying Manipur, which included several cases of rape and indiscriminate arrest and violence. It is a voluntary grass-roots vigilante women's movement organized in each locality, which has had some success in protecting citizens' basic rights.

22

Gender in the Critiques of Colonialism and Nationalism

Locating the 'Indian Woman'*

MRINALINI SINHA

K umkum Sangari and Sudesh Vaid's excellent analysis of the historical processes which reconstituted patriarchy in colonial India provides both a definition and an example of the potential of feminist historiography. They provide a definition of feminist historiography that goes much beyond an exclusively 'women's history'. According to Sangari and Vaid, 'a feminist historiography rethinks historiography as a whole and discards the idea of women as something to be *framed* by a context, in order to be able to think of gender difference as both structuring and structured by the wide set of social relations'.[1] Hence they argue, on the one hand, that feminist historiography is neither a choice, as in the choice of an area or field of study, nor a simple inclusion of women, nor an evaluation of their participation in particular movements, but rather a mode of questioning that must undergird all attempts at historical reconstruction. On the other hand, they also suggest that 'patriarchies are not . . . systems either predating or superadded to class and caste but are intrinsic to the very formation of, and changes within, these categories'.[2] Feminist historiography, conceived in these terms, recognizes that all aspects of reality are gendered and that the very experience of gender changes according to race, class/caste, nation and sexuality.

This double move is also being reflected in feminist theory in general. This is evident, for example, in the bid to go beyond the simple enumeration of gender, race, class/caste, nationality and sexuality, as parallel or co-equal axes along which oppression, identity, and subjectivity are organized, to a recognition of the ways in which these axes are mutually determining and necessarily implicated in one another. For, as Chandra Mohanty puts it, 'no one "becomes a woman" (in Simone de Beauvoir's sense) purely because she is female. . . . It is the intersections of the various systemic networks of class, race, (hetero) sexuality and nation . . . that position us as 'women".'[3] This, according to Teresa de Lauretis marks the crucial shift in feminist consciousness brought about by the interventions made by women of colour and lesbians. It has led, she suggests, to a redefinition of the feminist subject as 'not [just] *unified* or *simply divided* between positions of masculinity and femininity, but *multiply organized* across positionalities along several axes and across mutually contradictory discourses and practices'. This recognition of the interrelatedness and coimplication of various other categories, such as race, class, nation and sexuality, in gender and in one another, has made possible the redefinition of the 'feminist subject . . . as much less pure, as indeed ideologically complicitous with "the oppressor" whose position [the feminist subject] may occupy in certain sociosexual relations (though not in others), on one or another axis'.[4]

It is from within the challenges of feminist historiography as defined by Sangari and Vaid, and the redefinition of the feminist subject as outlined by Teresa de Lauretis, that I pose the problem of locating 'Indian womanhood' and the politics of feminism in colonial India. I will approach this question through a discussion of a particular historical controversy in India, occasioned by the 1927 publication of the American-born writer Katherine Mayo's *Mother India*.[5] *Mother India* was ostensibly an exposé of the condition of women in India. Although Mayo's book focuses on the various inequities imposed upon women, such as child marriage and premature maternity, by a patriarchal Hindu culture, it includes a more wide-ranging discussion of India's various social, economic and political ills, for which Mayo held Hindu culture responsible. Mayo arrived at the conclusion that far from being ready for political self-determination, India needed the continued 'civilizing' influence of the British. Her connections with the official British propaganda machine quickly discredited Mayo's credentials as a champion of women's issues in India. For nationalists, however, *Mother India's* attack on the political and cultural project of Indian nationalism, made under the pretext of a discussion of the condition of women in India, could not be left unchallenged.[6] Indeed, the book generated a tremendous controversy, the impact of which was felt in India, Britain and the United States.

My interest in this particular controversy as an Indian feminist grew out of an earlier effort to reconstruct the Indian woman as subject in the debate in which both sides used the Indian woman as the object of their starkly opposed evaluations of Indian society. My attempt was to highlight the contributions of individual women and of the women's movement in India to the *Mother India* debate. Here, I return to my earlier reading of the emergence in this controversy of what Sarojini Naidu and her other middle-class/upper-caste contemporaries identified as the 'authentic voice of modern Indian womanhood'[7] in order to explore the particular discursive strategies by which a subject position was created enabling the Indian woman to speak. I will explore the opportunity that such a reading offers for locating the Indian woman and the politics of middle-class Indian feminism.

My earlier inclination had been simply to read women's responses, following Joanna Liddle and Rama Joshi's analysis of the women's movement in India, as naturally occupying a space from which both male nationalist patriarchy and imperialist feminism could be critiqued in order to disrupt imperialist–nationalist invocations of the Indian woman in the *Mother India* controversy.[8] However, the responses of the individual women and of the organized women's movement were not readily amenable to such an analysis. A nationalistic critic of imperialism and/or imperialist feminism could very easily interpret the women's responses as a triumph of the general nationalist critique of *Mother India*. For a feminist critic of nationalism, however, the women's responses could be read just as easily as a co-optation of Indian women by nationalist politics.[9] Such possible interpretations proved to be inadequate in one crucial way. To paraphrase Chandra Mohanty, reading women's responses simply in terms of their 'achievements' or their 'failures' in relation to some ideal effectively removes them and the ideal from history, and freezes them in time and space.[10] I was forced to recognize that any interpretation that hoped to historicize women's responses or the ideals against which they are measured must refuse to take as given or self-evident either the gender politics of colonialism and nationalism which framed the *Mother India* controversy or the self-constitution of the Indian woman herself in women's responses to the controversy. Such a reading would have to take into account both the historical context which made possible the identity of the Indian woman and the particular strategies by which women learned to speak in the voice of the Indian woman.

The historical context in which the identity of the Indian woman emerged has been written about extensively, but comparatively little work has been done on women's own self-constitution within this context.[11] Here, therefore, my efforts to locate Indian womanhood and the politics of middle-class Indian feminism in the *Mother India* controversy will shift between a survey of some recent scholarship on the gender politics of colonialism and nationalism and an examination of the voice of Indian womanhood itself. This survey in no way pretends to be exhaustive, but touches primarily on those issues that may enhance a reading of Indian women's voices in the *Mother India* controversy. I will return to the responses of Indian women themselves via a brief discussion of gender in some critiques of colonialism and nationalism in India.

Chandra Mohanty's introduction to *Third World Women and the Politics of Feminism* identifies three symptomatic characteristics of imperial rule: the ideological construction and consolidation of white masculinity as normative, and the corresponding racialization and sexualization of colonized peoples; the effects of colonial institutions and policies in transforming indigenous patriarchies and consolidating hegemonic middle-class cultures in metropolitan and colonized areas; and the rise of feminist politics and consciousness in this historical context within and against the framework of national liberation movements.[12] These aspects of imperial rule mark both Mayo's *Mother India* and the imperialist-nationalist controversy following the book's publication. I will briefly make a note of some of these elements in the framing of *Mother India* and the subsequent controversy, but will focus mainly on the impact of imperial rule on the emergence of a hegemonic middle-class Indian culture and its implications for the mobilization of women in the *Mother India* controversy.

Ann Stoler, in an article on the colonial cultures of French Indo-China and the Dutch East Indies, makes the important point that the very categories of 'colonizer' and 'colonized', essential for the exercise of imperial authority, were never stable, but needed to be secured through various policies and practices that constructed and regulated particular, historically specific, gendered and racialized identities.[13] Stoler's analysis has implications for understanding why the construct of the 'manly Englishman' as the liberator of helpless Indian women and other oppressed groups becomes such a crucial element in Mayo's defence of imperial rule. Mayo's use of such old colonial stereotypes as the enlightened and reform-minded British official and the indolent and selfish Indian male who was the nemesis of helpless Indian women, however, also limited her discussion of Indian women. Consequently, in *Mother India* the Indian woman appears either as the object of the benevolent salvation of British imperialists or the object of the Indian male's cruel and barbaric practices.

Various scholars have also pointed out the collusion between imperialist and indigenous patriarchies in nineteenth-century debates over the 'woman's question' in India. Lata Mani's and Uma Chakravarti's analyses of debates about women in social-reform and protonationalist movements in India have provided illuminating insights into the simultaneous proliferation of discourses about women and their surprising marginalization in these same discourses.[14] Lata Mani's study of the official discourse on the regulation and the eventual abolition of the practice of widow immolation (sati) in the early nineteenth century clearly demonstrates that women were seldom the major concern of the various groups in this debate; instead, women were merely the sites on which competing views of tradition and modernity were debated. The legacy of these nineteenth-century debates about women was felt in many ways in the *Mother India* controversy. The understanding of tradition and modernity, for example, that framed the responses to child marriage and early sexuality were particularly colonial constructs; the arguments for and against the practice of child marriage were made, as Lata Mani has so brilliantly identified, in the context of the early nineteenth-century debate over sati, on the basis of a selective, textualized construct of Hindu culture and tradition. In such a context, the debate over child-marriage reforms shifted attention from the historical and material conditions for such practices to an evaluation of Indian culture. Both imperialists and nationalists invoked the position of the Indian woman to buttress their opposing evaluations of Indian culture. Uma Chakravarti, for example, has demonstrated that the upper-caste/class concept of the Indian/Arya woman was crucial to the modern reinvention of traditions for the protonationalist and nationalist project of national regeneration. Not surprisingly, therefore, the image of the Indian woman featured prominently in the *Mother India* debate: both sides invoked her in their battle over the nature of India.

The image of the Indian woman as simply the object of imperialist-nationalist debates, however, was further complicated by the broader nationalist agenda. The re-articulation of middle-class Indian womanhood had been necessary for the emergence of a new middle-class public and private sphere in colonial India; this same ideal of womanhood also offered a space for the mobilization of middle-class women themselves. The significance of the ideal of womanhood to the consolidation of a hegemonic middle-class culture has been examined by several scholars. Sangari and Vaid, drawing upon the works of Partha Chatterjee and Sumanta Banerjee, suggest that the definition of Indian womanhood was closely tied to the class polarization that accompanied the development of the middle class, and to the anxieties of colonial nationalism. Sumanta Banerjee argues that the need for sharper differentiation between the classes provided the context for the regulation of women's popular culture in the nineteenth century, and for the creation of a new public space for the respectable *bhadramahila* (new, educated middle-class woman) who was now defined in opposition to women from the lower economic strata.[15]

According to Partha Chatterjee, a re-articulation of Indian womanhood was crucial in the resolution of the 'constitutive contradiction' in the formation of an Indian identity.[16] The central problem for Indian nationalism, he suggests, was the problem of modernizing the nation on Western terms while at the same time retaining an essential national identity as the basis for a political claim to nationhood. Nationalist thought dealt with this contradiction by distinguishing the spiritual from the material and the inner from the outer. Nationalists could now afford to imitate the West in the outer or material sphere while retaining the spiritual or the inner sphere as an 'uncolonized space' wherein the essence of Indianness could be located. This dichotomy was related, he suggests, to the socially prescribed roles for men and women. Women as the guardians of the inner or spiritual sphere of the nation were now regarded as the embodiments of an essentialized 'Indianness'.

The re-articulation of the Indian woman for the self-definition of the nationalist bourgeoisie provided the context for the 'modernizing' of certain indigenous patriarchal modes of regulating women in orthodox Indian society.[17] Although the critique of orthodox indigenous patriarchy did afford a limited agenda for the emancipation and self-emancipation of women, its emancipatory politics were severely constrained within the modernizing project of Indian nationalism. The models for modernization, for example, drew upon notions of bourgeois domesticity and the ideals of Victorian womanhood introduced via British rule in India; yet they were crucially modified to suit the particular needs of the nationalist bourgeoisie. Dipesh Chakrabarty suggests, drawing upon Chatterjee's work, that the 'originality' of the Indian middle-class project of modernization was constituted by the nationalist 'denial of the bourgeois private': the cultural norm of a patriarchal, patrilineal, patrilocal extended family was counterposed to the bourgeois patriarchal ideals of companionate marriage.[18] This reconfiguration of the middle-class 'home', he suggests, was part of the history of the development of the modern individual in India. Indeed, it was central in marking the difference between what was 'Indian' and what was 'European/English'.

We can see the impact that nationalist modifications of bourgeois domesticity had on the construct of the Indian woman in Chakrabarty's analysis of the word 'freedom' in debates about women's education in nineteenth-century India. He suggests that while freedom in the West was defined as the right to self-indulgence, freedom in India was defined as the capacity to serve and obey voluntarily. Hence, unlike the ultra-free Western/Westernized woman who was selfish and shameless, the 'modern' Indian woman was defined as educated enough to contribute to the larger body politic but yet 'modest' enough to be unself-assertive and unselfish.[19] The ideological construct of the modern Indian woman as 'superior' to orthodox, uneducated women, to women of the lower castes/class, and to the Western/Westernized woman was key to the emerging social order in India, characterized by the consolidation of the nationalist bourgeoisie. At the same time, however, the construct of the modern Indian woman also created the climate both for women's reforms and for women's entry, under male patronage, to the male-dominated public sphere. The impact of this was evident in the unprecedented mobilization of middle-class women on behalf of the Gandhi-led nationalist movement, as well as in the all-India women's organizations and movements in the early twentieth century.

The question that we might legitimately raise at this point is that, given the ideological structures of domination outlined above, how can any reading of women's responses, as those in the *Mother India* controversy, hope to reconstruct the Indian woman as the subject of the controversy? In other words, do the ideological constructs that condition women's participation predetermine the nature of women's responses and make any interrogation of the consciousness and agency of women themselves irrelevant? I contend that a focus on the voice or the agency of women themselves does not have to be opposed to an examination of the ideological structures from which they emerged. I focus on women's responses during the *Mother India* controversy, not because they make visible the voice of the modern Indian woman that was always there, simply waiting to be expressed, but because these responses make visible the particular strategies by which a subject position was created, in a certain historical moment, from which the Indian woman could speak.

The question of the Indian woman's voice was clearly critical to the narrativization of the *Mother India* controversy. In the midst of the controversy, for example, *The Times* of London carried a piece with the provocative title: 'Indian Women: Are They Voiceless?'[20] Indian nationalists were happy to be able to give a resounding no to that question. The male author of *Sister India*, a book written in response to Mayo's *Mother India*, reported, with barely concealed satisfaction, that while Mayo considers herself a champion of women in India 'the women of India have held meetings in every part of India and have unanimously protested against *her* descriptions of their troubles'.[21] Prominent women leaders, such as Sarla Devi Chaudhrani, Latika Basu and Jyotirmoyee Ganguly, were conspicuously present at the large protest meetings held against the book.[22] In separate women's meetings, such as the Mahila Samitis in Bengal and similar women's associations all over the country, women met to discuss the 'insult' to Indian womanhood contained in *Mother India*. Fairly typical of resolutions passed at such meetings was one proposed by Mrs Mirza Ismail at the Mysore Women's Education Conference. The resolution declared Mayo's book to be 'at variance with the ideals of Indian womanhood, which inspire Indian women to lead much happier lives than appear to be led by women of other countries'.[23] Similarly, Maya Das's letter compared the nature and extent of the sexual exploitation of women in Britain unfavourably with the situation in India, provoking a long controversy in the *Pioneer*, a semi-official British newspaper in India.[24] Books written by women in response to *Mother India* also expressed feelings of nationalist outrage against Mayo. Chandravati Lakhanpal's *Mother India Ka Jawab* (A Reply to Mother India) and Charulata Devi's *The Fair Sex of India: A Reply to Mother India* pursued a line of argument also found in the numerous books written by men. Lakhanpal's, for instance, was a *tu quoque* response; she focused on the 'depraved sexuality' of Western societies just as Mayo had focused on sexual practices in India.[25] Charulata Devi, on the other hand, made no mention of Mayo or any of the points raised in *Mother India*, but simply provided sketches of eminent Indian women that countered Mayo's dismal portrait.[26]

The voices of women in India alluded to above may be read as contributing to the general nationalist outrage against *Mother India*. Of particular interest to me, however, are the discursive strategies through which a subject position was created for the Indian woman to speak. I turn, therefore, to the strategies that enabled the emergence of an 'authentic voice of modern Indian womanhood'. I will begin by examining the different strategies exemplified in the responses of four women: Cornelia Sorabji, Uma Nehru, Sarojini Naidu and Dhanvanthi Rama Rau. My aim in analysing the array of positions represented by these women is to identify the particular conditions that enabled a so-called distinctive Indian woman's position on the controversy—a position to be contrasted not only with the imperialist/imperialist-feminist positions, but also with the allegedly gender-neutral nationalist positions. I will also explore the emergence of a politics of middle-class Indian feminism in this context.

Cornelia Sorabji

Cornelia Sorabji was the only Indian woman who had been cited at some length in *Mother India*. Sorabji and Mayo maintained a warm relationship, through private communications, for years after the *Mother India* controversy. Yet Sorabji's complicated attitude towards Mayo's imperialist project precluded any possibility for the emergence of an Indian woman's position critical of either indigenous or imperialist patriarchy. At the time, Sorabji was one of the leading female legal practitioners in India and had developed a considerable reputation as the legal adviser to orthodox Hindu women in *purdanashin* (veiled seclusion).[27] Sorabji's main interest in the women's question was in social service, embodied in her scheme for an Institute for Social Service in India. Her role models came from an earlier generation of strong female reformers, such as Pandita Ramabai, Ramabai Ranade, and her own mother, Francina Sorabji. She was also an ardent supporter of the female ascetic Mataji Tapashwini who had started a school for women along orthodox Hindu lines in Calcutta.[28] Sorabji herself adopted a cautious, or even conservative, attitude towards female reform; she, for example, often defended the practice of purdah among upper-caste Hindu women. As a self-confessed loyalist of the British Raj, she was particularly sceptical of the new generation of women activists who, according to Sorabji, were advocating overly hasty political and social reforms for women. These women, in turn, regarded Sorabji as far too 'individualist' and far too critical of India.[29]

Despite Sorabji's close ties to Mayo and her prominence as an advocate for social reform in India, she remained a shadowy figure in the debate over *Mother India*. Apart from a review of *Mother India* which appeared in the Calcutta-based newspaper the *Englishman*, Sorabji's views on the book were confined to private communications to Mayo and to a handful of British women in Britain.[30] Even Mayo's efforts to portray Sorabji as an example of the 'enlightened' woman's position in India came to naught. Sorabji was forced to write to Mayo's secretary, Henry Field, urging him to request that Mayo refrain from using Sorabji's name in public. She later wrote to Mayo directly requesting that Mayo write to the Indian press absolving her of any complicity in the writing of *Mother India*. Mayo's disclaimer along these lines appeared in the Calcutta *Statesman* and in the Swarajist newspaper, the *Forward*.[31] Sorabji's sensitivity no doubt had been prompted by the flurry of criticism directed against her from nationalist quarters in India. She was publicly denounced at nationalist meetings held to protest Mayo's book. The *Forward* accused Sorabji of supplying Mayo with all her ammunition against India, while C.S. Ranga Iyer, a Swarajist member of the legislative assembly, denounced Sorabji in his *Father India*, written as a rejoinder to *Mother India*. Iyer had described Sorabji's work, from which Mayo had quoted extensively, as the 'vapourings of an unbalanced and unstructured mind'.[32] Even Sorabji's younger sister Dr Alice Pennell had disagreed with her sharply on her evaluation of Mayo's politics and on Mayo's contributions to the cause of Indian women, The most hurtful attack, one which Sorabji herself recorded with great bitterness, came from the young women graduates of the Federation of University Women in India, of which she was honorary president. The younger university women in India circulated a virulent petition, behind Sorabji's back, attacking her for her conciliatory stand towards Mayo's *Mother India*.[33]

If Sorabji's public position in the controversy was fraught, her private position was equally problematic. Even though Sorabji had praised Mayo for writing about the condition of women in India, she was, at first, careful to distance herself from Mayo's general political conclusions. This was in essence the position she had adopted both publicly, in her review of *Mother India*, and in her private communications with Mayo in which she expressed regret that Mayo had not eschewed all 'politics'. She even advised Mayo, although to no avail, to change the title of her book in subsequent editions so that it did not appear as an indictment of all of India or of Indian political aspirations.[34] As an advocate of social reform, Sorabji's initial concern was to use the controversy as an opportunity to draw attention to the need for a social service institute in which the conditions of women could be discussed in a less charged political atmosphere. This position, however, was abandoned quickly in favour of an anti-nationalist and pro-imperialist position. Later Sorabji, acknowledging her secret collaboration with Mayo, saw her role in the controversy only as a 'Scarlet Pimpernel', who supplied Mayo with information for her subsequent anti-Indian books. Sorabji's direct collaboration with Mayo, however, had to be kept a secret because, as she herself acknowledged, her association with such anti-Hindu diatribes, like that in Mayo's subsequent book *The Face of Mother India*, might end up alienating Sorabji's Hindu wards.[35]

Sorabji's role in the Mayo controversy was marked by contradictions and shrouded in secrecy. Sorabji found it impossible, from a position of support for Mayo and her imperialist politics, to articulate a subject position for/by the Indian woman in the controversy. Even Sorabji's initial sympathy for the Indian woman as the object of benevolent salvation, either by the British or by her own Institute for Social Service, provided only a limited appeal for an Indian woman's position in the controversy. Her subsequent endorsement of Mayo's pro-imperialist politics, moreover, caused her to abandon all efforts at trying to describe a space from which the Indian woman could become the subject of the controversy. The only other Indian woman to be cited in *Mother India*, Mona Bose, had recognized the impossibility of speaking either for or as an Indian woman from within Mayo's pro-imperialist politics. Bose, therefore, publicly denied the views that were attributed to her in *Mother India*.[36] In contrast, Sorabji learnt through bitter experience that her pro-imperialist defence of Mayo could not provide a subject position from which the Indian woman could address either the British or male nationalists in India.

Uma Nehru

For very different reasons, Uma Nehru also failed in her efforts to articulate a subject position for the Indian woman in the *Mother India* controversy. Although Nehru was an uncompromising critic of certain patriarchal assumptions in male nationalist discourse, she responded to Mayo's book from the general nationalist perspective. Indeed, her response to *Mother India* reflected the power of the nationalist discourse to contain even those voices that were critical of its particular nationalist resolution of the women's question. Nehru long had been a powerful advocate for women's rights through her articles in the Hindi journal *Stri Darpan* (Women's Mirror), edited by her sister-in-law Rameshwari Nehru. Her articles had addressed the hypocrisy of male nationalist discourse in prescribing models of ideal Indian womanhood for modern Indian women that were drawn from the legendary figures of Sita-Sati-Savitri.[37] Not surprisingly, Nehru was considered as far too 'Westernized', even in the anglicized Nehru family into which she was married.[38] Yet, in the imperialist–nationalist controversy over *Mother India*, Nehru responded to Mayo from the allegedly unmarked position of the 'Indian'.

Nehru's *Mother India Aur Uska Jawab* is a Hindi translation of Mayo's book meant, most probably, for Hindi-speaking women.[39] In the preface Nehru writes that her aim is 'to use this book meant to insult us to instil pride among us'. Her translation of *Mother India* was preceded by an imaginary dialogue with Mayo. *Mother India Aur Uska Jawab* was true to Nehru's earlier reservations about the nationalist ideal of modern Indian womanhood: it refrained from invoking the glorious tradition of Indian womanhood in responding to Mayo's criticism of the position of women in India. Deprived of the counter-vailing argument about the ideals of Indian womanhood, however, Nehru's dialogue with Mayo deals largely with the political and economic issues raised in *Mother India*. Nehru avoided discussing the particular implications of Mayo's book for the women's question. She missed, for instance, the opportunity to respond to Mayo's taunt to India's women leaders. In her second book on India, *The Slaves of the Gods*, Mayo had written that her aim was 'to awaken [Indian women's] intelligent patriotism and the consciousness of [their] men, by making inescapable the contrast between, on the one hand, florid talk of devotion and "sacrifice" poured out before an abstract figure, and, on the other hand, the consideration actually accorded to the living woman, mother of the race'.[40] Nehru's desire to present a strong nationalist argument against *Mother India*, even though she was herself critical of the attitudes towards women in male nationalist discourse, led her to avoid a detailed discussion of the special emphasis that Mayo had placed on women's issues in her attack on India. Nehru's critique of *Mother India*, therefore, was made from the supposedly neutral, or non-gendered, position of the Indian nationalist: it could not become the site for the elaboration of the gendered subject position of the Indian woman.

Sarojini Naidu

Ironically, the consolidation of a distinct Indian woman's position in the controversy could occur only within the male nationalist discourse. This is evident in the response of Sarojini Naidu, one of the most pro-minent women in the nationalist and the women's movements of the time. Naidu, by combining 'modern' political activism with 'traditional' Indian roots, embodied the nationalist ideals of middle-class Indian womanhood.[41] Her response to the *Mother India* controversy reflects the ways in which the Indian woman could arrogate a subject position for herself from which to address both the British and the male nationalists in India. In one of Naidu's earliest responses, she referred to *Mother India* only to urge Indian men to give up their prejudices against women and to educate their wives, mothers and sisters if they sincerely wished to neutralize the impact of Mayo's book. Mayo would later use extracts from this speech to endorse her own views about the hypocrisy of male nationalists.[42] Yet there was no mistaking Naidu's sharp criticism of Mayo's imperialist politics. Her telegram to the famous Calcutta Town Hall meeting, organized by the nationalist Mayor J.N. Sengupta, summed up her attitude towards Mayo: 'The mouths of liars rot and perish with their own lies, but the glory of Indian womanhood shines pure and as the morning star.'[43] Unlike some of her male colleagues, however, Naidu's main concern was not to prove that oppressive practices against women did not exist in India, but to show that the women of India were capable of redeeming themselves.

Naidu's invocation of the glorious ideals of Indian womanhood and her elaboration of the nationalist Sati-Savitri model for the Indian woman did not simply reflect a co-optation by male nationalist discourse, but was also critical in legitimating the interventionary practices of Indian women themselves. Naidu's challenge to Mayo was directed at the latter's right to speak for Indian womanhood. Naidu stated this in no uncertain terms in her 1928 Kamala Lectures at the Calcutta University Senate in a speech on the 'Ideals of Indian Womanhood':

> The women of India should answer all those who come in the guise of friendship to interpret India to the world and exploit their weakness and expose the *secrets of the home* [my emphasis], with the words 'whether we are oppressed, treated as goods and chattels and forced on the funeral pyres of our husbands, our redemption is in our hands. We shall break through the walls that imprison us and tear the veils that stifle. We shall do this by the miracle of our womanhood. We do not ask any friend or foe in the guise of a friend, to come merely to exploit us while they pretend to interpret, succour and solace our womanhood.'[44]

The accent on the 'secrets of the home' in Naidu's speech signals the ambivalence at the heart of the identity of the Indian woman. On the one hand, her speech recalls the nationalist effort at reformulating the new middle-class 'home' as an insulated space in which patriarchal authority remained intact and, on the other, its vigorous arguments for the potential of Indian woman's own agency in correcting the roots of their domination also leave open the possibility of challenging the patriarchal closure of the 'home' as a site for women's struggle.

Naidu's intervention demonstrates that although the nationalist ideal of the Indian woman ensured that middle-class women's entry into the public space was under male patronage, the same ideal also enabled a relatively liberal space for women at least partly of their own making. The popular representation of the nation as *Mother India* as well as the figure of the Indian woman as the essence of Indianness had also opened up new arenas for women's activism. The potential of such an ideal was evident in the radical claim that Naidu, as a prime example of the 'new woman' in India, had the unique distinction of representing, not only the Indian woman, but the entire Indian nation. Gandhi, for example, would recognize Naidu's claim as the unofficial ambassador for India/Indian women. In the wake of the *Mother India* controversy, he was persuaded to send Naidu to the United States as the spokesperson for India and the Indian woman. Officially Naidu was a representative of the All India Women's Conference at the Pan-Pacific Women's Conference in Honolulu, but as her extensive lecture tour demonstrates, her trip was meant to educate the American people about the 'real' Mother India.[45] Naidu lectured in the United States on 'The Interpretation of Indian Womanhood' and 'The Political Situation in India', topics on which she seemed uniquely qualified to speak. As the symbolic figure of nationalist India and of Indian women, she hoped to dispel the image of an unregenerate patriarchal Indian nationalism and of the downtrodden

Indian woman found in Mayo's book. Therefore, she felt no compulsion to debate the specifics of the book with a Western audience.[46] Despite the sustained efforts of Mayo and her supporters to discredit Naidu as simply a mouthpiece for Gandhi, her trip was an immense public relations success, especially with the more liberal US women's organizations.[47] Indeed, it was precisely because Naidu had offered a strategy for articulating the Indian woman's position within male nationalist discourse that she was able to appropriate a unique subject position for the middle-class Indian woman in the *Mother India* controversy.

How does a discourse of the Indian woman as a figure of essentialized Indianness, however, enable a subject position for the 'Indian woman'? To recall Partha Chatterjee's analysis, the modern Indian could create a subject position from which to address the British only by elaborating an ahistorical and essentialized notion of Indian womanhood. Chatterjee, for example, argues that a marked '*difference* in the degree and manner of westernization of women, as distinct from men' was essential for the subject position of the Indian.[48] However, the entry of women into the male-dominated public sphere in the early twentieth century made it increasingly difficult to maintain this essential difference in the westernization of women, and created new demands on the gendered subject position of the Indian. In the context of rapid westernization of women, modern/westernized women, like Naidu, could, through service to the nation, also appropriate a subject position from which to address the West as Indian. They did this by positing an essential difference in the degree and manner of westernization of the truly modern Indian woman, as distinct from the merely westernized Indian woman. The essential difference lay in the fact that the modern Indian woman, unlike her merely westernized counterpart, claimed 'traditional' ideals of Indian womanhood on *behalf of the modernizing project of nationalism*. Naidu's strategy of negotiation in the *Mother India* controversy, therefore, reflected the particular conditions under which even the modern/westernized woman could address the West as Indian. This particular moment of an Indian female subjectivity, however, rested on an uneasy resolution of the modern Indian woman as both subject and object of the nationalist discourse of essentialized Indianness.

Dhanvanthi Rama Rau

Dhanvanthi Rama Rau's interventions in the Mayo controversy further illustrate how a subject position for the modern Indian woman was assigned within male nationalist discourse. Rau's contributions to the controversy lay in her struggle to establish the claim of Indian women and their organizations, against the rival claims of Western women's organizations, as the legitimate crusaders for the rights of all women in India. The argument for the special role of the modern Indian woman received its legitimacy from a nationalist discourse that papered over the very real class/caste contradictions in the particular imagining of the national community.

Following *Mother India*, women's organizations, especially in the United States and in Britain, demonstrated a great interest in the 'upliftment' of women in India. In the United States it was the more conservative women's groups, like the Daughters of the American Revolution, which openly endorsed Mayo's book, and started a fund for the helpless child brides of India.[49] More direct intervention on behalf of the women in India was left to British women's organizations, especially under the direction of Eleanor Rathbone. Rathbone acknowledged a 'great tidal wave of responsibility' for the helpless women of India.[50] As an imperialist, Rathbone was equally impressed by the political implications of Mayo's revelations in *Mother India*. Rathbone, therefore, urged Mayo to issue a cheaper edition of her book to be distributed among members of the Labour Party in Britain which 'badly need the corrective of [*Mother India*] because of their tendency to espouse self-government anywhere'.[51] In response to Mayo's description of women in India, Rathbone petitioned the British parliament to appoint two members of the National Union of Societies for Equal Citizenship (NUSEC), of which she was president, to the parliamentary commission, popularly known as the Simon Commission. This all-white commission was later boycotted in India by all the major political parties and by the all-India women's organizations for its exclusion of Indians and of women. Rathbone's proposal to the commission, as it was about to undertake an inquiry into the political conditions in India, was that British women appointed to the commission could provide information about that part of Indian society 'hidden behind the veil'. Rathbone's scheme, however, was met with scepticism from some Indian women. The wife of a distinguished Muslim leader from India wrote to the London *Times*, 'Indian women are not voiceless. They received the franchise, and those among them who are able and willing to take advantage of it are aware of the needs of their own people.'[52]

The most sustained criticism of Rathbone's efforts to get British women's organizations to assume responsibility for the women of India, however, came from Dhanvanthi Rama Rau, an active member of three of the all-India women's organizations. Rathbone, inspired by the revelations made in Mayo's book, had organized two large conferences in London on 'Women in India'. At the second conference, which was held in Caxton Hall on 7 and 8 October 1929, Rau attacked the remarks of the various speakers at the conference as variations of the 'white man's burden', and hotly 'disputed the right of British women to arrange a conference on Indian social evils, when all the speakers were British and many of them had never even visited India'.[53] On the request of some prominent British feminists, Rathbone was forced to provide Rau a platform to present her views to the conference. In her speech Rau outlined the work being done in India by Indian women's organizations and reiterated that British women could give only moral support: the practical work had to be done in India and by Indians. Despite the interventions of Rau and other Indian women, the resolution that British women's organizations had a special responsibility for Indian women was passed with only a few Indian women present dissenting. Sir M.F. Dywer, a former British official in India, concluded that the 'great meeting of British Women's Association' held at Caxton Hall could do much good to improve the status of Indian women because, at present, the 'Hindu women [themselves] were Dumb'.[54]

Although frustrated by the outcome of the conference, Rau did not leave unchallenged the claim that British women's organizations had a special responsibility for the condition of women in India. Rau, along with some British and Indian women associated with the Lyceum Club in London, wrote a letter to *The Times* accusing Rathbone's conference of promoting 'racial cleavage'. She boldly reiterated that while 'India welcomes co-operation [she] will not tolerate any form of patronage or philanthropy which will rob her of her self-esteem'.[55] Rau's various interventions served to attack the patronizing politics of Western women's organizations, and to secure recognition for the role of the modern Indian woman as the true representative of all her oppressed sisters in India. Henceforth, Rathbone and the NUSEC would be forced to work through the modern Indian woman as the representative of the women of India.

The consolidation of the nationalist bourgeoisie in India allowed the women of this class to emerge as the true champion of all women in India. Hence the modern Indian woman came to be seen as the liberator of all other women in India. To paraphrase Dipesh Chakrabarty's observations made in a slightly different context, the Indian woman, as a member of the modernizing elite, stood for an 'assumed unity called the "Indian people" that is always split into two—a modernizing elite and a yet-to-be-modernized peasantry'.[56] Within the modernizing project of nationalism, therefore, the modern Indian woman was also always the subject of modernity, the transmitter of the fruits of modernization to all other women in India. The self-constitution of the 'Indian woman', as simultaneously the subject and the object of nationalist discourse, however, exemplifies the contradictions in the subject positions available to women in all patriarchies.[57]

The Women's Movement

The particular history of the self-constitution of the Indian woman in nationalist discourse also had implications for the politics of middle-class Indian feminism. The political struggles of the Indian women's movement in the *Mother India* controversy provided an arena for middle-class Indian women's engagement with feminism. For the fledgling women's movement, the controversy afforded an opportunity to consolidate a feminist agenda for women's issues. Women activists and the women's movement, therefore, admitted the urgent need for the reform of women's position in India, even as they challenged Mayo's description of the Indian woman in *Mother India*. Kamala Sathianadhan, editor of the *Indian Ladies Magazine*, wrote:

> We honour Miss Mayo for her courage in not caring for resentments and accusations; we congratulate her on her public spirit in 'shouldering the task' of 'holding the mirror' to that part of the human race which is a 'physical menace' to the world; we do not question her ability or her cleverness in writing this book; but we do deny her the presumption that she is 'in a position to present conditions and their bearing', and we do not for a minute admit her 'plain speech' as the 'faithful wounds of a friend': for she is no friend of ours.[58]

Women's organizations carefully distanced themselves from Mayo's imperialist propaganda, but used the attention that the controversy created to facilitate their own campaign for child-marriage reform and other legislation for women. The Women's Indian Association (WIA), a pioneer of the all-India women's movement, issued the following statement on Mayo's book: 'while we repudiate the book as a whole we must turn every ounce of our zeal towards the rooting out of those social evils which are undoubtedly in our midst'.[59] At Triplicane in Madras, the association organized the largest protest meeting of women against the book. This meeting was chaired by Dr Muthulakshmi Reddy, the first Indian woman to be nominated to the provincial legislatures. The meeting passed the following two resolutions: first, it denied that 'Indian womanhood as a whole is in a state of slavery, superstition, ignorance and degradation which Miss Mayo affirms'; and, second, they called upon the legislative assembly and legislative council to enact measures that would legally prohibit child marriage, early parentage, enforced widowhood, dedication of girls to temples and 'commercialized immorality'. This was also the position of *Stri Dharma* (Woman's Duty), the paper of the Women's Indian Association.[60]

An episode at the annual meeting of the Indian National Social Conference held on 27 December 1927 indicates the context in which women activists conducted their successful campaign for child-marriage reform.[61] At the conference prominent men and women, while advocating the urgent need for child-marriage reform, denounced Mayo's *Mother India*. Only one speaker introduced a discordant note. S.N. Arya, the only representative from the Non-Brahmin Youth League present, referred to Mayo as a champion of women's reform in India. Pandemonium broke out at the mention of her name. Arya's comments, despite the pro-imperialist politics which he shared with some groups in the Non-Brahmin Movement of the 1920s and 1930s, served to question the consensus over women's issues secured within the upper-caste/-class politics of the nation-state.[62] The politics of the nation-state, however, also privileged the understanding of women of dominant classes/castes on women's reforms, and allowed the middle-class women's movement to set the agenda for women's reform in India. Dr Muthulakshmi Reddy, who chaired the conference, persuaded the delegates to ignore Arya's disruption and redirected their attention to women's reform.

The issue around which the all-India women's organizations mobilized in the *Mother India* controversy, that of the upper-caste/-class child bride rather than the underpaid *dhai*, or midwife, also mentioned in Mayo's book, reveals the elitist character of the early women's movement. It also reveals, however, the special conditions under which women's organizations could conduct a successful political campaign for women. The issue of child-marriage reform was not fundamentally opposed to the 'modernizing' efforts of the social reform and nationalist movements. The legacy of such male-sponsored reforms meant that the women's movement could mount a campaign for the modernization of the Indian home by urging child-marriage legislation without necessarily attacking male authority in the home. Rameshwari Nehru, for example, who was active in the campaign for child-marriage legislation, considered herself to be an advocate of women's rights, but not an advocate of sexual equality in the home. She wrote: 'I do not think that the home should be made a forum for women's battles.'[63]

This should not, however, make us overlook the contributions of the women's organizations in getting child-marriage legislation passed in the face of governmental indifference and orthodox male opposition. The women's movement had an uphill battle to gain recognition for their own contributions in getting child-marriage legislation passed in India. The issue of child-marriage reform had been a major concern of the women's movement in India even before the publication of *Mother India*. The very first meeting of the All-India Women's Conference (AIWC) held in Poona in 1926 had committed its support, not only to a bill on the age of consent—then languishing in the legislative assembly partly due to official indifference—but also to the eventual abolition of child marriage in India. The Mayo controversy speeded up the women's demand for child-marriage reform.[64] On 11 February 1928 a delegation of 19 members of the AIWC led by the Rani of Mandi met the Viceroy and leaders of all the major Indian

political parties to urge the passage of the Sarda Bill in the legislative assembly. The delegation also secured the appointment of one of its members, Rameshwari Nehru, to the
age-of-consent committee appointed by the government on 25 June 1928. Rameshwari
Nehru later wrote that it was in dealing with private bills on age-of-marriage and consent
that the government had appointed this committee. Significantly, she made no mention
of the publicity created by the Mayo controversy.[65] The report of the committee, which
Mayo later used to write her sequel to *Mother India* and to validate the claims of
her previous book, testified to the need for marriage reforms.[66] Women witnesses to
the committee meetings were among the strongest advocates for the abolition of child
marriage.

Following the report of the age-of-consent committee, women activists launched
a lobbying effort with Indian legislators and British officials to ensure the passage of the
Sarda Child-Marriage Bill. Kamaladevi Chattopadhyay, on behalf of the AIWC, or-
chestrated the work of getting support for the bill from Indian legislators in Delhi.
Dhanvanthi Rama Rau, as secretary of the Child-Marriage Abolition League, worked
among the wives of British government officials urging them to persuade their husbands
to support the child-marriage legislation.[67] On the day of the final debate on the Sarda
Bill in the legislative assembly, approximately 300 AIWC activists attended to ensure
support for the measure. The AIWC would later see the passage of the Child-Marriage
Restraint Act in 1929 as a triumph of their own fledgling organization.

Yet the contributions of the Indian women's movement in getting child-marriage
reform in India did not receive automatic recognition. International opinion, for example, gave all the credit for the appointment of the age-of-consent committee and the
passage of the Sarda Bill to Mayo's *Mother India*. The *New York Times* even carried a
piece entitled 'Miss Mayo's Book on India Gets Action on Child Marriage'.[68] Mayo and
her supporters were in great part responsible for popularizing the view that Indians had
been shamed into supporting legislative reforms for women as a result of her brave
exposé in *Mother India*. A letter which Mayo received from India chided her for taking
credit for the passage of the child-marriage legislation:

> speaking for every woman in India, I want to say to you that when you claim for yourself
> the credit of an 'attempt to raise the marriage age of females', because the U.S., as you
> explain, had accepted your book as truth—that you have betrayed yourself into a perfect
> illustration of what Dr Besant, Dr Tagore, Gandhi and others have called your perversion
> of facts. Such attempts have been going on for a number of years now.[69]
>
> It should come as no surprise that the women actually involved in the campaign for
> child-marriage legislation make little or no mention of the role of Mayo or *Mother India*
> in getting the legislation passed.[70]

It is in the act of constructing themselves as the agents or subjects in the discourse
about Indian women that we can locate the origins of middle-class Indian women's
activism. Indian feminism emerged in the context of middle-class women's challenge
to orthodox indigenous patriarchy. The very success of this challenge, however, also
strengthened the new nationalist patriarchy and the class/caste stratification of Indian
society. This ambivalence has led some scholars, like Kumari Jayawardena, to the pes-
simistic conclusion that the nationalist struggle did not permit 'a revolutionary feminist
consciousness' in India.[71] Yet this desire for a 'pure' feminist consciousness or agency

serves, in the end, to remove the feminist subject from the history of her production within interconnected axes of gender, race, class/caste, nation, or sexuality. A more useful way of locating middle-class Indian feminism is offered in Sangari and Vaid's observation that 'nowhere can or have reforms been directed at patriarchies alone, but they have also been involved in realigning patriarchy with social stratification (both existing and emerging) and with changing political formations'.[72]

As R. Radhakrishnan points out, Sangari and Vaid's observation has the potential for the reconceptualization of historiography as a whole. According to Radhakrishnan, implicit in Sangari and Vaid's comment is the recognition that the categories of gender, race, nationality, sexuality, or class can neither be made to speak for the totality nor for one another, but are rather relationally implicated in one another. This notion of 'relational articulation', he suggests, makes a feminist, nationalist or class-based historiography, pursued entirely from within itself, highly questionable.[73] Discrete feminist, nationalist or class-based historiographies arbitrarily fix the boundaries of the 'totality' or the total social formation that is the object of their study according to the different priorities that each assigns to gender, nation or class as distinct categories. Radhakrishnan's notion of a truly critical historiography, however, suggests a new understanding of 'totality', not as the product of fixed or given boundaries, demarcated by distinct categories, but as the product of several different relational articulations. Hence, Sangari and Vaid's feminist historiography, conceived within such a radical rethinking of 'totality', does not claim to offer a new and improved paradigm for the flawed nationalist understanding of India, but locates its challenge clearly within that nationalist paradigm even as it critiques its very terms.

This reconceptualization of historiography not only emphasizes the need to historicize the conditions in which politics and identities emerge, but also draws attention to the writing of history itself as an interventionary practice that recreates the past for the present. It, therefore, opens up new possibilities for conceptualizing the problem of locating the Indian woman and the politics of middle-class Indian feminism. For example, such a reconceptualization enables me, as an Indian feminist, to see my reading of the 'Indian woman' and middle-class Indian feminism in the *Mother India* controversy as not just a retrieval of some lost historical past, but as an intervention in the historical present. The range of women's responses in the *Mother India* controversy indicates that there was nothing necessarily inevitable or predetermined about the voice of the modern Indian woman. In fact, the particular discursive strategies that gave rise to the subject position of the 'modern Indian woman' and the politics of middle-class Indian feminism were produced by, and meant to intervene in, a certain historical moment.

This understanding of the historical specificity of the Indian woman allows us to recognize an ideological continuity in the contemporary re-articulation of the Indian woman as the figure of some essentialized identity. In recent years, various communalist and nativist movements in India have engaged in constituting and reconstituting the Indian/Hindu woman as subjects and as objects of virulently anti-democratic discourses.[74] By insisting on historicizing the identity of the Indian woman, we can begin to critique the implications of the resurgence of an essentialized and ahistorical identity, divorced from the political and economic contexts in which it is produced and which it helps sustain.

Notes

1. Kumkum Sangari and Sudesh Vaid, 'Recasting Women: An Introduction', in K. Sangari and S. Vaid (eds.), *Recasting Women: Essays in Indian Colonial History* (New Brunswick, NJ, 1990), 2–3.

2. Ibid., 1.

3. Chandra Talpade Mohanty, 'Cartographies of Struggle' in C. Mohanty, A. Russo and L. Torres (eds.), *Third World Women and the Politics of Feminism* (Bloomington, Ind., 1991), 12–13.

4. Teresa de Lauretis, 'Displacing Hegemonic Discourses: Reflections on Feminist Theory in the 1980s', *Inscriptions*, 314 (1988), 136.

5. Katherine Mayo, *Mother India* (New York, 1927).

6. For a detailed study of Mayo's imperialist politics, see Manoranjan Jha, *Katherine Mayo and India* (New Delhi, 1971).

7. The actual quotation is from the foreword, written by Sarojini Naidu, one of the most famous Indian women of the time, for a collection of essays by Indian women, Evelyn C. Gedge and Mithan Choksi (eds.), *Women in Modern India, Fifteen Papers by Indian Women Writers* (Bombay, 1929).

8. See Joanna Liddle and Rama Joshi, 'Gender and Imperialism in British India', *South Asia Research*, 5/2 (Nov. 1985), 147–65.

9. This tendency of evaluating women's mobilization in India along one or another of these lines is referred to in Geraldine Forbes, 'The Politics of Respectability: Indian Women and the Indian National Congress' in D.A. Low (ed.), *Congress, Centenary Hindsights* (Delhi, 1988), 54–97.

10. Chandra Mohanty, 'Cartographies of Struggle', 5–6.

11. For some exceptions, see Himani Bannerji, 'Fashioning a Self: Educational Proposals for and by Women in Popular Magazines in Colonial Bengal', *Economic and Political Weekly* 26/43 (26 Oct. 1991), ws50–ws62, and Susie Tharu and K. Lalita, 'Literature of the Reform and Nationalist Movement' in *Women Writing in India*, vol. 1 (New York, 1991), 143–86. Also useful are Susie Tharu, 'Women Writing in India', *Journal of Arts and Ideas*, 20–1 (Mar. 1991), 49–66; and Lata Mani, 'Cultural Theory, Colonial Texts: Reading Eyewitness Accounts of Widow Burning' in Lawrence Grossberg, Cary Nelson and Paula Treichler (eds.), *Cultural Studies* (New York, 1992), 392–408.

12. Chandra Mohanty, 'Cartographies of Struggle', 15.

13. See Ann Stoler, 'Making Empire Respectable: The Politics of Race and Sexuality in 20th Century Colonial Cultures', *American Ethnologist*, 16/4 (Nov. 1989), 634–60. Also 'Rethinking Colonial Categories', *Comparative Studies in Society and History*, 31/1 (Jan. 1989), 134–61.

14. Lata Mani, 'The Production of an Official Discourse on Sati in Early 19th Century Bengal', *Economic and Political Weekly* (Apr. 1987), 32–40, and 'Contentious Traditions: The Debate on Sati in Colonial India', *Cultural Critique*, 7 (1987), 119–56. Uma Chakravorty, 'Whatever Happened to the Vedic Dasi? Orientalism, Nationalism and a Script for the Past', in Sangari and Vaid (eds.), *Recasting Women*, 27–87.

15. Sumanta Banerjee, 'Marginalization of Women's Popular Culture in Nineteenth Century Bengal', in Sangari and Vaid (eds.), *Recasting Women*, 127–79 and *The Parlour and the Streets* (Calcutta, 1989). For the following discussion, I have drawn from Sangari and Vaid, 'Recasting Women: An Introduction', 1–26.

16. Partha Chatterjee, 'The Nationalist Resolution of the Women's Question', in Sangari and Vaid (eds.), *Recasting Women*, 233–53, and 'Colonialism, Nationalism and Colonized Women: The Contest in India', *American Ethnologist*, 16/4 (Nov. 1989), 662–83. For Chatterjee's analysis of Indian nationalist thought in general, see *Nationalist Thought and the Colonial Indian World: A Derivative Discourse?* (London, 1986).

17. Sangari and Vaid in 'Recasting Women: An Introduction' distinguish between what they call the 'modernizing' of gender relations in the social reform and nationalist movements and the 'democratizing' of gender relations in mass peasant movements, 19–24.

18. Dipesh Chakrabarty, 'Postcoloniality and the Artifice of History: Who Speaks for "Indian" Pasts?', *Representations*, 37 (Winter 1992), 17.

19. Ibid., 11–14.

20. The article, written by a British doctor who had served in India, was reprinted in the *Calcutta Statesman* (30 Mar. 1928), 8.

21. World Citizen [S. G. Warty], *Sister India: A Critical Examination of and a Reasoned Reply to Miss Katherine Mayo's 'Mother India'* (Bombay, 1928), 143.

22. See *Bombay Daily Mail*, 5 Sept. 1927 in India, vol. 2 in folder no. 207, series 4, box 37, Katherine Mayo Papers, manuscript group no. 35 at Sterling Memorial Library, Yale University (henceforth KM Papers). For details of this meeting, see *Bengalee* (6 Sept. 1927), 3.

23. Cited in *Indian Social Reformer* in India, vol. 2 in folder 207, series 4, box 37 in KM Papers. For some examples of the women's protest meetings held all over India, see the report of the protest of 'ladies' at Noakhali in *Amrita Bazar Patrika*, 17 Sept. 1927, 5; Lahore 'ladies' protest, *Amrita Bazar Patrika*, 13 Dec. 1927, 10; protest of Comilla Mahila Samiti Meeting, *Bengalee*, 8 Sept. 1927, 3. Several other protest meetings were reported in the *Statesman*, *Bengalee* and *Amrita Bazar Patrika* during the period September to December 1927.

24. For the exchange occasioned by Maya Das's letter, see *Pioneer*, 5 May 1928; 10 May 1928; 18 May 1928; and 31 May 1928 in India, vol. 3 in folder no. 207, series 4, box 37, KM Papers.

25. Mrs C. Lakhanpal, *Mother India Aur Uska Jawab* (Dehradun, 1928). I was unable to trace this book; however, I had access to a brief translation of the book in a letter from Wolsey Haig to Mayo's secretary, Henry Field, letter, dated 22 June 1928 in folder no. 47, series I, box 6, KM Papers. Although Haig declares the book to be poorly written, the Indian papers give it a more favourable review. See *Bombay Daily Mail*, 14 Jan. 1928 in India, vol. 3 in folder no. 207, series 4, box 37, KM Papers.

26. Charulata Devi, *The Fair Sex of India* (Calcutta, 1929).

27. Mayo had quoted from Cornelia Sorabji's *Between the Twilights* (London, 1908). Biographical information on Sorabji is available in her prolific writings; see especially *India Calling: The Memoirs of Cornelia Sorabji* (London, 1934); *'Therefore': An Impression of Sorabji Kharshedji Langrana and His Wife Francina* (London, 1924); and *Susia Sorabji: Christian-Parsee Educator of Western India* (London, 1932). For a brief sketch of Sorabji's early career, also see Mrs E.F. Chapman, *Sketches of Some Distinguished Indian Women with a Preface by the Marchioness of Dufferin and Ava* (London, 1891), 121–38.

28. See Cornelia Sorabji, 'The Position of Hindu Women Fifty Years Ago' in Shyam Kumari Nehru (ed.), *Our Cause: A Symposium of Indian Women* (Allahabad, 1938). Also letter from Sorabji to Mayo, dated 29 Jan. 1927, in folder no. 36, series I, box 5, KM Papers.

29. For Sorabji's views on this matter, see her *The Purdanashin* (Calcutta, 1917) and *India Recalled* (London, 1937). For critical assessments of Sorabji by her female contemporaries, see Margaret Cousins, *Indian Womanhood Today* (Kitabistan, 1941), 145; Kamaladevi Chattopadhyay, *Indian Women's Battle for Freedom* (New Delhi, repr. 1983), 51; and for Kamala Sathianadan's view, see Padmini [Sathianadan] Sengupta, *The Portrait of an Indian Woman* (Calcutta, 1956), 41.

30. Cornelia Sorabji, 'Mother India—The Incense of Service: What Sacrifice Can We Make?' *Englishman*, pt. 1, 31 Aug. 1927, 6–9, and pt. 2, 1 Sept. 1927, 6–9.

31. Letter from Sorabji to Mayo, dated 21 Nov. 1928 in folder no. 50, series q, box 7, KM Papers. Mayo's letter to the *Statesman* appeared on 5 Mar. 1929, 18.

32. C.S. Ranga Iyer, *Father India: A Reply to Mother India* (London, 1928 repr.), 72–3. Ramananda Chatterjee, editor of the *Modern Review*, addressed a large gathering of Indians at which he accused Sorabji of providing Mayo with all her information on India, *Bengalee*, 8 Sept. 1927, 3; *Amrita Bazar Patrika*, 15 Nov. 1927, 5.

33. Letter from Sorabji to Mayo, 10 June 1928, in folder no. 47, series 1, box 6, KM Papers. For Alice Pennell's position, see the letter from Miss Hotz to Mayo, dated 1 Jan. 1936 in folder no. 78, series 1, box 10, KM Papers.

34. Letters from Sorabji to Mayo, dated 6 Sept. 1927 and 1 Sept. 1927 in folder no. 38, series 1, box 5, and letter of 10 June 1928 in folder no. 47, series 1, box 6, KM Papers.

35. Katherine Mayo, *The Face of Mother India* (New York, 1935); letter from Sorabji to Mayo, dated 2 May 1935 in folder no. 75, series 1, box 9, and 31 Dec. 1935 in folder no. 76, series 1, box 10, KM Papers.

36. Bose's denial appeared in an article written by a British YMCA official, in the *Indian Witness*, 7 Sept. 1927 cited in Henry Field, *After 'Mother India'* (New York, 1929), 140. For Mayo's concern about Bose's denial, see letter from Mayo to Ellen Stanton, 17 Dec. 1927 in folder no. 41 and Moyca Newell [Mayo's partner] to Col. Baltye, 25 Feb. 1928 in folder no. 43, series 1, box 6, KM Papers.

37. For a discussion of Nehru's journalistic contributions, see Vir Bharat Talwar, 'Feminist Consciousness in Women's Journals in Hindi, 1910–1920' in Sangari and Vaid (eds.), *Recasting Women*, 204–32. See also Uma Nehru, 'Whither Women', in S.K. Nehru (ed.), *Our Cause*, 403–19.

38. Nehru was married to the journalist Shyamlal Nehru, uncle of the famous Jawaharlal Nehru. For an assessment of Nehru as too 'westernized', see Vijaylakshmi Pandit (Uma Nehru's niece by marriage), *The Scope of Happiness: A Personal Memoir* (New York, 1979), 194–5 and interview with Indira Gandhi (Nehru's grand-niece) in Promilla Kalhan, *Kamala Nehru: An Intimate Biography* (Delhi, 1973), 133.

39. *Miss Mayo ki 'Mother India' (Sachitra Hindi Unuwad) jis me Srimati Uma Nehru likhit 'Bhumika' tatha paschimi samajyawad ke vishay me 'Miss Mayo se do do bate'* (Allahabad, 1928).

40. Katherine Mayo, *Slaves of the God* (New York, 1929), 237.

41. For a discussion of Naidu in these terms, see Geraldine Forbes, 'The Women's Movement in India: Traditional Symbols and New Roles' in M.S.A. Rao (ed.), *Sectarian, Tribal and Women's Movements*, ii. *Social Movements in India* (Delhi, 1979), 149–65; and Meena Alexander, 'Sarojini Naidu: Romanticism and Resistance', *Economic and Political Weekly*, 20/43 (26 Oct. 1985), ws 68–ws71.

42. Naidu's speech was reported in *The Times* (London), 5 Sept. 1927, 5. For an extract of Mayo's interview in which she quotes from Naidu's speech, see folder no. 38, series 1, box 5, KM Papers.

43. For Naidu's telegram to the Calcutta meeting, see *Forward*, 7 Sept. 1927 in India, vol. 2 in folder no. 207, series 4, box 37, KM Papers.

44. Quoted in the *Statesman*, 24 Jan. 1928, 6. See also *Hindi*, 24 Jan. 1928 in India, vol. 2 in folder no. 207, series 4, box 37, KM Papers.

45. See *Statesman*, 30 Jan. 1929, 10.

46. For Naidu's refusal to discuss Mayo in the USA, see Tara Ali Baig, *Sarojini Naidu* (New Delhi, 1974), 99–100; and Padmini Sengupta, *Sarojini Naidu* (Bombay, 1966), 209–11.

47. Naidu's triumphant US trip is covered in the *New York Times*, 14 Oct. 1928, 14; 28 Oct. 1928, 6; and 3 Mar. 1929, 15. For the efforts of Mayo and her supporters to sabotage Naidu's reception in the USA, see letter from Sulton to Mayo, dated 22 Sept. 1930 in folder no. 56 in series 1, box 8, KM Papers. Also see the publication of Henry Field's (Mayo's secretary), *After 'Mother India'* with its unfounded charge that Naidu had attempted to bribe an American woman who had been killed in a Gandhi-led demonstration in Bombay.

48. Chatterjee, 'The Nationalist Resolution', 243.

49. Mayo was now seen as an authority on Indian women in some women's circles abroad; she was invited by the League of Nations' Fellowship branch to head the Indian delegation on Child Health. See letter from Miss Gail Barker, dated 9 Sept. 1927, in folder no. 38, series 1, box 5, KM Papers. For the Daughters of the American Revolution, and other conservative women's groups' support for Mayo, see the Colony Club meeting of women's groups in the USA held on 27 Nov. 1927, letter from Field to Mrs Henry Loomis, 19 Oct. 1927, in folder 39, series 1, box 5; copy of the resolutions passed at this meeting, see folder 42, series 1, box 6, KM Papers.

50. Rathbone's sense of 'responsibility' for the condition of women in India is discussed in Barbara Ramusack, 'Cultural Missionaries, Maternal Imperialists, Feminist Allies: British Women Activists in India 1865–1945', *Women's Studies International Forum*, 13/4 (1990), 309–21. For the

significance of the condition of women in India for the self-identity of British feminism in the nineteenth century, see Antoinette Burton, 'The White Woman's Burden: British Feminists and "The Indian Woman", 1865–1915', *Women's Studies International Forum*, 13/4 (1990): 245–308.

51. Letter from Rathbone to Mayo, 24 Aug. 1927, in folder no. 37, series 1, box 5, KM Papers.

52. Mrs I. Ameer Ali's letter to *The Times* is quoted in *Statesman*, 14 Dec. 1927, 12. Ali's letter also provoked a response from a 'Rani of India' who argued that women behind the veil were indeed voiceless.

53. The second two-day conference was reported in *The Times*, 8 Oct. 1929, 9 and 9 Oct. 1929, 9. The report of the conference in the *Statesman* appeared under the heading 'Indian Women Lively', 9 Oct. 1929, 9. The details of the conflict between Rathbone and Rau is discussed in Mary D. Stocks, *Eleanor Rathbone: A Biography* (London, 1949), esp. 137, and Dhanvanthi Rama Rau, *An Inheritance: The Memoirs of Dhanvanthi Rama Rau* (London, 1977), esp. 170–2.

54. See his 'Mother India-Swaraj and Social Reform', *Fortnightly Review*, 122/633 (2 Jan. 1928), 182.

55. Letter signed by Dhanvanthi Rama Rau, Hannah Sen and others appeared in *The Times*, 22 Oct. 1929, 12. Rathbone's reply was published on 24 Oct. 1929, 12. A letter supporting Rathbone's complaint that Indian women were politicizing women's issues appeared under the name Eva Mary Bell on 31 Oct. 1929, 10.

56. Chakrabarty, 'Postcoloniality and the Artifice of History', 18.

57. This point has been made in the context of discourses about nineteenth-century property and marriage legislation in Britain in Rosemary Hennessey and Rajeshwari Mohan, 'The Construction of Women in Three Popular Texts of Empire: Towards a Critique of Materialist Feminism', *Textual Practice*, 3/3 (Winter 1989), 323–59.

58. Quoted in Sengupta, *The Portrait of an Indian Woman*, 179–80.

59. The statement of Margaret Cousins, an Irish woman and pioneer of the all-India women's organizations, on behalf of the WIA, was quoted in the *Indian National Herald*, 17 Sept. 1927 in India, vol. 2 in folder no. 207, series 4, box 37, KM Papers.

60. For the report of the WIA protest meeting, see *Hindu*, 29 Sept. 1927 in India, vol. 2 in folder 207, series 4, box 37, KM Papers.

61. The events of the meeting have been reconstructed from the *Bombay Daily Mail*, 27 Dec. 1927 and the letter-to-editor in the *Hindu*, 12 Jan. 1927 in India, vol. 3 in folder no. 207, series 4, box 37, KM Papers.

62. For a background of the Non-Brahmin movement, see Gail Omvedt, *Cultural Conflict in a Colonial Society: The Non-Brahmin Movement in Western India, 1873–1830* (Poona, 1976).

63. See Rameshwari Nehru, *Gandhi is My Star: Speeches and Writings of Smt. Rameshwari Nehru*, comp. and ed. Somanth Dhar (Patna, 1950), 52.

64. For a history of child-marriage and age-of-consent reforms, see Geraldine Forbes, 'Women and Modernity: The Issue of Child Marriage in India', *Women's Studies International Quarterly*, 2 (1979), 407–19. For a general history of the AIWC, see Bharati Ray, *Women's Struggle: A History of the All India Women's Conference 1927–1990* (New Delhi, 1990).

65. Rameshwari Nehru, 'Early Marriage', in R. Nehru (ed.), *Our Cause*, 256–67.

66. Katherine Mayo, *Volume 2* (London, 1931).

67. See Kamaladevi Chattopadhyay, *Inner Recesses, Outer Spaces: Memoirs* (New Delhi, 1986), 113–17, and Rau, *An Inheritance*, 151.

68. See *New York Times*, 10 Feb. 1928, 13.1 Papers in Britain, like the *Edinburgh Evening News*, 10 Feb. 1928; *Star*, 10 Feb. 1928; *Reynolds Illustrated News*, 12 Feb. 1928; among others, gave sole credit to Mayo's book, see Great Britain, vol. 2 in folder no. 207, series 4, box 38, KM. Papers. The view continues today; see the biographic entry on Mayo by William E. Brown Jr. in vol. 30 of *Encyclopedia of American Biographies*, 20, KM Papers. Historians also continue to differ in their evaluations of Mayo's contribution to women's reform: William W. Emilsen,

'Gandhi and Mayo's *Mother India*', *South Asia*, 10/1 (1 June 1987), 69–82, credits Mayo with the reform, ignoring entirely the women's movement in India. R.K. Sharma, *Nationalism, Social Reform and Indian Women: A Study in the Interaction between the National Movement and the Movement of Social Reform among Indian Women 1921–1937* (Patna, 1981), 198–212, argues that Mayo had no role in getting reform legislation passed.

69. Letter from Blanche Wilson, no date, in folder no. 42, series 1, box 6, KM Papers.

70. For some examples, see Jahan Ara Shahnawaz, *Father and Daughter* (Lahore, 1971), 97–8; Hansa Mehta, *Indian Women* (Delhi, 1981), 63; Amrit Kaur, *Challenge to Women* (Allahabad, 1946), 5; and the collection of essays in Kamaladevi Chattopadhyay et al. (eds.), *The Awakening of Indian Women* (Madras, 1939).

71. Kumari Jayawardena, *Feminism and Nationalism in the Third World* (London, 1986), 107–9. This point has been made in Mary John, 'Postcolonial Feminists in the Western Intellectual Field: Anthropologists and Native Informants', *Inscriptions*, 5 (1989), 49–74.

72. Sangari and Vaid, 'Recasting Women: An Introduction', 19.

73. R. Radhakrishnan, 'Nationalism, Gender and Narrative' in Andrew Parker et al. (eds.), *Nationalisms and Sexualities* (New York, 1992), esp. 79–82.

74. The importance that such questions hold for our sense of the contemporary historical situation in India is spelled out in Kumkum Sangari, 'Introduction: Representations in History', *Journal of Arts and Ideas*, 17 and 18 (June 1989), 3–7. For an excellent example of the currency of the Indian/Hindu woman in some contemporary communal discourses in India, see Tanika Sarkar, 'The Woman as Communal Subject: Rashtrasevika Samiti and Ram Janmabhoomi Movement', *Economic and Political Weekly*, 26/35 (31 Aug. 1991), 2057–62.

23

Jawaharlal Nehru and the Hindu Code

A Victory of Symbol over Substance?*

REBA SOM

If to Gandhi goes the credit of having drawn out Indian women from their cloistered protected environment to join the national movement for freedom, to Jawaharlal Nehru surely goes the credit for having recognized the need formally to grant equality between the sexes and to enshrine it in the Fundamental Rights drawn up at the Karachi Congress of 1931.

Analyses on Gandhi's role in the women's movement have veered from one extreme position, that he used the essential non-violent nature of women for the limited purpose of making the political strategy of non-violent, non-cooperation viable, to the other extreme that he revolutionized the Indian social scene by drawing women out of their protective shell. The truth, as always, lies in between. It is a fact that, as never before, Gandhi's call to women to participate in the movement had a dramatic impact. The physical presence of women engaged in picketing, boycott and other non-cooperative activities added a new dimension to the movement. But it is equally true to say that Gandhi had thought of women's participation in a limited sense. He was aware that the innate qualities of silent suffering, stoic resistance and non-violence in a woman would give credence to the underlying non-violent philosophy of his movement. But he was very wary of allowing women to take on roles other than what he prescribed. And so he was reluctant to allow women activists to participate in the salt protest marches lest they become victims of violence. In general, Gandhi sought to hold the women's discontent within the overall nationalist cause and direct it in such a way that it remained targeted at imperialism. Thus women's participation in the national struggle remained within the parameters of what Geraldine Forbes calls 'the politics of respectability'.[1]

In his construct of women Gandhi defined his concept of femininity within a prescriptive frame of reference. Intrinsically a believer in sex equality Gandhi declared: 'I am uncompromising in the matter of women's rights. In my opinion, she should labour under no legal disability not suffered by man.'[2] But, at the same time, he envisioned separate roles for men and women in society. As he put it, 'man and woman are equal in status but are not identical. They are a peerless pair being supplementary to one other; each helps the other.' Accepting the role differentiation between man and woman, Gandhi declared that their vocations must be different for 'equality of sexes does not

*From *Modern Asian Studies*, vol. 28, no. 1 (1994), pp. 165–94.

mean equality of occupation'.[3] While drawing women into the vortex of the national movement, Gandhi did not spell out any definite programme for women to achieve socio-economic equality, nor did he take up socially divisive issues along caste, religious and sex lines. Instead, he devised programmes such as spinning which would bind the various women's social groups together and give them a common agenda and also dwelt on self-effacement and silent suffering, the qualities of Sita which would give women the ideological boost and moral encouragement for sacrifice.

To Jawaharlal Nehru, women's participation in large numbers in the national struggle in response to Gandhi's call was a social revolution of sorts. It broke barriers of social restraint and gave women a new cause and sense of commitment. As he wrote in his *Discovery of India*, '. . . a remarkable thing happened. Our women came to the front and took charge of the struggle . . . Here were these women, women of the upper or middle classes, leading sheltered lives in their homes—peasant women, working class women, rich women—pouring out in their tens of thousands in defiance of government order and police lathi.'[4]

In his own family, Nehru realized the impact of Gandhi's call. Kamala Nehru was a total convert to the Gandhian philosophy of non-violent non-cooperation and threw herself into the fray with a zeal that took even Jawaharlal by surprise. In fact it was her total commitment that made it simpler for Jawaharlal to take the plunge into a full-time involvement in national politics. Explaining Kamala's involvement, Nehru simply explained: 'She wanted to play her own part in the national struggle and not be merely a hanger-on and a shadow of her husband. She wanted to justify herself to her own self as well as to the world.'[5]

To Jawaharlal the participation of women in the national movement was only the beginning of a larger process whereby women would struggle to find their proper identity in the Indian social milieu and enjoy equal rights with men. Nehru was perhaps one of the few leaders who sensed this inevitable turn in the women's movement and actually heralded it. He loudly proclaimed: 'I have the greatest admiration . . . for the women of India today. I have faith in them, I am not afraid to allow them freedom to grow, because I am convinced that no amount of legal constraint can prevent society from going in a certain direction. And if you put too much legal constraint, the structure breaks.'[6] It was this legal constraint, binding women in society, that Jawaharlal sought to remove but he realized that the process of doing so must be actively pursued by women. As he put it, 'no people, group, no community, no country has ever got rid of its disabilities by the generosity of the oppressor . . . the women of India will not attain their full rights by the mere generosity of the men of India. They will have to fight for them and force their will on the menfolk before they can succeed.'[7] While on the one hand Nehru was forthright in condemning the male-dominated society that India was where 'our civilization, our customs, our laws, have all been made by men and he has taken good care to keep himself in a superior position and to treat woman as a chattel and a plaything to be exploited for his own advantage and amusement',[8] on the other hand he was equally aware that the move to break the socio-legal restraints on women had to be cautiously taken. He explained: 'inheritance, marriage, divorce are all supposed to be parts of the personal law of various communities and this personal law is supposed to be part of religion. It is obvious that no change can be imposed from the top.'[9] He visualized that education of public opinion would ultimately rally around support to get the measures of socio-legal equality between man and woman passed. This, however, was easier said than done and it took Nehru several years before he finally realized the volume of orthodox opinion arrayed against him in his bid to carry forward progressive legislation affecting personal laws.

Although the women's involvement in the freedom struggle was channelled by the Congress in an approved direction, there is no doubt that for many women, political involvement spurred their feminism and it was their commitment to improving the status of women that kept going their involvement in the freedom struggle. Already as early as 1917, the Women's Indian Association had petitioned Montagu, the Secretary of State for India, for women's political representation through adult franchise without any special reservation of seats. Although the ensuing 1919 Government of India Act excluded women from the vote, the provincial assemblies were allowed to drop the exclusion clause if they wished, which many of them did, led by the Madras Legislative Assembly. Even though a property qualification disqualified most women, who had normally no independent share in family property, the significance of this move was remarkable and lauded specially by Jawaharlal Nehru. As he put it, 'We must not forget that our womenfolk have consistently refused special and reserved representation in the legislatures. They have even protested against the partial representation that has been given to them. That attitude must be appreciated by the nation as a whole.'[10]

In fact, it was in this spirit of appreciation that Congress at the behest of Jawaharlal Nehru decided to enshrine the principle of equal rights for men and women in the Fundamental Rights of the People at the Karachi Congress of 1931. In spelling out the economic content of the equal rights for women, Nehru was doubtless inspired by Leninist rhetoric. Introducing the egalitarian legislation between the sexes, Lenin had said: 'We may now say with pride and without any exaggeration that outside of Soviet Russia there is not a country in the world where women have been given full equal rights.' Acknowledging that much of Lenin's legislation remained on paper, Nehru went on to observe that its importance lay in its 'powerful effect on changing the mentality of the masses'.[11] To Nehru symbolism was very important and in the Karachi resolution he saw the symbolic victory of women in their fight for recognition of equal status and civic rights, a significant victory for which women of England had to fight with great bitterness for generations'.[12]

What is of great significance to note in the passing of the Fundamental Rights resolution in 1931 is that it was adopted without any great opposition. In the first place it was considered to be a Gandhian concession to Jawaharlal Nehru.[13] Secondly, the political elite gave their support readily because thereby they could show that they were more socially advanced than the British and could counter claims that they were too backward for self-rule. Also, women's suffrage was bound to help the nationalist cause, as any increase in India's political representation would be unfavourable to the British presence. But more importantly, no objection was raised because the rights were on paper and their realization remained in the unforeseeable future. Expressing his ominous misgivings Jawaharlal Nehru said: 'Many of them who silently voted for the Karachi resolution might not have meant what the resolution laid down. They might have had mental reservations. The question was bound to arise again.'[14]

Nehru's fears were confirmed in a worse form than he had ever imagined when the movement to introduce reforms in Hindu personal law was initiated.

Hindu law had evolved over the years on the basis of (a) customs with diverse applications in the different parts of the country, and (b) the works of commentators expressed through different schools of legal thought such as Dayabhaga and Mitakshara which had varied applications in the different regions of the country. The British policy of non-interference in indigenous personal law and the rigidness of the British judiciary had created a situation where the evolutionary growth of Hindu law had become arrested. As Pattabhi Sitaramayya explained, 'when custom became petrified, progress became impeded altogether, and for a hundred and fifty years our society has not been able to make much progress'.[15] Besides, the underlying principle of Hindu law in the pre-independence era was inequality, the inferior position of the woman in all matters governing personal law like marriage, maintenance, inheritance and guardianship. The fact that women were, to quote Nehru, 'shackled and unfree'[16] and the fact that the different High Court interpretations of legal texts created a sense of legal confusion, generated a need for bringing about a uniformity in legal practices through codification.

It was the passing of the Hindu Women's Rights to Property Act, otherwise known as the Deshmukh Act, in 1937 that brought out the legitimacy of this demand for codification. The Act, while securing for the widowed daughter-in-law legal rights equal to those of her son, to enjoy her husband's share in the joint family property, did not give her absolute and alienable rights of ownership. Nor did it mention the rights of the daughter. It was clear that piecemeal legislation could not meet the growing demands for modernizing the whole structure of the law. There were difficulties in interpreting the Act[17] and protests made from many strata of society including the All India Women's Conference.[18] Finally, the government ordered an investigation of the situation as a whole and placed the Act of 1937 together with other similar bills pending, before a specially formed committee for its detailed consideration.

The Committee, called the Hindu Code Committee, was set up in 1941 under the chairmanship of Sir B.N. Rau, a former judge of the Calcutta High Court. It distributed an elaborate questionnaire on various questions related to the codification and after an examination of the replies received, submitted a report in 1941 urging the government to go ahead with comprehensive legislation. It also suggested that instead of piecemeal legislation, a complete code should be prepared which should retain the distinctive character of Hindu law while introducing particular changes. After a study of the draft bills prepared by the Rau Committee, the government revived the activities of the Hindu Code Committee in 1944 under Sir B.N. Rau which now met to prepare a Draft Code dealing specifically with Succession, Maintenance, Marriage and Divorce, Minority and Guardianship and Adoption. This Code known popularly as the Hindu Code Bill was widely circulated after being translated into 12 regional languages. The Code Committee toured the country extensively examining witnesses and finally presented a revised Code, which was introduced into the Legislative Assembly in 1947. It was the intention of the government that the Code should become law on 1 January 1948. However, the whole project was temporarily suspended when, with independence, the Constituent Assembly was formed and the energies of the legislature were devoted to consolidate the new regime. In 1948, under Nehru's primeministership, the Draft Code was referred to a Select Committee under the chairmanship of the Law Minister, Dr B.R. Ambedkar. While introducing the Code in the Constituent Assembly, Ambedkar pointed out that the main aim of the Bill was 'to codify the rules of Hindu Law which are scattered in innumerable decisions of the High Courts and the Privy Council, which form a bewildering motley to the common man'.[19] He introduced several important changes in the Bill including equal property rights for women, abolition of customary law, and specification of grounds for divorce.

The reintroduction of the Bill in the Constituent Assembly with the major changes, created a most interesting situation. The founding fathers of the Constitution, who, a short while ago had passed the Constitution and accepted without discussion the principles of equality and absence of discrimination between the sexes, now in a total volteface opposed tooth and nail the Hindu Code Bill. Their opposition opened up the Pandora's box of age-old superstitions, complexes, patriarchal feelings and deep-rooted prejudices running along caste, class, religious and regional lines.

Matters came to such a pass that Nehru decided to break up the Code into four separate parts to facilitate their early passage. This was, however, not to be. Finally, in September 1951, B.R. Ambedkar resigned, a frustrated, ill and broken man. Nehru chose to bide his time and ultimately in May 1955, the Hindu Marriage Act was passed, followed by the Hindu Succession Act in May 1956, and the Hindu Adoption and Maintenance Act in December 1956 and the Dowry Prohibition Act in July 1961.

The voluminous debates on the Hindu Code brought into public focus a broad spectrum of ideas on social issues. An analysis of the dominant mentalities is crucial for an understanding of how Nehru had to dilute substantially his original position, resulting in a set of legislation which was more symbolic than substantial in character.

The major groups opposing the legislation were:

(a) the conservative hardliners within the Congress Party: veterans like Vallabhbhai Patel, Rajendra Prasad, J.B. Kripalani who had a completely different worldview from Nehru's and who had traditionally, through the 1920s and 1930s, been ranged against Nehru within the Congress, representing the conservative point of view. Rajendra Prasad entered into lengthy correspondence with Jawaharlal Nehru (copies of which he gave to Vallabhbhai Patel), trying to persuade him not to go through with the legislation and finally holding out the threat of refusing Presidential assent to the Bills, if passed. Patel, who was unmistakably opposed to the Bill[20] and shared Prasad's views, characteristically, did not have the inclination to argue the issue with Nehru. He simply disallowed time in the Parliament for discussion of the Hindu Code Bill and summarily dismissed it, saying: 'the Government do not propose to ask for any more days for the Hindu Code. It is unnecessary waste of time';[21]

(b) the Hindu fundamentalists within the Congress Party who were substantial in number, including the Deputy Speaker, Ananthasayanam Aiyangar, who had openly declared that monogamy per se was not good and that in the case of dearth of children, there was no harm in allowing polygamy.[22] The fundamentalists constantly opposed and sabotaged the attempts of Ambedkar to proceed with the legislation. The fact that Ambedkar was outside the Congress Party made it more difficult for him to manoeuvre the simmering party politics from within.

The fact that the Congress Party was itself divided on the question of the Code gave a certain lever to Rajendra Prasad who repeatedly pointed out to Nehru his procedural lapse in not having formally notified the Congress Working Committee or the AICC about the Bill. Stoically Nehru tried to defend himself. While accepting the charge that the AICC or Working Committee had not considered the matter, he said that there was no precedent for such matters to be placed before the Congress. If indeed any Congress member was inclined to raising the matter for discussion, he could surely have done so, since the issue had received so much publicity.[23]

(c) the Hindu Mahasabha and its women's wing, with representatives like Shyama Prasad Mukherjee, N.C. Chatterjee and others who opposed the Bills strongly for threatening the so-called religious foundations of Hindu society. By using inverse logic the Mahasabha leaders tried to suggest that the Hindu Code was, after all, a communal measure and a uniform Civil Code should have been made instead, to give effect to the secular ideals of the country. The real motives of the Mahasabha, however, were betrayed when Dr Shyama Prasad Mukherjee made the suggestion that the Hindu Code be made optional. Ambedkar was provoked into dismissing S.P. Mukherjee's remarks as not worth serious consideration since he had after all, as a member of Nehru's Cabinet, wholeheartedly supported the Code which he was now opposing. Ambedkar also pointed out that the innocuous suggestion that a uniform Civil Code be initiated seemed curious, as he wondered how could opponents of the Bill turn overnight into protagonists of a Civil Code;

(d) the Sikh group represented by men like Sardar Mann and Sardar Hukum Singh who resented being clubbed with the Hindus in the broad framework of reform. They considered the Bill to be a dubious attempt on the part of Hindus to absorb the Sikh community;

(e) the Muslim group with men like Naziruddin Ahmad (Bengal) who were obviously encouraged by the fundamentalist group within the Congress to tilt the scale of opinion in their favour. Claiming to speak from experience, Ahmad criticized at length the bid to end Mitakshara joint family which, he said, would lead to breakdown of families and result in property wrangles. The Hindu families would then have the same fate as Muslim families and become pauperized.[24] Many members were not convinced of his sincerity and Renuka Ray openly asked Ahmad why he was chary of denying Hindus the advantages which Muslim society enjoyed;

(f) the women parliamentarians, who, while being greatly appreciative of the legislation, very often criticized the measures for not going far enough. As Sucheta Kripalani speaking on the Hindu Marriage Bill put it, 'this is basically a halting and halfhearted measure. It does give relief to certain suffering elements in our society, but by no means am I prepared to call it . . . a wonderfully progressive measure.'[25] Hansa Mehta said that the Succession Bill did not go far enough as sons were regarded as being more equal than daughters.[26]

Although the focus of the Parliamentary debates tended to change periodically when the different bills and clauses came up for discussion, by and large the broad areas of opposition to the Bill, as expressed over more than a decade of debates and discussions, can be identified and the trends of thought highlighted.

A recurrent cry which appeared through the years of debate was that the Hindu shastras were hallowed by tradition and any attempt to tamper with them was presumptuous and undesirable. This was a view commonly shared by traditionalists, conservatives and many parliamentarians from the Akhil Bharatiya Hindu Mahasabha. N.C. Chatterjee, a Mahasabha member from Bengal, pointed out that the essence of Indian civilization which was 'the purity of family life, the great ideal of chastity and the great ideal of Indian womanhood' was being threatened to be sabotaged by the intended legislation. Describing Manu, Yagnavalkya and other lawmakers of India as 'God-given, God-intoxicated men, inspired by the highest ideals' he asked what right did the Prime Minister have to initiate revolutionary bills which would shake the roots of Indian civilization shaped by personal law which had stood the test of centuries and thousands of years.[27] The Hindu Mahasabha had consistently in various meetings and resolutions[28] condemned the proposed Code for subverting Hindu ideas, culture and religion. It also feared that the ideology of Jawaharlal Nehru would be a menace to the religious identity of India and bring about 'a Godless State'.[29]

There was, moreover, a strong undercurrent of resentment at the fact that the Muslim personal law remained untouched. N.C. Chatterjee challenged: 'Why not frame, if you have got the courage and wisdom to do it, one uniform Civil Code? Why are you then proceeding with communal legislation?'[30]

There was another view strongly articulated by Dr Rajendra Prasad that the bulk of the proposed legislation, which would affect 'the entire population by fundamental changes in the personal law Hindus', was not sufficiently discussed, circulated and presented for public opinion.[31] Moreover, whatever evidence had been analysed by the Rau Committee had gone overwhelmingly against the committee recommendations, as the note of dissent by Dr Dwarka Nath Mitter[32] and others had shown. Therefore, the matter should form part of the election manifesto instead of being hurriedly pushed through. Further, the Constituent Assembly which was elected for the special purpose of framing the Constitution of India was not competent to deal with legislation of such fundamental importance and controversial nature.[33] The views of Dr Prasad were widely shared. Concurring with the opinion of Dr Prasad, Pandit Thakur Das Bhargava (Congress U.P.) said that the sense of propriety and proportion demanded that the principles which had existed for thousands of years should not be hastily brushed aside by legislation.[34]

There was a strong feeling that the tradition of customary law had served well the purpose of effecting important socio-legal changes and, therefore, legislation would merely have a disruptive impact on almost all families.[35] As Rajendra Prasad put it, 'tremendous changes have come about without any legislation and are legalized under the sanction of custom which is ever-changing and ever-growing. I, therefore, do not see the necessity for hurried legislation.'[36] Many parliamentarians like Lakshmi Kanta Moitra (Bengal) tried to ridicule the whole effort of codification as being an unwise, unnecessary exercise, 'a simple intellectual pastime; Codification for the sake of Codification'.[37]

There was also the feeling that the intended codification would lead to the furtherance of the progressive ideas of a small, if not a microscopic minority. Many of the reforms intended, for example, divorce, existed in some form or the other in the customary laws and applied to 80% of the population. As Rajendra Prasad powerfully expressed it, by making it obligatory on all to have resort to a court of law caused unnecessary trouble, delay, expense and uncertainty to the majority of the population who, in any case, had always exercised the same right through simple, inexpensive and unquestionable caste customs.[38] Rohini Kumar Chaudhuri (Assam-General) pointed out that a large mass of people dependent on agriculture and agricultural property would remain outside the pale of legislation which would cater to the interests of the so-called 'enlightened section'[39] or what Naziruddin Ahmad sarcastically called, 'the ultra modern' section of society.[40]

Coming to the specific provisions of the Code there were long debates on the monogamy clause. Certain conservative elements pointed out that in any case the practice of polygamy had died down and if monogamy was enforced only on Hindus, they would be committing 'racial suicide'[41] as the Muslim population would multiply out of proportion to the existing Hindu ratio. Ananga Mohan Dam (Bengal-General) tried to clinch his argument by saying that compulsory monogamy would prove as disastrous as it had been for the Roman Empire where monogamy had led to concubinage on a large scale, leading to its fall.[42] Naziruddin Ahmad pleaded that 'polygamy is not as dangerous as it is supposed to be in point of view of abstract logic and abstract legislation'. Absolute prohibition of polygamy would be a 'defect and practical difficulty in the way of the Bill'.[43] He said there was comfort to be drawn from the fact that in effect having more than one wife was rare as 'one is costly and troublesome enough'.[44] Rajendra Prasad projected a new dimension to this debate by saying that while the number of polygamous marriages was in any case going down, it would be undemocratic to thrust the benefits of monogamy on a few 'against their will'. Ideally he recommended monogamy for a life-time even in the event of death or divorce of spouse.[45]

On the clause for divorce, there were considerable misgivings among traditionalists who felt that thereby the institution of marriage would be dealt a severe blow. Laboured attempts were made to quote from legal luminaries like Dr Radha Binode Pal saying that divorce would result in a miserable life for women since they would have to face injustice and cruelty with divorce. Lakshmi Kanta Moitra declared that the introduction of the divorce clause was the 'rudest possible shock' which was repugnant to Hindu notions of marriage which the shastras had rendered 'sacred and absolutely inviolable'.[46]

The recommendation for compulsory registration of marriages also caused deep resentment among many. P.B. Gole (Berar: Non-Mohammedan) argued that 'the very object of getting the marriage registered is to have a divorce'.[47]

Closely linked with the question of divorce was the provision for alimony. While welcoming the provision of alimony for women there was a sense of outrage among certain women members at the clause that alimony may be stopped if the woman had not remained chaste. Sucheta Kripalani feared that vague charges might be brought in the name of chastity to deprive women of property rights. As Renu Chakravarty put it, the chastity clause could well be the 'handle to beat the wife with'.[48] The question of alimony to be paid by women threw up interesting points of view. Although the principle was opposed by most men and women in the House, the reasons put forward betrayed deep-seated prejudices. Sucheta Kripalani pointed out that the provision that husbands can claim alimony was itself a shock to right thinking people as it had been purposely introduced with a vengeance on the plea of equality. Since women were economically not independent this provision had little meaning and demonstrated 'a monstrous kind of equality'.[49] Her husband Acharya Kripalani, interestingly enough, pointed out the flaw in women's argument, saying that when it was a question of alimony, women argued about not being economically independent, but how could they support themselves if divorced? He condescendingly advocated divorce rights only for women until true economic equality came to be established.[50]

To N.C. Chatterjee, the concept of men asking for alimony was unacceptable as it hurt his male pride. He called it 'unthinkable, revolting, preposterous . . . if any Hindu husband solemnly asks for alimony . . . he should be thrown out of the Hindu fold altogether'.[51] To that Pandit K.C. Sharma added, such a person would not be 'a manly man'.[52]

Perhaps the most vocal protests were articulated against the clause granting equal property rights to women for it threatened the well-entrenched economic rights of the male in society. As Pandit Thakur Das Bhargava put it, it was 'equality run mad'.[53] It was pointed out that women traditionally were brought up with the purpose of being given in marriage into another family. As Lakshmi Kanta Moitra put it, 'the girl is made for her husband's family; she is not to become a part and parcel of the family where she is born. That is the whole thing. And, therefore, no question of injustice or inequality arises.'[54] While women should be given rights, he emphasized that there was no question of giving her 'absolutely equal rights'.[55] It was feared that equal property rights for women would create family tensions within her paternal family. It would replace the relationship of affection between brother and sister by one of clashing economic interest.[56] Rajendra Prasad pointed out that the induction of daughters' husbands who were complete strangers into the family, to share property with the brothers, would result in 'a most heterogeneous conglomeration which would definitely lead to conflict and litigation'.[57] There was also the feeling that women, who had absolute rights over Stridhan (jewellery and valuables given at the time of marriage) and rights over their husbands' property, would now be given an unfair advantage with equal property rights in their fathers' property. As Ram Sahai (Gwalior State) pointed out, 'men are being subjected to the same injustice which has until now been done to the women'.[58]

There was a deep-seated fear that by granting equal property rights to women, the Mitakshara concept of joint family would be dealt a crippling blow which in turn would break the basic fabric of Hindu society. There would be excessive fragmentation and litigation or, as Prasad explicitly put it, 'open violent conflict among members family'.[59] As it is, the joint family system was gradually and surely breaking up and the legislation would add an unceremonious haste to the process.

Acharya Kripalani spoke forcefully about certain benefits that still came from the joint family system. It was 'an insurance against sickness, against unemployment, against old age and even against the "badmashi" of the young whether male or female'. It would be foolish to do away with the system without providing for some alternative social insurance for the people.[60]

As the different points of view on the various aspects of the codification began to emerge there was a tendency for prejudice to colour judgement. As Kripalani analysed, people came to be guided more by their passion than reason. Thus all those ranged on the side of the Bill were branded as ultra modern, westernized and not good Hindus, whereas those against the Bill were branded as being deeply religious, orthodox and reactionary.[61] Striking a note of caution on value judgements Rajendra Prasad said: 'I do not think anything and everything which some people regard as reactionary or conservative is necessarily bad and everything that they call progressive is necessarily good. We have to weigh how it will be received by the vast bulk of Hindu public against what foreigners outside and those who call themselves "progressive" would say.'[62]

However, as opinions were forcefully articulated and prejudices mounted there was considerable politicization of the issues. Thus in the constituency of Hindu Mahasabha leader N.C. Chatterjee, Renu Chakravarty alleged that there was active propaganda that if the Hindu Code Bill was passed there would be complete incestuousness and wives would marry sons or sons marry daughters.[63] So deep ran prejudices that the Akhil Bharatiya Mahila Hindu Mahasabha actually sent a representation to Lord Wavell the Viceroy, asking him to disallow Renuka Ray, the well-known western-educated woman activist, from sitting in the Constituent Assembly representing the women's view, on the ground that she was of the Brahmo Samaj and hence ill conversant with the Hindu law.[64] Mrs Jankibai Joshi, President of the All India Hindu Women's Conference, shared with Rajendra Prasad her fears that a class of people detached from the current Hindu life and enamoured with western ideas had appointed the Rau Committee to prepare a Code with which they would silently disrupt the Hindu society.[65] There were attempts to show the decadence of western society and point out that the proposed legislation was along the same permissive lines and the sins of the western society would now invade and disrupt the age-old balance and stability of the Indian social fabric.

There were slanted comments made in the course of the debates on the role of westernized women, social butterflies, frequenting the Connaught Circus circuits,[66] in pushing the legislation through. While protesting against such insinuations, women leaders like Renu Chakravarty warned at the same time against the attitude of exaggerated feminism which would do more harm to the cause of women. She pointed out that it would be absolutely wrong to believe that 'marriage was an anti-man affair' and that the passage of the Bill would immediately confer equality on women, for, without economic equality and education, legislation would have no effect.[67]

Very often the debates took such a turn that the latent regional prejudices tended to surface. A North–South divide in terms of culture, practice and custom was often apparent. Thus while discussing the question of divorce, there was mention that the customary laws of South India permitted the practice. Hindu Mahasabha leader S.P. Mukherjee was provoked into replying: 'I say good luck to South India. Let South India proceed from progress to progress, from divorce to divorce. . . . Why force it on others who do not want it?'[68] Or again, while discussions on women's property rights were on, it was evident that opponents of the measure based their logic on the basic principle that daughters are born to go out of the family. Making a mocking distinction between northern and southern Indian practices, Pandit Mukut Behari Lal Bhargava commented that in North India, 'the father or mother will not even take water in the house of the daughter' whereas the South with its more liberal customs seemed like 'an outside country'.[69]

A legal and constitutional angle to the debate was projected by Dr Rajendra Prasad, which proved to be the greatest challenge to the Nehru government's bid to see the legislation through. Prasad pointed out that the measure, owing to its controversial nature, should be incorporated into the election manifesto of the Party and placed before the electorate. Any attempt to push the measures through would, apart from rousing bitter feelings, 'affect the chances of the Congress at the next election'.[70] Finally, knowing that the Nehru government was determined to push the controversial Bill through, Rajendra Prasad, who had been opposing various aspects of the Bill, made it abundantly clear that as President, he might exercise his option and reserve his assent to the measure.[71]

Nehru's reaction and response to the proceedings of the debate on the Hindu Code Bill indicate a sense of hopelessness. In a candid letter to Vallabhbhai Patel he wrote: 'What is important is the difference in outlook between Parliament as a whole and me. They put up with me because of their friendliness towards me and their affection and a certain past record and habit of doing so. But they go farther and farther away from me in mind and heart. This produces unhappiness all round and frustration and work suffers.'[72]

To begin with, Nehru had been confident that following the easy acceptance of the Fundamental Rights resolution ensuring sex equality at Karachi 1931 and subsequently, in 1947, by the Constitution, the Hindu Code Bill would be easily passed. In 1949 he stated firmly: 'We stand committed to the broad approach of the Bill as a whole and the Government will stand or fall on it.'[73] The hornet's nest that was roused in the course of the debates took him by surprise. He painfully realized that while accepting the principle of sex equality on paper, there had been no serious contemplation of what it implied and hence the outburst on seeing the specific clauses of the Bill.

For Nehru the Hindu Code was a necessary reform measure which fitted into his larger perspective of all-round national development. As he put it, 'We talk about Five Year Plans, of economic progress, industrialization, political freedom and all that. They are all highly important. But I have no doubt in my mind that the real progress of the country means progress not only on the political plane, not only on the economic plane, but also on the social plane. They have to be integrated, all these, when the great nation goes forward.'[74]

The proposed reforms were not revolutionary to Nehru, since many of the customary laws had already adopted them in some form or other. To him they were 'a very moderate measure of social reform . . . indeed very largely a codification of the existing law'.[75] As the first Prime Minister it was important, he felt, to weave a certain pattern of uniformity into legal practices which would hold good throughout the land. He believed that Hindu society which was traditionally dynamic and vibrant instead of static and inflexible, would be able to absorb and integrate the changes proposed without any disruption. The changes envisaged were more than warranted by the swiftly changing socio-economic conditions. As he crisply put it, 'It is very unfair for Manu or Yagnavalkya or anybody else to be brought in as a witness as to what should be done in the present conditions.'[76] To him the Hindu Marriage Bill was of special symbolical value since it would be the first major crack on the age-old system of Hindu personal law.[77] Indeed, he felt confident that this Parliament would be remembered for that particular measure of social reform rather than any other legislative activity.[78]

Nehru felt disgusted by the repeated references to the pristine purity of the Hindu shastras and the exalted position given to Sita, Savitri, Damayanti and others. As he put it, 'I have a feeling that these echoes from the past are raised chiefly to hide our present deficiencies and to prevent us from attacking the root cause of women's degradation today.'[79] Why, after all, were men not reminded in the same manner of Ramachandra and Satyavan, and urged to behave like them.[80] Were they 'supposed to be perfect, incapable of any further effort or further improvement?'[81]

Nehru also strongly condemned the tendency that he noticed in the parliamentary debates constantly to run down western civilization in an attempt to praise one's own in comparison. As he put it, 'to make a parallel and say, "See how horrible the conditions in America are, and, if you pass this Bill, you will have the same conditions" is not only non-sequitor in logic but it is a bad way of approach.'[82] He explained that the large incidence of divorce and other family problems in the West was due to the impact of industrialization on human relationships and this was a trend which could well affect the developing world.

On several particular provisions of the Code, which caused acrimonious debate, for example the divorce issue, Nehru spoke very forcefully. He considered it absurd to put a halo round a sacramental marriage and call it inviolable. With powerful invective Nehru asked: 'does it mean that it is a sacrament to tie up people who bite, who hate each other, who make life hell for each other? . . . There is something rather fine in human relationships provided they are good relationships.'[83]

Throughout the prolonged course of the debates, Nehru's own interjections were not very many. This was probably because it became painfully clear to him that his worldview was so totally different from that of most fellow parliamentarians. On the question of allowing women equal property rights, for instance, Nehru's own views on the subject can be sharply contrasted with the views of those who bitterly opposed the measure. After the death of Motilal Nehru, Jawaharlal found himself heir to his father's sizeable property. He wrote to his sister Krishna, 'I can only consider myself as a joint sharer in father's property; the other sharers being mother and you. I am not including Nan, as she stands in no need of money. . . . Indeed mother and you are the real sharers. I am a trustee for the family property. . .'.[84]

Stemming from this major difference in mentalities was the practical problem of keeping the debates within manageable limits. Nehru realized that the absence of time limit in the speeches caused the debates to become tediously long and dilatory. There was also a feeling that deliberate filibustering prevented the measures being passed. For Nehru the position was particularly delicate because even the Deputy Speaker, Ananthasayanam Aiyangar, had pronounced views against the Hindu Code. So while Nehru did not desire to suppress full discussion, he was wary of all the motions brought in by various members in an attempt to postpone discussions and obstruct the measures.

He was also conscious of the fact that the Hindu Mahasabha was exploiting the situation for political purposes.[85] Nehru gradually came to accept the position that the Hindu Code Bill in its existing form could never secure Parliamentary approval. With its changes and recommendations, it had become very unwieldy—'a huge document of hundreds and hundreds of pages. . . . It was so big that we could never get through it.'[86] It was decided, therefore, to split the Bill into several parts and the first, dealing with Marriage and Divorce, was taken up.

In September 1951, there seemed to be little doubt that Jawaharlal Nehru was determined to steer the Marriage and Divorce Bill through. In a letter to Rajendra Prasad on 15 September 1951, Nehru took a tough legal stand and stated firmly that 'the President has no power or authority to go against the will of Parliament in regard to a

Bill that has been well-considered by it and passed. The whole conception of constitutional government is against any exercise by the President of any such authority.'[87] He declared his firm intention to enact the Marriage and Divorce part of the Bill as a separate Act before the current Parliament session ended. This deadline coincided with that accepted by Nehru's Law Minister, B.R. Ambedkar, who despite his ill health, had been determined to get the Marriage and Divorce Act passed in the September 1951 session of Parliament. Ambedkar had even requested Pandit Nehru to prepone Parliamentary discussions on the Hindu Code to 16 August so that it would be completed by 1 September and he could resume his medical treatment without any interruption. Nehru, however, felt he could not rush proceedings without harming the cause of reform. Requesting Ambedkar to be a little patient, he slated 17 September 1951 for the day when the Marriage and Divorce Bill would be taken up to be an Act by the time the session ended.

In effect, however, after only four clauses were passed, the Bill was dropped. As Ambedkar dramatically put it, after a life of four years in the House the Bill was 'killed and died unwept and unsung'. To Ambedkar it was 'a great shock—a bolt from the blue'.[88] He resigned his seat from the Cabinet on 27 September 1951 and in a Press Note dated 10 October 1951 declared in no uncertain terms: 'I got the impression that the Prime Minister although sincere, had not the earnestness and determination required to get the Hindu Code Bill through.'[89] The unavoidable impression at that time was that the Nehru government had proved weak kneed and failed to back up Ambedkar. As a journalist commented on Nehru at that time, 'he wrote like an angel and spoke like Poor Paul'.[90] Ambedkar himself ascribed the non-passage of the Bill to the inability of Nehru to persuade the chief whip of Parliament to limit the time taken on speeches so that filibustering could be avoided and the measure passed. As Ambedkar sarcastically put it, 'I have never seen a case of chief whip so disloyal to the Prime Minister and the Prime Minister so loyal to a disloyal whip. . .'[91] Ambedkar also laboured under the belief that the Nehru government had intentionally, over the years, not allowed sufficient time for the Hindu Code to be discussed in Parliament. Even at the September 1951 session other issues which Ambedkar felt could have been taken up later, for example the Benaras and Aligarh University Bills or the Press Bill, were given priority of discussion over the Hindu Code.

What was the truth that lay behind the inability of Parliament to pass the Hindu Marriage and Divorce Bill in September 1951? How valid was Ambedkar's indictment of Nehru?

The inescapable conclusion seems to be that Jawaharlal Nehru, in spite of his spirited stand before the President, tended to back pedal at the eleventh hour and there was the proverbial gap, as Ambedkar put it, between the 'promises and performances of the Prime Minister'.[92]

It seems likely that Rajendra Prasad's reply dated 18 September 1951 written with incisive legal logic, to Nehru's strong letter of 15 September had made a serious impression on Nehru. While reiterating that the Constitution conferred on the President in 'unequivocal terms' the right to confer or withhold assent to a Bill, Prasad went on to warn Nehru that with the general elections only four months away, Nehru by introducing the controversial legislation just then, would be taking a gamble on Congress chances in the election.[93] This logic weighed heavily on Nehru's conscience. Further, Prasad's charge that it would be undemocratic and morally wrong of the Nehru government to exploit the popularity that it enjoyed in Parliament, by getting a debatable measure passed, worried Nehru.[94] Prasad's strongly worded letter to Nehru was a calculated and desperate move to stall legislation. As Prasad confided to Dr K.N. Katju, 'I have written as strongly as I could . . . I could not have done more.'[95] Rajendra Prasad with his intimate association with Nehru in Congress politics must have known that Nehru's ideological stand on the issue would ultimately have to take into account the brutal logic of practical politics.

There was also another dimension to Nehru's dilemma posed by Ambedkar himself who, though he shared with Nehru a passionate zeal for social legal reforms, approached the problem in a totally different way demonstrating a complete difference in world-views. Being of the untouchable Mahar caste, Ambedkar took upon himself the task of getting the Bill through as a crusade against the bastions of the tyrannical upper-caste stranglehold over Hindu society. Ambedkar had researched deep into the shastras which he freely quoted to illustrate weaknesses in the Hindu social system and to ridicule many of its socio-religious practices.[96] Having publicly burnt the Manusmriti in 1927,[97] Ambedkar made the passing of the Hindu Code an article of faith. As his biographer put it, 'He was inspired by the thrilling idea that a Mahar would be reorganizing the basic framework of the Hindu society.' As Ambedkar put it, Hindu society had enslaved both Sudras and women, who had to be rescued by law so that society could move on.[98] Ambedkar's basic argument was that Hindu society was inert and static where the function of law machinery had been left to the Gods. For the first time, Hindu society was being encouraged to move in a positive direction and, therefore, all opposition, though substantial, had to be disregarded.[99] To him the pace of reform had to be fast and he was most reluctant at having had to agree to the original Code being split up. Ambedkar's messianic ardour and his aggressive stance provoked a lot of opposition. As a critic put it, Dr Ambedkar was 'bristling with barbed wire from the inside out, and no respector of persons'.[100] Parliamentarians became incensed with Ambedkar's loud denunciations of the Hindu social system, 'his abuses and invectives' and his attempts to 'vilify the Hindu religion'.[101] While Ambedkar was desperate to see at least the Marriage and Divorce Act through,[102] his opponents were equally determined that he should be denied the distinction of being called the 'Modern Manu'. Some members openly declared that as long as Dr Ambedkar was piloting the Bill, they would not allow it to pass.[103] Even those not opposing the measures per se became determined to vote down the Bill as an expression of anti-Ambedkarism. There were personal attacks on his background and even suggestions that his keenness to get the Marriage and Divorce Act passed was because he wanted to legalize his own marriage.[104] Dr Pattabhi Sitaramayya (Congress-Madras) denounced the 'professorial, pedagogic and pontifical attitudes' of Ambedkar which 'will only alienate attitudes that have almost been reconciled' or, as Naziruddin Ahmad said, 'perhaps call up an opposition where there is none now'.[105]

To Jawaharlal Nehru, Ambedkar's approach to the issue was a total anathema. Whereas Ambedkar dwelt on the static quality of Hindu society, Nehru was never tired of emphasizing its dynamism. 'Hindu law had never been rigid', Nehru said, 'Hindu law had a certain dynamic quality' which could easily absorb the prospective socio-legal changes.[106] As against the hurry with which Ambedkar tried to rush the Bills through,

Nehru felt that it would be tactically unsound to give a handle to opponents to say that they were gagged and not given an opportunity for discussion.[107] Pragmatically viewing the impasse created by the obstructionist and delaying tactics in Parliament, Nehru analysed: 'We may pass the Bill in spite of this opposition' but there would be great obstruction in the implementation of the Bill when passed. Large numbers of people might offer this obstruction in an organized way. 'It is always difficult to deal with this kind of thing.'[108] Although Nehru advocated tact and restraint, Ambedkar managed to make himself the focal point of controversy. Nehru's dilemma was complete. On the floor of the House he declared, 'I want to make it perfectly clear that I stand by every word that the Law Minister has said.'[109] And yet, the virulence of Ambedkar's opposition and the 'hurt caused by his provocative language'[110] created a situation when Nehru seriously considered resignation and reforming his Cabinet with a more congenial Law Minister.[111] It is not surprising, therefore, that Ambedkar's resignation did not cause any protest from Nehru. On the contrary, he was so apprehensive that Ambedkar's resignation speech in Parliament would stir up further controversy that he insisted on receiving a copy of the speech in advance. Ambedkar considered this gesture as tantamount to censorship and resigned in a huff and released his speech to the Press.[112]

Ambedkar's resignation was a setback to the pace of reform. Nehru's government had taken a beating—the reformers felt let down, the traditionalists felt elated, the women Parliamentarians felt that Nehru had been weak. Nehru admitted as much when he wrote to the Chief Ministers: 'We had to confess defeat for the moment at least.'[113] The painful experience was not without its lessons. The opposition, Nehru realized, could not be wished away. As he had explained to Ambedkar, 'With the best will in the world, we cannot brush aside this opposition and get things done quickly. They have it in their power to delay a great deal. We must, therefore, proceed with some tact.'[114] His tactics were simply to bide his time. His commitment to the cause of reform remained. As he wrote, 'Personally, I shall not give up this fight because I think it is intimately connected with any progress on any front that we desire to make.'[115] To committed women reformers like Renuka Ray and Durgabai Deshmukh, Nehru was most reassuring. He asked them to trust him to choose the opportune moment for the enactment of the legislation. ' If we come back [after the elections],' Nehru assured Renuka Ray, 'we shall not tolerate dilatory tactics and we will not allow impediments to the passage of this vital legislation.'[116]

With Congress success in the 1951 elections, Nehru was assured of a stronger support in Parliament to back his social reform legislation. Since the issue had dragged on for long, differences of opinion had been amply talked out. Law Minister C.C. Biswas would claim in 1954 that the delay in passing the legislation was 'fully justified' because over the years the bitter opposition to the Bills had died down.[117] Ambedkar's absence from the House had also removed the element of controversy which had previously crept into the debates and been much politicized by interested parties. Now that Parliament was freshly constituted with the mandate of the people, Congress veterans like Rajendra Prasad could also not raise further objections. Finally, the Bills themselves had been made more acceptable by whittling down the controversial points. As Sardar Hukum Singh put it, 'It is not the public opinion that has changed its attitude. . . . This is not the original Bill. . . . That Hindu Code has practically been given up by the Government.'[118] Even then, it took a few more years before the Hindu Marriage Act was passed in 1955, followed by the Hindu Succession Act, the Hindu Minority and Guardianship

Act and the Hindu Adoption and Maintenance Act, all of which were passed in 1956 and finally, the Dowry Prohibition Act passed in 1961.

To Nehru the passage of the Hindu Reform legislation marked a victory. To Aubrey Menen he remarked that they constituted the greatest real advance in his career.[119] In a report to his Chief Ministers, Nehru declared that the 'passage of this legislation marks an epoch in India' for 'it has pulled out Hindu law from the ruts in which it had got stuck and given it a new dynamism'.[120]

To what extent was this a victory of symbol over substance? Even after almost four decades since the epoch-making legislation was made, the condition of women in the country in general remains unequal. Broad demographic data show a decline in sex ratio, higher female infant mortality, continuing incidence of child marriage, rising rate of reported dowry deaths and bride burnings, low level of female literacy and workforce participation. Apart from many other factors, this predicament can also be traced to the fact that major loopholes had remained in the social legislation passed in Nehru's time and that, in the euphoria of having passed the legislation, a sense of false complacency had crept in and proper measures to enforce the legislation through a functioning infrastructure or attempts to bring in improving legal amendments were not undertaken. For both, Nehru and his government can be partially faulted.

Unlike customary law which had been simple, inexpensive and geared to local requirements, the separate Acts had nuances which were never fully explained or understood at the local level. Moreover, in many cases, those guilty of violating the laws could not be easily brought to book as the offence was very often not cognizable, as in the case of the Child Marriage Restraint Act. Also the compulsory registration of marriages recommended in the Hindu Marriage Act which would have been an excellent check on child and bigamous marriages remained ineffective since there was no clause threatening the validity of a marriage not registered.[121]

In the case of the Hindu Succession Act, there were several major compromises which many considered were a sell-out by the Nehru government. For example, the joint family system of the Hindus which Nehru had criticized as being 'a relic of a feudal age, utterly out of keeping with modern conditions'[122] was retained. The retention of the Mitakshara Coparcenary, whose membership was confined only to males, meant that sons would not only get a share of their father's property but also their own interest as coparceners in the joint family property. Daughters would only get an equal share in paternal property. V. Prasad Rao (MP, Congress-Hyderabad) called this a case of 'fractional justice'.[123] Moreover, the coparcener's right to will away this share in the joint family property and transform his self-acquired property into joint family property could negate or reduce the share of a female heir. This provision introduced in the last stages of legislation by Pataskar, the Law Minister, was widely perceived by the contemporary press to be a capitulation by the government to what an MP called, 'the fifth column of the Hindu Mahasabha within the ranks of the Congress'. Moreover, by excluding agricultural land from the pale of legislation relating to succession, its beneficial impact remained largely restricted. The distinction made in the right of inheritance in a dwelling house, between unmarried, widowed and married daughters was discriminatory against married daughters. As Lotika Sarkar put it explicitly, 'a daughter who is part of an ongoing marriage and subject to harassment and cruelty in her husband's home cannot claim even the right of residence in the family house'.[124] A woman who had deserted her husband was not to be given dwelling rights in the parental house either, the logic being that such women were not 'needy' and could have deserted only because they had thoughts of another marriage.[125] Moreover, those daughters (unmarried, widowed, separated) who had a right to residence could not demand partition until the brothers agreed to partition their share.[126] Finally, the unrestricted right of testation, that is, right to make a will, often led girls to be dependent on their father's good will for being provided for in life. In effect, many female heirs were deprived of their rights of inheritance. This clause was actually introduced to render property more mobile in the hands of individual male owners and prevent uneconomic fragmentation of urban family business or family agricultural holdings. In the same strain is the provision in the Hindu Minority and Guardianship Act making the father a natural guardian in preference to the mother. The maintenance provisions in the Adoption and Maintenance Act were woefully inadequate. Even Yagnavalkya had stipulated that the maintenance granted should amount to one-third of the husband's income. The Act, however, left the amount of maintenance to the individual discretion of the judge.

In the ultimate analysis it can be said that Nehru's victory was largely symbolic. He recognized that the legislation as drafted was not perfect. Yet, he was not willing to initiate changes which would shake up the social organization too drastically.[127] In fact, he wondered why the legislation could possibly be objected to by anybody since most of them were 'voluntary permissive pieces of legislation which people may or may not accept'.[128] To him, the Hindu Law Reform Bills were revolutionary in symbol rather than in substance which he claimed to be 'the outstanding achievement' of his time. As he explained, 'they are not in any way revolutionary in the changes they bring about and yet there is something revolutionary about them. They have broken the barrier of ages and cleared the way somewhat for our womenfolk to progress.'[129] Nehru's symbolical victory did help to establish the notion of women's equality as a desirable ideal to which the Indian polity was committed. It is important to note that all the Members of Parliament opposing equal rights for women, whether from the Congress or other parties, such as the Hindu Mahasabha, came to preface and end their speeches on the noble note of disclaiming any intention to oppose justice for women.[130] Even the Hindu Marriage Bill, the first in the series of the Hindu Code enactments, was ultimately passed by a near-total approval in the Houses of Parliament. The only dissident voice was that of V.G. Deshpande of the Hindu Mahasabha. As Pataskar said, replying to complaints that the Hindu Succession Act had proved inadequate, what was important was that 'henceforward daughters would have a *sense of property* irrespective of what actual property she would get under the law'.[131]

Without delving deep into the legal implications of the Acts themselves, Nehru was satisfied with the spirit behind the passage of the Hindu Code Bills. He was deeply conscious of the charges levelled against him that the Hindu social reforms did not amount to much. But as he candidly said, 'You have to make a beginning somewhere!' The gaps in the legislation 'no doubt could be changed. . . . The struggle to achieve these changes will have to continue.' What was important was that 'the essential principles underlying the changes were not given up'.[132] He linked this legal advance in the social domain with the advances in the political and economic areas for 'only by way of advance on these three separate lines and their integration into one great whole, will the people of India progress'.[133] By recognizing and accepting in principle the concept of woman's equality and forcefully advocating it in the face of opposition, Nehru was able to enunciate an emancipated and liberal point of view which was not only unique in the time when he lived but also has relevance for posterity.

The shortfalls of this idealistic position are obvious. Nehru comes across as being the visionary who could never match his expectations with his achievements. By harping on the symbolic value of the social reforms that were passed, he inadvertently lulled people into a sense of complacency and achievement. Although he considered a uniform Civil Code for the whole of India to be essential, he was afraid that any imposition on communities, before they were ready for such changes, would be unwise. Lack of uniformity, he felt, would be preferable to a situation where, because of ill will, laws passed were dead in their application.[134] Thus the uniform Civil Code which he had originally envisaged was never realized. It remained a pious hope, caught among the linguistic trappings of Article 44 of the Directive Principles of the Constitution. Muslim personal law remained untouched; the principles of protection to women workers and maternity leave benefits which had figured prominently among the Fundamental Rights of the Karachi Resolution were relegated to the Directive Principles of the Constitution and finally the principle of equal wages for equal work also enshrined in the Directive Principles, came to be passed only in 1976 by his daughter Indira Gandhi as a special gesture in the International Year of the Woman. As a critic aptly summed up, 'In the case of all leaders of men, there is an angle of refraction between ideas and achievements. In Nehru this angle has grown with the unfolding of his ideas. In their very acceptance, has disenchantment grown. That is at once the glory and the tragedy of Jawaharlal Nehru.'[135]

It is important to note, however, that it was not only in the field of social reform for women that this ambivalence in Nehru between thought and action can be seen. Even in the momentous decades of the national movement, Nehru would often take a principled stand on certain issues which later he would have to tone down in the face of Gandhian reaction within Congress. Thus, in the 1930s, when Nehru, fired by socialist thinking, spoke forcefully of doing away with the class structure and taking up the cause of worker and peasant, he was gently made to bow to Gandhian opposition within the Congress. Although he rebelled in speech, he could never rebel in action like Subhas Bose had done. He remained Gandhi's erring and truant child in politics who was always coming back to the fold. The Gandhian old guard consisting of Rajendra Prasad and Vallabhbhai Patel, who in the 1930s had seen Nehru through many crises when he would rebel and yet ultimately submit to the majority opinion, were able to predict his responses and reactions during the Hindu Code Bill crisis. The Congress old guard were against the passage of the Hindu Code legislation and were apprehensive of Nehru's determination to see it quickly through but they finally succeeded in slowing him down. Thus Nehru who began with the vision of a uniform Civil Code ended up by accepting the diluted version of a truncated Hindu Code. For him, it was not, however, a surrender of principles but merely the pragmatic recognition of the volume of opposition that was pitted against him.

To the credit of Nehru it must be said that he never gave up and without him the legislation would not have been passed at all. Parliamentarians like R.K. Chaudhuri, while differing with Nehru on the details of the legislation, conceded that to Nehru went the entire credit of having had the Hindu Code Bills passed.[136] Amrit Kaur said as much when she commented: 'The social reforms, that are now on the Statute Book would . . . have been talked out if it had not been for Jawaharlal's powerful advocacy of and insistence on them.'[137]

Notes

Abbreviations used:

CAD —Constituent Assembly Debates
LAD —Legislative Assembly Debates
LSD —Lok Sabha Debates (Parliamentary Debates)
SWJN—*Select Works of Jawaharlal Nehru*, edited by S. Gopal (New Delhi, 1972 onwards)
NMML—Nehru Memorial Museum and Library, New Delhi

1. Geraldine Forbes, 'The Politics of Responsibility: Indian Women and the Indian National Congress', in *The Indian National Congress, Centenary Hindsights*, edited by D.A. Low (1988).
2. M.K. Gandhi, *The Role of Woman*, edited by Hingorani (1964).
3. Ibid.
4. J. Nehru, *Discovery of India* (1982), p. 41.
5. Ibid.
6. Speech during debate on the Third Reading of the Hindu Marriage Bill, 5 May 1955. *LSD* 1955, vol. IV, pt II.
7. *SWJN*, vol. 3, p. 363; Speech at Mahila Vidyapith, Allahabad, 31 March 1928.
8. *SWJN*, vol. 6, p. 218. Address to Prayag Mahila Vidyapith, 24 Jan. 1934.
9. *SWJN*, vol. 11, pp. 316–18.
10. *SWJN*, vol. 7, p. 557.
11. *SWJN*, vol. 2, p. 441.
12. *SWJN*, vol. 7, pp. 313–14.
13. 'It was plain that Pandit Jawaharlal wanted it and that Mahatma Gandhi wanted to give Pandit Jawaharlal what he wanted.' *Amrita Bazar Patrika*, 3 April 1931.
14. *SWJN*, vol. 7, p. 236.
15. Pattabhi Sitaramayya, *CAD* 1948, vol. V.
16. *SWJN*, vol. III, p. 191.
17. J.D.M. Derrett, *Hindu Law Past & Present* (1957), p. 57.
18. Kamaladevi Chattopadhyay, *Indian Women's Battle for Freedom* (1983).
19. 9 April 1948, *CAD* 1948, vol. V.
20. Dhananjay Keer, *Dr Ambedkar, Life and Mission* (1962), p. 423.
21. 5 April 1949, *CAD*, 1949, vol. III.
22. *LAD* 1946, p. 340/.
23. Prasad to Nehru, 24 July 1948; Nehru to Prasad, 27 July 1948, in *Sardar Patel's Correspondence: 1945–50*, vol. VI, edited by Durga Das (1973) (hereafter, *SPC*, vol. VI).
24. *CAD* 1949, vol. III.
25. *LSD* 1955, vol. IV, pt II.
26. *CAD* 1948, vol. V.
27. N.C. Chatterjee, 26 April 1955, *LSD* 1955, vol. IV, pt. II.
28. Akhil Bharatiya Hindu Mahasabha Papers, File C-57, NMML.
29. *LSD* 1955, vol. IV, pt II.
30. Naziruddin Ahmad, *CAD* 1948, vol. V.
31. Note of Rajendra Prasad, 31 July 1948, *SPC*, vol. VI.
32. D.N. Mitter, ex-Judge Calcutta High Court, Member of Rau Committee, later became a critic of Code.
33. Note of Rajendra Prasad, 31 July 1948, *SPC*, vol. VI.

34. *CAD* 1949, pt II.
35. Notes of Rajendra Prasad, 31 July 1948, *SPC*, vol. VI.
36. Note from Rajendra Prasad to J. Nehru, 15 Sept. 1951, *Indian Constitutional Documents*, vol. I, edited by K.M. Munshi (1967) (hereafter, *ICD*, vol. I).
37. *CAD* 1949, pt II.
38. Note from Rajendra Prasad to J. Nehru, 15 Sept. 1951, *ICD*, vol. I.
39. *CAD* 1948, vol. V.
40. Ibid.
41. Ananga Mohan Dam, *LAD* 1944, vol. III.
42. Ibid.
43. Naziruddin Ahmad, *CAD* 1949, vol. III.
44. Ibid.
45. Note from Rajendra Prasad to J. Nehru, 15 Sept. 1951, *ICD*, vol. I.
46. *CAD* 1949, vol. II.
47. Gole; *LAD* 1947, vol. I.
48. *LSD* 1955, vol. IV, pt II.
49. Sucheta Kripalani, *LSD* 1955, vol. IV, pt II.
50. Acharya Kripalani, ibid.
51. N.C. Chatterjee, ibid.
52. Pandit K.C. Sharma, ibid.
53. *CAD* 1949, pt II.
54. Ibid.
55. Ibid.
56. N. Ahmad, *CAD* 1949, pt III.
57. Note from Rajendra Prasad to J. Nehru, 15 Sept. 1951, *ICD*, vol. I.
58. *CAD* 1948, vol. V.
59. Note from Rajendra Prasad to J. Nehru, 15 Sept. 1951, *ICD*, vol. I.
60. Acharya Kripalani, *LDS* 1955, vol. IV, pt II.
61. Ibid.
62. Rajendra Prasad to J. Nehru, 24 July 1948, *SPC*, vol. VI.
63. *LDS* 1955, vol. IV, pt II.
64. Petition of Jankibai Joshi, President, All India Hindu Women's Conference to Lord Wavell, Governor-General of India, 20 March 1944, Akhil Bharatiya Hindu Mahasabha Papers, File C-67, NMML.
65. Jankibai Joshi to R. Prasad, 4 Feb. 1955, Akhil Bharatiya Hindu Mahasabha Papers, File C-183, NMML.
66. N.C. Chatterjee, *LSD* 1955, vol. IV, pt II.
67. *LSD* 1955, vol. IV, pt II.
68. *CAD* 1951, vol. XV, pt II, p. 2716.
69. *CAD* 1949, vol. VI, pt II.
70. Rajendra Prasad to J. Nehru, 24 July 1948, *SPC*, vol. VI.
71. Note from Rajendra Prasad to Nehru, 15 Sept. 1951, ibid.
72. Jawharlal Nehru to Vallabhbhai Patel, 21 Feb. 1950, in *Dr Rajendra Prasad: Correspondence and Select Documents*, vol. 12, edited by Valmiki Chowdhury (1989).
73. *CAD* 1949, vol. VII, pt II, p. 784.
74. *LSD* 1955, vol. IV, pt II.
75. J. Nehru to R. Prasad, 15 Sept. 1951, *ICD*, vol. I.
76. *LSD* 1955, vol. IV, pt II.
77. 20 May 1955, Jawaharlal Nehru, *Letters to Chief Ministers 1947–64*, vol. IV (1988).
78. 17 Sept. 1951, Jawaharlal Nehru, *Letters to Chief Ministers 1947–64*, vol. II (1986).
79. *SWJN*, vol. 3, Speech at Mahila Vidyapith, Allahabad, 31 March 1928.
80. *Jawaharlal Nehru's Speeches 1953–57* (1958), p. 451.

81. 5 May 1955, *LSD* 1955, vol. IV, pt II.

82. Ibid.

83. Ibid.

84. Krishna Hutheesingh, *We Nehrus* (1967), p. 99.

85. The demonstration of over 500 people outside the Parliament House on 12 December 1949, burning Gandhi caps and effigies and chanting 'Down with the Hindu Code Bill' and 'Down with the Nehru Government' was for Nehru, a 'revealing' experience; 15 Dec. 1949, Jawaharlal Nehru, *Letters to Chief Ministers 1947–64*, vol. I (1985).

86. 5 May 1955, *LSD*, 1955, vol. IV, pt II.

87. J. Nehru to R. Prasad, 15 Sept. 1951, *ICD*, vol. I.

88. *Selected Speeches of B.R. Ambedkar*, vol. I, compiled by Bhagwan Das (1963).

89. Ibid.

90. Keer, *Dr Ambedkar: Life and Mission*, p. 431.

91. *Selected Speeches of B.R. Ambedkar*, vol. I.

92. Ibid.

93. Rajendra Prasad to J. Nehru, 18 Sept. 1951, *ICD*, vol. I.

94. President's Note on the Hindu Code Bill, in *Dr Rajendra Prasad: Correspondence and Select Documents*, vol. 12.

95. R. Prasad to K.N. Katju, 21 Aug. 1948, in *Dr Rajendra Prasad: Correspondence and Select Documents*, vol. 10, edited by Valmiki Chowdhury (1988).

96. He pointed out, for instance, the derogatory references to women in Manusmriti; he ridiculed the authority of Purushashukta in determining the caste system as 'the fantastic dream of a troubled mind'; he dismissed Krishna's illicit intimacy with Radha. B.R. Ambedkar, *Writings and Speeches*, vol. 3 (1987), compiled by Vasant Moon.

97. S.G. Barve, 'Dr B.R. Ambedkar' in *Thoughts on Dr Ambedkar*, compiled by Hoti Lal Nim (1969).

98. *CAD* 1951, vol. XV.

99. *CAD* 1948, vol. V.

100. Vincent Sheen, 'Dr Ambedkar', in *Thoughts on Dr Ambedkar*.

101. Dr C.D. Pande's observations, *CAD* 1951, vol. XV.

102. He wrote to J. Nehru that he attached the 'greatest importance to this measure and would be prepared to undergo any strain on my health to get the Bill through.' 10 Aug. 1951, *CAD*, 1951, vol. XVI, pt II.

103. Deogirikar, *Twelve Years in Parliament*, pp. 100–1.

104. Pandit Thakur Das Bhargava, *LAD*, vol. I, pt II.

105. *CAD* 1950, vol. VII.

106. *LSD* 1955, vol. IV, pt II.

107. J. Nehru to Ambedkar, 20 March 1949, *SWJN* Second Series, vol. 10.

108. J. Nehru to Ambedkar, 26 Feb. 1949, *SWJN* Second Series, vol. 10.

109. *CAD* 1950, vol. VII.

110. *LSD* 1956, vol. X.

111. Keer, *Dr Ambedkar: Life and Mission*, p. 426.

112. Ibid.

113. Jawaharlal Nehru, *Letters to Chief Ministers 1947–64*, vol. II (1986), 4 Oct. 1951.

114. Nehru to Ambedkar, 10 Aug. 1951, *CAD* 1951, vol. XVI, pt II.

115. Nehru to Ambedkar, 27 Sept. 1951, *CAD* 1951, vol. XVI, pt II.

116. Renuka Ray, *My Reminiscences: Social Development during Gandhian Era and After* (1982), p. 149.

117. *LSD* 1954, vol. V, pt II, pp. 6973–6.

118. Ibid., pp. 7253–4.

119. Aubrey Menen's account of his interview with Nehru, in Raloff Beny, *India* (London, 1969), p. 189.

120. Jawaharlal Nehru, *Letters to Chief Ministers 1947–64*, vol. IV (1988), 10 May 1956.
121. *Towards Equality: Report of the Committee on the Status of Women in India* (Ministry of Education, 1975), p. 114.
122. *SWJN*, vol. 3, p. 399.
123. *Hindustan Times*, 16 May 1956.
124. Lotika Sarkar, 'Empowering Women', in *Seminar*, Nov. 1989.
125. Pataskar, *LSD* 1956, vol. IV, pt II, p. 7567.
126. Lotika Sarkar, 'Empowering Women'.
127. Jawaharlal Nehru, *Letters to Chief Ministers 1947–64*, vol. II (1986), 4 Oct. 1951.
128. *Jawaharlal Nehru's Speeches 1953–57* (1958), p. 444.
129. Jawaharlal Nehru, *Letters to Chief Ministers 1947–64*, vol. IV (1988), 15 June 1956.
130. Madhu Kishwar, 'Hindu Code Bill—Myth & Reality', unpublished paper presented at Oxford University 1990.
131. *The Hindustan Times*, 16 May 1956 (emphasis mine).
132. Jawaharlal Nehru, *Letters to Chief Ministers 1947–64*, vol. II (1986), 4 Oct. 1951.
133. Jawaharlal Nehru, *Letters to Chief Ministers 1947–64*, vol. IV (1988), 10 May 1956.
134. *SWJN*, vol. II, pp. 317–18.
135. Ashok Mehta, 'Planning without Progress' in Rafiq Zakaria, *A Study of Nehru* (1988).
136. 29 April 1955, *LSD* 1955, vol. IV, pt II.
137. Amrit Kaur, 'A Friend without Friends' in Zakaria, *A Study of Nehru*.

PART B
Contemporary Documents

24

Tracts against Sati*

RAMMOHAN ROY

I

Advocate. I alluded, in page 18, line 18, to the real reason for our anxiety to persuade widows to follow their husbands, and for our endeavours to burn them pressed down with ropes: viz., that women are by nature of inferior understanding, without resolution, unworthy of trust, subject to passions, and void of virtuous knowledge; they, according to the precepts of the *Sastras*, are not allowed to marry again after the demise of their husbands, and consequently despair at once of all worldly pleasure; hence it is evident, that death to these unfortunate widows is preferable to existence; for the great difficulty which a widow may experience by living a purely ascetic life, as prescribed by the *Sastras*, is obvious; therefore, if she does not perform concremation, it is probable that she may be guilty of such acts as may bring disgrace upon her paternal and maternal relations, and those that may be connected with her husband. Under these circumstances, we instruct them from their early life in the idea of concremation, holding out to them heavenly enjoyments in company with their husbands, as well as the beatitude of their relations, both by birth and marriage, and their reputation in this world. From this many of them, on the death of their husbands, become desirous of accompanying them; but to remove every chance of their trying to escape from the blazing fire, in burning them we first tie them down to the pile.

Opponent. The reason you have now assigned for burning widows alive is indeed your true motive, as we are well aware; but the faults which you have imputed to women are not planted in their constitution by nature; it would be, therefore, grossly criminal to condemn that sex to death merely as a precaution. By ascribing to them all sorts of improper conduct, you have indeed successfully persuaded the Hindu community to look down upon them as contemptible and mischievous creatures, whence they have been subjected to constant miseries. I have, therefore, to offer a few remarks on this head.

Women are in general inferior to men in bodily strength and energy; consequently the male part of the community, taking advantage of their corporeal weakness, have denied to them those excellent merits that they are entitled to by nature, and afterwards they are apt to say that women are naturally incapable of acquiring those merits. But if we give the subject consideration, we may easily ascertain whether or not your

*Extracts from *A Second Conference between an Advocate for and an Opponent of the Practice of Burning Widows Alive* (Calcutta, February 1820; *Selected Works of Raja Rammohun Roy*, pp. 154–7.)

accusation against them is consistent with justice. As to their inferiority in point of understanding, when did you ever afford them a fair opportunity of exhibiting their natural capacity? How then can you accuse them of want of understanding? If, after instruction in knowledge and wisdom, a person cannot comprehend or retain what has been taught him, we may consider him as deficient; but as you keep women generally void of education and acquirements, you cannot, therefore, in justice pronounce on their inferiority. On the contrary, Lilavati, Bhanumati, the wife of the prince of Karnat, and that of Kalidasa, are celebrated for their thorough knowledge of all the *Sastras*: moreover in the *Brihadaranyaka Upanishad* of the *Yajur Veda* it is clearly stated that Yajnavalkya imparted divine knowledge of the most difficult nature to his wife Maitreyi, who was able to follow and completely attain it!

Secondly. You charge them with want of resolution, at which I feel exceedingly surprised: for we constantly perceive, in a country where the name of death makes the male shudder, that the female, from her firmness of mind, offers to burn with the corpse of her deceased husband; and yet you accuse those women of deficiency in point of resolution.

Thirdly. With regard to their trustworthiness, let us look minutely into the conduct of both sexes, and we may be enabled to ascertain which of them is the most frequently guilty of betraying friends. If we enumerate such women in each village or town as have been deceived by men, and such men as have been betrayed by women, I presume that the number of the deceived women would be found ten times greater than that of the betrayed men. Men are, in general, able to read and write, and manage public affairs, by which means they easily promulgate such faults as women occasionally commit, but never consider as criminal the misconduct of men towards women. One fault they have, it must be acknowledged; which is, by considering others equally void of duplicity as themselves, to give their confidence too readily, from which they suffer much misery, even so far that some of them are misled to suffer themselves to be burnt to death.

In the fourth place, with respect to their subjection to vile passions, this may be judged of by the custom of marriage as to the respective sexes; for one man may marry two or three, sometimes even ten wives and upwards; while a woman, who marries but one husband, desires at his death to follow him, forsaking all worldly enjoyments, or to remain leading the austere life of an ascetic.

Fifthly. The accusation of the want of virtuous knowledge is an injustice. Observe what pain, what slighting, what contempt, and what afflictions their virtue enables them to support! How many Kulin Brahmans are there who marry ten or fifteen wives for the sake of money, that never see the greater number of them after the day of marriage, and visit others only three or four times in the course of their life. Still amongst those women, most, even without seeing or receiving any support from their husbands, living dependent on their fathers or brothers, and suffering much distress, continue to preserve their virtue; and when Brahmans, or those of other tribes, bring their wives to live with them, what misery do the women not suffer? At marriage the wife is recognized as half of her husband, but in afterconduct they are treated worse than inferior animals. For the woman is employed to do the work of a slave in the house, such as, in her turn, to clean the place very early in the morning, whether cold or wet, to scour the dishes, to wash the floor, to cook night and day, to prepare and serve food for her husband, father, mother-in-law, sisters-in-law, brothers-in-law, and friends and connections! (for amongst

Hindus more than in other tribes relations long reside together, and on this account quarrels are more common amongst brothers respecting their worldly affairs). If in the preparation or serving up of the victuals they commit the smallest fault, what insult do they not receive from their husband, their mother-in-law, and the younger brothers of their husband? After all the male part of the family have satisfied themselves, the women content themselves with what may be left, whether sufficient in quantity or not. Where Brahmans or Kayasthas are not wealthy, their women are obliged to attend to their cows, and to prepare the cow-dung for firing. In the afternoon they fetch water from the river or tank, and at night perform the office of menial servants in making the beds. In case of any fault or omission in the performance of those labours they receive injurious treatment. Should the husband acquire wealth, he indulges in criminal amours to her perfect knowledge and almost under her eyes, and does not see her perhaps once a month. As long as the husband is poor, she suffers every kind of trouble, and when he becomes rich, she is altogether heart-broken. All this pain and affliction their virtue alone enables them to support. Where a husband takes two or three wives to live with him, they are subjected to mental miseries and constant quarrels. Even this distressed situation they virtually endure. Sometimes it happens that the husband, from a preference for one of his wives, behaves cruelly to another. Amongst the lower classes, and those even of the better class who have not associated with good company, the wife, on the slightest fault, or even on bare suspicion of her misconduct, is chastised as a thief. Respect to virtue and their reputation generally makes them forgive even this treatment. If unable to bear such cruel usage, a wife leaves her husband's house to live separately from him, then the influence of the husband with the magisterial authority is generally sufficient to place her again in his hands; when, in revenge for her quitting him, he seizes every pretext to torment her in various ways, and sometimes even puts her privately to death. These are facts occurring every day, and not to be denied. What I lament is, that, seeing the women thus dependent, and exposed to every misery, you feel for them no compassion, that might exempt them from being tied down and burnt to death.

II

Several essays, tracts, and letters, written in defence of or against the practice of burning Hindu widows alive have for some years past attracted the attention of the public. The arguments therein adduced by the parties being necessarily scattered, a complete view of the question cannot be easily attained by such readers as are precluded by their immediate avocations from bestowing much labour in acquiring information on the subject. Although the practice itself has now happily ceased to exist under the Government of Bengal,[1] nevertheless it seems still desirable that the substance of those publications should be condensed in a concise but comprehensive manner, so that enquirers may with little difficulty, be able to form a just conclusion, as to the true light in which this practice is viewed in the religion of Hindus. I have, therefore, made an attempt to accomplish this object, hoping that the plan pursued may be found to answer this end.

The first point to be ascertained is, whether or not the practice of burning widows alive on the pile and with the corpse of their husbands, is imperatively enjoined by the Hindu religion? To this question even the staunch advocates for concremation must reluctantly give a negative reply, and unavoidably concede the practice to the opinion of widows. This admission on their part is owing to two principal considerations, which it is now too late for them to feign to overlook. First, because Manu in plain terms enjoins a widow to '*continue till death* forgiving all injuries, performing austere duties, avoiding every sensual pleasure, and cheerfully practising the incomparable rules of virtue which have been followed by such women as were devoted to one only husband.' (Ch. V; p. 158).[2] So Yajnavalkya inculcates the same doctrine: 'A widow shall live under care of her father, mother, son, brother, mother-in-law, father-in-law, or uncle; since, on the contrary, she shall be liable to reproach.' (*Vide Mitakshara*, Ch. 1.)[3] Secondly, because an attempt on the part of the advocates for concremation to hold out the act as an incumbent duty on widows, would necessarily bring a stigma upon the character of the living widows, who have preferred a virtuous life to concremation, as charging them with a violation of the duty said to be indispensable. These advocates, therefore, feel deterred from giving undue praise to a few widows, choosing death on the pile, to the disgrace of a vast majority of that class preferring a virtuous life. And in consideration of these obvious circumstances, the celebrated Smartta Raghunandana, the latest commentator on Hindu Law in Bengal, found himself compelled to expound the following passage of Angira, 'there is no other course for a widow besides concremation,'[4] as 'conveying exaggerated praise of the adoption of that course.'[5]

The second point is, that in case the alternative be admitted, that a widow may either live a virtuous life, or burn herself on the pile of her husband, it should next be determined whether both practices are esteemed equally meritorious, or one be declared preferable to the other. To satisfy ourselves on this question, we should first refer to the Vedas whose authority is considered paramount, and we find in them a passage most pointed and decisive against concremation, declaring that 'from a desire, during life, of future fruition, life ought not to be destroyed.' (*Vide Mitakshara*, Ch. 1.)[6] While the advocates of concremation quote a passage from the *Vedas*, of a very abstruse nature, in support of their position, which is as follows: 'Oh fire, let these women, with bodies anointed with clarified butter, eyes coloured with collyrium and void of tears, enter thee, the parent of water[7] that they may not be separated from their husbands, themselves sinless, and jewels amongst women.'[8] This passage (if genuine) does not, in the first place, enjoin widows to offer themselves as sacrifices; secondly, no allusion whatever is made in it to voluntary death by a widow *with the corpse of her husband*; thirdly, the phrase 'these women' in the passage, literally implies women then present; fourthly, some commentators consider the passage as conveying an allegorical allusion to the constellations of the moon's path, which are invariably spoken of in Sanskrit in the feminine gender:—butter implying the milky path, collyrium meaning unoccupied space between one star and another, husbands signifying the more splendid of the heavenly bodies, and entering the fire, or, properly speaking, ascending it, indicating the rise of the constellations through the south-east horizon, considered as the abode of fire. Whatever may be the real purport of this passage, no one ever ventured to give it an interpretation as *commending* widows to burn themselves on the pile and with the corpse of their husbands.

We next direct attention to the *Smriti*, as next in authority to the *Vedas*. Manu, whose authority supersedes that of other law-givers, enjoins widows to live a virtuous life, as already quoted. Yajnavalkya and some others have adopted the same mode of exhortation. On the other hand, Angira recommends the practice of concremation, saying: 'That a woman who, on the death of her husband, *ascends the burning pile* with him, is exalted to heaven as equal to Arundhati.'[9] So Vyasa says: 'A pigeon devoted to her husband, after his death, *entered the flames*, and, ascending to heaven, she there found her husband.'[10] She who follows her husband to another world, shall dwell in a region of glory for so many years as there are hairs in the human body, or thirty five millions.'[11] Vishnu, the saint, lays down this rule: 'After the death of her husband, a wife should live as an ascetic or ascend his pile.'[12] Harita and others have followed Angira in recommending concremation.

The above quoted passages, from Angira and others, recommend concremation on the part of widows, as means to obtain future carnal fruition; and, accordingly, previous to their ascent on the pile, all widows invariably and solemnly declare future fruition as their object in concremation. But the *Bhagavad Gita* whose authority is considered the most sacred by Hindus of all persuasions, repeatedly condemns rites performed for fruition. I here quote a few passages of that book.

> All those ignorant persons who attach themselves to the words of the *Sastras* that convey promises of fruition, consider those extravagant and alluring passages as leading to real happiness, and say, besides them there is no other reality. Agitated in their minds by these desires, they believe the abodes of the celestial gods to be the chief object, and they devote themselves to those texts which treat of ceremonies and their fruits, and entice by promises of enjoyment. Such people can have no real confidence in the Supreme Being.'[13]
>
> Observers of rites, after the completion of their rewards, return to earth. Therefore they, for the sake of rewards, repeatedly ascend to heaven and return to the world, and cannot obtain eternal bliss.[14]

Manu repeats the same.

> Whatever act is performed for the sake of gratification in this world or the next is called *Pravartak*, as leading to the temporary enjoyment of the mansions of gods; and those which are performed according to the knowledge respecting God are called *Nivartak*, as means to procure release from the five elements of this body; that is, they obtain eternal bliss.[15]

The author of the *Mitakshara*, a work which is considered as a standard of Hindu Law throughout Hindustan, referring on the one hand to the authority of Manu, Yajnavalkya, the *Bhagavad Gita*, and similar sacred writings, and to the passages of Angira, Harita and Vyasa on the other hand, and after having weighed both sides of the question, declared that 'the widow who is not desirous of eternal beatitude, but who wishes only for a perishable and small degree of future fruition, is authorized to accompany her husband.'[16] So that the Smartta Raghu Smartta Raghunandana, the modern expounder of Law of Bengal, classes concremation among the rites holding out promises of fruition; and this author thus inculcates: 'Learned men should not endeavour to persuade the ignorant to perform rites holding out promises of fruition.'[17] Hence, concremation in their opinion, is the least virtuous act that a widow can perform.[18]

The third and the last point to be ascertained is whether or not *the mode* of concremation prescribed by Harita and others was ever duly observed. The passages recommending concremation [that] are quoted by these expounders of law, require that a widow, resolving to die after the demise of her husband, should *voluntarily ascend*[19] *and enter the flames*[20] *to destroy her existence*; allowing her, at the same time, an opportunity of retracting her resolution, should her courage fail from the alarming sight or effect of the flames, and of returning to their relatives, performing a penance for abandoning the sacrifice,[21] or bestowing the value of a cow on a Brahman.[22] Hence, as *voluntarily ascending* upon and *entering into the flames* are described as indispensably necessary for a widow in the performance of this rite, the violation of one of these provisions renders the act mere suicide, and implicates, in the guilt of female murder, those that assist in its perpetration, even according to the above quoted authorities, which are themselves of an inferior order. But no one will venture to assert, that the provisions, prescribed in the passages adduced, have ever been observed; that is, no widow ever voluntarily *ascended* on and *entered* into the *flames* in the fulfilment of this rite. The advocates for concremation have been consequently driven to the necessity of taking refuge in *usage*, as justifying both suicide and female murder, the most heinous of crimes.

We should not omit the present opportunity of offering up thanks to Heaven, whose protecting arm has rescued our weaker sex from cruel murder, under the cloak of religion, and our character, as a people, from the contempt and pity with which it has been regarded, on account of this custom, by all civilized nations on the surface of the globe.

Notes

1. The administration to which this distinguished merit is due, consisted of Lord W.C. Bentinck, Governor-General, Viscount Combermere, Commander-in-Chief, W.B. Bayley, Esq., and Sir C.T. Metcalfe, Members of Council.

2. आसीतमरणात् क्षान्ता नियता ब्रह्मचारिणी ।।
   यो धर्म एकपत्नीनां काङ्क्षन्ती तमनुत्तमम् ।।

3. पितृमातृसुत भ्रातृश्वश्रूश्वशुरमातुलैः ।
   हीना न स्यात् विना भर्त्री गर्हणीयान्यथा भवेत् ।।

4. नान्यो हि धर्मो विज्ञेयो मृते भर्त्तरि कहिंचित् ।

5. नान्यो हि धर्म इति तु सहमरणस्तुत्यर्थ ।

6. तस्मादिह न पुरायुषः स्वःकामी प्रेयात् ।

7. In Sanskrit writings, water is represented as originating in fire.

8. इमा नारीरविधवाः सुपत्नीरान्जनेन सर्पिषा संविशन्त्वनश्रवा अनमीरा सुरत्ना आरोहन्तु यामयो योनिमग्न ।

9. मृते भर्त्तरि या नारी समारोहेद्धुताशनम् ।
   सारुन्धती समाचारा स्वर्गलोके महीयते ।।

10. पतिव्रता संप्रदीप्तं प्रविवेश हुताशनम्
    तत्र वित्रंगदधरं भर्त्तारं सान्वपद्यत ।।

11. तिस्रः कोट्यर्द्धकोटी च यानि लोमानि मानवे ।
    तावन्त्यव्दानि सा स्वर्गे भर्त्तारं यानुगच्छति ।।

12. मृते भर्त्तरि ब्रह्मचर्य्यं तदन्वारोहणं वा ।

13. यामिमां पुष्पितां वाचं प्रवदन्त्यविपश्चितः ।
    वेदवादरताः पार्थ नान्यदस्तीतिवादिनः ।।
    कामात्मानः स्वर्गपरा जन्मकर्म्मफलप्रदाम् ।
    क्रियाविशेषबहुलां भोगैश्वर्य्यगतिं प्रति ।।
    भोगैश्वर्य्यप्रसक्तानां तथापहृतचेतसाम् ।
    व्यवसायात्मिका बुद्धिः समाधौ न विधीयते ।।

14. ते तं भुक्त्वा स्वर्गलोकं विशालं क्षीणे पुण्ये मर्त्यलोकं विशन्ति ।
    एवं त्रयीधर्म्ममनुप्रपन्ना गतागतं कामकामा लभन्ते ।।

15. इह वामुत्वा काम्यं प्रवृत्तं कर्म कीर्त्यते ।

निष्कामं ज्ञानपूर्वन्तु निवृत्तमुपदिश्यते । ।

प्रवृत्तं कर्म संसेव्य देवानामेति सार्ष्णिताम् । ।

निवृत्त सेवमानस्तु भूतान्यत्येति पंच वै । ।

16. अतश्च मोक्षमनिच्छन्त्या अनित्याल्पसुखरूपस्वर्गार्थिन्याः सहमरणानुमरणयोरधिकार इतरकाम्यानुष्ठानवत् ।

17. पण्डितेनापि मूर्खः काम्ये कर्म्मणि न प्रवर्त्तयितव्यः ।

18. Hindus are persuaded to believe that Vyasa, considered as an inspired writer among the ancients, composed and left behind him numerous and voluminous works under different titles, as *Maha-puranas, Samhitas, Smritis*, etc., to an extent that no man, during the ordinary course of life, could prepare. These, however, with a few exceptions, exist merely in name, and those that are genuine bear the commentaries of celebrated authors. So the *Tantras*, or works ascribed to Siva as their author, are esteemed as consisting of innumerable millions of volumes, though only a very few, comparatively, are to be found. Debased characters among this unhappy people, taking advantage of this circumstance, have secretly composed forged works and passages and published them as if they were genuine, with the view of introducing new doctrines, new rites, or new prescripts of secular law. Although they have frequently suceeded by these means in working on the minds of the ignorant, yet the learned have never admitted the authority of any passage of work alleged to be sacred, unless it has been quoted or expounded by one of the acknowledged and authoritative commentators. It is now unhappily reported that some advocates for the destruction of widows, finding their cause unsupported by the passages, cited by the author of the *Mitakshara*, by the Smartta Raghunandana, or other expounders of Hindu law, have disgracefully adopted the trick of coining passages in the name of the *Puranas* or *Tantras*, conveying doctrines not only directly opposed to the decisive expositions of these celebrated teachers of law, but also evidently at variance with the purport of the genuine sacred passages which they have quoted. The passages thus forged are said to be calculated to give a preference to concremation over virtuous life. I regret to understand that some persons belonging to the party opposing this practice, are reported to have had recourse to the same unworthy artifice, under the erroneous plea that stratagem justifies stratagem.

19. समारोहेद्धुताशनम् । Angira

20. पतिव्रता सम्प्रदीपतं प्रविवेश हुताशनम् । Vyasa

21. चितिभ्रष्टा तु या नारी मोहाद्विचलिता भवेत् ।

प्राजापत्येन शुद्धेत्तु तस्माद्धि पापकर्मणः । ।

22. प्राजापत्यव्रतासकृता धेनुं दद्यात् पर्यस्वनीम् ।

धेनोरभावे दातव्यं तुल्यं मूल्यं न संशयः । ।

25

The Woeful Plight of Hindu Women*

KAILASHBASINI DEVI

It is practically common knowledge that the women of our country are in a far sorrier situation than those of other civilized nations; and the root thereof lies in our evil-laden social mores. Enslaved by these, what hateful deeds do our noble sires, full of Hindu religious conceit, carry out; what pride they take in tossing out their daughters at a very tender age to unsuitable grooms so that their lofty family prestige may be preserved. O God the Lord, Exalted Ruler of the world! How long till we are rid of our sorrows? How long till the light of awareness shines forth in the land of Bengal, dispelling dark ignorance? O sisters of Bengal! How long till you bedecked in all virtues make Mother Bengal beauteous?

How Women of Bengal are Born

Thus the expectant mother thinks incessantly till the time she gives birth: 'Pray! If only the Good Lord grants me: a boy child, how happy I'll be, how my kin will love me.' But if, as fate may have it, a girl is born, the mother takes a look and sinks into unspeakable gloom—what is more—is often moved to tears, a sign of utter misery, and the kin shows great distress. Beating of drums, worship of brahmins, feeding the poor, doing propitiatory rites, giving away loads of gifts to prolong the son's life-span and conducting sundry sacred customs like sending the barber to carry the good tidings to relatives far and near—all these acts that follow the birth of a boy are omitted when a girl is born; rather, the opposite things follow. Lord have mercy! Are we so low that the times of our birth and death are equivalent? O social mores! Thy powers are indeed hypnotic! Caught in thy thrall, people are enveloped in confounding darkness. Alas! How long till the land of Bengal becomes the home of happiness and these hated mores are ousted altogether. O Ye Good Samaritan sirs! Pray be enterprising and root out this intolerable tyranny.

What the Girl Child Does and
How the Parents Treat Her

Let alone send his daughters to school for education, as he does so sincerely for his sons, the father says, on the contrary: 'What business do they have in getting educated? Will they work outside to earn money? Let them be fed and keep house.' Alas, Education! Art

*From Malini Bhattacharya and Abhijit Sen, eds, *Talking of Power: Early Writings of Bengali Women* (Kolkata: Stree, 2003), pp. 25–51. Originally published as *Hindu Mahilaganer Hinabastha* (Calcutta: Gupta Press, 1963).

thou there just for money, not for knowledge? Those who have no desire for earning money, will they be ever apart from thee and pass their earthly lives in ignorance? Thanks to you, O social mores!

The sire does not educate his daughters, so they engage themselves wholly in illusory pleasures and pointless games. They spend almost their entire childhood with pots, dolls, rags, dirt, leaves, vines, and so on. Pity! A matter of regret, indeed, that well-wishers like their parents and brothers have totally deprived these tenderhearted girls of the joys of education. Do they not spare even a stray thought on what lies ahead for these girls or how equipped they are to sustain life's journey? The patriarch has no sane counsel for his daughter as to how she, when at her in-laws' after marriage, should behave with her husband and his kin, nor any on infant care. Alas! If girls could have education and parental guidance—they would not then have to suffer so. O Mother Bengal! When will these miserable daughters of thine be replete with learning and virtue, when will this inferiority leave them and give way to knowledge, which will light thee up with its glow?

Oh, had our mothers been educated, we would not be in such a sorry state. These unlettered mothers teach their daughters exactly what they were taught themselves. They make their daughters perform various rituals and tell them what good these bring about—the daughters too accept the teachings as the word of God and follow them ever after.

The Prestige of the Clan

Our king Ballal Sen, of baidya descent, conferred prestige and title to the commoners of this country; the self-same prestige has now become a matter of national dishonour.[1] Whether desiring to immortalize his name or to conform to the prevailing practice of the Bengali people, he distinguished the kulins from the mouliks.[2] This, however, has led to much harm. Quite a few among the kulin offspring declare thus: 'Our God-given stature and respectability are quite enough for us. What use do we have for education? The homes we once visit become hallowed beyond measure.' Bloated with such self-importance, they express the utmost hatred for the mouliks, who in turn worship them as Gods. If a kulin visits a moulik on some work, the moulik is flattered no end. Oh, how unjust! Even though the moulik may possess every desirable quality; he gets less respect than a true-blue kulin and, if a father, finds it terribly difficult to marry off his children.

Compared to the middle class and the poor home-earners, however, the rich have less trouble in this regard since they are able to overwhelm all with large dispensations of money. To accomplish the same task, the poor and the middle class have to bear untold misery, implore countless people and visit myriad lands. To reach this goal, some even sell off whatever fixed or mobile assets they might have; meanwhile, if the daughter has turned ten or eleven, the parents, in a spate of hurry and without a care for propriety, give her hand to the first person they lay their eyes on. Having thus rid themselves of the burden of a daughter, scarcely less than the burden of parental after-death rites, they proceed on a blissful existence of food and frolic. But unending despair befalls the ones whose daughters are terribly ugly or physically disabled. They take great pains to marry off their daughters and spend huge amounts for the wedding. The groom goes through the nuptial rites and returns home with the dowry and the gifts. The girl stays back ever after at her father's place.

Among these people are some who for want of grooms organize marriage ceremonies with flowers or trees as grooms. Alas! Only they know what good such a marriage begets; and they reply, when queried on the issue, 'A daughter must be married off, or our parents' ancestors on both sides would be consumed in hellfire.' Mercy! Rather than be married so, girls had better be left unmarried, else married to a groom of similar disposition; otherwise such marriages are sheer delusion, no less. O Lord, great and compassionate! When wilt thou have pity on us and destroy these erroneous ways; when will our friends desist from such grossly unfair practices as marrying a daughter to a tree?

As regards family pedigree, all caste groups stand alike; only the brahmins and the kayasthas are special in certain ways, which, therefore, are documented separately.[3] Kayastha gentlemen of high pedigree, aiming to enhance their family status, arrange to marry their eldest sons to daughters of kulins, whom they pay hefty sums as bride price. Lusting for money; the girl's father sells her off. Having thus firmly secured their bonds of pedigree, these newly kulin gentlemen thereafter marry their sons for a second time to daughters of high-pedigree families; deeming such grooms to have godlike sanctity, these families give them their daughters' hands, along with hoards of jewels and ornaments. Pity! How lamentable that they wilfully drain this bitter cup of bigamy and forever endure the extreme agony that results.

How Kulin Gentlemen Treat their Children and What their Marriage Customs are

It would be good if kulin gentlemen do not hanker overly for money and, with due mercy for forthcoming generations, avoid being the prime cause of corrupting the family lineage (O everlasting misery!). Otherwise, terrible suffering awaits their descendants, poisoned by hereditary ills.

Those whose forefathers took care to preserve their individual worth and dignity are called 'naikashya' sons. The naikashya son first marries into a shrotriya family [highest in rank amongst the kulins], then, to preserve family honour, takes a kulin wife too. However, this wife forms no part of the man's family; she stays at her father's home for life, the children of her womb are denied any share of their father's wealth and they spend all their lives at their maternal homes. It is the shrotriya wife who becomes her husband's favourite. And it is the children of *her* womb who inherit his wealth. Goodness! How unjust of the man to wed the girl and make her conceive, yet not provide her and the children with means of sustenance. The children are reared uncaringly and amid great distress; in absence of a guardian, they fail to acquire education and intelligence. This leads to an extreme scarcity of means so, not having other ways out of it, they fall back upon the Ballal Sen hallmark. They marry daughters of an aristocratic stock in exchange of a goodly sum of money—this is called 'corruption of lineage'.

Ah! Is it not a matter of anguish that the young kulins indulge in immediate pleasures at the cost of future good? Alas! As fire brings about its own nemesis, so is it with the kulin progeny. As smoke from fire turns into cloud, which brings forth rain to destroy its own source, so does the kulin gentleman proceed to demolish his own lineage. The lineage is the fire, the kulin wife the smoke and her progeny the cloud; the fire-like lineage is totally devastated by corruption raining down from the cloud-like progeny. Alas! If only he did not wed the woman of kulin birth or, even if he did, brought her home and treated her on a par with the shrotriya wife, cared for, nurtured and educated her children and bequeathed them a part of his wealth; then might these children avoid the terrible danger of corruption of lineage.

The honour of naikashyas who have no sisters has a somewhat subdued glow; those who have, give the sisters away to families superior or equal to theirs in status. The same goes for their daughters. These marriages greatly enhance their glory, and the ones unable to do so are besmirched by the evil of deterioration of lineage. In order to preserve family prestige, these kulin worthies marry off their sisters and daughters to men who are horrendously ugly, blind, hump-backed, lame, dumb, deaf or even dying. Alas! What a cruel act! The unfairness they mete out to their sisters and daughters merely for self-gain is beyond words.

I heard that once, learning that someone of a pedigreed clan was on his deathbed, a naikashya man thought, 'This person comes from a lofty family, of a stature compatible with ours. If he dies, my daughters would have little chance of getting married and, in that case, my sons would lose their honour. Married to this person, however, they would soon be widows. Admittedly, they are kulin girls and it matters little whether they marry or not, or whether they are widowed. Nonetheless, this marriage is imperative since it would preserve my sons' honour.' So deciding, he married his daughters to that dying and affluent groom.

Hark, Ye Good Samaritan sirs! Judge for yourselves how far such incidents differ from a Sikh killing his daughter. Merely this much—he destroys at once, whereas these worthies kill slowly, by inches. Fearful of having a daughter to marry off and thus being looked down upon, the former engages in that heinous deed, while the latter carry out the detestable activities apprehending destruction of the family lineage.

I am reminded of another example in this regard. In a village on the west bank of the river Suratarangini, there lived a similar 'exalted' one with his only sister whom, he had decided, would marry his paternal aunt's stepson. It so happened that the girl fell seriously ill. When the illness had subsided somewhat, his paternal uncle paid them a visit. Whereupon the girl's mother, brother and other relatives pondered thus: 'This girl was so sick that she had hardly any chance of surviving; who knows when she would be at death's door again? No marriage in that case and devastation of family honour! So let us make no delay and marry her to the uncle.' Having conferred thus, they broached the proposal to that eighty-year-old groom. To which he replied with great irritation, 'Do not marry her to me. Why ruin her? Give her hand to my son who, upon my bidding, is on his way here.' But nothing could put them off and they proceeded to marry off the girl to the old man. The girl, once she came of age, started indulging in extremely despicable activities; her mother, brother and such close ones put up with this vice quite comfortably. Thus it went on until the old man's death, which caused a minor holdup in the girl's self-indulgent ways, so she left her brother's home and set up house on the riverbank. I remember having seen this groom in my early childhood days; he was exactly like a coconut-scraper in appearance.

An Account of Tri-kulin Daughters

A tri-kulin daughter is one born of a naikashya girl wedded to a man who has a naikashya father and a naikashya grandfather. Tri-kulin daughters usually stay unmarried. Like the fabled elderly virgins of *Mahabharata*, they are perpetually in the state of maidenhood. If, God willing, these kulin gentlemen come to hear of a groom having an equivalent

family status, they take the utmost care in fetching him and, giving up all sense of propriety, grant him the hand of their sister or daughter. The disproportionate difference
in age, resulting from such imprudence, is there for all to see and ridicule.

Once I came to know that the kin of a tri-kulin daughter, residing in a small village
on the bank of the Bhagirathi, brought for her a groom much advanced in years. The
girl refused to marry the aged groom, saying, 'Do not force me to observe the Ekadashi
rituals. I will stay unmarried.[4] However, if you really wish to see me married, marry me
to his son.' At this, her near-and-dear ones married off this woman of thirty, not to the
old man, but to his twelve-year-old son whom she then led away by his hand. Good
readers! Judge for yourselves how ludicrous the act was. Rather than the groom accepting
the bride's hand, it is she who takes him off by his hand! Many other similar incidents
are common with these people.

A tri-kulin daughter of high pedigree who lived in a village of Hooghly district, was
still unmarried at twenty-six. One day she told her mother, 'I shall turn wayward if you
do not arrange for my marriage.' 'I cannot possibly do such an audacious thing,' replied
her mother. 'Your stepbrothers would berate me roundly and their family honour would
be compromised; for scarcely any house can match ours in status. Should I, because of
you, let this greatness go to the dogs? And should I, sullied by the vice of trashing this
honour, earn infamy in the after-world as a denizen of Hell and in this world as a family-
wrecker? Do as you please then.' That was all the mother had to say. Later, when people
came to learn about this, a few gentlemen of the village got together and started looking
for a groom for the girl. In the end, they gave her away to the grandson of genteel folk
coming from a venerable family. The mother used to live at her maternal grandfather's
home. Her mother's uncle, much peeved by the whole affair, turned both mother and
daughter out of his home. After that, the persons who had arranged the girl's marriage
reached her to her husband's place.

Sometime after this incident, the girl's stepbrother arrived from Chittagong, accompanied by a prospective groom and a matchmaker. On seeing them, the mother was
in a great predicament and wondered how she would face his queries. 'Mother,' the man
asked presently, 'Where is my sister?' 'At her in-laws,' she responded, Instantly, he exploded like a fireball, 'What? My sister? At her in-laws? Who arranged her marriage?
Heavens above! Who has wrought this ruin upon me'? Who is it that has utterly blighted
the jewel, the honour that is as lifeblood to us?' And thus he went on lamenting and
striking his forehead, fit to bring tears to the eyes of all who saw or listened. In due course,
people tried to console him through various homilies, but he refused to be mollified and
kept saying over and over again, 'Please bring me my sister; I shall arrange to marry her
once more and preserve the family honour.' Upon which, the others told him that such
a thing was impossible—one who was legally married once cannot be given in marriage again. Frustrated, he said, 'Please then write a statement to the effect that she has
died; I shall spread word of my sister's death in my neighbourhood.' And they agreed
to this proposal.

There are innumerable such miseries these tri-kulin daughters have had to endure.
Unending grief befalls the ones who stay unmarried all their lives. Many bring dishonour to the family and taint the family name by taking the way of easy virtue, such
misdemeanour then leading to major sins like unwanted pregnancy. Pity! How sad
indeed that they take to such misdeeds only because they fail to get married.

On the 'Broken' Kulins of Bengal

Persons who crush and chew up sacred family honour on their own in this way may be called 'self-nihilists'. Self-nihilists receive limitless esteem; great is their power, like the mythical Ruler of the Three Worlds. They first break their stock by marrying into a well-to-do family of good stature and subsequently wed again a number of times—people are only too happy to offer them their daughters. Two generations of the sons of self-nihilists and three generations of their sons, thus the stock remains undamaged up to the fourth, fifth, sixth and seventh generations but withers away thereafter.

The kulins have a great many wives: to them, marriage is a profession. They start marrying when nine or ten years of age and only give up when they die. Like proselytizing gurus, they travel across lands with baggage and servant. Just as the gurus visit their new disciples to impart sacred knowledge and old disciples to collect their yearly dues, these gentlemen too land up at their in-laws of many years to seek their wives' services and at new homes to fix fresh marriages. Each maintains a record book, which lists the number of marriages, showing the name of each wife and the year of marriage. Those having a degree of affluence are not dependent upon their in-laws; they have a higher status, moreover. They do not set foot in the in-laws' home unless given ten or twelve pieces of silver coins as sacred offering. Most of the fathers-in-law, being petty householders, cannot afford such expense to take in the son-in-law, so the girls spend their lives in this state with their fathers; some, for want of their husbands' company, indulge in loath-some acts.

Many a noble-hearted kulin meets his wife for the second time only during his son's marriage; this is the moment too when the son first sees his sire. Heavens above! How hateful it is that these people, far from condemning such depravity, take pride in saying, 'Why should we, of kulin birth, feel ashamed of it? Mention one kulin family free of such doings. It has been common enough with our forefathers, so why should it be a slur on us? We kulins are as pure as the Ganges; just as the holy Ganges remains unpolluted even though nauseating stuff like excreta and corpses are dropped into Her, thus it is with us.' Mercy! How insensate they are that they care nothing even if their wives are wantons and their honour remains unsullied even if their sons are bastards. The lack of devout offerings from in-laws, however, upsets their applecart of prestige.

This reminds me of the story of a certain kulin householder, living in a village of Krishnanagar district, who once had his son-in-law visiting his house. No one was there but the daughter who, on seeing her husband after a long time, bestirred herself joyfully and welcomed him. The husband asked her, 'Well then, is there something you have for me?' At this his wife replied, 'What do I, a mere woman, receive that I can keep for you? It is the husband who provides for his wife's upkeep and gifts her jewellery and clothes. So tell me what you have brought for me?' Hearing these words spoken in jest, the husband left the place without a second thought and even his wife's earnest entreaties could not make him stay. Afterwards, deeply distressed, the woman contemplated thus:

'Since marriage, I have never laid my eyes once on my husband and I am almost twenty now. To him, my character is worth no consideration, he only desires money. Surely I shall have him if I ever get hold of some money.' Having reached this conclusion, she ditched her family honour and set up business in the city of Calcutta. Some time later, while she stood at her window looking down the street, she espied her husband and recognized him instantly. Upon which she instructed her maid to bring the brahmin in, which the maid did right away. The brahmin did not realize that it was a prostitute's house, so he entered and accepted her hospitality. Later, in the evening, the woman loaded a silver salver with a large number of coins and placed it before the brahmin. Seeing this, he was filled with great wonder and exclaimed, 'Who are you? And what makes you so generous to me? Spare me no detail.' To which the woman replied, 'I am Gourmani, daughter to so-and-so family of such-and-such locality.' These words plunged the brahmin into the depths of amazement and, silently ruing his misconduct, he prepared to leave. But the fallen woman proceeded to speak, 'I have let myself into this evil act only because of you. You refuse to cohabit with me unless you are given money, so take this money and keep me company.' At this, the brahmin was overcome by a pall of gloom and pledged that any of his descendants who married more than once would be deemed to have fallen from sanctity. Subsequently, when the brahmin departed for his home, the prostitute, too, spent all her money in good deeds and retired to the holiest of holy lands at Vrindavan.

Good readers! Think for yourselves how the events unfolded in this case—the sole cause was the so-called honour of the kulin dynasty.

What wrongs the kulins of the Rarhi category commit under the influence of this idea of kulin honour! They give away the girls, so dear to their hearts, to some gaunt and withered old man, on whose death the girls encounter a most terrible widowhood. Who does not know how wretched this condition is? As soon as they get hold of a kulin groom, the parents and other relatives, fully aware of what the girls' plight would be, sacrifice all of them—the daughter, the sister, the niece—to the same bull. Alas! It was none other than Ballal Sen who started all this. Had he not planted in Bengal the notion of clan-based hierarchy, a veritable poison tree, this land would not have been polluted by the resulting ills—the fruits borne by that tree.

On Kulin Descendants

Those born in a kulin dynasty but seven or more generations down the line, or those who, lacking foresight, give away their daughters to lesser families, lose their former prestige and respectability. From heaven, they land with a thud onto the earth and, instead of the dominance their forefathers enjoyed, they suffer its very opposite. The forefathers married many women and abhorred them, whereas the descendant spends much and pays obeisance to many for possessing just one woman. They treated their comely and virtuous wives with great scorn, whereas he, let alone get such a wife, gratefully accepts any unsightly specimen; many remain unsuccessful, even after hoarding lucre like honey bees all their lives, and finally breathe their last. Among the descendants some purchase three- or four-year-old girls at a few hundred rupees and kick the bucket before the girls reach twelve or thirteen. Some marry such children and bring home their mothers with them; not a bad arrangement—reaping immediate benefit from the tree even if the fruit gives none. Some sell off all their assets, fixed and mobile, to escape demonhood in future lives. Four or five brothers may have a Pandava-like marriage and the girl may have several unmarried elder brothers-in-law.[5] Quite a few, in a bid to propagate the dynasty, marry off their younger brothers and become bachelor brothers-in-law. Yet others trade off their daughters against their son's secure marriage.

Such marriages lead to untold misery—destruction of caste, loss of wealth, damage to esteem, and so on. Lusting for money, fraudulent matchmakers arrange to marry these sons of brahmins to low-caste girls whom they pass off as brahmin girls. The groom's father does little scrutiny; his joy knows no bounds on seeing that the girl is of age and inexpensive to boot. Later, when the deception is revealed, he finds himself in a sorry state. Greedy for wealth, kulin wives sell their daughters to families of kulin descent, thereby tainting their husbands' lineages. If, after marriage, the girl stays on at her father's, her near kin often puts her through a second marriage, keeping the family honour intact. Some set up a second marriage for want of money, others make a neat sum by giving away the seven- or eight-year-old girl to a groom who is seventy or eighty. The fact that the girl may be suffering from consumption or other illness is concealed and she exchanges hands for a few hundred rupees. In a few months she dies, devastating the ones who took her in.

A few incidents of kulin descendants' marriages come to my mind. I relate them here for the information of all and sundry:

I heard from someone that, in the village of West Debanandapur, Tribeni, a groom had just taken his seat for the ceremonial acceptance of his bride when she spoke thus:

'Do not marry me to a brahmin as I am of Sadgop stock.'[6] Those present were stunned at this and rewarded the matchmaker with a generous dose of thrashing.

A brahmin in a certain village married his son to a girl of ignoble caste, but was unaware of this for a long time. One day at the brahmin's home, the family inmates were preparing a sacred thread. The daughterin-law replied, 'Why do you weave the yarn thus? What kind of cloth will it make? My father never weaves that way.' At this, they asked her, 'Are you a weaver's daughter?' whereupon she fell silent. After a thorough investigation, they found that she was indeed born of a weaver.

A brahmin and his paramour defrauded a city householder by introducing themselves as husband and wife, and parading a barber's daughter as their own. The gentleman and his family were ignorant of this for quite a time. At some stage, she was down with a grievous illness, which caused someone in the house to remark, 'Good grief! What parents! It appears that they have sent her to exile. They have not once enquired about her, though she is as ill as could be.' The instant she heard this, the daughter-in-law said, 'My *parents*? Those people? They are brahmins whereas I am born of a barber.' To the people around, these words seemed like delirious blubbering. Later, when the girl had recovered, thorough enquiries revealed that she was indeed a barber's daughter. Nevertheless, being a pricey buy, she could not be turned out; she stayed in the house like a maid and subsequently gave birth to a number of children. Behold! A mixed breed is spawned. What name does one call it by?

Child Marriage

Who does not know that child marriage is the root of immense harm? It is one of the prime reasons for our wretched condition, the stepping-stone to our misfortune. O friends and well-wishers of our land! Before paying heed to any other issue, please first do away with this extremely harmful practice and bring succour to the masses. Ah me! The great anguish of child marriage is a matter of common knowledge. Who does not suffer its consequences? Who, in the land of Bengal, is not incensed about it? Oh! Would it that child marriage did not prevail here, how blissful would this land then be! Whether it be for pleasure of the eyes or whether it be for living happily and comfortably after a good job done, the parents cast their children into terrible and permanent danger by marrying them off when they are yet wholly immature. For a while, such a marriage does look agreeable to the relatives, but is nevertheless completely shattering to the wedded children since they have no say in the matter. Thus, when they grow up and are able to judge right and wrong, they spend their lives in utter misery, enduring each other's merits and demerits. Maybe the husband, overcome by the ills of stupidity and alcohol, causes distress to both families; or maybe the girl falls below her husband's expectations. As a result, far from being mutually affable, each feels intensely hostile towards the other. So it happens that in most homes marital discord makes its appearance.

Ah me! Would that one could have a spouse after one's own heart—boundless good fortune would then result. Pity! How unjust that the act of marriage is authorized only by the parents or some relative! How unfair that while the looks and qualities of the couple get little importance, the real aim is to secure the finest groom or the all-square wife and to link oneself maritally to a house of superior status, so as to boost one's own social prestige. They send matchmakers far and near in search of a suitable match. The matchmakers, greedy for money, proceed to delude them through falsehood and trickery, which sometimes leads to disaster. By nature, matchmakers are very crafty and are capable of anything by dint of their cunning; they charm both parties effortlessly and create havoc by adulterating the pure with the fake.

Alas! How regrettable that parents, ignoring their children's views, yoke them in that lifelong captivity called marriage, thinking only about their own prestige and glory; not the children's good or harm in the long run. It needs to be said that, even discounting marriage through mutual consent, parents and other close ones could take special interest in personally meeting the boys or the girls, and judging their nature and appearance carefully so that they might be married to their equals, thereby putting an end to the dastardly practice of match-making. Our good fortune would then know no bounds.

As mentioned before, there is little chance of accord on any issue unless the two are comparable in all respects. Of a married couple, if one is noble and the other mean, the one would most probably look down upon the other. If that be so, how would they unite in genuine warmth and true love and how, without that love, would they stay together all their lives? And how would they bear the fearsome torment, locked for life in that terrible prison? In case the husband is inferior to his wife, she suffers endlessly. If the wife is as ravishingly beautiful as a heavenly maiden, but the husband ugly and disfigured, or addicted to intoxicants and prostitutes, untold bad luck awaits her. If the husband is hideous and repulsive in looks, yet principled, intelligent and possessed of all virtues, he emerges even comelier than Cupid, the highest icon of beauty. On the other hand, if the husband is a cut above the wife in all respects, it is the wife who suffers the greater distress; for looks are a woman's strength and it is common knowledge that a plain visage does not make a wife desirable to her husband. A man, even though unsightly, can attain the heights of excellence through learning and knowledge, a feat that is impossible for a woman. Besides, so what if a woman is full of fine traits? She can never be of a comparable status to a man.

In truth! How gratifying would it be, had none of these unfair customs prevailed in our land. It is impossible for a man and a woman to find harmony unless they are closely matched—no other way can love take root. The surprising thing, however, is that, although well aware of such untoward situations occurring in every home, parents and the like never desist from this practice. They continue to marry their beloved, darling children to incompatible grooms and brides. Alas! What a matter of regret that parents put their children in wedlock without prior disclosure of their appearance and character. At that time, the bride and the groom have no option but to agree, but as they grow up and are able to sense right and wrong, both suffer much anguish. Some men proceed to take a new wife, thereby plunging the previous one in a sea of lifelong misery. Some, who are imperturbable and full of profound wisdom, make do with unattractive wives; indeed, some noble hearts are even observed to express a special affection towards them. But the woman finds it humiliating and so, instead of being pleased, she is hounded by remorse.

Thus, it is evident at every step that child marriage is the root of much evil. Unless child marriage is prevented, our land will never have happiness and prosperity, marital harmony will never be established and girl children will never escape the harrowing torment of widowhood; child marriage has emerged as one of the main reasons for the backwardness of Bengalis. Some men, having married early; become fathers even before they are sixteen or seventeen and, with no education, are unable to earn; this makes them crave for ways and means of sustaining their families. There are instances of twelve- or thirteen-year-old girls getting in the family way, thereby putting themselves in grave danger. Some leave this world along with the newborn, casting a pall of deep gloom over the families on both sides. Some escape this fate themselves but lose their beloved infants and, at such tender age, are distraught by heart-rending and unbearable sorrow. Indeed! These girls would not be suffering such intense agony, had there been no child marriage. Even the women who are fortunate enough to avoid such ill fate do not find unalloyed happiness. Maybe the new mother contracts post-natal maladies which cause extreme suffering; or else the infant is very sick and emaciated, adding to the parents' woes. Moreover, the mother, being immature herself and thus incapable of raising a child, goes through immense hardship. So, there remains no doubt that it is sorely necessary to put a stop to child marriage.

O friends, you who are social benefactors and purveyors of learning! Please put all your efforts to destroy this tyranny of child marriage, which hinders everything good and places thorns on the path of learning. So long as this practice prevails, how will you succeed in advancing the education of women? Girls are only nine or ten when they marry and, before they reach eleven or twelve, are sent to their in-laws, where they are engaged in domestic chores; how then would they develop their learning and intelligence? At ten, they are still immature and have little knowledge about any matter. How then, having received education only till that age, would they gain all-round skills and true knowledge of the facets of education? Consequently, efforts at imparting education are bound to fail unless the custom of child marriage is abandoned.

In ancient times, this harmful system of marriage was non-existent in our realm and the women of yore, not deprived, as we are, of the riches of education, did not pass their earthly lives in useless pursuits: this is borne out by ample evidence from our books on mythology and history. In present times too, therefore, great good would result if people took pains to have their daughters educated on various topics and, with due consideration for their appearance and merits, wedded them to their equals. The women, freed from their terrible predicament, would then pass their days in complete happiness. However, our marriage habits can never be the same as those of other countries; our country is warmer, so its inhabitants reach puberty earlier, and the age of marriage must be correspondingly lower. For boys, the right age to marry is twenty and for girls, thirteen or fourteen. At this age, having left childhood for youth, girls are competent to distinguish right from wrong and, having acquired some learning and sundry domestic skills, can avoid excruciating misery at their in-laws'.

A Woman's Passage to Her In-laws' Abode; Her Concurrent Feelings and Activities

After marriage, women spend some days at their fathers' and then leave for their in-laws' place; this is called *nabadhabagaman* (advent of the newly wed) or *dwiragaman* (advent of the couple). During the stay at her father's, a girl wishes to pass her time with her dear ones and is upset if she has to leave them for some reason even for a day. Would she then be willing to go to her in-laws' for an extended or a lifelong sojourn? During this time, she dreads hearing about the in-laws' place; this thought continues to smoulder day and night in the young girl's petal-soft heart and dims the attractive lustre on her lotus-like countenance. Pity! Instead of a joyous heart and a smiling face heightening the parents' pleasure, it is just the reverse. Ah! Seeing their beloved daughter's face clouded over, the parents become exceedingly anxious and start worrying about her ability to adjust at her in-laws' and to bear the intense pain of leaving her old home. Seeing her parents' distress, the daughter, in turn, grows increasingly restive. Oh, how painful it is finally for the parents to force the girl to go to her in-laws' and then continue to live in great wretchedness. The girl too, desolate at the separation from her kin, spends her lowly existence incarcerated in the inner sanctum of the in-laws' house, like one imprisoned for the crime of theft.

Mercy! The girl is but a child, unlettered in every respect; so she is as bereft of knowledge as a wild animal. Just as animals are trapped from the jungle by guile and force and brought to a human neighbourhood, where they are tamed through various ploys, similar wiles are used to bring the girl to submission. Like an animal, the girl is not subdued easily and behaves in the same way as a caged creature, which, forgoing food and sleep, continues to brood over its old habitat and keeps looking around the cage for a way of escape. Head draped in a veil, she keeps scanning the cage-like house and goes without food or sleep, pining constantly for her parental home and counting her days to be back there. During this time, she develops no affection for any of her in-laws, who are largely unfamiliar to her: after all, can fondness for unknown people come easily? Far from her having any warm feelings for the in-laws, the opposite is rather more likely. Just as a boy greatly resents his school and nurses a strong irritation for those who sent him there, the girl likewise expresses annoyance towards the in-laws and their home, while people at her parental home, being out of sight, grow dearer yet to her heart. Thus, she treats even a minor visitor from her parents' home as an intimate friend but is unable to convey such genuine warmth towards her closest relatives-in-law. What more is there to tell, even the husband—the most beloved one—receives less affection from her than do the birds, animals and trees at her parental home. During this period, the in-laws' palatial residence appears to her as a rocky range, devoid of people but abounding in fierce, marauding animals; articles of attire, ornaments and other exquisite physical embellishment seem to hurt as intensely as an adder's bite; the most delicious food tastes like foul venom; the alluring bed, as delicately soft as a layer of floating cream, feels as painful as a thorny field; even her husband's nectar-sweet words scorch as unbearably as a lightning bolt. On the other hand, she sees splendour in the ghastly hovel of her parental home and finds it far more appealing than any heavenly mansion; discovers deep pleasure in the few accessories she had in her childhood; relishes the meagre, plebeian fare at her father's as if it were some ambrosial delicacy; sleeps on the bare floor as though on a tender flower bed. How can the girl, pulled by such contradictory emotions during this time, settle down at her in-laws' home?

Untold distress befalls those of the girls who, born to affluent fathers, are married into middle class households, or, born to middle class fathers, are married into commoner families. Having enjoyed the best of luxuries at their parental homes, they land in deep trouble at their in-laws', where they get to eat the plainest food and wear the barest clothing, and must slog through the daily chores as befits a maid. Also, if perchance the chores get disrupted in any way, the family elders reward them with torrents of abuse. Ah! Who does not know how unbearable it is when sorrow follows happiness.

How Bengalis Treat their Wives

While on child marriage I have mentioned that unless a woman acquires all-round excellence, she cannot gain a place of esteem at her husband's side. Established though the fact is, there seems to be no easy way for her to reach such an elevated standing and, on that basis, ultimately to attain a state of empathic salvation, which would ensure her a prosperous family life. This is because she receives no guidance at her parents', nor is she made aware of it at the in-laws'; how then does she achieve importance? What knowledge is she supposed to gain, cooped up in the dark inner sanctum and staring at an assortment of pots, pans and bowls? Or mayhap like a plant, she would imbibe natural virtues. Having received no advice, she remains ignorant in all matters and is incapable of evaluating things that she sees or hears, believing impossible things as possible and ending up as a laughing stock of all concerned.

Asked to cite examples of an idiot, one mentions asses and women; sundry jibes on their inborn stupidity and ignorance are bandied about. A woman is supposedly the repository of all evil: her many traits are elaborated in this context. A contradictory approach is taken on all issues; for example, 'Why is a woman known as "*abala*"?[7] Because like an animal, she cannot speak for herself and is dominated by us, as are animals. Thus, there is no difference between a woman and an animal.' 'Why pray; is a woman called "*bama*"?[8] For her lop-sided thinking, of course.' Alas! The unspeakable woe! Not only in the current age, but in ancient times too, women were viewed with such enormous respect. Writers of past eras also have showered us with lavish praise; for example, 'Two-fold in eating, four-fold in cunning, six-fold in trading, eight-fold in mating, and so on.'

Love

Oh, how sweet this word is, but regrettably, soft as it sounds, its practice is as hard. Nothing can proceed without love and each expects it from others: a man from his friends and relatives, a wife from her husband. Thus, each hopes to be loved by others, but none cares to practise it sincerely. If no act is possible without love, can there be marital bliss in its absence?

In our realm, a woman ties the conjugal knot at a very tender age, so she cannot be blamed on this point; rather, it is the man who should bear the burden. Only if the husband displays his genuine affection for her and educates her well on a variety of topics, will she, having come of age, be able to observe and recollect her husband's worthy ways, and form a bond of unalloyed love. If this happens, she will succeed in undertaking the voyage of married life with supreme contentment, the devotion to her husband being the sacred feet of refuge. If not, would the unlettered woman, burning incessantly in the fire of her husband's misdemeanour, be prepared to walk that supreme path of devotion?

Nuptial love is about to disappear from our land. The vicious poison of conjugal discord has entered every home. True love in a married couple is rarely observed; the partners are vocal about their likes and dislikes of each other's external trappings and embellishment, uncaring towards each other's sentiments and unwilling to voice their own desires. Pity, that when they must stay together for life as one soul and go about the same business, how can true love emerge from a game of hide-and-seek? How indeed can women undertake the holy rites of devotional attachment to their husbands?

O Lord above! How long till the ladies of Bengal rid themselves of highly despicable and malicious feelings? How long till the soil of their minds is consecrated by the holy water of honesty? And till they are able to spend their conjugal lives in utmost bliss, committed and dutiful to their husbands? And till the full moon of their fame rises to brighten up all the corners of the firmament? O Lord of the destitute! Heed thou my mournful words! Save thou the women from this unbearable agony and turn upon them thy glance of compassion.

How Bengali Women School Themselves

Currently, women in every household have started receiving education; many of them are learning the native language, while some have read small English books like 'New Spelling'. Still, Heaven only knows how far they will succeed in this and to what extent enhance the prosperity of the nation; for most, reading means settling down somewhere quiet with a couple of fancy, entertaining books steeped in cloying verse and perusing these, just as a brahmin priest, innocent of Sanskrit semantics, mouths a religious text. Some find solace for their minds, as fickle as the Goddess of Wealth, by delving into the estimable *Battala* literature that drips with eroticism.[9] Some cleanse their intellect by watching the glamour of theatrical shows; some, with a dash of English and a flash of frills, bring disgrace to the marital casket of vermilion.[10]

Thus, these ladies, feeling self-important and trying to look sedate, expect a degree of deference from the populace. They shy away from authentic knowledge. Not that they are to blame though, since no one ever gave them the right counsel. Through self-education most have picked up a smattering of knowledge, which suffices them. It is not merely the lack of guidance that hinders their education—numerous other hassles too come in the way. The woman who takes up education becomes an eyesore of the entire family and thereby suffers great anguish. The elders constantly fret and fume in an effort to restrain her from this activity; female neighbours target her with a variety of taunts and forbid their daughters from speaking with her. For such reasons as these, no woman can readily set about educating herself.

We have not been able to fathom the underlying causes for such impediments; opinions vary widely on this subject. Some say a woman who receives education is liable to be widowed. According to others, once she gets to taste the joys of learning, she would eschew domestic work. Some noble souls declare that education would so unsettle her mind that, heedless to her husband, she would try to gain independence, write inviting letters to some man of her choice and make him her paramour. Yet others argue thus: 'Having gained the power of intelligence through education, women would start behaving like men, which would devastate our honour and prestige.' Ah me! Widowed on account of education? Can the might of knowledge kill a husband and deprive a woman of the apple of her eye? In truth! The Lord only knows wherefrom this utterance came forth. Probably the tale spread from the instance of Lilavati, daughter of Bhaskaracharya.[11] Be that as it may, what basis is there for the notion that on being educated a woman would turn wanton and shun family duties? Is learning such a vile thing that associating with it makes a woman fall into evil ways? And why should she neglect housework? Would she, on being educated, turn less affectionate towards her husband, children and other kin? And in what way would she be independent? Can we talk of freedom of the Bengali woman, seeing that she falls from honour the moment she steps out of the courtyard?

The Freedom of Bengali Women

Alas! A misleading turn of phrase indeed! So assert some exalted minds of Bengal. A woman who has education would not wish to stay confined in the inner sanctum, but rather stray around everywhere at her will, like her counterparts in other lands; and, assuming the air of European beauties, would set about conversing with men. Thus, having travelled extensively and seen aplenty, she would try to free herself of the shackles of submission. It is, therefore, in no way logical to educate women.

Ah! These noble folk, brimming with Hindu religious ardour—the logic they cite! What magnetic force resides in learning that would draw a woman out into the world? Also, what evidence is there that women would crave for freedom? Till now, women of no country have achieved freedom; why then would Bengali women seek it?

The disposition and ability the Lord has granted them amply demonstrate that the subordination of women is the will of God; so the *abalas* [weak ones] can never transform themselves into *sabalas* [strong ones] and acquire freedom. If one could be liberated by being educated and travelling about as one wished, the women of Europe would have inducted themselves long since into high positions in the government, thus enhancing the glory of their nation. Women, therefore, will never have freedom. It does not befit a woman to be without a safe haven. No one has any regard for a shelterless woman; so, if there is no freedom, what chances remain that a woman would roam about hither and thither at her will?

However, many among the modern gentlemen of the new order argue that the nation will never prosper unless our women, like those of other countries, are able to move around everywhere. True as this is, they alone know how they propose to get the women out in the open. For, given that our women lose their honour and status and face unanimous censure as soon as they cross the courtyard why would they readily agree to go out to, say, social meetings? And pray, what accoutrement would they suggest for the women on such trips? The splendour of a gathering would increase a hundred-fold if our women go there bedecked and bejewelled as they are used to; for the advent of such women of heavenly magnificence would make the congregation appear exactly as the court of Indra, the king of the Gods. So, while one can never allow women to step out dressed like a court dancer, it should be fairly acceptable if they appear before the populace in an Englishwoman's attire. Yet, consider how middle class gentry and common householders would fare if women, so attired, turn into *pucca memsahibs*.

If a system is to be put into practice, it needs to be applied to the common people or else its power is lost. Even if one popularizes this system, how does one maintain a balance? Since everyone is keen to experience something new, who would keep house and do the cooking and cleaning if both man and woman leave home to savour this experience? One could reply that education would impart immense capability, by virtue of which everyone could earn prodigious amounts of money, thus enabling them to accomplish any task. Ah! Were this to happen by the grace of the Most Benevolent One, it would be a matter of great good; but would the common people attain such capability? It does not seem possible, ever. And what if it does come about? Our people do not like living alone as the Europeans do and so cannot act likewise. They have to live in association with a number of relatives and their earnings do not match those of Europeans. Indeed, even the most powerful among them earn hardly a third of what a European earns. Thus, their wives can never be as enlightened as those of Europeans. However, if it so transpires that these women are equally at ease working with mud and cow dung as well as attending meetings, it would be excellent for us too.

It is true that in ancient times the Hindu woman had a modicum of freedom and could go about everywhere at will. If one opts for those mythological customs, one should go the whole hog; one cannot adopt some and ignore others. However, wrongful practices, then prevalent, cannot be acceptable now. To preserve the family lineage, some people arranged to have sons procreated through the help of others than the spouses concerned. A woman, even though an object of gratification of four or five males, could be renowned as utterly sacred and among the first to be revered.[12]

Yet, no one can act thus now. It follows that nothing is gained by adhering to ancient precepts.

The Agony of Widowhood

Ah me! No words can describe the intolerable anguish of widowhood. Alas! In the past, unable to bear this deadly pain, women used to follow their departed husbands through the harsh ritual or the sati thereby escaping the torture; but this custom no longer exists. As a result, widows these days, unable to rid themselves of this terrible, heart-rending grief, continue to be consumed in its fiery incandescence.

Ah! Happy indeed is the home where this vile poison of widowhood has not entered; but unfortunately widowhood has penetrated every household like wildfire and the flames of sorrow are incinerating many souls. Pity! Some people, with their sixteen-year-old daughters-in-law engulfed by the fire, see nothing but an all-pervasive void; others, watching the fire consume their darling daughters, beautiful beyond compare, suffer incessantly in an abyss of misery. Alas! Peace lies at the end of all strife, but this turmoil knows no relief. Pity! Who does not feel sorrowful at the sight of a widowed woman? In truth! The kin, that earlier used to be delighted by her charming vivacity, is now sunk in a morass of infinite gloom on seeing her in the widow's garb.

Alas! How regrettable that on being widowed, women renounce everything and adopt a life of extreme austerity. They lose their former radiance and place of honour. No one cares for widows; just as a hallowed flower pot, when broken, is turned into an urn for ashes, what shame that a widowed woman too faces the same predicament. Engaged in lowly housework, having one meal a day, they eke out their lives in a thoroughly piteous state.

More! On occasion, some wretches even have to crave for the day-end meal and a rag of clothing. Which heart is not moved by compassion as the suffering of Hindu widows comes to mind? Sooth! Even the toughest of hearts fill with pity to see them, on a cruel Ekadashi day in summer, thirst-ravaged and restless as a bush-fowl craving for rain.

Hail Hinduism! Thanks to you and also to the exalted one that created you, it is the widow who knows what fruits this religion has borne. The worthies that preached thus: 'A human being cannot be called so unless he is compassionate, those without compassion are like animals in human shape'—alas! Why do they now act contrariwise? An ascetic life for the widow, deadly punishment for breach of discipline like drinking water on an Ekadashi day and other such stringent decrees—did they introduce all these out of compassion for widows? Alas, a harrowing tale to tell! Perchance some wretch, severely ill, breathes her last on an Ekadashi day; her relatives, powerless to dispense holy water to her mouth for her well-being in the after-world, pour it into her ear instead. Pity! What a heartless act! For one, there is the unquenchable thirst that fever brings, then the dry fast to boot. Oh! God alone knows where lies the great sublimity of this religion. O ye friends that ponder the good of the country! Do take the initiative and come to the rescue of these women. O Good Lord, thou Timeless One! Be thou merciful and, through thy solace, deliver these hapless women from the terrible maelstrom of worldly existence.

(Translated by Kumardeb Bose)

Notes

Kailashbasini Devi (1837–?) was the wife of Babu Durgacharan Gupta who helped her to gain some education. She is known for three books: *Hindu Mahilaganer Hinabastha* (1863); *Hindu Mahilakuler Bidyabhyash o Tahar Samunnati*, where she talks about the degraded lives of Hindu women; and *Viswasobha*, which contains some verse compositions as well. She is bracketed with Bamasundari Devi as being one of the two women who were the first to write Bengali prose.

1. Ballal Sen belonged to the Sen dynasty of Bengal who ruled in the twelfth and thirteenth centuries. The Sens were Brahma-Kshatriya, deriving their lineage from dynasties in south India. They were patrons of Brahminism and brahminical influence flourished at that time. The baidyas mentioned by the author are like kayasthas, part of the upper echelons of the shudra community, and supposed to be descended from a mixture of castes. Sometimes it is said they are born of a brahmin father and a vaishya mother.

2. See 1, 'What Are the Superstitions That Must Be Removed for the Betterment of Our Country', n2 [Bhattacharya and Sen, eds, *Taking of Power*]; mouliks formed 79 groups and were supposed

to be the original descendants of non-brahmin shudra inhabitants of Bengal who were thus differentiated from the group of shudras who were invited to Bengal from north India and were therefore supposed to be of higher rank.

3. Kayasthas were non-brahmins who again observed Kulinism. The mouliks were also kayasthas but inferior in rank to the kayastha who had come from north India. They were quite a powerful group and were involved in judicial and administrative work.

4. The eleventh day after the new moon and after the full moon, that is, twice a month, when upper caste widows had to fast and observe very rigid customs They fasted without taking even a drop of water. Harrowing tales about child widows falling ill or even dying while observing these customs were cited by reformers agitating against child marriage.

5. Draupadi in the *Mahabharata* was married polyandrously to five brothers. The allusion suggests that among the banshajas there was a dearth of women of the same status within the caste.

6. One of the 14 caste-groups identified as nabasakh, who ranked beneath brahmins, baidyas and kayasthas but nonetheless were higher than the so-called untouchables.

7. A female who lacks strength or *bal*, a pun with *abola*, that is, a female who cannot speak, is intended.

8. Placed left, literally.

9. An area in Calcutta which in the early nineteenth century became the publication centre of low-priced literature. Although many eminent publications came out from Battala, its name began to be touted in a pejorative sense as the birthplace of lowbrow sensational literature.

10. The mark of vermilion worn by a married Hindu woman at the parting of her hair indicates her married status and her chastity. Thus the casket of vermilion is the symbol of conjugal loyalty and honour.

11. A brilliant mathematician who may have been born in the middle of the twelfth century AD, and was said to be the daughter of Bhaskaracharya, one of the most famous astronomers of ancient India. Lilavati is supposed to have been widowed immediately after her marriage. Trained in astronomy and mathematics by her father, she attained great fame for her mathematical calculations. The third part of *Siddhanta-Shiromani* attributed to Bhaskaracharya, is supposed to have been written by her; see also 11, Calcutta, 'The Worship of Women', this volume [Bhattacharya and Sen, eds, *Taking of Power*].

12. 'Daily remembrance of the holy quintet—Ahalya, Draupadi, Kunti, Tara and Mandodari—destroys the deadliest of sins' [this note is in the original text]. The allusion is to Draupadi who was married to the five Pandava brothers.

26

From *Stripurusha Tulana**

Tarabai Shinde

These days the newspapers are always writing about poor helpless women and the wicked things they do. Why won't any of you come forward and put a stop to these great calamities?

Just look now, how the custom of not remarrying widows has spread—in so many places, to so many castes, like a great sickness. It's hard to imagine the bitter despair all these hundreds and thousands of widows must suffer. And how many disasters come out of it. Because stridharma hasn't ever been saved just by making people sit at home and control their thoughts.[1] What they do with their minds and eyes can make them just as guilty. Where does it get you if you snatch away all the happy signs of a woman's marriage, if you chop off one woman's hair and wipe off another's kumkum from her forehead? Women still have the same hearts inside, the same thoughts of good and evil. You can strip the outside till it's naked, but you can't do the same to the inside, can you? In fact, what does stridharma really mean? It means always obeying orders from your husband and doing everything he wants. He can kick you and swear at you, keep his whores, get drunk, gamble with dice and bawl he's lost all his money, steal, commit murder, be treacherous, slander people, rob peoples' treasures or squeeze them for bribes. He can do all this, but when he comes home, stridharma means women are meant to think, 'Oh, Who's this coming now but our little lord Krishna, who's just stolen the milkmaids' curds and milk and tried to blame Chandravali for it.'[2] And then smile at him and offer their devotion, stand ready at his service as if he was Paramatma himself. But how can people go on believing this idea of stridharma once they've begun to think about what's good and bad? They'd change their ideas straightaway, wouldn't they? A man can run off with someone else's wife, but that's not against the rule of pativrata.[3] In fact, there are thousands of reasons for breaking the rule. You're supposed to worship your husband as if he were a god. But who is there nowadays that really does? There's that story of Savitri,[4] which sets out an example of pativrata. Would any woman now try to follow it all to the letter? Go on then, can you show us even one?

That story tells us that if a husband kicks you, you should just smile at him and say, 'Don't do that, my lord and husband: you'll hurt your foot.' And so saying, you should sit down and promptly start massaging his foot. You're not to cry if he lets you have it with his fist, even if he beats you with a stick. No, you've got to smile, fetch fresh butter

*Extracts from Tarabai Shinde, *Stripurush Tulna*, translated by Rosalind O'Hanlon. Copyright © Rosalind O'Hanlon 1993.

and rub it into his hands for him, saying, 'My lord, the palm of your hand must be burning from those blows.' And if there's no butter in the house, use the neighbour's, and if she's got none, run and get some from the market. But who'd do any of this nowadays? Far from stroking his hand, she'd more likely tell him to shove it in the stove. If he dislikes a particular sort of food, she's meant to avoid it too. It's just the opposite though—he throws it down and she picks it up straight. It's got to be something sweet though! If it's some ordinary old vegetable like carrots or gourd, then fine, she'll avoid them for life! But if it's mangoes the husband won't eat, will she give them up? Not a bit![5] If the husband asks for water, she's not standing ready with a clean brass vessel. Instead the lady will tell him, 'Oh yes, I'm dying for some water, there's some in that pot over there, get yourself some, and get me some while you're at it! What am I supposed to do? This child here just won't let me get up.'

The husband's only got to mention his bath and she's meant to lay out the stool, get a bucket of hot water and stand ready to scrub his feet. But actually she just calls out, 'Anyone out here? Come in here, Ramya boy, he wants to have a bath, fetch him water and fold his dhoti for him. If he asks for me, tell him I'm having my tea.' As soon as her husband comes in for dinner, she's meant to bring a stool, lay out vessels for drinking, serve him his favourite foods, then sit wasting her time entertaining him with talk till he's finished his feast. But nowadays he'll be saying, 'Have you finished in there or not? Come on, serve it up, it's nine o'clock!' And the answer comes from her: 'All right, I'm coming, it's nearly ready. Can't you even wait till the vegetables and lentils are done? What, do you want me to serve you uncooked rice? What a chore this business is, every bloody day at nine o'clock! Every day the same hurry!' Then comes the subject of his roll of betel nut, and off they go again.[6] He calls out, 'Make me some betel, will you? The dish is in that niche in the wall over there. No, no, not like that—can't you even roll betel nut properly? You take all the ingredients together in your hand, like this.' So the lord and master goes over to the dish and looks inside, only to find there's no lime. 'Look, there's no lime', he says. 'Go and get some, will you?' But all he gets out of her is, 'There's some supari nut in a little bag in that box up there. You eat your betel and get one of those out for me. Ugh—doesn't your mouth feel nasty when you finish eating?' Well now—isn't this much closer to the truth?

This is what pativrata means these days. If I was to tell you the whole of it from start to finish, it'd take a whole separate book. Who on earth really follows the shastras to the letter or expects anyone else to?[7] If the husband is really to be like a god to the wife then shouldn't he behave like one? And if wives are to worship them like true devotees, shouldn't husbands have a tender love for them in return, and care about their joys and pains like a real god would? When the gods see those who worship them, they feel happy and satisfied. Shouldn't husbands be the same? When husbands find virtues or faults in people devoted to them, shouldn't they take a proper account of them, accept their shortcomings and correct them with love? What woman could really treat her husband like a god, no matter how nasty he was? The Pandavas' uncle Dhritarashtra was blind, so his wife Gandhari tied a cloth over her eyes when they were married.[8] But what person with eyes could stand to be told to close them and carry on as if they were blind? Who'd have the self-control for that? I don't know anyone. All your big talk—you make it all up on the basis of the shastras. But in fact the people who wrote all these books ought to be ashamed of themselves, shastras, puranas, pothis and so on.[9] You ask me why? Well, when they picked out women from previous ages, some of them had gone wrong too, but there they are now, held up as first-class pativratas. That's good, is it? Take Drau-padi—she was a woman who had five husbands already, but that never stopped her from lusting secretly after Maharaja Karna, did it?[10] Ahalya sat in Surendra's lap, got turned to stone, then she became divine.[11] Satyavati and Kunti were supposed to be virgins, but they each had a son Vyas, the author of the Vedas, and Karna himself—but their names are still on the list. One of them believed what the sage told her because he got rid of the nasty smell on her body. The other just wanted to try out the magic mantra![12] Aren't all these gods and sages of yours wonderful? Each one better than the last! Each of them made a secret love marriage,[13] then went off and got hitched to Shantanu and Panduraja! So what else were they doing but marrying a second time? Then their kids Vyas and big-hearted Karna got so holy even the gods fell down at their feet. But when someone has kids like that these days they get called very different names. A female slave's child gets put into one class of bastard, a brahman widow's into another; then there are cases like Vidur.[14] Other people put kids like that down as just another source of expense. So tell me what we should call it when an unmarried girl has a child? Someone like Vyas gets to be a great expert in shastras and puranas and writes books like the Mahabharata. Does that make his mother and father all pure again too? I reckon Karna's mother only got her virtue back when he fought with the Pandavas on the battlefield of Kurukshetra.

Then there's the story of Tara, wife of Vali the monkey. Sugriva was Vali's younger brother, but Vali carried off his wife Ruma and drove Sugriva the black-faced monkey away, long tail and all. Then Sugriva met up with Maharaja Ramchandra himself. They found they were in the same boat. Ramchandra's wife was stolen by Ravana, and Sugriva's by his own brother. So what a good thing, they joined up together! Ramchandra felt sorry for Sugriva, so he killed Vali by a cunning trick and fixed it up for Sugriva to marry Tara. Poor Tara said to Ramchandra, 'Maharaj, how can you do this? Your husband's younger brother is like your own child. This looks all wrong to me.' So Ramchandra reassur-ed her: 'Don't you worry about it. You can marry a second time, even your husband's younger brother, and your name will still be counted among pativratas.'[15] All this went on. Then Shridhar Swami wrote a couple of extra lines saying it doesn't matter what the gods have done.[16] Of course, it doesn't mean that human beings are allowed to as well. But did the Swami never realize everyone would copy these examples and make them into models to be strictly followed? What else would they do? As for the Swami, he got carried away describing the crowds at Sugriva's coronation, all the confusion and extra-vagances and so on. Otherwise, he'd have probably written even more verses to put the fear of God into people!

Now, when that lad Ravana carried off the lady Sita he soon found he'd made a mistake. He got really besotted with her, sighing and groaning and all the rest. But if today's laws had been operating, the whole matter would have been settled quite simply. Ravana just would have handed over a few hundred thousand rupees to Rama towards his marriage expenses! The poor thing would have been left to live out his days happily, and people would never say of him that he lost his kingdom for a woman. But what was he to do? The god Brahma put a curse on him: 'If you lay violent hands on someone else's wife, your body will shatter into a hundred pieces.' He was terrified by the curse, and because of that he decided to die on the battlefield.[17] Otherwise, he'd have had to fork out money enough for ten weddings, and do his best to make sure Sita never saw Ayo-dhya again. He tried everything in his power, but he was finished. But wait—here's another example of pativrata. What is it? Ravana went to his wife Mandodari, and told her, 'You're a great pativrata—go and persuade Sita, make her believe she's like a sister to you—like a joint wife.' In those days, wives treated the command of a husband with great reverence. If you were carrying out the command of your husband, there was nothing wrong even in lying to another man's wife and procuring her for your husband, if that was what he wanted. Mandodari thought this was pativrata pure and blameless. So she went to see the lady, full of wise advice. 'See, Rama and Ravana are under the same sign of the zodiac. The first letters of his name are Ra; and Ravana's are just the same. And just look at everything our great demon Ravana's got—his feats of courage, his wealth and luxury, his great kingdom. Anyway, what would there be for you back there in Ayodhya? Nothing but living in the jungle, no house, no kingdom, nothing but disgrace.'[18] She lavished all this advice on Sita, but the lady wouldn't have any of it. Because Sita knew all about a different side to the story, about when the peasant woman humiliated Ravana in Baliraja's house, tying him upside down to Angada's cradle so he had to drink the child's pee, and the poor old chap couldn't do anything about it. So Sita told Mandodari some blunt home truths in return and sent her away.[19] That was the story of that little episode. But as for Mandodari herself, there was nothing wrong at all in obeying her husband's command to deceive someone else's wife with her devotion as a pativrata and deliver her over to satisfy his pleasure. Just the opposite, the names of people like Mandodari are celebrated all through the puranas. So this is really a story with two morals. The husband's happy because his wife carried out her great duty of seeing to his pleasures, and the wife's happy because she thinks she's done the proper thing. But it's poor old number three who falls in the snare for it, the first two don't care a damn! Oh, congratulations, all you gods! And three cheers for pativrata!

In fact, shouldn't we think of putting some of the blame on the gods themselves for all this? After all, what's the real truth here? Let the real truth be as it may—what our shastras tell us is that we shouldn't hesitate to kill a father or a brother if we find them against us on the battlefield. Seeing Lakshman strike Indrajit down, Ramchandra cried out, 'Lakshman, my brother, what are you doing? Oh, this dharma of warriors is so hard and heavy. To have regard for no one, not for your son-in-law, not even your own son.' At that point, and seeing Sulochana's devotion as a pativrata, Rama should have raised up Indrajit again and brought him back to life. But Rama listened to Maruti and Bibhishan stirring things up, so he just left that rare jewel of a woman to be thrown in the fire and be burnt.[20] Anyway, I just have to point out things like these, when they're true and there right in front of me. I'll say my prayers to the gods and ask them to excuse me if I've thrown a bit of blame on two or three of them here. They may forgive me, they may not; they'll go on being gods in any case. What about the sages of those days? One of them was born of a deer: that's Shringarishi; one of a bird, and that was Bharadvaj; one of an ass, Gardhabharishi; and one of a cow, Vrishabharishi.[21] So each of them ended up writing their names after the animals they were born out of. They're all gone now, but women are still stuck with living up to it all. And you, what remedy have you got for it?

Oh yes, you've got the courage of lions, you do labours as great as Bhagiratha, you're as wise as Jaimini; oh, you've become such brave and fearless heroes, defeating great unconquerable enemies and turning them loose as if they were mere goats.[22] You catch hold of a great fierce god of fire like Agni in your fist and make him work any way you want through machines for all types of purposes. Vayu the wind is even stronger than Agni;

you can see Agni with your eyes, sometimes even hold him in your hand, but you can't hold Vayu in your hand, you can't even see him, but you men have used your power to bring even him under control. Lightning is the mother of all, she lives high up in the infinite sky, surrounded by clouds where even the birds don't go. Yet you've dragged even her down, and put her to toil for you like a female slave. Seeing as you're such almighty heroes, why is it so impossible for you to pull poor widows out of this pit of shame? Why can't you break some caste rules, put the kumkum back on their foreheads and let them enjoy the happiness of marriage again?

Oh, all your superiority and courage—it never gets outside the house! It's just like when there's a blind old mother sitting in the middle with five or six little boys playing round her, and one of them says, 'I wanna be king!', and the second one says, 'Mummy, I'm the minister', and the third says, 'I'm the general of the army! Now, let's make a kingdom! This is the army! This is the king's court!' This is how you go on, all just floods of water in a mirage. Not one of you has really dared pick up the hero's challenge.[23] You're all just like the mice in council in Aesop's fables: 'Oh, we must tie the bell around the cat's neck, mustn't we?' This is so true: your mouths are full of talk about reform, but who actually does anything? You hold these great meetings, you turn up at them in your fancy shawls and embroidered turbans, you go through a whole ton of supari nut, cartloads of betel leaves, you hand out all sorts of garlands, you use up a tank full of rosewater, then you come home. And that's it. That's all you do. These phoney reform societies of yours have been around for thirty, thirty-five years. What's the use of them? You're all there patting yourselves on the back, but if we look closely, they're about as much use as a spare tit on a goat.

See now—God, who decides everything in this world, has used his great intelligence to fill the world with all sorts of fascinating things. But two things drag people's minds towards them strongest of all: wealth, and women. Out of these, women are even more piercing than money. They fill your lives with pleasures a thousand times greater than any money could give you. Just imagine—you could build a wonderful palace and live in it surrounded by luxury, with the most beautiful gardens, with all sorts of costly and exotic possessions, carriages, horses, chariots, palanquins, elephants, camels, armies, with servant retinues who waited on your every word, with all the pomp of the court. Would you set all this up for yourself, and leave out women? If you did, it would seem more like a burning ground than a palace, your stately golden couch and its warm bed of pillows just like a funeral pyre, and all that company of armies, companions and servants not friends but enemies. All your rich delicacies would feel bitter as lemons in your mouth, your fine robes and jewelled ornaments like snakes winding round you. It would send you crazy, all of it. Even if God himself came and stood before you, you'd drive him off that very instant, no doubt about it. Think how you'd feel, then ask yourself again—how can a woman be happy without men? She'd be in just the same state as you. Put her in whatever wonderful luxury you like, give her the whole world, but if she's alone, you just see what condition she'd be in. It's God's own wish that the two should be joined as a pair. Can't you see, God has created female in everything he's made, from the birds on down even to inanimate trees and plants. There's no grace or beauty in anything without matching pairs. No work gets done that's not done in pairs. Can you make your way in this wilderness of a world all on your own? Can you manage all the business of worldly life yourself? Can you really draw the plough over that great field all on your own, or live like a sanyasi[24] even for a month or two without seeing a woman's face? Without a woman by your side, your own uncle, even your father would hesitate to stand you up alongside a couple. Who cares about a stray solitary man all on his own?

If a man with a wife and children gets into difficulties through his vices or his virtues, if he falls out of favour with someone or gets in trouble with moneylenders, people say, 'Oh, but have a thought for his poor children.' No one really cares about the man him-self. People only let him off for the sake of his wife and children. Even Agastya refused to take his darshan of Ramchandra without Sita.[25] When Ravana carried her off, he car-ried off Rama's very own strength. All he could do was wander helplessly through the wilderness, crying piteously, 'Oh my love, oh daughter of Janaka, river of virtue, oh Sita, Sita.' This is the sort of victorious power women possess.[26] Now, you can attack a strong enemy with great armies, with powder and shot and all sorts of murderous weapons, and make your enemy just a slave in chains. Countless strong kings can fall around you and blood flow like a swollen river, so in the end victory smiles on you. You might be able to catch a tiger and throw it in a trap, even saddle up a fierce wild animal like a lion, put a bit in its mouth and ride it round like a horse. But all your bravery and your shining heroism shrivel up in front of this little slip of a woman and the piercing glance of her eyes, and you fall down licking her feet like a dog. Any fool can pick up a sword or some weapon and hurt someone, there's no great heroism in that. But it's something else to be able to look at someone from a distance and set them sighing, aah, aah, with just a glance.[27] Who's more powerful now then? That woman or you?

It's the same even with your mother. She loves you beyond what she cares for herself, she watches over your life in times of trouble even more than when you were a child. She flashes to your command quick as lightning, she takes care in all sorts of ways that no blows should land on your honour in this worldly life, and when you look up there she is at your service, a sweet saint who bears everything in times of sorrow or of joy, sweet to the end. The point is it's her, who's always trying to make you happy, that you're heap-ing all this blame on to—it's her you're trying to push down to the bottom of the earth.[28] Aren't you ashamed? Oh, you idiots, women are shy, delicate and foolish in their very natures. And you, what lords you are, naturally so bold, courageous, strong, learned—so there you are calling women all these names, even before your lips have touched the nectar from your mother's golden breast. But just because you happen to be strong, does that make it right? You label women with all sorts of insulting names, calling them utterly feeble, stupid, bold, thoughtless—you beat out the sound of their names in shame. You shut them up endlessly in the prison of the home, while you go about building up your own importance, becoming Mr, Sir and so on. So you think to yourselves: what's a wife matter, after all? 'The hunter's him who's got the rabbit in his hand', and everything else is just stupid nonsense.[29] Starting from your childhood you collect all rights in your own hands and womankind you just push in a dark corner far from the real world, shut up in purdah, frightened, sat on, dominated as if she was a female slave.[30] And all the while you go about dazzling us all with the light of your own virtue. Learning isn't for women, nor can they come and go as they please. Even if a woman is allowed to go outside, the women she meets are ignorant like her, they're all just the same. So how's she ever going to get any greater understanding or intelligence?

Can any of these ancestors of yours produce any evidence direct from God that it's best for a wife to die before her husband, or a husband before his wife? Who lives and who dies is all in the hands of the all-powerful Narayan. Next to him, what stones are in your hands to throw? Is there a law about young people dying or old people living? Isn't it true that some people die just as they're born, some in the full flush of youth, some not till they've lived to be a hundred and taken full experience of the world; that some die when they're at the very peak of happiness? Isn't it true that some kings abandon their thrones as soon as Yama's messenger calls them and leave it all behind, whether they enjoy having an all-powerful kingdom or just find it a heavy burden, that they go without a moment's waiting, leaving their women and children behind?[31] That some people are very happy to go, and others sad and unwilling? Do you think there's anyone who can change that? Even a mighty king can do nothing in front of Yama's messenger. So who's going to listen to a poor woman? She, she's an orchard only God looks after.[32] What can she do about it? As for your Mahabharata, where does it show a woman going to ask Brahma if she could have her dead husband back, and being specifically told by Bhagavan the creator himself, 'No woman, whoever she is, can marry a second time in this life, once she's lost her first husband'? Apart from that one woman Savitri, no one has gone to Yama to try and get back her position as a wife. All right, so she went, and she got her husband back, and all sorts of other favours besides. So, even though this Savitri was only a woman, she dared to go to Yama's court to bring her husband back to life. Have you ever heard of a man who even set out on such a journey to save his wife's life, let alone one who got as far as she did? Once women have lost their position as wives, they have to hide their faces as if they've committed some huge crime worse even than murder and spend the rest of their lives shut away in a dark corner. So why don't you hide your faces when your wives have died, shave off your beards and moustaches and go off to live in the wilderness for the rest of your lives? Oh no, not you—one wife dies, and you just get another on the tenth day itself.[33] Just show us the evidence then—that some wise god has really told you to do this? In fact, what's good for a woman ought to be good for a man as well. What's so different about you? What—are you all such noble heroes that God gave you this freedom as a special gift?

Oh, you get your fine reputations from these so-called noble qualities—so long as no one examines them too closely! In fact, we women don't even need someone like the Rani of Jhansi to show us how: just take four or five hundred women who are free from attachments, put bayonets in their hands, then see what a time they'd give you.[34] You wouldn't even find a place to hide near the stove. In the old days of the Maratha kingdom, there really were heroes of the sword, those men who rocked the ancient throne of Delhi. But now since English rule came all your wonderful powers have gone, all your pleasures are ruined. Like the old saying—'No one's going to praise me, so I'll have to do it myself!'—so call yourselves heroes then, but only at pushing pens! Who takes any notice of you? Better still, with the way things are, it should be heroes at stuffing yourselves with food, that's the name that really suits you!

If you're so good pushing pens, so clever, pious, charitable, compassionate, if you're a real battislakshani[35] graced with all the virtues, how come you've got no love in you for your fellow creatures? Isn't there even a crumb of love in you? Or perhaps you've given it all out on loan—to the tigers in the jungle?

According to you, our own lives ought to give us a way of understanding the lives of others. What's happened to your lives here then? Isn't a woman's life as dear to her as yours is to you? It's as if women are meant to be made of something different from men altogether, made of the dust from earth or rock or rusted iron, whereas you and your lives are made from the purest gold. To you, woman is just some utterly trivial form of life, like a louse or a flea—and your own experience tells you that this is all very fine and good.[36] You're asking me what I mean? I mean once a woman's husband has died, not even a dog would swallow what she's got to. What's in store for her? The barber comes to shave all the curls and hair off her head, just to cool your eyes. All her ornaments are taken away. All her beauty vanishes. She's stripped and exposed in all sorts of ways as if she belonged to no one, she becomes the widow-pot hidden in the corner.[37] She's shut out from going to weddings, receptions and other auspicious occasions that married women go to. And why all these restrictions? Because her husband has died. She's unlucky: ill-fate is written on her forehead. Her face is not to be seen, it's a bad omen. She's a sign now for all these things. Oh, but her husband's died! All right, who says he hasn't? But was it she who killed him? Did she make some private prayer to God, 'God take this husband from me quickly'? In fact, she might very well have felt like asking God to take pity on her, praying, 'Take this husband quickly, Oh God, release me from this torture.' But then, she'd have stopped herself out of fear of the unhappiness she'd suffer after his lordship had gone. Who's to say? No—who'd think such a thought? It's like the old saying: 'Narayan did the deed, but it's Keshav does the penance!'[38] The husband's life is at an end, all finished. His good and bad points have all been added up and he's gone. But why should his wife take the blame for it? All right then, let's say that she should. But if she's supposed to give up everything after her husband's gone, and sit lamenting, 'Hari, Hari, god, Oh god', why shouldn't the man do the same? Why should he go off and marry another woman and settle down happily with her? Did the authors of the shastras keep their savage glares just for women? Maybe there was some woman once upon a time who went and set fire to their houses or something. So just because of this one woman, they went and invented a law and applied it to all women.

It would have been all right if a similar law had been imposed on all men at the same time. But would we ever get them to do that? They really used their heads, those authors of the shastras, when they made all this up. All very comfortable for them. Absolutely excellent! But what if they laid it down today that 'No man can remarry after his first wife has died. If he does, it's like he's committed incest with his mother and should be thrown out of caste'? And then the next day one of these chaps' own wives suddenly fell down dead. People would say even of him, 'He's got bad luck written on his forehead—we don't want to see his face.' It would be him who would be shut out as a guest at marriages and be thrown out of the village into a math.[39] So isn't it quite obvious that these men were just thinking of their own comforts when they gave men permission to marry any number of wives? Then their fortunes flourished! If one wife died or the poor thing got ill, then our chap just moves straight on to another. And if he happens to be a rich man as well, that's one more stroke of good luck on top of all the others. It means he enjoys two sorts of power: one comes from his money, and the other just because he's a man. There's nothing to hold him back!

You even get shrivelled up old sinners of eighty years or more, and there'll still be some oily-faced hanger-on who'll tell him, 'What nonsense, sir, who says you're old? If anyone dares say so, I'll push their teeth in.' 'But look,' the old man says, 'What about my hair? Doesn't that spoil it?' 'No, no—you just take a bit of this cream, sir, rub it on, and tomorrow it'll look fine, nothing to it!' 'Well, that's good, that's my hair fixed then.

But my teeth—there's not a trace of one left in my head. Anything we could do about that, do you think?' 'No problem, my dear sir. Tomorrow I'll go along to a doctor I know who deals in teeth and I'll get you a brand new set, a full thirty-two. And next time you're washing your face, you just pull out any old bits of teeth still left and you'll be all ready, nothing to it. Even lads of twenty-five won't dare set themselves up alongside you. No, no, sir—these may be old bones, but does pepper ever fetch less than millet, even when it's a bit old and rotten?'[40] So it's all arranged and the old chap puffs up with pride, preening himself at the very thought. His few strands of hair on his bald head, his eyebrows and moustaches are all white, like bits of cotton wool, but he has his three rupee box of ointment brought to him and he rubs it in as instructed three times a day. Then he starts dressing himself up. He folds his dhoti and ties it up very tight. Then there's the turban with a gold border. And a shiny new jacket, which has to be forced on over his old bones. He finishes it off with a scarf over his shoulders and pops the borrowed set of teeth in his toothless mouth. Then he crushes up some betel for himself, to make his false teeth look good and red. Red sandals on his feet, and an imported walking stick in his hand in case he gets the shakes walking along. As for his diet, it's almond cakes, fried sweets, gourd sweets in syrup, ten times a day to fatten himself up. He inspects his ugly old face with its cheeks sunk in a hundred times in the mirror and struts about asking everyone, 'Well, hello there! How do you think I'm looking these days—pretty well, eh?' And then some mischief-maker will come along, and say, 'Tut, tut, sir, what's this about you being old? You don't look a day older than our Ganapati. You should find a wife! We don't have much fun at home these days ourselves, so how on earth do you manage? There's a saying, you know, "Money troubles and you need relatives, but if it's diarrhoea a wife's best!"'[41]

What next, then? The old man spends every minute of his time looking out for a woman, it's all he's got eyes for. Then it's done. The old corpse pays out a couple of thousand rupees and gets a pretty doe-eyed girl for himself, just like you buy a goat from the butcher and tie it up as bait to catch a tiger. Then out he goes one day and falls down dead, and it's all over. His worldly life is all finished and it's her again who's left to suffer. Right or not?

Do you ever find a woman going in for performances like these? Once the axe has fallen on her out of the sky, she accepts the burdens of widowhood, praises her husband's qualities good and bad and puts up with torments from the rest of the household till the day she dies. If a woman's husband has just a small illness her mouth dries up with terror. She watches him constantly, worrying for him more than her very life. It's out of devotion, you might say—or out of fear. She does everything just as he wishes. Of course, it's possible to be loving and open with someone, whether it's a man or a woman. But she has no choice but to be nice to him, however much she's got a mind of her own. So how can you tell her she's got to be all good and virtuous, when she just has to accept whatever you feel like handing out day after day? It's naturally from others that people learn how to behave, in good ways or bad. You can see this from your own experience. If you meet up with a cheat isn't it likely you'll become a ten times bigger cheat yourself?

It's just the same in this case. There's a saying in English, that compassion breeds compassion. So just as compassion is born from the belly of compassion, you should start off by thinking what comes out of your own mind, then think what it does to others. But even this won't work where men are concerned. If a man's wife is ill for a year or two, then His Majesty will be saying, 'When's she going to die and get it over with?' or 'I'm just sick and tired of having to feed her medicine'. Whatever a wife's circumstances, she can't say anything like that, out of shame at what people would think. The husband, he's got to be treated with reverence no matter what happens. It's like the Muslims, whatever you are they find something grand to call you—if a man's wealthy, he's an amir, if he's poor, he's a fakir and after he's died, they call him a pir![42] A man who isn't married is given the title of brahmachari; those who are married are called householders and family men.[43] Then, when a man's been through all the stages of life, he gives up the world and becomes a sanyasi, and that's the end! But what's the proper time of day for people to take the vow of sanyas? It's in the evening.[44] But you—you don't give up these worldly hopes till the very last moment, when the doctors have given up all hope of your life. Then and only then you'll take the vow to become a sanyasi, at some unearthly hour in the morning!

What a cunning lot of jackals you are then, real experts at it! If only God would preserve this English government forever! Since it began here, women have got the gift of education, and their minds made strong enough to face all sorts of mental and practical circumstances with courage. The ignorance that made its home in their hearts is all gone and they've begun to get some understanding of what's good for them and what isn't, of how they should behave to whom, of how they can best drive on this cart that's our life in the world; they have begun to get some understanding of truth, of dharma, of pativrata. Because of all this, things are going to change a lot in this land of Bharat. But there are some people who are enemies of women to their very bones, like the Pune Vaibhav newspaper. These people hate all the new things, or so it seems from one or two articles in the newspaper. These must have been appearing continually now for the last four or five months. Some widow by name of Vijaylakshmi got herself an abortion, or she might have had the child and sent it off to heaven herself—enquiries are going on about that at the moment.[45] So someone took up the poor widow's cause and wrote a letter to the government, saying widows ought to be married again. Then his lordship editor of the Vaibhav got into a furious rage over this and shouted his head off: 'The English government shouldn't ever put its hand in our religion!' But actually he's no different from all the other men. He doesn't look like a real reformer but he is one all the same, it's just that his reforms are all disguised. If you look at it, what religious differences are left now between European people and our own? There's only one difference left, and if you ask what, it's that people won't marry or have other sorts of physical connection with the women of another caste. That's all that's left now. For the rest, what customs of European people are there that you haven't taken on for yourselves?

You've started to wear clothes like theirs. You've made yourselves as learned as they are, if not more. You enjoy the things they eat to your hearts' content, like meat and alcohol. You keep on trying to be just like them, yet you go on about them not putting their hands in our religion! But how much of this religion is there left now? You go wherever you like in trains and boats, you dress just like them—a jacket on your back, a hat on your head, trousers, socks and shoes, a little handkerchief sprinkled with lavender water in your hand, a pipe in your mouth to finish it off. You turn yourselves into real live sahibs (the only difference being that they're white all over, and you're half white and half black, like a piebald horse!). You eat all sorts of forbidden foods just as your fancy takes you, you do all sorts of improper things, then you turn round and claim you're great defenders of dharma. Aren't you even slightly ashamed saying it?

Then you get into steamships, don't you, and go off to countries where there isn't a single member of your own caste. You mix with those people and spend year after year in close company with them. Then you just come back here, do a panchagavya penance, then there you are, all ready and proud to take your place at the communal table once more![46]

So you think that makes it all right, do you? But can you really wash out those intestines of yours which are stuffed full of things you shouldn't have eaten, by taking baths and special penances and rubbing cows' urine on your body? Why all these tears for your religion? In fact, wouldn't it be a far better way of defending our religion if the government did put its hand in and stopped you spending all that money on endless bottles of drink, and all those thousands of poor chickens and other birds and beasts being killed for you to eat? I quite agree with the old proverb that says, 'A stranger steps in, and harm comes to the house,' and I would have followed it in what I did if you hadn't taken on a single one of these people's habits, if you'd followed your own dharma to the letter.[47] Even the poor widows would have realized that their fortunes were never going to get better and would have kept quiet. But all that Manu, it's changed and gone now.[48] What's left of it? Those people are just better than you a thousand times over. Do they copy a single one of our people's customs on these worthless whims? Just the opposite, they look at these get-ups of yours and laugh. Oh, you asses, if someone from a distant land or one of your forefathers came back again to see, they wouldn't even be able to recognize this place. All these different arts and skills have come in the last fifty years and everything has changed, and if you came back like the black sheep in the family, you'd see what a change there's been! . . .

Notes

1. *Stridharma: Dharma* or 'right action' for women.
2. A reference to one of god Krishna's boyhood pranks, a central theme in the *puranas* and other early Sanskrit texts, carried over into vernacular and oral traditions. Chandravali is the leader of the *gopis*, the cowherd maidens whose hearts as well as their butter Krishna steals as a boy, and with whom he sports as a youth.
3. *Pativrata*: the ideal wife, who devotes herself to her husband and honours him as a god. There are supposedly five great examples: Ahalya, Draupadi, Sita, Tara and Mandodari.
4. Savitri: princess in the great epic *Mahabharata*, celebrated for her devotion to her husband: she followed him to the regions of the dead and won his soul back.
5. Another mark of ideal devotion in the pativrata is that she will only eat what her husband eats.
6. Betel or *pan*, rolled betel leaf and areca-nut (*supari*), often flavoured with spices, sugar, lime and other ingredients, taken after eating. Tarabai hints here knowingly that the wife's refusal to share a tender after-dinner pan with her husband suggests also a rejection of other kinds of post-prandial intimacy.
7. *Shastra*: a general term for Sanskrit digests of religious law.
8. The five Pandava brothers and their uncle Dhritrashtra, the blind king of Hastinapura, are central characters in the *Mahabharata*. Since her husband was blind, Gandhari herself always wore a bandage over her eyes. Their sons were the Kauravas, whose wars with the Pandavas form the main subject of the story.
9. *Purana*: texts, usually in verse, which post-date the epics and recount the deeds of gods and goddesses; *pothi*: a general term for a book or pamphlet often used to refer to vernacular versions of epic or puranic literature of the kind which Tarabai read. See note 16.

10. Draupadi: wife to the five Pandava brothers in the Mahabharata story. Her five husbands are explained rather apologetically: the Pandava prince Arjuna won her hand in an archery contest, and his mother Kunti told him to share whatever prize he won with his brothers, so out of deference to their mother's command Draupadi was married to all of them. She encountered Karna, son of Kunti's first marriage and bitter rival of Arjuna himself, at the contest. Karna himself later fought on the side of the Kauravas against the Pandavas on the battlefield of Kurukshetra.

11. Ahalya appears in the epic *Ramayana* as the beautiful wife of the sage Gautama, guru to the god Indra. Gautama caught Indra making love to his wife and cursed her so she turned to stone. In some versions Ahalya knows Indra and is flattered, in others Indra only gets his way by disguising himself as Gautama. Ahalya was eventually redeemed by Rama and restored to her husband, to become a great pativrata.

12. Satyavati: nymph, fishermaid and mother of some of the main characters in the *Mahabharata*. The sage Parashara saw her playing in a stream and told her she would give birth to a prodigy if they made love. She was half-willing, but embarrassed because she smelled of fish. He convinced her by changing her smell into fragrance. From the union she bore Vyasa, author of the Vedas, then went on to marry a king, Shantanu. Their two sons died childless, so Satyavati instructed Vyasa to provide the widows with sons. The sons so born were Dhritarashtra and Pandu, fathers of the Kauravas and Pandavas respectively. Kunti was a princess who so devoted herself to the sage Durvasa that he gave her a *mantra* or magic charm by which she could call gods and make them do her bidding. She called up Surya, the sun, and by him bore Karna, but had to give him away as she was unmarried. She went on to marry Pandu and bear the Pandavas.

13. Love marriage: *gandharva vivaha* is classified in Manu as one of the eight legitimate forms of marriage: see G. Buhler (ed.), *The Laws of Manu*, Delhi 1979, p. 81. It is so called because of the free love supposed to exist among these celestial beings.

14. Vidur: son of a union between Vyasa and a slave girl.

15. The story of Rama, incarnation of Vishnu and eldest son of Dasaratha, king of Ayodhya, forms the main theme of the *Ramayana*. Dasaratha banished his son at the instigation of one of his wives, Kaikeyi, who wished her own son Bharata on the throne. Rama's brother Lakshman and his faithful wife Sita accompanied him. During their exile the demon king Ravana abducted Sita, and she was eventually rescued from Lanka by Rama in alliance with Sugriva, king of the monkeys. Sugriva himself had been driven from his throne by his usurping half-brother, Vali. Rama helped Sugriva recover his kingdom and his wife, and after Vali's death arranged for his widow, Tara, to marry Sugriva himself.

16. Shridhar: a brahman of Pandharpur writing in the mid-sixteenth century, author of the *Ramavijaya*, Bombay 1876, and *Pandavapratapa*, Bombay 1868, Marathi versions of the *Ramayana and Mahabharata* respectively. These found a much wider and more popular audience than the Sanskrit originals, and their public or private reading was one means through which the unlearned had access to the epics. Editions were published in 1876 and 1868 respectively, but neither of the texts has ever been stabilized in a standard critical edition. Tarabai was familiar with both, and in many of her detailed references to episodes from the epics, used these Marathi versions rather than the Sanskrit originals.

17. Ravana's austerities led the gods to give him the boon of invincibility in battle, but a curse was laid on him that he would die through a woman's doing.

18. Ravana's wife Mandodari is celebrated in the *Ramayana* as a great pativrata. She warned him against seizing unwilling women and tried without success to get him to send Sita back. Tarabai follows Shridhar's Marathi version very closely here: see *Ramavijaya*, 24, 80–116. For these themes in twentieth-century women's folk-songs, see I. Junghare and J. Frater, 'The Ramayana in Maharashtrian Women's Folk-Songs', *Man in India*, vol. 56, 1976, p. 295.

19. Angada was the son of Vali the monkey king and his wife Tara. This episode does not appear in the published *Ramavijaya* that I have seen, and may likewise come from a different text or from oral versions of the story.

20. Indrajit was Ravana's son, slain when Lakshman cut his head off. His faithful wife Sulochana came to the enemy camp to ask for her husband's head back. Impressed by her devotion, Rama was about to bring Indrajit back to life. He was persuaded not to by the monkey army, who wished to see Bibhishan, estranged brother of Ravana and ally of Rama, placed on the throne of Lanka. Sulochana went as *sati* on Indrajit's pyre. This is Shridhar almost word for word: see *Ramavijaya*, 30, 174–6.

21. *Rishi*: a sage, of whom many appear in the epics and *puranas*, with a range of different stories about their parentage.

22. Bhagiratha: a son of the kings of Ayodhya, who laboured to bring the sacred river Ganges down from the celestial regions to earth. Jaimini: a disciple of Vyasa, and a celebrated sage.

23. Literally, 'not one of you picks up the hero's vida'. *Vida* is a roll of betel leaves. The phrase 'to pick up the vida' means to accept a challenge, and originates in the Maratha practice 'of throwing a *vida* into the midst of an assembly (as of warriors)': J.T. Molesworth, *A Dictionary of Marathi and English*, Bombay, 1857, p. 757.

24. *Sanyasi*: one who has abandoned all worldly ties, the last of the four ideal stages in the life of a high-caste Hindu man. This first three are *brahmachari, grhastha* and *vanaprastha*: celibate student, householder and forest-dweller. Tarabai's language here recalls the common metaphor of woman as the field in which man sows his seed. See Wadley, 'Women in the Hindu Tradition', in R. Ghadially (ed.), *Women in Indian Society*, New Delhi 1988, pp. 26–7.

25. *Darshan*: 'taking sight' of a god or shrine, which confers blessing in itself. Agastya: a celebrated sage who befriended Rama during his exile.

26. Tarabai uses the term *shakti* to describe this special power of women.

27. The power of women's eyes, piercing like arrows into the hearts of men, is a common motif at many cultural levels in South Asia—but employed here to make rather a different kind of point about the power of women.

28. Tarabai echoes an absolutely central theme in women's oral culture here, where mother's love, its innocence, its constancy, its sweet selfless depths, forms a very strong value in women's songs, often accompanied by bitter reproaches for those who hold mothers cheap. See A. Bhagwat, 'Maharashtrian Folk-Songs on the Grind-Mill', *Journal of the University of Bombay*, January 1942, pp. 138–62, and Mary Fuller, 'Marathi Grinding Songs', *New Review*, June 1940, p. 512.

29. I.e., 'Might is Right', 'Possession in Nine-tenths of the Law'.

30. Rights: I have translated the term *sikka* as 'rights', but it has a range of meanings rather different from its western sense. Sikka refers to a seal or stamp in general, but more specifically the royal signet or seal placed upon any grant of rights in pre-colonial Maharashtra.

31. Yama: the god of the dead, whose messengers summon the living and who sits in judgement on their souls in his city in the lower world.

32. A common phrase for someone that no one looks after or cares about: see Y. Date and C. Karve, *Maharashtra vakya-sampradaya kosha*, Poona 1932–8, vol. I, p. 145.

33. Ten days is the standard period of Hindu mourning for close relatives, during which no marriage or other auspicious ceremony is held.

34. Rani of Jhansi: Lakshmibai was queen of the small Maratha state of Jhansi, annexed in 1854 under Dalhousie's doctrine of lapse. She fought on the rebel side during the rebellion of 1857 and was killed in the siege of Gwalior in 1858. Her name became a byword for women's daring and courage.

35. *Battislakshani*: the 35 marks of excellence—i.e., someone so superior that they have them all. They refer to the proper proportions and colours of different parts of the body. See Date and Karve, *Maharashtra vakya-sampradaya kosha*, vol. II, p. 258. The term lends itself best to sarcasm, as is the case here.

36. Men's lack of affection compared to the devotion of wives and mothers is another theme in women's songs: see Mary Fuller, 'Maher', *Man in India*, vol. 22, 1942, p. 118; Bhagwat, 'Maharashtrian Folk-Songs', p. 171.

37. *Sandice khapara*, 'pot in the corner', a rich Marathi reference to a widow. The widow is a pot or vessel, a common symbol for the female, but she is no longer used by the family and so thrown aside into the corner. Anything which is 'in the corner' also has the implication of something improper, fit only for a secret place, reflecting the association of widows with illicit sex and prostitution.
38. I.e., the punishment for a crime visited on a party quite innocent.
39. *Math*: a monastery, community of Hindu ascetics and scholars.
40. I.e., superior goods will always be valued over inferior, no matter what condition they are in.
41. This proverb means that a wife's attention is worth most in times of real sickness or adversity.
42. I.e., if you're a man, you can always get some form of honour—*amir, fakir* and *pir* translate as lord, mendicant and saint respectively. A pointed proverb to the effect that men demand respect no matter what their rank or stage of life.
43. See note 24.
44. The joke here is that the ritual of man's become sanyasi should really begin with a sacrificial fire at sunset.
45. For Vijaylakshmi's crime and trial, see introduction [to O'Hanlon (ed.), *A Comparison Between Women and Men*], p. 1.
46. *Panchagavya* penance: a powerful rite of purification in which the offender consumes the five products of the cow (milk, curds, ghee, dung and urine). For liberals and reformers who had broken caste rules by travelling abroad, eating the wrong food or associating with the widow-remarriage movement, this was a common means of purifying themselves.
47. This proverb reflects the intense loyalty and protectiveness women are supposed to feel to their own homes and families, and equally intense reticence and suspicion towards outsiders.
48. Manu: Tarabai plays on the double meaning of this term. Manu is the author of the Institutes of Manu, most authoritative of orthodox Hindu law-books, but the name is also generic: each age has its Manu, and the passing of ages is measured by each one. Thus Manu also has the meaning of time, age or season, reflected in the emphasis here on the changes time has brought.

27

From *Miscellaneous Writings**

M.G. RANADE

I**

The past twelve months have been notably distinguished for the warmth and freshness of light thrown upon many of our most cherished social institutions by free discussion. As is usual in the case of all discussions on social evils, much declamation and invective have been employed on both sides, to supply the place of calm and critical investigation, and the merits of the questions really at issue have been obscured by clouds of words and figures, and empty boasts of self-satisfied complacency. These questions really reduce themselves to two points of inquiry, first, whether or not the institutions assailed produce on the whole more of evil than good, and secondly, whether the evil that is in them admits of a speedier and more effective remedy than is implied in the advice of those who would let things alone, and would drift along with the stream of events, but neither exert themselves, nor permit others to make an effort, to regulate the current and make it run steadier and stronger in the desired direction. On the first point, taking the general sense of those who have spoken out on both sides, there appears to be a general agreement. The dispute here is confined to the alleged extent of the evils, which are freely admitted to be so. On the second point, the difference of views is radical, and there does not appear to be any great likelihood of an agreement ever being arrived at which will satisfy both parties. When one sees how men, who had grown grey in the denunciation of these evils, turned round immediately a suggestion was made for practical action, and joined the orthodox majority in their praise of the existing arrangements, the Political Rishi's warning about the defects of Hindu character seems to be more than justified. There appears to be no ground for hope, under such circumstances, of seeing any genuine reform movement springing up from within the heart of the nation, unless that heart is regenerated, not by cold calculations of utility, but by the cleansing fire of a religious revival. However, there is really nothing strange in all this outcry. There will always be, and there always have been, as Lord Ripon in another connection observed, a clean and an unclean party in small municipal, as well as in large social, arrangements. If the population of our cities were entirely left to themselves, and each man's or woman's vote was as good as another's, the good sense

*M.G. Ranade, *Miscellaneous Writings* (1915; repr. New Delhi: Sahitya Akademi, 1992), pp. 70–85, 100–15, 150–70.

**Introduction to 'A collection by Mr Vaidya containing the proceedings which led to the passing of Act XV of 1856'. The book was published in 1885.

of the men of light and leading would no doubt prevail in the end, but, in the earlier stage of discussion and argument, we should doubtless hear many an appeal to the glory of our ancestors, their long life and vigour maintained, it might be proudly observed, in spite of, or in the absence of, municipal conservancy. Even in European countries, there are anti-vaccination doctors, Shakers, who take no medicine, but leave the body to cure itself, physical science pedants who still question the truth of the motion of the earth round its sun centre, and its motion round its own axis. A love of paradox is a weakness which clings to many great minds, grows with their other excellences like a parasitic excrescence. Leaving these unnatural developments aside, it is clear that there is a chance of producing a reasonable conviction among not the vast majority of those who do not think, but among the considerable minority who in every country lead opinion by informing it and setting it in proper form before the community in general.

Viewed in this light, there is abundant reason for hope that an historical study of these institutions will dispel many a false conception of the antiquity and sanctity of the existing arrangements.

The early celebration of child marriages, the forcible disfigurement of widows and absolute prohibition of remarriage in the higher castes, the occasional and local practices of polyandry and polygamy, are all admittedly corruptions of recent growth unknown to the best days of our country's history. The Hon. Rao Saheb V.N. Mandlik, who speaks with an authority which few will dispute, has freely admitted that the Hindu girl's marriageable age is 12, and that the corresponding age for boys has been reduced from time to time as the period of Brahmacharya studies was more and more curtailed. Taking the most narrow acceptation of the Grihya Sutra rules, this period could not well be legally curtailed below 12 years, thus making the marriageable age for boys 20 years. In regard to the question of widow marriage, it is admitted by the orthodox leaders of the opposition that the prohibition forms part of the Kali Nisheda, or prohibitions intended for the Kali Yug. The writings of Manu and Yajnavalkya show, what the Itihasas and Purans confirm, that monogamy is the natural condition of Aryan life, and that both polygamy and polyandry are disreputable excrescences. Nobody can, under these circumstances, contend that, on the strictest interpretation of the texts, the local usages which obtain at present agree with our best traditions of the past. Those who advocate a return to the old order of things are thus in good company, and are not foreign imitators.

We have to consider, next, how it came to pass that the Aryan population in course of time departed from the vigorous and healthy usages of their ancestors. Such an enquiry alone will enable us, who now aspire after a higher life, to trace our way back without risk of failure or disappointment. The Hindu community has always been self-contained, if not original, in its grasp of social matters, and no analogies drawn from Christian or Mahomedan nations can have any convincing force, unless they are supported by reasons and associations of our own venerable past.

The rise and fall of female rights and status in Hindu Aryan Society has a history of its own, at once interesting and suggestive in its analogies to the corresponding developments in the institutions of another kindred stock, the Roman Aryans, who have so largely influenced European ideas. Both began by a complete subordination of the women in the family to the men, and of the men themselves to the head of the family. In early Vedic times, the woman was, like the deformed or the sickly member of a family, devoid of rights, and, being incapable of self-protection, was disentitled to share the inheritance. The succession in a united family after the death of its chief went to the surviving male members, his sons and brothers, and in their default to the more distant agnate males.

The earlier Sutrakars, Baudhayana and Apasthamba, clearly reaffirmed this exclusion from inheritance and asserted the perpetual subjection of every woman to her father, her husband, and her son. Gradually, however, as the Aryans settled in the land, and the necessities of war gave place to the gentler virtues and victories of peace, the earlier Smritis found admission by express texts for the wife, the mother, the grand-mother, the daughter, and the sister, and finally to the female relations of the male Gotraja Sapinda. It is hardly necessary to follow this growth step by step. Corresponding with this re-cognition of the claims of family affection, a chivalrous regard for women, and for their personal comfort and liberty, was asserted in other ways. The women took equal part with the husbands in solemn religious rites, and as queens took their places in great reli-gious sacrifices and the deliberations of State on occasions of display and power. They were permitted at their choice to remain single and unmarried, and neither the father nor the mother would interfere by exercising their power of choosing husbands for them. They were poets, philosophers, and Rishis, and composed hymns and wrote works, and studied and argued with men on equal terms. This went on for many cen-turies, and the proofs of it are too numerous in all our Purans and Itihasas to admit of any hesitation on the part of even the most hostile critic. Marriage was optional with man as well as with woman. The text of the marriage ritual, the rule for selecting brides or rather bridegrooms, the practice of Swayamwar in mature age, the liberty to be married again on the death, or absence, or incurable impotency, of the first husband, both before and after consummation, the strictness of the monogamous tie, all these privileges were conceded to women in the natural growth of things.

Thus far there was no break of continuity, and all was smooth sailing. The analogies between the Roman and Hindu developments were complete so far. In course of time, the Aryans like the Romans, having overcome their enemies, fell to fighting among themselves, and long and murderous wars between Brahmins and Kshatriyas devastated the land. Under the pressure of these complicated difficulties, the strong love of the active virtues of fighting and hunting, chivalrous regard for women, and the enjoyment of the pleasures of life generally, gave way to a philosophy which regarded life and being itself as a pain and a calamity, the bustle of the arts of peace and war as unrelieved weeping and lamentation. And naturally weak woman, from being the soul of chastity and virtue, came to be described as a snare and a burden. The gods who had cheered the conquering and militant Aryans with their countenance, retired with the Rishis to the Himalayas and beyond. They could no longer be seen, and gave way to a fatalistic belief that man was the slave of his own miserable *karma*, and must bear it patiently till he learned how best to throw off this mortal coil. The great excess of bad passions which had deluged the land with fratricidal blood demoralized society, and lowered the status of women in the family, the state, and in the social arrangements generally. The Aryan ideals lost their charm, and a lower type of character and morality asserted its predominance as the down-trodden races, which had been driven to the hills, issued from their haunts, and fell upon the demoralized and disunited Aryan kingdoms on all sides. At the same time, a new race of invaders from Central Asia, partly Scythian and partly Mongolian in stock, entered India by the north-west, drove before them the old Aryans, and established their power and colonies in the Panjab, in Sind, in Rajputana, and Central India, Guzerat, and even parts of Maharashtra. This process of the upheaval of non-Aryan races, and the invasion and settlement of barbarian Scythian conquerors, was in active development for many centuries, and these ethnic and political forces have profoundly modified the institutions and usages of modern India. They brought to the surface races of men with a lower civilization, more patriarchal, and therefore less chivalrous, ideals of life. Polyandry has always been a normal institution of the non-Aryan or Scythian races. It derived new dignity from the rise to power of these backward races. The woman's lot has always been one of dependence and misery in barbarous countries. It could not be otherwise here. Women in these ruder races were bartered in marriage as chattels moveable or slaves. They were burned with their deceased lords, with his bows and arrows, his horse and weapons, to provide for his comfort in another world. When these races rose to power, the better minds were driven to seek shelter in asceticism and abandonment of the world which had for them no charms, and only misery, life-long and unrelieved, and instead of being the deity of peace and good will in the family, women became the symbol of corruption and vice. Optional celibacy and Swayamvar were out of the question. The old state of pupilage and dependence was reaffirmed. Late marriages, and the liberty of second marriage to widows, were denounced, though here and there they were allowed to associate with their husband's surviving brother for the purpose of procreating children for him. The well-marked four-fold divisions of life lost their meaning and their sanctity, and baby and child espousals could not but come into fashion, and bring in their train polygamy and concubinage. Things thus settled themselves on this lower level of barbarous usages.

Gradually the better and the Aryan portion of the community recovered from the surprise and discomfiture, and the dark clouds of the Middle Ages of Indian History, the dreaded Kali Yug of the Purans, began to clear up. The Aryan Religion, social polity, and marriage institutions were reformed on a footing of compromise, and those who guided the course of events tried their best to re-assert the dominion of the Vedas and of the Brahmins, who represented in their persons the highest civilization of the olden days. This form of restoration and renaissance was again interrupted by the Mahomedan invasions, which repeated for some centuries all the horrors of the previous dark period. Before the license of Mahomedan outrage, women shrank from public gaze, and it became necessary for their safety to secrete them within the dark recesses of the house. Polygamy and illicit concubinage became once more fashionable.

It will be clear from this review that internal dissensions, the upheaval of non-Aryan races, and the predominance acquired by barbarous Scythian and Mahomedan conquerors, degraded the condition of the female sex, deprived them of their rights of inheritance and freedom, and made woman dependent on man's caprice, instead of being his equal and honoured helpmate. Political and ethnic agencies of great power have wrought the evil, and we cannot afford to lose sight of this fact in our attempts to elevate the status of the female sex. Fortunately, the causes which brought on this degradation have been counteracted by Providential guidance, and we have now, with a living example before us of how pure Aryan customs, unaffected by barbarous laws and patriarchal notions, resemble our own ancient usages, to take up the thread where we dropped it under foreign and barbarous pressure, and restore the old healthy practices, rendered so dear by their association with our best days, and justified by that higher reason which is the sanction of God in man's bosom.

The next question is, as stated above, a more difficult one to deal with. How is this gentle revolution to be effected without breaking with the past, is a problem which admits of difference of views. There are two schools of thinkers among those who have discussed this subject. One set would utilize all the active and passive agencies which tend to encourage and vitalize reform; the other set would leave things to take their own course, firm in the confidence that the passive agencies at work would secure all our ends just as we desire, slowly but surely. Those who feel the full force of the ethnical and political causes mentioned above, and also feel how necessary it is at certain stages of man's progress to secure the assertion of right ideas by the highest sanctions, advocate to some extent the help of State regulation, as representing the highest and most disinterested wisdom of the times, working to give effect to the other tendencies, concentrating and popularizing them. Those who are not sufficiently alive to these considerations would trust to education and the gradual development of better ideas by their own internal force, to achieve all that we desire. It is needless to state that the publication to which these remarks are prefaced is intended to strengthen the hands of the first set of thinkers, and to show, by the example of what occurred in the past, that timely State regulation is not attended with the mischiefs which people attribute to it, and that it co-ordinates and vivifies the healthy action of the other agencies. It becomes, in this connection, necessary to consider briefly the several objections urged by the advocates of the let-alone school in their order of relative importance.

The first objection urged on this head is that these are social questions, which it is not the duty of the State to regulate. We answer that this argument is not open to those who welcome, as the vast majority of this class of opponents freely acknowledge, State regulation of *sati* and widow marriage, of infanticide, the self-murder of jogees on the Ganges, and hook-swinging before idol shrines, or to those who propose compulsory education, and compulsory vaccination, and sanitary precautions generally. Individual liberty of action is no doubt a great force, but this liberty has its limitations imposed by the fact that no man's liberty should encroach upon the liberty of those who surround him. Whenever there is a large amount of unredressed evil suffered by people who cannot adopt their own remedy, the State has a function to regulate and minimize the evil, if by so regulating it, the evil can be minimized better than by individual effort and without leading to other worse abuses. The State in its collective capacity represents the power, the wisdom, the mercy and charity, of its best citizens. What a single man, or a combination of men, can best do on their own account, that the State may not do, but it cannot shirk its duty if it sees its way to remedy evils, which no private combination of men can check adequately or which it can deal with more speedily and effectively than any private combination of men can do. In these latter cases, the State's regulating action has its sphere of duty marked out clearly. On this, and on this principle alone, can State action be justified in many important departments of its activity, such as the enforcement of education, sanitation, of State undertakings like the Postal service, or subsidizing private effort in Railway extension and commercial development. The regulation of marriageable age has in all countries, like the regulation of minority, or the fit age for contracts, been a part of its national jurisprudence, and it cannot be said with justice that this question lies out of its sphere. The same observation holds true of the condition of the widow rendered miserable in early life, and thrown helpless on the world. More legitimately than minors, the widows are the wards of the nation's humanity, and to the extent that the evil they suffer is remediable by man, it cannot be said that this remedy may not be considered by the State as fully within its proper function.

The next argument urged on the other side is that the evil is not so great as some people think, and that it really needs no State action. There can be no doubt that, to some extent, Mr Malabari has laid himself open to this side attack. The evils of child-marriage, and enforced widowhood, and unrestricted polygamy, are not quantitatively, and calculating them by statistical returns, so great as Mr Malabari described them to be. But this does not go to show that, after making due allowance for all exaggerations, the residue of unredressed wrong which calls for remedy is not sufficiently great to justify action. Much the same thing was said when it was proposed to prohibit Sati or Infanticide. Wherever there is undeserved misery endured in a large number of cases, there is a ground for State interference, always supposing that the interference will lead to the redress of the wrong, better than any individual effort can accomplish.

A third way of stating the same objection is that the parties who suffer do not complain of it, and strangers have therefore no business to intervene. This is a very old line of defence. It was urged as an argument against the abolition of slavery, as well as against the laws which rendered Sati and Infanticide crimes, and validated widow marriages. Perhaps the worst effect of injustice is that it depresses the down-trodden victims to such an extent that they lick the hand of the oppressor. The slaves fought on the side of the Southern planters against their Northern liberators. No wonder then, if the helpless women and widows side with the orthodox majority. If the State contemplated forcible action in spite of the wishes of the victims, the argument might be urged with some effect. But nobody in his senses can, or does, contemplate any such method of procedure. Widows and children are not the proper persons who can seek their own relief under the wrong that is done to them, and to society, and this argument therefore falls to the ground.

Fourthly, it is urged that admitting the fact that such regulation falls within the province of State action, and that these evils, after making all allowances for exaggeration, and the apathy of the victims, are still sufficient to justify State action, if such action can remedy the wrong without leading to other and greater abuses, and that it is not proper to wait till the victims rebel—it is urged that a foreign Government cannot be trusted with this power. This jealousy of foreign interference in social matters is not altogether a bad sign, and if the interference was of foreign initiation, the force of this argument would be irresistible. In this case, however, the foreign rulers have no interest to move of their own accord. If they consulted their selfish interests only, they would rather let us remain as we are, disorganized and demoralized, stinted and deformed, with the curse of folly and wickedness paralyzing all the healthy activities and vital energies of our social body. The initiation is to be our own, and based chiefly upon the example of our vene-rated past, and dictated by the sense of the most representative and enlightened men in the community, and all that is sought at the hands of the foreigners is to give to this res-ponsible sense, as embodied in the practices and usages of the respectable classes, the force and the sanction of law. These considerations weighed with our leaders in the past when they welcomed this co-operation in the abolition of Sati and Infanticide, and in the recognition of the validity of widow marriages. If we are to abjure such help under all circumstances, we must perforce fall back behind the Parsis, Mahomedans, and

Christians, who have freely availed themselves of the help in recasting their social arrangements. Further, as it is likely that foreign rule will last over us for an indefinite length of time, we reduce ourselves, by accepting this policy, to the extreme absurdity of shutting out a very useful help for many centuries to come. In such matters, the distinction of foreign and domestic rulers is a distinction without difference. It has a meaning and significance when foreign interests override native interests, but when the foreigners have no interest to serve, and the initiative is to be all our own, the recognition of State help is not open to the stock objection urged by those who think that we forfeit our independence by seeking such regulation on lines approved by us.

Fifthly—It is further urged in deprecation of State action that in this matter we must not lose sight of the fact that institutions, like constitutions, must grow, and cannot be made to conform with foreign ideals to order. There is a great force in this observation, and it would be a fatal objection if the argument for change were based on the ground that we must copy the foreign exemplar. The remarks which have been made above are, however, a sufficient answer to this allegation. The change is sought not as an innovation, but as a return and restoration to the days of our past history. Those who advocate it justify it on the authority of texts revered, and admitted to be binding to this day. The intermediate corruption and degradation was not of the nation's seeking. It was forced upon it by the predominance of barbarous influences, and by the intolerance of ruthless conquerors. That force having ceased to be operative, we must now return to the old order of things, if we are to grow to our old proportions. The history of the suppression of Infanticide and of Sati shows that these institutions, which had grown as excrescences upon the healthy system of ancient Hindu Society, were checked, and could be checked, only by the strong arm of Law, and once they were denounced as crimes, they disappeared from the face of the country. Before Government made up its mind to deal finally with these evils, the usual arguments that Institutions grow, and cannot be made to order were urged, and the duty of religious neutrality was held up *in terrorem* to frighten the timid and arouse the passions of the ignorant and the prejudiced. The diseased corruptions of the body cannot, and should not, be dealt with in the same way as its normal and healthy developments. The sharp surgical operation, and not the homoeopathic infinitesimally small pill, is the proper remedy for the first class of disorders, and the analogy holds good in the diseases of the body politic, as well as the material body as also in dealing with the parasitical growths of social degeneration.

Sixthly—The apprehensions against State legislation expressed in some quarters might have been most reasonable if, as a fact, Hindu society was really not governed by any law, and it was proposed for the first time to regulate these matters by subjecting them to the regulating action of the State. The fact, however, is that a law, a written law, and a very stringent one too, does regulate these matters, and it is enforced much in the same way as other laws. The courts are bound to give effect to that law, and decree personal rights and disabilities in strict accordance with it. What is now proposed is to substitute the more ancient and righteous law for a later corruption, cancel a law which is condemned by a law more reasonable, at least more amenable to reason, utilize the force of State sanction as a final support. No private understanding can prevail against the coercive power of this corrupt law. The new law proposed is itself not a foreign importation, but is only a revival of the ancient law of the country as laid down in the texts, and all that the Government is called on to do is to revert from the times of corruption to the times when Hindu Society was more healthy and vigorous.

There is another incidental and an important advantage likely to accrue in consequence of the change proposed. All progress in social liberation tends to be a change from the law of status to the law of contract, from the restraints of family and caste customs to the self-imposed restraints of the free will of the individual. Nay more, the present confusion of judicial authorities on ancient Hindu Law and custom furnishes the strongest argument for a definite pronouncement on the subject by the legislature. There is not a custom however absurd which cannot be defended by some strong text of law. The usual practice of reconciling texts intended for different ages and countries, and the loss of the spirit of true criticism, have benumbed the power of judgment. The liberation from superstitious thraldom, which will result from the changes proposed, is not likely to be the least of its benefits. It will be necessary to be very circumspect in graduating the change desired to meet exactly the extent of the evil crying for redress. The past century or half a century has effected a change in national sentiment, which, if not recognized to the extent it has gone, will only lead to a catastrophe and revulsion of feeling that will be simply irresistible, and may involve the ruin of many interests dear to the nation's heart.

There is only one more objection which we think deserves a passing notice. It is said that all previous legislation was directed against positive crimes, or was only of a permissive nature, while the evils now sought to be remedied are not crimes, and the remedies proposed are not of a permissive character. On the first point, we must urge that the practices now complained of are in some respects far more criminal than those which State action has checked. Sati was committed under temporary insanity caused by grief, while infanticide was in too many cases dictated by a similar mad impulse. They were both offences not committed in cold blood, and their effects spent themselves in a single act of violence, which inflicted the greatest shock on the perpetrator himself or herself. In most cases, enforced widowhood and disfigurement, the destruction of home sanctity by polygamous connections, the stupidity of baby marriages, are not impulsive acts, they are done in cold blood, and they inflict lifelong and undeserved misery on helpless victims, while the offenders suffer but little. So far as their moral heinousness is concerned, they are inflictions of injustice without any redeeming features, and the criminal responsibility of the nation is beyond all reprieve.

As regards the question of permissive *versus* compulsory legislation, we have no patience with those who can find consolation in empty words. The remedies proposed are in their nature permissive, and need give offence to nobody. If the law lays down strictly that no polygamous connections shall be entered into except for reasons specially permitted by the ancient law of Manu, we fail to see how such legislation is more compulsory than permissive. When the law lays down that no widow may disfigure herself except of deliberate choice, and at a fit time of life, say after she is 25 years old, where indeed is the compulsion? When the law lays down that marriages shall not be celebrated below a certain age, 12 for girls and 18 for boys, under penalty that earlier celebrations will not meet with the recognition of the Civil Courts in cases of disputes, where again is the compulsion?

We have thus noticed and answered all the usual objections urged by those who honestly support the continuance of the existing order of things. The question of principle is one which must first be argued out in all its bearings. Once the principle is recognized, the details of legislation may safely be left to the common sense of the community. It is with this view that the compiler of this publication has addressed himself to the task of placing before the public, in an accessible form, the literature of the subject in the shape of the debates that took place when the Widow Marriage Bill was just introduced in the Legislative Council 30 years ago. The arguments then urged and refuted have a curious family likeness to those we hear at present, and just as the apprehensions then entertained were disappointed, so surely we trust to see that all our ignorant prophecies will be falsified. The directions in which the marriage law needs reform have been already briefly indicated. Diwan Bahadur Raghunath Rao has already sketched out a draft Bill in which some of the reforms urgently required are set forth in full detail. The late Maharaja of Burdwan submitted 30 years ago a scheme for abolishing polygamy [. . .]. The views of those who have given thought to the subject on this side of India may be briefly thus summarized.

(1) We would fix 12 and 18 as the minimum ages of marriage for girls and boys. These periods are in full keeping with the most approved practice, and the more respectable orthodox sentiment of the present day. Even Rao Saheb V.N. Mandlik has stated 12 years for females as a permissible limit, and for boys we do not think he will regard 18 years as an unreasonable limit.

(2) Marriages contracted before this age should be discouraged not by pains and penalties of the criminal law, but by the attendant risk of making them liable to be ignored in case of disputes in the Civil and Criminal Courts.

(3) Marriage, unless consummated by actual cohabitation, should not be recognized as a perfect union before the limits laid down above are reached. Before such consummation, the girl should not be recognized as having become one with the husband in Gotra, Pinda, and Sutaka. This is the ancient law, and our reversion to it will do away with the superstition which paralyses the action of parents in dealing with the misery of child widows.

(4) We would on no account permit disfigurement except after 25 years, when the female is really alive to the circumstances of her position, and can choose deliberately the celibate course of life.

(5) Under no circumstances should one wife be superseded by a second connection, except under the safeguards, recognized by Manu and other writers.

(6) The widow's forfeiture of her husband's estate as a consequence of her second marriage should be done away with, and her life interest in her husband's inheritance should remain intact, whatever her choice of life might be.

These are the several reforms we advocate. We are fully aware that the details of legislation will not be easily settled, without suggesting many difficulties and doubts which will have to be provided against. The time, however, for suggesting these details has yet to come. . . .

28

The Worship of Women*

BEGUM ROKEYA SAKHAWAT HOSSAIN

'The honour that Hindus accord women is certainly laudable,' I said, leafing through an old issue of the periodical *Bharati*.[1] 'The honour that Hindus accord women is certainly laudable. In no other country is such respect shown towards woman. Woman is the Hindus' deity of worship.'

At my words the women present burst out laughing. I was slightly disconcerted. Jamila Begum said, protesting, 'Forgive me, Mrs Chatterjee! In this country, the role of a woman is not superior to that of a maidservant.'

Jamila is the wife of a famous lawyer; she is a great friend of Kusumkumari Ray. The other lady present, Amena Begum, is a widow; she lived in western India for ten years, and knows Urdu very well. She is also a dear friend of Kusum. They are so intimate with Mrs Ray that they address each other by their first names. It has been only two or three months since I became acquainted with these Muslim women, but Kusum is the same age as I am, and a childhood friend of mine.

It was in Kusum's sitting-room that I was sitting and leafing through *Bharati*. I had not been prepared for an argument—nevertheless, quite a debate ensued upon my remark. Amena Begum smiled a little and said, 'In this country women are a kind of personal property belonging to men.'

I: This is a mistake on your part. If Hindus did not respect women, they would not have viewed them as Goddesses. Most of their deities are women.

Amena: But we would wish to judge after seeing the practical results. Leave aside the myth making, and show us true events.

I: Kusum! Help me. Bring your *Mahabharata*. We shall show them historical events.

Kusum: I respect all of you equally, so I can't favour anyone. What is the good of the *Mahabharata* or history? You should discuss contemporary social events.

I (to the two Muslim ladies): Do you want to call Damayanti, Sita, Savitri, and other daughters of India mere serving maids?

Jamila: No, Sita and Savitri became famous because of their own good qualities. Sita was a virtuous person, but how did society 'worship' her during her lifetime?

I (not answering them): In ancient times there were many Goddesses. Such learned women as Lilabati and Khana are unique in the world.[2]

*Originally published as 'Nari-Puja', *Mahila* (December 1905–March 1906).

Amena: They were learned, and that virtue was their very own. But the discussion here is about the treatment of women by society. Khana was exceptionally proficient in astronomy. Even now, there isn't a farmer in the countryside who doesn't know a few of Khana's precepts. But—

I: But what? The fact that Khana's precepts are recited from village to village shows that Khana is worshipped by the mass of the people.

Amena: Forgive me, Mrs Chatterjee. Let me finish what I was saying. Khana may be worshipped now, but don't you know how she died? She was killed by having her tongue cut out, the tongue that gave birth to those precepts.

I: She was not killed. But, yes, her tongue was cut out.

Jamila: Why shouldn't we call that killing? After her husband cut her tongue out, Khana gazed at her husband silently, wept, and died.

Kusum: Leave aside these old matters. Let victory and defeat be decided by events of this century.

I: I am alone, while the Begum Sahibas are two. Victory belongs to the strong, so I shall accept defeat without war.

Kusum: What? Why should you abandon the argument so soon? Advance as far as you can.

Amena: Even if there are two of us, on the whole we are weaker than you are since you have received higher education (even if you have failed the F.A.![3]). You have gathered experience by seeing and hearing many things and by reading various books. And we live under strict purdah—we know only Kusum and you.

I: Well, all right, since you won't let me be! Kusum! Is not the present century fourteenth by the Bengali calendar? Wouldn't that mean the twentieth century of the Christian era?

Kusum: Be it the fourteenth or the twentieth century. Why don't you consider events that have occurred in the last hundred years?

I: Very well. Recently, with the creation of the Brahmo Samaj, women have reached the status of real Goddesses, this takes them beyond their earlier merely imagined deification.

Jamila: That is partly true. But take something else on board too—since you take pride in the Goddesses of Hindu society, you should also be prepared to take on board the faults of that society.

I: That is a very hard condition.

Kusum: It is just, even if it is hard. They have sealed off your escape from beforehand—do you get it, Prabha?

I: What sort of escape?

Kusum: Had they talked about the plight of some helpless woman belonging to a Hindu family, you might have said, 'But that sort of thing doesn't happen in our Brahmo Samaj.'

I: That is true. Can anyone say that helpless women are oppressed in the Brahmo Samaj?

Amena: If you go only by the Nababidhan sect of the Brahmo Samaj, then why drag in Hindu Goddesses? It is really unjust for you to come forward and accept praise for the virtues, and yet refuse to accept blame for the vices.

Jamila: Now I have understood why you were accepting defeat without war. Well, then, let's not discuss the worship of women, let's talk about something else.

At first, I was unsure as to what I should do next; a little while later I thought, 'Am I such a coward that I shall concede defeat without argument?' Outwardly, I said, 'No Begum Sahiba! Fear not—I shall not turn my back—let us go on!'

Everyone burst into laughter. To make them laugh had been precisely my intention. But for reasons of etiquette, they were no longer discussing social issues. I found this intolerable, so I remained adamant and said: 'Well, Begum Sahiba, you have not been able to tell the story of a single oppressed woman.'

Jamila: Why only one, one could tell many—who will count the hundreds of flames in that fire?

I: Show me at least one such flame!

Jamila: Very well. We can hear it in the voice of the Hindu women who are worshipped:

> Bravo, children of Hindus!
> Are your hearts made of stone? . . .
> You mangle the scriptures to kill girls. . . .
> They have no compassion and no religion,
> They cannot distinguish between deeds and misdeeds,
> They chew up girls, citing the scriptures.

What do you say to this? Shall I call those words a scream of anguish from a wounded heart, or a benediction given in pleasure at being worshipped?

I: That is a poet's composition—imagined anguish.

Jamila: You call the anguish of a child widow imagined pain?

Amena: It is not entirely imagined, rather, it is largely true.

Kusum: Absolutely true.

Amena: But it is the social custom, so one can be forced to put up with it. Leaving aside questions of poetic imagination, I shall show you right now with what ingredients India worships women—for examples of that we shall not have to go far. Have you seen the book *Heart-beats* by Pratapchandra Mozoomdar?[4]

My first thought was that the book discusses only spiritual things. I thought a little and then said bravely, 'Yes, I have seen it. It does not propound any theory about the oppression of women.'

Amena: Although it is not found in the book itself, one gets an example in Mr S.G. Barrow's biography of Mr Mozoomdar.[5]

I: An example of the oppression of a helpless woman? In the brief biography of the teacher?

Amena said in a steady voice: 'Yes, the incident of his mother's death. When Mr Mozoomdar's mother, suffering from cholera, was in her death throes, the head of the household was sleeping peacefully. If the cow belonging to the household had been ill, perhaps the master of the house would not have remained unworried. The treatment of widows by society comes through wonderfully in Mr Mozoomdar's words: re-read pages fourteen to sixteen in the biography. It breaks one's heart to read them. Even pet dogs and cats don't perhaps die without medical care; and yet the best among God's creations, the wife in a family, is restless in the pangs of sickness—and no one takes a second look at her! No one thought that a doctor should be called for the widow. Mozoomdar himself was about to go and interrupt the contented sleep of his uncle, but he was unable to enter the room inhabited by the master of the household. Even the servant would not go and call a doctor—even if he wouldn't, the son could not remain tranquil. Can anyone whose mother is saying farewell forever remain inert? No. He ran out into the street like a madman. He tried to call [the late] Keshabchandra Sen and some other friends. But everyone's door was closed at night. He went to the house of a certain doctor—but the doctor's servant turned the poor man out! The servant was after all an Indian man: he certainly knew how to worship women. So he thought that it was not right to disturb his master for the sake of a widow, and he turned away a son grieving for his mother.

In our mind's eye we can clearly see that nineteen-year-old boy running about in the streets, nearly maddened with grief because of his mother. And we can feel the yearning and the terrible anguish in his heart. Among the various blessings of God that we enjoy, a mother is the greatest blessing. Let happiness and prosperity be put on one side of a pair of scales, and the mother on the other side.

If you call this, the heartless, ruthless treatment of widows, the 'worship of women', then I have nothing more to say.

I: Such incidents are rare, not everyone can be deemed guilty because one widow has not been treated with care.

Kusum: No, Prabha! Such incidents are not rare—rather, it is the case that no one else records such scandalous stories as Mr Mozoomdar did, so we don't get to know of such incidents.

I (to Jamila Begum): And you? Do you know of any hair-raising incident?

Jamila: I have seen an incident with my own eyes—it is a long story.

I: Tell us, we shall listen.

Jamila: 'The little daughter of a rich man was ill. In their house, they had servants, a coach and horses, and every possible item of luxury. However, the little girl was not receiving medical treatment because girls were considered a curse.

There was no dearth of anything—the other children would toss around money in their play, yet this child, yet to be weaned, was dying without medical care. The mistress of the house could not bear this. With tears in her eyes, she entreated the head of the household to call a doctor, but he did not heed her. One day when the master was going to the doctor for his own sake, the mistress said, 'Do tell the doctor about our little girl's condition.' 'Do girls ever die?' said the master, and left.

Then the helpless lady, having no other recourse, took the ailing child in her lap and continued to weep silently. When the father langur tries to kill the baby male langur, the langur mother clasps the child to her bosom and saves its life by fleeing to the jungle. But where can a woman in purdah go to save her baby girl from a father's oppression? There are innumerable doctors in the city—nevertheless, how does that benefit the dweller of the 'inner apartments'?

I: Can man be so heartless? What happened in the end? Did the baby survive, or did she die of neglect?

Jamila: In the end the baby survived. When the mother was crying with her daughter in her lap, providentially the fortunate eldest son of that family had entered the inner apartments. He was not yet an adult, so his tender heart grieved, and he himself went to the doctor and brought some doses of medicine. He had brought the medicine only to console his mother! By the grace of God, the little girl survived by dint of that small amount of medicine. That rich family still lives there. That child, that father, mother, brother—all are living!

I: Is this family Hindu or Muslim?

Jamila: I shall not divulge that. What is the good of smearing ink on their faces? It is enough to say that they are Bengalis.

I: Look, the heinous custom of total purdah prevalent in this country is the root of all ills. Muslim society is steeped in this. Muslim women are utterly helpless because they don't even appear before servants. Purdah has made them inferior to and more helpless than animals such as the langur mothers.

III

Amena: Though the custom of total purdah is disgusting, it has become part of our flesh and bone. Until men learn to be decent and courteous, it won't be easy to leave purdah. If men had learnt to show due respect to women, then there would be no problem!

Kusum: I have heard that in other countries where Muslims are in the majority such a custom of purdah is absent. Then why did Muslims in India create this sort of purdah and make us captive along with their own wives and daughters?

Jamila: Who is the creator of purdah? No one has been able to determine that. When a Muslim brother writes in favour of purdah, he says, 'It is we who are the creators of purdah; the claim that our Hindu brothers make that they invented purdah is not correct.' And then again, the Hindu brother who writes in favour of purdah adduces arguments to say, 'Muslims have learnt the custom of purdah from non-Muslims.' In any case, whoever the creator of purdah may be, it is we who are suffering its consequences.

I: Why don't you gradually abandon purdah? We have done it.

Jamila: Your abandoning of purdah has hardly been lauded. You have had to hear a lot of vilification because of the way in which you have left purdah.

I: Why fear such vilification?

Amena: You may not fear it, but many have stepped beyond the limits of natural modesty, and in some cases the loss of purity—

I: Why did you stop? Go on.

Amena: I was about to say something unpleasant; anyway we have certain duties towards society as well, which we cannot neglect simply for our personal comfort.

I: Hindus vilify the Brahmo Samaj baselessly, and I see no need for heeding them.

Kusum: But one should be careful after listening to the negative things that the Brahmo Samaj itself says about leaving purdah. Perhaps Amena was about to report something which she had heard about the Brahmo Samaj.

Amena: You infer correctly.

I: But, on the whole, the degree of oppression of women that takes place in Muslim societies does not happen anywhere else. You spoke of Khana's death, but do you know the history of the Anarkali mausoleum in Lahore? Anarkali was buried alive on Akbar's orders.[6] Afterwards Emperor Jehangir had the beautiful mausoleum built over Anarkali's corpse. Who knows whether some sad story lies hidden inside the Taj Mahal as well?

Jamila: It is true that the Muslims oppress women, but they don't practise deception in public by saying 'we worship women'. Rather the wooden, orthodox mullahs of our country think that it is their religious duty to oppress women.

Amena: I think that Hindus have learnt the custom of purdah from us, and that the hardened mullahs have learnt to treat women more cruelly from the Hindus. Otherwise, if one goes by the prescriptions of the Koran Sharif, neither the oppression of women nor the custom of purdah is acceptable.

I: Do you believe that orthodox mullahs are in favour of an unjust system of purdah?

Jamila: Look, Amena, don't you go throwing stones at the beehive of the mullahs now.

Amena: Yes, you are right. Now I am not prepared to throw stones at the mullahs' beehive. Let's stop talking about mullahs, Mrs Chatterjee.

I: If you are afraid of bees, how will you gather honey?

Jamila: Before gathering honey, one takes care to light a fire and raise smoke in advance, and then one can bear the stings of one or two bees. But it would be childish foolishness to throw stones at the hive without making preparations for gathering honey. Here we are talking about the oppression of women, speak of that.

I: That is something that you will speak about, and I'll listen to.

Amena: There was of course so much to say—there is no end of such heart-rending stories. But today there is no more time. We will go now, Kusum.

So we returned to our respective homes.

(Translated by Barnita Bagchi)

Notes

About the Author: Begum Rokeya Sakhawat Hossain (1880–1932), a brilliant writer and social reformer far ahead of her time, was taught at home, learning English from her older brother. At 18, she married Sakhawat Hossain of Bhagalpur, who supported the education of women. Ten years later, after his death, she came to Calcutta and immersed herself in social reform, undertaking pioneering work within the Muslim community. In 1911 she founded the Sakhawat Memorial School in Calcutta with eight pupils. In 1916 she founded the Anjuman-Khawateen-i-Islam to work for the welfare and uplift of Muslim women. A fighter for social justice and social reform, her writings are relevant even today. This is especially so for 'Abarodhbasini' (Those Dwelling in Seclusion) and *Sultana's Dream*, which she wrote in English, a fantasy where women rule and men are secluded. *Motichur*, vols 1 and 2, comprise her prose writings. She also wrote a novel, *Padmarag*.

1. A literary magazine published from the Tagore household that had widespread influence on the literary world of Bengal (1877–1926). It was edited initially by Dwijendranath Tagore and subsequently by Rabindranath Tagore, Swarnakumari Devi, Sarala Devi Chaudhurani and Hiranmoyee Devi.

2. Lilavati, see Kailashbasini Devi, 'The Woeful Plight of Hindu Women', n12 [Chapter 25 of this volume].

   Khana was the wife of Mihir and the daughter-in-law of Varaha, two eminent astrologers in the court of Vikramaditya (fourth century AD), though some accounts state that Verahamihir was one person and one of the 'nine jewels' of the royal court. Khana, according to legend, surpassed both her husband and her father-in-law in astrological calculations, as a result of which she too was invited to join the court. Fearing that Khana's fame would eclipse theirs, Mihir is said to have cut out Khana's tongue upon the order of his father, which caused her death. In Bengali proverbs Khana is mentioned in connection with agricultural and seasonal lore.

3. First Arts or the examination held at the end of the first year of college.

4. P.C. Mozoomdar, *Heart-beats*. Biographical sketch by Samuel J. Barrows (Calcutta: Nababidhan Publishing Committee, 1935).

5. Pratapchandra Mozoomdar (1840–1905), joined the Brahmo Samaj in 1859, and after the Brahmo Samaj split, he remained with Keshabchandra's Nababidhan group. He travelled to many countries as a preacher and also attended the world conference on religion held in Chicago in 1893. He edited a number of newspapers and journals and was associated with the Calcutta University Institute, and was one of the biographers of Keshabchandra.

6. A court singer and dancer in the Mughal court and Prince Selim, the son and heir of Emperor Akbar, fell in love. In order to put an end to this relationship Akbar supposedly had Anarkali sealed up alive in a tomb. Whether true or not, a tomb exists in Lahore. This love story has stirred the imagination of folk poets through the ages.

Copyright Statement

CPSIA information can be obtained at www.ICGtesting.com
Printed in the USA
LVOW112355170313

324702LV00001B/2/P

9 780253 220493